RECORDS OF EARLY ENGLISH DRAMA

Records of Early English Drama

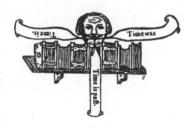

KENT: Diocese of Canterbury

EDITED BY JAMES M. GIBSON

1
Introduction
The Records
Alkham to Canterbury

THE BRITISH LIBRARY

and

UNIVERSITY OF TORONTO PRESS

© University of Toronto Press Incorporated 2002
Toronto Buffalo
Printed in Canada

First published in North America in 2002 by University of Toronto Press Incorporated
ISBN 0-8020-8726-4
and in the European Union in 2002 by
The British Library
96 Euston Road
London NW1 2DB

British Library Cataloguing in Publication Data
A catalogue record for this title is available from The British Library

ISBN 0-7123-4803-4

Printed on acid-free paper

T

National Library of Canada Cataloguing in Publication

Kent: Diocese of Canterbury / edited by James M. Gibson

(Records of early English drama)
Includes bibliographical references and index.
ISBN 0-8020-8726-4

1. Performing arts – England – Kent – History – Sources. 2. Theater – England –
Kent – History – Sources. 3. Music – Performance – England – Kent – History –
Sources. 4. Music – England – Kent – History and criticism. 5. Kent (England) –
History – Sources. 6. Church of England. Diocese of Canterbury – History – Sources.
I. Gibson, James M. II. Series.

PN2595.5.K45K45 2002   792'.09422'3   C2002-904528-2

The research and typesetting costs of
Records of Early English Drama
have been underwritten by the
National Endowment for the Humanities and the
Social Sciences and Humanities Research Council of Canada

Contents

Records of Early English Drama

The aim of Records of Early English Drama (REED) is to find, transcribe, and publish external evidence of dramatic, ceremonial, and minstrel activity in Great Britain before 1642. The executive editor would be grateful for comments on and corrections to the present volume and for having any relevant additional material drawn to her attention at REED, 150 Charles St West, Toronto, Ontario, Canada M5S 1K9 or s.maclean@utoronto.ca.

ALEXANDRA F. ROHNSTON University of Toronto DIRECTOR
SALLY-BETH MACLEAN University of Toronto EXECUTIVE EDITOR

Acknowledgments

Many people have contributed to the research and publication of these volumes. At the Kentish record offices all the staff, many of whom over the years have become both colleagues and friends, have answered my countless queries and requests for documents with professionalism and patience. At the Centre for Kentish Studies special thanks go to County Archivist Tricia Rowsby and for their help in the searchroom to Michael Carter, Libby Richardson, Helen Orme, Debbie Saunders, Margarete Kitcher, Mark Ballard, Allison Cresswell, Anne Atkinson, Alan Jordan, Alan Stubbs, Lucy Stroud, and Jonathan Barker; at the Canterbury Cathedral Archives, to former archivists Anne Oakley and Michael Stansfield, former librarian Sheila Hingley, and among the current staff Heather Forbes, Cressida Annesley, Mark Bateson, Elizabeth Finn, Sarah Griffin, Jackie Davidson, Sheila Malloch, and David Pilcher; and at the East Kent Archives Centre, to Lynne Bowden, Alison Cable, Pauline Davey, and Cerys Russell. Maureen Shaw answered many queries about the Hythe records, and Beryl Coatts shared her extensive knowledge of Lydd local history. The late Kathy Topping, former county archivist, guided the beginning of my Kent research in 1984 and never failed to show interest and to offer encouragement along the way. Staff at other record offices have also answered questions and helped with long-distance research: Steven Hogg and Stephen Roper at the British Library; Paul Botley, Gill Cannell, Helen Carron, Elisabeth Leedham-Green, and Malcolm Underwood at Cambridge libraries; Heather Wolfe and Georgianna Ziegler at the Folger Shakespeare Library; Melanie Barber at Lambeth Palace Library; Michael Heaney and Michael Stansfield at Oxford libraries; Alvan Bregman at the University of Illinois, Urbana-Champaign; Susy Marcon at the Biblioteca Nazionale Marciana; Muriel McCarthy at Marsh's Library; Magdalena Novakova and Jindriska Pospisilova at the National Library in Prague; and Ernst Petritsch at the Haus-, Hof- und Staatsarchiv in Vienna.

Other colleagues and friends of REED have provided expert assistance and advice. Alan Nelson helped with research in London and Cambridge, Eila Williamson in Scottish repositories, and Kirstie Jackson and Penny Tucker in London, Oxford, and Kent. Laetitia Yeandle and M.G. Brennan answered queries about the Dering manuscripts and Fiona Somerset about Nicholas Battely. Carolyn Barron and Benjamin Thompson answered questions about William Warham. Robert Tittler read the Historical Background section of the Introduction and made suggestions. Andrew Hughes and David Klausner read Appendix 4 and gave advice on liturgical drama. Tom Tate and Stephanie Martin provided computer assistance for the musical transcription in Appendix 4. Claire Breay, Nigel Ramsey, and Eileen White checked in situ many of the transcriptions from manuscripts that could not be microfilmed. William Edwards helped with the Anglo-Norman texts, transcriptions, and translations; Janet Ritch with the early-modern French; Dario Brancato, Konrad Eisenbichler, Margaret Loney, Kevin Reynolds, and Anne Urbancic with the Italian. The late Donald Gibson helped with some of the Latin translations. Andrew Butcher, Director of the Centre for Medieval and Tudor Studies at the University of Kent at Canterbury, answered many questions about manuscript sources and Kentish history. Postgraduate students in his history seminars also made useful suggestions. To Sheila Sweetinburgh I owe the reference to the Brookland play in James Hoggelyn's will, and to Graham Durkin I owe the market regulation for baiting bulls in Canterbury and several references to rough music.

At the REED office in Toronto the editorial staff, both past and present, have contributed greatly to production of these volumes. Tanya Hagen and Milton Kooistra helped with the chronicle research and the Select Bibliography. Ted de Welles and Miriam Skey have served as project bibliographers. Miriam Skey, along with Carolyn Black, also did the copy-editing. Between them they have corrected many inaccuracies in the Introduction and editorial apparatus. William G. Cooke helped with the palaeographical checking and prepared the English Glossary. Arleane Ralph also helped with the palaeographical checking, surveyed the Oxenden correspondence in the British Library, and, along with Marion Filipiuk, prepared the Index. Philip Collington helped with the proof-reading and checked the provincial and diocesan visitation articles. John Lehr, assisted by Agnes Ormsby and Jessie Sherwood, has researched the Patrons and Travelling Companies section. Patrick Gregory has checked the Latin Translations and the English and Latin Glossaries. Subash Shanbhag has produced the modern map of Kent. Gord Oxley has done the typesetting. Sally-Beth MacLean, executive editor, has guided the progress of the Kent volumes to the press with a sure blend of encouragement and requests for further information. Finally, associate editor Abigail Ann Young, whose name ought to be with mine on the title page, has prepared the Latin Glossary, checked the Latin Translations, and devoted her extensive knowledge and keen palaeographic skills to making these volumes far better than they would ever have been if I had been working on my own.

During the research for these volumes I have received grants from the American Philosophical Society and the British Academy and a fellowship from the American Council of Learned Societies. Special thanks go to Clifford Davidson, Roland Mushat Frye, Alexandra F. Johnston, and the late R.M. Lumiansky for their many letters of recommendation. The British Academy, the National Endowment for the Humanities, the Social Sciences and Humanities Research Council of Canada, and Father Edward Jackman and the Jackman Foundation have all given additional grants to REED for the editorial work and printing costs of these volumes.

The following record offices, organizations, and individuals have granted permission to publish excerpts from the records in their possession: the Biblioteca Nazionale Marciana, Venice; the British Library; the Canterbury Cathedral Archives; the Centre for Kentish Studies; the Cumbria Record Office (Carlisle); the East Kent Archives Centre; the Faversham Town Council; the Folger Shakespeare Library; the Haus-, Hof- und Staatsarchiv, Vienna; the Lambeth Palace Library; The Library, Imperial College at Wye; The Master and Fellows of Corpus Christi College,

Cambridge; The Master and Fellows of St Catharine's College, Cambridge; The Master, Fellows, and Scholars of St John's College, Cambridge; the Public Record Office; The Rector and Fellows of Exeter College, Oxford; the Vicar and Parish Records Society of St Margaret's, Bethersden; and the National Archives of Scotland.

To all these people and organizations I am indebted for their contributions, both large and small, toward the research and publication of these volumes. My deepest debt of gratitude belongs to the late R.M. Lumiansky, who long ago during his graduate seminar on the Chester mystery cycle at the University of Pennsylvania inspired my interest in medieval drama, introduced me to the mysteries of Elizabethan secretary hand, served as advisor for my doctoral dissertation in medieval liturgical drama, and encouraged me to embark on the Kent research for REED. To his memory I dedicate these volumes.

Historical Background

The Landscape

The county of Kent is located on the southeastern tip of England, bordered on the west by the ancient counties of Sussex, Surrey, and Middlesex and surrounded on the remaining three sides by the waters of the English Channel and the Thames estuary. Before the Local Government Act 1888 created county councils and transferred nine northwestern parishes to the London County Council, Kent ranked ninth in size among English counties, covering 971,991 acres and measuring sixty-eight miles from Deptford in the west to North Foreland on the Isle of Thanet in the east and thirty-eight miles from the Isle of Sheppey in the north to Dungeness in the south. Apart from its long and varied coastline, the most distinctive geographical feature of Kent is the North Downs, a long ridge of chalk hills running from northwest to southeast through the county, part of a much larger chalk formation that stretches eastward from Wiltshire across Salisbury Plain to meet the English Channel at the famed White Cliffs of Dover and continues on the French side of the Strait of Dover in the chalk hills of the Bas Boulonnais. Three river valleys break through these chalk hills, the River Stour running northeast to reach the sea near the Isle of Thanet, the River Medway rising in Sussex and cutting its way through the sandstone ridge and the North Downs to reach the Thames estuary between the Isle of Sheppey and the Isle of Grain, and the River Darent flowing into the Thames at Dartford. Two smaller rivers, the River Cray and the River Ravensbourne, rising on the north slopes of the downs west of the Darent also drain into the Thames. From an average elevation of 500 to 700 feet in the North Downs, the land slopes gently eastward through the fertile arable land of east Kent toward the Stour estuary and northward toward the Thames estuary and the marshlands along the north Kent coast. On the south slopes of the downs the land falls away steeply some 400 feet before rising gently to a parallel ridge of sandstone hill country two or three miles to the south. Predominantly wooded or covered with heath, this stony and less fertile hill country is often called chartland, meaning 'rough, rocky, sterile soil,' topographical features surviving in such place names as Wrotham Heath, Lenham Heath, and Charing Heath or Great Chart, Little Chart, and Chart Sutton. South of this sandstone ridge, which again drops away steeply on its southern slopes, lies the Low Weald or Vale of Kent and the High Weald, a heavily forested area between the North Downs and the parallel ridge of the South Downs that reach the sea at Beachy Head in East Sussex. Even in the early modern period the Weald was sparsely populated and, according to Kentish historian Edward Hasted in 1797, 'in former times nothing more than a waste desart and wilderness, not furnished with habitations, and peopled as the rest of the county was, but like a forest, stored with herds of deer and droves of hogs only.'[1] This forested landscape accounts for the many Wealden place names ending in -hurst, meaning 'a grove of trees, copse, or wood,' such names as Goudhurst, Hawkhurst, Penshurst, Sissinghurst, and Staplehurst, and the many place names ending in -den, meaning 'clearing or swine pasture,' such names as Benenden, Bethersden, Biddenden, Marden, Rolvenden, Smarden, and Tenterden. Finally, south and east of the Weald along the south coast lies the extensive marshland of Romney Marsh and Walland Marsh, where the rich alluvial soil, inned and drained with a network of dykes and ditches, provides plentiful pasture and grassland.[2]

Settlement History

Early settlement in Kent stretches back as far as the people of the Neolithic Age who constructed their long barrows near Chilham in the Stour Valley and their barrows guarded by megalithic standing stones at Kits Coty and Coldrum in the Medway Valley.[3] Numerous discoveries of Bronze Age pottery, implements, and coins and excavations of the Iron Age hilltop settlements at Oldbury near Ightham and at Bigbury near Canterbury also provide evidence of continuous occupation of Kent for at least 2,000 years before the Roman army under Julius Caesar first invaded Kent in 55 BC.[4] When the Romans returned to Kent under Claudius in 43 AD, the topography of the county largely influenced the pattern of Roman roads and Roman settlement. Walled towns were established at Canterbury (Durovernum) near the lowest fording point in the Stour estuary and at Rochester (Durobrivae) where the first bridge was constructed across the River Medway. Shore forts for the Britannic fleet were constructed at Reculver (Regulbium) and Richborough (Rutupiae) on the northeast coast inside the Wantsum Channel and at Dover (Dubris) and Lympne (Portus Lemanis) on the southeast coast where natural harbours protected the Britannic fleet. Within a few years after the invasion of Kent the eastern arm of Watling Street had connected Richborough with Canterbury, Rochester, and London along the north slope of the North Downs. Another road ran south from Richborough to Dover, while other roads radiated from the east Kent hub of Canterbury north to Reculver, southeast to Dover, southwest to Lympne, and a longer southwest road ran through Ashford to the iron-working district in the Weald. Further west another Roman road dropped south from Rochester along the Medway valley through the Roman settlements around the Maidstone area and on through Cranbrook toward Hastings on the south coast of Sussex. The ancient Pilgrims Way ran southeast from Maidstone below the south face of the downs through Lenham and Ashford to Lympne. Thus the downland of east Kent and the Low Weald of the Vale of Kent were furnished with a serviceable central road system from an early date. This did not hold true for west Kent and the High Weald. Although evidence of numerous Roman villas, farmsteads, and masonry buildings has been located north of the downs along Watling Street, in the Darent Valley, and in the Medway Valley, little Roman settlement beyond ironworks has been discovered in the Weald between the north-south Rochester to Hastings road and the north-south road further west connecting London with Lewes.[5]

After the Romans withdrew from Kent in the early fifth century, the Jutish colonization and settlement of Kent followed two distinct paths. The first was the establishment of trading settlements and towns along the Kent coast. All of the ancient Kent boroughs listed in the Domesday Book, except Canterbury, were directly related to the sea, a fact now disguised by the much altered coastline of Kent. On the north Kent coast a wide channel known as The Swale separated the Isle of Sheppey from the coast, providing a protected harbour for the royal ville of Faversham. An even wider channel known as The Wantsum separated the Isle of Thanet from the northeast coast where the trading settlement of Sandwich was located. The wide Stour estuary drained into The Wantsum, allowing navigation upriver as far as Fordwich, where another trading settlement was established as a port for Canterbury. On the southeast coast Dover had a natural harbour where the River Dour broke through the chalk cliffs to meet the sea. Further west along the coast the late Saxon trading seaports of Hythe and Romney were located at the east and west mouths of the River Limen, which flowed into a wide estuary of marshland and multiple water channels extending as far inland as Appledore and the Isle of Oxney.[6] During the later medieval period, however, the constant flow of shingle and sand on the flood tide running from the Atlantic through the English Channel to the North Sea gradually blocked many of these harbours with shingle banks, leading to the expansion of marshland as the river estuaries silted up and the once flourishing ports declined and became stranded inland.

The second path followed by the Jutes was the gradual colonization of the interior of the county, moving from the fertile downland in the north and northeast through the chartland to the Weald in the south and southwest. The earliest settlements in Kent were located along the fertile north coast downland near Watling Street, in the river valleys running inland from the north coast, or along the chartland at the foot of the North Downs close to the Pilgrims Way. From these areas herdsmen moved their herds of swine to summer pasture in the Weald along the ancient droveways running from northeast to southwest.[7] In time the drovedens in the Low Weald and High Weald led to permanent settlement, a long process of colonization lasting from the fifth century to the fourteenth century and leading to three distinct types of settlement in Kent: 'primary' settlements in the downland by a tribe or community leading to comparatively large parishes of 4,000 to 5,000 acres; 'subsequent' settlements during the later Anglo-Saxon period originating as isolated farms or dwelling places of single families, leading to small parishes of 1,000 to 2,000 acres, and accounting for some sixty place names in the higher downland and chartland ending in -stead, such settlements as Bearsted, Brasted, Chipstead, Elmstead, Nettlestead, and Stansted; and a third type of settlement arising after the Conquest from the settlement of the drovedens and the clearance of the Wealden forest and wooded chartlands, leading to sparsely populated, large parishes of 10,000 to 15,000 acres.[8] Two additional phases of colonization, driven by the increase in population and the expansion of the cloth and iron industries in the Weald between 1450 and 1650, led to further in-filling of the countryside with many new farms and hamlets in all parts of the county. By the early modern period settlement in Kent was characterized by the wide dispersal of population and the prevalence of small market towns and villages servicing these scattered outlying farms. Some parishes had no central village at all; others had only fifteen or twenty houses clustered around a church. Often villages of fifty or sixty houses surrounding a village green or lying along a single street served as a trading centre for two or three sparsely populated parishes. By the time that the first phase of the colonization of Kent was completed in the middle of the fourteenth century, eighty-one places in Kent held prescriptive market rights or had gained market charters, followed by an additional seventeen new market charters granted over the next two centuries as the population of the county increased.[9]

By the middle of the seventeenth century, however, about two-thirds of these markets had disappeared as the gradual improvement of roads and transport increasingly concentrated market activity in the larger town centres. On Philip Symonson's map entitled *A New Description of Kent*, first published in 1596,[10] the hub of roads in east Kent still radiated from Canterbury in the old Roman pattern. West of Canterbury along Watling Street, however, new connecting roads, following the old northeast to southwest droveways, linked Faversham with Lenham on the Pilgrims Way and Sittingbourne with Maidstone, now the A249. West of the Medway an additional northeast to southwest road ran from Strood through Cuxton and Halling to Trottiscliffe and Wrotham and Sevenoaks in the Weald. South of Maidstone another new road ran east from Cranbrook to Tenterden and Appledore and New Romney and then followed the coast northeast to Hythe and Folkestone and Dover. The chief difference between the old Roman road pattern and the early modern roads, however, came in west Kent. Instead of the single road of Watling Street along the north Kent coast connecting London with Rochester and east Kent, two new major routes had opened up the Weald. At Deptford, just inside the Kent border, Watling Street divided, the northern fork continuing east toward Rochester and the southern fork cutting southeast through the Weald to Sevenoaks and Tonbridge and Rye. A few miles further eastward at Lewisham, Watling Street divided again, sending a middle branch through Farningham and Kingsdown where the road again divided, one branch crossing the Medway north of Maidstone at Aylesford and the other crossing south of Maidstone at West Farleigh and continuing along the northern edge of the sandstone ridge to Loose, Langley and Lenham. Even with the improved transport and communication achieved by this road network, the population of early modern Kent remained generally dispersed in farms, villages, and market towns. There were in the early seventeenth century about twenty-five towns in Kent with 400 or more inhabitants, about two-thirds of which had a population of over 1,000. Dover, Maidstone, and Rochester each had about 3,000 inhabitants. Only Canterbury approached the middle rank of English towns with a population of around 6,000.[11]

Economic History

The topography of Kent influenced not only the history of its settlement and roads but also the history of its economy and the county's three principal industries of farming, fishing and coastal trade, and textiles. From the north Kent marshlands and North Downs to the forests of the Weald and the marshland on the south coast, the county's geography determined the agricultural produce of each area. Along the north Kent coast the fertile soils of the marshland were intensively farmed for hops, vegetables, and fruit, with much of the produce shipped directly to the London markets from the port of Faversham. It was here on the north Kent coast that Richard Harris established a cherry orchard at Teynham in 1533 at the command of

Henry VIII, leading to the county's renown for its hops and fruit by the middle of the seventeenth century. Directly south of this fertile marshland, where the North Downs ran across the county from northwest to southeast, the shallow soil on the southern slopes offered grass for sheep grazing and the deeper loam on the northern descending slopes provided rich soil for such corn crops as wheat, barley for the brewing industry as well as for bread, and oats or peas for fodder. Along the south-facing steep slopes of the downs from Folkestone in the east to Brasted in the west runs a narrow strip of scarpfoot land containing the worst soil in the county but still supporting in the sixteenth century a diversified agriculture of open heath, hops, apple, pear, and cherry orchards, and nut trees including filberts, hazels, sweet chestnut, and beech. South of the scarpfoot from Ashford in the east to Tonbridge in the west the Low Weald rises southward to the High Weald around Cranbrook. Covered by ancient woodland interspersed with small areas of grassland, the Weald supported smaller, mainly self-sustaining family farms devoted principally to livestock breeding, rearing, and fattening in contrast to the mainly arable downland of east Kent. Finally, on the south coast the rich alluvial soil of Romney Marsh, increasingly drained from the fifteenth century onwards by a network of dykes and ditches, protected by sea walls, and maintained by commissioners of the sewers, provided pasturage for cattle and sheep. This great diversity of agriculture, combined with the proximity of the ever-increasing London food markets, maintained the steady prosperity of farming in early modern Kent.[12]

The maritime industries of fishing and coastal trade were also influenced directly by the topography of Kent. The long coastline of Kent, surrounded on three sides by the English Channel and the Thames estuary, produced many towns and villages where fishing, coastal trade, or transport of passengers and goods to the Continent provided significant employment. Fishing and maritime trade had always been important for the Cinque Port towns; however, by the sixteenth century Fordwich, Lydd, and New Romney had lost their ports to the encroaching shingle banks and silted up river estuaries. At Folkestone, Hythe, and Sandwich maritime activity carried on with increasing difficulty. At Dover only extensive engineering works sponsored by the Tudor monarchs saved the harbour. At the same time, however, the smaller villages along the north Kent coast and in the Medway estuary became increasingly important centres of fishing and coastal trade. A survey of the Kent coast from Hythe to Dartford in 1566 revealed that most of the Kent fleet consisted of small boats, weighing twenty tons or less, employed principally in fishing or carriage of goods from one port to another, and concentrated in such villages as Ramsgate, Broadstairs, Margate, Whitstable, and Swalecliffe on the north Kent coast and Queenborough, Halstow, and Upchurch in the Medway estuary, where the ratio of mariners to households was far higher than in the once flourishing head ports of the Cinque Ports.[13] Fishing for herring and mackerel continued to be important during the sixteenth century at Folkestone and Hythe, while oysters were dredged at Faversham, Rochester, and Whitstable.[14] However, only three of the ancient coastal ports – Dover, Faversham, and Sandwich – and the Medway ports of Maidstone and Rochester continued to trade in the export and import of merchandise during the late sixteenth and seventeenth centuries, principally the import of coal and the export of corn, produce, and livestock from Kent's fertile farmland to the markets of London. During this period the London markets increasingly dominated the Kent coasting trade. Corn shipped from Kent ports to London by water increased from 14,500 quarters of cereals in 1579–80 to 42,000 quarters in 1615 and 100,000 quarters in 1638.[15] Between Christmas 1625 and Christmas 1626, 95 per cent of the total corn shipments from Kent ports went to London. Between Christmas 1649 and Christmas 1650, shipments of corn from Kent ports to London accounted for over half of all coastwise corn shipments arriving in the capital, including 179 shipments from Sandwich, 164 from Faversham, sixty-seven from Milton, sixty-six from Rochester, and forty-eight from Dover. All together Kent supplied more corn for the London market throughout the seventeenth century than any other county.[16]

In addition to maritime trade, fishing, and farming other industries also flourished in early modern Kent, including iron manufacture in the Weald, shipbuilding in the Medway estuary where royal dockyards were established in the Tudor period, paper mills at Dartford and Maidstone, the manufacture of copperas and gunpowder along the north Kent coast, and the quarrying of chalk and ragstone. Far outstripping this varied, but relatively minor, industrial output was Kent's textile industry, supported by the plentiful supply of wool from the Kent flock, the rich seams of fuller's earth near Maidstone, the proximity of continental markets, and the immigration of several thousand Flemish textile workers and cloth manufacturers into Kent during the later sixteenth century.[17] During the fourteenth and fifteenth centuries Kentish merchants not only exported wool to clothiers in Essex but also successfully established the clothmaking industry in the Weald, particularly in the parishes of Benenden, Biddenden, Cranbrook, Goudhurst, Hawkhurst, Headcorn, Staplehurst, and Tenterden. The clothiers of the Weald could easily procure wool from the sheep that grazed on Romney Marsh or on the downland of east Kent. Equally essential and advantageous was the local supply of fuller's earth, rare elsewhere in England, but found in rich seams near Boxley and along the Medway north of Maidstone.[18] By the end of the fifteenth century the Kentish cloth industry was expanding, participating in the flourishing international trade that saw the export of English cloth double between the 1470s and the 1550s and approach in peak years the value of nearly one million pounds sterling.[19] In the sixteenth and seventeenth centuries native Kentish clothmakers specialized in two main types of cloth: broadcloth, usually a yard and three-quarters wide and at least twenty-eight yards in length, often coloured russet or dyed in a variety of hues, and designed primarily for export; and to a lesser extent narrow cloth, or kersey, one yard in breadth and usually sixteen to seventeen yards in length, designed primarily for domestic consumption. In the mid-sixteenth century Kentish broadcloth accounted for just under 10 per cent of England's total woollen cloth exports.[20] During the second half of the sixteenth century Protestant refugees from the Netherlands and northern France were permitted to settle in Sandwich in 1561, Maidstone in 1567, and Canterbury in 1575. The immigrants were licensed to manufacture 'new draperies,' specializing at Sandwich in says and bays, a Flemish 'lightweight cloth made from long stapled fleece wool,' at Maidstone in linen thread, and at Canterbury in luxury textiles and such items as ribbons, lace, and 'silk rash,' a lightweight textile made from a combination of silk and wool. The Flemish and Walloon communities quickly expanded, reviving the flagging economies of both Canterbury and Sandwich.[21] The growing demand for lighter fabrics in the 1620s and 1630s and the competition from continental producers of the new draperies, however, brought a slump in demand for traditional English broadcloth and a general downturn in the Kentish textile industry.[22]

Administrative History

In early Anglo-Saxon times Kent was divided into administrative districts called lathes, which organized the payment of the king's rents, administered customary justice for pleas of trespass, theft, and bloodshed, and regulated the economic life of the peasantry in such matters as maintenance of sea defences and communal woods.[23] These early administrative districts of the kings of Kent grew out of the considerable Germanic settlement around the important Roman centres of Canterbury, Dover, Faversham, and Rochester and may well have retained the outline of the Romano-British administrative structure. The Saxon shore fort of Portus Lemanis near Dover, for example, became the territorial centre for the lathe of the Limenewara. Lands around Canterbury became the lathe of Borowara and around Rochester the lathe of Cesterwara.[24] The Domesday Book mentions seven lathes or half-lathes: the Lathe of Borough in the northeast of the county comprising the Isle of Thanet and the lower Stour valley with its centre at Canterbury, the Lathe of Eastry centred on the royal ville of Eastry, the Lathe of Lympne along the south coast, the Lathe of Milton centred on the royal ville of Faversham along the north Kent coast, the Lathe of Wye in central Kent, the Lathe of Aylesford along the Medway and the westernmost Lathe of Sutton at Hone.[25] In the thirteenth century the number of lathes was reduced to five: Milton and Wye were joined to form the Lathe of Scray, Borough and Eastry were joined to form the Lathe of St Augustine, and Lympne was renamed the Lathe of Shepway.

The lathes were also subdivided into hundreds probably during the tenth century. Closely connected with manorial feudalism, the hundreds of Kent were largely determined by the geography of the great ecclesiastical and royal estates. Manors and towns under the lordship of the king or the archbishop or the abbots of religious houses were grouped together regardless of the size of the territory. The five lathes were thus divided into sixty-seven hundreds, some comprising just one parish, others as many as seventeen parishes. Except for the hundreds that had an ancient royal seat of justice within their boundaries, most hundreds in Kent functioned primarily for the manorial view of frankpledge and for the apprehension and punishment of theft.[26] By the sixteenth century the hundred courts dealt mainly with nuisance and petty criminal cases, giving way in most other jurisdictions to the quarter sessions and assizes. During the early modern period, however, the administration of judicial and fiscal matters was still organized according to lathes and hundreds.[27] The county bench, for example, assigned responsibility for groups of hundreds to different justices of the peace.[28] Parliamentary taxes were also assessed and collected by commissioners in each hundred.[29]

Such central administration was carried out during the Middle Ages and early modern period chiefly by the most important county official, the sheriff, whose office in Kent dates back before the time of the Conquest. Originally appointed by the king at his pleasure from men of rank and power and then annually from the time of Richard II, the sheriff was accountable to the Crown for royal revenues and presided over the county court that met on Penenden Heath near Maidstone to levy royal fines, to hear actions for debt, and to return the county MPs to parliament.[30] During the sixteenth century the sheriff's function of recruiting and training the county militia was transferred to muster commissioners and then to the newly created office of lord lieutenant during the reign of Edward VI, an office filled during the sixteenth century by Sir Thomas Cheyne; Sir Henry Jerningham; Sir William Brooke, Lord Cobham; Sir Henry Brooke, Lord Cobham; and during the seventeenth century by Edward, Lord Wotton; James, duke of Lennox; Philip Herbert, earl of Montgomery; and Heneage Finch, earl of Winchilsea.[31] While the Crown appointed its officials to administer the county, the county in turn sent its representatives to parliament. The two knights of the shire were chosen by the leading gentry of the county from men who often held other positions of influence at court while maintaining political connections and landed estates in the county.[32] In addition to these two MPs who represented the county, MPs were also returned by Canterbury, Maidstone after the restoration of its charter in 1559, Rochester, and the Cinque Port towns of Dover, Hythe, New Romney, and Sandwich. These representatives tended to be wealthy citizens or gentry prominent in local government.[33]

The administration of justice in criminal or Crown indictments in Kent took place in two main courts: the assizes and the quarter sessions. After the Magna Carta (1215), various arrangements were established for assize trials and gaol delivery. During the early fourteenth century the counties had been grouped into six assize circuits, each circuit receiving two annual visitations from judges who normally presided over the courts of common law in Westminster. Kent, along with Essex, Hertfordshire, Middlesex, Surrey, and Sussex, belonged to the Home Circuit.[34] Twice yearly, usually in the Lent vacation during February and March and in the Trinity vacation during July and August, two common law judges or a judge and a serjeant rode the circuit. Armed with commissions of oyer et terminer and gaol delivery directed to the sheriff of the county, they were empowered to hear both Crown and common pleas and to administer justice in the king's name. The county sheriff, coroner, constables, and knights attended the assize courts; juries were impanelled; and cases were presented and tried, including felonies such as murder, burglary, and highway robbery. During the early modern period the usual assize towns for Kent were Canterbury, Maidstone, and Rochester, although gaol deliveries occasionally also took place in west Kent at Dartford, Gravesend, Greenwich, and Sevenoaks.[35]

In between the semi-annual assize courts the county quarter sessions courts met four times annually, usually alternating between Maidstone on the Wednesday after Epiphany, Canterbury on the Wednesday after Easter, Maidstone on the Wednesday after the feast of St James, and Canterbury on the Wednesday before Michaelmas. These courts were presided over by local magistrates or justices of the peace, who usually dealt with lesser criminal matters such as theft, trespass, and assault, as well as a host of administrative and regulatory matters including licensing of alehouses, maintaining highways and bridges, compiling muster rolls, and overseeing poor law administration. With powers to arrest suspects, take depositions, grant bail, or bind individuals to keep the peace, the magistrates held great power and influence in their local areas. Appointed usually for life by the lord chancellor from the wealthy and prominent dignitaries, landowners, professionals, and gentry of the county, the justices of the peace formed the permanent governing oligarchy in the county, sons or relatives of current magistrates often being appointed to fill vacancies as they occurred. The commissions of the peace for Kent appointed between thirty and thirty-five justices during the reign of Henry VIII, rising to fifty-six in the commission of 1562, seventy-six in 1584, 110 in 1608, ninety-seven in 1626, and eighty-five in 1636.[36] Since their remit included the enforcement of government policy and the maintenance of public order, as well as the punishment of criminals, magistrates sometimes questioned or prosecuted allegedly seditious players or disruptive minstrels and morris dancers, as, for example, at Harbledown in 1594, at New Romney in 1615, or at Canterbury following the passage of a city ordinance against public dancing in 1565.

In addition to the courts of assize and quarter sessions that administered the common law through representatives of the Crown and local magistrates, the church also administered canon law through its system of ecclesiastical courts.[37] All probate matters came under the jurisdiction of the archdeacon's court or the consistory court of the bishop. During the annual visitation of the archdeacon or bishop, the churchwardens of each parish also returned their answers to the visitation articles set for each diocese by the bishop. These articles ranged in content from the repair of the church fabric to the moral conduct of the parishioners. During the second half of the sixteenth century and the first half of the seventeenth century, they usually included sabbatarian articles prohibiting people from practising their trade or craft on Sunday and forbidding drinking in the taverns, dancing, minstrelsy, or plays during the time of divine service. Most of the cases prosecuted by the ecclesiastical courts in response to these visitation articles involved recusancy or some form of sexual immorality; however, between the 1560s and 1640s there were also over 120 cases involving dancers, minstrels, players, bearbaiting, morris dancing, and maypoles presented by churchwardens to the archdeacon's and consistory courts in the diocese of Canterbury.

When the churchwardens presented a parishioner for breaking one of the visitation articles, the court summoned the parishioner through a court official called the summoner or apparitor. If the defendant did not appear, he would be summoned again by ways and means, a process which involved fixing the summons to the door of his residence or to the door of the parish church. If he still did not appear, he would be declared contumacious and be excommunicated. A letter of excommunication would then be read by the vicar at the next service in the parish church. To lift the sentence of excommunication, the defendant would have to appear in court, submit to the judge a petition for absolution, and pay a fine to the parish poorbox. Then the case would continue where it had left off. When the defendant did appear, he could either plead guilty and submit to the correction of the judge or deny the charge and undergo compurgation. If he did plead guilty, he could be dismissed with a warning or required to perform penance, usually reading out a confession in church on the next Sunday or holy day while dressed in a white penitential garment and carrying a candle. A letter from the vicar or curate verifying the completion of penance had to be produced before the case could be dismissed. If he denied the charge, he had to swear an oath or produce compurgators, persons of honest reputation and good character in the parish, to verify his story. At any point in the proceedings, which often stretched over several months, the defendant could be declared contumacious if he did not cooperate and be excommunicated.[38]

All parishes in the county were subject to these diocesan courts; however, many parts of the county were exempt from both the county administration exercised by the sheriff, coroner, and lord lieutenant and the jurisdiction of the judges and magistrates in the assize and quarter sessions courts.[39] The cities of Canterbury and Rochester and the town of Maidstone after 1549 were protected by their charters, governed by a mayor, jurats, and commonalty, and allowed to hold their own courts within the boundaries of their liberties. The liberty of Romney Marsh, with its charter dating from 1492, operated much the same way as an urban corporation with its bailiff, jurats, and commonalty and its own court. In 1461 Edward IV had even granted county status to Canterbury with power to appoint its own sheriff and to hold its own quarter sessions courts. Chief among the liberties exempt from county administration and court jurisdiction, however, was the liberty of the Cinque Ports and Two Ancient Towns, a federation of Kentish and Sussex boroughs that provided ship service for the king in exchange for freedom of trade and freedom from taxation.[40] The boroughs of Dover, Hastings, Hythe, Romney, and Sandwich ranked as head ports; Rye and Winchelsea in Sussex were the Two Ancient Towns. To each town and port were joined corporate members – Pevensey and Seaford with Hastings, Tenterden with Rye, Lydd with Romney, Faversham and Folkestone with Dover, Fordwich with Sandwich – and non-corporate members – Denge Marsh, Old Romney, and Orlestone with New Romney; West Hythe with Hythe; Birchington, Kingsdown, Margate, and Ringwould with Dover; Deal, Ramsgate, Reculver, Sarre, and Walmer with Sandwich. Together they provided the king with fifty-seven ships for fifteen days of service each year, the charge for ship money being divided proportionally among all members according to the agreement known as the Ports Domesday. In return they received exemption from taxation and tolls and representation in parliament, rights extending back before the Conquest and enumerated in charters to the individual towns and in the general charters granted by Henry III in 1260 and Edward I in 1278. Administration of the Cinque Ports was conducted at the General Brotherhood, an ancient court that met at Dymchurch during the thirteenth and fourteenth centuries and after 1357 at the central head port of Romney, or at occasional separate meetings of the east and west ports with their members, known as Guestlings.[41] The General Brotherhood dealt with arrangements for ship service, matters relating to their ancient fishing rights along the Norfolk coast and the annual herring fair at Yarmouth, disputes with the exchequer over the protection of their liberties, and disputes concerning the process of withernam, an arrangement for settling suits of debt, covenant, and trespass among the ports or individual portsmen. As early as the reign of Henry II the Cinque Ports claimed exemption from the county assize courts and the right to plead in the Court of Shepway, a royal court comprised of jurats summoned from each port and presided over by the lord warden of the Cinque Ports. From the fourteenth and fifteenth centuries the importance of the Cinque Ports had begun to decline as many of the harbours were blocked by shingle and silt. When called to defend the coast against the Spanish Armada in 1588, the Cinque Ports could muster only seven small ships: the *Elizabeth* of Dover (120 tons), the *Reuben* of Sandwich (110 tons), the *William* of Rye (eighty tons), the *Ann Bonaventure* of Hastings (seventy tons), the *John* of Romney (sixty tons), the *Grace of God* of Hythe (fifty tons), and the *Hazard* of Faversham (thirty-eight tons).[42]

Religious History

Some evidence survives for the Romano-British church in Kent, but the history of Christendom in Kent really begins in 597 with the arrival of the mission of St Augustine sent by Gregory the

Great to convert the English people.[43] The well-known story related by Bede describes the arrival of Augustine on the Isle of Thanet and the invitation by Æthelberht for Augustine to enter Canterbury where his Frankish queen, Bertha, and her chaplain were already worshipping in the Romano-British church of St Martin's.[44] After the conversion of Æthelberht on Whitsun Eve in 597, Augustine established the first English diocese at Canterbury and was consecrated the first archbishop on 16 November 597. Augustine consecrated Justus the first bishop of Rochester in 604, securing for Kent the distinction of being the only English county with two medieval sees and two cathedrals. In addition to the royal abbey of St Peter and St Paul in Canterbury, founded by Augustine in 598 and later renamed St Augustine's Abbey, eight other royal monasteries were established with Anglo-Saxon royal patronage during the seventh century at Dover, Folkestone, Hoo, Lyminge, Minster (in Sheppey), Minster (in Thanet), Reculver, and Upminster, all but St Augustine's eventually destroyed by Viking raids during the ninth century. Augustine also established the priory of Christ Church at Canterbury Cathedral and the priory of St Andrew at Rochester Cathedral. From the missionary centres provided by these monasteries and nunneries, the conversion of the Kentish people led to the building of numerous parish churches in the two Kentish dioceses during the seventh and eighth centuries. Another period of extensive church building in stone followed the Conquest and the appointment of Lanfranc as archbishop of Canterbury in 1070.[45] By the late thirteenth century the Taxatio of Pope Nicholas in 1291 shows that the system of parishes and rural deaneries was well established in Kent with eleven deaneries in the diocese of Canterbury, stretching from Sittingbourne, Ospringe, Westbere, and Canterbury in the north to Charing, Lympne, Elham, and Dover in the south, from Sutton in the west to Bridge and Sandwich in the east, and four deaneries in the diocese of Rochester – Dartford, Malling, Rochester, and Shoreham. The *Valor Ecclesiasticus* in 1535 gives the same division of the two dioceses into deaneries and lists a total of 245 rectories, 172 vicarages, fifty-two chapels, and forty-one chantries, about two-thirds of which were located in the diocese of Canterbury.[46]

In addition to over 400 ancient parish churches in the two dioceses, many religious houses, friaries, hospitals and colleges were established in the county. Most of the Benedictine monasteries and nunneries founded by the Anglo-Saxon kings along the Kent coast were refounded after the Viking invasions. St Augustine's Abbey, along with the cathedral priory, was reformed and enlarged by Archbishop Dunstan in the tenth century. Other Benedictine houses in the diocese of Canterbury included Faversham Abbey, founded in 1147 by King Stephen, and the nunneries of St Sepulchre, Canterbury, in the late eleventh century and Davington Priory near Faversham in the twelfth century. Two other nunneries, Malling Abbey and Higham Priory, were established in the diocese of Rochester in the eleventh and twelfth centuries respectively. The Cluniac monastery of Monks Horton Priory and the Cistercian monastery of Boxley Abbey, both in the diocese of Canterbury, also date from the middle of the twelfth century. The Austin canons had six houses, four in the diocese of Canterbury at Bilsington, Combwell, Leeds, and St Gregory's in Canterbury, and two in the diocese of Rochester at Lesnes and Tonbridge. The Praemonstratensian canons, a reformed branch of the Austin canons, had two additional houses near Dover at Bradsole and West Langdon. Noteworthy among the county's religious houses were the numerous medieval hospitals spread throughout the county and the twelve friaries located at Canterbury, Lossenham, Maidstone, Mottenden, Romney, and Sandwich in the diocese of Canterbury and at Aylesford, Dartford, and Greenwich in the diocese of Rochester.[47]

Apart from St Augustine's Abbey at Canterbury, however, none of these religious houses appeared among the first rank of English monasteries. Only eight monastic houses in Kent survived the first Act of Dissolution in March 1536 that dissolved all abbeys with annual revenues under £200: in the diocese of Canterbury the two great abbeys of Christ Church and St Augustine's, Boxley Abbey, Faversham Abbey, and Leeds Priory, and in the diocese of Rochester the cathedral priory of St Andrew and the nunneries at Dartford and Malling. There were no surrenders in 1537 but the end came quickly in 1538 and 1539, spurred by the surrender of Boxley Abbey in January 1537/8 and the exposé of the abbey's celebrated shrine, the Rood of Grace, whose superimposed image was believed to have been miraculously gifted with movement and speech. In February 1537/8 Cromwell's agent exposed the image as a fraud in the market place at Maidstone. The bishop of Rochester later exhibited the image during a sermon at St Paul's Cross in London and then had it cut into pieces and burned. Faversham Abbey, where King Stephen was buried, surrendered on 8 July 1538, followed by St Augustine's Abbey, the oldest abbey in the country, on 30 July and Malling Abbey on 29 October. During September the shrine of St Thomas Becket in Canterbury Cathedral was destroyed. By the end of the year all of the friaries had also surrendered. Leeds Priory and Dartford Nunnery followed in 1539, leaving only the two cathedral priories, which were surrendered to the archbishop in March 1540 and refounded as secular chapters in 1541, bringing medieval monasticism in Kent to an end.[48]

The progress of the Reformation in the parishes of Kent, driven by Archbishop Thomas Cranmer, who protected radical preachers and appointed reforming Protestants to vacant benefices, kept pace with the Dissolution of the monasteries during the 1530s and early 1540s. In August 1536 Cromwell had issued a set of injunctions that required incumbents to provide Bibles in both Latin and English, to teach the Creed, the Lord's Prayer, and the Ten Commandments in English, and to discourage pilgrimages, cults of the saints, and veneration of images or relics. In September 1538 a second, more radical set of injunctions followed, condemning the lighting of candles before images and indeed requiring the removal of images. Although Henry condemned the cult of St Thomas Becket, the royal injunctions in November 1538 and the Act of Six Articles in June 1539 slowed the pace of reform.[49] As convocation and parliament debated the course of true religion during the early 1540s, the conflict between traditionalists and reformers in Kent set radical parishioners against conservative clergy in some parishes and radical clergy against traditional churchwardens and congregation in other parishes, as Cranmer and Christopher Nevinson, his commissary, used diocesan visitations to push for the removal of images and the suppression of such expressions of late medieval devotion as the distribution of holy water and Candlemas candles. Cranmer continued to drive the reform movement, where possible appointing reformers to key positions, including Nicholas Ridley as a canon of the new cathedral foundation and Thomas Brooke, Michael Drumme, Lancelot Ridley, and John Scory as four of the Six Preachers, a newly created office in the reformed cathedral arising from the fresh emphasis on the importance of preaching and biblical exposition in the reformed church. The majority of the new prebendaries were traditionalists, however, and in 1543 a coalition of conservative prebendaries and such influential gentry as Sir John Baker, Sir William Finche, and Sir Thomas Moyle joined in the Prebendaries' Plot against Cranmer, a plot that backfired when Henry VIII placed Cranmer himself in charge of investigating the accusations of his enemies. As the Henrician years came to an end, the mood of the county was balanced between a strong Protestant party, including Archbishop Cranmer, Bishop Henry Holbeach of Rochester, a substantial minority of parish clergy, and such influential magistrates as George, Lord Cobham; Thomas Culpeper; James Hales; Edward Wotton; and Thomas Wyatt on the one hand, and a strong traditionalist party of clergy and parishioners committed to defend traditional religious practices on the other.[50]

Under Edward VI the pace of the Reformation quickened in Kent with the suppression of the colleges of Maidstone and Wingham and the twenty-three chantry chapels in the diocese of Canterbury and sixteen in the diocese of Rochester following the passage of the Chantries Act in November 1547. In the parishes the depositions of witnesses in the consistory court books show the systematic destruction of shrines and images, the administration of both bread and wine at Communion, the sale of chantry lands and assets, the introduction of the English prayer book in 1549, the removal of altars and erection of Communion tables, and the sale of redundant vestments, plate, and other ornaments.[51] The extent of the iconoclasm during Edward's reign may be gauged by presentments in the consistory court books during the reign of Mary that show the required re-equipping of parish churches with altars, ornaments, vestments, and rood screens during the visitation of Nicholas Harpsfield, the new archdeacon of Canterbury, in August and September 1557.[52] The churchwardens' accounts at All Saints', Lydd, to cite the example of just one parish, show the taking down of tabernacles and images in 1547–8; the sale of the rood loft in 1548–9, the Easter sepulchre in 1550–1, and numerous vestments in 1552–3; and the purchase of a 'Table called the Lord's Table' in 1550–1. During the Marian revival the churchwardens erected a new altar and Easter sepulchre and purchased a new antiphoner, new candlesticks and cross for the altar, and a new holy water stock in 1553–4; constructed a new high altar with half a ton of timber in 1554–5; and purchased a new processional book and processional banners in 1555–6 and a new image of Allhallows with a tabernacle in 1556–7.[53] The extent to which Kent had become committed to the Protestant cause may also be gauged by the ease with which Sir Thomas Wyatt of Allington recruited between 2,000 and 3,000 supporters in his uprising of Kent sparked by the news in November 1553 of the impending marriage of Mary to Philip II.[54] The seriousness of the threat posed by Kent Protestants may be measured by the high enforced turnover of Kent clergy through deprivation and resignation during 1554 and 1555 and the number of heretics burned after the passage of the heresy bill in December 1554.[55] John Foxe, in *Acts and Monuments* (1563), relates the stories of the Marian martyrs, more numerous in Kent than anywhere else in England outside of London. Between July 1555 and June 1557 most of Kent's martyrs were burned at Canterbury but also seven at Maidstone, five at Rochester, two each at Ashford and Wye, and one each at Dartford and Tonbridge, over sixty in all, including Archbishop Thomas Cranmer, who was executed at Oxford in March 1556.[56]

The Marian revival ended with the deaths of Queen Mary and her archbishop, Cardinal Reginald Pole, both on 17 November 1558. Under Archbishop Matthew Parker (1559–75) the slow process of advancing Protestant faith and worship in the diocese of Canterbury began. During his first decade Parker concentrated on removing the visible practices of Catholicism. By 1569, when the archbishop made a visitation of the diocese, most parish churches had acquired the necessary service books and church furniture.[57] The shortage of trained Protestant clergy, however, hampered Parker's efforts to combat Catholic recusants and to eradicate the vestiges of popular Catholicism in the parishes. Churchwardens may have removed the rood loft, destroyed the images of saints, substituted a Communion table for the altar, and purchased copies of the homilies and the Bible in English, but many parishioners did not hear a Protestant sermon from one year to the next.[58] The shortage of clergy in the diocese also forced Parker initially to tolerate both conservative Marian clergy and the radical reformers who, forced into exile during the Marian persecution, had returned to push forward the Protestant agenda.

Protestantism gradually gained ground in Kent, supported by Protestant gentry and magistrates who joined forces with the clergy and churchwardens to suppress not only the perceived threat from recusants but also the ever-present threat to public order posed by disruption and disorderly behaviour.[59] As Puritan magistrates and aldermen increasingly controlled civic affairs in Canterbury, the attitude of the city oligarchy toward players and minstrels turned from benevolence to hostility. A Canterbury city ordinance in 1565 prohibiting public dancing in taverns and inns led to prosecutions in quarter sessions court. In May 1589 morris dancers were arraigned for dancing in front of the mayor's house. In March 1592 boys of the King's School were in trouble with the diocesan court of High Commission for going 'abrode in the cuntrey to play playes contrary to lawe and good order' (see p 228). In 1595 the burghmote court passed a sabbatarian ordinance prohibiting performance of plays on Sundays, limiting performances by travelling troupes to two consecutive days in any calendar month, and establishing curfews. Hythe passed a similar ordinance against players in 1615, curtailing performance and authorizing payments to players not to play. In Canterbury payments to players slowed, then ceased. From 1616 Canterbury chamberlains' accounts show routine payments to players not to play, as in 1634 when the court reimbursed the mayor 20s for 'putting off of certen players' in order 'to avoyed disorders and night walkyng which myght come therby' (see p 290). Chamberlains in Dover and Tenterden made similar payments. By 1635 payments of any kind to players had ceased to appear in the chamberlains' accounts anywhere in Kent except in Canterbury where the last gratuity payment was made in 1641. At Hythe the maypole was removed in 1615 and apparently also at Dover in 1619. Throughout the diocese churchwardens routinely presented minstrels and morris dancers during the archdeacon's visitations, as both town and village authorities moved to suppress popular games and public disorder.

During the final decades of the sixteenth century conformist Puritanism increasingly permeated the centre ground of Kentish society occupied by the governing oligarchies in both town and countryside. At the same time the radical, nonconformist Puritan minority continually pushed at the boundaries, attacking rituals and ceremonies and opposing episcopal authority. When Archbishop John Whitgift (1583–1604) came to the see of Canterbury, noncomformity had spread to most parts of the diocese.[60] Attempts to make Kentish clergy subscribe to certain articles of religion led to polarization between moderate and radical Puritans and charges of episcopal harassment of godly ministers. The seeds of presbyterianism had already been sown in the fertile soil of Kentish clergy and Kentish parishioners, producing in the seventeenth century the increasing polarization between the mainstream Puritanism practised by the county gentry and the more radical Puritanism that called for root and branch religious reconstruction. As the county and the country edged toward civil war, the logical conclusion of Kent's radical Protestantism came in August 1642, when the parliamentarian troops of Colonel Sandys vandalized Christ Church Cathedral, overturning the Laudian altar and smashing the altar rails. Following a parliamentary ordinance in August 1643 for the removal of all crucifixes, crosses, and images of saints from cathedrals, forces led by the Puritan minister Richard Culmer again attacked the cathedral, destroying the stained glass windows and pulling down the image of Christ from Christ Church gate.[61]

The Boroughs

Most of the ancient boroughs of Kent were located in the Diocese of Canterbury: Canterbury, Dover, Faversham, Folkestone, Fordwich, Hythe, Lydd, Maidstone, New Romney, Sandwich, and Tenterden. The ancient boroughs of Gravesend and Rochester and other towns and parishes in the Diocese of Rochester will appear in a separate collection in the REED series.

CANTERBURY

When the Romans first saw the ancient British settlement straddling the River Stour at the lowest crossing point east of the Forest of Blean plateau, they called it Durovernum Cantiacorum, or 'fort of the Kent people beside the swamp,' a name later altered by the Saxons to Cantwaraburh, or 'fort of the people of Kent.'[62] The Romans established a military presence in Canterbury during the first century and by the time of Trajan (98–117) and Hadrian (117–38) had developed the settlement into a large town with masonry buildings, including public baths, a temple, and a theatre. Rebuilt early in the third century, the theatre measured 250 feet across and was capable of seating around 7,500 spectators. The city walls dating from the late third century had gates opening on the main roads to London (Westgate), Reculver (Northgate), Richborough (Burgate), Dover (Ridingate), and Lympne (Worthgate). By the beginning of the fifth century, however, the Romans had abandoned the city, retreating from the invading Jutes and Saxons.[63]

For the next century the city most likely remained deserted, having been reoccupied only from the middle of the sixth century when the Saxons constructed their timber buildings among the Roman ruins. When Augustine arrived with forty monks to begin his mission in 597, he founded a church dedicated to St Martin in a building dating from the Roman occupation of the city and already being used by Queen Bertha as an oratory.[64] After the conversion of Æthelberht, Augustine began to build in the northeast section of the city the first Christ Church Cathedral, consisting of an apsidal chancel and a simple nave surrounded by porches. Outside the Roman walls of the city Augustine established in 598 an abbey dedicated to Sts Peter and Paul, which was consecrated in 613 by Archbishop Lawrence (607–19) and served during the seventh century as the burial place for the early archbishops and the royal family of the kingdom of Kent. Capital of the kingdom of Kent during the early Anglo-Saxon period, Canterbury developed into a major trading centre during the seventh century with a mint operating from as early as 630. Under Archbishop Theodore of Tarsus (668–90), who held regular synods and appointed bishops, the city also became the centre of Christianity in England. The school established by Augustine to train clerks to read the Latin scriptures and liturgy flourished under Archbishop Theodore and Abbot Hadrian.[65]

During the later Anglo-Saxon period the city's fortunes fluctuated. Although the city was sacked during the Viking raids of the later ninth century, by the mid-tenth century the city was flourishing again with markets along the newly established street running from Westgate to Newingate in the southeast. The city was administered by a portreeve, probably appointed by the king, who collected tolls and controlled the markets.[66] During the early ninth century Archbishop Wulfred (805–32) rebuilt Christ Church monastery. Massive enlargement of the cathedral took place during the ninth and tenth centuries, extending the nave westward and incorporating the porches into side aisles. Under the administration of Archbishop Dunstan (960–88) the monastic communities of the abbey and cathedral priory were both reformed under the discipline of the *Regularis Concordia*. The abbey was enlarged and rededicated to Sts Peter and Paul and Augustine. A new Benedictine community was established in the cathedral in 988, leading to the flowering of the Christ Church scriptorium during the late tenth and early eleventh centuries. During this same period, however, Canterbury suffered repeated raids by the Vikings, culminating in the sacking and burning of the city in 1011 and the following year in the capture and murder of Archbishop Alphege (1006–12). When England and Denmark were finally united under Cnut in 1016 and order was restored, the cathedral was repaired and enlarged by the rebuilding of the west end. The tombs of St Dunstan and St Alphege were established as shrines. By the end of the Anglo-Saxon period the cathedral measured some 100 feet in width and probably 300 feet in length, making it the largest church in England.[67] The city too had recovered from the Danish wars. The Domesday Book mentions about 450 burgesses and 187 urban properties, suggesting a population of about 6,000, making Canterbury one of the ten largest towns in England.[68]

In the century following the Conquest the city and its religious establishments flourished. Following the surrender of the city in October 1066, William the Conqueror built an early motte and bailey castle in the western part of the city, which was replaced by a Norman keep during the reigns of William II and Henry I. In 1155 Henry II granted the city a charter, formalizing the great measure of self-government recorded in the Domesday Book and recognizing the existence of a court or governing body. As an urbanized hundred the city had been divided into six wards, each headed by an alderman, and during the next century references begin to appear to the two bailiffs, twelve jurats, and six alderman.[69] The city prospered as the chief market town in east Kent. By the late twelfth century considerable extra-mural development, principally clustered around the six gates and along the approach roads, had expanded the city's economic boundaries.[70] Although a disastrous fire destroyed the cathedral in 1067, the city's religious establishments prospered under the energetic leadership of Archbishops Lanfranc (1070–89) and Anselm (1093–1109). By 1077 Christ Church Cathedral had been completely reconstructed in the Norman style with new cloisters. A Norman choir and transepts were added to the monastic church of St Augustine's. Outside Northgate Lanfranc founded in

1084 the new priory of St Gregory for secular canons and the hospital of St John the Baptist for sixty poor and infirm men and women.[71] To the west on the London road at Harbledown he founded the hospital of St Nicholas for lepers.[72] Archbishop Anselm enlarged the cathedral, building a new choir and crypt, and to the south of the city on the Dover road founded the priory of St Sepulchre for Benedictine nuns.[73] By the middle of the twelfth century the growing population of the city supported twenty-two parish churches.[74]

The defining moment for medieval Canterbury, the martyrdom of Archbishop Thomas Becket (1162–70), came on 29 December 1170. As chancellor, Becket had supported the legal reforms of Henry II; as archbishop, Becket opposed the Crown and supported the church. Having signed the Constitutions of Clarendon in 1164 that prohibited appeals from ecclesiastical courts to papal courts without royal assent, provided for state punishment for criminous clergy, and otherwise severely restricted the clergy and the ecclesiastical courts, Becket went into exile at the Abbey of Sens in France and obtained papal release from his promise. The rift deepened when Henry decided to crown his eldest son Geoffrey as his successor and instructed the arch-bishop of York to perform the ceremony, a ceremony that only the archbishop of Canterbury had the right to perform. After partial peace had been restored, Becket returned to England, landing at Sandwich on 1 December 1170. When Becket suspended the archbishop of York and excommunicated the bishops who had participated in the coronation ceremony, however, the quarrel between church and Crown erupted again. Provoked by the rash words of the king, the four knights Reginald Fitzurse, Hugh de Morville, William de Tracy, and Richard le Breton travelled from Normandy to Canterbury, where they murdered Becket just inside the north transept of the cathedral. Soon miracles were reported at the martyr's tomb, and in 1173 the pope announced that Becket had been canonized a saint. In the summer of 1174 Henry II himself performed penance, walking barefoot from St Dunstan's Church outside Westgate to the cathedral crypt, where he knelt and prayed by the tomb while the monks of Christ Church scourged him with rods.[75] Pilgrimages to Becket's tomb had already begun, some 665 pilgrims having been recorded between 1171 and 1177, including a large proportion of knights and nobility.[76] The destruction of the Romanesque cathedral choir by fire in 1174 led to the rebuilding of the choir in the Early English style and the construction of the magnificent shrine of St Thomas Becket. When Becket's relics were translated from the crypt to the shrine on 7 July 1220, the ceremony was attended by Henry III, twenty-four bishops, and most of the abbots from English monasteries.

For almost the next three centuries both the cathedral and the city benefited from the steady stream of pilgrims to the shrine of St Thomas. King and queens, nobility, and ordinary people visited the shrine and made their offerings. During the early years between 1198 and 1213 total offerings at the cathedral averaged £426 3s 7d per annum, rising to a total of £1,142 5s during the first jubilee in 1220. During the fourteenth century pilgrimages to the shrine reached their greatest popularity with offerings of £670 13s 4d during the third jubilee in 1320, £801 11s 0d in 1350, and £643 during the fourth jubilee in 1370. During the fourteen years between 1370 and 1383 annual offerings averaged £545 8s 10d. New inns were erected in the city to house the pilgrims, including The Chequer of Hope at the corner of the High Street and Mercery Lane built by the monks of Christ Church between 1392 and 1395. During the fifth jubilee in 1420 over 100,000 pilgrims flooded the city, leaving offerings totalling £644. Royalty were buried near the shrine, including the Black Prince in 1376 and Henry iv in 1413. Construction of a new cathedral nave in the Perpendicular style began under Archbishop Simon of Sudbury (1375–81) and was completed in 1405 under Archbishop Thomas Arundel (1396–1414). The southwestern transept and tower were rebuilt in the early fifteenth century. The great Bell Harry tower at the crossing of the transepts and the nave was begun in the 1480s and completed in 1497 under Archbishop Cardinal Morton (1486–1500). Christ Church Gate, begun under Cardinal Morton in 1500, was finished in 1517 by Archbishop William Warham (1504–32).[77]

Quite apart from martyrdom and medieval pilgrimages, the religious and civic life of Canterbury prospered during the later medieval period. A community of Franciscans, or Grey Friars, was established in 1224 near the River Stour, followed by the Dominicans, or Black Friars, in 1237.[78] The Austin Friars, or White Friars, arrived in 1318, settling first in the parish of Westgate and than moving to the parish of St George in the southeast of the city in 1324.[79] Both Christ Church Priory under the leadership of Prior Henry de Eastry (1285–1331) and St Augustine's Abbey under Prior Thomas Fyndon (1283–1309) expanded their wealth and influence. A new abbot's palace was constructed at St Augustine's. Many parish churches were enlarged as the city's population peaked during the early fourteenth century at 8,000.[80] In the taxation of 1334 the city ranked fifteenth in wealth among English provincial towns.[81] During the late fourteenth century the city walls were repaired and Westgate was rebuilt. The economic prosperity of the city was reflected in the rebuilding of the timber-framed Guildhall over its old twelfth-century stone vault in 1438, the erection of the market cross at the bull stake outside the cathedral precinct in 1446, and the construction of many of the surviving timber-framed buildings in the city. The city served as the principal trading centre of east Kent with fairs at the feasts of Pentecost, the Translation of St Thomas Becket (7 July), Michaelmas (29 September), and the Holy Innocents (28 December).[82] In 1234 the charter of Henry iii had granted the city the right to elect its own bailiffs; in 1448 a new charter of Henry vi provided for the annual election of a mayor in place of the two bailiffs. Elected annually on 14 September, the mayor was sworn into office on 29 September along with the twelve jurats, two chamberlains, a common clerk, and a common serjeant. In 1461 a further charter granted by Edward iv gave Canterbury county status to reward the city for its help during the War of the Roses. From that date Canterbury elected its own sheriff and administered its own court of quarter sessions, quite separate from the east and west Kent quarter sessions that alternated between Maidstone and Canterbury.[83]

By the beginning of the sixteenth century, however, Canterbury was suffering from economic decline. Pilgrims no longer crowded the city's streets, no longer supported the city's hostellers, victuallers, and blacksmiths, or left their offerings at the city's churches and religious houses. In spite of successful jubilee years in 1420 and 1470, offerings at the shrine had dwindled during the fifteenth and early sixteenth centuries to £66 15s in 1436, £25 6s 8d in 1444, £31 1s in 1453, and £25 6s 8d in 1455. In 1532, just six years before the destruction of the shrine, a note in one of the sacrist's books shows offerings of only £13 13s 3d.[84] Not even the civic marching watch with its pageant of St Thomas, begun in 1505 and paraded annually through the streets on the eve of the Translation, could reverse the trend. The age of pilgrimage had passed.

Demographic contraction further contributed to Canterbury's decline. Returns for the lay subsidies of 1524–5 reveal that the population of the city had fallen to about 3,000 and that the wealth of the city had dropped to seventeenth among English provincial towns.[85] In addition, the silting up of the Wantsum Channel and the River Stour affected the carriage of cargo upriver to the wharves at Fordwich just east of the city. A 1514 statute for dredging the River Stour declared that the city 'ys now of late in grete ruyne & decaye and the inhabytaunts therof enpoverysshid & many of grete mancyons in the same desolate.'[86]

The Dissolution of the monasteries further deepened the economic decline, abruptly ending the employment provided by the city's many religious houses. Both St Sepulchre's Nunnery and St Gregory's Priory were surrendered in 1536 under the statute that dissolved all abbeys with revenues under £200 per annum. On 30 July 1538 St Augustine's Abbey, the oldest abbey in the kingdom, was dissolved, followed by the destruction of the shrine of St Thomas Becket during September 1538 and the surrender of the three friaries to the bishop of Dover on 13 December 1538.[87] The cathedral priory itself was surrendered to Archbishop Cranmer on 20 March 1539/40 and reconstituted by letters patent on 8 April 1541 as the Dean and Chapter of Canterbury Cathedral.[88] Many monastic buildings, including the church of St Augustine's Abbey, were unroofed and destroyed. The abbot's palace became a royal palace for Henry VIII in 1539. At Christ Church Priory the dormitory, refectory, and kitchen were all unroofed and torn down; the chapter house was converted to a sermon house; other buildings were converted for use by the new prebendaries or by the newly endowed grammar school.[89]

The cult of St Thomas Becket was revived under Mary I, and the marching watch with pageants again paraded through the streets during her short reign.[90] No attempt, however, was made to re-establish the monasteries in Canterbury. By the time Elizabeth I visited Canterbury in 1573, the city had passed from a centre of religious life to the economic centre and chief market town of east Kent. Immigration, principally by the Walloons, who had established their silk weaving industry in the city, fueled population growth and the return to prosperity. The first Walloons arrived in 1575, their numbers quickly expanding to about 1,700 by 1582 and about 3,000 in the 1590s, nearly half of the city's population. The buildings near the River Stour formerly used by the Black Friars became a weaving factory for the Walloons. By the 1630s, when the centre of the cloth industry had shifted to the Weald, the foreign population of Strangers in the city decreased to 1,300 or about one-fifth of the total population. Overall, however, the city's total population continued to increase from about 3,500 during the 1560s, to 4,000 during the 1570s, over 6,000 in the early seventeenth century, and 6,500 by 1640.[91]

DOVER

About fourteen miles southeast of Canterbury, where the River Dour breaks through the white chalk cliffs to meet the sea, stands the town and port of Dover. Ruins of the town wall and remains of public baths discovered under the market square and nave of St Mary's Church show that the Romans founded a small walled town beside the natural haven at the river's mouth guarded by earthworks and the Pharos, or beacon-light, erected on Castle Hill to the east.[92] During early medieval times the town was located inside the walls of the old Roman-Saxon shore fort, where the churches of St Martin, St Peter, and St Mary clustered around the medieval market place. Before the middle of the tenth century there was a mint at Dover, the earliest of the Cinque Port mints, indicating a sizable trading community.[93] Perhaps because the town was destroyed by fire shortly after the Conquest, the Domesday Book does not list the properties or enumerate the burgesses, making it impossible to form any estimate of the Anglo-Saxon population. Nevertheless, the survey does identify Dover as an important and strategic port, listing the standard charges for transporting the king's messengers across the Channel and noting that the town provided twenty ships, each manned by twenty-one men, for fifteen days' annual ship service for the king.[94]

The Domesday Book also establishes Dover as a borough by prescription acting without a charter of incorporation, for in exchange for ship service the king had endowed the town with independent jurisdiction and free courts. The town's earliest charter, granted by Henry II but known only from its confirmation by John in 1205, confirms the liberties that Dover had held in the time of Edward the Confessor, William I and II, and Henry I.[95] In Norman times Dover was governed by a portreeve; however, the first mayor appears in the records as early as 1257. The custumal, drawn up in 1356, describes the ancient customs for the annual election of the mayor and jurats by the commonalty, a practice altered only in 1556 with the election of thirty-seven freemen from the commonalty to form the common council, who then proceeded to elect the mayor and jurats. Throughout the medieval period the commonalty had gathered annually at St Peter's Church and later at St Mary's on 8 September, the Nativity of St Mary the Virgin, to elect the town officers and receive the chamberlains' accounts, but by the early seventeenth century the town had erected its own court hall.[96]

Marking the strategic position of Dover as a head port of the Cinque Ports and the main port for trade and transportation to and from the Continent, the imposing walls of Dover Castle towered over the town. After 54 BC the Romans had built fortifications on Castle Hill, including the Pharos and a square tower. Henry II strengthened the fortifications, providing the constable of Dover Castle and eight knights with endowed estates in 1166 and building a Norman keep in 1188. By the beginning of the thirteenth century the lord warden of the Cinque Ports also served as the constable of Dover Castle, while the main administrative responsibility for the castle was vested in the office of lieutenant of Dover Castle.[97] Guarded by the strong towers of the castle atop the white chalk cliffs, ships sailed in and out of Dover harbour conveying passenger traffic to the Continent and transporting both overseas and coastal trade. The Roman harbour had been located up the Dour valley, the medieval harbour on the northeast side of the bay under the Castle Cliff, and the sixteenth-century harbour at the foot of the Western Heights. Like the other Cinque Ports Dover struggled with the perennial problem of protecting its harbour; however, unlike the other Cinque Ports Dover attracted royal support. Silting up of the eastern harbour led to the construction of a new harbour on the western side of the bay under the patronage of Henry VIII in 1534 and further work under Elizabeth I in 1583, described in Holinshed's *Chronicle* (see pp 474–6), to construct The Pent to dam up water from the Dour and The Great Sluice to flush the shingle from the harbour mouth. At the height of operations in the 1580s, 1000 men with 500 carts were at work under the direction of engineer Thomas Digges. In 1606 the warden and assistants of the Dover Harbour Board were established by royal charter.[98] Although Dover harbour suffered from the constant assault of silt and shingle, the town and port prospered during the sixteenth and seventeenth centuries. Markets were held in the town on Wednesdays and Saturdays. An annual fair lasting nine days began on 11 November, the feast of St Martin. Other fairs were held on 25 July, the feast of St James, and 24 August, the feast of St Bartholomew.[99] The 1566 survey showed 358 houses in the town and twenty ships in the harbour employing 130 men in trading and fishing, suggesting a total population of 1,700.[100] During the seventeenth century Dover ships increasingly supplied the London markets with corn and other produce.[101] Between 1570 and 1670 Dover's population increased to 3,000, placing Dover twenty-third in the ranking of English provincial towns between 1660 and 1670.[102]

Supplementing its long history as a commercial port and head port of the Cinque Ports, Dover also has a long history as a religious centre with three religious houses and seven pre-Reformation parish churches. Sometime before his death in 640 Eadbald, king of Kent, had established twenty-two secular canons to serve in the church of St Mary within Dover Castle. Wihtred, king of Kent (690–725), later transferred the canons to St Martin's Church, erected near the market place in the centre of the town. Referred to in later centuries as St Martin's the Less, the church was destroyed in the fire of 1066 but rebuilt after the Conquest by Odo, bishop of Bayeux, and subsequently known as St Martin's le Grand. In 1130 Henry I transferred the church to the monks of Christ Church, Canterbury, but in 1131 also granted it to the archbishop and the cathedral for the foundation of a reformed monastery of canons regular. This double grant led to a long struggle between the monks and the archbishop; however, a new monastery for Benedictine monks was eventually constructed outside the walls of the town and dedicated to St Mary and St Martin. Building work began under Archbishop Corbeil and was completed by Archbishop Theobald in 1139. Along with the greater part of the town the priory was burned when the French landed at Dover in 1295 but was rebuilt and continued as a cell of Christ Church, Canterbury, until its surrender in November 1535.[103] A second religious house, the Hospital of St Mary or the Maison Dieu, was founded by Hubert de Burgh in the early thirteenth century, was granted numerous royal charters by Henry III beginning in 1227, and was administered by a master and brethren of the hospital. Devoted to the maintenance of the poor and infirm and the provision of hospitality for the many travellers and pilgrims that passed through the town, the Maison Dieu was eventually surrendered to the Crown in December 1544.[104] A third religious house, the Praemonstratensian Abbey of St Radegund, located less than three miles southwest of Dover along the Dover to Folkestone road, was founded in 1191 and suppressed in 1538.[105]

In addition to these religious houses Dover also supported seven pre-Reformation parish churches. The Domesday Book mentions four churches, probably the churches of St Martin, St Peter, and St Mary near the medieval market place, and St Mary de Castro situated on Castle Hill east of the Roman lighthouse. The latter church, incorporating part of the Roman fortifications in its west tower, probably dates from the late tenth or early eleventh century with considerable alterations in the late twelfth century.[106] The parishes of St James, St Mary, and St Peter are mentioned in a charter granted by Archbishop Richard of Dover around 1180.[107] Under a unique arrangement among Kentish parishes, the church of St Martin le Grand contained three parishes under one roof after the twelfth-century removal of the priory from the Norman church in the market place to the new site outside the town walls. The parishes of St John the Baptist, St Martin, and St Nicholas served separate areas of the town but all maintained separate altars under the roof of the former abbey church, as described by John Leland in the sixteenth century: 'The towne is deuided in to .vj. paroches, wherof .iij. be under one rofe at .S. Martines yn the hart of the town.'[108] During the medieval period there was a close relationship between the corporation of Dover and the ecclesiastical authorities at St Martin's. The churchyard served as the market place for the weekly market and the site of the annual St Martin's fair held under the jurisdiction of the prior of Dover.[109] Common assemblies were held in the church, the muniment box of the corporation was kept in the church, and the sexton of the church was paid by the corporation. By the time of Archbishop Warham's visitation in 1511, however, St Martin's had fallen into disrepair.[110] In 1536 the church was pulled down, the fabric sold, the stone reused for the new court hall and harbour fortifications, and the site leased for grazing land.[111]

FAVERSHAM

The market town and port of Faversham are located along the Swale on the north Kent coast just north of Watling Street. The mouth of Faversham Creek opens into the Swale, part of the Thames separating Kent from the Isle of Sheppey and in medieval times the usual passage along the north Kent coast for all vessels to London. When John Leland visited Faversham in the sixteenth century, he noted: 'Ther cummeth a creke to the towne that bereth uessels of .xx. tunnes, and a mile fro thens north est is a large key cawled Thorn to disscharge bygge uessels.'[112] As early as 811 a charter of Cenwulf, king of Mercia, had identified Faversham as a royal ville or town.[113] At the time of the Domesday survey the town still belonged to the king and possessed a market, a mill, and seventy households.[114]

In 1147 King Stephen founded the abbey of St Saviour at Faversham for an abbot and twelve monks taken from the monastery of Bermondsey, east of Southwark, and endowed it with the manor of Faversham. Both Stephen and Queen Maud were later buried in the abbey church.[115] As early as the time of Edward the Confessor, however, the barons of Faversham had also functioned as a member of the Cinque Ports associated with the head port of Dover. A charter of Henry III in 1252 recognized Faversham as a corporate member of the Cinque Ports, granted the town a mayor and twelve jurats, and confirmed their ancient privileges of freedom of trade, freedom from fines and taxation, and the liberty not to plead in the hundred or shire courts.[116] Nevertheless, the town remained answerable to the abbot of Faversham Abbey, who also served as lord of the manor of Faversham, appointed a bailiff, and audited the town chamberlains' accounts. These overlapping royal grants and jurisdictions led to frequent conflict between the abbot and the town. A dispute concerning election of the mayor following the 1252 charter, for example, finally led to an agreement in 1258 under which the town submitted three names to the abbot who then appointed the mayor. At the beginning of the fourteenth century further litigation in the king's court in Westminster eventually ended in an agreement in 1310 to release the town from certain manorial customs in consideration of an annual payment to the abbot of £10.[117] Until the suppression of the monastery in 1538, however, the oath of the mayor and the jurats still contained a pledge to maintain the freedom and rights of the monastery.[118] In 1546

Henry VIII granted the town a new charter, confirmed by Edward VI in 1547. The government of Faversham, formerly in the hands of the mayor, jurats, and abbot, was given to the mayor, twelve jurats, and forty-four freemen, along with the right to hold a court of portmote, a court of piepowder, a gaol, and the power to make by-laws. The market and the fairs, which had previously belonged to the abbey, also passed to the town.[119]

In addition to these important changes in local government following the surrender of Faversham Abbey in 1538, the Reformation also affected the town in other ways. In 1527 Dr Cole, a warden of All Souls College in Oxford, had given money and lands to the abbot and monks to establish a grammar school in Faversham; however, the school had not been successfully launched before the dissolution of the abbey. A petition to Queen Elizabeth eventually resulted in the foundation and endowment by royal charter in 1576 of the Free Grammar School of Elizabeth Queen of England, in Faversham.[120] A second religious house, the nearby Hospital of St Mary, called Maison Dieu, on Ospringe Street, founded by Henry III for a master and three friars of the order of the Holy Cross to provide hospitality to pilgrims and travellers, had been granted to St John's College, Cambridge, in 1516 by Henry VIII.[121] Also in 1539 the Faversham parish church of St Mary of Charity finally passed out of monastic control following the surrender of St Augustine's Abbey, Canterbury, which had owned the advowson of the church since 1070, an arrangement that over the years had led to additional conflict between the town and monastic authorities (see Appendix 3).[122]

The economy of the town in the late sixteenth and seventeenth centuries was based primarily on its local markets and its port. A market house, supported on pillars, was erected at the north end of the market place in 1574 with three rows of shambles for weekly markets on Wednesdays and Saturdays.[123] Two fairs, each lasting seven days, were held annually on 14 February, St Valentine's Day, and 1 August, Lammas Day.[124] A trading guild named the Mercers Company, comprising fifty-two different trades and appointing a master, warden, clerk, and beadle, was established by by-laws in 1616. No one was allowed to trade in the town unless apprenticed to a guild member or admitted to the company by gift or fine.[125] From the time of Elizabeth the town specialized in the manufacture of gunpowder; however, the town derived most of its income from coastal trading and fishing, the Swale having been the site of an ancient oyster fishery.[126] In 1566 the survey of the Kent coast revealed 380 houses in the town and eighteen ships in the estuary employing fifty men in maritime trade and fishing.[127] During the early seventeenth century Faversham carried on an extensive shipping trade, supplying the London market with corn and fruit from the fertile arable land of northeast Kent.[128] The population increased from about 1,510 in 1563 to about 1,630 in 1671.[129] In the late sixteenth century the town also became famous for the notorious murder of its former mayor, Thomas Arden, by his wife's lover in 1551, a tale related by Holinshed in his *Chronicle* in 1586 and dramatized in the anonymous tragedy *Arden of Feversham* in 1592.[130]

FOLKESTONE

On the south coast of Kent about five miles southwest of Dover and three miles east of Hythe stands the Cinque Port town of Folkestone. Numerous Roman ruins, perhaps built over earlier

Celtic remains, indicate that the site was occupied from the first century until the late fourth century, probably by a small military or naval detachment of the 'Classis Britannica,' or British fleet, connected with coastal defence.[131] In 630 King Eadbald, son of Æthelberht, founded a nunnery on the cliff close to the seashore for his daughter Eanswithe, the first abbess, and endowed the monastery with the manor of Folkestone. Like other royal monasteries on the Kentish coast, the Folkestone abbey was attacked and destroyed by the Danes. In 927 King Athelstan restored the nunnery, which in 1052 was again destroyed by Earl Godwin. In 1095 the abbey of St Mary and St Eanswithe was refounded as a Benedictine foundation. When relentless erosion of the sea cliffs threatened the monastic buildings, William de Averenches, lord of the manor of Folkestone, granted the monks permission in 1137 to remove the monastery to the current site, where a new priory and parish church of St Mary and St Eanswithe were erected. Rebuilt in the thirteenth century, the parish church was enlarged and rebuilt again in the Perpendicular style during the fifteenth century. The abbey was surrendered on 15 November 1535.[132]

During the Saxon and early Norman periods Folkestone was governed by the lord of the manor, who held the advowson of the parish church, had custody of the priory when the abbacy was vacant, and controlled the affairs of the manor in his five manorial courts.[133] Through the influence of successive lords of the manor, Folkestone developed as a market town and trading centre. In 1205 Geoffrey fitz Peter, lord justiciar, obtained the right to hold a market in Folkestone every Thursday, a right that was renewed to William de Averenches in 1215. During the fourteenth century the status of Folkestone as a market town increased with the grant in 1349 of a second weekly market on Tuesdays. In 1390 Sir John de Clinton obtained the further grant of a Wednesday market and a yearly fair on the feast of St Giles, 1 September.[134] The town's income derived principally from its stone quarries, from fishing, and from the weekly markets.

From at least the twelfth century Folkestone had also been designated a limb of the Cinque Ports attached to the head port of Dover. A now lost charter of Stephen (1135–54) exempted the men of Folkestone from tolls and customs 'as my men of Dover have been.'[135] The royal wardrobe accounts for 1299–1300 show Folkestone contributing a cock-boat toward the ship service required by Edward I.[136] In 1313 Edward II granted a charter to the Barons of the Town of Folkestone, a name later altered to the Mayor, Jurats, and Commonalty of the Town of Folkestone. Each year at the blowing of the brazen horn on 8 September, the feast of the Nativity of St Mary the Virgin, the freemen of the town assembled at the cross in the churchyard of St Mary and St Eanswithe. After the town custumal was read, the freemen elected a mayor and twelve jurats and, after 1545, also twenty-four councillors to govern the town. Like the other Cinque Port towns Folkestone enjoyed freedom from taxation and tolls and administered its own courts, its freemen being exempt from litigation in the hundred and shire courts.[137]

In spite of its status as a market town and corporate member of the Cinque Ports, Folkestone remained a small town throughout the medieval and early modern periods. Domesday Book reports just over 300 households of tenant farmers and smallholders living in the manor of Folkestone.[138] The 1566 survey of the Kent coast reported only 120 houses in the town and twenty-five ships in the harbour with seventy men employed in fishing.[139] During the late sixteenth and seventeenth centuries Folkestone remained a small fishing town with a total population of about 350 in 1563 rising to about 500 in 1671.[140]

FORDWICH

Along the banks of the River Stour about three miles east of Canterbury stands the town of Fordwich. Situated at the former tidal limit of the Stour estuary, Fordwich during the Anglo-Saxon period developed into a small trading centre that functioned as the port for Canterbury under the governance of a portreeve. First mentioned in a charter of King Hlothhere in 675, Fordwich appears in subsequent toll charters of the eighth century, producing a 'substantial income from tolls for the Kentish kings.'[141] In Domesday Book the town is described as a 'parvus burgus,' ie, a small fortified town with ninety-six 'manurae terrae' or dwelling plots, although as Tim Tatton-Brown notes: 'Despite being called a *burh*, Fordwich never had its own defences and the use of the word *burgus* must here have denoted a purely administrative function.'[142] The estimated population at the time of the Conquest was at least 400.[143]

In 1055 Edward the Confessor gave two-thirds of the land in Fordwich to St Augustine's Abbey. The remainder passed to the abbey after the Conquest, remaining in its possession until the Dissolution in 1538. In the same charter Edward the Confessor gave to the abbot 'the right to levy a toll on all merchandise brought to Fordwich by water together with anchorage, lastage and bulkage of vessels.'[144] In the twelfth century a charter of Henry II, quoted in the town custumal, granted the town a merchants' guild and freedom from tolls.[145] Economic rivalry between the freemen of Fordwich and the Abbey of St Augustine's eventually led to an alliance between the town of Fordwich and the Cinque Port town of Sandwich. As early as 1229 Fordwich was designated a member of the Cinque Ports and a corporate limb of Sandwich liable to provide one ship for its head port.[146] The general charters of Henry III in 1260 and Edward I in 1278 enumerating the liberties of the Cinque Ports may have inspired reorganization of local government in Fordwich, for by 1292, when the mayor is first mentioned, the borough was being referred to as the Mayor, Jurats and Commonalty of the Town and Port of Fordwich.[147] From that time forward the town was governed by a mayor and twelve jurats elected on the first Monday after the feast of St Andrew, when the church bell of St Mary the Virgin tolled and the commonalty assembled. Serving as justices of the peace within the bounds of the liberty, the mayor and jurats held unlimited jurisdiction in criminal and civil cases, coroner cases, and matters of probate. After this reorganization of local government the abbot of St Augustine's, who continued to appoint his own bailiff until the Dissolution, submitted his appointees to the mayor for approval.[148]

The town's income came principally from quay dues, bridge tolls, land rents, and its fishery, stretching for nine miles along the river – Fordwich trout from the River Stour being reckoned a great delicacy. As the River Stour and the Wantsum gradually filled with silt and the Stour estuary became dry land during the fifteenth and sixteenth centuries, however, Fordwich lost its shipping trade and went into decline. The continual renegotiations for ship service paid to Sandwich and the meagre rewards paid to travelling entertainers during the sixteenth century all testify to the town's terminal decline.[149] In 1563 the estimated population had dropped to 120.[150] Only the church of St Mary the Virgin, the sixteenth-century court hall, and a modest collection of houses on the banks of the River Stour, now ten miles inland from the Stour mouth at Pegwell Bay, still remain of this once thriving Cinque Port town.

HYTHE

In Roman and Saxon times the ancient River Limen crossed the north side of Romney Marsh flowing eastward to reach the sea near the present day town of Hythe on the south coast of Kent.[151] A long harbour or haven, protected by shingle banks, provided safe anchorage for the original Roman settlement and fort Portus Lemanis about three miles west of Hythe where the Roman military road from Canterbury terminated and where the old sea cliffs and Roman ruins may still be traced along the northern edge of what is now Romney Marsh. During the Saxon period the settlement had migrated a mile eastward to West Hythe and by the Conquest even further eastward to the present site of the town, as the drift of shingle and the silting up of the river estuary progressively destroyed the harbours.[152] By the late eleventh century the Saxon town of Hythe was an urban trading centre of strategic importance, already performing ship service for the late-Saxon kings. Domesday Book records 231 burgesses in Hythe with an estimated population of over 1,000 people.[153] A head port of the Cinque Ports, Hythe still owns a copy of the general charter of the Cinque Ports granted by Edward I in 1278. An earlier charter of Henry II in 1156 confirms the town's rights and liberties extending back to William the Conqueror, for whom Hythe was obligated to provide five ships.[154] Hythe was also a market town, holding a market each Saturday and fairs annually on St Peter's Day (29 June) and the feast of St Edmund the King (20 November).[155]

During the fourteenth and fifteenth centuries, however, the ancient harbour of Hythe gradually filled with silt and the fortunes of the town declined. In his Collectanea John Leland commented: 'Hithe hath bene a uery great towne yn lenght, and conteyned .iiij. paroches that now be clene destroied, yat is to say .S. Nicolas paroche, our Lady paroch, S. Michaels paroche, and our lady of Westhithe, ye which is with yn lesse then half a myle of Lymme hille. And yt may be well supposed that after the hauen of Lymme and the great [h]old town there fayled that hithe strayte therby encresed and was yn price. Finally to cownt fro Westhyue to the place wher the substans of the towne ys now ys .ij. good myles yn lenght, al along on the shore to the which the se cam ful sumtyme, but now by bankinge of w[h]oose and great casting up of shyngel the se ys sumtyme a quarter, sumtyme di. a myle fro the old shore.'[156] When Leland visited Hythe in the 1530s, the town still had its harbour or haven. Fifty years later in 1586, however, Camden commented about Hythe: 'neere to Sandgate, Hith is situated, one of the Cinque ports, whereof it assumed that name, which in the English Saxons tongue signifieth an haven or harbour: although hardly it maintaineth that name now, by reason of sands, and the Sea withdrawing it selfe from it.'[157] As the sea retreated, the population decreased. The 1566 survey of the Kent coast registered only 122 houses in the town, thirty-three boats, and 160 men engaged in shipping or fishing.[158] The surviving evidence of Hythe wills indicates that a large proportion of the town's population during the fifteenth and early sixteenth centuries still earned its living from the sea; however, by the end of the sixteenth century the decay of the haven brought the end of commercial shipping at Hythe, although fishing from smaller boats that could be drawn up on the shingle beach continued to be the mainstay of Hythe's economy.[159] The 1563 diocesan survey suggests a population of about 550 rising slightly to about 750 in 1663.[160]

From Saxon times the town of Hythe had been attached to the manor of Saltwood. In 1036 during the reign of Cnut the manor was given to Christchurch, Canterbury, and came into the possession of Archbishop Lanfranc after the Conquest. Until the sixteenth century the town was governed by the archbishop's bailiff and twelve jurats, who met in the chapel of St Edmund in the north transept of St Leonard's Church to conduct the business of the town. In 1541, when Archbishop Thomas Cranmer exchanged the manor of Saltwood for other lands belonging to Henry VIII, the town passed into the hands of the Crown. In 1575 Elizabeth I granted a charter to the Mayor, Jurats, and Commonalty of the Town and Port of Hythe, who then met annually at Candlemas in the room above the south porch of St Leonard's Church to elect twenty-four commoners, twelve jurats, and the mayor.[161]

From the late fourteenth century St Leonard's was the only church still in use in Hythe. The Norman chancel was pulled down early in the thirteenth century and a new chancel built in the Early English style with a flight of steps separating the choir from the nave. During the fourteenth century the nave aisles were raised and Decorated windows inserted.[162] Chapels and altars were maintained in the chancel for St Leonard, in the south choir aisle for St Mary, in the north choir aisle for St Catherine, in the north transept for St Edmund, king and martyr, and in the south transept for St James. Lights were also kept burning before images of St John the Baptist, St John the Evangelist, St Anthony, Corpus Christi, St Mary of the Assumption, and St Christopher. During the fifteenth and early sixteenth centuries there were also fraternities or brotherhoods of St John and St Catherine.[163] Perched on the steep slope of the cliffs above the two or three streets that ran parallel to the sea, the imposing church of St Leonard during medieval times, as it does still today, dominated the Cinque Port town of Hythe.

LYDD

Now a small Cinque Port town located well inland on the marshland bordering the southern Kentish coast, about three miles southwest of Romney, the former Roman settlement of Lydd once stood on the estuary of the River Rother and probably derived its name from the Latin word 'litus,' or seashore. In Saxon times Lydd, or 'Hlida' as it was then known, belonged to the archbishop of Canterbury, having been granted to Archbishop Jaenberht by King Offa in 774, and was governed by his bailiff.[164] Remains of a Saxon aisled basilica incorporated in the north and west walls of the Lydd parish church of All Saints may date from the late eighth or early ninth century, in which case the church no doubt was plundered when the Danes sailed up the River Rother and wintered in Appledore in 893, or from the middle of the tenth century, built after peace had been restored.[165]

Lydd is not mentioned in Domesday Book, which mentions only the hundred of Langport in which the town is situated; however, shortly after the Conquest Lydd began to appear in the Cinque Port charters.[166] The earliest surviving Lydd charter granted by Edward III in 1364 confirms an earlier charter granted to Lydd by Edward II in 1313, a general charter granted to the Cinque Ports and letters patent granted to Lydd by Edward I in 1290, and an even earlier charter of Henry II recognizing Lydd as a corporate member of the Cinque Ports and a limb of the head port of Romney and declaring them as free from toll and tax 'as they have been in the time of

King Henry our grandfather,' that is, in the time of Henry I.[167] In exchange for the privileges and liberties of the Cinque Ports, Lydd provided a fifth part of the ship service levied on the men of Romney. Lydd reached its height as an active port in the twelfth and thirteenth centuries. In 1287, however, a disastrous storm redirected the River Rother southwest to reach the sea at Rye, leaving both Lydd and Romney stranded inland as silt and shingle gradually filled the Rother estuary during the fourteenth and fifteenth centuries and the coast moved southward. When the antiquary John Leland visited Lydd in the early sixteenth century, he noted that 'the townesch men use botes to the se, the which at this tyme is a myle of.'[168] During the sixteenth century Lydd had a weekly market on Thursdays and an annual fair on 11 July, the Translation of St Benedict; however, the economy of the town continued to contract. In 1563 the diocesan survey showed an estimated population of only 750.[169] Memoranda in the earliest town account book suggest election of town officials at irregular intervals, but after 1476 the bailiff and jurats were elected and the accounts audited annually on 22 July, the feast of St Mary Magdalene, the same day on which the churchwardens of All Saints' Church were elected.

In the thirteenth century the parish church of All Saints was rebuilt, the present nave, chancel, and aisles all dating from the Early English period. The west tower, soaring 132 feet in height, was probably added between 1435 and 1450. Numerous side chapels, lights, and fraternities demonstrate the late medieval devotion of the parishioners of Lydd during the fifteenth and early sixteenth centuries. The church had altars and chapels dedicated to St John the Baptist, St Nicholas, and the Virgin Mary and further altars dedicated to St James, St Peter, and the Holy Trinity. Lights were kept burning before the images of the Virgin Mary, All Saints, St George, St Catherine, St John the Baptist, and St Peter. Fifteenth-century guilds or fraternities of parishioners included those dedicated to the Holy Trinity, All Saints, St James, St John the Baptist, St Catherine, St Mary, St Peter, and St George, the latter perhaps having inspired the parish play of St George.[170]

MAIDSTONE

Seven miles south of Rochester along the River Medway stands the county town of Maidstone. Extensive remains of coins, burial urns, and ruined villas and cemeteries indicate Roman settlement in the Maidstone area dating from AD 75–380 along the north-south Roman road from Rochester to Hastings, evidence also surviving in the modern day place names of Week Street (deriving from the Old English 'wīc' and Latin 'vicus') and Stone Street still forming the main north-south route through the town.[171] Little evidence survives for Anglo-Saxon settlement in the Maidstone area; however, Domesday Book records that the manor of Maidstone belonged to the archbishop and lists eighty-eight households of tenant farmers and smallholders.[172] The presence of a minster church, always located in Kent on royal or archiepiscopal estates, may suggest the archbishop's control of the area as early as the seventh century.[173]

During the twelfth and thirteenth centuries Maidstone gradually developed into a populous market town and administrative centre. The manor of Maidstone included the surrounding parishes of Boxley, Detling, East Farleigh, East and West Barming, Linton, Loose, and part of the parishes of Bearsted, Hunton, Marden and Staplehurst. Maidstone served not only as the administrative centre of the archbishop's manor but also as the centre of the hundred of Maidstone, one of fifteen hundreds or half-hundreds in the lathe of Aylesford.[174] Nearby Penenden Heath, the traditional meeting place for the county, also served as the site of the sheriff's court.[175] In 1261 Archbishop Boniface obtained a charter for a weekly market on Thursdays, although there is some evidence for a market in the town at a much earlier date.[176] As well as serving the local area at its weekly market, Maidstone from an early date also specialized in the production, working, and export of stone from its quarries.[177] By the beginning of the fourteenth century the population of the town was around 2,000, falling to about 1,700 after the Black Death in 1349. Poll tax returns revealed a population of 844 inhabitants over the age of fourteen in 1377.[178]

During the fourteenth and fifteenth centuries the town also developed into an ecclesiastical centre. Archbishop Stephen Langton had acquired the Maidstone rectory as a residence early in the thirteenth century. Rebuilt and extended by successive archbishops during the fourteenth century, it became the principal residence for Archbishop Courtenay (1381–96), who obtained a licence from Richard II on 2 August 1395 to establish a college of secular canons and to convert the parish church of St Mary into the collegiate church of All Saints with a master and twenty-four chaplains and clerks. The building work was completed by Archbishop Arundel in 1398. The first stone bridge across the Medway may have also been built around this time.[179] About the same time the principal residents of Maidstone formed the guild or fraternity of Corpus Christi, one of several chantries at the parish church of All Saints. Officially confirmed by letters patent in 1445, the fraternity had been functioning as early as 1422, when it acquired the hall in Earl Street where the annual feast was held on Corpus Christi Day, and formed the focus of the late medieval civic and cultural life of the community.[180]

The Reformation altered not only the religious, but also the civic, life of Maidstone. The College of All Saints was dissolved in 1547, followed by the suppression of the fraternity of Corpus Christi. From ancient times the archbishop had appointed a portreeve who, assisted by his twelve brethren, had governed the town and presided over a court called a portmote. In July 1549, however, Maidstone was incorporated by a charter of Edward VI as the Mayor, Jurats, and Commonalty of the Town of Maidstone. This first charter of incorporation provided for government by a mayor and twelve jurats elected at Michaelmas and granted the town a common seal, a grammar school, and power to pass by-laws and hold courts. In 1549 the corporation also founded a grammar school in the hall of the dissolved Corpus Christi fraternity and endowed the school with the fraternity's estates. In 1554, after the town petitioned Mary to retain the Protestant religion and supported Sir Thomas Wyatt of Allington Castle in his rebellion against Mary, the town's charter was forfeited. Seven of Kent's sixty-seven Marian martyrs were burned in the town centre. In 1559, however, the town received a new charter from Elizabeth I, confirming the town's earlier charter and granting Maidstone the right to return two burgesses to parliament.[181] As a visible symbol of the power and authority of the town's new civic oligarchy, Maidstone built its first court hall during the first decade of the seventeenth century.[182]

During the late sixteenth and early seventeenth centuries Maidstone became the chief market town and administrative centre for central Kent. Its Edwardian and Elizabethan charters had confirmed the town's weekly market and its four fairs held annually at Candlemas (2 February) and the feasts of Sts Philip and James (1 May), St Edmund (9 June), and St Faith (6 October).[183] During the time of Elizabeth there were five craft guilds: Artificers, Cordwainers, Drapers, Mercers, and Victuallers. A further boost to the town's economy came during the 1560s and 1570s from the settlement in the town of the Walloons, who established the manufacture of linen and woollen textiles. The seventeenth century also saw the growth of paper making and the brewing trade. During the latter half of the sixteenth century Maidstone was well established as the quarter sessions town for west Kent, and by the early seventeenth century Maidstone had also established itself as the county assize town.[184]

During the same period the population of Maidstone also increased. The 1548 chantry return showing 1,440 communicants suggests a total population of about 2,100. The return for the 1557 ecclesiastical visitation gives 1,600 communicants for the urban part of the parish, indicating a population of around 2,400, and 1,776 communicants in the whole parish, indicating a total population of 2,600. The parish registers show a drop to 2,000 during the 1560s, due to an outbreak of the plague, and then a steady rise to 2,300 in the 1570s, 2,700 in the 1580s, 2,900 in 1590s, and possibly 3,000 by the turn of century. During the early seventeenth century the population continued to rise, reaching about 3,500 to 3,600 inhabitants in the 1610s and 1620s and perhaps 4,000 by the end of the 1630s, before falling back closer to 3,000 after the Civil War.[185]

NEW ROMNEY

Romney Marsh and the southern coastline of Kent have altered considerably over the centuries. During Roman times the coast line formed a concave arc from Hythe in the east to Fairlight in Sussex in the west. Degraded remains of the chalk cliffs along the ancient sea coast can be seen at Lympne and as far inland as Appledore and the Isle of Oxney where the ancient River Limen or Rother opened into a wide estuary of marshland, mud flats, and multiple river channels to the sea.[186] A channel from Appledore eastward to Port Lympne and West Hythe was in use during the Roman period but had progressively silted up from the fourth century onwards. Although mentioned in Romney Marsh charters as late as the ninth and tenth centuries, the channel probably was not navigable by that time.[187] During the Saxon period another channel flowed around the Isle of Oxney from Appledore southward toward Rye and then eastward to the sea at Romney, separating Old Romney and New Romney on the northern shore from Lydd on the southern shore, a channel large enough to allow the Viking fleet to sail up as far as Appledore in 892.[188] A smaller channel also flowed southward from Appledore through Snargate and Brenzett to Romney.[189] As shingle banks built up along the coastline, the marshland of Romney Marsh and Walland Marsh was gradually inned and drained and reclaimed for pasture and cultivation.[190]

In the mid-thirteenth century several violent storms flooded the marshes and diverted the course of the River Rother.[191] A patent roll dated 21 June 1258 notes that 'the port of Rumenal is perishing, to the detriment of the town of Rumenal,' because of the diversion of the river from its ancient course, and provides for the extension of the artificial channel for the Rother known as the Rhee Wall. This channel consisted of a watercourse from fifty to 100 feet wide between the Romney Marsh Wall on the east and the Walland Marsh Wall on the west, extending for seven miles along the distributary from Appledore to New Romney.[192] Yet another disastrous storm in February 1286/7, however, dealt the decisive blow to the port of Romney, raising the ground level of the town by three feet through a great deposit of shingle and diverting the course of the Rother so that it flowed southwestward to the sea at Rye rather than southeastward to Romney.[193] In spite of the Rhee Wall system, the days of New Romney's port were numbered. Numerous references appear in the New Romney records during the late fourteenth and early fifteenth centuries to 'digging in the Ree'; however, that channel too eventually silted up and by 1427 the space between the walls of the Rhee was let for pasture.[194]

The history of settlement at Romney, comprising the adjacent parishes of Old Romney and New Romney, is equally complex.[195] The first reference to settlement appears in an Anglo-Saxon charter dated 741, granting to the royal nunnery of Lyminge the fishing rights and land containing the houses of fishermen and the oratory of St Martin at the mouth of the River Limen, land which eventually passed to the archbishop after the destruction of the nunnery by the Danes.[196] The name 'Romney' first appears as Rumenea, meaning 'spacious river or estuary' in a charter dated 895.[197] The first evidence for a town at Romney is the establishment of a mint at the beginning of the eleventh century, by which time Romney was already a flourishing port.[198] Four different entries in the Domesday Book show a total of 156 burgesses at Romney already providing ship service to the king, a total implying a population in the town of at least 800.[199] Until the mid-twelfth century the historical record does not distinguish between 'Old Romney' and 'New Romney.' The settlement now known as New Romney was always referred to as 'Romene' or 'Romenel' or 'Rumenal' and continued to be referred to simply as Romney as late as the fifteenth century. The earliest mention of the name Old Romney ('de Veteri Romenal') first appears in 1140, the settlement now known as Old Romney having originally been referred to as 'Afettune' or 'Offetane' or 'Offeton.' From the thirteenth century onwards the prefix 'old' was always added to distinguish that part of Romney from the remainder of the town, and the name Afettune dropped out of use.[200] The consistent use of the names New Romney and Old Romney beginning in the fifteenth and sixteenth centuries has given rise to the suggestion that the town had moved to a new location during the early Middle Ages due to the silting up of the harbour at Old Romney.[201] The documentary and archaeological evidence of the ancient churches within the liberty of Romney further complicates the complexity of the town's development.[202] St Nicholas' Church at New Romney dates from the early twelfth century, while St Clement's Church at Old Romney dates from the late twelfth century.[203] Two further parish churches, St Laurence's and St Martin's, were also established in New Romney by the early twelfth century; however, a now destroyed church of St Laurence was still standing at Old Romney in the late thirteenth century along with a possible church of St Michael.[204] A chapel of St Martin of Northne, part of Old Romney, is also mentioned in the thirteenth-century register of town clerk Daniel Rough as a separate chapelry distinct from both the church of St Martin and the hundred of St Martin in which the town was located.[205] Whatever geologists, archaeologists, and historians may eventually conclude about the settlement history of the town and port of Romney, however, there is little doubt that by the sixteenth century Romney had entered terminal decline. During the 1530s John Leland noted: "ºRumeney a .iiij. myles or more from Lymmehil.º. Rumeney is one of the .v. portes and hath bene a metely good hauen yn so much that withyn remembrance of men shyppes haue cum hard up to the towne and cast ancres yn one of the chyrchyardes ⟨.⟩ the se is now a .ij. myles fro the towne so sore therby now decayed that where there wher .iij. great paroches and chirch[es] sumtyme is now scant one wel mayteined.'[206] The 1563 diocesan survey revealed an estimated population of only 200.[207]

As a town and port Romney had reached its height of commercial prosperity and architectural activity between the twelfth and fourteenth centuries. The poll tax returns for 1377 and 1382 show eighty-nine adults in Old Romney and 941 in New Romney assessed for tax, implying a total population of 133 in Old Romney and 1,412 in New Romney in addition to priests and paupers, who were exempt from the tax.[208] The assessments show that during the 1380s the town was divided into the thirteen wards of Holyngbroke, Bochery, Hospital, Codde, Joce, Sharle, Bartelot, Highmell, Hammersnoth, Olbord, Colbrand, Deme, and Hope, although the location of most of these cannot now be traced.[209] In addition to the fishing and trade carried on in the port, the town held a weekly market on Saturdays and an annual fair at the feast of St Laurence (10 August).[210] The commercial prosperity of the town was reflected in its architectural activity. During the second half of the twelfth century, the early twelfth-century church of St Nicholas was enlarged by the addition of aisles and a west tower. During the thirteenth century the aisles were widened, followed in the fourteenth century by the extension of the chancel with side chapels dedicated to St Mary and St Stephen. Guilds or brotherhoods were established for St Catherine, St Clement, St Edmund, St George, St John, St John the Baptist, and St Stephen. The late twelfth-century church of St Clement at Old Romney was also enlarged during the thirteenth and fourteenth centuries and maintained chapels dedicated to St Mary and St Catherine and brotherhoods of St Catherine, St Margaret, and St Mary.[211] Two other parish churches testified to the prosperity of the town. In the southwest area of the town stood the church of St Laurence, where side altars and lights were maintained to St Catherine, St John the Baptist, and the Holy Trinity. The oldest church in Romney, located in the northern part of town, was dedicated to St Martin and also maintained a side chapel and fraternity dedicated to St Mary.

By the early sixteenth century, as the prosperity of the town declined, many of these churches became surplus to requirements and fell into disrepair. The church of St Laurence in Old Romney had disappeared in the late thirteenth century. The visitation of Archbishop Warham in 1511 noted that the chancels of St Martin's and St Laurence's were in danger of falling down. Worship in these churches had ceased by 1539, when the sale of plate is recorded from both churches. In 1549, after town officials petitioned Archbishop Cranmer to allow them to pull down either St Martin's or St Nicholas' since the town was too small to support both churches, the archbishop authorized the destruction of St Martin's.[212] Two other religious institutions in the town also failed to survive the decline of the fifteenth century: the Hospital of St John the Baptist, defunct by 1495, and the Hospital of St Stephen and St Thomas, founded in the twelfth century for the maintenance of lepers, refounded as a chantry for two priests in 1363, and probably disbanded by 1481 when the property passed to Magdalen College, Oxford.[213]

In spite of its economic decline and the loss of its port, New Romney continued to maintain its privileges and responsibilities as a head port of the Cinque Ports. Since the ninth or tenth centuries, when the town passed into the control of the archbishop, Romney had been governed by a bailiff appointed by the archbishop and jurats elected annually by the commoners at the feast of the Annunciation. As the archbishop's officer in the town, the bailiff presided in the town and hundred courts, examined felons, and acted as coroner. Above all he swore an oath to uphold the liberties and customs of the town granted to Romney by the charter of Henry II in 1161, confirming liberties granted to the men of Romney in the time of Henry I. In exchange for the provision of five ships for the king, Romney like the other ports enjoyed freedom from taxation, freedom of trade, the right to hold their own courts, and the right to representation in parliament, liberties described in great detail in the general charter of Edward I to the ports in 1278.[214] When town clerk John Forsett translated the town custumal in 1564, the town was still following the same basic rules established in its early charters and its fourteenth-century custumal. The only major change in local government came that same year when Queen Elizabeth granted the town a new charter, confirming its ancient liberties and providing for the election of a mayor by the jurats and commoners. Since the middle of the fourteenth century the town of Romney also functioned as the administrative centre of the Cinque Port court of Brotherhood, which met twice annually in the town on the Tuesday in Easter Week and the Tuesday after the feast of St Margaret (20 July).[215]

SANDWICH

Sandwich first appears in the records as a seventh-century trading settlement near the Saxon shore fort of Richborough at the eastern end of the Wantsum Channel, then an arc-shaped stream of tidal water separating the Isle of Thanet from the mainland of Kent. Geological evidence demonstrates that the Wantsum once had a breadth of two miles and a depth of forty feet; however, the relentless deposit of shingle at Stonar on the south coast of Thanet opposite Sandwich eventually blocked the eastern end of the Wantsum Channel, reducing the tidal flow of the Wantsum and encouraging the deposit of silt from the Stour estuary, which drained into the Channel. By the eighth century Bede estimated the width of the Wantsum Channel at only three furlongs, or three-eighths of a mile. By the seventeenth century the northern arm of the Wantsum Channel had been largely reduced to a system of dykes and marshes, the eastern arm fed primarily by the meandering course of the River Stour separating Sandwich from Stonar. Despite numerous schemes presented to Elizabeth I, James I, and Charles I to save the harbour, the port of Sandwich failed as the Wantsum dwindled and filled with silt, leaving behind a small market town two miles from the sea.[216]

In addition to their doomed battle against geological forces, Sandwich suffered from the invasions of the Danes, who repeatedly burned and pillaged the town between the mid-ninth and mid-eleventh centuries. It was at Sandwich where Olaf's fleet of ninety-three Viking ships was based in 994 and where the English fleet of Æthelred gathered to oppose the Danes in 1006. In 1015 Cnut landed at Sandwich and defeated Æthelred to become king in 1016, followed by Harthacnut, who came to Sandwich with sixty ships after the death of Cnut and was made king by agreement of the Danes and English in 1035. Nevertheless, Sandwich thrived as a port during the late Saxon period. The town expanded. The new parishes of St Mary's on the west side of the town and St Clement's on the east side of the town were probably created in the early eleventh century to supplement the parish of St Peter's in the town centre. By the Conquest Sandwich was a thriving trading centre of 383 houses, three parish churches, and an estimated population of about 2,000, the fourth largest town in the kingdom after London, Norwich, and Ipswich.[217]

During the Danish wars, sometime between 959 and 975, Edgar had granted the town and port of Sandwich to the monks of Christ Church, Canterbury, a grant confirmed in 979 by Æthelred and again in 1023 by Cnut, who also granted the manor of Stonar to the monks of St Augustine's, Canterbury, thus initiating fierce economic rivalry between the monasteries for lucrative import duties. The town was governed by a portreeve appointed by the prior. During the exile of Christ Church monks resulting from the contested election of Archbishop Stephen Langton in 1207, control of the town passed from the priory to King John and remained in dispute until the priory conceded control to Edward I in 1290. The first mayor and town officials were elected during this power struggle between Christ Church and the Crown in the thirteenth century. In 1301, in response to the *quo warranto* proceedings against the town by Edward I, the town clerk, Adam Champneys, recorded the customs of the town in the first custumal, including the election of a mayor and jurats at the sound of the common horn on the Thursday next after St Andrew's Day (30 November), when the townspeople assembled at St Clement's Church.[218] A second power struggle, that between King John and the barons, also affected Sandwich in the early thirteenth century, when the French summoned to assist the barons landed in Thanet and sacked the town in May 1216. Returning in 1217, the French burned Sandwich before being defeated in a sea battle off the town on St Bartholomew's Day (24 August), a victory commemorated by the enlargement of St Bartholomew's Hospital from a resting place for travellers and pilgrims to a permanent shelter for sixteen poor people of the town.[219]

The fortunes of Sandwich fluctuated during the fourteenth and fifteenth centuries. The town reached its peak as a trading centre between 1377 and 1400, when there were 810 inhabited houses and an estimated population of over 3,000.[220] Markets were held in the town on Wednesdays and Saturdays, and an annual fair was held on St Clement's Day, 23 November.[221] The town supported three parish churches. St Clement's Church in the southern part of town maintained brotherhoods of the Corpus Christi, Holy Trinity, St Peter, and St George, who also had a chapel in the south aisle and a procession around the town on his feast day. St Peter's Church in the town centre had a chantry dedicated to St Thomas the Martyr, and beginning in the fourteenth century it maintained brotherhoods of Corpus Christi, St Erasmus, St Mary, and St John of Bridlington, who was canonized in the late fourteenth century. St Mary's Church on the south side of Strand Street had chapels and images dedicated to St Christopher, St James, St John the Evangelist, St Laurence, and St Ursula and a brotherhood of St Christopher. Other religious foundations included the Hospital of St Bartholomew founded about 1190, the Hospital of God and St John the Baptist dating from the reign of Edward I, the Hospital of St Thomas for support of poor persons, founded in the fourteenth century, and a Carmelite friary founded in 1268 and suppressed by Henry VIII in 1538.[222]

In 1385, after Richard II issued a royal order for enclosing and fortifying the town, a stone wall was built to the east along the River Stour. A moat with a steep bank and wooden palisade, broken by four gates, surrounded the town on the other three sides. In spite of these fortifications, the French again attacked the town with a force of sixty ships and 4,000 men in 1457, destroying all but the ancient town centre before aid from the other Cinque Port towns forced the French to retreat.[223] Recovery from this devastating attack was slow, compounded by the severe decline of the harbour in the late fifteenth and sixteenth centuries. By 1560 the population had fallen to about 1,500. The 1563 diocesan survey revealed an estimated population of only 1,010; the 1566 survey showed only 420 houses in the town and only seventeen ships in the harbour employing sixty-two men in trade and fishing.[224] The depression of Sandwich continued until the coming of the Walloons fleeing the religious persecution of Philip II. In 1561 Queen Elizabeth licensed the settlement in Sandwich of twenty-five families of Flemish and Dutch immigrants who were to be engaged in 'making saes, bay and other cloth, which hath not used to be made in this our realme of Englonde, or for fishing in the seas.'[225] The immigrant community quickly increased the population to over 2,000 people, necessitating the removal of the French-speaking Walloons to Canterbury in 1575. The town's population reached a peak of 4,000 during the late sixteenth century, fueled primarily by immigration, before falling back to about 3,200 by 1640.[226] In spite of the economic boost from the Flemish immigration, Sandwich never regained the prominence it had enjoyed in the thirteenth and fourteenth centuries.

TENTERDEN

The Wealden market town of Tenterden is situated eighteen miles southeast of Maidstone and ten miles north of the Sussex town of Rye. Tenterden derives its name from the Anglo-Saxon phrase 'Tenetwara denn,' or 'the denn or swine-pasture of the Thanet people,' for throughout the Saxon period and for long after the Conquest the town was part of the manor of Minster (in Thanet).[227] The earliest surviving Anglo-Saxon charter for Tenterden, dating from 968, confirms this connection with Thanet, for it conveyed land in the parish at Heronden adjacent to the 'Tenetwara brocas,' or the 'meadows of the men of Thanet.'[228] The Anglo-Saxon connection with Thanet also explains the unusual dedication of the Tenterden parish church to St Mildred the Virgin, one of only four Kent churches that bear this dedication. Although Hugo Norman, the first vicar to appear in the records, was presented to the parish church of Tenterden by the abbot of St Augustine's, Canterbury, during the reign of Richard I, the parish church had been established centuries before, probably during the eighth century when the royal abbey of Minster flourished on the Isle of Thanet. Founded in the late seventh century by Egbert and dedicated to the Virgin Mary, the abbey was rededicated to St Mildred the Virgin sometime after 733 to commemorate Mildryth, or Mildred, the second abbess and granddaughter of Egbert. In 840 the manor was looted and the monastery destroyed by the Danes. During the successive Danish invasions of the ninth and tenth centuries, when Thanet was periodically pillaged by the Danes, the manor of Thanet was held by the king until 1027, when Cnut granted it to the Abbey of St Augustine and the relics of St Mildred were transferred to the abbey in 1030. From then until the Dissolution, St Augustine's Abbey owned the manor of Thanet including the parish of Tenterden.[229]

The present church building at Tenterden dates from the second half of the fifteenth century, when the town began its rise to prominence. During the fourteenth and fifteenth centuries the Wealden parishes of Cranbrook, Goudhurst, Hawkhurst, Headcorn, and Tenterden had become centres of clothmaking, taking advantage of the local supplies of fuller's earth and the plentiful supply of wool from the flocks of sheep that grazed on Romney Marsh.[230] On 1 August 1449 Tenterden was incorporated by charter of Henry VI under the title, 'The Bailiff and Commonalty of the Town and Hundred of Tenterden,' and was designated a corporate member of the Cinque Ports and a limb of the Ancient Town of Rye, to which it was connected by the River Rother. The town was governed by a bailiff elected annually by the commonalty on 29 August, the Feast of the Decollation of St John the Baptist. On 16 August 1600 Queen Elizabeth granted Tenterden a new charter that changed the name of the corporation to 'The Mayor, Jurats, and Commons of the Town and Hundred of Tenterden,' provided for government by a mayor and twelve jurats, and removed its administrative ties to Rye. As a result of its membership in the Cinque Ports, Tenterden was granted its own court, presided over by the bailiff. The inhabitants became exempt from all tolls and taxes levied by the shire. In return, using the nearby port of Smallhythe on the River Rother, Tenterden accepted liability for ship duty, rebuilding the 400-ton royal ship, *The Grand Masters*, in 1549 and providing twenty-four men at the time of the Spanish Armada in 1588.[231] In spite of its status as a corporate member of the Cinque Ports and a centre of the Wealden broadcloth industry, Tenterden was never a populous town, the population of the wider parish comprising some 1,200 people in the 1560s, but the town reaching only perhaps 1,000 inhabitants by 1600 and declining to around 500 by the 1660s.[232] Several bequests were made during the 1520s for the establishment of a free grammar school in the town. From the mid-sixteenth century various references to the schoolhouse and schoolmaster appear in the records; however, the school did not thrive and by the early nineteenth century had been absorbed into the National School.[233]

Nobility and Gentry

In 1576 William Lambarde in *A Perambulation of Kent* fostered the notion that the nobility and gentry of Kent were largely recent in origin and heavily influenced by the county's proximity to London: 'The Gentlemen be not heere (throughout) of so auncient stocks as else where, especially in the parts neerer to London, from which citie (as it were from a certeine rich and wealthy seedplot) Courtiers, Lawyers, and Marchants be continually translated, and do become newe plants amongst them.'[234] More recent analysis, however, has shown that the topographical features that determined the settlement and economic development of Kent, rather than the county's proximity to London, exerted greater influence over the location and structure of its ruling class during the Tudor and Stuart periods.[235] Although the county does border London, its peninsular shape placed much of the county beyond the influence of London in the medieval and early-modern periods, leading to a ruling class increasingly indigenous and insular as the distance from London also increased. Nearest to London, in northwest Kent, nearly half of the gentry were Stuart in origin and less than a third were indigenous. Further south around Sevenoaks four-fifths of the gentry had settled in Kent in Tudor or pre-Tudor times, only one-fifth having arrived in Kent during the Stuart period. In the isolated parts of the High Weald nearly all the gentry were Kentish in origin. Further east around Faversham, Ashford, and Canterbury 85 per cent of the gentry were indigenous to Kent. Typical of the gentry in this area was Sir Edward Dering, who maintained his family seat at Surrenden in the parish of Pluckley and traced his Kentish ancestry back to the Domesday Book.[236] Only 3 per cent of the gentry in east Kent were Stuart in origin. It is instructive to remember that Canterbury is as far from the centre of London as is Cambridge or Oxford or Brighton; a circle with a thirty-mile radius, centred in London, reaches only as far east as Maidstone, leaving most of the county untouched. In spite of the county's proximity to London, then, all together only one-eighth of the Kent gentry were Stuart in origin, one-eighth entered the county during the Tudor reign, and the remaining three-quarters were indigenous to the county, including nearly three-quarters of the knights and four-fifths of the peers.[237]

These indigenous county families, such as the Culpepers, Derings, Oxendens, Sondeses, Scotts, and Twysdens, had emerged during the early colonization of the county in the thirteenth and fourteenth centuries, beginning as freeholders and gradually extending their holdings and wealth through marriage and land purchases. By the sixteenth century the Kentish gentry and yeomen families were known for their wealth. In tax returns during the reign of Henry VIII, Kent was surpassed only by Middlesex in the amount of tax per square mile.[238] In 1640–60 the county's peers enjoyed an average annual income of £4,089 (28 per cent of gentry income); baronets received an average of £1,405 (20 per cent), knights £873 (24 per cent), and untitled gentry £270 (28 per cent).[239] It is not surprising, moreover, to find that the county's wealth was related both to the longevity of its gentry families and the location of their family seats. During the 1640s the indigenous gentry and nobility enjoyed average annual incomes of £719 (72 per cent), families of Tudor origin averaged £602 (14 per cent), and families of Stuart origin £683 (11 per cent). The more wealthy gentry families tended to be located in the easternmost lathes of the county where early settlement had begun on the rich loam soil of the lathe of St Augustine or the wooded chartland to the south of the downs in the lathe of Shepway. In contrast the part of the westernmost lathe of Sutton at Hone closest to London contained few county families and only 9 per cent of the county's wealth.[240]

The dispersal of gentry throughout the county followed the pattern of dispersed settlement generally in isolated farms and homesteads with enclosed fields. This ancient colonization of the county by gentry families may be traced in the typical domestic architecture of Kentish manor houses: most country seats began as medieval farmhouses on Saxon or Norman sites with Tudor additions and Jacobean embellishments added to by successive generations of the family. Instead of large landholdings, most gentry families in Kent owned only one or two manors, with many parishes having five or six gentry families with holdings the size of Henry Oxenden's 600 acres at Great Maydekin. This relatively small size of landholdings among the Kent gentry was due partly to the general dispersal of the population and partly to the Kent custom of gavelkind, or partible inheritance, that divided estates equally among male heirs rather than the more usual practice in English common law of male primogeniture. The potential fragmentation of estates over successive generations tended to be counterbalanced by the second principle of gavelkind, the free alienation of lands during the owner's lifetime, which led to a constant flux of buying and selling of land and the increase and decrease of landholding.

Gavelkind tenure, with its division of large estates among family members, did, however, over time produce another distinctive feature of Kentish society, the existence of clans or families with many separately established branches. The Boyses, for example, included two knightly and eight untitled families; the Finches had one peer, one knight, and seven untitled heads of household.[241] The fragmentation of large estates due to partible inheritance and the concomitant development of clans with separately established branches of county families in turn tended to produce a largely immobile, insular, and conservative society. A large majority of Kentish families not only owned no land outside the county but also owned land only in one or two parishes. This insularity in landholding was reinforced by marriage connections between families, with two-thirds of Kentish gentry marrying among their neighbours. Here again the insularity of gentry families increased in direct proportion to the distance from London. 'In the environs of London only one-sixth of them married into Kentish families; along the Upper Stour, where nearly one quarter of all the gentry were seated, 72 per cent; and in east Kent, where more than a further quarter lived, 85 per cent.'[242] Although gentry families often had some family connections in London, the family members who established themselves as London merchants or professionals rarely maintained significant connections with the county where their families maintained their ancient family seats.

During the early modern period the social and political structure of Kentish society, then, was controlled by generally wealthy and largely indigenous county families, dispersed throughout the county but concentrated east of the Medway, grouped in perhaps twenty or thirty clans with separately established family branches, and connected by marriage ties and shared parochial and county responsibilities. Unlike some counties where a single great family or two or three rival families dominated county affairs, there were no great peers in Kent with the possible exception of the Brookes, Lords Cobham with their seats at Cooling Castle and Cobham Hall, and the Nevills, Lords Abergavenny at Birling, both located in west Kent. The Sackvilles at Knole and the Sidneys at Penshurst, who both rose to prominence in the later sixteenth century, were also located in west Kent. In east Kent the largest landowners from early Anglo-Saxon times had been the archbishop, the prior of Christ Church, and the abbot of St Augustine's. The church owned a larger share of land in Kent – as much as one-third of all agricultural land – than it did in other counties. Even before the Dissolution of the monasteries, however, the gentry in 1530 had owned 815 out of 1,348 manorial estates in the county compared to 370 owned by the church, sixty owned by the nobility, and forty-nine owned by the Crown. By 1640, after many of the monastic and Crown estates had been dispersed by gift, sale, and enforced exchange, the gentry owned 1,100 of these manors.[243] Although some gentry families, like the Bakers of Sissinghurst and the Wottons of Boughton Malherbe, accumulated large land holdings after the Dissolution of the monasteries, no one family dominated the social and political landscape of east Kent.[244]

The one exception to this general picture of Kentish gentry and nobility, interconnected by family and social ties and acting communally to control the affairs of the county, was the lord warden of the Cinque Ports and constable of Dover Castle. Most of the ancient boroughs and many smaller towns in east Kent were linked in the federation of the Cinque Ports and Two Ancient Towns, thus extending the lord warden's authority far beyond the four head ports in Kent. The lord warden, moreover, wielded great power and influence, not only within the liberties of the Cinque Ports but also within the county at large, often taking his place on the commissions of the peace, participating in the county quarter sessions, sitting on other special commissions in the county, organizing with the lord lieutenant the defence of the county, and representing the portsmen to the Crown.

Some lord wardens, such as Humphrey Stafford, duke of Buckingham and lord warden 1450–60, Richard Neville, 16th earl of Warwick and lord warden 1461–70, or William Fitz Alan, 21st earl of Arundel and lord warden 1470–87, were appointed from outside the county because of their prominence in national affairs. Few of these lord wardens maintained residences in the county or had much effect on the county outside of their official duties. Other lord wardens, particularly during the sixteenth century, were appointed from within the county families of Kent, thereby increasing their natural sphere of influence in the county. For example, James Fiennes, 1st Lord Saye and Sele, whose seat was at Knole near Sevenoaks, held numerous prominent county offices, including sheriff of Kent from November 1436 to November 1437, MP for Kent throughout the 1440s, and lord warden from 1447 to 1450. During the minority of Henry VIII, who had been appointed lord warden as an infant, Edward Poynings, whose seat was at Westenhanger near Hythe, served first as lieutenant of Dover Castle from 1496 and then as constable of Dover Castle and deputy lord warden from 1505 and lord warden from 1509 to 1521. George Nevill, 5th baron of Abergavenny, whose seat was at Birling in west Kent, acted as lord warden in the absence of Edward Poynings between 1512 and 1515. Sir Edward Guildford, whose seats were at Halden and Hempstead, was constable of Dover Castle and warden of the Cinque Ports from 1521 to 1534. George Boleyn, Lord Rochford, of Hever Castle in west Kent briefly held the two offices between 1534 and 1536, before being tried for treason and beheaded following the downfall of his sister Anne Boleyn. Sir Thomas Cheyne, lord warden from 1536 to 1558, who also held positions in the royal household as well as numerous other appointments in Kent, used his influence to gain more ex-Crown land in Kent after the Dissolution than any other grantee except the archbishop, particularly benefiting from lands formerly belonging to Boxley Abbey, Faversham Abbey, and Minster (in Sheppey) near his residence at Shurland on the Isle of Sheppey.[245] If any lord warden could be singled out as the leader of the Kent gentry and nobility during the sixteenth century, it would be William Brooke, 10th Lord Cobham, a favourite of Queen Elizabeth, who more than once entertained the queen at Cobham Hall and held not only the offices of lord warden of the Cinque Ports, constable of Dover Castle, and lord lieutenant for Kent from 1559 until his death on 6 March 1596/7, but also the office of lord chamberlain of the household from 8 August 1596 until his death. Henry, 11th Lord Cobham, succeeded his father in the offices of lord warden, constable of Dover Castle, and lord lieutenant for a short time until he was arrested for treason and imprisoned in the Tower in 1603. During the seventeenth century, however, many of the lord wardens once again were appointed from outside the county, thus reducing the effect of the office on the indigenous county families.

Drama, Music, and Ceremonial Customs

Travelling Minstrels and Players

The most striking feature of the *Kent: Diocese of Canterbury* entertainment records is the large number of payments to professional travelling minstrels and players. From the earliest recorded payment to 'histrionibus' by the monks of Christ Church Priory on the feast of St Thomas Becket in 1272 until the last recorded payment in Puritan Canterbury on 22 July 1641 'in dischardge of a Companie of plaieres out of Towne by master maiores appointment,' the surviving monastic and borough records of the diocese of Canterbury contain just over 2,400 payments to professional travelling minstrels and players.[1] This figure, although high, represents only part of the actual number of performances by these minstrels and players. The uneven survival of monastic records and several significant gaps in the borough accounts mean that for many years there are few or even no extant records. During some years for which records have survived there are only summary payments for entertainment, such as the payments at Faversham in 1546–7 'to diverse pleyers & Mynstrels' or 'to dyvers noble mens players' in 1569–70. Often medieval and early modern accountants entered individual payments in their rough accounts but then summarized them in their revised accounts at the end of the accounting year, as in the summary payment at Dover for 42s 4d 'geven this yere in Rewarde to sundry noble mens pleyers mynstrelles and other as in the paumflet apperythe' in 1539–40, a year for which 'the paumflet,' or paper booklet containing the itemized rough accounts, has perished and only the summary accounts have survived. Even when fully itemized rough accounts do contain payments to minstrels or players, the official payments made by the mayor or the chamberlain may not represent the only performances by the minstrels or players in a given place. Travelling minstrels and players probably performed as many times as possible in the streets and inns of the town before moving on to the next location.[2] At Canterbury in 1574, for example, the earl of Leicester's players played 'before Master Mayer & his bretherne at the Courte halle' on 3 December and again on 7 December before the dean and chapter of Christ Church Cathedral; however, other probable performances in the town between these dates have gone unrecorded because no official payments were made. Similarly, at Canterbury in 1608–9 the city chamberlains paid for a performance by the queen's men and paid gratuity payments to Lord Chandos' players and Lord Berkeley's players not to play. These three official payments notwithstanding, the diary of Thomas Cocks, auditor to the dean and chapter of

Canterbury Cathedral, includes six payments that same year for 'goynge in to the playe.' The following year, when no official payments by the chamberlains survive, Cocks paid 'for goynge into the playe twise.' Such payments beg the question of which players were playing in the city during those years. The inescapable conclusion must be that the historical record with all its hundreds of payments to players and minstrels preserves only a fraction of all payments for performance. Nevertheless, the surviving payments in the monastic and borough records do contain valuable evidence about professional travelling minstrels and players during the late medieval and early modern periods.

First of all, the borough and monastic accounts distinguish between two types of performers.[3] Of the 2,400 total payments approximately 950 payments were made to players, variously described in the Latin records as 'lusores,' 'ludentes,' or 'homines ludentes,' or in English simply as 'players.' Usually, although not exclusively, these Latin performance terms were used as synonyms for performers who produced mimetic or dramatic entertainment. This category also includes payments for interludes and payments for 'ludi' or plays. The remaining approximately 1,450 payments were made to minstrels, variously described in the Latin records as 'ioculatores,' 'histriones,' 'mimi,' or 'ministralli,' and in the English records as 'jugglers,' 'jesters,' or 'minstrels.' These various medieval Latin performance terms were generally employed throughout the late medieval monastic and borough accounts as synonyms for performers who produced a wide variety of musical and mimetic entertainment. A small number of payments to travelling musical performers described as 'harpers,' 'lute players,' 'pipers,' or 'fiddlers' has also been included here under the general category of minstrels. Sometimes these Latin terms were equated in summary payments for entertainment as, for example, in the payment to 'histrionibus harpatoribus & aliis menestrallis diuersis' in the 1286–7 treasurer's accounts of Christ Church Priory. At other times one term was used in the rough accounts and another in the revised accounts, as at New Romney in 1474–5 when payments in the rough accounts to 'le menstrelis' of the earl of Arundel and the duke of Clarence and the 'Mynistrys' of the king all appear in the revised accounts as 'Mimis.'[4] Often the same performers were described by different terms in different towns. The queen's performers in 1479–80, for example, were described in Canterbury as 'histrionibus domine Regine,' in Dover as 'the quenys Mynstrell',' and in Lydd and New Romney as 'Mimis Regine.'

Whichever term late medieval accountants chose to describe these performers and whatever the exact nature of the entertainment they performed, the records do distinguish between these minstrels on the one hand and players on the other hand. At Dover the chamberlains used the terms 'ministralli' and 'ludentes,' at Hythe, 'ministralli' and 'lusores,' at Lydd, 'mimi' and 'lusores,' at Sandwich, 'histriones' or 'ministralli' and 'homines ludentes.' From the distant perspective of several centuries the exact distinctions between these late medieval and early modern minstrels and players remain blurred. Players may have employed music in their plays; minstrels may have employed mimetic activity in their performances. There is usually no way of telling. Indeed, to audiences at that time the distinction may occasionally also have been blurred, for some payments even seem to equate minstrels and players, as in the payment in the Christ Church Priory treasurer's accounts in 1447–8 for 'Ministrallis & alijs lusoribus,' a description also used in summary accounts at Dover in 1433–4. Nevertheless, most of the time there must have been a discernible difference. At Folkestone in 1543–4 (an accounting year that saw payments both to minstrels of the king and the queen and to players of the lord warden and the prince), the accounts include a payment to 'the lord wardens [pleyers] ⌜Menstrelles⌝.' Here the warden first wrote the word 'players' and then deliberately altered it to 'minstrels.' The payment at Dover in 1502–3 for 'the Kynges [Mynstrelles] Players' shows the correction of the opposite mistake.

If these distinctions made by medieval and early modern accountants between minstrels and players are accepted at face value, clear historical trends do emerge from the hundreds of payments to these travelling performers. As Figure 1 illustrates, payments to travelling minstrels in the monastic and borough accounts in the diocese of Canterbury began in the late thirteenth century and continued through the first quarter of the seventeenth century. The low number of payments during the late fourteenth and early fifteenth centuries reflects the lack of sources rather than the lack of minstrel activity. A gap in the Dover borough records between 1384 and 1423 and the change in accounting procedures at Christ Church Priory (the daybook of the prior with its frequent expenses for entertainment was after 1378 no longer copied into the treasurers' accounts) mean that the total payments for these years are artificially low. Throughout the remainder of the fifteenth century the sporadic survival of the priors' daybooks and priors' account rolls again depresses the otherwise high number of payments that reached their peak in the last quarter of the fifteenth century. During the sixteenth century the number of payments to minstrels across the whole range of borough accounts dropped steadily until the last recorded payments early in Elizabeth's reign: to the lord warden's minstrels in 1558–9 at Faversham and Lydd and to 'Mr cheynyes servantes beyng mynstrells' at Dover in 1561–2. After these two payments there were no further payments to professional travelling troupes of minstrels. Occasional payments to individual minstrels and jesters appear in later accounts, such as the payment to

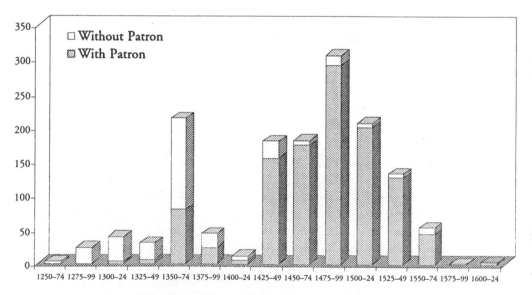

Figure 1: Payments to Travelling Minstrels in Monastic and Borough Accounts

Walter, the queen's jester, during her visit to Canterbury in 1573 (see p 201), the payment at Dover 'to Blynde will*ia*m the musician' in 1599 (see p 486), and seventeenth-century payments at Canterbury 'to ffenner Iester to the lady Elizabeth the xx^th of Aprill 1613 toward losse of his clothes and mony whearof he said he lost and was here robbed' (see p 261), again at Canterbury to the court jester during the visit of Charles I in 1625, and at New Romney in 1620–1 to 'the kings Iugler in reward that he should not shew his tricks in this Towne.' Although these scattered payments testify to the continued presence of individual minstrels and jesters, particularly in the Elizabethan and Stuart courts, the heyday of organized troupes of travelling minstrels came in the century between 1425 and 1525 with 61 per cent of all surviving payments to travelling minstrels falling during that period.[5]

The other significant aspect revealed by the surviving records of payments to minstrels in the monastic and borough accounts is the high percentage of minstrels travelling under the patronage of royalty and nobility. Overall 78 per cent of the minstrels receiving payment in these accounts had patrons. During the century between 1425 and 1525 that figure rises to 94 per cent. Although some payments to minstrels without patrons do appear throughout the period covered by these accounts, most such payments occurred during the late thirteenth and fourteenth centuries when the treasurers' accounts at Christ Church Priory often recorded only the feast day on which the performance occurred, such as the payments in 1308–9 to 'ystrionib*us* die translac*io*nis *sancti* th*ome*' or 'ystrionib*us* die *sancti* mich*ae*lis,' rather than noting whether or not the minstrels had a patron. Although it is impossible to know for certain, this clerical peculiarity may explain the large number of minstrels otherwise travelling without patrons during these years.

Minstrels of the king or queen or prince received 42 per cent of all payments to minstrels with patrons during the century between 1425 and 1525. Although minstrels of most noblemen prominent in national or court politics also visited Kent during that century, over half of all other payments were made to minstrels of the lord warden of the Cinque Ports, who wielded more influence and power over the towns of east Kent than any other nobleman. Minstrels of Humphrey, duke of Gloucester and lord warden from 1415 until 1447, for example, were paid forty-six times in the borough accounts of Canterbury, Dover, Hythe, Lydd, and New Romney between 1423 and 1447. Minstrels of Lord Saye and Sele, lord warden for less than three years, received eight payments between 1447 and 1450. Minstrels of Humphrey Stafford, duke of Buckingham and lord warden from 1450 to 1460, received seventeen payments for performance, and minstrels of Richard Neville, earl of Warwick and lord warden from 1461 to 1470, received nineteen. Minstrels of William Fitz Alan, earl of Arundel and lord warden from 1470 to 1487, were paid sixty-four times. Minstrels of Henry Tudor, who was created lord warden while still an infant in 1492, performed in Kent twenty-four times between 1492 and 1509. Minstrels of Sir Edward Poynings, who served as deputy lord warden from 1505 to 1509 during the minority of Prince Henry and then as lord warden from 1509 to 1521, received forty-two payments, including many individual payments to his lute player named Thurrold. Finally, minstrels of Sir Edward Guildford, lord warden from 1521 to 1534, were rewarded twenty-five times. Altogether during these years payments to the lord wardens' minstrels totalled 245 performances or 30 per cent of all payments to minstrels with patrons.

If the century between 1425 and 1525 was the heyday of professional travelling minstrels, the century between 1525 and 1625 was the heyday of professional travelling players. As Figure 2 indicates, payments to travelling players extend from the final quarter of the fourteenth century to the second quarter of the seventeenth century. Of all the payments in monastic and borough records to these players, however, 81 per cent fall in the century between 1525 and 1625. As payments to travelling minstrels dropped steadily during the sixteenth century, payments to travelling players increased steadily during the same period. In the last quarter of the fifteenth century there were 306 payments to minstrels and forty to players; in the first quarter of the sixteenth century, 216 payments to minstrels and sixty to players; in the second quarter, 143 payments to minstrels and 144 to players; and in the third quarter, fifty-four payments to minstrels and 178 to players. In the last quarter of the sixteenth century, when the borough accounts record only one payment to minstrels, there were 256 payments to travelling companies of players. Payments to players then declined to 194 during the first quarter of the seventeenth century before dropping sharply to just twenty-seven payments to travelling players between 1625 and 1642.

Just as most minstrels travelled under the patronage of royalty or nobility so most professional travelling players also had patrons. Some payments to players without patrons were made throughout the period between 1375 and 1642. During the fifteenth century, however, many of these payments were summary payments, such as the payment at Christ Church Priory in 1446–7 to 'diuersis lusoribus ludentibus coram domino Priori' or the payment by the Dover wardens in 1440–1 to 'diuersis hominibus ludentibus in ludis.' During the seventeenth century payments to players without patrons tended to be gratuity payments to unspecified players, such as the payment at Canterbury in 1639–40 'to a Company of plaiers,

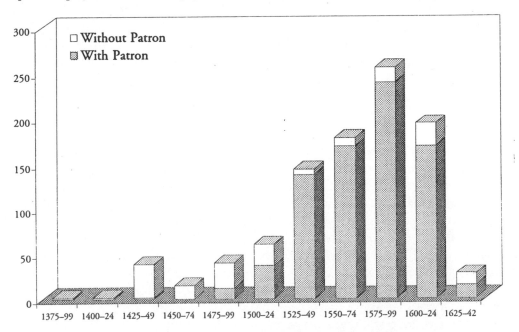

Figure 2: Payments to Travelling Players in Monastic and Borough Accounts

not to play' or the payment at Dover in 1630–1 'to Players, who were sent out of Towne.' The vast majority of payments to specific companies of players, however, did mention patrons. Overall the figure for payments to players with patrons is 82 per cent, rising to 93 per cent during the century between 1525 and 1625.

The first unambiguous payment to players with a patron appears in the 1477–8 Dover borough accounts where separate payments were made to the minstrels and the players of William Fitz Alan, earl of Arundel and lord warden of the Cinque Ports.[6] During the peak of minstrel activity in the remainder of the fifteenth century and the first quarter of the sixteenth century, most payments to performers with patrons were still made to minstrels; however, the payments to players with patrons increased dramatically during the second quarter of the sixteenth century. Henry VIII, for example, maintained both a travelling troupe of waits or minstrels and a travelling troupe of players, as did the lord wardens Sir Edward Guildford and Sir Thomas Cheyne. Just under half of all payments to players with patrons between 1525 and 1625 went to players of the king, queen, or prince, with players of most noblemen prominent in national or court politics also playing in Kent during that century.

When minstrels or players travelling under royal or noble patronage visited the towns of the diocese of Canterbury, they seem to have been rewarded according to the prestige of their patron rather than the quality of their performance.[7] The Canterbury chamberlains' accounts for 1477–8, for example, include payments of 6s 8d to the king's minstrels, 5s each to the queen's minstrels and the duke of Gloucester's minstrels, and 3s 4d to the minstrels of the duchess of York. Similar gradations in entertainment payments appear in the accounts of every borough in almost every year. In addition to the reward for their performance the performers often received additional payments for their expenses or for food and drink. In 1477–8 the Canterbury chamberlains made additional payments for wine given to visiting minstrels: 8d for the king's minstrels, 8d for the queen's minstrels, 4d for the duke of Gloucester's minstrels, and 4d for the duchess of York's minstrels. Payments to travelling players in the sixteenth century followed a similar pattern of carefully calibrated rewards. At Lydd in 1589–90, to cite just one example, players of the earl of Sussex received 6s, players of the earl of Essex and players of the lord admiral each received 10s, and the queen's players received 20s.

Travelling minstrels and players moved with relative ease along the well-developed system of main roads radiating from Canterbury and connecting the towns of east Kent. In some cases sufficient payments survive in the town accounts to enable the reconstruction of the probable itineraries of these travelling performers. During the 1588–9 accounting year, for example, payments to the queen's players appear in the chamberlains' accounts at Faversham dated 30 January, at Canterbury 'aboute candlemas,' at New Romney on 14 February, and at Lydd on 15 February. Additional undated payments are found at Folkestone, Hythe, Maidstone, and Rye.[8] At Dover during the last payment period of the accounting year in September 1589 expenses were submitted for money 'given vnto the quenes players at Christmas laste.' This suggests a tour of Kent, perhaps starting at Maidstone, moving through Faversham, Canterbury, and Dover, then westward along the coast through Folkestone, Hythe, New Romney, Lydd, Rye, and the west.[9] A second tour by the queen's men during the summer of 1589 is indicated by further payments in the 1588–9 accounts to the queen's players at Canterbury, at Dover 'at their laste beynge heare,' at Faversham, at Maidstone dated 'the ij of august,' at Rye, and in the 1589–90 accounts at Hythe, Lydd, and New Romney.[10] Payments during 1588–9 at Dover, Hythe, Lydd, New Romney, and Rye also indicate a similar tour by the players of the earl of Essex.

The changing political and religious mood of the country during the seventeenth century led to the decline and eventual disappearance of travelling players in Kent.[11] As early as 1565 Sandwich had passed a sabbatarian ordinance prohibiting the performance of plays on Sunday. Canterbury had followed suit in 1595 with an ordinance prohibiting Sunday performance, limiting engagements by any troupe to two consecutive days in any calendar month, establishing a nine o'clock evening curfew for the completion of a play, and prescribing severe penalties for disobedience – innkeepers accommodating players who had exceeded their two days or the nine o'clock curfew would be fined 40s and the players themselves would be forbidden to play in the city ever again. Hythe passed a similar ordinance against players in 1615. Players of the king, queen, or prince were limited to two, or at most three, plays; players of other nobility, after showing their commission, were confined to one or two. A curfew of eight o'clock in winter and nine o'clock in summer was imposed, fines were levied against innkeepers or householders entertaining players who did not abide by the decree, and the mayor was authorized to pay players a gratuity not to play. Although it is difficult to measure the success of these restrictive ordinances, Puritan disapproval of drama did certainly end the official payments by town chamberlains for performances. In the eighteen years following the 1595 ordinance the Canterbury chamberlains paid for only eight performances in the city and after 1616 began to make routine payments to players not to play. Dover, Fordwich, Hythe, New Romney, and Tenterden paid similar gratuities, such as the payments at Tenterden in 1635–6 to 'a Companie of players because they should not playe in Towne' and at Dover in 1640–1 to 'the Princes players for a gratuitie who presently thervppon departed the Toune.' The last payments for performance were made in 1613 at Canterbury and Maidstone, in 1620–1 at Folkestone, in 1624–5 at New Romney, in 1632–3 at Fordwich and Sandwich, in 1633 at Hythe, in 1635–6 at Dover and Faversham, and in 1636 at Lydd and Tenterden. Thereafter, only gratuity payments appear in the chamberlains' accounts, culminating in the last gratuity payment in Canterbury in 1641 'in dischardge of a Companie of plaieres out of Towne by master maiores appointment,' ending the long tradition of performance by professional travelling players and minstrels that stretched back to the first recorded payment to 'histrionibus' in 1272.

Amateur Players

BOROUGH AND PARISH PLAYS

During the fifteenth and early sixteenth centuries many boroughs and parishes of the diocese of Canterbury sponsored their own amateur players and sent their own bann criers throughout the countryside to promote their plays. Always described in the records as 'lusores,' 'ludentes,' or 'homines ludentes,' these players were clearly distinguished in the fifteenth-century records from the 'ioculatores,' 'histriones,' 'mimi,' and 'ministralli' travelling under royal or noble patronage.

Apart from a few isolated sources, however, our knowledge of these amateur plays and players comes only from payments in the borough accounts of Lydd and New Romney and to a lesser degree in those of Canterbury, Dover, Folkestone, Hythe, and Sandwich. The Lydd accounts, for example, show payments to bann criers from the nearby towns and parishes of Appledore, Brookland, Folkestone, Hythe, Ivychurch, New Romney, and Stone and to players from Benenden, Bethersden, Chart, Dymchurch, Goudhurst, Hamstreet, Lympne, Ruckinge, Tenterden, and Wittersham. From farther afield in Kent players came to Lydd from Dover, Faversham, Herne, Maidstone, Rochester, and Sittingbourne, from Billericay in Essex, and from Lewes, Rye, and Winchelsea in Sussex. Most of these players and bann criers, as well as players from Hastings and bann criers from High Halden, Lydd, and Wye, also performed in New Romney. Similar evidence of widespread parish drama survives in east Kent where the Dover accounts include payments to players from Boughton, Canterbury, Elham, Faversham, Folkestone, Herne, Hythe, Sandwich, Sittingbourne, Sturry, and Thanet, and the Sandwich treasurers' accounts for 1462 include payments to players from Ash, Canterbury, Deal, and Herne. Altogether players and bann criers from thirty-five different boroughs and parishes in the diocese of Canterbury are mentioned in these accounts. Over half of these players and bann criers, as well as those from the Kentish parishes of Ashford, Bonnington, Cranbrook, East Malling, Frittenden, Harrietsham, Lydden, Mersham, Newenden, Reading Street, and West Malling, are also mentioned in the accounts of the nearby Sussex town of Rye.[12] The records range from just two performances between 1488 and 1490 in Rye by the players of the parish of Frittenden to twenty-five performances between 1494 and 1534 in Dover, Hythe, Lydd, New Romney, and Rye by the bann criers and players of the parish of Brookland, the payment for at least one performance having been designated 'to players of Brokland for the Reparacions of the Church ther' (see p 399).

Except for Bethersden, Lydd, and New Romney, however, none of the boroughs or parishes mentioned in the account books of the Cinque Port towns has significant records of its own players. Few fifteenth- or early sixteenth-century churchwardens' accounts have survived; those that have rarely mention plays or players. The only other references in the Kent records to the players of Brookland and Frittenden, for example, are found in a bequest of 12d to William Ealdishe in the will of James Hoggelyn of Old Romney in 1527 'if he playe yn brokeland playe on penticost next commyng to the makyng of his hoses' and a bequest in the will of Richard Bannoke of Faversham in 1522, giving to his son Nicholas 'my sute of playing garmentes that the men of fretynden hath yn kepyng.' Players of Dover were paid at Lydd in 1527–8 and at Rye in 1506–7 and 1508–9; however, the only record of these players in the Dover wardens' accounts are rewards paid 'to players of the towne of Douorre' in 1522–3 and again in 1523–4.[13] Even such slim supporting evidence has not survived for most of the other borough and parish plays. The Christ Church Priory treasurer's accounts in 1444–5 include a reward to 'parochianis sancte Mildrede in coexibicionem ludi'; however, no further evidence of this play survives in the parish records of St Mildred's, Canterbury. The Boughton under Blean churchwardens' accounts include a receipt for money gathered in 1535 at the 'Corpus christi play'; however, no further evidence of this play survives in the parish records of Sts Peter and Paul, Boughton under Blean. Not even in the boroughs of Faversham, Folkestone, or Hythe does evidence survive of their own town or parish players. The borough accounts of Canterbury, Dover, Hythe, Lydd, New Romney, and Sandwich record seven performances by the players of Faversham between 1446 and 1527, twelve performances by the bann criers and players of Folkestone between 1473 and 1534, and fourteen performances by the bann criers and players of Hythe between 1387 and 1533, yet none of these three towns has any record of its own plays or players. Given the scarcity of supporting evidence for these borough and parish plays, what conclusions can be drawn about this once thriving dramatic tradition?

The surviving evidence suggests that these amateur borough and parish plays were primarily saints' plays and biblical plays encouraged by the piety of late medieval religious guilds and fraternities, dedicated at least in part to raising parish funds, and brought to an abrupt end by the sustained attack on the veneration of saints during the early Henrician Reformation. As Figure 3 indicates, payments in the borough accounts of the diocese of Canterbury for perform-ances by borough and parish bann criers and players rose steadily throughout the fifteenth century, reaching their peak during the early sixteenth century. Payments to fifty-three travelling troupes, or 29 per cent of all payments to bann criers and players, were made in the last quarter of the fifteenth century and fifty-five payments, or 30 per cent, in the first quarter of the sixteenth century.[14] During the next decade between 1525 and 1534 the number of performances proportionally increased even further with twenty-seven payments, or 15 per cent of all pay-ments, being made during this decade alone. After the 1534–5 accounting year, however, pay-ments for borough and parish plays virtually disappeared with only the payment in Canterbury to players of Hadlow in 1537–8 and the payment in New Romney to players of Rochester in 1539–40 falling during the second half of the decade.[15] After that date there are no further pay-ments to bann criers and players from boroughs and parishes in the diocese of Canterbury.

Why did the performances of borough and parish plays disappear so abruptly in 1535? The surviving evidence points to the content of the plays. Apart from a single reference to the 'Robyn hod playes' of Hythe in 1532 (see p 770), all other named plays in the records are miracle plays or

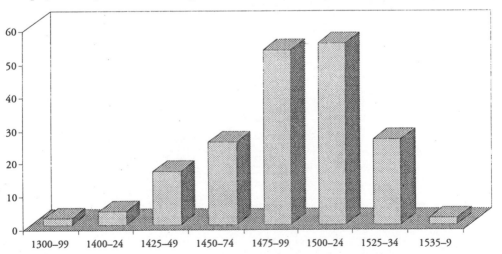

Figure 3: Payments to Borough and Parish Bann Criers and Players

saints' plays. In 1408–9 the bursar of Boxley Abbey, for example, rewarded six men for playing 'vnum miraculum de sancta Maria.' At Bethersden in 1521–2 playwardens' accounts survive for the play of St Christina. Judging from the payments for swords and axes the heroine was probably the fourth-century virgin and martyr honoured in both Eastern and Western churches for suffering a series of tortures after her refusal to sacrifice to pagan gods. At Lydd between 1456 and 1534 the town chamberlains' accounts and churchwardens' accounts contain scattered references to the parish play of St George, the last performance of which was recorded in 1532–3. None of these saints' plays, however, survived the sustained attack on the veneration of saints during the early 1530s that culminated in an act of parliament for the abrogation of numerous feast days and saints' days in September 1536.[16] Under the protection of Thomas Cromwell and Archbishop Thomas Cranmer radical preachers like Hugh Latimer, who was appointed Lenten preacher to the king in 1534, campaigned against pilgrimages to shrines, the superstitious veneration of relics, the lighting and adornment of images of saints, and the invocation of saints. After the break with Rome in March 1533 traditional piety in pulpit and parish had become associated with dissatisfaction with the Crown and support of the papacy. Under the watchful eye of the archbishop of Canterbury performance of traditional parish plays celebrating the miracles of the saints had suddenly become far too dangerous.

The only exception to the sudden disappearance in 1535 of traditional borough and parish plays in the diocese of Canterbury was the passion play of New Romney where evidence of performance continues as late as 1568. In 1539 the New Romney chamberlains paid for 'expences at the rehersyng of the play in lent.' Other play expenses occur in the New Romney accounts during the 1540s and 1550s. In December 1555 three recognizances, listing most of the players and binding them to learn their parts before the feast of Pentecost, appear in the New Romney court book. Both the court books and chamberlains' accounts contain extensive records concerning the production of the play in 1560. The Lydd accounts for this year include a reward to the bann criers of New Romney. Evidence in the New Romney quarter sessions records, as well as a payment to the New Romney players in the Dover accounts, indicates a performance in 1562 while an enigmatic memorandum in the New Romney chamberlains' accounts may indicate a further performance in 1568.

This survival of the New Romney passion play well into the first decade of Elizabeth's reign resulted from the solid support of the play by the wealthy and powerful men of the town's oligarchy.[17] Comparison of the names on a tax assessment of New Romney residents levied on 1 April 1559 with the names of players on the 1555 recognizances and the names of townsmen who agreed on 18 February 1559/60 to help produce the play at Whitsuntide shows a high correlation between wealth, as measured by the amount of tax paid, and support of the town's play.[18] In the lower tax bands 58 per cent of residents did not participate in the play; in the higher tax bands 76 per cent of residents did. Furthermore, most of the influential men who served as the churchwardens, jurats, or bailiff of New Romney, who held the offices of town clerk, chamberlain, or serjeant, or who represented the town in the Brotherhood meetings of the Cinque Ports or in parliament also were involved in the proposed revival of the passion play at Whitsuntide in 1556 or the production of the play in 1560 (see pp 1362–3, endnote to EKAC: NR/JB 6 ff 215–16, and pp 1363–4, endnote to EKAC: NR/JB 7 ff 40–1). These men not only joined together to produce the passion play but also used their influence to ensure its success and survival. The 1555–6 accounts, for example, include a payment to Christopher Coucheman, who had served over the years as jurat, churchwarden, bailiff, mayor, and MP, 'for his charges in Rydyng to our lorde warden to have his good wyll touchyng our playe.'

For a town suffering from economic decline, the reputation of the passion play brought increased revenue and boosted civic pride. The play had always attracted large audiences, drawing many spectators from the surrounding towns and villages. So many people from nearby Lydd came to see the play in 1465–6 that the Lydd town chamberlains had to pay 'iiij Waychemen þe first sonday att þe play of Romene.' Similarly, in 1516–17 they paid 'for the labor of v. men wacchyng the towne at the play day of Romene.' The receipts from the four play days in 1560 on Whit Monday, 14 July, 3 August, and one other unspecified date amounted to £25 12s 10d, which at the probable gate price of a penny a head meant at least 6,000 people descending on the innkeepers, hostelers, and victualers of the town. The proposed revival of the play at Whitsuntide in 1556 also drew actors from the surrounding towns and villages of Brenzett, Brookland, Dymchurch, Lydd, Old Romney, and perhaps other locations, attracted by the prestige of playing in the town's renowned play (see pp 1362–3, endnote to EKAC: NR/JB 6 ff 215–16).[19]

Although the playbook has not survived, the probable characters, structure, and staging of the New Romney passion play may be reconstructed from the surviving evidence of the fifteenth-century playwardens' account fragment (see pp 745–50), the 1555 recognizances listing the actors and the part or parts played by each (see pp 779–82), and various memoranda and accounts relating to the 1560 performances (see pp 783–94).[20] Most of the dramatis personae of the passion play are mentioned in these records. Three recognizances sworn before bailiff Richard Bunting and the jurats of New Romney on 27 December 1555, binding the actors to learn and rehearse their parts, form a nearly complete cast list. On the first appear Herod, accompanied by two knights and a messenger, Pilate and his messenger, Caiaphas and his messenger, Annas and his handmaid, the second devil, and six tormentors: Mischaunce, Falce at Nede, Untrust, Faynthart, Unhappe, and Evyll Grace. The second recognizance lists the blind man, his boy, his mother and father, Sts Peter, Simon, Matthew, Andrew, John, James, James the Less, Thomas, Philip, Bartholomew, and Jude, Judas the traitor, two Pharisees, Lazarus, Martha, Mary Magdalene, Martha's servant, a neighbour, and another Jew. The third adds a doctor, the Virgin Mary, three princes, Malchus, Mary Salome, the Third Devil, and Simon of Cyrene. Other characters emerge from payments in the 1560 chamberlains' accounts for 'A sho set on the centuryons horsse' (see p 787), 'payntyng of St Iohn baptistes coote' (see p 789), and 'shepeskynnes for ye godheddes coote for the iiij[th] playe' (see p 789). Notable absentees from the recognizances, however, include the first and second soldier, the first and second thief, the angel, the first devil, and Jesus.

The surviving records also reveal hints about the passion play's structure and staging. The accounts refer to four separate plays within the passion play, and other memoranda and payments for properties suggest further division of these four plays into several scenes. A 1560 memorandum, for example, appoints builders for seven stages: 'Pylates ∧⌜& princes⌝ Stage,' 'Annas stage & the Tormentours,' 'the Pharises stage,' 'herodes stage,' 'heaven,' 'the Cave' including 'the iij cross*es*,' and 'hell' (see p 794). In the same year Thomas Starre was paid 'for dressing of the pascall lambe at o*u*r last play' (see p 789), a payment that may signify a perform-ance of the Last Supper. In the playwardens' account fragment a payment for 'ij. halters for the asse' (see p 747) indicates a performance of the triumphal entry. These memoranda and accounts, together with the characters mentioned in the recognizances, permit a conjectural reconstruction of the New Romney passion play as a cycle of four plays, each with two or more scenes.

The first play, a sequence of five scenes mostly unique to the Gospel of John, covered the ministry of Christ, focusing on his confrontation with the Pharisees: the baptism of Jesus and choosing of the disciples (John 1), the woman of Samaria (John 4), the healing of the blind man (John 9), the raising of Lazarus (John 11), and the triumphal entry (John 12). The sequence probably opened with John the Baptist baptizing Jesus. The various payments in the accounts for the coat of John the Baptist, the recognizances that include the twelve disciples and two Pharisees, and the memorandum that mentions the Pharisees' stage, all point toward the version of Jesus' baptism narrated in John 1 where John debates with the Pharisees before baptizing Jesus and then sends to Jesus two of his own disciples, who subsequently recruit the rest. The second scene in the sequence, a unique appearance in the cycle plays of the Samaritan woman at the well, may be deduced from the payment in 1560 to Richard Hawkyns 'for a dayes worcke to set vp the cytye of samary' (see p 788), an allusion to the Vulgate's 'civitatem Samariae' in John 4.5. This story, in which Jesus offers water and forgiveness to the Samaritan woman, also includes parts for the disciples and the two Pharisees. Cast lists for the next two scenes, the healing of the blind man and the raising of Lazarus, both appear in the 1555 recognizances. Again each story features a confrontation with the Pharisees, who plot the death of Lazarus and the death of Jesus just before the triumphal entry narrated in John 12, suggesting that both scenes were played on the Pharisees' stage. The entry of Jesus into Jerusalem, deduced from the payment in the playwardens' account fragment for 'ij. halters for the asse,' concludes the ministry sequence at a triumphal moment for Jesus, as the Pharisees exclaim to themselves in John 12.19, 'Perceive ye how ye prevail nothing? behold, the world is gone after him.' Structurally, then, the first play, or ministry sequence, pits the Pharisees against Jesus in a series of confrontations drawn from the Gospel of John, rising to a climax in the triumphal entry and preparing the way for the reversal of action in the Passion sequence of the second play.

The second play, The Betrayal and Buffeting, portrays the arrest and trial of Jesus. Payments in the 1560 accounts 'for dressing of the pascall lambe' (see p 789) suggest that the play opened with the Last Supper. The remaining scenes, deduced from the recognizances and from the list of stages, follow the traditional sequence of events found in all the gospels although the inclu-sion of Malchus in the cast list indicates that the compiler of the play was probably still relying principally on the Gospel of John, since only John names the servant of the high priest whose ear was cut off and restored during the arrest. The trial scenes take place successively on Annas' stage with Caiaphas and Annas, dressed as the bishops mentioned in the account fragment, and their servants; on Pilate's stage with Pilate, his messenger, who also doubled as Caiaphas' messenger, and the three princes; and on Herod's stage with Herod and his two knights, the second of whom also doubled as his messenger. Most notable here are the six personified tormentors – Mischaunce, Falce at Nede, Untrust, Faynthart, Unhappe, and Evyll Grace – who shared the stage with Annas and Caiaphas. As in Thomas Preston's *Cambises*, Bale's *King John*, and other sixteenth-century hybrid plays, these abstract personifications rubbed shoulders with concrete historical or biblical characters, depicting in stylized form emotions that later sixteenth-century dramatists learned to show realistically through speech and action.[21] When Jesus appeared before Annas, the tormentors objectified or portrayed outwardly the torment he must have felt inwardly: Falce at Nede portrayed the denial of Peter, Untrust the betrayal of Judas, Faynthart the desertion of the disciples, Evyll Grace the mockery of Annas and Caiaphas, and Mischaunce and Unhappe the misfortune of scourge and thorns and nails.

The third play, depicting Christ's death and descent into hell, probably consisted of three scenes, each with its own stage or centre of action noted in the 1560 memorandum listing the builders of the stages. Three crosses are specified for the Crucifixion scene. The recognizances include parts for Simon of Cyrene, the three Marys, and John. No soldiers are listed but the 1560 accounts include payments for swords and for the shoeing of the centurion's horse. If the playwright was still following the Gospel of John, then Pilate, Annas, Caiaphas, and the two Pharisees would have swelled the group around the cross. A burial scene in 'the cave,' featuring Nicodemus and Joseph of Arimathaea, who also appear in the Gospel of John, may have followed although neither character appears in the recognizances. The harrowing of hell may be safely inferred both from the hell stage and from the mention of the second and third devils, the former having doubled as Annas in the second play. Among other stage properties the fifteenth-century account fragment calls for 'Campanis pro inferno' (see p 747), or hell's bells, probably morris bells strapped to the arms and legs of the devils.

The last play, 'ludi de resureccione' (see p 737), is the only play specifically mentioned by name in the New Romney records. The action here revolves around two centres – 'the cave' for the Resurrection scene and 'heaven' for the Ascension. The former may have featured Mary Magdalene, mentioned in the recognizances, as does the Resurrection account in John 20. The latter scene apparently featured both God the Father and God the Son appearing on the heaven stage, for the 1560 accounts include payments 'for makyng of the fyrst godheddes Coote' (see p 786) and 'for skynnes for the ij^d godheddes Coote & for makyng' (see p 787), as well as a payment for half a dozen sheepskins 'for ye godheddes coote for the iiij^th playe' (see p 789). Altogether the payments for these two costumes totalled 7s 4d.

These numerous hints about the passion play's content, structure, and staging drawn from the surviving New Romney records, then, reveal a fully developed passion play performed on fixed staging, dramatizing scenes from Christ's baptism to his ascension, and probably based on the Gospel of John. Together with the surviving records of the Bethersden play of St Christina and the Lydd play of St George, the records of the New Romney passion play also give fascinating glimpses into the administration of these borough and parish plays. All three plays were administered by playwardens. The 1521 Bethersden play accounts were submitted by four play-wardens. The wardens of the St George play are mentioned in the Lydd chamberlains' accounts for 1526–7. The churchwardens' accounts for the same year refer to 'ij of the wardens of Saynt Georges playe,' implying that there were others as well. At New Romney the playwardens were elected by the bailiff, jurats, and commonalty. A memorandum in the chamberlains' accounts for 1516–17 reports that three jurats – Richard Stuppeny, MP, Christopher Hendfeld, and Robert Paris – and two commoners – John Bunting and William Beadell – were chosen to be playwardens for that year. In April 1560 jurats Robert Kennett and Thomas Ederyck and commoners John Parker and Richard Godfrey were elected.

The playwardens or the town clerk kept custody of the playbook and arranged for parts to be copied and distributed to the players. In preparation for the proposed performance of the New Romney play at Whitsuntide in 1556, for example, town clerk John Forcett was paid 'for wryting owt the *partes* for the playe At m*aste*r Bailif Comavndement.' The parts were distributed to the all-male cast on 27 December 1555 when recognizances were to be sworn before bailiff Richard Bunting, committing the players to learn their parts by Pentecost and to come to New Romney for every rehearsal of the play. The failure of many players to sign the recognizances, however, may indicate that the play was not in fact played that year as proposed. The New Romney playbook itself remained in the custody of the town clerk and appears in inventories of the town records in February 1554/5 and February 1556/7. Whenever it was needed for rehearsing of the play, careful records were made of its borrowing and return. At Bethersden the parts were also presumably copied from the playbook, for the playwardens' accounts contain a payment 'to the Clerke for Wryty*n*g.' At Lydd numerous tantalizing references to the playbook appear in the chamberlains' accounts. In 1520–1 payments are made to Thomas Bunting for writing 'the boke of the pley' and 'for brengyng of the seid boke of Saynte Georgis pley in to the Custody of the towne ageyne where as it was in the kepyng of other men.' In 1526–7 the chamberlains paid 'for a new Bookc for the lyfe of Saynt George' and again in 1533–4 'for wrytyng of the pley boke.' Between 1526 and 1533 the wardens of the St George play consulted New Romney resident Richard Gibson, who served as serjeant of the tents for Henry VIII, about the costumes for the St George play. In 1530–1 they carried 'the olde pley boke' to London for Gibson to review.

Production of the play in both Bethersden and New Romney seems to have been a communal effort under the direction of a deviser or producer. At Bethersden the payment of £3 10s 'to the devyser for h*is* labor' represents a significant part of the total play expenses of £6 5s 11d ob. Numerous other smaller payments for food and drink, for construction of the stage, and to various people whose contribution is not specified indicate the involvement of a sizable group of people. At New Romney a similar significant payment of £4 was made in 1560 'to Gover m*ar*tyn o*ur* devysour for his s*er*uyce at o*ur* play,' an additional 16s 5d 'for certen necessaryes bought by hym for o*ur* playe' (see p 787), and 20s 'for ˄⌈his labor at⌉ the iiij^th play' (see p 789), although the first two of these payments may correspond to the bill submitted by Gover Marten totalling £4 11s 5d for provisions 'bought At London for o*ur* playe' (see pp 791–2). As at Bethersden numerous townsmen of New Romney were involved in the production of the play. The 1555 recognizances name forty-four actors. The 1560 list of New Romney inhabitants 'agreynge that the playe of New Romney shall be playd at wytsontyde next folowynge & what eu*er*y man wyll do & gyue towardes it' (see pp 783–5) includes the names of sixty people, each volunteering labour or money. Other names not on either list emerge from payments in the 1560–1 chamberlains' accounts. Although some names appear on both lists, altogether 103 different people are named as building stages, organizing costumes and props, collecting and disbursing money, or performing in the 1556 and 1560 performances of the play. In addition to the deviser, the actors, and the many inhabitants who played backstage and administrative roles, both Bethersden and New Romney hired musicians for their plays. The playwardens' accounts at Bethersden include a payment 'to the menstrel*es* the ij*d* pleye daye.' In the fifteenth-century playwardens' accounts at New Romney there are several payments for minstrels and in the 1560–1 accounts payments 'to the wayte of Rye for his *seruyce* at *our* ij*de* play day' (see p 787), 'to the mynstryll*es* that played at o*ur* iij*de* playe' (see p 788), 'to the drom player for his paynes' (see p 788), and 'to A mynstryll at o*ur* iiij*th* play' (see p 789).

As the play day drew near, bann criers travelled to surrounding towns and villages to proclaim the banns of the play. For the 1521 performance the Bethersden playwardens paid for 'Wat*er* at nashe to Ryde w*ith* our banys.' Similarly, Lydd chamberlains paid 20d in 1466–7 'in Exspenc*es* of our*e* Bane cryar*es* of our*e* play.' These banns were apparently separate from the play and comprised an official announcement that summarized and advertised the play.[22] This practice explains the expenses submitted by the New Romney town clerk in 1560 for writing out the playbook, writing out the parts, and writing the '*pro*claymynge of the playe' (see p 790). Often the players who read this proclamation or cried the banns were dressed in costume. Before the 1560 performance of the New Romney passion play, for example, the deviser spent 10s in London for 'iiij beard*es* & heare*s* for the bane cryers & A heare & beard for the ffoole' (see p 791). Usually, the bann criers were rewarded with donations toward play expenses and were often entertained with food and drink. In 1508 bann criers for the Bethersden play of St Christina were paid 3s 4d for the proclamation of their banns in New Romney and 4s in Rye.[23] During their promotion of the St George play Lydd bann criers were paid at Hythe in 1503–4, at New Romney in 1476–7, 1478–9, 1486–7, 1493–4, 1494–5, 1503–4, 1509–10, and 1532–3, and at Rye in 1502–3 and 1508–9.[24] According to the fifteenth-century playwardens' account fragment, New Romney bann criers collected 3s 4d each from Ivychurch and Brookland, 5s from Folkestone, and 6s 8d each from Hythe and Lydd (see p 748). In other years the New Romney bann criers were paid at Dover and Lydd in 1479–80, at Hythe in 1497–8 and 1503–4, at Rye in 1502–3, at both Lydd and Rye in 1516–17, 1525–6, and 1539–40, at Dover in 1547–8, and at Hythe, Lydd, Rye, and Tenterden in 1560.[25]

The finances of the plays were usually administered by the playwardens, as at Bethersden in 1521 and at New Romney in the 1480s; however, in other years the town chamberlains seem to have accounted directly for the receipts and expenses, as at Lydd in 1532–3 and New Romney in 1560. Apart from using the money collected by the bann criers in advance of the performance, the playwardens apparently paid the majority of expenses for rehearsals, costumes, and properties from loans that were then repaid from the play's receipts. At New Romney in 1503, for example, the playwardens received a loan directly from the town chamberlain; in 1497 and again in 1505 the chamberlain reimbursed various townspeople who had themselves loaned money to the playwardens. In 1560 the chamberlain accounted for a total of 35s from various inhabitants 'gyven toward*es* o*ur* playe w*hich* afterward*es* was paid ageyne' (see p 785). At Lydd in 1532–3 the town chamberlain repaid bailiff John Cawston in several instalments for money 'whiche is owing to hym for the pley' (see p 687). In 1533–4 the Lydd chamberlain was still paying off the play debts from the previous year, including 13s 4d to the town serjeant John Mighell 'of old dett for the pley' and the same amount to jurat Thomas Attye 'of old dett of the towne for the pley.' At the performance itself money gatherers collected money from the audience. The Bethersden playwardens paid 12d 'for their Sopper*es* that were gether*es* þe ij^d pleye' and another 4d 'for the gether*es* dennar the iij^d playe daye.' The fifteenth-century New Romney playwardens' account fragment shows receipts from five money gatherers at the second play day (see p 746); in 1560 the total receipts are given for each play day (see pp 785–6). The Bethersden play-wardens' accounts also give the receipts for each of three play days during the 1521 performances. After all expenses had been paid the Bethersden playwardens then apparently paid over the remainder to the churchwardens. In the churchwardens' accounts for the previous year a memorandum notes that 'the remayn to the Cherch of the pley aboue all thyng*es* Cownted and alowyd xlv s. vj d.'

MONASTIC PLAYS

From Christ Church Priory in Canterbury comes the earliest evidence of liturgical drama in England: the only two extant medieval manuscripts of the *Regularis Concordia* dating from the late tenth and mid-eleventh centuries and written in the Christ Church scriptorium.[26] The *Regularis Concordia*, an agreement designed to regulate monastic life and practice at Benedictine houses throughout England, was drawn up at the council of Winchester sometime between 965 and 975 under the direction of St Dunstan, the archbishop of Canterbury (960–88), and St Æthelwold, bishop of Winchester (963–84). The agreement combined Anglo-Saxon monastic customs with continental liturgical innovations from Fleury, where Æthelwold had studied, and from Ghent, where Dunstan had studied, including detailed performance practice for the Easter liturgical play, the *Visitatio Sepulchri*, with its famous *Quem quaeritis in sepulchro* dialogue (see pp 1262–3, endnote to *Regularis Concordia*).[27] These liturgical innovations were introduced in Canterbury by Archbishop Dunstan as part of his reform of both St Augustine's Abbey and the cathedral priory where he had established new communities of Benedictine monks. The music for the *Quem quaeritis in sepulchro* dialogue does not appear in the contemporary eleventh-century Canterbury troper (BL: MS. Cotton Caligula A.xiv) due to a missing leaf at the beginning of the Easter tropes. The Canterbury troper, however, was copied from the late tenth-century Winchester troper, which does contain the *Quem quaeritis in sepulchro* dialogue, and there is little doubt that the music was known and the liturgical play performed at Christ Church (see Appendix 4).

A second liturgical drama in the diocese of Canterbury was performed by the Trinitarian friars of Mottenden, who maintained a religious house in the parish of Headcorn until it was suppressed by Cromwell in 1538.[28] An account of this liturgical drama, performed as part of their patronal festival on Trinity Sunday, appears in the second and subsequent editions of *A Perambulation of Kent* by the Kentish historian William Lambarde (1536–1601). Although Lambarde's description is not free from Protestant bias, it does appeal to the eyewitness who remembered the solemn procession of the friars and the liturgical pageant, which involved someone dressed like the devil who attempted to join the procession and steal the cross from the crucifer. At each attempted attack the friars repulsed the devil by sprinkling him with holy water (see pp 910–11).

HOUSEHOLD PLAYS

Sir Edward Dering (1598–1644), antiquary and politician, was educated at Magdalene College, Cambridge, knighted on 22 January 1618/19, and created a baronet on 1 February 1626/7. Appointed lieutenant of Dover Castle in 1629, he devoted his early years to antiquarian study and the accumulation of an extensive library and collection of manuscripts. He inherited the family property at Surrenden Dering near Pluckley in 1636 and during the later part of his life became involved in politics, serving as MP for Hythe in 1625 and representing the county of Kent in the Long Parliament. The household account book kept by Sir Edward between 1617 and 1628 records many expenses for paying fiddlers and other itinerant performers during his travels and for seeing plays at Maidstone and London. The account book also contains numerous payments for buying and binding playbooks. Notable purchases in December 1623 were two copies of Shakespeare's first folio at £1 each and a copy of Ben Jonson's collected plays for 9s. Other plays mentioned by name include Francis Beaumont's *The Woman Hater* (1607) and *Band, Cuff, and Ruff*, a comedy he probably first saw performed in 1615 at Cambridge. More significant for the history of drama in Kent are the performances of plays organized by Dering in his own household at Surrenden. A fragmentary cast list in Sir Edward's handwriting survives for a private production of John Fletcher's *The Spanish Curate*, c 1622. In January 1622/3 he also paid for a manuscript copy of the conflation of Shakespeare's *1 Henry IV* and *II Henry IV* (now Folger: MS. V.b.34) that he had prepared for performance at Surrenden.[29]

Other evidence for the performance of plays in private households in Kent survives from Shurland on the Isle of Sheppey, the country residence of Philip Herbert (1584–1650), nephew and namesake of Sir Philip Sidney. A royal favourite, Herbert had become a gentleman of the privy chamber in May 1603, a Knight of the Bath later that year, and in 1605 a gentleman of the bedchamber. Having been created Baron Herbert of Shurland in the Isle of Sheppey and the 1st earl of Montgomery in May 1605, Herbert gained a variety of honours at court, eventually succeeding his brother as lord chamberlain of the household in August 1626. During the reign of James I Herbert was a prominent figure in court tournaments and masques. A letter from Sir William Browne to William Trumbull, dated 1 October 1610, describes how the earl entertained the court of James I at Shurland, where a four-day feast featured performances of comedies and tragedies by the king's men.

SCHOOL PLAYS

Evidence for school drama, both in the monastic almonry schools and in later sixteenth-century schools influenced by humanistic educational reforms, comes from Canterbury and Sandwich. Scattered references to school plays between the fifteenth and seventeenth centuries suggest a long-standing tradition of school drama in Canterbury. The monastic records of Christ Church Priory record a payment in 1447–8 to the boys of Thomas Ware, master of the almonry school at Christ Church, for playing before Prior John Elham. A similar payment in the 1515–16 Sandwich treasurers' accounts to 'the Children of saint Augustyn of Canterbury when they playde in the Courthall' refers to the boys of the abbey's almonry school in Canterbury.[30] Later references occur in the dean and chapter records of the reformed cathedral. In 1562 during the tenure of playwright John Bale as a prebendary of Canterbury Cathedral, the dean and chapter approved the performance of tragedies, comedies, and interludes at Christmas by boys of the King's School and authorized the expenditure of £3 6s 8d by Anthony Rushe, school-master from 1561 to 1565 (see p 191). A further payment the following year to Canterbury painter John Johnson 'yn tyme of the playe' (see p 193) may indicate the preparation of scenery for a Christmas performance in 1563 as well. Although no evidence survives for school plays during their time at the school, Elizabethan playwright Stephen Gosson attended the King's School between 1566 and 1569, and Christopher Marlowe was a student in 1578–9 (see Appendix 1). In 1592 a court case brought before the court of High Commission involved the enticement of boys from the King's School 'to go abrode in the cuntrey to play playes contrary to lawe and good order' (see p 228) and may have been an attempt by William Symcox, later one of the duke of Lennox' players, to recruit boys for a company of players.[31] More firm evidence for drama at the King's School during the seventeenth century comes from payments by the treasurer of the dean and chapter between 1629 and 1632 for students playing in comedies and from a letter by Henry Oxenden written on 6 February 1637/8 that mentions 'a comedie acted to night in Lattin at the Deanery' (see p 927) in the cathedral precincts. In the eighteenth century William Gostling in *A Walk in and about the City of Canterbury* notes that the dean's great hall was 'demolished by the zealous puritans, for being profaned by the King's scholars having acted plays there.'[32] Elsewhere in east Kent the 1580 foundation statutes for The Free Grammar School of Roger Manwood in Sandwich provide for 'one Commodie or tragedie of chaste matter in latin to be plaied' at Christmas time 'yf the Master do thinck mete.'

Performance Spaces

OUTDOOR PERFORMANCE

Archaeological records provide evidence of outdoor theatrical performance dating from the Roman occupation of Kent. In 1849 archaeologists discovered at Richborough the remains of a Roman amphitheatre, an elliptical structure, measuring 200' by 166' with entrances on the south, west, and north and a view extending past the south side of the Isle of Thanet across the Channel to the white cliffs in the distance between Calais and Boulogne.[33] Investigation of war-damaged areas of Canterbury by the Canterbury Excavation Committee following World War II and more recent work by the Canterbury Archaeological Trust have produced archaeological evidence of a second Roman theatre at the intersection of St Margaret's Street, Castle Street, and Watling Street. Originally constructed in the late first century and rebuilt early in the third century, the theatre measured 250' across and was capable of seating around 7,500 spectators.[34]

More recent evidence of outdoor performance comes from the later medieval records of borough and parish plays and payments to travelling entertainers. In some communities an open area of land was specifically designated as 'the playing place' and was used by travelling bann criers, players, and other entertainers in the late medieval period. At Lydd, for example, entries in the early sixteenth-century rent book of the manor of Aldington for '*Tenementes* lyeng on the sowthewest *pa*rte of strete ledyng from the church to the harmytage' refer in passing to land known as 'the playing place' (see pp 672–3), formerly an open area bordered by the High Street, Park Street, and New Lane but now covered with buildings. At Linsted in 1482 the will of John Weston contains a bequest to the churchwardens of a piece of land in Church Field for making a place called 'apleying place' for use by parishioners on feast days and holy days. In other communities payments were made for outdoor performances in the streets or markets or other open areas. In the 1484–5 accounts the Lydd chamberlains paid a reward 'to the Playres in the hyghe strete.' At nearby New Romney in 1441–2 the chamberlains rewarded the men of Wittersham for showing their parish play 'sup*er* le Crokhill' and other men playing 'sup*er* le Crokhill,' an elevated open space on the western side of New Romney, southwest of Church Road, known also as Crocky Green or Crockley Green. At Sandwich in 1520–1 the treasurers paid the king's players for a performance 'in the fishem*ar*ket openly,' and at Dover in 1550–1 the wardens paid for 'players that played in the markett place one estre mundaye.'

INNS AND PUBLIC HOUSES

Occasionally, payments in the borough chamberlains' accounts to travelling players and minstrels or to civic musicians mention inns or public houses as the performance venue or the place where the entertainers were rewarded with food and drink after their performance. Particularly in Canterbury, where some seventeenth-century vintners' licences have survived, many of these locations can be identified. The Chequers Inn, for example, where the mayor and his brethren rewarded the prince's players after their performance in 1546–7, was located on the northwest corner of the High Street and Mercery Lane in St Andrew's parish. Vintners' licences for this inn survive from 1667.[35] During the early seventeenth century The Chequers Inn is mentioned as a performance venue for the queen's men in 1608–9, for the city waits at the annual accounting dinners in 1609–10 and 1610–11, at the entertainment of the French ambassador in 1624–5, at the eating of venison sent by the countess of Winchilsea in 1632–3, and at the gunpowder treason dinner on 5 November 1638. The Crown Inn, where the city waits entertained the mayor and aldermen at the dinner on 5 November 1612, was located in the parish of St Mary Bredman on the southwest side of the High Street, not far from the guildhall. During the early seventeenth century The Crown is mentioned as the site of further civic entertainment by the city waits at the annual accounting dinner in 1613 (see p 263). One seventeenth-century vintner's licence survives from 1685.[36] The Red Lion Inn, where the mayor and his brethren rewarded the king's minstrels in 1505–6, was situated on the High Street immediately east of the guildhall. Demolished in 1806 to allow for construction of Guildhall Street connecting Sun Street with the High Street, The Red Lion had often catered for civic functions at the adjacent guildhall, the requirement to provide 'one gallon of good claret wine to the mayor at every sessions dinner' actually appearing in surviving vintners' licences from the seventeenth century.[37] During the later sixteenth and early seventeenth centuries, The Red Lion is frequently mentioned in records of performances by the city waits: on the Queen's Day in 1587 and 1599; at sessions dinners in 1597–8 and 1600–1; at the annual accounting day dinners in 1600–1, 1607–8, 1611–12, 1612–13, 1627–8, 1628–9, 1629–30, and 1634–5; on 5 November 1635; at the dinner for Lord Cobham in 1598–9; at the dinner for Lord Wotton in 1607–8; and during the entertainment of Prince Charles in April 1613. The Sun, where the waits entertained the mayor and aldermen on 17 November 1597, is located on Sun Street in St Alphege's parish, just outside Christ Church gate. The Sun is also mentioned in the records as the site of further entertainment by the waits on the King's Day, 24 March 1608/9. Vintners' licences survive from 1666.[38] Finally, The Three Kings, where the city waits entertained the mayor and aldermen at the sessions dinner during Michaelmas term in 1609, was located in All Saints' parish, a short distance northwest of the guildhall. One seventeenth-century vintner's licence for this inn survives from 1686 but gives no further details about the inn's exact location.[39] No information has survived either about The Swan, where the entertainers of the king played in the presence of the mayor and aldermen in 1486–7, or about The Fleur de Luce, where the Canterbury waits performed at the Christmas quarter sessions dinner in 1601 and at two further civic dinners in 1608–9.

Elsewhere in the diocese of Canterbury there are scattered references in other borough records to inns and public houses as performance spaces. At Maidstone, for example, the queen's players played during Christmas 1587 at The Star, the town's principal inn, now the site of a shopping plaza known as the Royal Star Arcade. Occupying the area between the High Street and Earl Street, The Star had numerous rooms, stables, and yards including a great county room, known as the justice chamber, where the justices of the peace met for debate during the quarter sessions and assizes, a room which may have been the venue for this performance.[40] In other towns public houses mentioned in the borough records have disappeared without a trace. At Hythe the chamberlains rewarded the king's minstrels in 1484–5 and players in 1499–1500 at The Swan; at Sandwich in 1518–19 the treasurers paid for players at The Bull. At New Romney in 1520–1 Adam the bearward was given food and drink at The Crown; at Folkestone the prince's players were given food and drink at The Chequers Inn in 1543–4. No records of these public houses survive. Even more elusive are the probable alehouses referred to only by the vintner's name, such as the payment for 'a pley at Mr ffl*uces*' in Dover during 1520–1, the reward to the players of Brookland 'att Buntyng*es*' in New Romney during 1521–2, or 'a drynkyng then at pellams' with the lord warden's minstrels in New Romney during 1554–5. Many such payments occur in the borough records for performance spaces that can no longer be traced.

TOWN HALLS

During the second half of the sixteenth century many performances by travelling players took place indoors in the town hall or court hall before audiences that included the mayor and aldermen of the town.[41] At Canterbury, for example, the court hall, or guildhall, is frequently mentioned in the records as a performance space during the sixteenth and seventeenth centuries: for the king's players in 1546–7, the lord protector's players in 1547–8 and 1548–9, the earl of Leicester's players in 1574–5 and 1576–7, the queen's players in 1582–3, Lord Strange's players in 1591–2, the lord admiral's players in 1599–1600, and Lord Chandos' players in 1607–8. The guildhall was located on the northeast side of the High Street in the parish of St Mary Bredman adjacent to The Red Lion Inn. Newly built in 1439 on the site of the hall of the old merchants' guild, the guildhall was described in the original specification as a three-storey building, measuring 41' 10" in length, and consisted of an open courtroom with a high bench on a dais and two oak side benches. At the High Street or south end of the hall there were two chambers with a jettied chamber above and at the north end another chamber with a jettied chamber above.[42] In 1806 the adjacent Red Lion Inn was demolished to allow for the construction of Guildhall Street between the High Street and Sun Street, and the eastern wall of the guildhall was rebuilt with a side entrance and windows. An interior plan of the building in 1828 shows semicircular rows of seats at the north end, an open court in the centre, and two serjeants' rooms on either side of the High Street entrance with a gallery above reached by two staircases from the open court. The dimensions on the plan, however, are much greater than the 41' 10" specified in the original contract, suggesting that the building had been extended and remodelled. In November 1950, due to the poorly constructed roof having over the centuries steadily pushed the walls outward, the building was declared unsafe and was demolished.[43] At Sandwich the ancient court hall or guildhall near St Peter's Church, where the children of St Augustine's, Canterbury, performed their play in 1515–16, was demolished in 1579. The current guildhall, erected about that time on the corner of Cattle Market and New Street, may have served as a performance venue as well, although the surviving treasurers' accounts contain no payments. At Faversham, where the town hall was constructed around 1575, there is one surviving payment 'to players at the Corte hale' in 1577–8. Other towns in the diocese of Canterbury also built town halls during the sixteenth and early seventeenth centuries, including Dover in 1605–6, Fordwich c 1540, and Maidstone in 1608.[44] No payments for players performing in these town halls, however, appear in the surviving town records.[45]

CHURCHES

Apart from the *Visitatio Sepulchri* presumably performed in Christ Church Cathedral, only two, or possibly three, other performances in churches are documented in the Kent records.[46] The first performance is mentioned in a payment in the Dover wardens' accounts for 1477–8 'to playeres in Sent Martyns Cherche,' the large church formerly located on the west side of the market square and frequently used by the town for civic purposes until it was destroyed during the Reformation. A possible second performance, mentioned in Thomas Cromwell's account book, took place at 'saynt Stephens besydes Caunturbury,' where John Bale's troupe played before Cromwell on 8 September 1538. Because St Stephen's was routinely used as the name of the village or parish of Hackington north of Canterbury, however, the performance referred to in this payment need not have taken place in the church building.[47] Nor does the payment specify the play that was performed. It may have been a performance of Bale's play *The Chief Promises of God* or, judging from the large payment of 40s, possibly a combined performance of that play with his other two biblical plays, *John Baptist's Preaching in the Wilderness* and *The Temptation of Our Lord by Satan*, all described on title page or colophon as 'compiled in 1538.'[48] The third church mentioned as a performance space in the records of the diocese of Canterbury is the parish church of St Mary Magdalene, Stockbury, where 'an Enterlude or playe' was performed in the chancel on the afternoon of 22 July 1600. The play was disrupted by servants of the Catholic Sir Edmund Baynham, who forced their way into the church, began a brawl with the players, and two months later ended up in the arch-deacon's court.[49]

The Stockbury church, which stands on the North Downs near the remains of a Norman motte and bailey castle, was a part of the ancient possessions of the Priory of Leeds and passed to the dean and chapter of Rochester following the Dissolution of the monasteries. Mentioned in the Domesday Book, the church was rebuilt in the thirteenth century with further alterations dating from the fifteenth and nineteenth centuries. There are four bays in the nave with a blanked clerestory above and narrow aisles on either side. The chancel, where the play was performed, has four more bays with arches resting on marble columns along the north and south sides of the chancel and with access on either side into the transepts through the western-most two arches. A large arch separates the nave from the chancel, and smaller arches separate the side aisles from the transepts. The north transept (16' 2" square) and the south transept (21' by 18' 6") are asymmetrical, causing the arches separating the chancel and transepts from the nave to run at an angle across the church, making the possible performance space in the chancel 36' 10" on the north, 37' 8" on the south, and 16' 2" on the east and west. The rood screen originally stretched across the nave through the fourth bay; however, the screen has now been removed and the stairway to the rood loft in the north aisle blocked up. An opening or squint in the south wall of the chancel, which originally provided sight of the main altar from the south transept, has also been blocked up. Screens, which may have been part of the rood screen, now separate the north and south transepts from the chancel. It is not known whether these screens were in place in 1600, when the interlude or play was performed in the chancel on 22 July, the patronal festival of St Mary Magdalene.

Professional Travelling Musicians

In addition to the payments to travelling minstrels and players, the borough records of the diocese of Canterbury also contain many payments to professional travelling musicians. These performers fall into two general classes: ceremonial musicians and civic musicians. In the first class belong the drummers, fife players, and trumpeters who usually accompanied royalty and the great magnates on their travels, heightening their impressive entrances or departures with trumpet fanfares or the beating of drums. When Henry VIII and Jane Seymour visited Dover in 1536, for example, the Dover wardens paid a reward to 'the kynges Trompettes' (see p 433) as well as rewards to the royal footmen. Two years later, when the king accompanied by the lord warden again visited Dover to inspect the harbour fortifications, the Dover wardens paid not only the king's trumpeters but also the lord warden's drum and fife. Similar payments to these ceremonial musicians appear in the borough accounts of Canterbury, Dover, Faversham, Folkestone, and Sandwich whenever there was a royal visit (see pp lxxxii–lxxxiv). These ceremonial musicians also travelled separately on behalf of their masters with proclamations. For example, when Henry VIII and Ferdinand formed an Anglo-Spanish alliance to counter the threat of French military expansion in October 1515, royal trumpeters accompanied the king's messengers who brought the news. The Dover wardens that year paid a reward 'to the Trvmpett*es* in reward at the *p*roclamac*io*n of the peax betwene the kyng and the *p*rince of Castell.' Other royal trumpeters were paid at Dover and Faversham at the proclaiming of the accession of James I in 1603 and again in 1625 at the accession of Charles I. Occasionally, the king's trumpeters seem to have accompanied the king's men, as suggested by the payment in the 1605–6 Maidstone chamberlains' accounts 'to the king*es* player*es* by m*aste*r maior & to the trompettors.' Both the king's players and the king's trumpeter were also paid during the same year at Faversham.

In the second class of professional travelling musicians are the civic musicians or waits, identified by their home location, who travelled to Kent from outside the county. Many of these musicians seem to have been hired to perform for particular occasions. For the Midsummer marching watch at Canterbury in 1506, for example, the chamberlains paid 'the wait*es* of londen on seint Thomas Night goyng before the wacche' and made similar payments in 1505, 1507, and 1510. Likewise, the wardens of the New Romney passion play in 1560 paid 'the wayte of Rye for his s*er*uyce at o*ur* ij^de play day.' Other waits from outside the county seem to have toured widely, performing in Kent several times over a period of years. The waits of Calais, for example, performed at Dover in 1467–8, at New Romney in 1539–40, and at Lydd in 1540–1. The waits of Hertford were paid at Lydd in 1538–9 and 1541–2, and at New Romney in 1539–40. Other travelling waits included the waits of Norwich at Sandwich in 1515–16, the waits of Harwich at Lydd in 1516–17, the waits of London at Faversham in 1519–20, the waits of Colchester at Lydd in 1541–2, and the waits of Lincoln at Canterbury in 1549–50.

Civic Musicians

WAITS AND MINSTRELS

The best documented tradition of civic waits or minstrels within Kent comes from Canterbury. Variously referred to as 'histriones,' 'uigiles,' 'musicians,' 'waits,' or 'minstrels,' the waits of Canterbury appear in the city records from 1401 until 1641, wearing the city's livery, entertaining the mayor and aldermen at civic feasts, and playing in the streets. The chamberlains' accounts record the purchase of silver scutcheons in 1401–2 and in 1416–17 the awarding of scutcheons to the minstrels John Langle, Thomas Wodelond, and William Fordmell. Similar notices appear periodically thereafter, whenever a scutcheon was returned after the death or dismissal of a wait and a replacement was chosen. Often the weight of each scutcheon in ounces of silver is noted, pledges are taken from third parties or bonds are given for the safe return of the scutcheons, and the names of the musicians are carefully recorded.

The composition of the company of city waits and the terms of their remuneration varied over the years, often becoming a disputed matter demanding resolution in burghmote court. In the fifteenth century there were usually three men; in the early sixteenth century, three men and a boy serving an apprenticeship; in the later sixteenth century, four men and a boy; and in the seventeenth, four men and two boys. Reflecting the increased size of their company, the three silver scutcheons were melted down and recast at the expense of the waits in 1584 to make five smaller ones. During most years between 1429–30 and 1594–5 the waits each received an annual grant of three yards of russet or buff cloth for their livery and thereafter the periodic renewal of the crimson silk ribbons for their silver scutcheons. In the fifteenth and early sixteenth centuries they also received an annual wage and during the later sixteenth and seventeenth centuries frequent payments for performing at various civic feasts, such as quarter sessions dinners and audit dinners, and at various civic ceremonies, such as the payment for 'playing the lowd musycke on the topp of All Saintes church in the highe streate' to welcome Prince Charles, Princess Elizabeth, and her husband the palsgrave in April 1613 (see p 262).

In addition to their official civic duties the city waits played music in the streets in the mornings, taking 'the good wylles of euery man within the liberties of the Cytty in reward towardes their paynes & travell' (see p 211), and also performed at various private functions, such as the annual dinners of the Drapers' and Tailors' guild. Numerous payments to the Canterbury waits or minstrels at Dover between 1433 and 1551, at Folkestone in 1539–40, at Lydd between 1518 and 1540, at New Romney between 1528 and 1555, and at Sandwich in 1497–8 demonstrate that the waits travelled outside the city. During the seventeenth century payments in the dean and chapter accounts reveal that at least some of the city waits also played their cornets and sackbuts in the cathedral on major feast days and their vigils.

In 1544, during the mayoralty of John Alcock, the city waits, along with all other minstrels living in Canterbury, were incorporated into the 'ffelowshyp of the Craft & mystery of Mynstrelles' (see pp 160–2). The incorporation deed regulates the hiring of apprentices and journeymen and the conduct of minstrels in the city. The hierarchy was carefully established. No town minstrels were to interfere with the city waits when they played for the aldermen or mayor or common council, nor could they interfere with fellow minstrels who were playing for weddings or May games. Travelling minstrels from other towns must give place to Canterbury minstrels at weddings, dedications, child ales, May games, or garlands. No minstrel was to call another 'knave or any other vyle wordes' either 'in sport or in malice' on pain of forfeiting 12d. And foreshadowing the changes to come, the deed included a sabbatarian clause forbidding minstrels to play on Sunday during the time of mass or evensong.

In spite of such regulations the city waits still had their share of reprimands from burghmote court. In October 1571 the court decreed 'that there shalbe appoynted a company of discrete & mete men & such as are able & quyet personez to be the waytes of the Cytty as in tyme paste hathe byn vsed/ ffor the worship of the Cytty' (see p 200). In March 1575 Edmund Nicholson was directed to reorganize the waits and 'to take to hym the other [foure] musysyons that served before yf they wyll serve reasonably & vsyng them selves well' (see p 206). In November 1631 controversy about the number of apprentices that should share in the proceeds of the company required the attention of a burghmote committee of aldermen. In April 1638, when two rival groups both petitioned the burghmote court for the honour of being named city waits, again the dispute was referred to a committee. In their report the committee recommended a compromise, choosing some players from each group, but in January 1639/40 the issue again came before the court when William Matheres, the chief wait, objected to the arrangement for dividing the money and 'did refuse to be [at] one of the waites of this Cittie vnles he may haue his owne will & a full share for his boy.' The waits were still wrangling in February 1640/1 when the court voted to disband the company: 'It is ordered that in respect of the misdemenor of this Citty musick the Escutchons of the Citty shalbe called in by master Chamberleyn & if they refuse to deliuer the same then to be sued for them by master Chamberlyn & the said Citty musick & company are hereby absolutely dischardged & dissolued.' Not until after the Restoration did the city waits again play in Canterbury.

The records of Dover, Faversham, Lydd, and Sandwich also contain evidence of civic minstrels or waits. At Dover payments to the wait, called 'fistulator' or 'piparius' in the Latin accounts and 'piper' or 'wait' in the English accounts, appear routinely in the town accounts from 1365 to 1571. Along with the town clerk, town serjeant, mayor's serjeant, and other civic officers, the wait is named at the beginning of the annual rough accounts. Occasionally, two musicians served together but usually only one held the post, receiving an annual stipend for livery and a quarterly wage of 5s, rising to 6s 8d by the mid-sixteenth century. After 1570–1 all mention of the wait disappears from the town records until 1605 when the assembly act book notes that Matthew Woodden volunteered to serve as wait free of charge without either wages or livery. At Faversham, in contrast to the extensive evidence of town waits at Dover, only two references appear in the chamberlains' accounts: a payment in 1561–2 'to the waites of the Town for ther wages for one hole yere' and a payment in 1572–3 for the 'aperile of waittes.' At Lydd there is only one reference to waits in the chamberlains' accounts: a reference in 1517–18 'for the wages of the wayte betwene alhalowyn & Cristemasse.' At Sandwich references in the town year books and in the surviving account rolls, although sporadic, suggest a civic tradition of town musicians throughout the fifteenth and sixteenth centuries. In 1468–9 the waits received 40s for their wages and 16s for their livery. In 1476–7 John Watson, William Watson, and William Scarlett were appointed waits by the mayor and jurats and were granted the scutcheons of office. In 1489–90 the treasurers paid for remaking a silver collar for one of the waits. Further payments for wages and for livery appear in the accounts for 1482–3, 1489–90, and 1536–7. Few accounts survive for the later sixteenth century; however, the year book does contain an order in January 1567/8 for paying the wages of the town wait. As in Canterbury the Sandwich waits played for the public as well as for the mayor and jurats, for reference is made in 1536–7 'to the Mynstrelles gowing euery morning about the Town piping,' a custom that Bavarian envoy, Leo of Rozmital, had noted during his visit to Sandwich in February 1465/6. Like the Canterbury waits the Sandwich waits also travelled and performed outside the town. The Sandwich minstrels or waits received numerous payments for performing at Dover between 1381 and 1492, as well as payments at Canterbury in 1402–3, at Hythe in 1483–4, and at New Romney in 1478–9 and 1491–2.

HORN BLOWING

Medieval and early modern Kentish towns also paid civic musicians for blowing the brazen horn to assemble the townspeople for meetings or to defend the town in times of danger. The surviving custumals of Dover, Faversham, Folkestone, New Romney, and Sandwich all describe the custom of blowing the town horn at various locations in the town to signal the freemen to assemble for the annual mayoral election. At Hythe, where the custumal does not survive, the account books contain payments in 1582–3 and 1619–20 for blowing the horn for the election at Candlemas. An agreement in 1258 between the abbot of Faversham Abbey and the men of Faversham specified certain other occasions for blowing the horn of Faversham: for meetings of the burghmote, for the death of a man, for the command of the king, for fire, and for setting of watch against criminals or invasion. Records of purchase and repair of town horns also demonstrate their common use in Kentish towns. Canterbury, in one of few references to horn blowing, paid 'for amending the Burghmot horne' in 1615–16. Dover purchased two horns 'pro vigilatoribus' in 1370–1 although the town had a horn as early as February 1297/8, when the horn was blown to call the townsmen to prevent the archbishop's messengers from delivering a summons for town officials to appear in the ecclesiastical courts. Over the years the Dover wardens paid for periodic repairs, including payments in 1551–2 'to Robard the tynker for mendyng of the towne horne' and in 1601–2 'for Sodering the Brasen horne.' Faversham paid for mending its horn in 1540–1, 1552–3, 1565–6, and 1636–7; Lydd purchased two horns 'pro le wachemen' in 1436–7 and a third in 1454–5; and New Romney, where frequent payments for blowing the town horn appear in the records between 1432 and 1608, bought a new horn in 1614–15. In addition payments to various town officials for blowing the horn further demonstrate its common use in Kentish towns although in some cases the responsibility for blowing the town horn seems to have been included in the job description of the town wait or town serjeant and therefore was not especially noted in the accounts. That appears to have been the case in Canterbury where, apart from a single payment to the town crier in 1637, no payments for horn blowing appear in the accounts. At Dover, however, payments appear almost annually between 1367 and 1609 for horn blowing. Originally, the town wait received a reward of 2d for each horn blowing in addition to his regular quarterly stipend; however, in 1538 the job passed to the town serjeant. At Folkestone the town serjeant also performed the duty, receiving during the 1540s an annual fee of 14d, rising to 24d during the seventeenth century. At Sandwich the town serjeant, or common wardman, received an annual supplement to his wages of 16d in the early sixteenth century and 4s during the seventeenth century for blowing the town horn.

RINGING THE BASIN

Public punishment in medieval and early modern towns often included the carting of wrong-doers through the streets of the town to the mocking cacophony of clashing cymbals or the beating of metal basins. In the Kent records this custom of rough music, or charivari, first appears in the Sandwich records where it is the punishment for scolds prescribed in a fourteenth-century custumal. Women guilty of brawling or quarrelling in the streets or other public places were to be led through the town, carrying a mortar and preceded by the wait or another minstrel making some sort of rough music (see p 823). At the end of this spectacle the wait was to receive 1d from the woman for his trouble. The surviving accounts include no particular payments for this punishment, probably since the accused was responsible for paying the wait; however, a memorandum in the Sandwich assembly book in 1638 does describe ringing the basin during the punishment of a 'leud wench' who had abused the mayoress, 'calling her by many ill termes, and saying she cared not a fart for her.' A similar clause for the punishment of scolds appears in the fifteenth-century Fordwich custumal, which was based on the Sandwich custumal. No early accounts survive in Fordwich; however, the mayor's accounts for 1578–9 do contain a payment to two boys for 'leadinge of a cart & Ringinge a bason.' During the second half of the sixteenth century numerous payments appear in the Canterbury chamberlains' accounts for carting and basin ringing. The crime most often mentioned was sexual immorality, as in the payment in 1562–3 'ffor a Cart & one yat Range ye basson beffore a harlott,' but basin ringing was also used to punish seditious speech in 1558–9 and witchcraft in 1571–2. Typical punishment included ringing the basin while leading the guilty person through the streets in a horse-drawn cart, the crime written on a placard and displayed on his or her head. Sometimes the punishment also included whipping, as in the 1576–7 payment 'to hym that was in the devylles clothes that whypped the man & the woman' and in the 1585–6 payments for carting, writing of papers, ringing the basin, and for 'hym that dyd whyp the woman.' During the seventeenth century the Dover court records and account books also relate in great detail both the sexual crimes and their punishment that culminated in ringing the basin in 1604–5, 1606–7, 1610–11, 1611–12, 1614–15, and 1619–20. As in Canterbury a paper, usually bearing the words 'for whoredome,' was placed on the head of the guilty party or parties as they were carted through the streets with the discordant serenade of rough music.

DRUMS AND DRUMMING

In addition to the discordant rough music of ringing the basin, the clarion call of the brazen horn, and the sound of cornets, sackbuts, and shawms played by the town waits in the streets, the beating of drums also filled the urban air of early modern Kent. During the sixteenth and seventeenth centuries militia bands marched and trained to the music of fife and drum; however, drumming in Kent was not limited to military activity. At Canterbury in 1554 and 1555 drummers beat their drums in the marching watch with pageants on the eve of the Translation of St Thomas Becket. At Dover throughout the early seventeenth century and at Sandwich in 1625–6 the town drummers called people to work at the harbour and to work on the highways. Town drummers welcomed visiting royalty, as at Faversham in 1573 during the progress of Elizabeth I or at Sandwich in 1641 during the visit of the prince of Orange. Town drummers even drummed on holidays. At Lydd there are payments in 1579 for 'playing vppon the drom in ye Easter Hollidaies' and 'in whitson Holidaies' and in 1588 'for playeng vppon our droms on the queenes daye' on 17 November. At Dover in 1589 there is a payment 'for playeng the dromme to give warning vnto the tounsmen agaynst may day.'

All of the ancient towns in the diocese of Canterbury, with the possible exception of Fordwich, owned their own drums. Numerous payments for the purchase and repair of drums appear throughout the second half of the sixteenth century and the first half of the seventeenth century. Canterbury purchased drums in 1569–70, 1587–8, 1608–9, and 1639–40. Dover spent 10s on a drum in 1557–8, 14s in 1568–9, 12s in 1584–5, 7s 6d in 1588–9, £2 for two drums bought in London in 1623–4, and £3 13s for two more drums bought in London in 1635. An inventory of the court hall in 1634–5 lists three drums and three pairs of drumsticks. Faversham levied a cess to buy a drum for the town in 1557–8. In 1588–9 Hythe paid 18s for a new drum and in 1622–3 an additional £1 15s 'for a Newe Drumme a Drumme Case & drumme heades.' Lydd spent 33s 4d for a drum in 1582–3; thereafter, town records refer to both 'the great drome' and 'the lyttle drome' (see p 702). No record survives of the purchase of a drum at Maidstone; however, in 1575–6 Maidstone chamberlains paid for 'newe hedynge of the townes drume.' New Romney spent £2 10s for a new drum in 1608–9 and £2 3s for a drum in 1620–1. Sandwich paid £1 2s 4d 'to Iohn the Ioiner for A drum for the townes vse' in 1628–9 and bought two more drums in 1634–5 and 1641–2. Tenterden purchased a new drum and a drum case in 1635–6. Scores of payments also appear in the records for mending broken drums, for heading the drums, and for supplying new hoops, new cords, new braces, new snares, new drumsticks, and new drum cases.

In addition to purchasing and repairing their town drums all of the ancient towns in the diocese of Canterbury except Maidstone employed their own town drummers, paying them a quarterly wage along with the other town officers in addition to any specific payments made to them for military musters. Some towns, such as Dover, Faversham, Fordwich, and Lydd, had employed drummers during the 1580s, perhaps in response to the growing threat of invasion by the Spanish Armada. During the seventeenth century these towns, as well as Canterbury, Folkestone, Hythe, New Romney, and Tenterden, were making regular payments to town drummers. At Lydd, for example, a memorandum in the 1618–19 chamberlains' accounts states 'that Markes [Sq] Skinner the dromme of the Towne shall yearly soe long as he Contineweth the said place have by the yeare for exercisinge the said place eight shillinges.' In 1623–4 another memorandum raised his salary 'for beatinge of the drvmme' to 20s. Town chamberlains made annual payments for his wages during the 1620s and 1630s. The most elaborate arrangements for civic drumming were made at Dover where the activities of the town's drummers were most extensive. After receiving occasional payments over several years for drumming, Henry Barnes petitioned the mayor and jurats in September 1617 for an annual stipend to cover his drumming 'at the seuerall dayes of Musters, Trayninge of Souldiors, Calling of labourers to work at the high wayes or at the havens mouth or at the walles of the harbour or pent and for all other service for his Maiestie, or the Townshipp.' The mayor and jurats agreed to pay him an annual stipend of 20s and allowed him to run a victualling house 'ffree of the payment of ij d. the Barrell for drawing of Beere,' on the condition that he both perform his duties and undertake to instruct three boys nominated by the town 'to play or Beate the drvm perfectly.' Quarterly payments, rising to 10s a quarter in the late 1630s, continued to be paid through 1642 to Henry Barnes or his apprentices and successors for drumming in Dover.

Civic Ceremonial Customs

PROCESSIONS AND MARCHING WATCHES WITH PAGEANTS

Throughout late medieval and early modern England people were on the march during late May and June. In many places Corpus Christi processions, often with pageants or plays, took place between 21 May and 24 June. Other towns and cities marked Midsummer on 24 June not only with traditional bonfires but also with marching watches and processions that included dancers, musicians, and pageants.[50] John Stow in *A Survey of London* (1598), for example, describes the marching watches formerly held on the vigils of the feasts of St John the Baptist (23 June) and Sts Peter and Paul (28 June), civic parades by torchlight that included not only the mayor and aldermen marching with soldiers, drummers, and trumpeters, but also minstrels, morris dancers, pageants, and giants.[51] In Canterbury during the early sixteenth century the Midsummer marching watch with giants, morris dancers, torches, and pageants was held on 6 July, the eve of the Translation of St Thomas Becket. Expenses for the Canterbury marching watch and pageants began in 1505 and continued through Midsummer 1522. Between 1523 and 1529 the city chamberlains' accounts contain payments only for storage of the St Thomas pageant wagon; however, full expenses for the marching watch resumed in Midsummer 1530. Two undated ordinances for the resumption of the marching watch and the Corpus Christi play probably date from this time. The ordinance for the marching watch notes that 'summe Maiers in ther yere haue full honourably kepte the seide wacche and summe Maiers none' (see p 139) and establishes a fine of £10 for any mayor failing to keep the watch during his year. The ordinance for the Corpus Christi play also notes that 'nowe of late daies it hath bene lefte & laide aparte to the grete hurte & decay of the seide Cite' (see p 139) and orders that all crafts and mysteries in the city should be incorporated 'for the sustentacion & contynuance of theseide play' (see p 140). An order for the marching watch in 1532–3 during the mayoralty of Thomas Bele describes the Canterbury procession and pageants: giants, morris dancers, musicians, the mayor and aldermen processing in their scarlet gowns or in armour, firelight flashing from seventy-eight cressets, over 300 marching militia men brandishing handguns, bills, bows, morris pikes, and two-handed swords, and the five pageants of the Annunciation, the Nativity, the Assumption, St George, and St Thomas Becket.

Expenses for the St Thomas pageant first appeared in the city chamberlains' accounts for 1504–5, including construction of a pageant wagon, forging the armour for the knights, hire of a sword, and painting the alb and head of St Thomas. Routine expenses for the pageant included payments for horse hire, payments for food and drink for the children who played the knights and the men who carried the pageant, payments for washing the costumes and storage of the pageant, and numerous payments for silver foil, gold foil, glue, thread, needles, wire, and repair of the head of St Thomas. Occasional improvements for the St Thomas pageant included the painting of an angel in 1513–14 and in 1519–20 the painting of 'an ymage of our lady with ij angelles gylt to hang ayenst the ymage of seynt Thomas vppon the auter' (see p 118). In 1514–15 payments began for a mechanical device called 'the vyce,' described more fully the following year as 'the vyce of ye angell,' that needed three yards of wire, a man to turn it, and a

'candell to lyght the turner of the vyce' (see p 113). In 1520–1 an entirely new pageant wagon
was constructed. Other general expenses for the procession included payments for gunpowder
and for fetching the guns from the storehouse, payments for the waits of London who for
several years marched in the procession, and in 1521–2 payment 'for a staf & a baner to bere
byfore the Mores pyk*es* ⌈& the gunners⌉ on seynt Thomas eve' (see p 129). No expenses appear
in the city accounts, however, for the remaining four pageants of the Annunciation, the
Nativity, the Assumption, and St George. Nor have any records of these pageants survived in
churchwardens' accounts or guild records in the city, with the possible exceptions of a receipt in
the St Andrew's churchwardens' accounts in 1520 for torches supplied to 'the wardens of the
Grocerr*es* paieaunte' (see p 120) and expenses incurred in 1556–7 by the Drapers' and Tailors'
guild for torches, candles, and 'caryng the pagent' (see p 178). Who performed and paid for the
Canterbury pageants of the Annunciation, the Nativity, the Assumption, and St George remains
a tantalizing mystery.

After the eve of the Translation of St Thomas Becket in 1538, the annual Canterbury
marching watch with pageants became embroiled in the national and local power struggle
between reformers and conservatives in the Henrician Reformation.[52] Against the background
of the 1536 injunctions of Cromwell that discouraged pilgrimages and the veneration of relics
of the saints, as well as the forthcoming September 1538 injunctions that would require the
removal of images, Henry VIII moved during the summer of 1538 to end the veneration of
St Thomas Becket. On 24 April 1538 St Thomas had been formally cited before the king's
council. On 11 June, St Thomas having been cited and no one having defended him, the
council pronounced its sentence: 'Judgment is given that in his life time he disturbed the realm,
and his crimes were the cause of his death, although the people hold him for a martyr. He is
therefore never to be named martyr in future, his bones are to be taken up and publicly burnt
and the treasures of his shrine confiscated to the King.'[53] Following the publication of this edict
in London and in Canterbury, the sentence was executed in September 1538, when the shrine
was destroyed, the gold and silver and precious stones confiscated, the relics publicly burnt, and
the ashes scattered. In the royal proclamation published in November 1538 Henry proclaimed
Becket a rebel: 'His pictures throughout the realm are to be plucked down and his festival shall
no longer be kept, and the services in his name shall be razed out of all books.'[54] The city
complied with the king's order, selling 'the Cart of Bysshop beket*tes* pageant' in 1539–40 (see
p 152) and removing the saint's image from the city's seal in 1541. In July 1541 the city kept
the marching watch without the pageants, paying 'for fetchyng of Gyaunt*es* & the gonnes from
ye store house' (see p 153). In 1542 and 1543 the city put on a play requiring a stage and
costumes for four tormentors, possibly another re-enactment of the martyrdom of St Thomas
Becket, but then sold the stage in 1543.

No further expenses for a St Thomas Becket play or pageant appear in the city records until
the veneration of the saint was revived during the reign of Queen Mary I. Again St Thomas
Becket served as a political touchstone for the Canterbury establishment. In July 1554 the
marching watch marched again with morris pikes, guns, drums, and torches, with the trumpeter
of the lord warden of the Cinque Ports and the trumpeter of Dover Castle leading the procession. During the following year a new pageant wagon was constructed for the St Thomas

pageant in the marching watch on 6 July 1555. No marching watch with pageants was held on 6 July 1556; however, burghmote court agreed on 22 September not to fine the outgoing mayor £10 for neglecting to keep the watch during his year. There is an unfortunate gap in the city accounts between Michaelmas 1555 and Michaelmas 1557; however, expenses in the account book of the Drapers' and Tailors' guild may indicate a watch with pageants on 6 July 1557. No watch was held on 6 July 1558. During the following year on 13 June 1559 burghmote court decreed 'that the comon wacche vsed to be kept on seynt Thomas Evyn next shall not be then done with pageantes.'

In 1561, looking back on those days when the city kept the marching watch with pageants, prebendary of the cathedral John Bale wrote, 'As the preachers haue bene in the pulpett, with a very small numbre of hearers afore them, the cytie neuerthelesse beynge populouse and great, they haue mocked them with their maye games, troubled them with their tombrelles, greued them with their gunnes, and molested them with their other mad mastryes: they settynge fourth those vnruly pageauntes, whose dewtye it had bene, to haue seane best rule, and vpon the sondaye to haue sought the glorye of God with edifycatyon of sowle.' Perhaps under the new Protestant monarch the mayor and aldermen agreed with Bale, for on 19 May 1564 burghmote court repealed the marching watch order and sold the pageant wagon for the final time.

TRIUMPHS AND FESTIVE CELEBRATIONS

Early modern towns throughout England often celebrated significant political events, such as military victories or royal marriages and births, with bell ringing, drumming, music, fireworks, bonfires, civic feasts, and special prayers.[55] Such celebrations featured prominently in the Tudor and Stuart civic life of the town of Dover and to a lesser extent in the town of Sandwich, where political news from London was frequently marked by religious processions, torches, bonfires, distribution of bread and beer, and musical entertainment. In 1537, for example, Dover celebrated with a 'triumphe for Ioye that quyne Iane is with childe.' On that occasion the Dover wardens paid for a bonfire, wine, beer, bread, trumpeters, and the singing of the *Te deum*. Later that same year on 20 October, when a yeoman of the guard came with news of the birth of Prince Edward, another triumph included a general procession, festival mass, and singing of the *Te deum* at St Martin's Church followed by a bonfire with wine, beer, ale, and bread in the market square. At Sandwich 'the Triumphe of the princes birth' included payments for a procession, bread, drink, and the firing of guns. Other civic celebrations at Dover included 'a Tryvmphe doon by the kinges Commaundment for Marryage of hys doghter' in 1507–8, a triumph for 'the byrth of the prynce' in 1510–11, 'the tryhumphe when tydynges came that the Kyng of Scottes was slayne' in 1513–14, 'the tryhumphe of the coronation of the kynges maiestie' in 1546–7, another 'tryuhmphe of the coronation of our soueraing lord the kynges Edward the Syxt' in 1547–8, 'the trymhmphe at the proclamacion of quyne maryes grace' in 1552–3, 'the tryhowmphe of the proclamatione of quene elisabethe' in 1558–9, and trumpeters, bell ringing, and bonfires 'when the king was proclaymed' in 1602–3 and again in 1624–5 'att the proclamation of the king.'

In addition to these ad hoc civic celebrations Tudor and Stuart monarchs also encouraged the commemoration of royal anniversaries, partly to compensate for the reduction in religious holidays after the Reformation and partly to reinforce the importance of the royal dynasty. Throughout the country the accession of Elizabeth I on 17 November, variously called the Queen's Day, Coronation Day, or the Queen's Holiday, was commemorated by the ringing of church bells, religious services, civic feasting, bonfires, and pageants.[56] Many Kentish parishes rang their church bells on 17 November. In Canterbury the mayor and aldermen marked the day with a civic feast for the town officers at which music was usually provided by the city waits. In Dover the more populist celebration included civic bonfires, bell ringing, distribution of bread to the poor, and musical entertainment provided by the town wait. In 1602 the Dover wardens paid for 'Certen songes (geven to the maior Iurattes and Comon Counsell) to be songe at the Coronacion daie.' In 1588 the Lydd chamberlains paid two drummers 'for playeng vppon our droms on the queenes daye.' Even more elaborate celebrations on 17 November were staged during the 1580s in Maidstone, where the chamberlains paid for feasting on venison and ox, fireworks, torches, bell ringing, trumpeters, musicians, and a pageant. The pageant was performed by boys of the Maidstone Grammar School and supervised by the new schoolmaster Thomas Symonson, who had been appointed in 1585.[57] Expenses included payments in 1586 for 'makinge the Scaffold for the Children,' in 1587 for 'makinge the scaffold and carienge the pagiant,' and in 1588 for costumes, a stage, and a reward 'paid vnto Mr Simosone for his paynes takinge one the coronation daye.' Omission of any reference in the town accounts to parts or playbooks, however, suggests more tableau or spectacle than drama.

After 1603 civic celebration continued on 24 March, commemorating the accession of James I. At Maidstone annual bell ringing continued throughout the king's reign. At Dover the usual expenses for the bonfire, bell ringing, and distribution of wine and bread included in 1604 a payment to the town wait 'for musick at the meeting this day.' At Canterbury the civic dinners on 24 March for the mayor, aldermen, and officers included entertainment by the city waits in 1605 and in 1612. Beginning on 5 November 1606 the Canterbury establishment, like many other towns throughout the country, also added another feast to the civic calendar with the commemoration of the delivery of King James from the Gunpowder Plot of Guy Fawkes.[58] The marching watch, which had been abandoned in 1564 early in Elizabeth's reign, marched again through the streets of Canterbury, although without pageants, on Guy Fawkes Day. On 5 November 1638 'the shott of the selected band' dined with the city officers at The Chequers Inn; in 1611 mistress mayor and the aldermen's wives joined the mayor and aldermen for the annual feast at The Swan. Again the city waits usually provided entertainment for these dinners on 5 November.

In addition the waits also played their music for the city oligarchy during the other secular feasts in the Canterbury civic calendar. The rhythm of civic life in Canterbury during the Elizabethan and Stuart years was marked four times a year by the quarter sessions dinners at Christmas, Lady Day, Midsummer, and Michaelmas and by the annual audit or 'countie' dinner usually during November or December after the annual accounts had been read and approved. Gifts of venison from county magnates for these regular civic feasts and other occasional dinners emphasized and enhanced the prestige of the city oligarchy. In 1597, for example, the newly appointed lord lieutenant, Henry Brooke, Lord Cobham, sent a 'fate dowe' for the annual dinner on the Queen's Day on 17 November. In 1618 the feast on 5 November featured another 'ffatt dooe' sent by Edward, Lord Wotton, the lord lieutenant of the county, 'to ma*ster* maior and the rest of the Company.' In 1607–8 '4 great pasties of venison' were made from a deer given by the lord treasurer. In the same year the preparation of venison pasties from another deer sent by the lord lieutenant required two bushels of flour, twenty pounds of suet, thirteen pounds of butter, one pound of pepper, and fifty eggs. Altogether at that dinner the city chamberlains spent £5 14s 8d for the food, drink, and entertainment of thirty invited knights and gentlemen plus the serjeants, officers, and waits of the city (see pp 250–1).

VISITS OF ROYALTY AND NOBILITY

The status of the civic oligarchy in the east Kent towns of Canterbury and Dover, and to a lesser extent in Faversham and Sandwich, was further enhanced by the frequent visits of royalty and nobility to the county. Medieval monarchs, such as Edward I in 1299 or Edward II in 1310, came to Canterbury to visit the shrine of St Thomas Becket and to confer with the archbishop, the prior of Christ Church, or the abbot of St Augustine's. Other monarchs, such as Henry VI in 1452, Edward IV in 1482, or Henry VIII in 1513, visited both Canterbury and Dover on their way to wage war in France or to inspect the fortifications along the Kentish coast. During the 1530s and 1540s Henry VIII made almost annual visits to these towns. Often monarchs welcomed foreign dignitaries at the ports of Dover or Sandwich, entertained them at Dover Castle or at Canterbury, and then escorted them to London, passing along Watling Street through Faversham and Rochester. In 1539, for example, Anne of Cleves landed at Deal near Sandwich and was entertained by Archbishop Cranmer at Canterbury before meeting Henry at Rochester. In 1555 and twice during 1557 Philip passed through Faversham, Canterbury, and Dover on the way to and from the Netherlands. In 1582 Elizabeth I accompanied the duke of Alençon through Faversham and Canterbury to Sandwich, where he embarked for France. In 1625 Charles I met his bride, the French princess Henrietta Maria, at Dover and entertained her at Canterbury before continuing to London. Altogether almost every monarch from Edward I to Charles I was entertained with music, drama, or civic ceremony in the towns and ports of Kent, during which period Canterbury and Dover each registered over thirty visits.[59]

The usual entertainment of visiting royalty included payments for food, drink, and rewards to officials and entertainers travelling with the monarch. During June 1470, for example, while pursuing Warwick and Henry VI who had fled to France, Edward IV came to Dover to discuss the defence of the town with William Fitz Alan, the earl of Arundel and lord warden of the Cinque Ports. Town officials provided wine and halibut for the king and paid rewards to the lord warden's minstrels and to the king's minstrels, trumpeters, and footmen (see pp 345–6). During a similar visit the previous year, the Dover chamberlains not only paid the usual rewards to the lord warden's minstrels and the king's minstrels, trumpeters, and footmen but also provided wine, halibut, and eighteen capons for the king and paid several men for fishing for the king (see p 344). In 1500, when Henry VII passed through Dover on his way to Calais for trade talks with Archduke Philip, Dover officials supplied four dozen quails, ten sheep, and an ox to entertain the royal party in Dover Castle and paid rewards to the king's footmen, the king's minstrels, and the queen's minstrels. Such occasions often involved delicate diplomacy on the part of town officials. In 1515, for example, after the death of Louis XII, when Henry VIII's sister Mary returned from France determined to marry the duke of Suffolk, Henry had dispatched Edward Stafford, duke of Buckingham, to meet the couple in Dover. Canterbury officials sent a messenger to Dover 'to know the Dukys pleasur how Maister Mayer shoulde receyve the frenche quene comyng oute of ffraunce to Canterbury.' After this consultation the town clerk and one of the aldermen rode to Dover to meet the queen, presented her with an elaborate 'dysshe of ffysshe' including ten lobsters and three turbots, and paid rewards to Mary's footmen and the duke of Buckingham's minstrel. The occasion evidently passed off successfully since the chamberlains later paid 4d 'for a potell of white wyne for Master Mayer & the aldermen after they had received the ffrenche quene.'

On other occasions the entertainment was more elaborate. Before Henry VIII met Francis I at the Field of the Cloth of Gold in June 1520, the emperor Charles V came to Kent to consult with the king. Henry, Katherine, and Wolsey travelled to Canterbury, stopping along the way in Faversham where the town officials entertained them with spiced bread, wine, beer, and ale and paid rewards to the king's footmen, the queen's footmen, the cardinal's footmen, and the king's minstrels. Charles arrived in Dover on 26 May, where he and his retinue were met by Wolsey and Henry and entertained by Dover officials (see pp 414–15) before being conducted to Canterbury, where the emperor was received at the archbishop's palace by his aunt, Queen Katherine. The city chamberlains' accounts show that as early as 16 April Canterbury officials had consulted with the lord warden and the lord chief justice about arrangements for the king's visit. New livery was purchased for the city officers. During the visit rewards were paid to the footmen of the king and queen and cardinal, the king's trumpeters, and the king's waits (see pp 118–19). Letters written by the Venetian ambassadors during the visit describe a mass celebrated by Cardinal Wolsey in the cathedral followed by an elaborate banquet for over 200 lords and ladies lasting four hours, a masque involving lovers, and dancing in the Spanish style (see pp 120–2). On 29 May Henry accompanied Charles to Sandwich, where the emperor embarked for Flanders (see pp 120–1), and on 31 May Henry, Katherine, and Wolsey sailed for Calais from Dover, where town officials paid for further wine and rewards to the various noblemen, the lord admiral's minstrels, the lord warden's minstrels, the king's trumpeters, and other members of the king's household (see p 415).

On her progress through Sussex and Kent during August and September 1573, Elizabeth I visited Dover, Sandwich, Canterbury, and Faversham. On 25 August the archbishop, accompanied by many knights and gentlemen, met the queen on Folkestone Down and escorted her to Dover, where she was welcomed by an orator, presented with a cup, and then conducted to Dover Castle surrounded by the sound of ringing bells and discharging ordnance.[60] On 31 August the queen proceeded to Sandwich, where she was greeted at the town gates by the mayor, dressed in his scarlet gown, who presented her with the town mace to the accompaniment of drumming and the discharge of ordnance and muskets. Richard Spycer, vicar of St Clement's Church, welcomed her with an oration and presented her with a Greek New Testament and a golden cup worth £100. Entertainment the following day included a mock sea battle in the harbour and an assault on a specially erected fort at Stonar on the other side of the River Stour (see pp 857–9). Similar civic ceremony on 3 September marked the queen's arrival in Canterbury, where the mayor and aldermen in their scarlet gowns met the queen on horseback, an oration was delivered, and a gift was presented, and on 16 September in Faversham, where the queen was greeted by an honour guard of militia men, drums, and flutes, an oration was delivered by a child from a stage, and a cup purchased in London was presented to the queen. Both the Canterbury and Faversham chamberlains paid rewards to various royal servants, including the queen's trumpeters, drummers, musicians, jester, and bearward. At the cathedral the dean and chapter also presented the queen with a gift of gold coins and her trumpeters and musicians with rewards. At the archbishop's palace the archbishop entertained her at a banquet that concluded with music and dancing.

BULLBAITING AND BEARBAITING

In addition to the civic ceremony celebrating royal visits and other special events, another common custom in Tudor Kentish towns was watching bullbaiting and bearbaiting. In the bull-rings of Canterbury, Dover, Faversham, and Sandwich snarling and snapping dogs were pitted against bulls that gored and tossed the dogs on their horns and trampled them under their hooves. Market regulations in Canterbury forbade the city's butchers from selling beef until the bulls 'be chasyd or baytid at the Bulstake' (see p 87). Fines for butchers who had killed unbaited bulls began in 1489 and continued as late as 1601 although for most years in the late sixteenth and early seventeenth centuries no fines were levied. That bulls were routinely baited before butchering in Canterbury during this period, however, may be deduced from the frequent payments between 1501 and 1641 for paving and repairs at the bullstake. In 1547–8 the city paid 14d 'for makyng of dyuerse fourmes for the markett folkes to sett on' and in 1570–1 8s 'ffor ij Ioyned fformes ffor ye aldermenn to set on at the bulstak.' Other occasional expenses included 3s 10d in 1601–2 for bricks, lime, sand, and a mason's labour 'for to vnderpyn the bulstacke,' a total of £7 8s in 1602–3 for repairing the penthouse roof of the bullstake and setting up the pinnacles and vanes (see pp 241–3), another 2s in the same year 'for makinge 4 new fourmes at Bulstake & for legginge the old' (see p 243), and 20s in 1624–5 'for newe painting the armes at the Bulstacke' (see p 276). Altogether between 1501 and 1641 the city chamberlains made 151 separate payments totalling over £32 for repairs and improvements at the Canterbury bullstake. Such extensive evidence for bullbaiting does not survive in the records of other east Kent towns; however, the Dover records do show fines for unbaited bulls in 1552–3 and 1555–6, a market regulation dated 1446 forbids the slaying or selling of unbaited bulls in Faversham, and the Sandwich records include payments in 1462–3 for baiting bulls and in 1518–19 'for Tymbre and Iron worke to amende the bulring.'

The routine entertainment provided by bullbaiting in the markets of the larger east Kent towns was supplemented in most Kentish towns during the fifteenth, sixteenth, and early seventeenth centuries by bearbaiting provided by bearwards travelling under royal and noble patronage. Payments for bearbaiting appear in the records of every Kentish town except Tenterden, where the early records do not survive, and Fordwich, whose poverty evidently curtailed professional entertainment. Although Maidstone chamberlains made no official payments to bearwards, they did pay a total of £2 18s 4d for paving 'at the place comonly called the bere stake' in 1574–5 and 2s 6d for 'making cleane the crosse & bearstake' in 1594–5. Elsewhere, from the earliest payment to bearwards in Lydd in 1445–6 to the last recorded payment in Faversham in 1615–16, over 200 payments to bearwards appear in the records of Kent towns. Visits of travelling bearwards often provided the occasion for official civic entertainment as, for example, at Dover in 1513–14, when the wardens paid 'for expences of Master Maire and his Brethern at a Soper then beyng there the kynges Bereward' or at Sandwich in 1519–20, when the treasurers paid not only a reward to the duke of Suffolk's bearward but also 'for wyne for Master Mayer & his brethren drynking with the said berward.' Nor was bearbaiting restricted to urban entertainment provided by professional bearwards. In 1610 the churchwardens of the parish of Molash presented before the archdeacon's court one Ralph Knowles of the neighbouring parish of Boughton Aluph 'for bayting of the Beare in our parishe vpon sondaye in Evening prayer tyme.' Bearbaiting reached its peak of popularity in Kentish towns during the first half of the sixteenth century with 36 per cent of all payments to bearwards falling in the first quarter of the century and 21 per cent in the second quarter. During the late fifteenth century patrons of travelling bearwards in Kent included such noblemen as George Plantagenet, duke of Clarence; Thomas Stanley, earl of Derby; John de Vere, earl of Oxford; and Richard Grey, earl of Kent. During the reign of Henry VIII other patrons included Henry Percy, earl of Northumberland; Charles Brandon, duke of Suffolk; and Edward Stanley, earl of Derby. From the mid-1540s onwards, however, payments in the Kent records were made almost exclusively to bearwards of the king or queen, including forty-five payments to the bearwards of Elizabeth I between 1560 and 1593 and twelve payments to the bearwards of James I between 1604 and 1616. Payments declined sharply even to these royal bearwards during the late sixteenth and early seventeenth centuries but continued in most towns, except in Hythe and Sandwich, where there are gaps in the records, and in Canterbury, where the Puritan establishment increasingly restricted entertainment. In March 1597 John Bly was called before Canterbury magistrates 'for a noyinge the Queenes hey way with the solege of Tow beares.'

Other animal sports and exhibits in Tudor towns merit a minor mention. There is one recorded payment in Canterbury during 1518–19 for the traditional Shrovetide sport of cock-fighting. A dromedary was exhibited at Lydd in 1466–7. Payments were made for the king's lion at Canterbury in 1474–5 and at Dover in 1484–5, for a keeper of lions at Dover in 1483–4, for a dancing bear at Sandwich in 1516–17, for an ape at Lydd in 1539–40, and for a bearward who also showed a wolf at Folkestone in 1541–2.

Popular Mimetic Customs

From year to year the late medieval and early modern towns of east Kent sponsored the organized civic ceremonial customs of bearbaiting and bullbaiting, entertaining visiting royalty and nobility, celebrating royal anniversaries and political developments with bonfires, music, drumming, bell ringing, pageants, and feasting, and at Canterbury displaying the military preparedness and civic pride of the city in the annual marching watch with pageants. Supplementing these official ceremonial events were numerous informal popular customs observed in the towns and parishes throughout the diocese of Canterbury. Such popular customs usually involved feasting, music, and dancing, often with a mimetic component such as disguising, role reversal, or the acting out of folk rituals. Just as the civic ceremonial customs followed the rhythm of the civic year so these popular mimetic customs followed the rhythm of the church year and the natural cycle of the seasons. Beginning with Advent and Christmas and continuing through the major Christian festivals of Epiphany, Easter, Ascension, and Whitsun, the celebrations of the church year mingled and merged with the natural rhythm of the seasons: Christmas festivity with Midwinter wassail, Whitsun ales with May games and morris dancing, Corpus Christi processions with Midsummer bonfires and marching watches.

The surviving evidence for popular mimetic customs is far more fragmentary and dispersed than the evidence for the dramatic, musical, and ceremonial activity that is concentrated in the annual records of the larger Kentish towns. Few official records were kept of informal celebrations. Summer games may have escaped official notice unless they involved expenditure by parish churchwardens or borough chamberlains or unless they involved disorder or damage to property and came to the notice of the ecclesiastical courts or magistrates. Maypoles may have been noticed in the records only when they needed repair or when they were erected or taken down. Other long-standing customs, such as wassailing the apple trees on New Year's Eve or Twelfth Night at Fordwich, were mentioned only when they were interrupted for some reason or when they were discontinued. Many of these popular mimetic customs were doubtless performed for years or decades without ever appearing in official records. The caveat that absence of evidence is not evidence of absence is nowhere more pertinent than in attempts to assess the extent and longevity of these popular mimetic customs. As always the available information also depends on the survival of the relevant manuscripts. Nevertheless, considerable evidence does survive in the Kent records for popular mimetic customs, even though most of them cannot be routinely documented from year to year.

THE TWELVE DAYS OF CHRISTMAS

During the medieval and early modern periods the twelve days between the feast of Christmas on 25 December and the feast of Epiphany on 6 January were celebrated with general feasting, entertainment, and merriment in monasteries, in towns, and in parishes alike.[61] At Boxley Abbey, for example, surviving bursars' accounts between 1353 and 1409 include payments for players before the abbot and monks on the feasts of Christmas and the Circumcision (1 January). In Canterbury the treasurers' accounts show that the prior and monks of Christ Church in the thirteenth, fourteenth, and fifteenth centuries also frequently paid for entertainers, minstrels, pipers, and players on the feasts of Christmas, St Stephen (26 December), the Martyrdom of St Thomas Becket (29 December), the Circumcision (1 January), and Epiphany (6 January). During the 1445 festive season, for example, there were payments for interludes at Christmas in the presence of the lord cardinal, for players playing before the lord prior, for the cardinal's minstrels, and for other minstrels (see pp 66–7). The few surviving fifteenth-century accounts from St Augustine's Abbey show that the abbot and monks also paid for minstrels or players on Christmas Day and on the feast of St Thomas Becket. Fewer payments in town records than in monastic records are dated by feast days; however, in 1501–2 the Canterbury city chamberlains' accounts include expenses for a 'bankett in the Courte hall' and the performance of a play of 'the iij kynges of Coleyn' on Twelfth Night (see pp 95–6). At Dover the wardens' accounts show frequent expenses between the fourteenth and sixteenth centuries for entertainers, minstrels, players, and wine at Christmas, including payments in 1452 for 'hominibus de herne ludentibus coram Maiore &c tempore Natalis Christi,' in 1481 'for playeres at christemasse,' in 1492 for players and wine when Dover officials entertained the mayors of Folkestone and Faversham at Christmas, in 1535 for 'my lord lyles players in wyne on christmas daie,' and in 1588 for a reward 'given vnto the quenes players at Christmas laste.' At Fordwich in 1592 the mayor paid for 'players in the Cristmas tyme.' At Sandwich the treasurers' accounts also show the custom of celebrating Christmas and Twelfth Night with plays, including payments in 1458 for 'diuersis hominibus ludentibus ad festum Natalis domini,' in 1497/8 for 'the waites of Canterbury on xijthe day,' in 1505 'for a player a fore the Mayer at Crestmas,' and in 1521 'for a play at the Bull in Crystmas.' Although most prosecutions of minstrels and dancers in the quarter sessions and ecclesiastical courts involved disorderly behaviour during summer games, the churchwardens of Elmstead did present a minstrel in 1584 for 'occupienge his instrumente to daunsinge' on a Sunday 'beinge St Iohns daye in Christmas.'

The entertainment, merriment, and festivity of the twelve days of Christmas also incorporated the inversion of order in such mimetic customs as the lord of misrule and the St Nicholas bishop.[62] During the sixteenth century such controlled disorder seems to have flourished particularly in the towns and parishes of Romney Marsh and the south coast of Kent. In 1525 the lord of misrule of Old Romney was entertained at New Romney. In Lydd the churchwardens' accounts show receipts in 1534 and again in 1537 for money gathered at Christmas by the lord of misrule and his retinue for 'the maynteynyng of the light of Seynt george' in the parish church of All Saints (see pp 689, 690). It is possible that at Lydd these 'lordes of mysrule in Cristmas tyme' may have been a group of morris dancers since there are six names listed in the churchwardens' accounts and six was the traditional number of dancers for the morris. In 1542 the Folkestone wardens' accounts include payments for bread, beer, and wine for the lord of misrule of Folkestone and the lord of misrule of nearby Sandgate. In 1550 the Dover wardens paid for 'a baynckett made to the Lorde of mys Rull of Sandwiche in full contentation and payment of his demand.' The 'diskeysers of Caunterbury' paid at Sandwich in 1489 and the payment by Sir Edward Dering at Surrenden Dering 'to some fellowes that came a maskinge hither' at Candlemas in 1620 may also be related to the traditions of festival disguise and lords of misrule.

In monasteries, cathedrals, colleges, and parish churches the boy bishop or St Nicholas bishop customs on St Nicholas' Day (6 December) or the feast of the Holy Innocents (28 December) provided a similar opportunity for disguising and role reversal, involving parody by choirboys and students of their teachers and masters. At Christ Church, Canterbury, the earliest references to St Nicholas clerks, or boys in the priory's almonry school who were in minor orders and hence referred to as clerks, appear in the treasurers' accounts in 1367 and again in 1377 (see p 1267, endnote to LPL: MS. 243 f 143 col 2). The archbishop's school, the forerunner of the present day King's School in Canterbury, also kept the custom of the St Nicholas bishop during the fifteenth century, for its omission in 1464 and its resumption in 1466, when the monks of St Augustine's dined in the hall of the prior of Christ Church 'in presen|cia episcopi sancti Nicolai,' were both noted by John Stone in his chronicle of Christ Church Priory. Scattered references to the custom appear in other monasteries and churches throughout the diocese of Canterbury. In his will dated 1417 John Wotton, the first master of the collegiate church of All Saints, Maidstone, bequeathed vestments for the St Nicholas bishop at All Saints'. Maidstone had a St Nicholas bishop long before 1417, however, for the bursars' accounts of Boxley Abbey include a payment for a ring given to 'Episcopo sancti Nicholai de Maydynstane' in 1355. A parish inventory of St Dunstan's, Canterbury, in 1500 lists 'A vestment, for Saint Nicholas tyme, with crosyar and myter'; an inventory of church goods at Faversham parish church in 1512 lists two vestments 'for seynt Nycolas with ij Course Mitours'; and at the Priory of Sts Mary and Sexburga, Minster (in Sheppey), an inventory taken at the dissolution of the monastery in 1536 lists a cope and 'ij olde Mytars for saynt nycholas.' At Dover Priory the one surviving prior's account roll lists a payment in 1530 'in reward to the St Nicholas clerks.' By far the best documented observance of the St Nicholas bishop festivities in the diocese of Canterbury was at St Nicholas' Church in New Romney. Although no reference to the custom survives either in the New Romney town records or in the parish records of St Nicholas' Church, the fifteenth-century chamberlains' account book in the nearby town of Lydd shows annual payments between 1428 and 1485 to the boy bishop and his retinue from New Romney. On 6 December the boy bishop of New Romney, usually accompanied by the men of the town, made his episcopal visitation of Lydd, where he and his company were often rewarded with bread and wine and beer. By royal proclamation Henry VIII finally abolished the St Nicholas bishop festivities in July 1541.

Another mimetic custom during the twelve days of Christmas featured the singing of wassail carols, drinking from the wassail bowl or cup, and the election of a king and queen to preside over the festivities on New Year's Eve or on Twelfth Night (5 January).[63] At Fordwich the surviving borough records begin in the mid-sixteenth century just in time to record the end of this popular mimetic custom. In 1565 expenses appear in the mayor's accounts for making and mending of the apparel for the king and queen. In 1566 an inventory of apparel 'appertaynyng to the kyng & the Quene of fordwiche' lists a cloak trimmed with velvet, a velvet jacket trimmed with lace, breeches embroidered with lace, two velvet caps, a velvet jerkin, red satin sleeves, and two kirtles. A later memorandum in 1579 mentions tables, forms or benches, tablecloths, and an ornamental bowl or drinking cup. Whatever ceremony surrounded the Twelfth Night king and queen at Fordwich was stopped in 1579 by a town ordinance that decreed the sale of 'the apparell & other thinges of the late supposed kinge & Quene within the sayd towne.'[64] The wassail festivities at Fordwich had also included the related custom of wassailing the apple trees of the east Kent orchards on New Year's Eve and Twelfth Night. This folk custom, known also in the orchards of Sussex and Devon, involved 'hoode boyes' singing and rapping the trees with sticks in order to increase the apple crop.[65] In January 1576/7, however, the ecclesiastical commissioners instructed the mayor and jurats of Fordwich to end this 'superstycious or old custome or fond order contynewyd or maynteyned vnder collour of boyes pastyme.'

HOCKTIDE GAMES

Hocktide, the Monday and Tuesday after Easter week, was commonly supposed to celebrate either Æthelred's defeat of the Danes on 13 November 1002 or the death of Harthacnut, hated king of the Danes whose occupation of Kent came to an end on 8 June 1042. Sixteenth-century Kentish historian William Lambarde notes in *A Perambulation of Kent*, 'that euer after, the common people in ioy of that deliuerance, haue celebrated the annuall day of Hardicanutus death (as the Romanes did their feast of Fugalia, or chasing out of the Kings) with open pastime in the sstreetes, calling it, euen til this our time, Hoctyde.'[66] Whatever its specific origin, by the fifteenth century Hocktide had evolved into a national folk custom in which the men chased and captured the women on Hock Monday and the women chased and captured the men on Hock Tuesday, or vice versa, charging their captives for release and contributing the proceeds to parish funds.[67] Sometimes the custom was practised only by the women, emphasizing the reversal of social norms that held most women in positions of social subservience the rest of the year. In many parishes this popular mimetic custom made a great contribution to parish funds or was used to maintain candles and lights in the parish church. In Canterbury receipts for Hock Monday and Hock Tuesday appear regularly in the churchwardens' accounts in St Andrew's and St Dunstan's parishes between 1485 and 1559. At St Andrew's in 1547 the usual receipt also mentions a communal Hocktide supper: 'gatheryd at hoktyde at the suppr in the Corne markett.' Elsewhere in the diocese of Canterbury the collection of money at Hocktide is mentioned at Lydd in 1445, 1538, and 1545, at Chart Sutton in 1511, at Little Mongeham also in 1511, and at Birchington in 1540. Hock lights in parish churches, for which money at Hocktide was presumably collected, are also mentioned in wills at River, St Lawrence in Thanet, Seasalter, Staple, Stourmouth, Sturry, Tilmanstone, Whitfield, and Whitstable.[68] During the second half of the sixteenth century, however, this custom ceased to appear in the Kent records.

ST GEORGE'S DAY

The festival of St George, military saint and patron of England, was celebrated on 23 April. Although English monarchs as early as Henry III and Edward I had displayed the red cross of St George on their banners, the English veneration of St George primarily flourished during the fourteenth and fifteenth centuries under the royal devotion of Edward III, Henry V, and Henry VI, leading to the establishment of numerous religious guilds dedicated to the saint and the celebration of his feast day with religious and civic processions. During the sixteenth century many of these processions included torches, minstrels, banners, and mimetic portrayal of the battle between St George and the dragon. Following the royal injunctions of November 1538, however, St George processions were curtailed and, during the reign of Edward VI, eventually suppressed along with the St George guilds. Although St George processions and guilds enjoyed a brief revival under Mary I and although the festival was retained by Elizabeth I in the list of feast days published in 1560, the veneration of the saint never regained its pre-Reformation popularity.[69]

In Kent a St George brotherhood or fraternity was established during the fifteenth century at St Nicholas' Church in New Romney where an image of the saint was erected with great ceremony in 1481.[70] A similar religious guild was founded at All Saints' Church in Lydd to maintain the image of the saint there.[71] After the guild was suppressed and the statue removed during the Reformation, the churchwardens' accounts for 1549 contain receipts for the sale of the 'Saynt george curtaynys,' the 'seelynge of sayncte George skaffold,' and the 'borde that the george dyd stande on.'[72] At St Clement's Church in Sandwich there was a brotherhood of St George, which maintained the image of St George in the chapel in the south aisle and carried it through the streets in procession on St George's Day.[73] Most of the surviving Sandwich treasurers' account rolls before the Reformation have a standard payment of 6s 8d to the wardens of St George 'toward the charge of beryng of saint George this yere.'[74] At St George's Church, Canterbury, the saint's image 'was borne in procession on St. George's day in the honor of God and the King, with Mr. Mayor, the aldermen, their wives, with all the commons of the same going in procession.'[75]

Except at Lydd, where a St George play was performed during the fifteenth and early sixteenth centuries (see pp lvi–lxv), this religious devotion apparently did not extend to dramatic re-enactment. There is some evidence in Kent, however, for popular mimetic customs associated with the veneration of St George. At Lydd the lords of misrule, who may have formed a group of morris dancers, collected money at Christmas in 1534 and 1537 to maintain the lights burning before the image of St George in All Saints' Church. At Sandwich in 1535 the St George procession extended beyond Sandwich and beyond St George's Day, for the 1534–5 Dover chamberlains' accounts include a payment for 'men of Sandwyche that dauncyd the Mores on seint Mark*es* daie (*ie*, 25 April) at the beryng of seint George.' Dover may also have marked 23 April with more than religious observance, for in 1504 the waits of Canterbury were also paid for performing on St George's Day in Dover.

MAYPOLES AND MAY GAMES

In Tudor England May Day celebrations began early in the morning with the gathering of flowers and greenery to decorate streets and houses and continued with revelry and dancing to mark the official beginning of summer. Celebrations were not limited to the day itself, however, for May Day ushered in a period of merry-making that lasted until Midsummer. Variously known as May games, summer games, May ales, Whitsun ales, or church ales, these summer revels were kept on any date between May Day and Midsummer and included dancing around maypoles decorated with boughs and greenery, crowning of a king and queen to preside over the festivities, and the brewing and selling of beer to augment parish funds. The dance most often associated with May games or summer games was the morris dance. Often these summer revels featured a Robin Hood game or play in which the gallant outlaw and Maid Marian took the place of the summer king and queen. In a later Tudor variant of the game Robin Hood and Maid Marian took part in the morris dancing, often accompanied by two additional characters playing the fool and the hobby horse.[76]

All these popular customs associated with maypoles and May games appear in the Kent records. Although there are no systematic records of summer games, scattered references do occur in the town chamberlains' accounts and assembly books, in parish churchwardens' accounts, and in judicial records of the quarter sessions and the ecclesiastical courts. Among these disparate references to summer revelry there are glimpses of official support and sponsorship, of corporations that paid for maintenance of maypoles and catered for communal celebrations. There are also inevitable attempts by civic and ecclesiastical authorities either to control the licence and disorder often connected with May games or to suppress the games outright. Overall the picture that emerges from these disparate records shows a flourishing folk tradition, both favoured and feared, both supported and suspected by authority, a folk tradition that flourished during the early Tudor period and that could not entirely be suppressed during the more austere Elizabethan and Stuart periods.

Communal celebration on May Day appears in town records as early as 1424, when the New Romney chamberlains paid for the expenses of entertaining the men of Lydd 'when they came with their May,' and 1432, when they again entertained the men of Lydd 'in the showing of the May.' At Dover in 1476 the wardens paid for 'þe May of Mongeham.' At Sandwich in 1517 the town treasurer paid for 'Costes of the May.' Again at Dover in 1549 there are payments for 'a breckfast made one maye daye,' 'a banket that the comynes made at maye daye,' and 'a hoghed of bere spent one maye daye'; in 1550 payments for '⌈bere⌉ spent one the hill one may daye' and for a 'bankett one may daye made by a grett nomber of the honest comynes'; and in 1589 a payment 'for playeng the diomme to give warning vnto the tounsmen agaynst may day.' At Fordwich during the 1550s and 1560s the mayors' accounts contain payments for baking wheat and malt, brewing beer, and hiring minstrels for the annual Easter ale or give ale until it was abolished by ordinance of the mayor and jurats in 1569.

Maypoles also appear in the records of several Kentish towns and villages, including references to their erection, repair, and removal. At Dover a flag was purchased for the maypole on 18 May 1560. In 1587 a total of 9s 4d was spent to repair the Dover maypole, including splicing the pole, binding it with iron bands, painting it, and setting it up again. In 1619–20, when May games were suppressed in Dover, the wardens paid 1s 2d 'for pavinge the ground wher the Maypole did stand.' In 1567–8 the Faversham chamberlains paid 'for mendyng of the benche of the may pole,' the same year in which the Maidstone chamberlains paid for taking their maypole down. The Maidstone maypole was evidently re-erected, for after a storm in 1585–6 the chamberlains received money for selling 'a peece of the Maypole' and two trees 'blowne downe in the great wynd.' A maypole was also erected in 1589 at Sandwich, where on 20 May the mayor and jurats, who had assembled in the councell chamber 'forr Reformacion of divers disorders lately spronge vpp within this Towne,' committed three men to gaol for threatening to cut down the maypole 'Lately sett vpp by consent of the said maior & Iurates.' At Birchington the churchwardens paid to take down the maypole in 1606 and thirty years later, following the publication of *The Book of Sports*, to set it up again in 1636. At Hernhill in 1611 zealous parishioners were also in trouble for attacking the maypole. The churchwardens presented Thomas Baker and John Steven to the consistory court for digging up the parish maypole and using the bell ropes from the church tower to lower the pole 'in most Contemptious

manner not regardeing the kinges maiestyes ecclesiasticall lawes.' In their defence Baker alleged
'that the same pole was before that tyme Cut verry much and thereby in danger to fall to the
hurte of the howses neere adioyning there and of people that might be there at the tyme of the
ffall thereof.' Finally, in 1616 Hythe authorities ordered that their maypole be taken down and
paid 'for fillinge vp ye hole where ye maypole stoode.'

Scattered references in the Kent records also support the traditional association of Robin
Hood and Maid Marian with May games and morris dancers. In the midst of Henry VIII's
divorce proceedings in June 1528 an order from Sir Edward Guildford, lord warden of the
Cinque Ports, to the mayors, bailiffs, and jurats of all the Cinque Port towns and their
corporate members forbade large gatherings of people, no doubt to forestall any possible public
demonstrations of discontent. The order specifically banned any 'stage pley Robyn hoodes pley
wacches or wakes yeveales or other such lyke playes.' 'Robyn hoodes pley' here probably refers
to May games or morris dances involving Robin Hood; 'wacches or wakes,' held throughout
the year on the eve of saints' days and festivals, refer in the first instance to the traditional
Midsummer bonfires and dances that would soon be held on St John's Eve and St Peter's Eve;
and 'yeveales,' a variant spelling of 'give ales,' refers to traditional Kentish summer ales or church
ales, such as the give ale in Fordwich. Issued on 3 June in the middle of the summer games
season to all the towns in the Cinque Ports network, the order testifies to the widespread
practice of these summer revels in Kent. Four years later in 1532–3 the New Romney accounts
also mention the 'Robyn hod playes' of Hythe and include payments for the reward and entertainment of the men of Hythe. In 1577, after morris dancers including Maid Marian and a
fool visited Elmstead, the churchwardens presented minstrels Thomas Rolfe and John Collyns
to the archdeacon's court for leading 'abowte the contrye a companye of morres daunvers with
their mayde marryon, representynge a whore, vsynge vngodly tryckes with their foles bable.'
On 4 June 1570 'serten morrys daunsers off the cuntre' were paid by the mayor of Canterbury;
however, in May 1589, when another group of morris dancers 'with mayd maryon being a boy
in womans apparell' danced in front of the mayor's house, they were arrested and arraigned
before Canterbury magistrates. Depositions from the dancers revealed that Maid Marian was
played by a twelve-year-old boy 'dressed in womans apparell for mayd marryon with out any
breches with Breyded here.'

This evidence for Robin Hood games, maypoles, and the communal celebration of May Day,
primarily drawn from the town records, is supplemented by numerous references to summer
games, morris dancers, and minstrels in the ecclesiastical records. The earliest prohibition of
these summer revels appears in the statutes of Wye College in 1448 forbidding the priests and
chaplains of the college from attending 'ludos vocatos Somergamys.' Other references to
summer games are found in the presentments of churchwardens to the archdeacon's and
consistory courts in response to the visitation articles set by the archbishop of Canterbury.
Tudor and Stuart visitation articles usually contained general prohibitions against drinking and
disorderly conduct in the church or churchyard. Archbishop Edmund Grindal's visitation
articles for 1576, however, included a specific question directed against summer games:
'Whether the Minister and Churchwardens haue suffered any Lordes of Mysrule, or Summer
Lordes or Ladies, or anye disguysed persons, or others in Christmasse, or at Maygames,

or any Morrice dauncers, or at any other tymes, to come vnreuerently into the Church or Churchyarde, and there to daunce, or play any vnseemely partes, with scoffes, ieastes, wanton gestures, or ribalde talke, namely in the time of common prayer. And what they be that commit such disorder, or accompanie or mayntaine them?' (see p 931). Similar questions appeared in Grindal's visitation articles reissued in 1577, 1580, and 1582. Archbishop Richard Bancroft's visitation articles in 1604, repeated in 1607 and 1610, prohibited suppers, church ales, and drinkings in the church or churchyard and requested the names of minstrels and other parishioners 'that vpon the Sundaies and Holidaies goe to other parishes to Play or Daunce' (see p 940). In 1621 the visitation articles of Archbishop George Abbot asked, 'Whether haue any Lords of Misrule, Dauncers, Players, or any other disguised persons beene suffered to enter the Church, Chappell, or Churchyard with their sports?' and 'whether doe any use dauncing or such like sports on the Sabaoth day before the end of all diuine Seruice appointed for that day?' (see p 934). In response to these articles over 100 presentments of minstrels and dancers survive in the ecclesiastical court records of the diocese of Canterbury, most defendants having been accused of playing or dancing on Sunday during the time of divine service and drawing the youth of the parish away from attendance at church. Not all of these presentments give dates for the alleged offences; however, many either specifically mention morris dancers and May games or give dates that fall within the summer games season. In 1577, for example, the Elmstead churchwardens presented two minstrels for playing at 'a soleme daunsynge' on 12 May, the Sunday before Ascension Day. In 1579 the Waltham churchwardens presented a total of twenty-six people for attending 'a may game or morres dance' on 3 May, the second Sunday after Easter. In 1583 the minstrel Thomas Younge of Headcorn 'verie disorderlie & Lewdelie vpon the Sabothe day did play vpon his fedle aboute the Churcheyarde & certeine morris daunsers beinge disgised followinge of him to the great offence of manie.' In 1592 Elizabeth Curling and Joan Hockman of Orlestone were presented for dancing during evening prayer at Snave 'one sunday in May last past' (see p 874). In 1607 Edward Taster, a victualer at Preston near Wingham, held a garland with 'certeine fidlers or musitions playeing … whereto a great company resorted & there dawnced & keepte ill rule' both on 14 May, Ascension Day, and on 17 May, the following Sunday. Often the secular authorities joined the ecclesiastical authorities in attempts to control May games. In May 1594, for example, the parishioners of Harbledown presented Richard Bridges to the justices of the peace for 'comynge in company with diuers youthes which were assembled in a mawrice daunce,' and on 20 May 1611 Robert Thorne, fiddler, and John Elgar and William Richardson, dancers, appeared before the mayor and jurats of Dover and were fined 'for playing yesterday beyng Sunday and beyng absent from the Church.'

MIDSUMMER WATCHES AND WAKES

Midsummer marked the end of the summer game season that had begun two months earlier on May Day. It was celebrated in late medieval and early modern England with bonfires, music, and dancing and in the larger towns and cities with a Midsummer marching watch and pageants. In pre-Christian Britain Midsummer had originally been observed on 21 June, the summer solstice, but in the Christian calendar Midsummer gradually became linked with the feast of the Nativity of St John the Baptist on 24 June. As at Midwinter people decorated their doors with boughs and greenery, made bonfires in the streets in front of their houses, and invited their neighbours to share their food and drink. Traditional bonfires on St John's Eve included both bones and wood to commemorate the martyrdom of St John the Baptist, whose tomb had been desecrated and bones burned during the time of Julian the Apostate. The proximity of a second major saint's feast, St Peter's Day on 29 June, provided one last opportunity for more bonfires, music, and dancing on St Peter's Eve as the season of summer revelry finally drew to a close.[77]

The major organized Midsummer celebration in Kent before the Reformation had been the Canterbury marching watch with torchlight and pageants, which was celebrated a week later on 6 July due to the proximity of the feast of the Translation of St Thomas Becket (see pp lxxviii–lxxx). Dover also frequently provided entertainment at Midsummer, just as it did at Midwinter during the twelve days of Christmas. In 1375, for example, the minstrels of the lord warden were paid 'contra festum Nat*iuitatis* sancti Iohannis Bapt*iste*.' In 1429 the mayor paid 'vj hom*inibus* luden*tibus* in vigil*ia* sancti petri.' In 1435 there were payments for wine given to the minstrels of the earl of Warwick at Midsummer and in 1440 payments to 'diuers*is* lud*is* coram maiore in festo Natal*is* dom*ini* Nat*iuitatis* sancti Iohannis & Sancti Petri.' At Lydd on St Peter's Eve in 1432 the players of New Romney were rewarded for showing their play and entertained with bread, wine, and beer. At Sandwich payments appear in the treasurers' accounts for civic bonfires on St John's Eve and St Peter's Eve.[78] Elsewhere in the diocese of Canterbury, even after the Reformation, Midsummer on St John's Eve and St Peter's Eve was observed with the traditional bonfires, music, and dancing. As with the celebration of May games much of the evidence for this popular custom survives in the presentments of churchwardens to the ecclesiastical courts and as a result documents only the occasions on which disorder or disobedience came to the notice of the authorities. At Elmstead in 1577, for example, Arthur Baker of Wye insisted on playing his taber 'bothe the sonday beinge St Iohns even & also St Iohns day.' In their presentment the churchwardens noted, 'no warninge wolde stay him.' At Stone in 1579 the minstrel Stephen Helyard missed church because he was playing on 28 June, St Peter's Eve, and at Great Chart in 1582 another minstrel Peter Waterman missed church because he 'went out of our parish on St Peters day last.' At Wormshill in 1586 it was one of the churchwardens who was in trouble for failing to collect the usual 12d fines from 'such as playd and daunsed in the tyme of common prayior vpon St Peters day last.' At Chislet in 1600 it was the alehouse keeper who was in trouble for keeping 'a garlond with a minstrell plaieinge' in his public house during service time 'about Midsomer last past.' At Cranbrook in 1606 another innkeeper, James Riche, was presented 'for keeping disorder in his house vpon ye Sabboath day in the time of devine service, as fydling, pyping, & as we suspect dauncing.' When he appeared before the court Riche admitted that 'a sevennight before midsomer last' he had a firkin of beer and about twenty people in his house during time of divine service. At Preston near Wingham in 1608 churchwarden John Phillips presented the other churchwarden, John Allen, who had kept a garland in his house on Midsummer Day and again on St Peter's Day 'and then and there suffered playeing vpon instrument*es* & daunceing all the said two holie dayes whollie without intermission.' At Benenden on St Peter's Day in 1612 Edward Morlene was presented because he kept 'a blynde Alehouse & suffereth danceing in his howse on the holydaies in service tyme,' Philip Marten was presented 'for playeing vpone his fiddle vpone vnlawfull tymes, as vpone St Peeter*es* daye laste paste, whereby to drawe the yownger sorte of people, to spende those tymes vnlawfullye,' and four parishioners were all presented for dancing in Edward Morlene's alehouse on St Peter's Day while Philip Marten played 'to the offence of god contrarye to the kinges Ma*ie*sties eccl*esia*stical lawes and evill exsample of other*es*.' Finally, at Walmer on St Peter's Day in 1629 alewife Bridget Cooper was presented 'for keeping and suffering divers p*er*sons in her howse eating drinking and daunsing in time of divine service one the xxix[th] day of Iune last' and William Swaine and William Neame, minstrels from Sandwich, were presented for 'playing to many there dawnsing.' As with May games the persistence of these charges over a fifty-year period suggests that the popular folk custom of celebrating at Midsummer with music and dancing was never successfully stopped by Puritan opposition during the Elizabethan and Stuart years.

The most vivid description of the Midsummer bonfires, music, and dancing comes from the dedicatory epistle to John Bale's intended reply to James Cancellar's *The pathe of obedience, righte necessarye for all the king and quenes maiesties louing subiectes* (*STC*: 4564), where Bale describes the customary vigils on St John's Eve and St Peter's Eve in Canterbury in 1561 and the more disorderly protest on St Peter's Night. Bale was a prebendary of the reformed dean and chapter of Canterbury Cathedral. Like other zealous Protestant reformers he attacked the popular custom of celebrating Midsummer, both because its association with St John and St Peter connected it to the old rites of the church and because of the generally held superstitious belief in the efficacy of bonfires on St John's Eve to purge evil vapours from the air. As usual on Midsummer's Eve in 1561, however, there were bonfires in the streets of Canterbury, even in front of some aldermen's houses, as Bale observes, 'doubtlesse in contempte of the Christen religyon, and for vpholdynge the olde frantyck supersticyons of papistrye' (see p 188). The following day on St John's Day in a sermon in the cathedral Simon Clarke, one of the Six Preachers of the cathedral, condemned these 'superstityouse bonefyers' (see p 188). As a result on the following Saturday night, which was St Peter's Eve, there were twice as many bonfires as on Midsummer's Eve. On Sunday, St Peter's Day, Richard Beseley, former radical Protestant protégé of Thomas Cromwell and also one of the Six Preachers, exhorted the mayor and aldermen to abolish 'suche superstitiouse and mocky*n*ge customes' (see p 188). This sermon sparked an even larger protest bonfire at the bullstake outside Christ Church gate on St Peter's Night at the instigation of the minstrel Richard Borowes, who with more than a hundred boys following him marched about the streets beating a drum and collecting fuel. The civic and religious establishment did not unanimously join in Bale's condemnation of traditional Midsummer bonfires, for several city officers, including Philip Lewes, sheriff of Canterbury, contributed toward the fuel. The evening finished, says Bale, with Borowes and his boys dancing 'abought the fyer as in processyon, with burchyne bowes in their handes, syngynge most fylthie songes of baudrye' (see p 189).

The Midsummer bonfires at Canterbury in 1561 illustrate perfectly the persistence of many popular customs in Kent amid opposition and condemnation both by radical reformers and the increasingly powerful Puritan presence in the civic and religious establishment of Kentish towns and parishes. They illustrate, too, the ambivalence of civic authorities who often tolerated traditional customs yet attempted to control the ever-present threat of disorder. Perhaps nothing sums up the resulting tension better than two surviving records from the parish of Linsted. In 1482 John Weston bequeathed a field called Church Field to the parishioners of Linsted for making 'apleying place' for use forever on feast days and holy days. Just one hundred years later in 1581, however, during the archdeacon's visitation the churchwardens of Linsted presented the minstrels Henry Norman and Timothy Canon, who 'vppon a Sabothe daye dyd play in lynsted.'

The Documents

The document descriptions and the transcriptions have been arranged in six sections: Boroughs and Parishes, Religious Houses, Households, County of Kent, Province of Canterbury, and Diocese of Canterbury. The first three sections are subdivided alphabetically by place and, where appropriate, further subdivided by types of record: civic records, ecclesiastical records, guild records, miscellaneous records, and antiquarian records. In the document descriptions that follow no notice has been taken of individual documents that do not contain entertainment records, even though their omission may disturb an unbroken series of documents.

Boroughs and Parishes

ALKHAM

Archdeacon's Court Books

Canterbury, Cathedral Archives, DCb/J/X.2.1; 1577–85; English and Latin; paper; iii + 184 + ii, gathered in 8s; 305mm x 205mm, average 30 lines; contemporary ink foliation 1–96, continued in modern pencil 97–184; modern brown cloth binding. Contains comperta and detecta presentments for Elham and Dover deaneries.
   This book also supplies entries for Elmstead and Waltham.

Canterbury, Cathedral Archives, DCb/J/X.5.4; 1609–18; English and Latin; paper; i + 186 + v, gathered in 12s; 295mm x 192mm, average 36 lines; contemporary ink foliation 1–178, continued in modern pencil 179–86; original parchment binding. Contains comperta and detecta presentments for Dover and Elham deaneries.

ASHFORD

Archdeacon's Court Book

Canterbury, Cathedral Archives, DCb/J/X.2.2; 1577–82; English and Latin; paper; iii + 189 + i, gathered in 8s; 305mm x 205mm, average 30 lines; contemporary ink foliation 1–154, continued in modern pencil 155–89; modern brown cloth binding. Contains comperta and detecta presentments for Charing deanery.

This book also supplies an entry for Biddenden.

Nehemiah Wallington, Historical Notes and Meditations

The Puritan artisan Nehemiah Wallington (1598–1658) was a freeman of the Company of Turners and a resident of the London parish of St Leonard's, Eastcheap. By his own account Wallington wrote some fifty volumes of notebooks, journals, and commonplace books, mostly on religious, historical, or autobiographical subjects, six of which survive in the British Library.[1] The commonplace book entitled 'Historical Notes and Meditations,' which quotes or refers to over 300 tracts and pamphlets on religious and political topics covering the history of the civil war and ending with the beheading of Charles I, was published in the nineteenth century: Nehemiah Wallington, *Historical Notices of Events Occurring Chiefly in the Reign of Charles I*, Rosamond Anne Webb (ed), 2 vols (London, 1869).

London, British Library, Additional MS. 21,935; 1588–1646; English; paper; ii + 281+ i; 200mm x 150mm (195mm x 135mm); modern pencil foliation replacing imperfect contemporary ink foliation (1 unnumbered blank leaf following f 1); 19th-c. tooled green leather binding, title on spine: 'N. Wallington, Historical Notes and Meditations, 1588–1646, Autograph.'

BARHAM

Archdeacon's Court Book

Canterbury, Cathedral Archives, DCb/J/X.5.8; 1612–24; English and Latin; paper; i + 279 + vi, gathered in 12s; 295mm x 205mm, average 21 lines; contemporary ink foliation; original parchment binding. Contains comperta and detecta presentments for Bridge deanery.

This book also supplies an entry for Stodmarsh.

BENENDEN

Archdeacon's Court Book

Canterbury, Cathedral Archives, DCb/J/X.5.5; 1610–15; English and Latin; paper; ii + 285 + viii, gathered in 12s, with numerous loose pages of confessions pinned in; 298mm x 200mm, average 29 lines; contemporary ink foliation; parchment binding, modern brown cloth case. Contains comperta and detecta presentments for Charing deanery.

BETHERSDEN

The ancient parish church of St Margaret in Bethersden was given by Archbishop Lanfranc in 1086–7 to the Priory of St Gregory, which he had founded outside Northgate in Canterbury in 1084 or 1085. This deed of gift firmly establishes that the church was dedicated to

St Margaret of Antioch, virgin and martyr, since St Margaret of Scotland did not die until 1093. The church, however, has Anglo-Saxon origins, since it is mentioned in the Domesday Monachorum, a manuscript written shortly after 1100 listing churches in the diocese of Canterbury that by ancient custom paid money to the archbishop at Easter. The ancient church was enlarged in the fourteenth and fifteenth centuries, when the early fifteenth-century Perpendicular windows were added.

Churchwardens' accounts survive from 1515 but only the first volume, which also includes playwardens' accounts, contains any record of parish entertainment. The early churchwardens' accounts were rendered towards the end of December, those after 1520 on the next Sunday after the feast of St Nicholas, and those after 1546 on the Sunday after the feast of St Mark. The playwardens' accounts are dated only by regnal year.

St Margaret's Churchwardens' Accounts

Bethersden, St Margaret's Church; 1515–73; Latin and English; paper; iv + 216 + iv, in irregular gatherings; 288mm x 205mm, average 24 lines; modern pencil pagination; vellum binding.

Archdeacon's Court Book

Canterbury, Cathedral Archives, DCb/J/X.1.11; 1571–2; English and Latin; paper; ii + 173 + i, gathered in 8s; 308mm x 205mm, average 27 lines; contemporary ink foliation; modern brown cloth binding. Contains comperta and detecta presentments.

This book also supplies an entry for Headcorn.

BIDDENDEN

Archdeacon's Court Book

See under Ashford for CCA: DCb/J/X.2.2.

BIRCHINGTON

The ancient parish church of All Saints, Birchington, has a remarkably rich collection of parish records, perhaps resulting from its administrative responsibilities as a non-corporate limb of the Cinque Ports town of Dover. Parish registers survive from 1538, churchwardens' accounts from 1531, and overseers' assessments and disbursements from 1611. The parish even holds rare copies of the Solemn League and Covenant, signed by parish officers in 1643, and the Solemn Vow and Covenant, dating from 1644. Among these records only the churchwardens' accounts contain any record of parish entertainment, a record supplemented by two cases from the diocesan consistory court. The sixteenth-century accounts may have run from Michaelmas to Michaelmas; however, in 1598 the accounting year was altered to begin and end on Annunciation Day.

All Saints' Churchwardens' Accounts

Canterbury, Cathedral Archives, U3/76/5A/2; 1531–87; English; paper; ii + 200 + ii; dimensions vary from 210mm x 150mm to 190mm x 140mm, average 25 lines; modern ink pagination; modern white vellum binding.

Canterbury, Cathedral Archives, U3/76/5A/3; 1587–1680; English; paper; 189 leaves, gathered in 32s; 295mm x 200mm, average 37 lines; modern ink pagination; hardback vellum binding with old parchment cover bound inside.

Consistory Court Books

Canterbury, Cathedral Archives, DCb/J/Z.4.2; 1621–2; English and Latin; paper; ii + 227 + xi, gathered in 12s; 305mm x 205mm, average 30 lines; contemporary ink foliation; modern brown cloth binding incorporating original parchment covers. Contains comperta and detecta presentments.

Canterbury, Cathedral Archives, DCb/J/Z.4.5; 1627–30; English and Latin; paper; i + 276 + xi, gathered in 12s; 293mm x 190mm, average 21 lines; contemporary ink foliation; modern brown cloth binding. Contains comperta and detecta presentments.

BONNINGTON

Consistory Court Book

Canterbury, Cathedral Archives, DCb/J/X.8.8; 1569–70, 1593–5; English and Latin; paper; ii + 259 + i, gathered in 16s; 305mm x 200mm, average 26 lines; contemporary ink foliation 1–109, 200–67 ('109' apparently misread as '199' as no folios are missing), continued in modern pencil 268–349; modern brown cloth binding and case. Contains comperta and detecta presentments.

This book also provides an entry for the parish of St Alphege, Canterbury.

Archdeacon's Court Book

Canterbury, Cathedral Archives, DCb/J/X.3.3; 1587–97; English and Latin; paper; part 1: i + 184 + iv, part 2: i + 179 + vii, both gathered in 10s; 295mm x 195mm, average 37 lines; contemporary ink foliation; modern brown cloth binding and case. Contains comperta and detecta presentments for Lympne deanery.

This book also provides entries for Lympne and Snave.

BORDEN

Archdeacon's Court Book

Canterbury, Cathedral Archives, DCb/J/X.2.4; 1582–9; English and Latin; paper; ii + 443 + i, gathered in 8s; 295mm x 195mm, average 26 lines; modern pencil foliation; modern brown cloth binding and brown case. Contains comperta and detecta presentments for Charing, Sittingbourne, and Sutton deaneries.

This book also provides entries for Boughton Monchelsea, Great Chart, and Headcorn.

BOUGHTON MONCHELSEA

Archdeacon's Court Book

See under Borden for CCA: DCb/J/X.2.4.

BOUGHTON UNDER BLEAN

Sts Peter's and Paul's Churchwardens' Accounts

The churchwardens' accounting year ran from 2 November to 2 November.

Canterbury, Cathedral Archives, U3/221/5/1; 1530–1656; English; paper; iii + 179 + ii; 302mm x 215mm, average 31 lines; modern pencil foliation; repaired and rebound in 19th-c. brown leather binding.

Complaint against Samuel Smith

London, British Library, Additional MS. 26,785; 9 February 1640/1; English; paper; bifolium; 295mm x 190mm (252mm x 185mm); good condition; endorsed '9 Febr 1640 proofes for Boughton Blean.' Now foliated 137–8v, mounted on guard, and bound with other correspondence to and from Sir Edward Dering dated 1639–41 in c 19th-c. fabric on board covers with leather corners and spine, raised bands, and gilding on spine.

BOXLEY

Archdeacon's Court Book

Canterbury, Cathedral Archives, DCb/J/X.2.9; 1584–93; English and Latin; paper; part 1: ii + 188, part 2: i + 192 + i, both gathered in 10s; 300mm x 195mm, average 27 lines; contemporary ink foliation; original parchment binding with modern brown case. Contains comperta and detecta presentments for Sutton deanery.

This book also supplies an entry for Wormshill.

BRABOURNE

Archdeacon's Court Book

Canterbury, Cathedral Archives, DCb/J/X.4.7; 1602–9; English and Latin; paper; ii + 190 + vi, gathered in 12s; 295mm x 200mm, average 25 lines; contemporary ink foliation; original parchment binding, modern brown cloth case. Contains comperta and detecta presentments for Elham and Dover deaneries.

This book also supplies an entry for Elham.

BREDGAR

Consistory Court Book

Canterbury, Cathedral Archives, DCb/J/X.8.10; 1577–81; English and Latin; paper; ii + 270 + xii, gathered in 10s; 297mm x 205mm, average 23 lines; contemporary ink foliation with folios misnumbered as follows: 1–229, 300–9, 400–9, 500–9, 600–9, 700; original parchment binding. Contains comperta and detecta presentments.

This book also supplies an entry for Hollingbourne.

Archdeacon's Court Book

Canterbury, Cathedral Archives, DCb/J/Y.4.18 pt 2; 1578–81; English and Latin; paper; iii + 198 + iii, gathered in 8s; 305mm x 205mm, average 27 lines; contemporary ink foliation; modern brown cloth binding. Contains comperta and detecta presentments for Sutton deanery.

This book also supplies entries for Goudhurst, Milton next Sittingbourne, Queenborough, and Sittingbourne.

BROOKLAND

Will of James Hoggelyn of Old Romney

Maidstone, Centre for Kentish Studies, PRC 17/17; 1523–7; English and Latin; paper; vi + 365 + v, in irregular gatherings; 312mm x 215mm, average 48 lines; modern foliation; modern yellow cloth binding.

CANTERBURY

The Canterbury documents have been arranged in five major sections. The civic records include accounts, burghmote minutes and orders, and quarter sessions court presentments and papers. The ecclesiastical records include documents from Christ Church Priory, the dean and chapter of Christ Church Cathedral, St Augustine's Abbey, various Canterbury city parishes, and archdeaconry and consistory court proceedings. The guild records include records of the Minstrels' guild and the Drapers' and Tailors' guild. The fourth and fifth sections include a variety of correspondence and other miscellaneous records.

Civic Records

The city of Canterbury possesses an impressive collection of civic records, including a series of fifty-eight charters from Henry II (1155) to James I (1622), burghmote minutes from 1429, subsidy rolls from 1591, account books from 1393, lease books from 1575, and judicial records of the borough court of pleas from 1300, the court of piepowder ('curia pipedis puluerisati' that dealt with cases of debt, theft, and assault) from 1459, and the court of quarter sessions from 1465. Among these records the account books, burghmote minutes and orders, and the records of the quarter sessions court proved the most fruitful for records of ceremonial activity, minstrelsy, and dramatic entertainment. The account books contain an almost unbroken series from 1393 to 1642, beginning with jurats' accounts and, after a change in city administration, continuing with the accounts of two chamberlains in the latter third of the fifteenth century and a single chamberlain in the sixteenth century. In the list of accounts below, CC/FA 2, which covers the years 1445 to 1505 and spans this change in accounting procedure, has been designated simply as 'Civic Accounts.' Many of these account books also include occasional accounts for the city bailiffs and the common serjeant.

The assembly or burghmote minutes have many gaps before 1542 and a missing volume between 1603 and 1629. From 1542 to 1602 and from 1630 to 1642, however, the minute books record in detail the fortnightly meeting of the court of burghmote. The Canterbury court of quarter sessions was established in 1461, when the Yorkist Edward IV created the city of Canterbury a county in return for its financial and loyal support against Henry VI during the Wars of the Roses. Four court sessions were held annually until 1972, when the county borough and city of Canterbury was abolished by the Local Government Reorganization Act of 1972. Although Canterbury regained city status in 1974, as one of forty-seven new cities established by royal charter that year, it did not regain its power to hold a quarter sessions court. Early quarter sessions document bundles include sheriff's oaths, jury lists, calendars of prisoners, writs, bills, indictments, bonds, recognizances, presentments from wards for such offences as theft, murder, assault, and riots; in the seventeenth century the quarter sessions records also include such typical poor law material as apprenticeship indentures and bastardy papers. Many of the quarter sessions records were lost after flooding in 1929, including all court records for 1461–4, 1466–8, 1469–73, 1476–84, 1487, 1489–99, 1501, 1502, 1507, 1517, 1526–8, 1531, 1535, 1537, 1543–52, 1559, 1574, 1583, 1586, 1598, 1620, 1625, 1633, 1636, and 1641.

City Jurats' Accounts

Canterbury, Cathedral Archives, CC/FA 1; 1393–1445; Latin and English, paper; 313 leaves in irregular gatherings; 403mm x 275mm, average 46 lines; contemporary roman foliation in groups of 50 folios, superseded by modern pencil arabic foliation; original leather binding.

Canterbury, Cathedral Archives, CC/FA 3; 1394–1404; Latin; paper; ii + 42 + ii, in irregular gatherings; 282mm x 217mm, average 38 lines; modern pencil foliation (ff 31–42, containing 1394–8 accounts, bound out of chronological order); repaired and rebound in modern red cloth binding.

Canterbury, Cathedral Archives, CC/FA 4; 1459–64; Latin and English; ii + 43 + ii, in irregular gatherings; 285mm x 210mm, average 29 lines; modern pencil foliation in arabic replacing several discontinuous series of roman foliation (ff 30–43, containing 1459–61 accounts, bound out of chronological order); rebound in modern red cloth binding.

Civic Accounts

Canterbury, Cathedral Archives, CC/FA 2; 1445–1505; Latin and English; paper; 454 leaves, gathered in 24s; 430mm x 295mm, average 41 lines; modern pencil foliation in arabic replacing several discontinuous series of roman foliation; original white sheepskin binding, title on spine: 'Accounts 1445–1506.'

City Chamberlains' Accounts

Canterbury, Cathedral Archives, CC/FA 5; 1465–79; Latin and English; paper; ii + 232 + ii, in irregular gatherings; 295mm x 218mm, average 36 lines; modern pencil foliation in arabic replacing several discontinuous series of roman foliation; modern red cloth binding.

Canterbury, Cathedral Archives, CC/FA 6; 1479–83; Latin; paper; ii + 44 + ii, in 1 gathering of 46 (last 2 leaves with part of 1482–3 accounts wanting); 297mm x 210mm, average 41 lines; modern pencil foliation in arabic replacing several discontinuous series of roman foliation; first 2 leaves repaired; bound in modern red cloth binding.

Canterbury, Cathedral Archives, CC/FA 7; 1483–97; Latin; paper; iii + 254 + i, in irregular gatherings; 286mm x 205mm, average 36 lines; foliated in original ink to f clxxxv, continued in modern arabic pencil numbering; modern red cloth binding.

Canterbury, Cathedral Archives, CC/FA 9; 1505–10; Latin and English; paper; ii + 191 + ii, in irregular gatherings; 313mm x 220mm (290mm x 200mm), average 25 lines; modern pencil foliation; bound in modern red cloth. Accounts for 1505–6 (ff 36–80), 1506–7 (ff 1–36), 1507–8 (ff 80–113), 1508–9 (ff 144–91), and 1509–10 (ff 113–43) bound out of chronological order.

Canterbury, Cathedral Archives, CC/FA 10; 1512–20; English and Latin; paper; ii + 414 + ii, in irregular gatherings; 310mm x 195mm, average 27 lines; modern pencil foliation; modern red cloth binding.

Canterbury, Cathedral Archives, CC/FA 11; 1520–8; English; paper; ii + 455 + ii, in irregular gatherings; 320mm x 215mm, average 25 lines; modern pencil foliation; modern red cloth binding.

Canterbury, Cathedral Archives, CC/FA 12; 1528–38; English and Latin; paper; ii + 395 + i, in irregular gatherings; 315mm x 220mm, average 26 lines; modern pencil foliation (ff 260–5 mistakenly repeated); modern red cloth binding.

Canterbury, Cathedral Archives, CC/FA 13; 1539–45; English; paper; ii + 286 + ii, gathered in 44s; 310mm x 210mm, average 30 lines; modern pencil foliation; modern red cloth binding.

Canterbury, Cathedral Archives, CC/FA 14; 1546–52; English; paper; i + 248 + i, gathered in 42s; 415mm x 210mm, average 21 lines; modern pencil foliation; red cloth binding, title on spine: 'ACCOUNTS 1546–53.'

Canterbury, Cathedral Archives, CC/FA 15; 1553–5; English; paper; iv + 91 + ii, in 2 unequal gatherings; 302mm x 205mm, average 32 lines; contemporary foliation ff 1–22, modern pencil foliation thereafter; rebound in modern red cloth binding, title on spine: 'ACCOUNTS 1553–58' (but accounts for 1557–8 appear in CC/FA 16).

Canterbury, Cathedral Archives, CC/FA 16; 1557–68; English; paper; i + 466 + i, in irregular gatherings; 310mm x 215mm, average 29 lines; modern pencil foliation; modern red cloth binding.

Canterbury, Cathedral Archives, CC/FA 17; 1568–77; English; paper; i + 410 + i, gathered in 48s; 310mm x 210mm; modern pencil foliation (several blank leaves cut out of each gathering sometime before foliation); modern red cloth binding.

Canterbury, Cathedral Archives, CC/FA 18; 1577–87; English; paper; ii + 472 + i, in irregular gatherings, 1 for each year; 305mm x 205mm, average 36 lines; modern pencil foliation; modern red cloth binding.

Canterbury, Cathedral Archives, CC/FA 19; 1587–92; English; paper; ii + 217 + ii, gathered mainly in 48s; 313mm x 205mm, average 36 lines; modern pencil foliation replacing inconsistent contemporary foliation (several blank leaves cut out of each gathering before foliation); modern red cloth binding.

Canterbury, Cathedral Archives, CC/FA 20; 1592–1602; English; paper; i + 491 + i, in irregular gatherings, 1 for each year; 305mm x 205mm, average 34 lines; modern pencil foliation correcting and completing inconsistent contemporary foliation; some marginal headings appear in display scripts; modern red cloth binding.

Canterbury, Cathedral Archives, CC/FA 21; 1602–10; English; paper; i + 346 + i, in irregular gatherings, 1 for each year; 315mm x 210mm, average 36 lines; modern pencil foliation; some marginal headings appear in display scripts; modern red cloth binding.

Canterbury, Cathedral Archives, CC/FA 22(1); 1610–19; English; paper; i + 405 + i, in irregular gatherings, 1 for each year; 310mm x 205mm, average 37 lines; modern pencil foliation; some marginal headings appear in display scripts; modern red cloth binding.

Canterbury, Cathedral Archives, CC/FA 22(2); 1619–20; English; paper; i + 46 + i, in 1 gathering (42 with 4 separate leaves); 342mm x 236mm, average 36 lines; numbered 406–51 in modern pencil foliation as a continuation of CC/FA 22(1); bound in modern red cloth separately from CC/FA 22(1) due to the difference in dimensions between this annual account booklet and those bound in CC/FA 22(1).

Canterbury, Cathedral Archives, CC/FA 23; 1620–30; English; paper; i + 510 + i, in irregular gatherings, 1 for each year; 315mm x 210mm, average 37 lines; modern pencil foliation; some marginal headings appear in display scripts; modern red cloth binding.

Canterbury, Cathedral Archives, CC/FA 24; 1630–40; English; paper; i + 488 + i, in irregular gatherings, 1 for each year; 330mm x 212mm (305mm x 202), average 28 lines; modern pencil foliation;
modern red cloth binding.

Canterbury, Cathedral Archives, CC/FA 25; 1640–50; English; paper; i + 539 + i, in irregular gatherings, 1 for each year; 340mm x 215mm (285mm x 180mm), average 30 lines; modern pencil foliation;
modern red cloth binding.

Burghmote Court Minutes

Canterbury, Cathedral Archives, CC/AC 1; 1419–1542; Latin and English; paper; ii + 108 + ii;
430mm x 298mm (261mm x 72mm), average 21 lines; modern pencil foliation; leaves of irregular
size much repaired and stitched in irregular gatherings; half-vellum modern binding.

Canterbury, Cathedral Archives, CC/AC 2; 1542–78; English; paper; ii + 346 + i; 303mm x 204mm,
average 25 lines; contemporary ink foliation (ff 326–34 misbound after f 346); many leaves repaired;
modern blue and black half-leather binding.

Canterbury, Cathedral Archives, CC/AC 3; 1578–1602; Latin and English; paper; i + 418 + ii,
gathered in 16s; 285mm x 210mm, average 40 lines; contemporary ink foliation; contemporary brown
leather binding.

Canterbury, Cathedral Archives, CC/AC 4; 1630–58; English; paper; xi + 472 + i, gathered in 12s;
345mm x 225mm, average 37 lines; contemporary ink foliation; modern half-leather binding.

Burghmote Orders

Canterbury, Cathedral Archives, CC/AB 1; 1487–1608; English; paper; ii + 129 + ii, in irregular
gatherings; 277mm x 210mm; modern pencil foliation; leaves repaired; rebound in original rough
calf binding.

Ordinance for Regulating the Markets

London, British Library, Stowe MS. 850; 1489–90; Latin and English; paper; 4 leaves consisting
of 1 bifolium and 2 separate leaves; 292mm x 210mm; now numbered as ff 15–18 of a composite MS containing various documents of the reigns of Henry VII and Henry VIII; brown morocco
binding.

Order of the Marching Watch

Canterbury, Cathedral Archives, Literary MS C13; 16th c.; Latin and English; paper; ii + 204 + iv,
in irregular gatherings; 292mm x 210mm, 29 lines; 2 series of foliation, 1 in contemporary ink in
roman numerals beginning with ij and continuing to ccxxix with many gaps, 1 in modern pencil
in arabic numerals for ff 1–127 (followed here); 16th-c. leather binding.

Quarter Sessions Jury Presentments

Canterbury, Cathedral Archives, CC/J/Q/366; 1566–7; English; paper; bifolium; 310mm x 210mm; unnumbered; faded and mutilated by damp, but repaired. One of a file of 3 documents.

Canterbury, Cathedral Archives, CC/J/Q/370; 9 July 1571; English; paper; 2 bifolia (f [4] blank); 310mm x 210mm; unnumbered; damaged by damp, but repaired. One of a file of 11 documents.

Canterbury, Cathedral Archives, CC/J/Q/374/i; 1574–5; English; paper; 4 sheets, attached at the top; 415mm x 308mm; writing on 1 side only; modern pencil foliation.

Canterbury, Cathedral Archives, CC/J/Q/396(a); 1596–7; English; paper; single sheet; 300mm x 200mm.

Canterbury, Cathedral Archives, CC/J/Q/428/ii; 1628–9; English; paper; 5 sheets, attached at top; 397mm x 305mm; writing on 1 side only; roll repaired; modern wrapper.

Quarter Sessions Examinations

Canterbury, Cathedral Archives, CC/J/Q/388; 10 May 1589; English; paper; single sheet; 306mm x 206mm; damaged by mildew, but now repaired.

Canterbury, Cathedral Archives, CC/J/Q/388; 10 May 1589; English; paper; bifolium; 306mm x 204mm; modern pencil foliation; damaged by mildew and damp, but now repaired.

Quarter Sessions Recognizance

Canterbury, Cathedral Archives, CC/J/Q/405/vii/28; 1605–6; English and Latin; paper; single sheet; 304mm x 203mm.

Ecclesiastical Records

This section describes the records of the three great ecclesiastical foundations in Canterbury: Christ Church Priory, the dean and chapter of Christ Church Cathedral, and St Augustine's Abbey. Christ Church Priory, whose long history stretched back to the arrival of St Augustine in 597, ceased to exist on 8 May 1540, when the last medieval prior, Thomas Goldwell, surrendered the monastery to a royal commission headed by Archbishop Thomas Cranmer. By royal charter dated 8 April 1541 the cathedral establishment was refounded as the dean and chapter of Christ Church Cathedral, consisting of a dean, twelve prebendaries, six preachers, twelve minor canons, musicians such as lay clerks and choristers, and various other officials. Reflecting this historical break between the medieval monastery and the reformed new foundation, the records relating to the prior and monks of Christ Church Priory have been described separately from those relating to the dean and chapter of the new foundation.[2]

The Venerable Bede in *The Ecclesiastical History of the English People* relates how Augustine also erected a monastery in Canterbury in the year 598. The monastic church, endowed by king Æthelberht and dedicated to Sts Peter and Paul, was eventually consecrated in 613 by Archbishop Lawrence. In 978 the church was rededicated by Archbishop Dunstan in honour of Sts Peter and Paul and St Augustine. The story of this wealthy and influential monastery, which reached its peak of prosperity at the beginning of the thirteenth century, is primarily known through the chronicles of its own historians Goscelin, Thomas Sprott, and particularly William Thorne, who revised and expanded the earlier chronicles and related the history of the abbey from its foundation to 1397. At the Dissolution the monastery was finally surrendered on 30 July 1538 by Abbot John Essex and thirty monks.[3]

Christ Church Priory

Regularis Concordia

The *Regularis concordia Anglicae nationis monachorum sanctimonialiumque* or 'Agreement of the Rule of the Monks and Nuns of the English Nation,' designed to reform and regulate monastic life and practice at Benedictine houses throughout England, was drawn up at the council of Winchester in the latter half of the tenth century. St Dunstan, archbishop of Canterbury (960–88), St Æthelwold, bishop of Winchester (963–84), and King Edgar (d. 975) are all associated with the text, making a date of *c* 970 the usual date assigned to the council. The *Regularis Concordia* survives in two manuscripts, both connected with Christ Church, Canterbury: BL: Cotton Faustina B.III, ff 159–98 *(F)*, dating from the end of the tenth century; and BL: Cotton Tiberius A.III, ff 3–27v *(T)*, dating from the first half of the eleventh century. The latter manuscript contains an Anglo-Saxon gloss of the Latin text and is probably the book described in the fourteenth-century Christ Church catalogue as 'Consuetudines de faciendo seruitio divino per annum glosata Anglice.'[4] Since both manuscripts contain numerous erasures, corrections, and errors in the Latin text, neither is followed exclusively for the edition of the *Visitatio Sepulchri*. All substantive variants in either Latin text are given in the collation notes. The Anglo-Saxon interlineation is given in full from *T*.

London, British Library, Cotton Faustina B.III; late 10th c.; Latin; parchment; iii + 280 + ii, gathered in 8s; 245mm x 170mm, average 25 lines; modern pencil foliation; brown leather binding. The Regularis occupies ff 159–98.

London, British Library, Cotton Tiberius A.III; mid-11th c.; Latin and Old English; parchment; ii + 180 + xv; 285mm x 225mm, average 24 glossed lines; modern pencil foliation; use of rustic capitals for some proper names, as GREGORII on f 21; brown leather binding. The Regularis occupies ff 3–27v; ff 177–7v is the final folio of text missing from the Cotton Faustina B.III text.

Christ Church Priory Treasurers' Accounts

The prior was the central administrative and executive head of Christ Church Priory; however, the central accounting figure, dating back to the 1160s, was the treasurer, whose duties were carried out by usually two and often three monks. They received the revenues of the monastery and redistributed them to the obedientiaries. Treasurers' accounts from the thirteenth and fourteenth centuries also record the expenses of obedientiaries and monastic officials, including the prior, whose expenses were often recorded in rough form in daybooks and then copied into the treasurers' accounts in blocks of entries. During the late fourteenth century the prior took over some of this central accounting role. Surviving priors' accounts from this later period list receipts from arrears, manors, churches, obedientiaries, and oblations, and expenses for obedientiaries and other officials, repairs, taxation, and travel. Separate account rolls also survive for the following obedientiaries and monastic officers: almoner, anniversarian, bartoner, cellarer, chamberlain, feretrar, granger, infirmarian, monk warden, prior's chaplain, receiver, sacrist, sheep warden, and treasurer.[5] Payments for entertainment at festivals and feast days were usually made by the prior or prior's chaplain and were typically entered first in the prior's daybook and then copied into the prior's account rolls or the treasurers' accounts.

The monastic accounting year, like the Canterbury civic accounting year, ran from Michaelmas to Michaelmas.

London, Lambeth Palace Library, MS. 242; 1257–1326; Latin; vellum; i + 370 + i; dimensions of leaves vary from 300mm x 243mm to 250mm x 188mm; modern pencil foliation; individual leaves tipped into guard book with 2 leaves of thick skin which originally formed covers at each end; calf binding, title on spine: 'Accounts of Christchurch Canterbury.'

London, Lambeth Palace Library, MS. 243; 1327–91; Latin; vellum; ii + 224 + i; dimensions of leaves vary from 350mm x 295mm to 320mm x 230mm; modern pencil foliation; brown calf binding, title on spine: 'Accounts of Christchurch Canterbury.'

Canterbury, Cathedral Archives, DCc/Miscellaneous Accounts 4; 1444–9; Latin; paper; i + 230 + i, gathered in 20s; 285mm x 205mm, average 36 lines; modern pencil foliation; edges of pages charred; parchment binding. Regular use of accounting marks (+) next to nearly every entry.

Christ Church Priors' Daybook

This daybook includes rough accounts of Richard de Oxenden (prior 1331–8) and Robert Hathbrande (prior 1338–70).

Canterbury, Cathedral Archives, DCc/DE 3; 1331–43; Latin; paper; iii + 54 + iii, in irregular gatherings; 400mm x 145mm; modern pencil foliation; final 4 folios faded and mostly illegible, entries and whole pages of rough accounts frequently crossed out; modern maroon leather binding.

Prior Goldston's Daybook

Canterbury, Cathedral Archives, Literary MS E6; 1450–1; Latin; paper; 75 leaves, gathered in 12s; 205mm x 137mm, average 32 lines; modern pencil foliation; original parchment binding.

Christ Church Priors' Accounts

Canterbury, Cathedral Archives, DCc/Prior 22; 1372; Latin; paper; 2 sheets serially attached; 444mm x 152mm, 290mm x 152mm; fragment of draft account, expenses only.

Canterbury, Cathedral Archives, DCc/Prior 7; 1436–7; Latin; parchment; 4 mbs serially attached; 776mm x 266mm; modern wrapping.

Canterbury, Cathedral Archives, DCc/Prior 6; 1442–3; Latin; parchment; 4 mbs serially attached; 790mm x 264mm; heading missing; modern wrapping.

London, British Library, Sloane MS. 4074; 1452–3; Latin; parchment; single mb; 630mm x 283mm; expense account fragment, written on 1 side only, repaired with 130mm strip of parchment attached to top, forming outside of roll.

Canterbury, Cathedral Archives, DCc/Prior 9; 1453–4; Latin; parchment; 4 mbs serially attached; 760mm x 278mm; modern wrapping.

Canterbury, Cathedral Archives, DCc/Prior 10; 1455–6; Latin; parchment; 5 mbs serially attached; 702mm x 281mm; modern wrapping.

Canterbury, Cathedral Archives, DCc/Prior 15; 1456–7; Latin; parchment; 5 mbs serially attached in order 1, 3, 4, 2, 5; 670mm x 306mm; roll repaired, heading wanting; modern wrapping.

Canterbury, Cathedral Archives, DCc/Prior 16; 1467–8; Latin; parchment; 2 mbs serially attached; 735mm x 293mm; fragment of expense accounts only; modern wrapping.

Canterbury, Cathedral Archives, DCc/Prior 11; 1468–9; Latin; parchment; 4 mbs serially attached; 728mm x 246mm; mbs repaired; modern wrapping.

Canterbury, Cathedral Archives, DCc/Prior 12; 1472–3; Latin; parchment; 4 mbs serially attached; 700mm x 278mm; mbs repaired; modern wrapping.

Canterbury, Cathedral Archives, DCc/Prior 14; 1473–4; Latin; parchment; 4 mbs serially attached; 725mm x 281mm; mbs 3 and 4 written on both sides; roll repaired, heading wanting; modern wrapping.

Christ Church Chronicle

This manuscript contains various memoranda and accounts of Christ Church, including the weekly accounts of the dean of the seven priests serving in the almonry chapel during 1424 (ff 37–51). Folios 20v, 21, 31, 34, and 35 comprise an anonymous chronicle of Christ Church Priory during the fourteenth and early fifteenth centuries from the time of Prior Henry de Eastry (1284–1331) to the third year of Prior John Wodnesburgh (1414).

Canterbury, Cathedral Archives, Literary MS C14; early 15th c.; Latin; paper; ii + 51 + i, in irregular gatherings; 294mm x 110mm, average 40 lines; modern pencil foliation; brown leather binding. Writing on f 31 is reversed.

John Stone's Chronicle of Christ Church Priory

John Stone made his monastic profession at Christ Church on 13 December 1417. Serving variously as refectorer, master of ordinands, subsacrist, and third prior, he best served the monastery by maintaining a chronicle and obituary record of the Christ Church community between 1415 and 1471. Stone himself died *c* 1480.

Cambridge, Corpus Christi College, MS. 417; 1415–72; Latin; paper; 103 leaves in irregular gatherings; 213mm x 148mm, average 21 lines; foliated in pencil (ff 94–6, 98–103 do not carry folio numbers but belong to the folio sequence, as shown by the fact that f 97 is marked appropriately); condition excellent; modern binding, half-leather over boards.

Register of Christ Church Penitentiarian

This register of the penitentiarian of Christ Church, Canterbury, was kept by William Ingram, who made his profession as a monk in 1483 and served as warden of martyrs (1503–11) and as penitentiarian (1511–32). In addition to his accounts for these offices, the manuscript also contains expenses arising from the entertainment of guests, expenses arising from the care of almonry school boys whom he may have tutored, and a number of inventories, including an inventory of the personal possessions of Henry Arundel made when Ingram succeeded Arundel as penitentiarian following the latter's death on 7 June 1511.[6]

Canterbury, Cathedral Archives, Literary MS C11; 1500–33; English and Latin; paper; iv + 157 + iii, in irregular gatherings; 410mm x 110mm, average 57 lines; modern foliation; modern brown cloth binding.

Dean and Chapter of Christ Church Cathedral

New Foundation Treasurers' Accounts

After the cathedral establishment was refounded as the dean and chapter of Christ Church Cathedral in 1541, two canons were elected annually to the posts of receiver and treasurer. The receiver accounted for the collection of revenues from the dean and chapter's estates. The treasurer accounted for disbursements for repairs, alms, fees, and the salaries of the dean and prebendaries, stipends of the preachers, minor canons and lay clerks, master of the choirboys and choristers, headmaster of the grammar school, the grammar school boys, the twelve bedesmen, and various workmen. The New Foundation treasurers' accounts from 1541 to 1642 consist of a series of rough account booklets, now bound together to form the two composite volumes DCc/Miscellaneous Accounts 40 and DCc/Miscellaneous Accounts 41, and a second series of revised account rolls DCc/TA 1–DCc/TA 47, which with some gaps covers the same period.

Canterbury, Cathedral Archives, DCc/Miscellaneous Accounts 40; 1541–76; English; paper; iv + 463 + iv, in irregular gatherings; 310mm x 212mm, average 19 lines; modern pencil foliation; 19th-c. brown half-leather binding.

Canterbury, Cathedral Archives, DCc/Miscellaneous Accounts 41; 1576–1643; English and Latin; paper; iv + 597 + iv, in irregular gatherings (composite volume of annual account booklets often with parchment covers still intact); 320mm x 198mm, average 29 lines; modern pencil foliation; 19th-c. brown half-leather binding.

Canterbury, Cathedral Archives, DCc/TA 7; 1572–3; Latin and English; paper; 11 sheets, attached at top; 412mm x 314mm; written on both sides and foliated 89–99 in accounts series.

Canterbury, Cathedral Archives, DCc/TA 8; 1576–7; Latin and English; paper; 11 sheets, attached at top; 422mm x 307mm; written on both sides and foliated 104–14 in accounts series.

Canterbury, Cathedral Archives, DCc/TA 9; 1578–9; Latin and English; paper; 11 sheets, attached at top; 403mm x 317mm; written on both sides and foliated 115–25 in accounts series.

Canterbury, Cathedral Archives, DCc/TA 10; 1589–90; Latin and English; paper; 10 leaves in stitched booklet; 397mm x 268mm; written on both sides and foliated 126–35 in accounts series.

Canterbury, Cathedral Archives, DCc/TA 19; 1610–11; Latin and English; paper; 8 sheets, attached at top; 465mm x 370mm; written on both sides and foliated 199–206 in accounts series.

Canterbury, Cathedral Archives, DCc/TA 38; 1629–30; Latin and English; paper; 6 sheets, attached at top; 445mm x 343mm; written on both sides.

Canterbury, Cathedral Archives, DCc/TA 39; 1630–1; Latin and English; paper; 5 sheets, attached at top; 445mm x 340mm; written on both sides.

Canterbury, Cathedral Archives, DCc/TA 40; 1631–2; Latin and English; paper; 4 sheets, attached at top; 435mm x 340mm; written on both sides.

Canterbury, Cathedral Archives, DCc/TA 43; 1635–6; Latin and English; paper; 5 sheets, attached at top; 450mm x 360mm; written on both sides.

Cathedral Chapter Act Book

Canterbury, Cathedral Archives, DCc/CA 1; 1561–8; English; paper; ii + 86 + vii; 315mm x 240mm, average 37 lines; modern pencil foliation supersedes original ink foliation; MS badly damaged by fire; repaired and rebound in black leather with original parchment cover bound in at back of volume.

St Augustine's Abbey

Most of the financial manuscripts of the monastery were lost after the Dissolution, leaving only a handful of fifteenth-century treasurers' accounts to hint at the abbey's once thriving patronage of medieval musicians and entertainers. The monastic accounting year ran from Michaelmas to Michaelmas.

St Augustine's Treasurers' Accounts

London, British Library, Harley Roll Z 19; 1406–8; Latin; parchment; 9 mbs serially attached; 550–600mm x 250mm; modern pencil numbering; receipts on front, expenses on dorse; heading torn and repaired with 240mm head mb.

Canterbury, Cathedral Archives, DCc/Charta Antiqua A 218a; 1431–2; Latin; parchment; 7 mbs serially attached (roll is attached backwards: expenses are on the front, receipts on the dorse); 800mm x 255mm; modern pencil numbering; parchment much faded and repaired.

London, Lambeth Palace Library, Estate Document 2058; 1446–7; Latin; parchment; 5 mbs serially attached; 800mm x 262mm; modern pencil numbering; written on both sides, expenses begin on dorse.

London, Lambeth Palace Library, Estate Document 298; 1459–60; Latin; paper; 28 leaves in 1 stitched gathering (last 6 cut away); 303mm x 230mm, average 30 lines; modern pencil foliation; repaired and rebound.

Canterbury, Cathedral Archives, DCc/Charta Antiqua A 66e; 1464–5; Latin; paper; iv + 45 + iv, in irregular gatherings; 310mm x 220mm, average 30 lines; modern pencil foliation; bound in brown half-leather binding, title on spine: 'Treasurer's Accounts of St Augustines Abbey. 1469–70.' The manuscript contains three separate accounts: full accounts for 1468–9 (ff 1–21), fragmentary accounts for 1464–5 (ff 22–37), and a further undated fragmentary account (ff 38–45).

Canterbury, Cathedral Archives, DCc/Charta Antiqua A 66d; 1468–9; Latin; paper; iv + 45 + iv, in irregular gatherings; 310mm x 220mm, average 30 lines; modern pencil foliation; bound in brown half-leather binding, title on spine: 'Treasurer's Accounts of St Augustines Abbey. 1469–70.' The manuscript contains three separate accounts: full accounts for 1468–9 (ff 1–21), fragmentary accounts for 1464–5 (ff 22–37), and a further undated fragmentary account (ff 38–45).

William Thorne's Chronicle of St Augustine's Abbey

Little is known about the life of William Thorne, monk of St Augustine's Abbey, except that he was a candidate for the abbacy in 1375 and that he subsequently served as attorney for Abbot Michael Peckham and his successor, William Welde. He is remembered today primarily for his chronicle of St Augustine's Abbey, which survives in two manuscripts: a late fourteenth-century manuscript (Cambridge, Corpus Christi College: MS. 189), which is used in the Records and Appendix 3, and an early fifteenth-century manuscript (BL: Additional MS. 53,710), which once belonged to Sir Roger Twysden, who edited Thorne's Chronicle in the seventeenth century.[7] Printed editions include *Chronica Guill: Thorne Monachi S. Augustini Cant.*, cols 1753–2296, in Roger Twysden and John Selden, *Historiae Anglicanae Scriptores X* (London, 1652; Wing H2094), and A.H. Davis (trans), *William Thorne's Chronicle of Saint Augustine's Abbey, Canterbury* (Oxford, 1934).

Cambridge, Corpus Christi College, MS. 189; late 14th c.; Latin; parchment with paper flyleaves (probably 18th c.); v + 202 + v, gathered mostly in 12s; 290mm x 200mm, average 40 lines; variously paginated and foliated, but ink foliation (often very faint) is followed here; paragraph marks, important names or topical words, enlarged initial capitals of chapters, and running titles in red; 18th-c. leather binding, largely perished, over boards covered with reused parchment. Thorne's chronicle occupies ff 45–190 according to the ink foliation.

London, British Library, Additional MS. 53,710; early 15th c.; Latin; vellum with paper flyleaves; v + 384 + iv, primarily gathered in 10s; 277mm x 190mm, average 36 lines; later ink pagination; original brown leather binding. Manuscript also contains two charters of Æthelberht to the Abbey of Sts Peter and Paul, Canterbury (pp 382–3), and memoranda of bonds for the ransom of Alfonso de Villena of Aragon, son of the count of Denia, held hostage in England for his father after the battle of Najera in 1367 (p 384).

Parish Records

St Andrew's Churchwardens' Accounts

The ancient parish church of St Andrew's, Canterbury, was situated in Middle Row in the High Street between the crossing of Mercery Lane and St Margaret's Street on the west and Butchery Lane to the east until it was pulled down in 1763. Churchwardens' accounts survive with some gaps from 1485 until 1625 and have been published in a series of articles by Charles Cotton in *Archaeologia Cantiana*.

For much of the first half of the sixteenth century the accounting year ran from Michaelmas to Michaelmas; however, during the early sixteenth century and throughout the Elizabethan and Jacobean periods the accounting year was highly irregular, beginning and ending at different times of year and often extending for periods longer than one year.

Canterbury, Cathedral Archives, U3/5/4/1; 1485–1625; English; paper; 215 leaves, gathered in

10s; 305mm x 215mm, average 30 lines; modern pencil foliation; brown leather 17th-c. binding with clasps.

St Dunstan's Churchwardens' Accounts

The ancient parish of St Dunstan's, Canterbury, was located outside of Westgate along the London Road. Churchwardens' accounts survive from 1485 until 1580 and have been published in a series of articles by Joseph Meadows Cowper in *Archaeologia Cantiana*.

The St Dunstan's accounting year during this period was highly irregular, beginning and ending at different dates and extending for different intervals.

Canterbury, Cathedral Archives, U3/141/4/1; 1485–1563; English; paper; 31 leaves in 1 stitched booklet; 290mm x 205mm, 31 lines; 19th-c. ink pagination 1–62. Many gaps in the accounts.

Canterbury, Cathedral Archives, U3/141/5/1; 1505–56; English; paper; 17 leaves in 1 stitched booklet; 282mm x 195mm, average 28 lines; modern pencil pagination 1–34.

Canterbury, Cathedral Archives, U3/141/5/2; 1508–50; English; paper; 14 leaves (formerly in a stitched booklet but now separate and repaired); 295mm x 210mm, average 28 lines; paginated 35–62 as continuation of U3/141/5/1.

Canterbury, Cathedral Archives, U3/141/5/3; 1537–58; English; paper; 19 leaves; 215mm x 155mm, average 21 lines; 19th-c. ink pagination; parchment cover.

St Dunstan's Church Inventory (A)

This inventory of church goods belonging to St Dunstan's, Canterbury, survives only in antiquarian copies. It was sent to *The Gentleman's Magazine* in 1837 by J.B. Bunce, the vicar of St Dunstan's, with the following note: 'I send you the following, if you feel disposed to rescue from oblivion the fading contents of an old (and I may say) curious manuscript, employed for its last office as a covering of an ancient book of accounts, containing a Schedule of the Goods of the Parish Church of St. Dunstan, near Canterbury; as set forth in an instrument dated 1st May A.D. 1500, and made between Master Clement Hardyng, Vicar, Master John Roper, with others of the Parishioners, and the Wardens of that Church, then having the custody of those goods ... V.S.D. [Vicar of St. Dunstan's].' The inventory appeared in *The Gentleman's Magazine*, and was reprinted by J.M. Cowper, in 'Accounts of the Churchwardens of St. Dunstan's, Canterbury, A.D. 1484–1514,' *Arch. Cant.* 16 (1886), 312–16. The manuscript may once have served as the cover for the churchwardens' accounts, which survive in unbound paper booklets, but the cover has since disappeared.

V.S.D., 'Church Goods of St. Dunstan's, Canterbury, 1500,' *The Gentleman's Magazine*, ns, vol 8 (July–December, 1837), 569–71.

Ecclesiastical Court Books

Examinations in John Bale con. Richard Ugden

Canterbury, Cathedral Archives, DCb/J/X.10.7; 1560; Latin and English; paper; i + 358 + i, in irregular gatherings; 300mm x 200mm, average 29 lines; modern pencil foliation; modern brown cloth binding.
    This book also supplies an entry for Appendix 1.

Consistory Court Book

See under Bonnington for CCA: DCb/J/X.8.8.

Actes du Consistoire

In 1575, by order of the privy council, the Walloon refugees were moved from Sandwich to Canterbury. By 1576 the French-speaking congregation had begun to worship in the cathedral crypt and to hold their own consistory courts to discipline their members. For further background, see p 1289, endnote to CCA: U47/A1 p 31.

Canterbury, Cathedral Archives, U47/A1; 1576–8; French; paper; 63 leaves; 210mm x 155mm, average 20 lines; modern pencil pagination 1–126; original manuscript has been disbound and individual leaves tipped into modern binding interleaved with guard pages; parchment binding over hard boards, wording on spine: 'Actes du Consistoire de l'Eglise Wallonne 1576–1578.'

Canterbury, Cathedral Archives, U47/A2; 1581–4; French; paper; ii + 62 + i, in irregular gatherings; 298mm x 100mm, average 50 lines; modern pencil foliation supersedes inaccurate pencil pagination; parchment binding over hard boards, title on front: 'Actes du Consistoire de L'Eglise Francaise a Canterbury 1581 to 1584.'

Archdeacon's Court Book

Canterbury, Cathedral Archives, DCb/J/X.5.2; 1608–15; English and Latin; paper; ii + 272 + ix, gathered in 16s; 287mm x 195mm, average 20 lines; contemporary ink foliation; modern binding incorporating original parchment covers in a brown clothbound case. Contains comperta and detecta presentments for Canterbury deanery.

Guild Records

Minstrels' Guild Deed of Incorporation

Two copies of the incorporation deed for the Fellowship of the Craft and Mystery of Minstrels survive in the city archives: the city's copy of the deed (cca: CC/Woodruff's List liv/20), still bearing a fragment of the common seal, and the counterpart deed (cca: CC/Woodruff's List liv/18), sealed with two personal seals presumably belonging to two of the waits. Neither deed nor counterpart is signed. In the transcription, the text follows that of the deed with variants in the counterpart deed listed in the collation notes.

Canterbury, Cathedral Archives, CC/Woodruff's List liv/20; 1544–5; English; parchment; single sheet; 295mm x 466mm; fragment of the common seal attached; display script at opening and at beginning of successive clauses.

Canterbury, Cathedral Archives, CC/Woodruff's List liv/18; 1544–5; English; parchment; single sheet; 300mm x 473mm; 2 private seals attached; display script at opening and at beginning of successive clauses.

Drapers' and Tailors' Memoranda Book

Canterbury, Cathedral Archives, U12/A1; 1544–1672; English; paper; iii + 135 + iii, gathered in 8s; 409mm x 145mm, average 47 lines; modern pencil foliation; manuscript repaired and rebound in modern parchment binding.

Correspondence

Summaries of Letters from the Venetian Ambassadors

These summaries were entered in the 1 October 1519–30 June 1520 volume of an extensive collection of diaries kept by the Venetian diarist and historian Marino Sanuto (1466–1535).

Venezia, Biblioteca Nazionale Marciana, Cod. It. vii, 256 (=9243); 28–9 May 1520; Italian; paper; i + 395 + i; average 330mm x 225mm; contemporary ink foliation; good condition; early 20th-c. binding over boards with leather spine and clasps.

Letter from Antonio Maria di Savoia to the Bishop of Arras

This letter from Antonio Maria di Savoia, one of Philip ii's courtiers, was written to Antoine Perrenot de Granvella (1517–86), bishop of Arras since 1540, minister of King Philip ii of Spain, and later the archbishop of Malines in 1560 and cardinal in 1561.

Wien, Haus-, Hof- und Staatsarchiv, England, Varia 4; 25 December 1554; Italian; paper; bifolium; 316mm x 206mm; originally unnumbered. Now foliated 5–6 in a composite manuscript containing the correspondence of the bishop of Arras.

Letters from the Privy Council to the Mayor and Aldermen

Canterbury, Cathedral Archives, CC/Woodruff's List LII/29; 27 June 1557; English; paper; single sheet; 296mm x 197mm.

Canterbury, Cathedral Archives, CC/Woodruff's List LII/27; 11 August 1557; English; paper; single sheet; 305mm x 207mm.

Letter from Sir Lewis Lewknor to Sir Edward Conway

Sir Lewis Lewknor was knighted in 1603 and served as MP for Midhurst (1597–8), as MP for Bridgnorth (1604–11), and as master of the ceremonies to James I from 1603. A principal secretary to James I, Sir Edward Conway was knighted in 1618, served as MP for Warwick (1624–5) and Yarmouth and Isle of Wight (1626), and was created 2nd Viscount Conway in 1631.[8]

London, Public Record Office, SP 14/146; 14 June 1623; English; paper; original bifolium; 308mm x 205mm; now repaired, outer panels dirty; addressed: 'For his Maiesties especiall affaires To the right Honourable Sir Edward Conwey Knight one of the Principall Secretaries to his Maiestie at Courte hast hast Post hast hast hast From [Douer] ⌈Canterburie⌉ Saterday 14th of Iune past 9 of ye clocke at night *(signed)* Lewes Lewkenor' ('9' has been corrected from '8') and endorsed 'Sir Lewis Lewkenor The Manner of reception, and entertaynment of the Spanish Ambassador vp⟨..⟩ his Landinge, in his passage through Kent, and at Canterb⟨...⟩.' Formerly item 88, now foliated 107–8v and mounted with other state papers in a guardbook.

Letter from Mayor James Nicholson to Archbishop William Laud

London, Public Record Office, SP 16/317; 25 March 1636; English; paper; original bifolium; 300mm x 180mm; addressed 'To the most reverend father in God William Lord Archbishop of Canterbury his grace' and endorsed 'Received March 26. 1636. From the Maior of Canterbury: the abuses of ye players thar thiss Lent.' Formerly item 15, now foliated 27–8v and mounted with other state papers in a guardbook.

Letter from the Privy Council to Mayor James Nicholson

London, Public Record Office, SP 16/317; 29 March 1636; English; paper; single sheet; 345mm x 235mm; draft letter endorsed '29. march 1636. A lettre to the Maior of Canterbury/. Examinatur.' Formerly item 58, now foliated 155 and mounted with other state papers in a guardbook.

Letter from Mayor James Nicholson to the Privy Council

London, Public Record Office, SP 16/318; 5 April 1636; English; paper; original bifolium; 305mm x 213mm; addressed 'To the right honorable the Lordes and otheres of his Maiesties most honorable prevy Counsell' and endorsed 'Rec*eived* Aprill 6: 1636 from ye Mayor of Can*terbury* touching Players/.' Formerly item 25, now foliated 51–2v and mounted with other state papers in a guardbook.

Miscellaneous Records

O Quantum in Rebus Inane

This account of the feasting following William Warham's enthronement as archbishop of Canterbury (*STC*: 25073) was probably printed by J. Cawood in 1570, according to the *STC*. There are now no known perfect copies of this work, although Bodl.: Bodley Rolls 8 was formerly a complete copy made up of ten broadsheets pasted together to form a continuous paper roll, with *STC*: 18482.5 (*The great feast at the intronization of ... George Neuell, archbishop of Yorke*) on the verso of sheets 4–8. This copy, once mounted in a composite roll with three other broadsheets – *STC*: 3419.5, *STC*: 6836.5, and *STC*: 19286 – is now no longer complete; however, the original, undamaged Bodley Rolls 8 is preserved in the UMI *STC* microfilm series, reels 78 and 159. In addition, there are three other imperfect copies of *STC*: 25073: a second Bodleian copy, Douce W 273; a copy at Canterbury Cathedral Archives containing sheets 3–8 (sheet 3 imperfect) with *STC*: 18482.5 on the verso of sheets 4–8; and another in Lambeth Palace Library containing sheet 9 and a fragment of sheet 10. This last copy, the only surviving copy of the 'Provisiones & Emptiones' sheet, has been tipped into LPL: MS. 959, a composite manuscript which consists of the printed pages of Matthew Parker's *De Antiquitate Britannicae Ecclesiae* (*STC*: 19292) interleaved with various manuscript and printed material and bound in two volumes. The *STC*: 25073 fragment is now between pp 208 and 209 of the printed pages of *STC*: 19292.

Two eighteenth-century antiquarians, apparently independently, noticed and printed *O Quantum*. The first was Nicholas Battely, in the Appendix to *Cantuaria Sacra*, the second part of his revised and enlarged 1703 edition of William Somner's *Antiquities of Canterbury* (*STC*: 22918). Excerpts appear on pp 20–9, with the enthronement expenses on pp 27–8. On p 20 the whole excerpt is headed 'Out of a Printed Roll in the Archives of the Church.' A comparison of Battely's text with the CCA and LPL copies shows this must have been a roll comprising those now separate fragments of *STC*: 25073, already missing sheets 1–2 and part of sheet 3. Thomas Hearne, giving his source as 'out of an old paper roll,' printed the contents of the entire composite Bodley Rolls 8, with a description, in an appendix to his second edition of John Leland's *Collectanea*, *Iohannis Lelandi Antiquarii De Rebus Britannicis Collectanea*, vol 6 (London, 1774), pp 2–40, with the list of expenses at William Warham's enthronement on pp 30–1.

O quantum in rebus inane. | ¶ INTRONIZATIO VVIL- | helmi VVarham, Archiepiscopi | Cantuar. Dominica in Passione. Anno Henrici 7. | vicesimo, *& anno Domini.* 1504. | *nono die Marcij*. *STC*: 25073.

Charles V's Visit to Canterbury

This description of the emperor's visit to Canterbury was entered in the 1 July 1520–28 February 1520/1 volume of an extensive collection of diaries kept by the Venetian diarist and historian Marino Sanuto (1466–1535).

Venezia, Biblioteca Nazionale Marciana, Cod. It. VII, 257 (=9244); 27–8 May 1520; Italian; paper; i + 402 +ii; average 330mm x 225mm; contemporary ink foliation; good condition; early 20th-c. binding over boards with leather spine and clasps.

Thomas Cromwell's Accounts

This account book of Thomas Cromwell, kept by Thomas Avery, covers three calendar years from 1 January 1536/7 to 31 December 1539. Receipts month by month for 1537 appear on ff 3–30v, for 1538 on ff 31–58v, and for 1539 on ff 59–81v. Payments for 1537 follow on ff 82–115, for 1538 on ff 116–48v, and for 1539 on ff 149–181.

London, Public Record Office, E 36/256; 1537–9; English; paper; ii + 183 + ii; 284mm x 195mm, average 26 lines; modern pencil foliation, original parchment cover bound in as f 1; repaired and rebound in green half-leather binding.

Depositions Concerning Henry Totehill of London

London, Public Record Office, SP 1/142; 10 January 1538/9; English; paper; bifolium; 308mm x 221mm. Originally enclosed in an otherwise unrelated letter of Archbishop Thomas Cranmer to Thomas Cromwell, chief minister of Henry VIII, now foliated 35–6 and mounted in a guardbook.

John Bale, 'A retourne of James Canceller's raylinge boke'

This holograph manuscript of John Bale, radical Protestant playwright and prebendary of Christ Church Cathedral, was intended as a reply to *The pathe of obedience, righte necessarye for all the king and quenes maiesties louing subiectes* (STC: 4564) by James Cancellar, theological writer and priest in Queen Mary's chapel. Bale's manuscript was entered in the Stationers' Register by the printer, John Day.[9] Folios 1–2 were marked up for printing but the book never appeared in print. The dedicatory epistle was addressed to Francis Russell, 2nd earl of Bedford, and was dated Canterbury, 6 July 1561. For further biographical records of John Bale, see Appendix 1 (pp 945–54).

London, Lambeth Palace Library, MS. 2001; 1561; English; paper; iv + 45, gathered in 4s; 198mm x 135mm; foliated i–iv (a prefatory epistle), 1–7, 7A, 8–44 (f 7 is tipped in and smaller than original leaves; 7A is the original 7); modern cloth binding with 13th-c. vellum wrapper bound inside. Holograph manuscript of John Bale entitled 'A retourne of Iames Canceller's raylinge boke upon hys owne heade, called the path of obedyence: to teach hym hereafter how he shall sedicyously gyve fourth a pernicyouse disobedyence agaynst the crowne of thys realme, in stede of true obedyence.'

Probate Inventory of Robert Betts

For further information on Robert Betts, see p 1288, endnote to CCA: DCb/PRC 10/6 f 91.

Canterbury, Cathedral Archives, DCb/PRC 10/6; 1571–3; English; paper; iv + 331 + iv, gathered in 8s; 295mm x 225mm, average 29 lines; contemporary ink foliation; original parchment binding.

The Life of Archbishop Matthew Parker

London, British Library, Printed Book C.24.b.6; 1573; Latin; 23 leaves; unnumbered; title: De | Antiquitate | Britannicæ Ecclesiæ | & Priuilegiis Ecclesiæ | Cantuariensis, cum | Archiepiscopis | eiusdem | *70.* | *AN. DOM.* | *1572.* | ¶ *Excusum Londini in ædibus* | *Iohannis Daij* (STC: 19292). The text of the Life was added by hand following sig II.ij verso. Text ends with the departure of Queen Elizabeth I from Canterbury in 1573 with a copyist's note: 'In originali hic, [sic] spacium ^⌈relictum⌉ fuit, culpa, an Impressoris emissunt, [necnon] necne, mihi incertum est.'

Court of High Commission Act Book

Canterbury, Cathedral Archives, DCb/PRC 44/3; 1584–1603; Latin and English; paper; 101 leaves, gathered in 8s; 300mm x 205mm, average 36 lines; modern pencil pagination; bound in 2 volumes in modern hardback cloth binding.

Diary of Thomas Cocks

Thomas Cocks, auditor to the dean and chapter of Canterbury Cathedral from the late sixteenth century until his death on 15 October 1611, lived in the archbishop's palace in Canterbury. His diary, containing daily receipts and expenses between 25 March 1607 and 1 January 1610/11, records numerous payments for players and for the music of the Canterbury waits.

Canterbury, Cathedral Archives, Literary MS E31; 1607–10/11; English; paper; 54 leaves in 1 gathering; 310mm x 203mm, average 46 lines; modern pencil foliation supersedes original ink pagination; manuscript repaired and rebound in original parchment binding.

Privy Council Warrant

London, Public Record Office, PC 2/33; 1625–6; English; paper; ii + 472 + ii; 403mm x 270mm; contemporary ink foliation; condition generally good; binding damaged, with remains of 19th-c. stamped leather over boards, title on spine: 'Charles I | Vol. I. | Council Register. | 27 Mar. 1625 to 17 July 1626.' Volume includes contemporary unfoliated subject index and 19th-c. paginated indices of subjects and places.

CHART SUTTON

Visitation Proceedings

London, Lambeth Palace Library, Register of Archbishop William Warham, vol 1; 1503–32; Latin and English; parchment with modern paper flyleaves; iv + 216 + iv; 420mm x 330mm; modern arabic pencil foliation supersedes contemporary roman ink foliation (both series irregular); modern binding.

This book also supplies an entry for Little Mongeham.

CHISLET

Archdeacon's Court Book

Canterbury, Cathedral Archives, DCb/J/X.2.6; 1584–1601; English and Latin; paper; part 1: ii + 188, part 2: 309 + xiv, both gathered in 12s; 295mm x 195mm, average 19 lines; contemporary ink foliation; modern brown cloth binding and case. Contains comperta and detecta presentments for Ospringe and Westbere deaneries.

This book also supplies entries for Faversham and Whitstable.

Quarter Sessions Examinations

See under Canterbury for CCA: CC/J/Q/388.

CRANBROOK

Archdeacon's Court Books

Canterbury, Cathedral Archives, DCb/J/X.1.10; 1570–2; English and Latin; paper; 128 leaves, gathered in 8s; 305mm x 205mm, average 27 lines; modern pencil foliation; parchment binding with modern brown cloth case. Contains comperta and detecta presentments for all deaneries.

Canterbury, Cathedral Archives, DCb/J/X.4.11; 1606–8; English and Latin; paper; ii + 229 + vii, gathered in 12s; 296mm x 187mm, average 20 lines; contemporary ink foliation; original parchment binding. Contains comperta and detecta presentments for Charing deanery.

DENTON

Archdeacon's Court Book

Canterbury, Cathedral Archives, DCb/J/X.3.1; 1585–99, 1632–6; English and Latin; paper; part 1: ii + 191, part 2: 55 + viii, in irregular gatherings; 296mm x 200mm, average 36 lines; contemporary ink foliation; parchment binding. Contains comperta and detecta presentments for Dover and Elham deaneries.

DOVER

Civic Records

The town and port of Dover has a fine collection of ancient records now kept at the East Kent Archives Centre. During the nineteenth century, however, many other Dover records, including wardens' accounts, assembly minutes, and records of the borough court of pleas, passed out of the town's possession and may be found today among the Egerton MSS and Additional MSS in the British Library. All civic records that do include evidence of ceremonial and dramatic activity have been described in detail below.

Dover's mayoral and accounting year officially began and ended on 8 September, the feast of the Nativity of St Mary the Virgin, but in practice for most of the sixteenth century the accounting year actually began on the following Sunday or Monday, since the traditional weekly payment date was Saturday and the outgoing chamberlains continued to make payments during the week in which the feast day fell and occasionally for one or more additional weeks. When the account terms differ from the 8 September–8 September pattern, the dates appear in the records as given in the account books.

Wardens' Accounts

There are three series of borough wardens' or chamberlains' accounts, two in the British Library and one in the East Kent Archives Centre. These three series contain a mixture of rough accounts, revised accounts, and summary accounts, but between them present an almost unbroken record of Dover financial expenditure from 1365 to 1642.

London, British Library, Additional MS. 29,615; 1365–79, 1423–36, 1452–3; Latin; paper; ii + 220 + ii; 280mm x 215mm, average 34 lines; modern foliation; leaves repaired; rebound in modern red cloth binding. Contains a mixture of rough and summary accounts.

London, British Library, Egerton MS. 2091; 1381–1424; Latin; paper; iii + 96 + iii; 300mm x 218mm, average 22 lines; modern pencil foliation; leaves repaired; rebound in modern red cloth binding with parchment spine. Contains rough wardens' accounts for 1381–4 and miscellaneous town ordinances, and records of the mayor's court.

London, British Library, Additional MS. 29,810; 1434–58; English and Latin; paper; ii + 83 + ii; 278mm x 205mm, average 30 lines; modern pencil foliation; leaves repaired; rebound in 19th-c. green half-leather binding. Contains a mixture of rough and summary accounts.

London, British Library, Additional MS. 29,616; 1462–85; English and Latin; paper; iii + 264 + iii; 298mm x 198mm, average 34 lines; modern pencil foliation; leaves repaired; rebound in 19th-c. green half-leather binding. Contains mostly rough accounts.

London, British Library, Egerton MS. 2090; 1465–79; English and Latin; paper; iii + 174 + iii;

310mm x 220mm, average 37 lines; modern pencil foliation; leaves repaired; rebound in 19th-c. green leather binding. Contains mostly summary accounts.

London, British Library, Egerton MS. 2107; 1485–1508; English and Latin; paper; i + 120 + i; 295mm x 215mm, average 33 lines; modern pencil foliation; leaves repaired; rebound in 19th-c. green half-leather binding. Contains mostly summary accounts.

London, British Library, Additional MS. 29,617; 1485–1509; English; paper; iii + 357 + iii; 295mm x 215mm, average 35 lines; modern pencil foliation (ff 160–77 bound out of chronological order); leaves repaired; rebound in 19th-c. green half-leather binding. Contains mostly rough accounts.

London, British Library, Egerton MS. 2092; 1509–46; English and Latin; paper; iii + 569 + iii; 315mm x 220mm, average 33 lines; modern pencil foliation; leaves repaired; rebound in 19th-c. green half-leather binding. Contains a mixture of rough and summary accounts.

London, British Library, Additional MS. 29,618; 1509–46; English and Latin; paper; iv + 216 + iii (29,618A) and iii + 183 + iv (29,618B); 287mm x 195mm, average 30 lines; modern pencil foliation: ff 1–216 (29,618A) and ff 217–399 (29,618B); leaves repaired; rebound in 1988 in 2 volumes bound in green half-leather binding. Contains a mixture of rough and summary accounts.

Chamberlains' Accounts

Whitfield, East Kent Archives Centre, DO/FCa 1; 1546–58; English and Latin; paper; vi + 342 + iii, in irregular gatherings; 315mm x 205mm, average 35 lines; foliated at time of binding; brown half-leather binding with title: 'Dover Corporation Accompts | Edward VI | Queen Mary | 1546–1558.' Contains a mixture of rough and summary accounts.

Whitfield, East Kent Archives Centre, DO/FCa 2; 1558–81; English; paper; iv + 499 + iii, in irregular gatherings; 305mm x 205mm, average 38 lines; foliated at time of binding; brown half-leather binding with title: 'Dover Corporation Accompts | Elizabeth | 1558–1581.' Contains a mixture of rough and summary accounts.

Whitfield, East Kent Archives Centre, DO/FCa 3; 1581–1603; English; paper; iv + 506 + iii, in irregular gatherings made up of annual booklets of unequal length; 305mm x 205mm, average 40 lines; foliated at time of binding; brown half-leather binding with title: 'Dover Corporation Accompts | Elizabeth | 1581–1603.' Contains a mixture of rough and summary accounts.

Whitfield, East Kent Archives Centre, DO/FCa 4; 1603–25; English; paper; vi + 686 + iii, in irregular gatherings; 310mm x 195mm, average 40 lines; foliated at time of binding; 19th-c. brown half-leather binding with title: 'Dover Corporations Accompts | James 1st | 1603–1625.' Contains a mixture of rough and summary accounts.

Whitfield, East Kent Archives Centre, DO/FCa 5; 1625–60; English; paper; iv + 540 + vi, in irregular gatherings; 340mm x 230mm, average 47 lines; foliated at time of binding; some leaves damaged by damp but repaired; bound in green and brown half-leather binding with title: 'Dover

Corporation Accompts | Charles 1st. | Interregnum | 1625–1660.' Contains a mixture of rough and summary accounts.

Assembly Books

The common assembly minutes are also divided between the British Library and the borough collection at the East Kent Archives Centre. Egerton MS. 2095 and Additional MS. 28,036 are draft versions of the DO/AAm 2.

Assembly Book of Orders and Decrees

British Library, Egerton MS. 2093; 1520–47; English and Latin; paper; iii + 219 + iii; 301mm x 214mm; average 30 lines; modern pencil foliation; MS repaired and each sheet tipped individually into green morocco binding; original parchment covers labelled 'Liber vocatus C' bound in.

Assembly Book

Whitfield, East Kent Archives Centre, DO/AAm 2; 1603–73; English; paper; 451 leaves, gathered in 16s; 435mm x 285mm, average 55 lines; contemporary ink foliation in 2 series: 1–205 (front section, here designated F, containing acts of mayors' court) and 246–1 (back section, here designated B, containing decrees and ordinances); black leather binding.

Town Custumal (A)

When Roger Mortimer, earl of March, was appointed constable of Dover Castle and lord warden of the Cinque Ports, he ordered the five ports and two ancient towns to provide for his use in the Court of Shepway copies of their custumals by Michaelmas 1356. Having been transcribed in 1689 by order of Sir Basil Dixwell, lieutenant of Dover Castle, the surviving custumals were again copied and published by John Lyon in *The History of the Town and Port of Dover and of Dover Castle*. Lyon's transcription of the now-lost earlier copies of the Dover custumal has been subsequently reprinted by John Bavington Jones in *The Records of Dover* (Dover, 1920), prefaced by a short discussion (pp 97–8) of these antiquarian copies. A further antiquarian version of the custumal, based on the medieval original but not copied from it, was compiled in the sixteenth century and survives in the Stowe manuscripts in the British Library.

John Lyon, *The History of the Town and Port of Dover and of Dover Castle; with a short Account of the Cinque Ports*, 2 vols (Dover, 1813–14).

Usages and Customs of Dover

London, British Library, Stowe MS. 850; early 16th c.; English; paper; 10 leaves; 310mm x 200mm;

individual leaves repaired and tipped into brown morocco binding. Now numbered ff 133–42 of a composite MS containing various documents of the reigns of Henry VII and Henry VIII.

Ecclesiastical Records

Order to the Mayor and Commonalty about a Riot

London, Lambeth Palace Library, Register of Archbishop Robert Winchelsey; 1294–1313; Latin; parchment on guards (flyleaves and Ducarel's synopsis, paper); ii +354 + ii; 310mm x 235mm (Ducarel's synopsis, 220mm x 185mm); contemporary but irregular ink foliation (first 8 leaves unfoliated); modern binding, title on spine: 'Winchelsey 1294.' The first seven leaves consist of Ducarel's synopsis of the register followed by an unfoliated limp parchment cover.

St Martin's Prior's Account

The priory of Dover, originally established by King Eadbald of Kent as a house of secular canons in the seventh century, was refounded in the twelfth century as a Benedictine cell of Christ Church, Canterbury, and was eventually surrendered on 16 November 1535. The only surviving financial record is the account of Prior Thomas Lenham for the year ending at Michaelmas 1531.[10]

London, British Library, Additional MS. 25,107; 1530–1; Latin; paper; iv + 16 + iv; 306mm x 210mm, average 36 lines; modern pencil foliation, 19th-c. brown half-leather binding.

St Mary's Churchwardens' Accounts

Like many of the early Dover civic records now in the Egerton MSS or Additional MSS in the British Library, these early Dover churchwardens' accounts passed at some point into private hands. A note on the flyleaf of these accounts says, 'purchased at Rob. Cole's sale, 30 July 1861.' The surviving accounts of the St Mary's churchwardens in the parish collection deposited in the Canterbury Cathedral Archives begin in 1888. The accounting 'year' for these sixteenth-century accounts is highly irregular, starting and ending at different months of the year and lasting for irregular intervals.

London, British Library, Egerton MS. 1912; 1536–58; English; paper; iv + 91 + iv, in irregular gatherings; 305mm x 215mm, average 29 lines; modern pencil foliation; 19th-c. green morocco binding.

Miscellaneous Records

Holinshed's Account of a Workmen's Song from Dover

THE | First and second | *volumes of Chronicles,* | comprising | 1 The description and historie of

England, | 2 The description and historie of Ireland, | 3 The description and historie of Scotland: | First collected and published by Raphaell | Holinshed, William Harrison, | and others: | Now newlie augmented and continued | (with manifold matters of singular | note and worthie memorie) | to the yeare 1586. by | Iohn Hooker *aliàs* Vowell Gent. | and others. | With conuenient tables at | the end of these | volumes. | *Historiæ placeant nostrates ac peregrinæ.* STC: 13569.

Draft Letter from George Villiers to the King of France

George Villiers, 4th duke of Buckingham (1592–1628), was a favourite of James I and Charles I and received a variety of court and political appointments including gentleman of the bedchamber from 1615, master of the horse from 1616, lord high admiral from 1619, and lord warden of the Cinque Ports from 1624. Knighted in 1615, he was created earl of Buckingham in 1617, marquis in 1618, and duke in 1623. He was instrumental in arranging the marriage between Charles I and Henrietta Maria, daughter of King Louis XIII of France.

Edinburgh, National Archives of Scotland, GD24/1/825; June 1625; French; paper; single sheet; 292mm x 195mm. Now bound as item 107 in a composite manuscript.

Privy Council Warrant

See under Canterbury for PRO: PC/2/33.

EGERTON

Consistory Court Books

Canterbury, Cathedral Archives, DCb/J/X.9.2; 1600–2; English and Latin; paper; i + 229, in irregular gatherings; 295mm x 200mm, average 18 lines; contemporary ink foliation; original parchment binding with modern brown cloth case. Contains comperta and detecta presentments.

Canterbury, Cathedral Archives, DCb/J/X.9.3; 1602–4; English and Latin; paper; 235 leaves, gathered in 12s; 296mm x 200mm, average 27 lines; contemporary ink foliation; original parchment binding with modern brown cloth case. Contains comperta and detecta presentments.

ELHAM

Archdeacon's Court Book

See under Brabourne for CCA: DCb/J/X.4.7.

ELMSTEAD

Archdeacon's Court Books

Canterbury, Cathedral Archives, DCb/J/X.10.17; 1576–7; English and Latin; paper; part 1: ii + 199, part 2: 162 + 1, both gathered in 8s; 297mm x 200mm, average 21 lines; part 1: contemporary ink foliation 1–188 continued in modern pencil 189–99, part 2: contemporary ink foliation 1–150 continued in modern pencil 151–62; modern brown cardboard binding and case. Contains comperta and detecta presentments for all deaneries.

See also under Alkham for cca: DCb/J/X.2.1.

FAIRFIELD

Quarter Sessions Presentment

Maidstone, Centre for Kentish Studies, Q/SRp; 1630–1; Latin and English; parchment; 8 mbs attached at top with parchment tag; dimensions vary from 659mm x 310mm to 684mm x 317mm; original ink numbering; writing on both sides.

FAVERSHAM

Faversham records form one of the largest collections of borough records in Kent. The borough custumal survives from the early fifteenth century. Wardmote minutes survive from 1448, containing annual lists of jurats and officers, admissions of freemen, memoranda, and orders of the wardmote. Draft accounts of the chamberlains, overseers, surveyors of the highways, churchwardens, and other town officers survive in rolls and files from 1569. Revised accounts appear from the early sixteenth century in the first wardmote book, FA/AC 1, and in the account book FA/FAc 197. Judicial records include fines in the borough court of record dating from 1295–1640; pleas, depositions, bonds, and recognizances dating from 1560–1666; and quarter sessions rolls and papers dating from 1571–1641 containing such customary sessions business as inquests, indictments, recognizances, and judgments for theft, piracy, and assault. Among these records only the town custumal and the accounts contain evidence of civic musicianship and dramatic activity. The mayoral and civic accounting year in Faversham began and ended at Michaelmas.

Civic Records

Town Custumal

Faversham, Alexander Centre, Borough Custumal; c 1400; Latin, Anglo-Norman, and English; parchment; 54 leaves, gathered in 8s (first gathering in 6, fifth gathering in 10); 195mm x 140mm, average 31 lines; contemporary ink foliation; modern white sheepskin binding.

Wardmote and Account Book

The town's civic year ran from 29 September until the following 29 September. Each year at Michaelmas new town officers were elected and their names were entered in the wardmote book. Sometime after Michaelmas the annual accounts for the previous year were gathered together by the previous year's chamberlains and presented to the auditors. These annual accounts (usually identified by the names of the chamberlains and mayor) were then entered in the wardmote book after the list of officers' names for the year in which those accounts were rendered, rather than after the list of officers' names for the year in which the accounts were created.

    This ordering has created a confusion about dating in the secondary sources, a confusion that has been compounded by the accountants' actual errors in co-ordinating regnal years with years of grace. The mayors' list in Edward Jacob, *The History of the Town and Port of Faversham, in the County of Kent* (London, 1774), for example, is inaccurate: some mayors are omitted while others, not mentioned in the wardmote book, are included. Some of his dates do not agree with the manuscript. As well, some of Giles Dawson's dates in *Collections* 7 are not accurate. The arrangement and dating of FA/AC 1 are so problematic that for reference I append the following corrected list of mayors and chamberlains of Faversham from 1543 to 1582. Specific dating problems affecting material excerpted in the Records are discussed in detail in the Endnotes.

Year	Mayor	Chamberlains	Officers' list begins:	Accounts begin:
1543–4	John Bringborn	John Paulyn, John Gyll	f 38	f 39v
1544–5	John Bringborn	Richard Bond, Nicholas Gaunt	f 38v	——
1545–6	John Seth	John Goff, Thomas Hill	f 41v	f 42
1546–7	Thomas Dunkyn	John Casslock, Ralph Deaton	f 44	f 44
1547–8	Simon Auncelme	Francis Swan, Thomas Oldefield	f 47	f 50v
	(Auncelme died in office and was succeeded by Thomas Arden, elected 26 March 1548)			
1548–9	John Best	John Strensham, Robert Bowgrove	f 51v	f 52v
1549–50	John Wrewke	Thomas Norton, Richard Johnson	f 53v	f 54
1550–1	William Marshall	Richard Smithe, William Neale	f 58	f 59
1551–2	John Seth	Thomas Tenaker, Thomas Muster	f 61	f 62
1552–3	Thomas Gate	Jeffrey Goodwyn, Robert Elfrythe	f 62	f 64v
1553–4	John Dryland	Bartholomew Baull, Thomas Lytell	f 64v	f 66
1554–5	Thomas Strensham	Thomas Belke, Edmund Curtall	f 66	f 68v
1555–6	John Dryland Jr	Christopher Amyas, Henry Bond	f 68	f 70v
1556–7	John Webbe	Richard Wood, John Melhale (or Robert Coldwell)	f 70	f 72v
1557–8	Thomas Strensham	William Comber, Bartholomew Amys	f 72	f 75
1558–9	John Best	Robert Avale, Richard Lawrance	f 74v	f 79v

1559–60	Joseph Beverley	Humphrey Atkynson, John Maycott	f 79	f 83
1560–1	Willam Neale	Michael Allen, John Stone	f 82v	f 86
1561–2	Thomas Norton	Robert Rye, Ambrose Hewlett	f 85v	f 93
1562–3	George Strensham	John Elfrythe, Francis Curteis	f 92v	f 103v
1563–4	Edward Blackwell	Thomas Barton, Hugh Booth	f 103	f 107v
1564–5	Harry Philpott	William Hampton, Robert Lam	f 107	f 111v
1565–6	Thomas Oldefield	Thomas German, Thomas Post	f 111	f 114v
1566–7	John Maycott	William Bennett, Edward Harrys	f 114	f 117v
1567–8	John Best	John Skyrre, Richard Tyllman	f 117	f 120v
1568–9	Bartholomew Amys	William Okenfolde, Thomas Cool	f 120	f 123v
1569–70	Thomas Belke	John Neale, William Pecocke	f 123	f 126v
1570–1	Robert Fagg	Thomas Barlyng, Thomas Waterman	f 126	f 139v
1571–2	Thomas Oldefield	John Tyndale, William Cadman	f 139	f 144v
1572–3	Richard Balle	Thomas Furmynger, Thomas Rye	f 144	f 154v
1573–4	John Finch	Edmund Masterson, Leonard Fidge	f 154	f 165v
1574–5	John Skyrre	William Saker, William Rockerye	f 165	f 176v
1575–6	Thomas Cool	William Tode, Christopher Potter	f 176	f 187v
1576–7	John Keyes	Nicholas Upton, John Casslock	f 187	f 198
1577–8	Christopher Finch	John Upton, Thomas Harte	f 197	f 212
1578–9	Christopher Finch	John Philpott, Abraham Snoode	f 211	f 229v
1579–80	Thomas Barmynge	John Denard, William Chattbourne	f 228v	f 238
1580–1	Richard Tyllman	William Besbeeche, John Elfrythe	f 237	f 246
1581–2	Edward Harrys	Simon Greenstrete, Nicholas a Dye	f 245	——

Faversham, Alexander Centre, FA/AC 1; 1436–1605; Latin and English; paper; ii + 282 + i, gathered in 24s; 404mm x 282mm; 16th-c. ink foliation; originally bound in parchment, rebound in modern half-leather binding. Includes chamberlains' accounts for 1514–15 to 1580–1.

Chamberlains' Accounts

Maidstone, Centre for Kentish Studies, FA/FAc 197; 1581–1621; English; paper; ii + 315 + i; 427mm x 275mm, average 45 lines; modern pencil foliation; manuscript repaired and rebound in modern red cloth binding and case with some leaves bound out of chronological order.

Town Accounts

The original accounts from which the Wardmote and Account Book and the Chamberlains' Accounts, described above, were copied usually took the form of annual account rolls made up of the reckonings of various town officials, such as the mayor, chamberlains, serjeants, and churchwardens. These subsidiary accounts were kept in a variety of formats, mixing single sheets with stitched or unstitched booklets, and then combined by contemporary auditors or accountants to create the annual account rolls. Booklets were opened flat before being joined with sheets and other booklets to form rolls. Such original accounts do not survive for every year, some having apparently perished after being copied into one of the two account books. The following booklets, rolls, and papers have provided relevant material.

Maidstone, Centre for Kentish Studies, FA/FAc 1/1; 1569–70; English; paper; 1 bifolium and 4 folios in 1 gathering, forming an unstitched booklet of 6 leaves; 312mm x 220mm, average 34 lines; modern pencil foliation. Now kept in folder with file of chamberlains' papers comprising 26 numbered sheets, attached at top left. Contains mayor's accounts.

Maidstone, Centre for Kentish Studies, FA/FAc 1/2; 1569–70; English; paper; roll of 26 sheets attached at top left; dimensions vary from 60mm x 155mm to 345mm x 265mm; modern pencil numbering; sheets 13–14 constitute a flattened, stitched booklet of 4 leaves produced from a single sheet folded twice (sheets [2v–4v] remain blank and sheets [3–4] uncut); modern wrapping.

Maidstone, Centre for Kentish Studies, FA/FAc 2/1; 1571–2; English; paper; roll of 10 sheets originally attached at top middle; 420mm x 312mm; modern pencil numbering; edges torn and much decayed by mildew.

Maidstone, Centre for Kentish Studies, FA/FAc 4; 1573–4; English; paper; 4 leaves in stitched booklet; 308mm x 210mm, average 38 lines; contemporary ink foliation. Now among loose sheets gathered together to form an artificial bundle (Bundle 4) of annual accounts.

Maidstone, Centre for Kentish Studies, FA/FAc 5; 1574–5; English; paper; single sheet; 395mm x 305mm, 37 lines. Now kept in a folder of unnumbered loose chamberlains' papers and booklets (Bundle 3). Contains list of outstanding debts owed by the town to former mayor John Finch (1573–4).

Maidstone, Centre for Kentish Studies, FA/FAc 7; 1576–7; English; paper; roll of 21 sheets originally attached at top left; 420mm x 303mm; modern pencil numbering; written on one side only.

Maidstone, Centre for Kentish Studies, FA/FAc 9; 1577–8; English; paper; roll of 52 sheets originally attached at top; dimensions vary from 410mm x 300mm to 205mm x 155mm; modern pencil numbering.

Maidstone, Centre for Kentish Studies, FA/FAc 12; 1581–2; English; paper; 6 leaves in stitched gathering; 405mm x 155mm, average 43 lines; modern pencil foliation. Now rolled in bundle with loose papers and account roll. Contains unlabelled chamberlains' accounts.

Maidstone, Centre for Kentish Studies, FA/FAc 13; 1582–3; English; paper; roll of 32 sheets originally attached at top; 415mm x 305mm; contemporary ink numbering; written on one side only.

Maidstone, Centre for Kentish Studies, FA/FAc 14; 1583–4: English; paper; roll of 16 sheets originally attached at top; 410mm x 305mm; modern pencil numbering; sheet 6 written on both sides.

Maidstone, Centre for Kentish Studies, FA/FAc 15; 1584–5; English; paper; 10 leaves in stitched gathering; 300mm x 210mm, average 23 lines; modern pencil foliation; originally flattened and attached at top left to chamberlains' account roll but now folded and rolled inside paper roll of 12 separately numbered sheets.

Maidstone, Centre for Kentish Studies, FA/FAc 17; 1587–8; English; paper; roll of 37 sheets originally attached at top middle; 410mm x 310mm; modern pencil numbering; written on one side only.

Maidstone, Centre for Kentish Studies, FA/FAc 18; 1588–9; English; paper; roll of 29 sheets originally attached at top; 405mm x 315mm; modern pencil numbering; sheets 7–17 constitute a flattened booklet of 11 leaves.

Maidstone, Centre for Kentish Studies, FA/FAc 19; 1589–90; English; paper; roll of 21 sheets originally attached at top; 410mm x 300mm; modern pencil numbering; sheets 4–7 constitute a flattened booklet with sheet 6 written on one side only and sheet 7 blank.

Maidstone, Centre for Kentish Studies, FA/FAc 20/1; 1590–1; English; paper; roll of 21 sheets originally attached at top; 403mm x 305mm; modern pencil numbering; written on one side only.

Maidstone, Centre for Kentish Studies, FA/FAc 21; 1591–2; English; paper; roll of 24 sheets originally attached at top; dimensions vary from 403mm x 307mm to 205mm x 304mm; modern pencil numbering; sheets 4 and 8–14 written on both sides.

Maidstone, Centre for Kentish Studies, FA/FAc 22/1; 1592–3; English; paper; roll of 25 sheets originally attached at top; dimensions vary from 397mm x 296mm to 257mm x 153mm; modern pencil numbering; sheets 4 (flattened bifolium) and 15–21 (flattened booklet of 7 leaves) written on both sides.

Maidstone, Centre for Kentish Studies, FA/FAc 23/1; 1593–4; English; paper; roll of 23 sheets originally attached at top middle; dimensions vary from 403mm x 300mm to 355mm x 130mm; modern pencil numbering; sheets 4–13 constitute a flattened stitched booklet of 10 leaves.

Maidstone, Centre for Kentish Studies, FA/FAc 24; 1594–5; English; paper; roll of 24 sheets originally attached at top; dimensions vary from 430mm x 160mm to 400mm x 305mm; modern pencil numbering; sheets 4–6 (flattened, unstitched booklet of chamberlains' expenses) and sheets 11–18 (folded, stitched booklet containing expenses of overseer of the poor) written on both sides.

Maidstone, Centre for Kentish Studies, FA/FAc 25; 1595–6; English; paper; roll of 25 sheets originally attached at top; dimensions vary from 405mm x 305mm to 200mm x 115mm; modern pencil numbering; sheets 5–6 and 11–14 (flattened booklets) and 21 (flattened bifolium) all written on both sides: this flattening has produced appearance of having been laid out in 2 columns.

Maidstone, Centre for Kentish Studies, FA/FAc 26; 1596–7; English; paper; roll of 28 sheets originally attached at top; dimensions vary from 405mm x 305mm to 141mm x 149mm; modern pencil numbering; sheet 5 written on both sides; now includes 4 additional, unnumbered, loose sheets containing accounts of churchwardens and receiver of school lands.

Maidstone, Centre for Kentish Studies, FA/FAc 27; 1597–8; English; paper; roll of 26 sheets originally attached at top; 405mm x 310mm; modern pencil numbering; sheets 4–5 written on both sides (flattening of these sheets has produced appearance of having been laid out in columns), sheets 3–6 constitute flattened stitched booklet of 4 leaves containing chamberlains' expenses.

Maidstone, Centre for Kentish Studies, FA/FAc 28; 1598–9; English; paper; roll of 27 sheets originally attached at top; 400mm x 303mm; modern pencil numbering; sheets 5 and 18 (flattened bifolium) written on both sides, sheets 4–6 constitute a flattened booklet.

Maidstone, Centre for Kentish Studies, FA/FAc 29; 1599–1600; English; paper; roll of 26 sheets originally attached at top; dimensions vary from 405mm x 305mm to 200mm x 148mm; modern pencil numbering; sheets 4–5 written on both sides.

Maidstone, Centre for Kentish Studies, FA/FAc 30; 1600–1; English; paper; roll of 19 sheets attached at top with original fastening; 405mm x 304mm; modern pencil numbering; written on one side only.

Maidstone, Centre for Kentish Studies, FA/FAc 31; 1601–2; English; paper; roll of 14 sheets attached at top with original fastening; 410mm x 310mm; modern pencil numbering; written on one side only.

Maidstone, Centre for Kentish Studies, FA/FAc 33; 1602–3; English; paper; roll of 12 sheets attached at top with original fastening; 405mm x 300mm; modern pencil numbering; written on one side only.

Maidstone, Centre for Kentish Studies, FA/FAc 35; 1604–5; English; paper; roll of 15 sheets tied at top; 405mm x 305mm; modern pencil numbering; sheet 14 (flattened bifolium) written on both sides.

Maidstone, Centre for Kentish Studies, FA/FAc 36; 1605–6; English; paper; roll of 12 sheets attached at top; dimensions vary from 395mm x 300mm to 325mm x 135mm; modern pencil numbering; sheets 4 and 6 written on both sides, sheets 4–5 (bifolium) and 6 (single sheet) now loose from roll.

Maidstone, Centre for Kentish Studies, FA/FAc 38; 1607–8; English; paper; roll of 11 sheets attached at top with original fastening; 397mm x 308mm; modern pencil numbering; sheets 2–3 (bifolium entirely reversed when attached) written on both sides. Now rolled up with 8 sheets and 1 bifolium, all unnumbered.

Maidstone, Centre for Kentish Studies, FA/FAc 39; 1608–9; English; paper; roll of 9 sheets attached at top with original fastening, and fragmentary booklet of 8 leaves; 405mm x 310mm (roll), 200mm x 205mm (booklet); booklet only numbered in modern pencil; mutilated and decayed by damp. Contains chamberlains' expenses.

Maidstone, Centre for Kentish Studies, FA/FAc 40; 1609–10; English; paper; roll of 10 sheets attached with original fastening at top; 407mm x 307mm; modern pencil numbering.

Maidstone, Centre for Kentish Studies, FA/FAc 41; 1610–11; English; paper; roll of 10 sheets attached at top with original fastening and 2 unattached bifolia; 405mm x 310mm (roll), 395mm x 155mm, average 41 lines (bifolia); bifolia only numbered in modern pencil. Contains chamberlains' expenses.

Maidstone, Centre for Kentish Studies, FA/FAc 42; 1611–12; English; paper; roll of 9 unnumbered sheets attached at top with original fastening, single sheet, and 2 bifolia, unattached but kept at beginning of roll; 405mm x 310mm (roll), 410mm x 155mm, average 53 lines (booklet); 2nd bifolium only numbered in modern pencil; torn and badly repaired fragment. Contains chamberlains' expenses.

Maidstone, Centre for Kentish Studies, FA/FAc 46; 1615–16; English; paper; roll of 9 sheets attached at top middle with original fastening, and unattached bifolium; dimensions vary from 410mm x 310mm to 396mm x 153mm (roll), 205mm x 190mm, average 31 lines (bifolium); bifolium only numbered in modern pencil; badly repaired. Contains chamberlains' expenses.

Maidstone, Centre for Kentish Studies, FA/FAc 48; 1617–18; English; paper; 6 leaves in stitched booklet; 395mm x 155mm, average 61 lines; modern pencil foliation; repaired and bound in protective grey cover.

Maidstone, Centre for Kentish Studies, FA/FAc 50; 1619–20; English; paper; roll of 8 sheets attached at top with original fastening, and 8 leaves in stitched booklet, a single sheet, and a bifolium; 410mm x 310mm (roll), 308mm x 202mm, average 42 lines (loose accounts); loose accounts only numbered in modern pencil; badly damaged by damp.

Maidstone, Centre for Kentish Studies, FA/FAc 51; 1620–1; English; paper; roll of 7 sheets attached at top with original fastening, and 1 bifolium; 405mm x 310mm (roll), 307mm x 200mm, average 36 lines (bifolium); bifolium only numbered in modern pencil. Contains chamberlains' expenses.

Maidstone, Centre for Kentish Studies, FA/Fac 52; 1621–2; English; paper; roll of 6 sheets attached at top with original fastening, 2 single sheets, 1 bifolium, and 22 leaves in a stitched booklet (mostly blank); 395mm x 305mm (roll), 405mm x 155mm, average 52 lines (booklet); booklet only foliated in modern pencil; badly damaged by damp at bottom.

Maidstone, Centre for Kentish Studies, FA/FAc 53; 1624–5; English; paper; 8 leaves in stitched booklet; 415mm x 155mm, average 73 lines; modern pencil foliation. Now in a folder with a flattened roll of 6 sheets attached at the top with the original fastening.

Maidstone, Centre for Kentish Studies, FA/FAc 54; 1625–6; English; paper; 8 leaves in stitched folder; 400mm x 150mm, average 44 lines; modern pencil foliation; damaged by damp. Now in a folder with a flattened roll of 5 sheets attached at the top with the original fastening.

Maidstone, Centre for Kentish Studies, FA/FAc 55; 1626–7; English; paper; roll of 13 sheets attached at top with original fastening; dimensions vary from 390mm x 305mm to 154mm x 200mm, average 40 lines; sheets numbered consecutively in a combination of original ink and modern pencil foliation (sheet 1 modern pencil, sheets 2–4 original ink, sheets 5–13 modern pencil).

Maidstone, Centre for Kentish Studies, FA/FAc 56; 1627–8; English; paper; roll of 11 sheets originally attached at the top; dimensions vary from 405mm x 310mm to 205mm x 153mm, average 34 lines; modern pencil foliation. Now rolled up loosely with a bifolium and 3 single sheets.

Maidstone, Centre for Kentish Studies, FA/FAc 57; 1628–9; English; paper; 4 leaves in stitched booklet; 200mm x 155mm, average 30 lines; modern pencil foliation. Now rolled loosely with a roll of 5
sheets attached at the top with the original fastening.

Maidstone, Centre for Kentish Studies, FA/FAc 59; 1630–1; English; paper; roll of 7 sheets attached
at top with original fastening; dimensions vary from 395mm x 295mm to 160mm x 270mm, average
42 lines; modern pencil foliation.

Maidstone, Centre for Kentish Studies, FA/FAc 62; 1635–6; English; paper; 14 leaves in stitched
booklet; 400mm x 151mm, average 42 lines; parchment covers. Now in a folder with a flattened roll
of 5 sheets attached at the top with the original fastening.

Maidstone, Centre for Kentish Studies, FA/FAc 63; 1636–7; English; paper; bifolium; 395mm x
153mm, average 57 lines; modern pencil foliation. Now rolled loosely with a roll of 9 sheets attached
at the top with the original fastening.

Assembly Book of Orders and Decrees

See under Dover for BL: Egerton MS. 2093.

Ecclesiastical Records

The ancient Faversham parish church, dedicated to St Mary of Charity, belonged to the
abbot and monks of St Augustine's Abbey, Canterbury, until the Dissolution of the abbey in
1539. The earliest surviving churchwardens' accounts begin in 1732.

Inventory of Church Goods

Canterbury, Cathedral Archives, U3/146/6/6; 1512; English; paper; roll of 4 sheets attached serially;
dimensions vary from 425mm x 290mm to 395mm x 300mm; unnumbered; writing on both sides.

Archdeacon's Court Books

Canterbury, Cathedral Archives, DCb/J/X.1.12; 1574–6; English and Latin; paper; ii + 194 + i, in
irregular gatherings; 298mm x 205mm, average 27 lines; contemporary ink foliation; modern brown
cardboard binding. Contains comperta and detecta presentments.
    This book also supplies entries for Molash, Newington, Oare, and Sheldwich.

Canterbury, Cathedral Archives, DCb/J/X.1.14; 1578–84; English and Latin; paper; iii + 161 + ii,
gathered in 8s; 290mm x 200mm, average 25 lines; contemporary ink foliation 1–115, continued in
modern pencil 116–61; modern brown cloth binding. Contains comperta and detecta presentments to
the archdeacon's court for Ospringe and Westbere deaneries.
    This book also supplies entries for Linsted and Stalisfield Green.

See also under Chislet for CCA: DCb/J/X.2.6.

Miscellaneous Records

Will of Richard Bannoke

Maidstone, Centre for Kentish Studies, PRC 17/15; 1521–3; English and Latin; paper; v + 290 + v, in irregular gatherings; 312mm x 215mm, average 38 lines; modern pencil foliation; modern yellow cloth binding. Contains register of wills in archdeacon's court.

The Murder of Thomas Arden

This document is included in a manuscript containing the collections of the chronicler John Stow (1525–1605), almost all written in his own hand.

London, British Library, Harley MS. 542; late 16th c.; English; paper; v + 168 + iv; 200mm x 155mm; modern pencil foliation; single sheets and gatherings tipped into brown leather binding.

Deposition Concerning Thomas Napleton of Faversham

This deposition appears among a series of depositions and petitions (PRO: SP 14/90, items 111, 139, 140, 141, 142; SP 14/91, items 7, 8; SP 14/96, item 101; and SP 14/104, item 132) relating to an allegedly seditious remark by Thomas Napleton. Only this deposition mentions the performance of a play.

London, Public Record Office, SP 14/90; 14 February 1616/17; English; paper; bifolium; 304mm x 200mm; originally item 66, now numbered 66 and bound with other state papers in a guardbook.

FOLKESTONE

Few early manuscripts have survived at Folkestone. Of these only three have entertainment records: a fragmentary chamberlains' account from the sixteenth century, a seventeenth-century book of corporation minutes and chamberlains' accounts, and a volume of church-wardens' accounts from the parish church of Sts Mary and Eanswithe covering the years 1489 to 1590. During the nineteenth century, however, several antiquarians saw and used many other ancient Folkestone records. In his preface to *A Descriptive and Historical Account of Folkestone and Its Neighbourhood*, Mackie writes, 'I have had often to describe antiquities that no longer exist, and customs and events long since forgotten; to wade through piles of old manuscript accounts, to extract a few historical facts disseminated through masses of petty expenses and municipal memoranda.' Between 16 September 1882 and 9 June 1883, John English, the printer and publisher of *The Folkestone Express*, printed in the weekly newspaper a series of thirty-two articles entitled 'Folkestone in Olden Times. Gleanings from the Municipal Records.' In the opening article he described the records as he found them in 1882: 'In the muniment chests stowed away in the Town Hall, there are piles and piles, and volumes and volumes of documents and records, most religiously guarded and cared for by the Town Clerk, which contain the history of Folkestone for the past four hundred years. They have been from time to time perused by antiquarians and historians, and fragmentary portions have now and then been published. But very few Folkestonians know the extent of these archives, and what a vast fund of information relating to by-gone times and ancient customs they contain.' In addition to these local historians, the antiquarian and biographer of Shakespeare, J.O. Halliwell-Phillipps, sometime before his death in 1889 saw Folkestone chamberlains' accounts extending from 1563 to 1601 and made numerous excerpts of payments to travelling entertainers. Fifteen years later, however, when Ernest George Atkinson of the Public Record Office reported on the Folkestone archives, most of the early Folkestone records had disappeared. Such entertainment records that do exist for the latter part of the sixteenth century, therefore, have been quoted from these nineteenth-century antiquarian sources.

The Folkestone civic and accounting year began and ended on 8 September, the feast of the Nativity of St Mary the Virgin.

Civic Records

Wardens' Accounts

Whitfield, East Kent Archives Centre, FO/FC1/1; 1512–15, 1540–6; English; paper; ii + 49 + ii, in irregular gatherings; 308mm x 207mm, average 28 lines; modern pencil foliation; modern cloth binding. Contains accounts for the years 1542–5 and fragmentary accounts for several other years.

Folios 8–48 have been repaired and rebound in a confused sequence. Fortunately, at least three different hands appear in the manuscript and the present binding is flexible enough to permit identification of gatherings and conjugate leaves. The present sequence of gatherings is the following: ff 2–7 and 8–13 (gathered in 6s), ff 14–15 (gathered in 2), ff 16–21 (gathered in 6), ff 22–39 (gathered in 18), and ff 40–8 (gathered in 10 with one folio wanting between f 44 and f 45). However, ff 22–39 should be placed inside ff 14–15; ff 40–8 should be placed between f 18 and f 19 and that whole gathering folded the opposite way and placed around ff 14–15; this new gathering then belongs between f 10 and f 11 to make one large gathering. This revised sequence produces a smooth chronological account from 1540–6: ff 8–9, expense fragment for 32 Henry VIII; ff 9v–10 and 45–7, receipts for 33 Henry VIII; ff 48 and 19–21, expenses for 33 Henry VIII; ff 14 and 22–5, receipts for 34 Henry VIII; ff 25v–8v, expenses for 34 Henry VIII; ff 29–33, receipts for 35 Henry VIII; ff 33v–6, expenses for 35 Henry VIII, ff 36v–9v, receipts for 36 Henry VIII; ff 15–18 and 40, expenses for 36 Henry VIII; ff 40v–4, receipt fragment for 37 Henry VIII; ff 11–13, undated receipts fragment without heading or total, probably more of 37 Henry VIII. When the folios are arranged in this sequence, the subtotals at the foot of each page tally with the totals at the end of each year; the hands are consistent within each year; and the refolding of conjugate leaves produces one large gathering instead of six irregular ones.

Whitfield, East Kent Archives Centre, FO/AM1/1; 1604–40; English; paper; ii + 320 + ii, gathered in 16s with first 2 folios wanting; 337mm x 215mm, average 46 lines; contemporary foliation;

manuscript repaired and rebound in original parchment binding with the following heading on the front cover: 'No 4 Minutes of Proceedings of Corporate Meetings Sessions of the Peace & Chamberlains Accounts from 2nd Ja*mes* 1st to 11th Chas 1st (1635).'

Assembly Book of Orders and Decrees

See under Dover for BL: Egerton MS. 2093.

Antiquarian Records

Wardens' Accounts (AC)

John English, printer and publisher of *The Folkestone Express*, made excerpts from the borough records in a series of thirty-two articles that appeared in the newspaper between 16 September 1882 and 9 June 1883 under the title 'Folkestone in Olden Times. Gleanings from the Municipal Records.' Two of these, 11 (from 25 November 1882, p 5) and 15 (from 30 December 1885, p 5) are relevant for our Records. In August 1883 the series was revised and reprinted in book form by J. English along with the second edition of S.J. Mackie's history of the town, *A Descriptive and Historical Account of Folkestone and Its Neighbourhood*, first published in 1856. Among the volumes that English saw were three volumes of minutes of the sessions and hundred courts and accounts of the chamberlains from 1547–95, 1596–1625, and 1635–60.

James Orchard Halliwell-Phillipps (1820–89), indefatigable antiquarian, book collector, and energetic contributor to such Victorian literary societies as the Camden Society, the Percy Society, and the Shakespeare Society, is chiefly remembered today as a biographer of Shakespeare. In 1848 he was the first historian to make use of the Stratford records in his *Life of William Shakespeare, including many particulars respecting the poet and his family never before published*, marking the beginning of a lifetime study that culminated in the four editions of *Outlines of the Life of Shakespeare* published between 1881 and 1887. Many of his letters and literary scrapbooks were bequeathed to the library of the University of Edinburgh. The Shakespearian collections, including many volumes of 'literary scraps,' were sold at auction after his death and now reside in the Folger Shakespeare Library.

John English, *Gleanings from the Municipal Records of the Corporation of Folkestone, from the Reign of Edward III to the Present Time* (Folkestone, [1883]).

Washington, D.C., Folger Shakespeare Library, W.b.141, 147, 173, 174, 176, 200, 203; 19th c.; English; paper; each scrapbook contains viii + 84 (some volumes have pages cut out); 310mm x 180mm; pagination by stamping machine, pages divided on both sides into double columns, many pages trimmed after writing; each volume bound in red or blue half-calf with matching marbled boards, series and volume titles stamped in gold on spine. Title page [ii]: LITERARY SCRAPS: | CUTTINGS FROM NEWSPAPERS, EXTRACTS, | MISCELLANEA, ETC. | "They are abstracts and brief chronicles of the time. **** To I show virtue her own feature, scorn her own image, and the very age and I body of the time his form and pressure." I SHAKESPEARE. I LONDON: I JOHN CAMDEN HOTTEN, 74 & 75 PICCADILLY. The volume numbers do not correspond with their order of compilation and may have been added after Halliwell-Phillipps' death in 1889; he referred to the volumes by individual titles.

Volumes 147, 173, and 203 also supply entries for New Romney.

Town Custumal (A)

The original Folkestone custumal was based on the charter granted to the jurats and commonalty of Folkestone by Edward II in 1313. In the nineteenth century, when the Commissioners on Public Records inquired into the ancient Folkestone records, Ralph Thomas Brockman, the town clerk, described in his return to the commissioners a parchment roll 'containing the customs of the town,' which he supposed from the style of writing to have been written during the time of Henry VIII.[11] In September 1882, while making excerpts from the borough records for his series of newspaper articles, John English saw and described that roll as 'four large parchment sheets endorsed "Customs of Court." A modern endorsement styles it a "Roll containing an account of the ancient privileges and customs of the town." It is also marked "1st Edward 3rd." Whether or not these four sheets formed part of the charter granted at that date, or whether they are only a copy, it is difficult to say. Most probably the latter, as there are here and there blank spaces, which seem to indicate that the copyist could not decipher the original. There are twenty sections.'[12] A copy of the custumal was also apparently made for the Municipal Corporation Commissioners and labelled 'Copy of The Customal of Folkestone from a parchment Scroll in the Town Chest temp. 1 Edw 3rd.' The parchment scroll, whether dating from the time of Edward III or Henry VIII, subsequently disappeared from the town chest, but sometime during the 1880s a further antiquarian copy was made for the town from the antiquarian copy then in the Public Record Office. That second copy, now among the borough records at the East Kent Archives Centre, remains the best available source for the Folkestone custumal.

Whitfield, East Kent Archives Centre, FO/AL/1; 1880s; English; paper; 17 loose sheets; 335mm x 210mm, average 34 lines; modern pencil foliation; damaged by damp but now repaired.

Ecclesiastical Records

Sts Mary's and Eanswithe's Churchwardens' Accounts

The churchwardens' accounting year ran from 25 December to 25 December.

Canterbury, Cathedral Archives, U3/88/4/1; 1489–1590; English; paper; 240 leaves in irregular gatherings; 305mm x 220mm, average 31 lines; contemporary ink foliation; original parchment binding with old reference number 'U3/20/5' on spine, now kept in box labelled 'U388/4/1.'

FORDWICH

The borough of Fordwich dates from Anglo-Saxon times, its earliest charter having been granted in 1055 by Edward the Confessor. Records of the mayor's court survive from the thirteenth century and mayors' accounts from the sixteenth century. Quarter sessions records begin in the seventeenth century. Borough elections were held in the parish church, and perhaps due to the general intermingling of parish and borough affairs in this sparsely populated borough, one volume of churchwardens' accounts, dating from 1510–37, survives with the town records. The borough of Fordwich ceased to exist by act of parliament in 1883, when the borough archives and lands were placed in the hands of the Trustees of the Fordwich United Charities. The archives continued to be kept in a wooden chest in the medieval guildhall in Fordwich until 1956, when the trustees deposited them in the Canterbury Cathedral Archives.

The Fordwich mayoral and accounting year began and ended on the Monday next after the feast of St Andrew (30 November). This means that the initial and terminal dates of the civic year fell between 1 December and 7 December according to the day of the week on which the feast of St Andrew fell.

Town Custumal

Canterbury, Cathedral Archives, U4/26; 15th c.; English, Latin, and Anglo-Norman; parchment; 123 + i, gathered in 8s; 250mm x 162mm, average 27 lines; modern pencil pagination; decorated red and blue initial capitals head each clause; 16th-c. leather binding.

Ancient Book of Decrees

Canterbury, Cathedral Archives, U4/19; 1433–1736; 174 leaves in irregular gatherings; 305mm x 205mm, average 35 lines; modern pencil foliation supercedes partial ink foliation; vellum binding, bound out of chronological order with many folios missing; title on front cover: 'The ancient Booke of Decrees of the Towne of Fordwich.' Contains orders of the mayor and jurats mostly dating from the 16th and 17th centuries.

Assembly Book of Orders and Decrees

See under Dover for BL: Egerton MS. 2093.

Borough Court Minute Book

Canterbury, Cathedral Archives, U4/20/1; 1560–1621; English; paper; 423 leaves, gathered in 6s; 300mm x 205mm, average 29 lines; modern pencil foliation; original leather binding.

Mayors' Accounts

Canterbury, Cathedral Archives, U4/8/29; 1559–60; English; paper; 6 leaves in 2 stitched gatherings; 313mm x 200mm, average 31 lines; modern pencil foliation.

Canterbury, Cathedral Archives, U4/8/30; 1560–1; English; paper; bifolium; 305mm x 203mm, average 25 lines; modern pencil foliation.

Canterbury, Cathedral Archives, U4/8/31; 1565–6: English; paper; 4 leaves in 1 gathering; 240mm x 345mm, average 30 lines; modern pencil foliation.

Canterbury, Cathedral Archives, U4/8/35; 1566–7; English; paper; 4 leaves in 1 stitched gathering; 309mm x 212mm, average 25 lines; modern pencil foliation.

Canterbury, Cathedral Archives, U4/8/36; 1567–8; English; paper; 4 leaves in 1 gathering with attached memoranda and receipts; 320mm x 205mm, average 37 lines; modern pencil foliation.

Canterbury, Cathedral Archives, U4/8/37; 1568–74; English; paper; 12 leaves in 1 stitched gathering; 300mm x 208mm, average 34 lines; modern pencil foliation; incomplete at beginning and ending. Apparently copied from annual rough accounts.

Canterbury, Cathedral Archives, U4/8/34; 1570–1; English; paper; 4 leaves in 1 stitched gathering; 305mm x 207mm, average 33 lines; modern pencil foliation.

Canterbury, Cathedral Archives, U4/8/38; 1571–2; English; paper; bifolium; 305mm x 200mm, average 36 lines; modern pencil foliation.

Canterbury, Cathedral Archives, U4/8/45; 1577–84; English; paper; 10 leaves in stitched gathering, and single loose sheet of accounts; 298mm x 207mm, average 39 lines; modern pencil foliation; torn and mutilated by damp in upper left corner and incomplete at beginning.

Canterbury, Cathedral Archives, U4/8/41; 1578–9; English; paper; 2 bifolia; 315mm x 207mm, average 31 lines; modern pencil foliation.

Canterbury, Cathedral Archives, U4/8/40; 1581–2; English; paper; bifolium; 305mm x 200mm, average 36 lines; modern pencil foliation.

Canterbury, Cathedral Archives, U4/8/43; 1582–3; English; paper; 4 leaves in 1 pinned gathering; 303mm x 205mm, average 37 lines; modern pencil foliation.

Canterbury, Cathedral Archives, U4/8/44; 1583–4; English; paper; 2 bifolia in stitched booklet; 305mm x 205mm, average 27 lines; modern pencil foliation.

Canterbury, Cathedral Archives, U4/8/45A; 1584–7; English; paper; 10 leaves originally gathered in 6s

(2 leaves now missing at beginning); 298mm x 207mm, average 39 lines; modern pencil foliation; damaged by mildew and mutilated in upper left corner.

Canterbury, Cathedral Archives, U4/8/46; 1585–6; English; paper; bifolium; 308mm x 205mm, average 36 lines; modern pencil foliation.

Canterbury, Cathedral Archives, U4/8/50; 1587–8; English; paper; 4 leaves in 1 gathering with 2 leaves pinned in between the 3rd and 4th leaf, making a booklet of 6 leaves; 280mm x 174mm, average 32 lines; modern pencil foliation.

Canterbury, Cathedral Archives, U4/8/49; 1590–1; English; paper; 4 leaves in 1 stitched gathering; 308mm x 205mm, average 43 lines; modern pencil foliation.

Canterbury, Cathedral Archives, U4/8/50A; 1591–2; English; paper; 4 leaves in 1 stitched gathering; 291mm x 205mm, average 32 lines; modern pencil foliation.

Canterbury, Cathedral Archives, U4/8/51; 1592–3; English; paper; 8 leaves in 1 stitched gathering; 305mm x 201mm, average 38 lines; modern pencil foliation.

Canterbury, Cathedral Archives, U4/8/54; 1604–5; English; paper; 2 bifolia in stitched booklet; 305mm x 200mm, average 34 lines; modern pencil foliation.

Canterbury, Cathedral Archives, U4/8/55; 1606–7; English; paper; 4 leaves in 1 stitched gathering; 305mm x 200mm, average 38 lines; modern pencil foliation.

Canterbury, Cathedral Archives, U4/8/56; 1608–9; English; paper; 6 leaves in 1 stitched gathering; 306mm x 209mm, average 40 lines; modern pencil foliation.

Canterbury, Cathedral Archives, U4/8/57; 1613–14; English; paper; 4 leaves in 1 stitched gathering; 312mm x 203mm, average 43 lines; modern pencil foliation.

Canterbury, Cathedral Archives, U4/8/58; 1614–15; English; paper; 4 leaves in 1 gathering; 310mm x 200mm, average 38 lines; modern pencil foliation.

Canterbury, Cathedral Archives, U4/8/59; 1616–17; English; paper; 4 leaves in 1 stitched gathering; 309mm x 202mm, average 47 lines; modern pencil foliation.

Canterbury, Cathedral Archives, U4/8/60; 1620–1; English; paper; 4 leaves in 1 stitched gathering; 308mm x 205mm, average 42 lines; modern pencil foliation.

Canterbury, Cathedral Archives, U4/8/64; 1632–3; English; paper; 6 leaves in 1 stitched gathering; 305mm x 202mm, average 36 lines; modern pencil foliation.

Canterbury, Cathedral Archives, U4/8/65A; 1639–40; English; paper; 7 leaves in 1 stitched gathering; dimensions vary from 305mm x 195mm to 140mm x 115mm; modern pencil foliation.

Antiquarian Accounts

Mayors' Accounts (AC)

Although Giles Dawson saw the chamberlains' accounts for 1507–8 when editing *Collections* 7 for the Malone Society, the booklet has subsequently been mislaid and could not be traced in the Canterbury Cathedral Archives, where the rest of the Fordwich manuscripts are stored.

Dawson, Giles E. (ed), *Collections* 7, Malone Society (Oxford, 1965).

GODMERSHAM

Consistory Court Book

Canterbury, Cathedral Archives, DCb/J/X.9.7; 1608–9; English and Latin; paper; i + 183 + ii, gathered in 16s; 290mm x 195mm, average 22 lines; contemporary ink foliation; original parchment binding and modern brown clothbound case. Contains comperta and detecta presentments to the consistory court.

GOODNESTONE

Letter of Richard Culmer to Sir Edward Dering

Radical Puritan preacher Richard Culmer (d. 1662) was born on the Isle of Thanet, attended the King's School in Canterbury, and received the degrees of BA in 1618 and MA in 1621 from Magdalene College, Cambridge. Culmer was suspended by Archbishop Laud from his first parish, Holy Cross, Goodnestone next Wingham. In 1643, however, he was appointed rector of Chartham and shortly thereafter made vicar of St Stephen's, Hackington, followed by a further preferment to Harbledown. Everywhere he went he made himself unpopular by his attempts to suppress sabbath sports and drunkenness. In 1643 he was appointed by parliament one of the ministers to detect and demolish the superstitious inscriptions and idolatrous monuments in Canterbury Cathedral, and in *Cathedral News, or Dean and Chapter News from Canterbury* (1644) Culmer relates how he 'rattled down proud Becket's Glassie bones' from the great north window of the Martyrdom Chapel. On 4 October 1644 he was made one of the Six Preachers of Canterbury Cathedral, and in the same year parliament appointed him vicar of St Mary's, Minster (in Thanet), a post he held until he was deprived of the living after the Restoration in 1660.[13]

London, British Library, Additional MS. 26,785; 8 January 1640/1; English; paper; original bifolium; 203mm x 195mm, 24 lines; addressed 'To the Right Wor*ship*full, and my Worthy freind, Sir Edward Deering, at his house in St Martins lane, neer the Church, pr*es*ent these' and endorsed by recipient '1640 11 Ian*uary* Mr Culmer.' Now foliated 84–5v, mounted on a guard, and bound with other correspondence to and from Sir Edward Dering dated 1639–41 in *c* 19th-c. fabric on board covers with leather corners and spine, raised bands, and gilding on spine.

GOUDHURST

Archdeacon's Court Books

Canterbury, Cathedral Archives, DCb/J/X.8.5; 1561–3; English and Latin; paper; i+139, gathered in 48s; 320mm x 210mm, average 33 lines; contemporary ink foliation 1–95 continued in modern pencil to 139; original parchment binding. Contains comperta and detecta presentments.

See under Bredgar for CCA: DCb/J/Y.4.18 pt 2.

GREAT CHART

Archdeacon's Court Book

See under Borden for CCA: DCb/J/X.2.4.

HARBLEDOWN

Parishioners' Petition to Quarter Sessions

Maidstone, Centre for Kentish Studies, QM/SB 37; 21 May 1594; English; paper; single sheet; 414mm x 303mm.

HEADCORN

Archdeacon's Court Books

See under Bethersden for CCA: DCb/J/X.1.11 and under Borden for CCA: DCb/J/X.2.4.

HERNE

Quarter Sessions Examinations

See under Canterbury for CCA: CC/J/Q/388.

HERNHILL

Consistory Court Book

Canterbury, Cathedral Archives, DCb/J/X.9.11; 1611–13; English and Latin; paper; i + 264, gathered

in 12s; 302mm x 195mm, average 33 lines; contemporary ink foliation; original parchment binding and modern brown cloth-bound case. Contains comperta and detecta presentments to the
consistory court.

HOATH

Quarter Sessions Examinations

See under Canterbury for CCA: CC/J/Q/388.

HOLLINGBOURNE

Consistory Court Book

See under Bredgar for CCA: DCb/J/X.8.10.

HYTHE

For many years the Hythe borough records, along with the parish records of St Leonard's
Church, were stored in cupboards over the south porch of the church, where many of them
suffered from damp and decay. In the 1930s they were moved to the newly established Hythe
Museum. A *Catalogue of Documents*, prepared by the vicar of Hythe, the Rev. Herbert Dixon
Dale, was published in 1937. The borough records are now stored at the East Kent Archives
Centre. Although many of the damaged records have been repaired, they have not been
recatalogued. Many of the boxes contain numerous unlabelled fragments, some repaired, some
unfit for production. To distinguish between various accounts in the same box, all bearing the
same H number in the current catalogue, I have used the designation [Item A] and [Item B]
for accounts in the boxes labelled H 1056, H 1060, and H 1061a.

Apart from a few fifteenth-century accounts that yielded no entertainment records, the
main body of Hythe churchwardens' accounts does not begin until 1675. Court books,
containing pleas of debt, trespass, detention of goods, and breach of pledge, survive from
c 1358 through the seventeenth century but have not yielded any entertainment records.
However, the borough accounts, which survive with many gaps from 1412, do contain many
payments for musicians, players, and other entertainers. The surviving fifteenth- and early
sixteenth-century Hythe accounts appear in three different formats: individual accounts of
the jurats and other residents for maletots assessed and for monies spent on the town's behalf,
rendered usually in January preceding the close of the main town account but sometimes
as late as the following June; summary accounts of ward collectors, sometimes given ward
by ward and sometimes with two wards grouped together; and summary chamberlains'
accounts.

The civic and accounting year in Hythe began and ended on 2 February, the feast of the
Purification of St Mary the Virgin.

Jurats' Accounts

Whitfield, East Kent Archives Centre, H 1055; 1441–53; Latin; paper; iv + 195 + iv, in irregular gatherings; 295mm x 215mm, average 25 lines; contemporary ink foliation; leaves damaged by damp; manuscript much repaired and rebound in modern parchment binding.

Whitfield, East Kent Archives Centre, H 1019; 1454–66; Latin; paper; iv + 152 + iv, in irregular gatherings; 300mm x 215mm, average 25 lines; contemporary ink foliation; many leaves faded and damaged by damp; repaired and rebound in modern parchment binding and cloth box.

Whitfield, East Kent Archives Centre, H 1058; 1468–84; Latin; paper; iv + 301 + v, in irregular gatherings; 297mm x 218mm, average 22 lines; 19th-c. ink foliation; good condition; 20th-c. parchment binding with clasps.

Whitfield, East Kent Archives Centre, H 1060 [Item A]; 1484–91; Latin; paper; 98 leaves in 1 gathering of 48 plus many loose leaves; 295mm x 210mm, average 20 lines; modern pencil foliation; mutilated and faded by damp, but now repaired; stored unlabelled in a box designated H 1060 with various other unlabelled account fragments from the reigns of Edward III, Richard II, Richard III, and Henry VII including [Item B].

Whitfield, East Kent Archives Centre, H 1060 [Item B]; 1494–5; Latin; paper; 21 leaves originally gathered in 32 with 11 leaves lost; 310mm x 225mm, average 20 lines; modern pencil numbering; now stored unlabelled in a box designated H 1060 with various other unlabelled account fragments from the reigns of Edward III, Richard II, Richard III, and Henry VII including [Item A].

Whitfield, East Kent Archives Centre, H 1059 [Item 6]; 1495–6; Latin; paper; 35 leaves originally gathered in 38 with 3 leaves missing; 285mm x 200mm, average 21 lines; modern pencil foliation; now stored in box designated H 1059 with other court and account fragments.

Whitfield, East Kent Archives Centre, H 1062; 1497–1503; English and Latin; paper; 129 leaves in irregular gatherings, each gathering devoted to 1 year's accounts; 290mm x 205mm, average 22 lines; modern pencil foliation; manuscript damaged by worms and damp; fragment of original parchment binding remains on spine and back.

Whitfield, East Kent Archives Centre, H 1056 [Item B]; 1532–3; English and Latin; paper; 11 leaves originally gathered in 14 with 3 leaves lost; 310mm x 210mm, average 28 lines; modern pencil foliation; mutilated by damp, but now repaired; stored unlabelled in a box designated H 1056 with various other unlabelled fragments of jurats' accounts including [Item A].

Chamberlains' Accounts

Whitfield, East Kent Archives Centre, H 1061a [Item A]; 1467–8; Latin; paper; 3 sheets serially attached; 420mm x 153mm; modern pencil numbering; writing continues on sheet 2v; stored unlabelled in a box designated as H 1061a with various other unlabelled account fragments from the reigns of Edward IV to Elizabeth I including [Item B].

Whitfield, East Kent Archives Centre, H 1056 [Item A]; 1480–1; Latin; paper; 2 sheets formerly serially attached; 430mm x 185mm; modern pencil numbering; heading is mutilated and entire roll is damaged by damp, but now repaired; stored unlabelled in box designated H 1056 with various other unlabelled fragments of jurats' accounts including [Item B].

Whitfield, East Kent Archives Centre, H 1061a [Item B]; 1562–3; English; paper; 10 leaves in 1 gathering; 310mm x 205mm, average 23 lines; modern pencil foliation; condition delicate, faded and mutilated by damp; stored unlabelled in a box designated as H 1061a with various other unlabelled account fragments from the reigns of Edward IV to Elizabeth I including Item [A].

Assembly Book of Orders and Decrees

See under Dover for BL: Egerton MS. 2093.

Assembly Books and Chamberlains' Accounts

Whitfield, East Kent Archives Centre, H 1208; 1580–91; English; paper; iii + 309 + i, gathered in 28s; 308mm x 205mm, average 41 lines; 19th-c. ink foliation; 19th-c. brown leather binding.

Whitfield, East Kent Archives Centre, H 1209; 1608–42; English; paper; iii + 253 + ii; 306mm x 200mm, average 39 lines; 19th-c. ink foliation; display script used in some marginal headings and openings of decisions; 19th-c. brown leather binding.

Whitfield, East Kent Archives Centre, H 1210; 1624–35; English; paper; ii + 153 + ii; 307mm x 210mm, average 42 lines; 19th-c. ink foliation; 19th-c. brown leather binding, repaired and rebound in 1968.

Town Accounts

Whitfield, East Kent Archives Centre, H 1061; 1483–1509; English and Latin; paper; 162 leaves, gathered in 8s; 390mm x 285mm, average 28 lines; 19th-c. ink foliation; leaves faded and damaged by damp; manuscript repaired and bound in 19th-c. brown half-leather binding. Contains revised chamberlains' and ward collectors' accounts.

LINSTED

Will of John Weston

Maidstone, Centre for Kentish Studies, PRC 32/2 vol 2; 1475–84; Latin; paper; v + 310 + v, in irregular gatherings; 295mm x 215mm, average 38 lines; foliated 324–633 in modern pencil; modern hardback cloth binding.

Archdeacon's Court Book

See under Faversham for CCA: DCb/J/X.1.14.

LITTLE MONGEHAM

Visitation Proceedings

See under Chart Sutton for LPL: Register of Archbishop William Warham, vol 1.

LYDD

Civic Records

In 1364 a charter of Edward III, confirming an earlier charter of Henry II dated 1155, recognized Lydd as a corporate member of the Cinque Ports and a limb of Romney responsible for every fifth penny of ship duty levied on Romney. Town accounts survive from 1428 with gaps from 1485–1511, 1542–9, and 1575–8. Plea books for the borough court of record survive with some gaps from 1507–49 and quarter sessions books from 1566–1685, but neither of these latter two classes of records yielded any evidence of entertainment.

After 1476 the bailiff and jurats were elected and the accounts audited annually on 22 July, the feast of St Mary Magdalene, the same day on which the churchwardens of All Saints' Church were elected. A general intermingling of religious and civic affairs in the town has resulted in the survival of two volumes of early churchwardens' accounts in the borough records covering the years 1519–59, 1560–77, and 1589–1613, but only the first preserves any record of communal entertainment.

Chamberlains' Accounts

Whitfield, East Kent Archive Centre, Ly/2/1/1/1; 1428–85; Latin and English; paper; iii + 185 + iii; 285mm x 210mm; modern ink foliation (f 15 is numbered twice, 1 unnumbered leaf appears between f 54 and f 55, and several leaves are loose, with some numbered out of chronological order); bound in parchment.

Until 1476, the first volume of accounts was kept by the twelve jurats representing Lydd and Denge Marsh but from 1477 by two chamberlains. Accounts for the following years have been bound out of chronological order: 1429–30: ff 8, 153, 10; 1430–1: ff 9, 11; 1441–2: ff 28–9; 1442–3: f 131; 1443–4: ff 131v–2v; 1444–5: ff 132v–6; 1445–6: ff 29v–31v; 1446–7: f 29v; 1447–8: ff 32–3v, 178, 176v; 1448–9: ff 178v, 34–5v; 1467–8: ff 99v–102v, 184v; 1468–9: ff 184, 103–5v. At least one folio containing part of the 1442–3 accounts is missing, and the expenses for that year continue on f 131. No payments are recorded for players in this year. Accounts for 1475–6 are incomplete. Most of the 1481–2 account is missing.

Whitfield, East Kent Archive Centre, Ly/2/1/1/2; 1511–42; English and Latin; paper; 129 leaves, gathered in 14s; 280mm x 200mm, average 25 lines; modern pencil pagination; some initial leaves missing (1 stored separately as a loose fragment in an envelope labelled 'Fragment from second account book'), final leaf repaired; originally bound in parchment, now in modern cardboard archival binding. The separately-stored leaf appears to be a fragment of the 1511–12 accounts.

Whitfield, East Kent Archive Centre, Ly/2/1/1/3; 1549–75; English and Latin; paper; ii + 230 + xxxiii, gathered in 16s; 286mm x 205mm, average 35 lines; modern pencil pagination; some leaves repaired; rebound in modern cardboard archival binding.

Whitfield, East Kent Archive Centre, Ly/2/1/1/4; 1578–9; English and Latin; paper; 4 leaves in 1 gathering; 315mm x 210mm, average 45 lines; modern pencil pagination; all leaves repaired; modern cardboard archival binding.

Whitfield, East Kent Archive Centre, Ly/2/1/1/5; 1580–1; English and Latin; paper; 4 leaves in 1 gathering; 310mm x 210mm, average 45 lines; modern pencil pagination; modern cardboard archival binding.

Whitfield, East Kent Archive Centre, Ly/2/1/1/6; 1581–2; English and Latin; paper; 4 leaves in 1 gathering; 290mm x 210mm, average 37 lines; modern pagination (last 3 pages blank); modern cardboard archival binding.

Whitfield, East Kent Archive Centre, Ly/2/1/1/7; 1582–1612; English and Latin; paper; 193 leaves in irregular gatherings; 283mm x 198mm, average 38 lines; modern pencil pagination 1–382 with first 2 pages and last page unnumbered (pp 9–89 also foliated in contemporary ink 1–41); bound in parchment.

Whitfield, East Kent Archive Centre, Ly/2/1/2/2; 1589–90; English and Latin; paper; 10 leaves in 1 gathering; 305mm x 205mm, average 35 lines; modern pencil pagination; unbound. Contains rough accounts.

Whitfield, East Kent Archive Centre, Ly/2/1/2/4; 1596–7; English; paper; single sheet; 282mm x 190mm, average 39 lines long. Contains fragment of rough accounts.

Whitfield, East Kent Archive Centre, Ly/2/1/2/5; 1597–8; English and Latin; paper; 6 leaves; 287mm x 185mm, average 38 lines; modern pencil pagination; edges tattered on all sides; unbound. Contains rough accounts.

Whitfield, East Kent Archive Centre, Ly/2/1/1/8; 1617–36; English and Latin; paper; 279 leaves; 292mm x 195mm, average 47 lines; modern pencil pagination 1–325 (pp 35–6, 53–4, 81–2, 120, 142, and 190–236 blank; pp 1–16, 231–58, and 58 unnumbered leaves at the end torn out); bound in parchment.

No records are extant for 1612–17. Page 17 begins near the end of the 1617–18 accounting year. The 1627–8 accounts begin on p 189 but stop half way down the page. Pages 190–230 are blank and the next gathering, pp 231–58, has been torn out. The remaining fragments of the gathering show that pages 231–6 were blank and that pages 237–58 contained accounts. Page 259 begins in the middle of the 1630–1 accounts. After p 325 the remainder of Ly/2/1/1/8 has been torn out, leaving only mutilated fragments of accounts.

Whitfield, East Kent Archive Centre, Ly/2/1/2/7; 1628–9; English; paper; 12 leaves in 1 gathering; 320mm x 200mm, average 34 lines; modern pencil pagination; unbound. Contains rough accounts.

Whitfield, East Kent Archive Centre, Ly/2/1/2/13; 1635–6; English; paper; single sheet; 272mm x 165mm, 44 lines. Now kept in a folder of draft accounts and vouchers. Contains rough accounting of 'Mr Thomas Stroughill Bayliffe his ⟨.....⟩ of mony owinge him by the Towne.'

Whitfield, East Kent Archive Centre, Ly/2/1/2/15; 1639–40; English; paper; 10 leaves in 1 gathering in stitched booklet; 195mm x 145mm, average 26 lines; modern pencil pagination. Now kept in a folder containing assessments, vouchers, and draft accounts. Contains the rough accounts of chamberlain John Potten.

Assembly Book of Orders and Decrees

See under Dover for BL: Egerton MS. 2093.

Ecclesiastical Records

All Saints' Churchwardens' Accounts

Whitfield, East Kent Archive Centre, Ly/15/2/1/1; 1519–59; English and Latin; paper; 147 leaves, gathered in 20s; 303mm x 215mm, average 31 lines; modern pencil pagination 1–268 (1 leaf cut out between p 64 and p 65, 2 between p 172 and p 173 containing accounts for 1542–3, and 9 between p 258 and p 259); original parchment binding.

Miscellaneous Records

Aldington Manor Rent Book

The Manor of Aldington, one of several manors in the parish of Lydd, was granted by King Offa to Archbishop Jaenberht in 774 and in the Domesday Book was still recorded among the possessions of the archbishop.

Whitfield, East Kent Archive Centre, Ly/15/1/1; early 16th c.; English; paper; iv + 48, in irregular gatherings; 310mm x 210mm, average 25 lines; first 4 folios numbered in modern pencil, followed by second foliation series in contemporary ink; final leaves mutilated; modern paper binding over limp parchment front cover on which is written: 'The Rent booke commonly called Allington Rent otherwise called Bishopp rent and a boundary of all the lands and tenements lying in Lydd and midley which are holden of the manor of Allington.'

LYMPNE

Archdeacon's Court Books

See under Bonnington for CCA: DCb/J/X.3.3 pt 2.

Canterbury, Cathedral Archives, DCb/J/X.4.2; 1597–1609; English and Latin; paper; part 1: vii + 175 + vii, part 2: i + 191 + vii, both parts gathered in 12s; 305mm x 185mm, average 35 lines; contemporary ink foliation; original parchment cover pasted onto modern cardboard binding with modern brown cloth case. Contains comperta and detecta presentments to the archdeacon's court for Lympne deanery.

This book also supplies an entry for Shadoxhurst.

MAIDSTONE

Civic Records

Maidstone was incorporated in 1549 by charter of Edward VI as the Mayor, Jurats, and Commonalty of the Town of Maidstone. Because the town supported the rebellion of Sir Thomas Wyatt the Younger, it lost its charter in 1554 but received a second charter from Elizabeth in 1559. The burghmote minute books begin in 1561, although no relevant entertainment records appear in the first volume. The chamberlains' accounts survive from 1562 with the following gaps: 1564–7, 1569–70, 1571–5, 1579–81, 1582–3, 1601–2, 1607–8, 1614–20, 1625–40. No churchwardens' accounts of the ancient parish of All Saints, Maidstone, survive before 1667.

Maidstone's accounting year began either on All Saints' (1 November) or on All Souls' (2 November).

Burghmote Book

Maidstone, Centre for Kentish Studies, MD/ACM1/2; 1604–43; English; paper; x + 205; 315mm x 207mm, average 36 lines; modern pencil foliation; parchment binding. Contains burghmote minutes, annual lists of officers, registration of apprenticeship indentures, and lists of freemen.

Chamberlains' Accounts

Maidstone, Centre for Kentish Studies, Md/FCa1/1568; 1567–8; English; paper; 4 leaves in 1 unstitched gathering; 310mm x 213mm, average 35 lines; modern pencil foliation.

Maidstone, Centre for Kentish Studies, Md/FCa1/1569; 1568–9; English; paper; 8 leaves in 1 stitched gathering; 318mm x 212mm, average 25 lines; modern pencil foliation.

Maidstone, Centre for Kentish Studies, Md/FCa1/1571; 1570–1; English; paper; 6 leaves in 1 stitched gathering; 308mm x 210mm, average 30 lines; modern pencil foliation.

Maidstone, Centre for Kentish Studies, Md/FCa1/1575; 1575; English; paper; 4 leaves in 1 stitched gathering; 310mm x 210mm, average 24 lines; modern pencil foliation.

Maidstone, Centre for Kentish Studies, Md/FCa1/1576/1; 1575–6; English; paper; 8 leaves in 1 stitched gathering; 412mm x 155mm, average 59 lines; modern pencil foliation.

Maidstone, Centre for Kentish Studies, Md/FCa1/1584; 1583–4; English; paper; 5 leaves in 1 stitched gathering; 410mm x 155mm, average 39 lines; modern pencil foliation.

Maidstone, Centre for Kentish Studies, Md/FCa1/1585; 1584–5; English; paper; 9 leaves in 1 stitched gathering; 415mm x 150mm, average 57 lines; modern pencil foliation.

Maidstone, Centre for Kentish Studies, Md/FCa1/1586; 1585–6; English; paper; 8 leaves in 1 stitched gathering; 412mm x 155mm, average 47 lines; modern pencil foliation.

Maidstone, Centre for Kentish Studies, Md/FCa1/1587; 1586–7; English; paper; 12 leaves in 1 stitched gathering; 410mm x 155mm, average 48 lines; modern pencil foliation.

Maidstone, Centre for Kentish Studies, Md/FCa1/1588; 1587–8; English; paper; 6 leaves in 1 stitched gathering; 415mm x 153mm, average 67 lines; modern pencil foliation.

Maidstone, Centre for Kentish Studies, Md/FCa1/1589; 1588–9; English; paper; 9 leaves in 1 stitched gathering; 410mm x 155mm, average 48 lines; modern pencil foliation.

Maidstone, Centre for Kentish Studies, Md/FCa1/1590; 1589–91; English; paper; 12 leaves in 1 stitched gathering; 408mm x 155mm, average 48 lines; original ink foliation in 2 series: 1589–90 account foliated 1–8 and 1590–1 account foliated 1–4 from back to front with booklet reversed.

Maidstone, Centre for Kentish Studies, Md/FCa1/1592; 1591–2; English; paper; 8 leaves in 1 stitched gathering; 407mm x 150mm, average 66 lines; modern pencil foliation.

Maidstone, Centre for Kentish Studies, Md/FCa1/1593; 1592–3; English; paper; 6 leaves in 1 stitched gathering + single sheet (unnumbered); 408mm x 152mm, average 52 lines (booklet), 226mm x 198mm (single sheet); modern pencil foliation. Single sheet contains late accounting to 1592–3 chamberlains from Thomas Frankleyn for expenditures on behalf of town when Frankleyn was mayor, 1591–2.

Maidstone, Centre for Kentish Studies, Md/FCa1/1594; 1593–4; English; paper; 6 leaves in 1 stitched gathering; 425mm x 168mm, average 70 lines; modern pencil foliation.

Maidstone, Centre for Kentish Studies, Md/FCa1/1595; 1594–5; English; paper; 6 leaves in 1 stitched gathering; 400mm x 150mm, average 57 lines; modern pencil foliation.

Maidstone, Centre for Kentish Studies, Md/FCa1/1596; 1595–6; English; paper; 9 leaves in 1 stitched gathering; 520mm x 200mm, average 46 lines; modern pencil foliation.

Maidstone, Centre for Kentish Studies, Md/FCa1/1598; 1597–8; English; paper; 20 leaves in 1 stitched gathering; 405mm x 142mm, average 50 lines; modern pencil foliation.

Maidstone, Centre for Kentish Studies, Md/FCa1/1603; 1602–3; English; paper; 8 leaves in 1 stitched gathering; 400mm x 150mm, average 46 lines; modern pencil foliation.

Maidstone, Centre for Kentish Studies, Md/FCa1/1605; 1604–5; English; paper; 8 leaves in 1 stitched gathering; 380mm x 148mm, average 64 lines; modern pencil foliation; paper covers.

Maidstone, Centre for Kentish Studies, Md/FCa1/1606; 1605–6; English; paper; 8 leaves in 1 stitched gathering; 404mm x 153mm, average 65 lines; modern pencil foliation; paper covers.

Maidstone, Centre for Kentish Studies, Md/FCa1/1607; 1606–7; English; paper; 4 leaves in 1 stitched gathering; 415mm x 155mm, average 67 lines; modern pencil foliation.

Maidstone, Centre for Kentish Studies, Md/FCa1/1610; 1609–10; English; paper; 6 leaves in 1 stitched gathering; 337mm x 142mm, average 51 lines; modern pencil foliation.

Maidstone, Centre for Kentish Studies, Md/FCa1/1612; 1611–12; English; paper; 8 leaves in 1 stitched gathering; 397mm x 150mm, average 70 lines; modern pencil foliation; paper covers.

Maidstone, Centre for Kentish Studies, Md/FCa1/1613; 1612–13; English; paper; 10 leaves in 1 stitched gathering; 410mm x 155mm, average 60 lines; modern pencil foliation.

Maidstone, Centre for Kentish Studies, Md/FCa1/1614; 1613–14; English; paper; 8 leaves in 1 stitched gathering; 400mm x 155mm, average 59 lines; modern pencil foliation.

Miscellaneous Records

Will of John Wotton

John Wotton, canon of Chichester and rector of Staplehurst in 1393, was the first master of the Collegiate Church of All Saints, Maidstone, serving from the completion of the college in 1397 until his death on 31 October 1417. His will, dated 30 September 1417 and proved on 26 November 1417, appears in the register of the archbishop of Canterbury, Henry Chichele, who was the patron of the collegiate church.

London, Lambeth Palace Library, Register of Archbishop Henry Chichele, vol 1; 1414–43; Latin; parchment; i + 497; 375mm x 275mm; contemporary but irregular ink foliation; stamped leather binding on wooden boards, title on spine: 'Chicheley 1414.'

Privy Council Agenda

London, Public Record Office, SP 16/278; December 1634; English; paper; bifolium; 335mm x 235mm; repaired, foliated 257–8v in modern pencil and mounted with other state papers in a guardbook; endorsed with date and 'Mr Dickenson's note of Busines depending before the Lords for the moneth of Nouember'; title on spine: 'Domestic I Charles I. I 1634 I December.'

The Life and Death of Mr Thomas Wilson

Thomas Wilson (1601–53) graduated at Cambridge with a BA in 1621–2 and MA in 1625. After serving pastoral charges at Capel in Surrey, Farlington in Hampshire, and Teddington in Middlesex, he was collated the curate of Otham in 1631. Suspended by Laud for refusing to read *The Book of Sports* but later reinstated, he was chosen by parliament to represent the diocese of Canterbury at the Westminster Assembly in 1643. In 1644 he was appointed perpetual curate of Maidstone, where he ministered until his death on 23 March 1652/3.

[George Swinnock.] THE | LIFE | AND | DEATH | OF *Mr.* | Tho. Wilson, | MINISTER OF | MAIDSTONE, | In the County of *Kent*, | *M.A.* | [rule] | *Printed in the Year* 1672. Wing: S6277.

MILTON NEXT SITTINGBOURNE

Archdeacons' Court Books

Canterbury, Cathedral Archives, DCb/J/X.1.5; 1564; English and Latin; paper; iv + 187 + iii, gathered in 8s; 305mm x 205mm, average 26 lines; modern pencil foliation; modern brown cloth binding. Contains comperta and detecta presentments for all deaneries of Canterbury diocese.

Canterbury, Cathedral Archives, DCb/J/X.4.10; 1605–20; English and Latin; paper; part 1: ii + 266 + vii, part 2: i + 223 + viii, both parts gathered in 12s; 296mm x 185mm, average 29 lines; contemporary ink foliation; parchment covers mended with brown tape. Contains comperta and detecta presentments to the archdeacon's court for Sittingbourne deanery.

See also under Bredgar for CCA: DCb/J/Y.4.18 pt 2.

MOLASH

Archdeacon's Court Books

Canterbury, Cathedral Archives, DCb/J/X.4.1; 1596–1612; English and Latin; paper; part 1: ii + 278 + vi, part 2: 230 + viii, both parts gathered in 12s; 295mm x 190mm, average 22 lines; contemporary ink foliation; modern brown cardboard binding. Contains comperta and detecta presentments to the archdeacon's court for Bridge deanery.

This book also supplies an entry for Preston near Wingham.

See also under Faversham for CCA: DCb/J/X.1.12.

NEWENDEN

Archdeacon's Court Book

Canterbury, Cathedral Archives, DCb/J/X.4.5; 1600–3; English and Latin; paper; ii + 182 + viii, gathered in 14s; 290mm x 195mm, average 20 lines; contemporary ink foliation; parchment binding with modern brown cloth case. Contains comperta and detecta presentments to the archdeacon's court for Charing deanery.

NEWINGTON

Archdeacon's Court Book

See under Faversham for CCA: DCb/J/X.1.12.

NEW ROMNEY

The ancient Town and Port of Romney was governed in medieval times by twelve jurats and a bailiff appointed by the archbishop. In 1563 a new charter granted by Queen Elizabeth provided for the annual election of a mayor and twelve jurats. Town records begin with the register of town clerk, Daniel Rough (1353–80). A series of civic accounts and assessments begins in 1379 and continues with some gaps until 1635. The minutes of the borough court of record and hundred court begin in 1429, broken only by gaps from 1442–53, 1483–1519, and 1610–15. Common assembly books, containing minutes of common assembly meetings, ordinances, elections, impositions of scots and fines, leasing of town lands, and admission of freemen, begin in 1577 and continue unbroken through 1642. Court of quarter sessions files of presentments survive from 1590, along with a collection of several hundred loose process papers including examinations, depositions, summonses, and indictments, but few of these have yielded any entertainment offences.[14]

The civic year in New Romney began and ended on 25 March, the feast of the Annunciation to St Mary the Virgin.

Civic Records

Town Custumal

Daniel Rough served as town clerk of New Romney between 1353 and 1380. In 1356 he prepared a now lost copy of the New Romney custumal for Roger Mortimer, the lord warden of the Cinque Ports, and about 1359 entered this copy of the custumal in his own register. A further copy of the custumal, dating from the second half of the fourteenth century and now designated DCc/Charta Antiqua R38 in the Canterbury Cathedral Archives, has been collated with the text transcribed from Rough's register.

Cambridge, St Catharine's College, G.V.69; 1353–*c* 1377; Latin and English; parchment (ff 1–105), paper (ff 106–20); i + 120+ i; 203mm x 148mm; foliation (ff 94–6, 98–103 have no folio numbers but belong to the folio sequence); excellent condition; early 17th-c. leather binding over boards with clasps, arms of New Romney stamped in gilt on front and back, rebacked.

Canterbury, Cathedral Archives, DCc/Charta Antiqua R38; late 14th c.; Anglo-Norman and Latin; parchment, 3 mbs attached at top; dimensions vary from 700mm x 225mm to 533mm x 218mm; writing on both sides; modern pencil numbering; manuscript headed: 'Ces sount les vsages vsque en la vile de Romene de temps dount memorie ne court.' This MS has been dated by CCA cataloguers as '2nd half of 14th cen' on paleographic grounds.

Chamberlains' Accounts

Whitfield, East Kent Archives Centre, NR/FAc 1; 1381–4; Latin; vellum; 20 leaves; 325mm x 224mm, average 45 lines; modern ink foliation; leaves repaired and mounted on larger parchment leaves 465mm x 340mm, interleaved with paper sheets containing English translation, and rebound in black leather binding.

Whitfield, East Kent Archives Centre, NR/FAc 2; 1384–1446; Latin; vellum; iv + 136; 425mm x 300mm, average 45 lines; contemporary ink foliation superseded by 19th-c. ink foliation; repaired, then interleaved with blank pages and rebound in black leather binding.

Whitfield, East Kent Archives Centre, NR/FAc 3; 1448–1527; Latin and English; parchment; 138 leaves; 465mm x 330mm (width variable), average 47 lines; contemporary ink foliation; first leaf wanting, f 110 bound between f 107 and f 108, final leaves much repaired; unbound, then interleaved with blank pages and rebound in late 19th-c. black leather binding.

Whitfield, East Kent Archives Centre, NR/FAc 4; 1469–92; Latin and English; paper; viii + 319 + ii; 306mm x 220mm, average 30 lines; ink foliation; final 15 leaves (much repaired) contain fragmentary accounts out of chronological order (ff 71–4 missing); leaves repaired on all sides and tipped individually into late 19th-c. binding.

Whitfield, East Kent Archives Centre, NR/FAc 5; 1492–1516; Latin and English; paper; iv + 196 + ii, in irregular gatherings; 312mm x 222mm, average 32 lines; contemporary ink foliation; manuscript repaired and rebound in 19th-c. vellum binding, title on spine: 'Romney Corporation. | Assessment Book. | 1492–1516.'

Whitfield, East Kent Archives Centre, NR/FAc 6; 1516–70; Latin and English; paper; iv + 153 + ii, in irregular gatherings (ff 1–56 missing, many leaves blank); 305mm x 218mm, average 30 lines; contemporary ink foliation; edges repaired on all sides; 19th-c. vellum binding, title on spine: 'Romney Corporation. | Assessment Book. | 1516–1522.' Contains miscellaneous accounts, assessments, and memoranda.

Whitfield, East Kent Archives Centre, NR/FAc 11; 1527–8; English; paper; single sheet; 310mm x 217mm. Contains chamberlain's expenses and receipts.

Whitfield, East Kent Archives Centre, NR/FAc 7; 1528–80; English; paper; iv + 286 + ii, in irregular gatherings (several leaves wanting at the end and many leaves blank); 307mm x 215mm, average 32 lines; contemporary ink foliation; fragment of f 289 clipped in; rebound in late 19th-c. vellum binding, title on spine: 'Romney Corporation | Chamberlains | Account Book | 1528–80.'

Whitfield, East Kent Archives Centre, NR/FAc 13; 1550–1; English; paper; 2 bifolia; 307mm x 207mm; modern pencil foliation; mutilated at top and first folio torn vertically. Contains chamberlain's expenses.

Whitfield, East Kent Archives Centre, NR/FAc 8; 1587–1627; English; paper; 256 leaves gathered in 16s; 295mm x 198mm, average 41 lines; contemporary ink foliation, an additional gathering paginated A–J has been inserted after f 204 and a second gathering paginated A–H after f 205; many marginal dates and other annotations in display script; vellum binding.

Whitfield, East Kent Archives Centre, NR/FAc 14; 1591–2; English; paper; 12 leaves in 1 gathering; 310mm x 205mm, average 33 lines; modern pencil foliation; unbound, labelled: 'The Accompte of william Kempe Chamberlayne Anno Domini 1591.'

Whitfield, East Kent Archives Centre, NR/FAc 15; 1634–5; English; paper; i + 10, in 1 gathering; 305mm x 195mm, 36 lines; contemporary ink foliation; unbound, labelled: 'The Bill of Acompt of Smith Tookey Chamberlaine ffrom 22th of March 1633 to the 25 1634.'

Jurats' Record Books

Whitfield, East Kent Archives Centre, NR/JB 2; 1454–82; Latin; paper; ii + 260 + ii, in irregular gatherings; 395mm x 280mm, average 17 lines; contemporary ink foliation; original leather binding.

Whitfield, East Kent Archives Centre, NR/JB 6; 1552–9; Latin and English; paper; 228 leaves in irregular gatherings; 298mm x 203mm, average 37 lines; contemporary ink foliation; repaired and rebound in modern maroon cloth binding.

Whitfield, East Kent Archives Centre, NR/JB 7; 1559–68; Latin & English; paper; 273 + i, in irregular gatherings; 294mm x 203mm, average 30 lines; contemporary ink foliation; original parchment binding.

Assembly Book of Orders and Decrees

See under Dover for BL: Egerton MS. 2093.

Quarter Sessions Presentment

Whitfield, East Kent Archives Centre, NR/JQp 1/4; 1562; English; paper; bifolium; 318mm x 210mm; modern pencil foliation; badly damaged.

Examination of Stephen Ketchpole

Whitfield, East Kent Archives Centre, NR/JQp1/28/3; 1615; English; paper; single sheet; 285mm x 170mm.

Antiquarian Records

Chamberlains' Accounts (AC)

See under Folkestone for Washington, D.C., Folger Shakespeare Library, W.b.147, 173, 203.

Miscellaneous Records

The Book of Notte

Whitfield, East Kent Archives Centre, NR/JBr 1; 1548–1612; Latin and English; paper; 170 leaves; 315mm x 210mm, average 42 lines; modern pencil foliation; much damaged by damp, extensively repaired, and rebound in stiff parchment binding. Mixed volume containing wills, pleas, rents, and proceedings of common assembly.

White Book of the Cinque Ports

Whitfield, East Kent Archives Centre, CP/B1; 1432–1571; English and Latin; paper; vi + 267 + iii; 420mm x 290mm, average 52 lines; repaired and bound in parchment binding and case.

OARE

Archdeacon's Court Books

Canterbury, Cathedral Archives, DCb/J/X.5.6; 1610–27; English and Latin; paper; part 1: ii + 283 + vii, part 2: i + 288 + viii, both parts gathered in 16s; 297mm x 190mm, average 24 lines; contemporary ink foliation; modern brown cloth binding. Contains comperta and detecta presentments for Ospringe and Westbere deaneries.

See also under Faversham for CCA: DCb/J/X.1.12.

PRESTON NEAR WINGHAM

Archdeacon's Court Book

See under Molash for CCA: DCb/J/X.4.1 pt 2.

QUEENBOROUGH

Archdeacon's Court Book

See under Bredgar for CCA: DCb/J/Y.4.18 pt 2.

RECULVER

Quarter Sessions Examinations

See under Canterbury for CCA: CC/J/Q/388.

RUCKINGE

Archdeacon's Court Book

Canterbury, Cathedral Archives, DCb/J/X.1.7; 1566–7; English and Latin; paper; i + 228 + i, in irregular gatherings; 297mm x 200mm, average 33 lines; modern pencil foliation; modern brown cloth binding, Contains comperta and detecta presentments.

SANDWICH

The civic history of the ancient Town and Port of Sandwich is contained primarily in the unsurpassed series of Year Books beginning in 1431 and preserving an unbroken record of common assemblies, resolutions, ordinances, and elections of officers for over 400 years. Records of the borough court of record, dealing with such matters as pleas of debt, trespass, and breach of covenant, survive from 1456. Court of quarter sessions records, including presentments, recognizances, and indictments, survive only from 1640. Financial records of the town treasurers (sometimes called chamberlains) survive in a series of account rolls from 1375 to 1550 with many gaps and in bound volumes from 1625 to 1663. The town custumal survives in several versions, the earliest dating from *c* 1375 based on the lost original custumal of 1301. There were three ancient parishes in Sandwich. Churchwardens' accounts survive from St Mary's for the period 1444–1582 (CCA: U3/11/5/1) and from St Peter's for the period 1592–1696 (CCA: U3/12/5/1); however, neither contains any entertainment records. Accounts for St Clement's begin in 1667.

The civic year in Sandwich began and ended on the first Thursday in December.

Civic Records

Town Custumal

According to its introductory paragraph, the Sandwich custumal was originally compiled by Adam Champneys in 1301. Although the original custumal has been lost, six additional copies of the custumal survive from the period before 1642: SA/LC 1, *c* 1375, appears to be a fair copy of the original; SA/LC 2, *c* 1450, is a working copy of either SA/LC 1 or of the original; SA/LC 3, *c* 1563, is an often inaccurate transcription with paragraph by paragraph English translation; SA/LC 4, *c* 1571, is a miscellaneous volume of customs and precedents, including the custumal; SA/LC 5, *c* 1625, contains a complete copy of SA/LC 2 with additions; and SA/LC 6, 1631, contains various customs and orders of court proceedings compiled by Robert Jager, who became town clerk in 1640. SA/LC 2 has been chosen as the base text for the excerpts given in the Records, and the collation notes give for each excerpt the substantive variants from SA/LC 1 *(A)* and SA/LC 3 *(C)*. The lost custumal of 1301, on which all of these later custumals are based, is preserved in an antiquarian transcription by William Boys, *Collections for an History of Sandwich in Kent* (Canterbury, 1792), 493–580.

Whitfield, East Kent Archives Centre, SA/LC 1; *c* 1375; Latin; parchment; xi + 141 + v, gathered in 8s; 170mm x 105mm, average 25 lines; original ink foliation; leather binding.

Whitfield, East Kent Archives Centre, SA/LC 2; *c* 1450 with additions up to 1562; Latin; parchment; iii + 77 + iii, gathered in 8s; 165mm x 248mm, average 32 lines; contemporary ink foliation 1–72 with 4 unnumbered parchment leaves before f 1 and 1 after f 72; repaired and rebound in original oak boards.

Whitfield, East Kent Archives Centre, SA/LC 3; *c* 1563; Latin and English; paper; iv + 128 + xv, gathered in 4s; 280mm x 215mm, average 28 lines; original foliation; original leather binding. Contains a 16th-c. copy of the medieval custumal alternating paragraph by paragraph with an English translation.

Treasurers' Accounts

Whitfield, East Kent Archives Centre, SA/FAt 2; 1454–5; Latin; paper; 5 sheets serially attached; 397mm x 293mm; modern pencil numbering; written on one side only; writing faded, roll repaired.

Whitfield, East Kent Archives Centre, SA/FAt 3; 1458–9; Latin; paper; 5 sheets serially attached; 420mm x 293mm; modern pencil numbering; written on one side only; part of sheet 1, including heading, is missing.

British Library, Additional MS. 33,511; 1462–3; Latin; paper; 6 bifolia; 295mm x 214mm, average 29 lines; modern pencil foliation. Booklet now numbered ff 3–12 and tipped individually into a guard book with brown half-leather binding containing the Sandwich treasurers' accounts, muster books, and court papers.

Whitfield, East Kent Archives Centre, SA/FAt 4; 1464–5; Latin; paper; 8 sheets serially attached; 415mm x 306mm; modern pencil numbering; written on one side only; writing very faded, roll repaired.

Whitfield, East Kent Archives Centre, SA/FAt 5; 1465–6; Latin; paper; 11 sheets serially attached; 410mm x 312mm; modern pencil numbering; written on one side only; edges repaired.

Whitfield, East Kent Archives Centre, SA/FAt 6; 1468–9; English; paper; 5 sheets serially attached; 405mm x 315mm; modern pencil numbering; written on one side only except for last mb; heading faded, roll repaired.

Whitfield, East Kent Archives Centre, SA/FAt 7; 1480–1; English; paper; 6 sheets serially attached; 370mm x 300mm; modern pencil numbering; written on one side only, sums underlined within account paragraphs; badly faded, heading missing.

Whitfield, East Kent Archives Centre, SA/FAt 8; 1482–3; English; paper; 9 sheets serially attached; 427mm x 315mm; modern pencil numbering; written on one side only except for sheet 2, sums underlined within account paragraphs; heading damaged.

Whitfield, East Kent Archives Centre, SA/FAt 9; 1489–90; English; paper; 17 sheets serially attached; dimensions vary from 362mm x 292mm to 142mm x 212mm; modern pencil numbering; written on one side only, sums underlined within account paragraphs; sheet 1 damaged.

Whitfield, East Kent Archives Centre, SA/FAt 11; 1496–7; English; paper; 8 sheets serially attached; 370mm x 287mm; sheets numbered 1B, 2B, 3B, etc, in modern pencil numbering; written on one side only; very faded and damaged by damp.

Whitfield, East Kent Archives Centre, SA/FAt 12; 1497–8; English; paper; 10 sheets serially attached; 370mm x 298mm; modern pencil numbering; written on one side only, sums underlined within account paragraphs; part of heading and first sheet missing.

Whitfield, East Kent Archives Centre, SA/FAt 13; 1498–9; English; paper; 5 sheets serially attached; 410mm x 314mm; modern pencil numbering; written on one side only, sums underlined within account paragraphs; first sheet with heading missing.

Whitfield, East Kent Archives Centre, SA/FAt 14; 1502–3; English; paper; 4 sheets serially attached; 405mm x 305mm; modern pencil numbering; written on one side only; much repaired, beginning missing.

Whitfield, East Kent Archives Centre, SA/FAt 15; 1505–6; English; paper; 3 sheets serially attached; 415mm x 313mm; modern pencil numbering; written on one side only; first sheet missing.

Whitfield, East Kent Archives Centre, SA/FAt 16; 1506–7; English; paper; 6 sheets serially attached; 388mm x 288mm; modern pencil numbering; written on one side only, writing very faded.

Whitfield, East Kent Archives Centre, SA/FAt 17; 1507–8; English; paper; 2 separate rolls (7 and 3 sheets respectively), each serially attached but numbered continuously; 392mm x 285mm (sheets 1 7), 425mm x 182mm (sheets 8–10); modern pencil numbering; written on one side only; first sheet mutilated.

Whitfield, East Kent Archives Centre, SA/FAt 18; 1509–10; English; paper; 5 sheets serially attached; 400mm x 290mm; modern pencil numbering; written on one side only; repaired, but badly faded.

Whitfield, East Kent Archives Centre, SA/FAt 19; 1510–11; English; paper; 6 sheets serially attached; 410mm x 295mm; modern pencil numbering; written on one side only; repaired, heading defective.

Whitfield, East Kent Archives Centre, SA/FAt 20; 1512–13; English; paper; 15 sheets serially attached; 420mm x 315mm; modern pencil numbering; written on one side only; roll repaired, but badly faded and first sheet damaged.

Whitfield, East Kent Archives Centre, SA/FAt 21; 1515–16; English; paper; 5 sheets serially attached; 402mm x 340mm; modern pencil numbering; written on one side only; heading missing, manuscript damaged throughout.

Whitfield, East Kent Archives Centre, SA/FAt 22; 1516–17; English; paper; 11 sheets serially attached; 420mm x 320mm; modern pencil numbering; written on one side only; heading defective, manuscript repaired.

Whitfield, East Kent Archives Centre, SA/FAt 23; 1517–18; English; paper; 5 sheets serially attached; 453mm x 355mm; modern pencil numbering; written on one side only; heading missing, manuscript repaired, but badly faded.

Whitfield, East Kent Archives Centre, SA/FAt 24; 1518–19; English; paper; 10 sheets serially attached; 390mm x 310mm; modern pencil numbering; written on one side only; first sheet repaired, heading missing.

Whitfield, East Kent Archives Centre, SA/FAt 25; 1519–20; English; paper; 8 sheets serially attached; 415mm x 308mm; modern pencil numbering; written on one side only; first sheet repaired, heading missing.

Whitfield, East Kent Archives Centre, SA/FAt 17A; 1520–1; English; paper; 7 sheets serially attached; 350mm x 285mm; modern pencil numbering; written on one side only; first sheet defective, heading missing.

Whitfield, East Kent Archives Centre, SA/FAt 27; 1521–2; English; paper; 10 sheets serially attached; 415mm x 313mm; modern pencil numbering; written on one side only; roll repaired.

Whitfield, East Kent Archives Centre, SA/FAt 28; 1527–8; English; paper; 21 sheets serially attached; 408mm x 318mm; modern pencil numbering; written on one side only; first sheets damaged, heading missing.

Whitfield, East Kent Archives Centre, SA/FAt 29; 1531–2; English; paper; 9 sheets serially attached; 402mm x 302mm; modern pencil numbering; written on one side only except final sheet; beginning of roll incomplete.

Whitfield, East Kent Archives Centre, SA/FAt 30; 1533–4; English; paper; 2 separate rolls (8 and 7 sheets respectively), serially attached; first roll (expenses): 413mm x 310mm, second roll (receipts): 402mm x 302mm; modern pencil numbering; written on one side only.

Whitfield, East Kent Archives Centre, SA/FAt 32; 1536–7; English; paper; 11 sheets serially attached; 382mm x 286mm; modern pencil numbering; written on one side only; receipts missing.

Whitfield, East Kent Archives Centre, SA/FAt 33; 1537–8; English; paper; 28 sheets serially attached; 392mm x 315mm; modern pencil numbering; written on one side only; roll repaired.

Whitfield, East Kent Archives Centre, SA/FAt 34; 1538–9; English; paper; 12 sheets serially attached; 381mm x 301mm; modern pencil numbering; written on one side only; heading defective, roll repaired, but faded.

Whitfield, East Kent Archives Centre, SA/FAt 35; 1549–50; English; paper; 16 sheets serially attached; 383mm x 329mm; modern pencil numbering; written on one side only; heading missing.

Whitfield, East Kent Archives Centre, SA/ZB4/12; 1574–5; English; paper; 54 leaves in 1 gathering (1 leaf missing); 312mm x 205mm; average 33 lines; modern pencil pagination. Now bound as article 12 in a guard book containing various Sandwich records from the 16th to 18th centuries.

British Library, Additional MS. 33,511; 1576–7; English; paper; 6 sheets; 303mm x 215mm, average 46 lines; modern pencil foliation. Now numbered ff 51–6 and tipped individually into a guard book with brown half-leather binding containing Sandwich treasurers' accounts, muster books, and court papers.

Whitfield, East Kent Archives Centre, SA/ZB4/9; 1620–1; English; paper; 12 leaves in 1 gathering; 312mm x 192mm, average 40 lines; modern pencil foliation. Now bound as article 9 in a guard book containing various Sandwich records from the 16th to 18th centuries.

Whitfield, East Kent Archives Centre, SA/FAt 38; 1625–38; English; paper; iii + 296 + ii, in irregular gatherings; 304mm x 200mm, average 32 lines; modern pencil foliation; modern sheepskin binding.

Whitfield, East Kent Archives Centre, SA/FAt 39; 1639–63; English; paper; i + 650, in irregular gatherings; 410mm x 240mm, average 47 lines; contemporary ink pagination (pp 559–75 numbered in error 1559–75, last 75 pages unnumbered); original vellum binding.

Year Books

Whitfield, East Kent Archives Centre, SA/AC 1; 1432–87; Latin and English; paper; iii + 318 + iv, gathered in 14s; 390mm x 280mm, average 40 lines; contemporary ink foliation; 19th-c. black leather binding. Also known as the Old Black Book.

Whitfield, East Kent Archives Centre, SA/AC 3; 1527–51; English; paper; ii + 251 + vi, gathered in 12s (first 2 pages wanting); 390mm x 275mm, average 39 lines; original ink foliation in roman numerals; laid out with mayors' names as running heads; black leather binding with original cover bound in. Also known as the Old Red Book.

Whitfield, East Kent Archives Centre, SA/AC 4; 1552–67; English; paper; v + 376 + v, gathered in 14s; 337mm x 226mm, average 42 lines; original ink foliation in a mixture of roman and arabic numerals: i–cccxxvij, ccc28–9, cccxxx–cccxxxi, ccc32–9, cccxl, ccc41–9, cccl, ccc51–2, cccliij, ccc54–9, ccclx, ccc61–9, ccclxx, ccc71–6; laid out with mayors' names as running heads; black leather binding with original cover bound in. Also known as the Little Black Book.

Whitfield, East Kent Archives Centre, SA/AC 5; 1568–82; English; paper; vi + 279 + ii, gathered in 12s; 395mm x 275mm, average 39 lines; contemporary ink foliation; laid out with mayors' names as running heads, display script used in marginal headings; red leather binding. Also known as the New Red Book.

Whitfield, East Kent Archives Centre, SA/AC 6; 1582–1608; Latin and English; paper; vii + 379 + viii, gathered in 14s; 425mm x 285mm, average 35 lines; original ink foliation; laid out with mayors' names as running heads, display script used in marginal headings; black leather binding with original covers bound in.

Whitfield, East Kent Archives Centre, SA/AC 7; 1608–42; Latin and English; paper; iii + 441 + iii, gathered in 16s; 420mm x 275mm, average 53 lines; original ink foliation; laid out with mayors' names as running heads; black leather binding. Also known as the New Black Book.

Assembly Book of Orders and Decrees

See under Dover for BL: Egerton MS. 2093.

Miscellaneous Records

Statutes for Sir Roger Manwood School

Sir Roger Manwood (1525–92) entered the Inner Temple in 1548 and was called to the bar in 1555. During his legal career he served as recorder of Sandwich 1555–66, MP for Sandwich in 1558, 1559, 1563, 1571, and 1572; serjeant-at-law from 1567, a justice of the court of Common Pleas from 1572, lord chief baron of the Exchequer from 1578, and member of the court of Star Chamber from 1581. In 1563 he obtained from Queen Elizabeth letters patent for the foundation and endowment of The Free Grammar School of Roger Manwood in Sandwich. This volume contains copies of title deeds, charters, ordinances, deed of endowment, commission of inquisition, and correspondence relating to the school's foundation.[15]

Whitfield, East Kent Archives Centre, EK/Ch10M/A1; 1572–1641; Latin and English; paper; 246 leaves, in irregular gatherings; 298mm x 196mm, average 42 lines; 1 unnumbered folio followed by contemporary ink foliation 1–32, continued in modern pencil to f 60, rest unnumbered blanks. On the first unnumbered folio is written: 'A book, Wherin is Contayned All the Charters, Writinges, Recordes and Mynimentes, towchinge and Concerning the Scholehowse, Viz The ffree schole of Sandwich.'

Travels of Leo of Rozmital

Between 1465 and 1467 the Bavarian envoy Leo of Rozmital travelled through Germany, Flanders, England, France, Spain, Portugal, and Italy. Contemporary records of his travels were written in Czech by his squire Schaseck and in German by Gabriel Tetzel. The latter manuscript survives at Munich (Bayerische Staatsbibliothek: Cod. Germ. 1279), but the former survives only in a Latin translation printed at Olmütz in 1577, the sole surviving copy of which is now Prague, Narodní Knihovna (National Library): 50.F.13. Both the German text of Tetzel and the Latin translation of Schaseck were published by the Stuttgart Literarischen Vereins in *Des böhmischen Herrn Leo's von Rozmital Ritter-, Hof- Und Pilger-Reise durch die Abendlande 1465–1467. Beschrieben von zweien seiner Begleiter. Itineris a Leone de Rosmital nobili Bohemo annis 1465–1467 per Germaniam, Angliam, Franciam, Hispaniam, Portugalliam atque Italiam confecti, Commentarii coaevi duo* (Stuttgart, 1844); and an English translation was published by the Hakluyt Society in *The Travels of Leo of Rozmital through Germany, Flanders, England, France, Spain, Portugal and Italy 1465–1467*, Malcolm Letts (trans) (Cambridge, 1957).

COMMEN- | TARIVS BREVIS, ET | IVCVNDVS ITINERIS AT- | que peregrinationis, pietatis & reli- | gionis causa susceptæ, ab Illustri & | Magnifico Domino, Domino Leo- | ne libero Barone de Rosmital et Blat- | na, Iohann*æ* regin*æ* Bohemi*æ* fratre germano, | Proauo Illustris ac Magnifici Domini, Do- | mini Zdenco Leonis liberi Baronis de Ros- | mital & Blatna, nunc supremi Marchio- | natus Morauiæ Capitanei: Ante cen- | tu*m* annos Bohemice co*n*scriptus, & | nunc primum in latina*m* linguam | translatus & editus. | Ex consensu Reuerendissimi Domini, Do- | mini Ioannis Olomucensis Episcopi. | Anno Domini: | M. D. LXXVII. | [device].

Book of Orphans

Whitfield, East Kent Archives Centre, SA/FOa 1; English; 1589–1655; paper; ii + 146, gathered in 12s; 300mm x 200mm, average 37 lines; modern pencil foliation 1–33, rest unnumbered; contemporary vellum binding.

Antiquarian Records

A Suit by the King and his Bailiff against the Mayor and Jurats (A)

London, British Library, Lansdowne MS. 276; early 17th c.; English and Latin; paper; i + 210 + ii, in irregular gatherings; 300mm x 210mm, average 37 lines; modern pencil foliation; red half-leather binding.

SHADOXHURST

Archdeacon's Court Book

See under Lympne for CCA: DCb/J/X.4.2 pt 1.

SHELDWICH

Archdeacon's Court Book

See under Faversham for CCA: DCb/J/X.1.12.

SITTINGBOURNE

Archdeacon's Court Book

See under Bredgar for CCA: DCb/J/Y.4.18 pt 2.

SNAVE

Archdeacon's Court Book

See under Bonnington for CCA: DCb/J/X.3.3 pt 1.

STALISFIELD GREEN

Archdeacon's Court Book

See under Faversham for CCA: DCb/J/X.1.14.

STOCKBURY

Archdeacon's Court Book

Canterbury, Cathedral Archives, DCb/J/X.3.6; 1591–1605; English and Latin; paper; part 1: i + 184 + v, part 2: 296 + i, both gathered in 16s; 294mm x 195mm, average 24 lines; contemporary ink foliation; original parchment cover and modern brown cloth case. Contains comperta and detecta presentments for Sittingbourne deanery.

This book also supplies an entry for Tunstall.

Consistory Court Book

Canterbury, Cathedral Archives, DCb/J/X.9.1; 1598–1600; English and Latin; paper; i + 286, gathered in 16s; 300mm x 200mm, average 24 lines; contemporary ink foliation; original parchment binding, modern brown cloth case. Contains comperta and detecta presentments.

STODMARSH

Archdeacon's Court Book

See under Barham for CCA: DCb/J/X.5.8.

STONE

Archdeacon's Court Book

Canterbury, Cathedral Archives, DCb/J/X.1.17; 1578–86; English and Latin; paper; ii + 181 + i, in irregular gatherings; 285mm x 200mm, average 23 lines; modern pencil foliation supersedes partial contemporary ink foliation; modern brown cardboard binding and case. Contains comperta and detecta presentments for Lympne deanery.

This book also supplies an entry for Willesborough.

SUTTON VALENCE

Archdeacon's Court Book

Canterbury, Cathedral Archives, DCb/J/X.5.1; 1608–20; English and Latin; paper; part 1: ii + 180 + viii, part 2: i + 226 + viii, both gathered in 16s; 302mm x 185mm, average 28 lines; contemporary ink foliation; original parchment cover and modern brown case. Contains comperta and detecta presentments for Sutton deanery.

TENTERDEN

Tenterden was incorporated by charter of Henry VI in 1449. Most of the medieval and early modern borough records, however, were destroyed in a Court Hall fire in 1661. Only the current and semi-current records in the possession of the town clerk, the custumal kept by the mayor, and one sixteenth-century court book survived. The extant chamberlains' account rolls begin in 1634. Churchwardens' accounts for the parish church of St Mildred survive from 1614 but contain no records of parish entertainment.

The Tenterden civic year began and ended on 29 August.

Civic Records

Assembly Book of Orders and Decrees

See under Dover for BL: Egerton MS. 2093.

Chamberlains' Accounts

Maidstone, Centre for Kentish Studies, TE/FAc 2; 1634–5; English; paper; 8 sheets, fastened at the top in original format; 415mm x 300mm; modern pencil numbering.

Maidstone, Centre for Kentish Studies, TE/FAc 3; 1635–6; English; paper; 9 sheets, fastened at the top in original format; dimensions vary from 390mm x 303mm to 358mm x 225mm; modern pencil numbering.

Maidstone, Centre for Kentish Studies, TE/FAc 4; 1636–7; English; paper; 10 sheets, fastened at the top in original format; dimensions vary from 400mm x 300mm to 360mm x 210mm; modern pencil numbering.

Maidstone, Centre for Kentish Studies, TE/FAc 5; 1637–8; English; paper; 10 sheets, fastened at the top in original format; 390mm x 305mm; modern pencil numbering.

Maidstone, Centre for Kentish Studies, TE/FAc 6; 1638–9; English; paper; 10 sheets, fastened at the top in original format; 400mm x 305mm; modern pencil numbering.

Maidstone, Centre for Kentish Studies, TE/FAc 8; 1640–1; English; paper; 9 sheets, fastened at the top in original format; 385mm x 305mm; modern pencil numbering.

Maidstone, Centre for Kentish Studies, TE/FAc 9; 1641–2; English; paper; 9 sheets, fastened at the top in original format; 400mm x 320mm; modern pencil numbering.

Miscellaneous Records

Bill of Complaint and Plea in Elliot et al v. Whitfield

For the background of these proceedings in the court of Star Chamber brought by James Skeets and John Elliott against George Whitfield and Herbert Deering, see pp 1377–8, endnote to PRO: STAC 8/132/6 mb 2.

London, Public Record Office, STAC 8/132/6; 1607/8; English; parchment; 2 mbs attached at left margin; 275mm x 498mm and 395mm x 545mm; modern pencil numbering; bill (mb 2) endorsed: 'Lune Octavo ffebruarij Anno Quinto Regni Iacobi Regis &c | *(signed)* Will*elmu*m Mill/ | R*etornatus.* 8 ffeb*ruarij.*'

Bill of Complaint in Elliot et al v. Deering

London, Public Record Office, STAC 8/138/5; 1609; English; parchment; single mb; 576mm x 640mm at greatest extent; damaged on the right hand side, resulting in a ragged edge and the loss of words at the end of every line of the complaint and the end of every line of the fifth column of the appended verses; endorsed: 'Lune vicesimo sexto Iunij Anno Septimo Iacobi Regis | *(signed)* Edw*ard* Iones | Re*tornatus.*'

TEYNHAM

Archdeacon's Court Book

Canterbury, Cathedral Archives, DCb/J/X.2.7; 1584–96; English and Latin; paper; part 1: ii + 190, part 2: i + 186 + 1, both gathered in 10s; 300mm x 200mm, average 25 lines; contemporary ink foliation; modern brown cardboard binding and case. Contains comperta and detecta presentments for Ospringe deanery.

This book also supplies an entry for Westwell.

TUNSTALL

Archdeacon's Court Book

See under Stockbury for CCA: DCb/J/X.3.6 pt 2.

WALMER

Archdeacon's Court Book

Canterbury, Cathedral Archives, DCb/J/X.5.7; 1611–39; English and Latin; paper; part 1: i + 213 + viii, part 2: 284 + vii, both gathered in 12s; 290mm x 195mm, average 22 lines; contemporary ink foliation; modern brown cloth binding. Contains comperta and detecta presentments for Sandwich deanery.

WALTHAM

Archdeacon's Court Book

See under Alkham for CCA: DCb/J/X.2.1.

WARDEN

Archdeacon's Court Book

Canterbury, Cathedral Archives, DCb/J/X.1.13; 1576–7; English and Latin; paper; i + 189 + i, in irregular gatherings (1 gathering of 12 unnumbered folios inserted between f 46 and f 47); 297mm x 200mm, average 21 lines; contemporary ink foliation 1–118, modern pencil foliation 119–28, 61 unnumbered leaves (mostly blank) after f 128; modern brown cardboard binding and case. Contains comperta and detecta presentments for Charing, Ospringe, Sittingbourne, and Sutton deaneries.

WESTWELL

Archdeacon's Court Book

See under Teynham for CCA: DCb/J/X.2.7 pt 2.

WHITSTABLE

Archdeacon's Court Book

See under Chislet for CCA: DCb/J/X.2.6.

WILLESBOROUGH

Archdeacon's Court Book

See under Stone for CCA: DCb/J/X.1.17.

WORMSHILL

Archdeacon's Court Book

See under Boxley for CCA: DCb/J/X.2.9 pt 1.

Religious Houses

BOXLEY

The Cistercian abbey of St Mary, Boxley, was founded in 1146 and suppressed in 1538. Numerous obedientiary accounts from the fourteenth and fifteenth centuries survive in the Public Record Office, including accounts of the bursar and the chaplain that contain many payments for entertainment.[16]

Bursars' Accounts

London, Public Record Office, SC 6/1253/4; 13 October 1353–23 June 1356; Latin; parchment; roll of 3 rotulets attached at foot, each rotulet composed of 2 mbs serially attached; rotulet [1]: 380mm x 245mm and 650mm x 252mm, rotulet [2]: 250mm x 220mm and 535mm x 240mm, rotulet [3]: 260mm x 277mm and 745mm x 277mm; rotulets unnumbered but mbs numbered 1–6 in modern pencil; rotulets written front to back in chronological order but attached and mbs numbered in reverse order as follows: rotulet [3] mbs 5–6 (13 October 1353–24 June 1354), rotulet [2] mbs 3–4 (24 June 1354–14 June 1355), rotulet [1] mbs 1–2 (14 June 1355–24 June 1356); repaired.

London, Public Record Office, SC 6/1253/12; 1 November 1360–3 June 1363; Latin; parchment; roll of 4 rotulets attached at foot, rotulet [1] composed of 4 mbs serially attached, rotulets [2]–[4] composed of 1 mb each; rotulet [1]: 375mm x 255mm, 625mm x 235mm, 395mm x 230mm, and 260mm x 236mm, rotulet [2]: 495mm x 218mm, rotulet [3]: 495mm x 220mm, rotulet [4]: 620mm x 225mm; rotulets unnumbered but mbs numbered 1–7 in modern pencil in reverse chronological order; rotulets written front to back and attached in chronological order as follows: rotulet [1] mbs 4–7 (1 November 1360–25 December 1361), rotulet [2] mb 3 (24 June–29 September 1362), rotulet [3] mb 2 (29 September–24 December 1362), rotulet [4] mb 1 (25 December 1362–3 June [1363]); repaired.

London, Public Record Office, SC 6/1253/15; 1363–6; Latin; parchment; roll of 4 rotulets attached at head, rotulet [1] composed of 3 mbs serially attached, rotulet [2] composed of 1 mb, rotulet [3] composed of 2 mbs serially attached, rotulet [4] composed of 3 mbs serially attached; rotulet [1]: 737mm x 220mm, 223mm x 223mm, and 247mm x 215mm, rotulet [2]: 725mm x 230mm, rotulet

[3]: 490mm x 195mm and 520mm x 205mm, rotulet [4]: 537mm x 235mm, 590mm x 237mm, and 600mm x 245mm; rotulets unnumbered but mbs numbered in modern pencil 1–9 in reverse chronological order; written front to back but rotulets attached in reverse chronological order with rotulet [4] apparently reversed as follows: rotulet [4] dorse (3 June 1363–22 February 1363/4), rotulet [4] (22 February 1363/4–11 August 1364), rotulet [3] (11 August 1364–2 February 1364/5), rotulet [2] (2 February 1364/5–29 June 1365), rotulet [1] (29 June 1365–22 February 1365/6).

London, Public Record Office, SC 6/1253/16; 22 February 1365/6–22 February 1366/7; Latin; parchment; 2 mbs serially attached; 450mm x 245mm and 485mm x 255mm; written on both sides; modern pencil numbering; repaired.

London, Public Record Office, SC 6/1253/19; 25 December 1371–16 April 1372; Latin; parchment; single mb; 650mm x 250mm; written on both sides; repaired.

London, Public Record Office, SC 6/1253/20; 16 April–29 September 1372; Latin; parchment; single mb; 685mm x 258mm; written on both sides.

London, Public Record Office, SC 6/1254/1; 29 September 1372–29 September 1373; Latin; parchment; 2 mbs serially attached; 695mm x 258mm and 415mm x 245mm; written on both sides; modern pencil numbering.

London, Public Record Office, SC 6/1254/5; 1 November 1376–1 May 1377; Latin; parchment; single mb; 670mm x 258mm; written on both sides.

London, Public Record Office, SC 6/1254/14; c 1 July 1380–1 June 1383; Latin; parchment; single mb; 433mm x 176mm; written on both sides; repaired.

London, Public Record Office, SC 6/1255/9; 1385; Latin; parchment; single mb; 560mm x 180mm; written on both sides; text legible despite loss and spotting of parchment.

London, Public Record Office, SC 6/1254/13; c 1385–97; Latin; parchment; single mb; 685mm x 240mm; written on both sides; repaired. Account is for a single term, 1 January–1 April, but the exact year cannot be determined.

London, Public Record Office, SC 6/1256/8; 29 September 1400–29 September 1401; Latin; parchment; single mb; 667mm x 240mm; written on both sides; damaged by damp but now repaired.

London, Public Record Office, SC 6/1256/10; 22 February 1403/4–January/February 1405/6; Latin; parchment; roll of 3 rotulets attached at foot, each rotulet composed of 2 mbs serially attached; rotulet 1: 595mm x 230mm and 245mm x 230mm, rotulet 2: 330mm x 235mm and 750mm x 235mm; rotulet 3: 550mm x 230mm and 715mm x 230mm; modern pencil numbering; written front to back in chronological order but attached and numbered out of order as follows: rotulet 1 (22 February 1403/4–1 October 1404), rotulet 1d (1 Oct 1404–1 January 1404/5), rotulet 3 mb 1 (1 January 1404/5–1 April 1405), rotulet 3 mb 2 (1 April 1405–1 July 1405), rotulet 3 mb 1d–2d (1 July 1405–1 October 1405), rotulet 2 (1 October 1405–January/February 1405/6); condition poor with some tearing and loss of text from rubbing and wear.

London, Public Record Office, SC 6/1256/13; 1408–9; Latin; parchment; single mb; 510mm x 188mm; written on both sides; repaired.

Chaplains' Accounts

London, Public Record Office, SC 6/1255/1; 1 March 1380/1–1 October 1381; Latin; parchment; single mb; 354mm x 264mm; written on both sides; repaired.

LEEDS

The Augustinian priory of Sts Mary and Nicholas, Leeds, founded in the early twelfth century, comprised a prior and twenty canons at the visitation of Archbishop William Warham in the early sixteenth century. No monastic accounts have survived the suppression of the monastery in the late 1530s; however, evidence of the sacrist and cellarer's indulgence in illicit entertainment does survive from the visitation of Leeds by Archbishop Simon Langham in 1368.[17]

Archbishop Simon Langham's Visitation

London, Lambeth Palace Library, Register of Archbishop Simon Langham; 1366–8; Latin; parchment with paper flyleaves; i + 148 + i; 360mm x 254mm; contemporary but irregular ink foliation; stamped leather binding over boards, title on spine: 'Langham 1366.'

MINSTER

The Priory of Sts Mary and Sexburga at Minster on the Island of Sheppey was founded in about 670 by Seaxburg, the Anglo-Saxon queen of Kent, who endowed the new abbey and became the first abbess. Attacked by the Danes in 835 and 855 and again by Earl Godwin in 1052, the monastery was probably abandoned during part of the ninth and tenth centuries during the Viking invasions. The priory was restored in 1130 by the archbishop of Canterbury, William Corbeil, and continued to function until it was surrendered in 1536. Taken by Sir Thomas Cheyne, lord warden of the Cinque Ports, this inventory lists the contents of the monastery at the time of the Dissolution.[18]

Inventory of Monastic Goods

London, Public Record Office, E 36/154; 1536; English; paper; v + 245 + iv; 303mm x 205mm; average 35 lines; modern pencil pagination; modern brown half-leather binding over green cloth boards. Composite volume containing separate returns for different monasteries.

MOTTENDEN

The Trinitarian friars of Mottenden, established in the early thirteenth century and suppressed by Cromwell in 1538, maintained a house in the parish of Headcorn comprised of seven inmates – the minister, three clerks, and three lay brethren.[19] An account of their liturgical drama performed on Trinity Sunday appears in the second and subsequent editions of *A Perambulation of Kent* by historian of Kent, William Lambarde (1536–1601). Trained at Lincoln's Inn, Lambarde was appointed a justice of the peace for Kent in 1579, a master in Chancery in 1592, and keeper of the rolls in Chancery Lane in 1597; in 1601 Queen Elizabeth made him keeper of the records in the Tower. In addition to *A Perambulation of Kent*, which went through five editions between 1576 and 1656, Lambarde wrote a number of other books, including *Eirenarcha: or of the Office of the Justices of the Peace*, a useful manual which was first printed in 1581 and reprinted eleven times between 1582 and 1619.

William Lambarde, *A Perambulation of Kent*

A Perambulation | of Kent: | Conteining the De- | scription, Hystorie, and | *Customes of that* | *Shyre.* | Written in the yeere 1570 by | *William Lambarde of Lincolne's* | Inne Gent: first published in | *the yeere 1576 and now increa-* | *sed and altered after the* | *Author's owne* | *last Copie.* | [device] | *Imprinted at London*, by Edm. Bollifant. | 1596. *STC*: 15176

OSPRINGE

The Hospital of St Mary at Ospringe, founded by Henry III and endowed with various lands in Kent, consisted in the early sixteenth century of a master and three brethren professed of the order of the Holy Cross, and two secular clerks. Since Henry VIII had granted the advowson of the hospital in mortmain to St John's College, Cambridge, in 1516, the hospital and its assets eventually came into the possession of the college. Although many of the hospital's records have survived in the college archives, the accounts yield only one payment for entertainment.[20]

St Mary's Hospital Accounts

Cambridge, St John's College Archives, D2.1.7.a; 1369–70; Latin; parchment; 4 mbs serially attached; 720mm x 246mm; written on both sides.

WYE

On 27 February 1431/2 John Kempe, then archbishop of York, obtained a licence from Henry VI for the establishment of a college of secular priests near his family home at Wye, Kent. Elevated to the position of cardinal in 1439 and finally made archbishop of Canterbury in 1452, Kempe during his ecclesiastical career endowed the college with considerable estates. In 1447 by instrument under his great seal he converted the parish church of Wye into the College of Sts Gregory and Martin consisting of a number of chaplains and priests.[21]

On 14 January 1447/8 Kempe drew up the statutes for the college. The highly ornate decoration of the manuscript suggests that it was probably Kempe's official copy made for the foundation of the college. According to a note written in a seventeenth-century hand on the last folio, on 17 April 1613 the manuscript was presented by John Budden, Regius Professor of Law at Oxford, to Merton College, where Kempe had been a fellow. On 13 June 1947 the fellows of Merton College returned the manuscript to Wye College, now merged with Imperial College at Wye, University of London, on the occasion of the five-hundredth anniversary of the foundation of the college.[22]

Statutes

Wye, Wye College; 14 January 1447/8; Latin; parchment; 20 leaves in 1 gathering with first 2 leaves cut away; 380mm x 290mm, average 40 lines; unnumbered; illuminated border on folios [1] and [2], red and blue decorated capitals and section headings in red display script throughout manuscript; original parchment cover mounted on boards, title displayed on front cover: 'Statuta Coll*egi* de Wy in Cantio de fundatione Io*han*nis Cardinalis et Archiep*iscopi* Eborac*i*.'

Households

DERING OF SURRENDEN DERING

The library and family archive of the Dering family of Surrenden owes much to the efforts of the antiquarian and scholar, Sir Edward Dering (1598–1644), who was a personal friend of Sir Robert Cotton, Sir William Dugdale, Sir Christopher Hatton, and Sir Thomas Shirley. Writing at the end of the eighteenth century, Kentish historian Edward Hasted noted about Sir Edward: 'He was the founder of the library at Surrenden, for which he collected a great number of books, charters, and curious manuscripts, and caused others to be transcribed with great labour and expence; among which were the registers and chartularies of several of the dissolved monasteries in this county, and a series of deeds and muniments relating not only to the family of Dering, but to others connected at different times with it.'[23] Even in Hasted's day, however, the dispersal of the family collection had begun, for Hasted adds, 'but most of these valuable manuscripts have been unwarily, not many years since, dispersed into other hands.'

Following the decline in the family fortunes in the mid-nineteenth century, several large sales of manuscripts took place with many documents going to the British Library and the Phillipps Collection. A further disposal took place in 1928, when Sir Henry Dering sold the estate; and in 1951 a miscellaneous accumulation of documents discovered in the attics was acquired by Commander C.D. Stephenson of Little Chart. The break-up of the Phillipps Collection in the twentieth century resulted in an additional dispersal of Dering documents. The main collection of Dering family and estate papers now at the Centre for Kentish Studies comprises a valuable group of medieval deeds mainly for Pluckley, a collection of original correspondence dating from 1607 to 1737, and Sir Edward Dering's collection of transcripts, genealogical and historical notes deposited by Mrs C. Langworthy and Mrs Sturgess, daughters of Sir Henry Dering. In the surviving Dering family archive only the following documents have yielded records of entertainment.

Sir Edward Dering's Household Accounts

Maidstone, Centre for Kentish Studies U 350 E4; 1617–28; English; paper; 95 leaves gathered in 14s; 447mm x 173mm, average 68 lines; modern pencil foliation; original vellum binding.

Cast-List for The Spanish Curate

Washington, D.C., Folger Shakespeare Library, MS. V.b.34; 1623; English; paper; half-sheet; 80mm–94mm x 163mm; bottom of original sheet now torn away but remainder in good condition. Contains an 8-line addition to Act 1, Scene 1 of Sir Edward Dering's revision and abridgment of Shakespeare's Henry IV, parts 1 and 2, written on the reverse of the cast-list. Now inset into a leaf measuring 295mm x 200mm (same dimensions as the rest of the play MS) and stitched together with the text of Henry IV so that those added lines face f 1 of the play (this MS currently unbound although it used to have a 19th-c. morocco binding, gilt-stamped around the edges with marbled endpapers).

Sir Edward Dering's Pocket Diary

London, British Library, Additional MS. 47,787; 1637–9; Latin and English; paper; iv + 75 + v, gathered in 6s; 97mm x 75mm, average 20 lines; modern pencil foliation; modern brown leather binding with gold tooling and cloth case. Includes miscellaneous accounts, memoranda relating to sales and purchases of land, debts, books and manuscripts, and notes of furnishings for his house in Surrenden.

HERBERT OF SHURLAND

Before succeeding his brother as earl of Pembroke, Philip Herbert was 1st earl of Montgomery and Baron Herbert of Shurland, in the Isle of Sheppey. It was at the latter estate that he entertained James I with plays as described in this letter.

Letter from Sir William Browne to William Trumbull

London, British Library, Additional MS. 72,339; 1 October 1610; English and French; paper; bifolium; 318mm x 205mm; originally unnumbered; good condition with surviving red wax seal on f 131v; endorsed: '1. of October 1610 from Sir William Browne.' Now numbered ff 130–1v and bound up with other correspondence to and from Trumbull in a composite manuscript (text on f [1] only, address on f [2v]).

OXENDEN OF GREAT MAYDEKIN

Henry Oxenden (1608–70), student of law and Latin poet, was born in Canterbury on

18 January 1607/8, educated at Corpus Christi College, Oxford, and admitted to Gray's Inn on 7 June 1632. His Latin poetry includes *Religionis Funus et Hypocritae Finis* (1647), *Jobus Triumphans* (1651), *Carolus Triumphans* (1660), and *Eikon Basilike*. He is best known today for his letters. The extensive correspondence of Henry Oxenden and other members of his family and circle, ranging in date from 1589 to 1710, is now in the British Library, Additional MSS 27,999–28,005. Selected letters have been published by Dorothy Gardiner (ed), *The Oxinden Letters 1607–1642: Being the Correspondence of Henry Oxinden of Barham and his Circle* (London, 1933), and Dorothy Gardiner (ed), *The Oxinden and Peyton Letters 1642–1670: Being the Correspondence of Henry Oxinden of Barham, Sir Thomas Peyton of Knowlton and their Circle* (London, 1937).

Henry Oxenden's Letter to his Mother

London, British Library, Additional MS. 27,999; 6 February 1637/8; paper; bifolium; originally unnumbered; 204mm x 150mm (196mm x 120mm); good condition, bottom right hand corner of f [1] torn with no loss of text, Oxenden red wax seal still attached in 2 pieces on f [2v]; addressed: 'To his uery louing Mother Mrs Katherine Oxinden at Mr Thomas Barrowes at the Signe of the Maydenhead at the upper end of Cheapside in London.' Now numbered ff 282–3 and mounted in a guardbook (text on f [1]; ff [1v–2] blank; address f [2v]).

County of Kent

Christ Church Priory Register

Canterbury, Cathedral Archives, DCc/Register I; 1275–1325; Latin and French; parchment; vi + 477 + vii, gathered in 10s; 245mm x 175mm, average 37 lines; modern pencil foliation; 18th-c. binding of burgundy leather-covered boards.

Privy Council Order against May Games

London, Public Record Office, PC 2/7; 1553–7; English; i + 427 + i; 360mm x 270mm; contemporary ink pagination; generally good condition; bound in 19th-c. stamped leather over boards.

Province of Canterbury

The Church of England is divided into the province of Canterbury and the province of York, each headed by its own archbishop. The province of Canterbury before 1642 included the following dioceses in southern England and Wales: Bangor, Bath and Wells, Bristol (created out of Worcester in 1542), Canterbury, Chester (created out of Coventry and Lichfield in 1541), Chichester, Coventry and Lichfield, Ely, Exeter, Gloucester (created out of Hereford and Worcester in 1541), Hereford, Lincoln, Llandaff, London, Norwich, Oxford (created out of Lincoln in 1542), Peterborough (created out of Lincoln in 1541), Rochester, St Asaph, St David's, Salisbury, Westminster (created out of London in 1540 and returned to London in 1550), Winchester, and Worcester. As metropolitan bishop, the archbishop of Canterbury exercised spiritual authority not only over the diocese of Canterbury but also over all the dioceses in the province of Canterbury. In this capacity then the medieval and renaissance archbishops of Canterbury issued statutes and visitation articles applicable not only to the diocese but also to the province.

ARCHIEPISCOPAL STATUTES

Statute for Stipendiary Priests

This statute was attributed during the later Middle Ages to Archbishop Robert Winchelsey and, if genuine, would have been issued during the archbishop's visitations between 1299 and 1305.[24] The edition of the statute in Powicke and Cheney (eds), *Councils and Synods*, vol 2, pt 2, pp 1382–5, is based primarily on Exeter College, Oxford: MS. 31, f 238v, with selected variants given from a further four principal manuscripts: Balliol College, Oxford: MS. 158, f 165; Trinity College, Dublin: MS. E.2.22, p 130; Gonville & Caius College, Cambridge: MS. 38, f 124; and BL: Cotton Faustina A.VIII, f 117v. Since no variants occur in clause nine, the prohibition forbidding clergy to attend plays, the edition of this clause in the Records relies only on Oxford, Exeter College MS. 31.

Exeter College, Oxford, MS. 31; late 15th c.; Latin; parchment with paper flyleaves; ii + 289 + ii; 355mm x 250mm; modern pencil foliation, superseding both older pencil foliation and erratic contemporary ink pagination; some blue and red decoration; generally good condition with some tears; bound in stamped leather over boards. Contains statutes and decrees.

Statute on Church Ornaments

This statute was likely issued (or reissued) by Archbishop Walter Reynolds (1313–27) for the province of Canterbury based on various synodal statutes collected by his predecessor, Archbishop Robert Winchelsey.[25] The statute survives in eighteen manuscripts, most of which omit the final prohibition forbidding performance of plays in the church or churchyard. The edition of this statute in Powicke and Cheney (eds), *Councils and Synods*, vol 2, pt 2, pp 1387–8, is based primarily on BL: Cotton Faustina A.I, f 217, extensively emended by reference to Balliol College, Oxford: MS. 158, f 184; Cumbria Record Office: DRC/1/2, p 379; and St John's College, Cambridge: MS. D.13 (James MS. 88), f 55. Of these four principal texts, however, only the last two contain this prohibition. The bishop's register from the diocese of Carlisle (Cumbria Record Office: DRC/1/2, p 379 col 2) has been chosen as the base text, and the collation notes give the substantive variants from St John's College, Cambridge: MS. D.13 (James MS. 88), f 55, marked by the siglum *(S)*.

Carlisle, Cumbria Record Office, DRC1/2; c 1313; Latin; parchment; ii + 473+ ii; ink pagination, probably 17th c., replacing several earlier sequences of foliation; 335mm x 263mm; mostly good condition; rebound in leather in the 18th c. with some displacement of gatherings. Contains the registers of three bishops of Carlisle diocese, 1352–92, and two sections of canonical texts and statutes.

Cambridge, St John's College MS. D.13 (James MS. 88); 14th c.; Latin; vellum; 97 + ii, in irregular gatherings; 258mm x 185mm, average 46 lines in double columns.

PROVINCIAL VISITATION ARTICLES

These visitation articles for the province of Canterbury have been divided into three sub-groups: articles that mention a particular archbishop, general visitation articles, and deanery visitation articles.

Archbishop Matthew Parker's Visitation Articles

London, Lambeth Palace Library, Register of Archbishop Matthew Parker, vol 1; 1559–72; Latin; parchment; i + 413 in irregular gatherings; 425mm x 350mm; foliation contemporary but irregular; stamped leather binding on wooden boards. The articles for the archbishop's 1560 metropolitical visitation of the province of Canterbury appear on ff 302–3. They subsequently appeared in print under the following title: ARTICLES | for to be inquired of, in the | METROPOLITICAL | visitation of the moste Re- | uerende father in GOD | MATTHEW, | by the sufferaunce of GOD, Arche- | bysshop of Canterbury, Pri- | mate of all England, and | Metropolitane: | In the second yeare of oure soueraingne Ladye | QVENE ELIZABETH, | by the grace of GOD Quene of | England, Fraunce, and | Ireland, Defendor of | the faith. &c. | M. [device] C. | *Anno Domini M.D.L.X.* STC: 10151.

ARTICLES | to be enquired of in the visi- | tation of the moste Reuerend fa- | ther in God, MATTHEW, by the | sufferaunce of GOD Archebyshop | of Canterbury, Primate of all Englande, | and Metropo- | litane, | In the year of our Lorde GOD, | M,D.LXIII. | [device] | M [device] A | Imprinted at Lon | don by Reginalde Wolfe, | *Anno Domini M,D.LXIII.* STC: 10152.

Archbishop Edmund Grindal's Visitation Articles

Articles | to be enquired of, within the Prouince | of Canterburie, in the Metropoliticall | *visitation of the most reuerende father* | in God, Edmonde Archbishop of Can- | terburie, Primate of all Englande, | and Metropolitane. | In the .xviij. yeare of the reigne of our most gracious | souereygne Ladie Elizabeth, by the grace of God, | Queene of Englande, Fraunce and Ire- | lande, defender of the fayth. &c. | [device] | ¶ Imprinted at London, by | *Willyam Seres.* | *Anno.* 1576. STC: 10155.

Articles | to be enquired of, within the Province of | *Canterburie, in the Metropoliticall visitation of the moste* | reuerende Father in God, Edmonde Archbishop of | Canterburie, Primate of all Englande, | and Metropoli- | tane. | In the xviij. yeare of the reygne of our most gracious soue- | reygne Ladie Elizabeth, by the grace of God, | Queene of Englande, Fraunce, and Ire- | lande, defender of the | fayth, &c. | [device] | ¶ Imprinted at London by | Willyam Seres. | Anno. 1577. STC: 10155.3.

Articles to be enqui- | red of, within the Prouince of Canterbu- | rie, in the Metropoliticall visitation of | the most reuerende father in God, Edmond | Archbishop of Canterburie, Primate | of all England, And Me- | tropolitane. | *In the xxii yeere of the reigne of our most* | gracious souereigne Ladie Elizabeth, by | the grace of God, Queene of England, | Fraunce and Ireland, defender of | the faith, &c. | [device] | Imprinted at London by Christo- | pher Barker, Printer to the Queenes | Maiestie. | 1580. *STC*: 10155.7.

Articles to be enqui- | red of, within the Prouince of Canter- | burie, in the visitation of the most | Reuerend father in God, Edmond | Archbishop of Canterburie, Pri- | mate of all England, and Me- | tropolitane. | *In the xxiiii. yeere of the reigne of our most* | gracious Soueraigne Lady Elizabeth, by | the grace of God, Queene of Englande, | Fraunce and Ireland, | defender of | the faith, &c. | [device] | *Imprinted at London by Christopher* | Barker, Printer to the Queenes Maiestie. | 1582. *STC*: 10157.

Archbishop Richard Bancroft's Visitation Articles

Articles to be inquired | Of, in the first Metropoliticall Visitation | of the most Reuerend Father: *Richarde* | by Gods Prouidence, Archbushop of Canterbu- | ry, and Primat of all ENGLANDE: in, & for, all thiese Diocesses | following, (Viz.) Exeter Norwich, Chichester, St. Dauids, | Landaffe, Heriford, Worcester, Bristol, Bath & Welles | and Couentrie & Litchfielde, in the yeare of our | Lorde God, 1605. and in the first yeare of his | Graces Translation. | [device McKerrow 298 with I.W. voided] | ¶ At London Printed by Ralph Blower, for | Thomas Pavier, and are to be solde at his Shop | neare the Royall Exchaung An. Dom. 1605. *STC*: 10158.

Archbishop George Abbot's Visitation Articles

[device] | ARTICLES | To be inquired of, in the | first Metropoliticall visitation, of the most | Reuerend Father, GEORGE, by Gods pro- | *uidence, Arch-Bishop of Canterbury, and Primate of all* | England; in, and for the Dioces of *(blank)* in the yeare of | our Lord God, *(blank)* and in the fifth yeare of his | Graces Translation. | [device McKerrow 283] | LONDON, | Printed by VVilliam Iaggard. *STC*: 10147.4. The *STC* assigned a date of 1615 to these articles because they are said to have been issued in the fifth year of Abbot's translation.

[device] | ARTICLES | To be inquired of, in the | first Metropoliticall visitation, of the most | Reuerend Father, GEORGE, by Gods pro- | *uidence, Arch-Bishop of Canterbury, and Primate of all* | England; in, and for the Dioces of *(blank)* in | the yeare of our Lord God, 1616. and in the sixt | yeare of his Graces Translation. | [device McKerrow 283] | LONDON, | Printed by VVilliam Iaggard. *STC*: 10147.5.

Archbishop William Laud's Visitation Articles

ARTICLES | *TO BE* | ENQVIRED OF | IN THE METROPOLITICALL | *VISITATION OF THE MOST* | REVEREND FATHER, | VVILLIAM, | By GODS Providence, Lord Arch-Bishop of | *Canterbury, Primate of all England; and* | METROPOLITAN: | In and for the Dioces of *(blank)*, In the yeere of our | LORD GOD 163*(blank)*, And in the first yeere | of his Graces Translation. | [device McKerrow 417] | Printed at *London*, by *Richard Badger.* | 1633. *STC*: 10147.7.

ARTICLES | *TO BE* | ENQVIRED OF | IN THE METROPOLITICALL | *VISITATION OF THE MOST* | REVEREND FATHER, | VVILLIAM, | By GODS Providence, Lord Arch-Bishop of | *Canterbury, Primate of all England; and* | METROPOLITAN: | In and for the Dioces of *(blank)*, In the yeere of | our LORD GOD 1634, And in the first yeere | of his Graces Translation. | [device McKerrow 417] | Printed at *London*, by *Richard Badger*. | 1634. *STC*: 10147.8. In the extant copy (in the Bodleian Library) the name of the diocese has been filled in as 'lincolne' and the final numeral of the first date has been written over apparently with '6.'

ARTICLES | TO BE | INQVIRED OF | THE METROPOLITICALL | ⟨..⟩*ISITATION OF THE MOST* | REVEREND FATHER, | WILLIAM | By Gods Providence, Lord Arch-Bishop of | *Canterbury, Primate of all England; and* | METROPOLITAN: | In and for the Dioces of *(blank)*, In the yeere of | our LORD GOD 163*(blank)*, And in the *(blank)* yeere | of his Graces Translation. | [device McKerrow 417] Printed at *London*, by *Richard Badger*. | 163*(blank)*. *STC*: 10147.8A. The *STC* has assigned a date of *c* 1635 to these articles since the Folger copy has been filled in with that date.

GENERAL ARTICLES FOR VISITATIONS

ARTICLES | to be enquired of by the Churchwar- | *dens and Sworne men within the (blank)* | *(blank)* and the trueth thereof | to be by them vpon their othes certainely presented to the | *(blank)* | with peculiar answer to euery Article, *Anno. Dom. (blank)* | and in the *(blank)* yeare of the Raigne of our most gratious | soueraigne Lady Elizabeth by the grace of God Queene | of England, France and Ireland, defender of the faith, &c. | [device] | *LONDON* | Printed by Felix Kingston. | 1597. *STC*: 10133.7. The extant copy (in the British Library) has been filled in for the deanery of Shoreham and was apparently used in a 1597 visitation.

ARTICLES | ECCLESIASTICAL TO | be enquired of by the Church- | wardens and Sworne-men with- | in the *(blank)* | In the Visitation of the *(blank)* | *And in the (blank) yeere of the Reigne of our* | *most dread Soueraigne Lord* | *King* IAMES.) | [rule] | [device] | LONDON | Printed by IOHN BILL. | 1621. *STC*: 10133.9. The extant copy has been annotated by a contemporary hand and was apparently used in visitations of the archdeaconry of Hereford in 1622 and 1623.

ARTICLES | Given by *(blank)* | *(blank)* and delivered to the Church-wardens | to be considered and answered in his visitation | holden in the yeare of our Lord God *(blank)* | WHEREVNTO THE SAID | Church-wardens and sidemen are | vpon their oathes to answere | truly and particularly. | [device (Oxford University coat of arms)] | *AT OXFORD*. | Printed by *William Turner* Printer to the Famous | University, *Anno, Dom. (blank)*. *STC*: 10134. The *STC* has assigned a date of *c* 1635 on the basis of its similarity to a dated series of articles.

DEANERY VISITATION ARTICLES

Archbishop William Laud's Deanery Visitation Articles

ARTICLES | *TO BE* | ENQVIRED OF | IN THE METROPOLITICALL | *VISITATION OF THE MOST* | REVEREND FATHER, | VVILLIAM, | By GODS Providence, Lord Arch-Bishop of | *Canterbury, Primate of all England; and* | METROPOLITAN: | In and for the Deany of *(blank)*, In the yeere of I our LORD GOD 163*(blank)*, And in the *(blank)* yeere I of his Graces Translation. I [device McKerrow 417] I Printed at *London*, by *Richard Badger.* I 163*(blank)*. *STC*: 10147.10. The Bodleian Library copy (Pamph C32 (6)) contains the following additions: the deanery name and the dates have been added in ink, the deanery given is Shoreham, '4' was added to the two year dates to give the year '1634,' and the archiepiscopal year was identified as Laud's first. The *STC* assigned a date of *c* 1634 to these articles on the basis of these additions to the Bodleian copy.

Visitation Articles for the Deanery of Canterbury

ARTICL⟨..⟩ I TO BE ENQUIRED ⟨..⟩ I By the Minister, Churchwardens, and I Sidemen of euery Parish and Chappelry, I within the Deanry of *(blank)* I In the Yeere of our Lord God 16*(blank)* and I Presentment to bee made by them, con- I taining a particular answer to I every Article. I [rule] [device] [rule] I Printed at LONDON, by I.B. I 16*(blank)*. *STC*: 10147.11. The Bodleian Library copy (Pamph C35 (13)) contains the following additions: the deanery name and the dates have been added in ink, the deanery given is Shoreham, and '37' was added to the two year dates to give the year '1637.'

Diocese of Canterbury

DIOCESAN STATUTES

Archbishop Stephen Langton's Diocesan Statutes

These statutes of Archbishop Stephen Langton, issued before the Fourth Lateran Council and now the earliest surviving set for any English diocese, originated between the archbishop's return from exile in June or July 1213 and the lifting of the interdict on England on 2 July 1214. The statutes survive in three manuscripts and one printed text, all of which are imperfect. The statute on the behaviour of priests appears in all four texts, but due to the damaged state of the manuscripts only two contain the statute prohibiting plays in churches and churchyards. The printed version, *Thesaurus Novus Anecdotorum*, which contains both of the statutes, has been chosen for the base text. The collation notes give the substantive variants from Pembroke College, Cambridge: MS. 62, f i col 1 *(B)*; BL: Additional MS. 16,170, ff 162v–3, 167 *(H)*; and Bodl.: Rawlinson A.423, f 51 *(R)*.[26]

Thesaurus Novus Anecdotorum Tomus Quartus. In Quo Continentur Varia Concilia, Episcoporum Statuta Synodalia, Illustrium Monasteriorum Ac Congregationum edita præsertim in capitulis generalibus DECRETA. F. Martène and R. Durand (eds) (Paris 1717). Cols 147–50 give the text of these statutes, unattributed, from a now lost manuscript from Corbie Abbey (diocese of Amiens).

Cambridge, Pembroke College, MS. 62; 12th c.; Latin; parchment; ii + 71 + ii; 278mm x 177mm; infrequent foliation in modern pencil; excellent condition except for torn final leaf; modern half-leather binding over boards. Folios i–ii contain a partial text of Langton's statutes; ff 1–[67v] contain a commentary on Daniel; f [68] is a Prologus Hieronimy; f [69] consists of pencil notes on recto only; ff [70–1], bound as back flyleaves, are from a 13th-c. manuscript of canon law, and the lower right corner of f [70] carries 15th-c. verses on the number of Christ's wounds.

London, British Library, Additional MS. 16,170; 15th c.; Latin; paper and parchment; iii + 200 + iii, in irregular gatherings; 225mm x 145mm, average 31 lines; modern pencil foliation; 19th-c. brown leather binding. These statutes are on ff 162–7.

Oxford, Bodleian Library, Rawlinson A.423; 15th c.; Latin and English; parchment with paper flyleaves; i + 79 + xi; average dimensions 190mm x 136mm; foliated i–ix, 12 unnumbered blank leaves, 1–57, x–xi; frequent use of red letter with red, blue, and gilt illumination of major capitals; condition generally good except for occasional trimming of folios; bound in vellum over boards with title on spine: 'Miscellanea An. & Latina M.S.' Contains commentaries, constitutions, and glosses; ff 50–3 contain the statutes.

Archbishop Stephen Langton's Synodal Statutes

This second set of statutes of Archbishop Stephen Langton for the diocese of Canterbury, issued after the Fourth Lateran Council, survives in three manuscripts. BL: Cotton Julius D.II, a mid-thirteenth-century register of St Augustine's Abbey, Canterbury, has been chosen as the base text. The collation notes give the substantive variants from Bodl.: Hatton 67, ff 76v, 82, an early thirteenth-century miscellaneous manuscript of unknown provenance, here designated *(G)*, and from Bodl.: Rawlinson A429, f 105, an early fifteenth-century volume of theological tracts of unknown provenance, here designated *(J)*.[27]

London, British Library, Cotton Julius D.II; 13th c.–15th c.; Latin; parchment mounted on guards with some paper flyleaves; iv (i–ii paper) + 264 + ii; 180mm x 130–5mm; modern ink foliation replacing various incomplete earlier foliations; red and blue decorated initials to f 172, with occasional rubricated headings thereafter; rebound in 1961 in modern cloth with gilt coat of arms, leather corner trims and spine, raised bands, green compartments and gilt on spine. This register of St Augustine's, Canterbury, also contains other material of interest to the monks, such as the Rules of Sts Benedict and Augustine.

Oxford, Bodleian Library, Hatton 67; late 13th or 14th c.; French and Latin; parchment with paper flyleaves; i + 83 + i; dimensions vary from 210mm x 141mm (ff 1–46) to 195mm x 113–40mm (ff 47–83); foliated in modern pencil; red lettering from f 51; generally good condition with some browning and rubbing; bound in stamped leather over boards, probably late 19th c. Contents vary and include chronicles, French sermons, pastoralia, and statutes.

Oxford, Bodleian Library, Rawlinson A.429; 15th c.; Latin and English; paper; iv + 134 + i; 209mm x 144mm; contemporary ink foliation to 132 continued in modern pencil; rubricated; generally good condition; bound in stamped leather over boards, probably in 18th c. Contains pastoralia, including some legislation, and medical writings.

DIOCESAN VISITATION ARTICLES

These visitation articles for the diocese of Canterbury have been divided into three sub-groups: articles that mention a particular archbishop, general visitation articles, and archdeaconry visitation articles.

Cardinal Reginald Pole's Visitation Articles

℃ Articles to be enquy- | red in thordinary visitacion of the most re- | uerende father in GOD, the Lorde Car- | dinall Pooles grace Archebyshop | of Caunterbury wythin hys | Dioces of Canterbury. | In the yeare of our | Lorde God. | m.v.c.lvi [device]. *STC*: 10149.

Archbishop Matthew Parker's Visitation Articles

ARTICLES | to be enquired of within the | Dioces of Canterbury, in the Me- | tropoliticall and Ordinary visita- | tion of the moste Reuerend father in God, | MATTHEW, by the prouidence of God, | Archebyshop of Canterbury, Primate | of all Englande, and Me- | tropolitane, | In the yeare of our Lord GOD, | M.D.LXXIII. | [device] | M [device] C | Imprinted at London, | by Reginalde Wolfe. *STC*: 10153.

Archbishop Richard Bancroft's Visitation Articles

Articles to be inquired | of, in the first Metropoliticall Visitation, | of the most Reuerend Father: *Richard* | by Gods prouidence Arch-bushop of Can- | terbury, and Primat of all ENGLAND, | in, and for the Dioces of CAVNTERBURY, in the | yeare of our Lord God 1607. and in the third | yeare of his Graces Translation. (. * .) | [rule] | [device] | [rule] At London printed by Raph. Blower, | ANNO DOMINI, 1607. *STC*: 10159.

Archbishop William Laud's Visitation Articles

ARTICLES | *TO BE* | ENQVIRED OF | IN THE METROPOLITICALL | *VISITATION OF THE MOST* | REVEREND FATHER, | VVILLIAM, | By GODS Providence, Lord Arch-Bishop of | *Canterbury, Primate of all England; and* | METROPOLITAN: | In and for the Dioces of *Canterbury*, In the yeere of our | Lord God 163*(blank)*, And in the *(blank)* yeere | of his Graces Translation. | [device (McKerrow 417)] | Printed at *London*, by *Richard Badger*. 16*(blank)*. *STC*: 10167. The *STC* has assigned a tentative date of 1633 to these articles because the only extant copy (at Emmanuel College, Cambridge) has the blanks on its title page filled in as '1634,' 'the firste yeere,' and '1635' respectively.

ARTICLES | *TO BE* | INQVIRED OF | IN THE FIRST TRIENNIALL | *VISITATION OF THE MOST* | REVEREND FATHER, | VVILLIAM, | By GODS Providence, Lord Arch-Bishop of | *Canterbury, Primate of all England; and* | METROPOLITAN: | In and for the Dioces of *Canterbury*, In the yeare of | our LORD GOD 1637, And in the fourth yeere | of his Graces Translation. | [device McKerrow 417] | Printed at *London*, by *Richard Badger*. *STC*: 10169.7.

Visitation Articles for the Diocese of Canterbury

[device] | ARTICLES | To bee enquired of by the | Churchwardens and Sidemen of | euery Parish

within the Diocesse of Can- | terbury, wherunto by vertue of their oathes | they are to make answere seuerally | to euery Article. | [device] | Printed at London by Thomas Este. *STC*: 10157.5. A series of handwritten changes in ink has been made to the title page in the Bodleian Library copy (Antiq f.E.112): 'Diocesse' on the fifth line was crossed out and replaced with '‚ˆ⌐archdeaconrie⌐,' the full stop after 'Article' on the eighth line was made into a comma, and the phrase 'and to present ye same to the Archdeacon or his Officiall.' was added following that comma. The *STC* assigns a date of *c* 1604 to these articles on the basis of internal evidence.

ARTICLES | to be inquired of by | *the Church wardens and Sidemen of* | euerie parish within the Diocesse of Can- | terburie, wherunto by vertue of their othes | they are to make answere seuerally | to euerie Article. | (˙ * ˙) | [device McKerrow 244] | AT LONDON, | Printed by *Thomas Haueland*. *STC*: 10159.2. The *STC* assigned a date of *c* 1610 to these articles.

Visitation Articles for the Archdeaconry of Canterbury

[device] | ARTICLES | *TO BE* | ENQVIRED OF BY | THE CHVRCHVVAR- |DENS and SIDEMEN | of every Parish; | *Within the Arch-deaconry of* Canterbury: | *Whereunto, by vertue of their* Oathes, *they* | are to make Answere severally, to | *every ARTICLE.* | [device McKerrow 265] | Printed at London, by *Richard Badger.* | 1636. *STC*: 10171.

Editorial Procedures

Principles of Selection

This edition attempts to include all records of dramatic, musical, and ceremonial activity before 1642 in the diocese of Canterbury: records of professional travelling players and minstrels; records of amateur town and parish plays, liturgical plays, household plays, and school plays; records of musical performance by professional travelling musicians and by civic musicians, including waits and people responsible for horn blowing, drumming, and rough music; records of civic ceremony incorporating musical or mimetic activity, including marching watches with pageants, triumphs and festive celebrations, royal visits, bullbaiting, and hearbaiting; and ceremonial customs incorporating mimetic or minstrel activity, such as the boy bishop celebrations, Hocktide rituals, and summer games. Appendix 1 contains biographical details of the playwrights John Bale, Stephen Gosson, and Christopher Marlowe and the producer Richard Gibson found in the records of the dean and chapter of Christ Church Cathedral, the city of Canterbury, and the town of New Romney. Otherwise, strictly biographical details not related to performance by minstrels and players have been omitted.[1]

Although most dramatic, musical, and ceremonial activities pose few problems of selection, some need further comment here. Ceremonial activity, whether liturgical or secular, has been included only when it involved mimetic or musical activity. Liturgical drama, for example, is included but purely liturgical rituals, such as sepulchre watching, torches for liturgical processions, or vigils on the eve of feast days, have been omitted unless mimetic or musical activity was clearly specified as in the processions in Sandwich on St Bartholomew's Day. Routine payments in churchwardens' accounts for torches used in festival processions are excluded, whereas the sale of torches in Canterbury in 1519–20 to the wardens of the Grocers' pageant is included. Hocktide rituals in Canterbury and elsewhere have been included; however, bequests for hock lights In parish churches have been omitted. Some secular ceremonies or customs, such as royal visits, civic feasts, and parish ales, were often, but not always, accompanied by entertainment. Again I have recorded such activities only when they clearly included mimetic or musical activity. At the annual Fordwich giveale, for example, I have recorded expenses only when minstrels are known to have performed and have ignored such peripheral items as repairs to the giveale house or rents from the giveale lands. In Canterbury, as Puritans increasingly shunned dramatic performance, the city fathers turned to civic feasting on quarter session days and audit days, often paying the city waits to perform. When no evidence of such entertainment occurs, I have ignored these feasts. Similarly, numerous payments appear in borough accounts for visiting magnates and royalty – payments ranging from rewards for royal retainers to gifts of food and wine to elaborate ceremonies of welcome. I have included only the visits that involved mimetic or musical activity; however, when such mimetic or musical activity is explicitly indicated, I have included all payments related to the visit in order to place the entertainment payments in context. Routine bell ringing on coronation days is not included; however, bell ringing to mark a royal visit is, if the visit also included entertainment. Finally, only those expenses appearing in provincial accounts for royal visits are included; expenses appearing in the royal household accounts, which could not be systematically searched, are not.

Some civic musical activities also pose their own selection problems. The head ports and limbs of the Cinque Ports followed the custom of summoning the men of the town by blowing a brazen horn. Directions for sounding the common horn appear in the town custumals. Payments for purchase and repair of the horns and payments to the town wait or the town serjeant for horn blowing throughout the year routinely appear in many of the town accounts. Often the town accounts, however, included payments only for the annual wages of the serjeant rather than specific payments for horn blowing, which formed only one of his numerous duties. I have included serjeants' wages when horn blowing was specifically mentioned. Beginning with the threat of invasion during the 1580s and continuing throughout the seventeenth century, the Cinque Port towns also employed civic drummers for military musters, for summoning the residents to their required labours on the harbours or fortifications, or even for entertainment on holidays. Most towns purchased their own drums and paid annual salaries to town drummers. Payments for the routine maintenance and occasional replacement of these civic drums appear throughout the town accounts. Since it is not always possible to distinguish between military exercises and musical entertainment, particularly in such matters as the purchase and repair of instruments and the payment of annual salaries to town musicians, all payments for civic drums and drumming have been included, except where payments for drumming or drum repair are clearly related to musters. In such cases the annual totals of muster-related drumming are given in the Endnotes.

Rough and Revised Accounts

A particular problem of selection arises in borough accounts when two versions of the accounts survive for the same year. Typically, the town chamberlains or wardens kept rough accounts in paper booklets or rolls with expenses entered daily or weekly in order of payment, often with later corrections or deletions. At the end of the accounting year these rough accounts were revised, often with similar payments grouped together, quarterly payments added up to produce annual totals, and payments that had been disallowed by the auditors omitted, before a fair copy was made for the official town records. Usually, only one version or the other has survived, but in Canterbury, Dover, Faversham, and New Romney both rough and revised accounts exist for certain years. In Canterbury two series of chamberlains' accounts survive between 1393 and 1505. Two large folio volumes, CC/FA 1 (1393–1445) and CC/FA 2 (1445–1505), form the first series. These two account books contain a mixture of revised and summary accounts, often preserving the only record for a given year. The second series forms an incomplete run of rough accounts: CC/FA 3 (1394–1404), CC/FA 4 (1459–64), CC/FA 5 (1465–79), CC/FA 6 (1479–83), and CC/FA 7 (1483–97). Faversham also has a double series of borough accounts. The first consists of two volumes: the wardmote book (Alexander Centre: FA/AC 1), which contains accounts from 1514 to 1581, and the continuation of the chamberlains' accounts from 1581 to 1621 (CKS: FA/FAc 197). The second series consists of an incomplete run from 1569 to 1641 of rough account rolls, booklets, and loose papers sorted into annual bundles (CKS: FA/FAc 1–FA/FAc 65). During some thirty years the two series contain duplicate entertainment expenses. At New Romney a series of three rough account books for the years 1469–92 (EKAC: NR/FAc 4), 1492–1516 (EKAC: NR/FAc 5), and 1516–20 (EKAC: NR/FAc 6) parallels a large folio volume of revised accounts from 1448 to 1527 (EKAC: NR/FAc 3). Sometimes these accounts are identical; at other times entertainment expenses appear only in one version or the other. In general the rough accounts, being closer to the actual date of performance, take precedence over the more formal revised accounts. Where duplicate payments occur, I have transcribed the payment from the rough accounts and given the reference in an endnote for the revised account, calling attention to significant differences in entertainment details or terminology between the two accounts. No notice has been taken of minor variations in spelling or expansion of abbreviations, nor has any attempt been made to collate all the variants. In the years for which the revised accounts provide the only record or contain payments not included in the rough accounts, I have transcribed these additional payments from the revised accounts.

The duplicate Dover accounts need further comment. Covering, with some gaps, nearly three centuries between 1365 and 1642, they fill ten manuscripts in the British Library and five in the East Kent Archives Centre. During this period the wardens of the corporation of Dover employed four different systems of accounting: rough accounts entered in chronological order of payment in the 'pamflett boke,' rough accounts grouped under ledger headings, revised accounts showing some grouping of similar payments and some annual totals of quarterly payments, and summary accounts listing only the subtotals of the ledger headings in the second system above. During the fourteenth and fifteenth centuries the wardens used the first system of rough accounts, entering expenses week by week as they occurred. In the rough accounts for 1476–7 (BL: Additional MS. 29,616), for example, payments to players and minstrels occur at irregular intervals throughout the year's accounts. Often the date of payment is entered in the margin. Payment to the wait is entered at quarterly intervals along with the wages for the other officers of the town. In these rough accounts the names of the wait and the other officers usually appear at the beginning of the year's accounts. At the end of the year the wardens revised these rough accounts. The revised accounts for the same year (BL: Egerton MS. 2090) give the wait's wages as an annual sum of 20s instead of four quarterly payments of 5s and group together the payments to minstrels and players in consecutive entries. In 1522 the wardens began to organize the rough accounts under ledger headings, such as ordinary payments, repairs, gifts, wines and pleasure, and travelling expenses on behalf of the town. For example, the 1534–5 rough accounts (BL: Egerton MS. 2092) list the individual payments for entertainment on a separate folio under the heading 'Rewardes to the kynges Mynstrelles berewardes players & other.'

The revised accounts for the same year (BL: Additional MS. 29,618, f 299) simply give the subtotals from each division of the rough accounts, producing the less than informative entry: 'Item paied for rewardes to Mynstrelles berewardes and players as apperith in the pamflett v s. x d.'

Unfortunately the Dover manuscripts do not fall neatly into two categories of rough and revised accounts. When the manuscripts were rebound in their characteristic green leather bindings in the nineteenth century, the accounts were incorrectly sorted, revised and rough accounts often being bound together in the same manuscript. The earliest Dover account book (BL: Additional MS. 29,615), for example, has a mixture of revised and rough accounts with many folios bound out of order. From 1465 to 1479 the rough accounts appear mainly in BL: Egerton MS. 2090 and from 1485 to 1509 in BL: Additional MS. 29,617, while the revised accounts from 1462 to 1485 appear mainly in BL: Additional MS. 29,616 and from 1485 to 1508 in BL: Egerton MS. 2107. Nevertheless, in 1490–1 the revised accounts appear in the former series and the rough accounts in the latter. Similarly, BL: Egerton MS. 2092 contains mainly the rough accounts from 1509 to 1546, and BL: Additional MS. 29,618 mainly the summary accounts for the same period, yet eight times the annual accounts are reversed. After 1546 only one version, sometimes rough, sometimes revised, survives for each accounting year.

When both rough and revised accounts do survive, they often contain different information. In 1467–8, for example, the revised accounts give both more and less detail than the rough accounts. The revised accounts that year include payment for the wait's livery and his annual fee of 20s, while the rough accounts give only partial payment for wages on two of the four quarter days and no payment for livery. The revised accounts mention the king's minstrels while the rough accounts do not. On the other hand several specific payments to named minstrels and players in the rough accounts are simply lumped together in one general summary payment in the revised accounts. In the transcription of the Dover accounts, therefore, I have where possible preferred the rough accounts and given the full reference to the revised accounts in an endnote along with significant variations in entertainment details and terminology. I have ignored minor variations of form, such as the annual 20s payment to the wait in the revised accounts versus the quarterly 5s payments in the rough accounts, unless there is a discrepancy in the total amount. When payments occur in the revised accounts but not in the rough, I have included these additional expenses alongside the rough accounts.

A final word of explanation must be made about the Hythe accounts. In a unique accounting system, encountered in no other borough in Kent, the annual accounts are entered ward by ward – East Ward, Middle Ward, West Ward, Market Ward, and West Hythe – with each freeman residing in that ward listing his 'maletot' or tax assessment due to the town less allowances for his expenses on behalf of the town. Sometimes these expenses are totalled ward by ward or the totals for several wards are combined; other times no totals are given. Entertainment expenses, then, appear sometimes under one ward, sometimes under another, depending on the residence of the jurat who paid the bill. In 1477, for example, there are thirteen payments to minstrels and players made by ten different jurats living in three different wards. The identities and wards of the residents who made payments for entertainment, when not given in the entries, have been supplied in the footnotes. In many cases the small sums suggest that the entertainment bill may have been split by two or more jurats, such as in 1471–2 when Thomas Stace and John Edewy each paid 8d to the minstrels of the earl of Arundel. Whether these payments represent two visits by the same minstrels or partial payments by two jurats for one visit is impossible to determine.

Dating

Few of the entertainment records in this edition give the exact date of performance. Civil and ecclesiastical court cases were sometimes dated according to when the proceedings began, not according to when the alleged musical or dramatic performance occurred. Although the latter date was sometimes referred to within the presentment or deposition, it was often not given. The proceedings themselves, however, were carefully dated as the case continued from one court day to the next, making these dates the most reliable point of reference. Most of the payments to players and minstrels transcribed from churchwardens' accounts or borough accounts can be firmly assigned to a fiscal year. In borough accounts this year was usually the same as the annual term of the civic officers. For example, the translation of a typical fifteenth-century account heading at Lydd begins, 'Account of John Kempe and Thomas Holdernesse, Chamberlains of Lydd, in the time of Thomas Gros, bailiff there, from the feast of St Mary Magdalene in the eighteenth year of the reign of King Edward ɪᴠ until the same feast in the nineteenth year of the said lord king.'[2] When the saint's day and regnal years are converted into modern usage, these accounts run from 22 July 1478 until 22 July 1479, giving terminal dates for any entertainment expenses during that year. Since the borough chamberlains or treasurers rendered up their accounts at an annual audit day, before handing over the finances to their successors, expenses rarely ran over from one year to the next. If unpaid bills were carried over, they were clearly identified, as illustrated by this payment for entertainment in the 1495–6 Canterbury chamberlains' accounts: 'Item sol*utum* Edwardo Bolney nup*er* Maiori *pro* histrionib*us* do*m*ini Regis *pro* annis ix & x° R*egis* nunc xiiij s. iiij d.' Although Edward Bolney paid these players while serving two terms as mayor between 29 September 1493 and 29 September 1495, he was not reimbursed by the town chamberlain until the 1495–6 accounting year. For almost all payments, however, the beginning and end of a town's accounting year give the terminal dates for the dramatic performance.

The exact date of a performance within these terminal dates usually remains unknown. A typical entry in the chamberlains' accounts, such as 'Item paid in reward to the king's players vj s. viij d.,' can refer to a performance given any time during the town's accounting year. Not even the order of payments gives reliable clues. Players were often paid by the mayor or one of the jurats, who were then reimbursed by the chamberlain at a later date. Some chamberlains seem to have paid bills in weekly or fortnightly batches, for marginal dates in the rough accounts often seem to refer to blocks of payments. Thus the payment date most likely differs from the performance date. Occasionally, individual payments are dated by saint's day or festival day, such as 'Item dat*um* istrionib*us* die passion*is* *sancti* thom*e* mart*iris* vj s. viij d.' (see p 39), or by a specific date, such as 'Item payd to the quenes players the 27 of marche 1588 xx s.' (see p 220). Even here it is difficult to tell whether the date refers to the date of performance, the date of payment, or to both.

Although the accounting year, then, represented the primary unit of dating, not all accounting years were equal. Throughout Kent the beginning of the borough, parish, and monastic fiscal year ranged from February to December. Hythe began its year on Candlemas (2 February), New Romney on Annunciation Day (25 March), Lydd after 1477 on the feast of St Mary Magdalene (22 July), Dover and Folkestone on the feast of the Nativity of St Mary the Virgin (8 September), Canterbury and Faversham on Michaelmas (29 September), Maidstone on All Saints' (1 November) or All Souls' (2 November), Fordwich on the Monday after St Andrew's Day (1 December–7 December), and Sandwich usually on the Thursday after St Andrew's Day (1 December–7 December). In any given accounting year only the two months of December and January overlapped in all the boroughs throughout the county, making all dramatic activity in a given year in Kent difficult or even impossible to determine. The most common terminal dates, however, were Michaelmas to Michaelmas, appearing in many monastic and parish accounts as well as in the boroughs of Canterbury and Faversham. In the records that follow, then, an accounting year running from Michaelmas to Michaelmas is assumed unless different initial and terminal dates are given in editorial parentheses following the folio, page, or membrane number. When parish or guild accounts followed a different accounting year than that followed by the borough accounts, they have been sorted under the civic year and the actual dates of the account term have been given in the subheading.

All regnal years, saints' days, or dates of moveable feasts in account headings have been converted into modern usage. For reference purposes dates of all fixed festivals mentioned in the Records are listed in Appendix 5; dates of moveable feasts are identified in the footnotes. When documents do give day, month, and year, they almost always follow the practice, which continued to be used in England much later than 1642, of beginning the new year on 25 March, Annunciation Day, rather than on 1 January. This means, for example, that records dated 1 January–24 March 1579 in the original manuscripts should be dated 1 January–24 March 1580 according to modern usage. A court case that began on 20 March 1579 and continued until 27 March 1580 really lasted only one week. To avoid confusion in the editorial apparatus and in the headings in the Records, dates between 1 January and 24 March indicate both the contemporary and modern usage by a slash date. For example, when the minstrel John Collyar was presented in the archdeacon's court for playing in Bredgar during service time, the transcription includes court proceedings on 26 January 1579 and 9 February 1579 but the date in the heading reads 1579/80.

Editorial Conventions

The transcriptions of documents appear with a minimum of editorial interpretation. The layout of the documents generally follows that of the manuscripts in the placement of headings, marginalia, and columns, except for lineation in prose texts and the shifting of right marginalia in the manuscripts to the left margin in the transcription where it has been marked by the symbol ®. The text of the documents also follows that of the manuscripts even when the chances of some sort of scribal error are high. Editorial corrections are given in footnotes, except for the frequent correction of the wrong number of minims in Latin text where the corrected text is printed and the error noted in a footnote. The small number of transcriptions from the Halliwell-Phillipps scrapbooks for Folkestone and New Romney have not preserved accidental features that resulted from the trimming of the notebook page or his underlining of the abbreviations 's.' and 'd.' In transcription of manuscript sources the original orthography, word division, and punctuation have been retained. Insofar as possible, initial majuscules have been rendered as upper-case letters and minuscules as lower-case, but when it was unclear whether majuscule or minuscule was intended, a lower-case letter has been used. Capital 'I' and 'J' are not distinguished unless a printed source is being followed. 'ff' is retained for 'F.' Raised letters are silently lowered except after numbers, as in 'xo' or 'xxti.' All other inserted material is enclosed between ⌈ ⌉ if written above the line and between ⌊ ⌋ if written below. Square brackets ([ ]) enclose material cancelled in the original. Angle brackets (⟨ ⟩) indicate damaged or illegible text, with the number of enclosed dots showing the number of letters omitted. Where there is extensive damage, the matter is discussed in an endnote. Text in different handwriting from that of the rest of the text is enclosed in bubbles (° °). Space left blank by a clerk for matter that has not been supplied is indicated by *(blank)*.

Abbreviations have usually been expanded in italics. When a printed or manuscript text uses italics or any other special lettering, it is replaced by roman type. The abbreviation 'l' is expanded as '*lord*' when it clearly functions as a particular clerk's standard abbreviation. The abbreviation 'coem' for the Latin word '*commun*em' was often also used by clerks for the English word '*commen*.' In such cases the final 'm' has been silently changed to 'n.' Abbreviations whose meanings are obvious to the modern reader, such as 'Mr' or 'viz,' or which stand for sums of money, such as 'li.,' 's.,' 'd.,' 'ob.,' and 'qa.,' have not been expanded. Expansion of abbreviations that requires unwarranted editorial guessing has been avoided. For example, when payments are made to 'ministrall'' with no indication of whether the form is singular or plural, the conventional apostrophe replaces expansion. Although this problem is more common in Latin records, it is occasionally also encountered in some of the early Dover and Lydd accounts in English.

Manuscript punctuation has been preserved when the mark is still in use. Virgules are printed as slashes (/). Decorations, line fillers, and flourishes, such as the otiose superior letter 'a' in the deed of incorporation for the Canterbury Minstrels' guild, have been ignored. Braces are not usually reproduced except in those cases where their presence contributes to the sense of the record. In the few cases where such marks may be of some use in interpretation, an endnote describes the situation.

Notes

Historical Background

1 Hasted, *County of Kent*, vol 1, p 294.
2 Kentish writers as early as William Lambarde, *A Perambulation of Kent*, pp 200–1, have described these prominent geographical features of the county. For more recent examples see C.W. Chalklin, *Seventeenth-Century Kent: A Social and Economic History* (London, 1965), 7–10; Ronald Jessup, *South East England* (London, 1970), 15–23; and Alan Everitt, *Landscape and Community in England* (London, 1985), 66–9.
3 Peter Drewett, David Rudling, and Mark Gardiner, *The South East to AD 1000* (London and New York, 1988), 24–62; Jessup, *South East England*, pp 27–112.
4 Drewett, Rudling, and Gardiner, *The South East to AD 1000*, pp 63–177, especially 158–62.
5 Drewett, Rudling, and Gardiner, *The South East to AD 1000*, pp 181–6; Frank W. Jessup, *A History of Kent* (Chichester, 1974), 21–5.
6 For a general discussion of these Anglo-Saxon boroughs and a plan showing the coastline, see Tatton-Brown, 'The Towns of Kent,' pp 1–4.
7 Everitt, *Landscape and Community*, pp 61–91.
8 Everitt, *Landscape and Community*, pp 83–6.
9 Chalklin, *Seventeenth-Century Kent*, pp 23–4; Everitt, *Landscape and Community*, pp 113–14, 126.
10 Henry Hannen, 'An Account of a Map of Kent Dated 1596,' *Arch. Cant.* 30 (1914), 85–92, argues for an earlier date of 1576.
11 Everitt, *Landscape and Community*, p 115; C.W. Chalklin, 'South-East,' *The Cambridge Urban History of Britain*, vol 2, Peter Clark (ed) (Cambridge, 2000), 51–2; Chalklin, *Seventeenth-Century Kent*, p 24; John Patten, *English Towns 1500–1700* (Folkestone, 1978), 116.
12 This sixfold division of the county's geography and agriculture is developed by Joan Thirsk, 'Agriculture in Kent, 1540–1640,' *Early Modern Kent 1540–1640*, Zell (ed), pp 75–103. See also Joan Thirsk, 'The Farming Regions of England: South-Eastern England,' *The Agrarian History of England and Wales, vol 4, 1500–1640*, Joan Thirsk (ed) (Cambridge, 1967), 55–64; and Joan Thirsk, *The Rural Economy of England* (London, 1984), 225–6.

13 James M. Gibson, 'The 1566 Survey of the Kent Coast,' *Arch. Cant.* 112 (1994 for 1993), 341–53.

14 Chalklin, 'South-East,' pp 54–5; Chalklin, *Seventeenth-Century Kent*, pp 150–1.

15 Michael Zell, 'Landholding and the Land Market in Early Modern Kent,' *Early Modern Kent 1540–1640*, Zell (ed), p 73.

16 T.S. Willan, *The English Coasting Trade 1600–1750* (Manchester, 1938), 137–8.

17 Jane Andrewes, 'Industries in Kent, c. 1500–1640,' *Early Modern Kent 1540–1640*, Zell (ed), pp 105–39.

18 Thirsk, *The Rural Economy of England*, pp 218, 225; Mavis Mate, 'The Occupation of the Land: Kent and Sussex,' *The Agrarian History of England and Wales, vol 3, 1348–1500*, Edward Miller (ed) (Cambridge, 1991), 135; Andrewes, 'Industries in Kent, c. 1500–1640,' *Early Modern Kent 1540–1640*, Zell (ed), p 108; Ethel M. Hewitt, 'Fuller's Earth,' *VCH: Kent*, vol 3, pp 396–7.

19 Kenneth R. Andrews, *Trade, Plunder and Settlement: Maritime Enterprise and the Genesis of the British Empire, 1480–1630* (Cambridge, 1984), 6.

20 Andrewes, 'Industries in Kent, c. 1500–1640,' *Early Modern Kent 1540–1640*, Zell (ed), pp 110–13.

21 Andrewes, 'Industries in Kent, c. 1500–1640,' *Early Modern Kent 1540–1640*, Zell (ed), pp 115–24; Francis W. Cross, *History of the Walloon and Huguenot Church at Canterbury* (London, 1898), 183–206.

22 B.E. Supple, *Commercial Crisis and Change in England 1600–1642: A Study in the Instability of a Mercantile Economy* (Cambridge, 1959), 55, 130.

23 F.M. Stenton, *Anglo-Saxon England*, 2nd ed (Oxford, 1947), 291.

24 J.N.L. Myres, *The English Settlements* (Oxford, 1986), 124–5.

25 The Domesday assessment for Kent was stated in terms of yokes (fifty acres) and sulungs (four yokes or 200 acres). J.E.A. Jolliffe, *Pre-Feudal England: The Jutes* (Oxford, 1933; rpt London, 1962), 39–72, has demonstrated that the Kentish lathes consisted of one or more groups of eighty sulungs, ie, a geographical unit consisting of 16,000 acres.

26 J.E.A. Jolliffe, 'The Origin of the Hundred in Kent,' *Historical Essays in Honour of James Tait*, J.G. Edwards, V.H. Galbraith, and E.F. Jacob (eds) (Manchester, 1933), 155–68; Jolliffe, *Pre-Feudal England*, p 121.

27 Patricia Hyde and Michael Zell, 'Governing the County,' *Early Modern Kent 1540–1640*, Zell (ed), pp 11–12.

28 William Lambarde, *A Perambulation of Kent*, pp 31–5.

29 Lambarde, *A Perambulation of Kent*, pp 36–59.

30 Hyde and Zell, 'Governing the County,' *Early Modern Kent 1540–1640*, Zell (ed), pp 12–15. See also Hasted, *County of Kent*, vol 1, pp 177–206, for a list of sheriffs taken from the pipe rolls.

31 Hyde and Zell, 'Governing the County,' *Early Modern Kent 1540–1640*, Zell (ed), pp 23–5. See also Hasted, *County of Kent*, vol 1, pp 231–2, for the list of lords lieutenant.

32 J. Cave-Browne, 'Knights of the Shire for Kent from A.D. 1275 to A.D. 1831,' *Arch. Cant.*

21 (1895), 198–243; Hasted, *County of Kent*, vol 1, pp 235–47; S.J. Bindoff, *The House of Commons 1509–1558*, vol 1 (London, 1982), 112–18.

33   Hyde and Zell, 'Governing the County,' *Early Modern Kent 1540–1640*, Zell (ed), pp 25–8. For lists of MPs, see J.M. Russell, *The History of Maidstone* (Maidstone, 1881; rpt Rochester, 1978), 409; Frederick Francis Smith, *A History of Rochester* (Rochester, [1928]; rpt 1976), 499–501; John Bavington Jones, *Annals of Dover* (Dover, 1916), 365–83; John Stokes, 'The Barons of New Romney in Parliament,' *Arch. Cant.* 27 (1905), 44–63; Hasted, *County of Kent*, vol 8, pp 241–2, 452–3; vol 10, pp 172–4; and vol 11, pp 45–55; Bindoff, *The House of Commons 1509–1558*, vol 1, pp 112–18.

34   J.S. Cockburn, *A History of English Assizes 1558–1714* (Cambridge, 1972), 15–22.

35   Cockburn, *A History of English Assizes*, pp 23–8.

36   J.H. Gleason, *The Justices of the Peace in England 1558 to 1640* (Oxford, 1969), 8–30, 123–44; Michael L. Zell, 'Early Tudor JPs at Work,' *Arch. Cant.* 93 (1977), 125–43; Michael L. Zell, 'Kent's Elizabethan JPs at Work,' *Arch. Cant.* 119 (1999), 1–43.

37   For jurisdiction of the ecclesiastical courts, see Brian L. Woodcock, *Medieval Ecclesiastical Courts in the Diocese of Canterbury* (London, 1952), 6–29.

38   Woodcock, *Medieval Ecclesiastical Courts*, pp 68–71, 93–102.

39   Hasted, *County of Kent*, vol 1, pp 256–9, lists eighteen liberties in the county. See also Hyde and Zell, 'Governing the County,' *Early Modern Kent 1540–1640*, Zell (ed), pp 9–11.

40   This account is based on K.M.E. Murray, *The Constitutional History of the Cinque Ports* (Manchester, 1935) and Felix Hull (ed), *A Calendar of the White and Black Books of the Cinque Ports 1432–1955* (London, 1966), ix–xxxvii.

41   The name 'Brodhull,' sometimes spelled 'Brodhelle' or 'Brodhyll,' was in use for this court from the thirteenth century onward. During the reign of Henry VII it sometimes appeared as 'Brothereld' or 'Brotherweld' or 'Brotherheld.' The term 'Brotherhood' first appeared in 1577 and gradually replaced the older term 'Brodhull.' See Murray, *The Constitutional History of the Cinque Ports*, p 140.

42   Jessup, *A History of Kent*, p 75.

43   G.M. Livett, 'Ecclesiastical History: Part I (to death of Lanfranc),' *VCH: Kent*, vol 2, pp 1–2.

44   Bede, *Ecclesiastical History*, Book 1, chapters 25–6, in C. Plummer (ed), *Venerabilis Baedae Opera Historica*, vol 1 (Oxford, 1896), 44–7; Livett, 'Ecclesiastical History: Part I,' pp 2–10.

45   Nicholas Brooks, *The Early History of the Church of Canterbury* (Leicester, 1984), 8–11, 202.

46   M.E. Simkins, 'Ecclesiastical History: Part II,' *VCH: Kent*, vol 2, p 110.

47   R.C. Fowler, 'The Religious Houses of Kent,' *VCH: Kent*, vol 2, pp 112–13; see also the useful map facing p 112 showing both rural deaneries and religious houses according to the *Valor Ecclesiasticus* of 1535.

48   Michael Zell, 'The Coming of Religious Reform,' *Early Modern Kent 1540–1640*, Zell (ed), pp 196–200, 205–6; R.C. Fowler, 'The Abbey of Boxley,' *VCH: Kent*, vol 2, p 154.

49   Eamon Duffy, *The Stripping of the Altars: Traditional Religion in England c. 1400–c. 1580* (New Haven and London, 1992), 398–423.

50 Duffy, *The Stripping of the Altars*, pp 433–45; Zell, 'The Coming of Religious Reform,' *Early Modern Kent 1540–1640*, Zell (ed), pp 192–6, 200–4; Peter Clark, *English Provincial Society from the Reformation to the Revolution: Religion, Politics and Society in Kent 1500–1640* (Hassocks, 1977), 57–66.

51 C. Eveleigh Woodruff, 'Extracts from Original Documents Illustrating the Progress of the Reformation in Kent,' *Arch. Cant.* 31 (1915), 92–106; Michael Zell, 'The Establishment of a Protestant Church,' *Early Modern Kent 1540–1640*, Zell (ed), pp 207–15.

52 Woodruff, 'Extracts from Original Documents,' pp 106–10; Zell, 'The Establishment of a Protestant Church,' pp 224–6; Duffy, *The Stripping of the Altars*, pp 555–64.

53 Finn (ed), *Records of Lydd*, pp xxv–xxvi.

54 Zell, 'The Establishment of a Protestant Church,' pp 218–22; Clark, *English Provincial Society*, pp 87–97.

55 Zell, 'The Establishment of a Protestant Church,' pp 222–4.

56 Zell, 'The Establishment of a Protestant Church,' pp 226–32, 242–4.

57 Zell, 'The Establishment of a Protestant Church,' pp 234–5.

58 Clark, *English Provincial Society*, pp 152–63; Zell, 'The Establishment of a Protestant Church,' pp 236–7.

59 Clark, *English Provincial Society*, pp 162–6; Gibson, 'Stuart Players in Kent: Fact or Fiction?', pp 1–12.

60 Clark, *English Provincial Society*, pp 169–78.

61 Patrick Collinson, 'The Protestant Cathedral, 1541–1660,' *A History of Canterbury Cathedral*, Patrick Collinson, Nigel Ramsay, and Margaret Sparks (eds) (Oxford, 1995), 194–7.

62 Eilert Ekwall, *The Concise Oxford Dictionary of English Place-Names*, 4th ed (Oxford, 1960), 85; Tim Tatton-Brown, *Canterbury: History and Guide* (Stroud, 1994), 1, 16.

63 Tatton-Brown, *Canterbury: History and Guide*, pp 1–9; P. Bennett, 'The Topography of Roman Canterbury: A Brief Re-Assessment,' *Arch. Cant.* 100 (1984), 47–56.

64 Bede, *Ecclesiastical History*, Book 1, chapter 26, in Plummer (ed), *Venerabilis Baedae Opera Historica*, vol 1, pp 46–7.

65 Tatton-Brown, 'The Towns of Kent,' pp 5–10; Tatton-Brown, *Canterbury: History and Guide*, pp 10–15; Nicholas Brooks, 'The Anglo-Saxon Cathedral Community, 597–1070,' *A History of Canterbury Cathedral*, Patrick Collinson, Nigel Ramsay, and Margaret Sparks (eds) (Oxford, 1995), 1–37. For archaeological excavations of St Augustine's Abbey, see R.U. Potts, 'The Latest Excavations at St. Augustine's Abbey,' *Arch. Cant.* 35 (1921), 117–26; R.U. Potts, 'A Note on the Plan of St. Augustine's Abbey Church,' *Arch. Cant.* 40 (1928), 65–6; R.U. Potts, 'The Plan of St. Austin's Abbey, Canterbury,' *Arch. Cant.* 46 (1934), 179–94; and D. Sherlock and H. Woods, *St. Augustine's Abbey: Report on Excavations, 1960–78* (Maidstone, 1988).

66 William Urry, *Canterbury under the Angevin Kings* (London, 1967), 80–7.

67 Tim Tatton-Brown, 'The Anglo-Saxon Towns of Kent,' *Anglo-Saxon Settlements*, Della Hooke (ed) (Oxford, 1988), 228–9; Tatton-Brown, *Canterbury: History and Guide*, pp 16–21; Brooks, *The Early History of the Church of Canterbury*, pp 256–310; Brooks, 'The Anglo-Saxon Cathedral Community, 597–1070,' pp 26–37.

68   Philip Morgan (ed), *Domesday Book: Kent* (Chichester, 1983), 2a; Tatton-Brown, 'The Anglo-Saxon Towns of Kent,' *Anglo-Saxon Settlements*, Hooke (ed), p 229. H.C. Darby and Eila M.J. Campbell, *The Domesday Geography of South-East England* (Cambridge, 1962), 548, suggest a much lower population of 2,500; however, Brooks, *The Early History of the Church of Canterbury*, p 32, also places the population at the Conquest around 6,000, the number having fallen from a population of around 8,000 before the destruction of the city by the Vikings in 1011.

69   Urry, *Canterbury under the Angevin Kings*, pp 88–104.

70   See D.J. Keene, 'Suburban Growth,' *The Medieval Town: A Reader in English Urban History 1200–1540*, Richard Holt and Gervase Rosser (eds) (London and New York, 1990), 102, fig 2 for a map of Canterbury showing the built up areas in the twelfth century.

71   R.C. Fowler, 'The Priory of St. Gregory, Canterbury,' and 'The Hospital of St. John the Baptist, Northgate, Canterbury,' *VCH: Kent*, vol 2, pp 157–9, 211–12; Tatton-Brown, *Canterbury: History and Guide*, p 29.

72   R.C. Fowler, 'The Hospital of Harbledown,' *VCH: Kent*, vol 2, pp 219–20; Tatton-Brown, *Canterbury: History and Guide*, pp 30–1.

73   R.C. Fowler, 'The Priory of St. Sepulchre, Canterbury,' *VCH: Kent*, vol 2, pp 142–4; Tatton-Brown, *Canterbury: History and Guide*, p 31.

74   Tatton-Brown, *Canterbury: History and Guide*, pp 22–32; Urry, *Canterbury under the Angevin Kings*, pp 207–13.

75   Marcus Crouch, *Canterbury* (London, 1970), 72–85.

76   Jonathan Sumption, *Pilgrimage: An Image of Mediaeval Religion* (London, 1975), 122–3.

77   Tatton-Brown, *Canterbury: History and Guide*, pp 33–54; Sumption, *Pilgrimage*, p 150, maintains that the popularity of pilgrimage to Canterbury declined sharply after the middle of the thirteenth century, but this assertion is countered by the above statistics gathered by C. Eveleigh Woodruff, 'The Financial Aspect of the Cult of St. Thomas of Canterbury,' *Arch. Cant.* 44 (1932), 13–32.

78   A.G. Little, 'The Franciscan Friars of Canterbury,' and 'The Dominican Friars of Canterbury,' *VCH: Kent*, vol 2, pp 190–4, 177–80.

79   A.G. Little, 'The Austin Friars of Canterbury,' *VCH: Kent*, vol 2, pp 199–201.

80   Tatton-Brown, *Canterbury: History and Guide*, pp 40, 42.

81   Patten, *English Towns 1500–1700*, p 42. W.G. Hoskins, *Local History in England*, 3rd ed (London, 1984), 277, ranks Canterbury as fourteenth.

82   Hasted, *County of Kent*, vol 11, p 104n. Lambarde, *A Perambulation of Kent*, p 64, gives 27 July instead of 7 July and 29 December (Martyrdom of St Thomas Becket) instead of 28 December.

83   Hasted, *County of Kent*, vol 11, pp 9–29.

84   Woodruff, 'The Financial Aspect of the Cult of St. Thomas of Canterbury,' *Arch. Cant.* 44 (1932), 23–5.

85   Patten, *English Towns 1500–1700*, p 42. Hoskins, *Local History in England*, p 278, however, ranks Canterbury ninth in this list, a discrepancy due to how many of the

suburbs of the city are counted. See also Jacqueline Bower, 'Kent Towns, 1540–1640,' *Early Modern Kent 1540–1640*, Zell (ed), p 144, and Peter Clark and Paul Slack, *English Towns in Transition 1500–1700* (London, 1976), 161, for a map showing that the population had fallen and Canterbury was no longer one of the larger towns of 4,000 or above.

86 'Acte concernyng the Ryver in Caunterbury,' 6 Henry VIII, c. 17, *The Statutes of the Realm*, vol 3 (London, 1817), p 134.

87 Zell, 'The Coming of Religious Reform,' *Early Modern Kent 1540–1640*, Zell (ed), pp 196–200, 205–6.

88 R.C. Fowler, 'The Cathedral Priory of The Holy Trinity or Christ-Church, Canterbury,' *VCH: Kent*, vol 2, p 119; Collinson, 'The Protestant Cathedral, 1541–1660,' *A History of Canterbury Cathedral*, Patrick Collinson, Nigel Ramsay, and Margaret Sparks (eds), pp 159–62.

89 Tatton-Brown, *Canterbury: History and Guide*, pp 55–60.

90 C. Eveleigh Woodruff and William Danks, *Memorials of the Cathedral and Priory of Christ in Canterbury* (London, 1912), 301–3; Woodruff, 'Extracts from Original Documents Illustrating the Progress of the Reformation in Kent,' *Arch. Cant.* 31 (1915), 114–15.

91 Laura Hunt Yungblut, *Strangers Settled Here Amongst Us* (London, 1996), 89–90; Peter and Jennifer Clark, 'The Social Economy of the Canterbury Suburbs: The Evidence of the Census of 1563,' *Studies in Modern Kentish History*, Alec Detsicas and Nigel Yates (eds), Kent Archaeological Society (Maidstone, 1983), 66; Bower, 'Kent Towns, 1540–1640,' *Early Modern Kent 1540–1640*, Zell (ed), pp 145, 160; Chalklin, *Seventeenth-Century Kent*, pp 31–2.

92 Canon Puckle, 'Vestiges of Roman Dover,' *Arch. Cant.* 20 (1893), 128–36; Canon Puckle, 'The Ancient Fabric of the Church of St. Mary the Virgin, Dover,' *Arch. Cant.* 20 (1893), 119–27.

93 Tatton-Brown, 'The Towns of Kent,' pp 22–3; Tatton-Brown, 'The Anglo-Saxon Towns of Kent,' *Anglo-Saxon Settlements*, Hooke (ed), p 227.

94 Morgan (ed), *Domesday Book: Kent*, 1a–1d; Darby and Campbell, *The Doomesday Geography of South-East England*, p 546.

95 Murray, *The Constitutional History of the Cinque Ports*, p 234.

96 John Bavington Jones, *Annals of Dover* (Dover 1916), 225–47; Hasted, *County of Kent*, vol 9, p 513; Robert Tittler, *Architecture and Power: The Town Hall and the English Urban Community c. 1500–1640* (Oxford, 1991), 164.

97 Jones, *Annals of Dover*, pp 1–78; F.W. Hardman, 'Castleguard Service of Dover Castle,' *Arch. Cant.* 49 (1938), 97–8.

98 Jones, *Annals of Dover*, pp 79–140; Alec Hasenson, *The History of Dover Harbour* (London, 1980), 17–32; Alec Macdonald, 'Plans of Dover Harbour in the Sixteenth Century,' *Arch. Cant.* 49 (1938), 108–26.

99 Lambarde, *A Perambulation of Kent*, pp 62–3, 65; Hasted, *County of Kent*, vol 9, p 516.

100 Gibson, 'The 1566 Survey of the Kent Coast,' *Arch. Cant.* 112 (1994 for 1993), 346–7; Bower, 'Kent Towns, 1540–1640,' *Early Modern Kent 1540–1640*, Zell (ed), p 151.

101 Willan, *The English Coasting Trade 1600–1750*, pp 137–9.

102 Bower, 'Kent Towns, 1540–1640,' p 151; Chalklin, *Seventeenth-Century Kent*, p 30; Patten, *English Towns 1500–1700*, pp 42, 106.

103 F.C. Plumptre, 'Some Account of the Remains of the Priory of St. Martin's and the Church of St. Martin-Le-Grand, at Dover,' *Arch. Cant.* 4 (1861), 1–26 (including plan of priory facing p 26). See also Charles Reginald Haines, *Dover Priory* (Cambridge, 1930), 111; Jones, *Annals of Dover*, pp 169–80; and R.C. Fowler, 'The Priory of Dover,' *VCH: Kent*, vol 2, pp 133–7. Gordon Ward, 'Saxon Abbots of Dover and Reculver,' *Arch. Cant.* 59 (1946), 19–28, offers an alternative view of the early history of the priory, arguing from the evidence of Anglo-Saxon charters that St Martin's was a monastery with abbots from at least 761 to about 890 and a college of canons only from sometime before 1017.

104 Edward Knocker, 'On the Municipal Records of Dover,' *Arch. Cant.* 10 (1876), cxxxv; R.C. Fowler, 'The Hospital of St. Mary, Dover,' *VCH: Kent*, vol 2, pp 217–19.

105 W.H. St. John Hope, 'On the Praemonstratensian Abbey of St. Radegund, Bradsole in Polton, near Dover,' *Arch. Cant.* 14 (1882), 140–52 (includes plans); and S.E. Winbolt, 'St. Radegund's Abbey, Dover,' *Arch. Cant.* 43 (1931), 187–98.

106 Tatton-Brown, 'The Anglo-Saxon Towns of Kent,' *Anglo-Saxon Settlements*, Hooke (ed), pp 227–8; Tatton-Brown, 'The Towns of Kent,' pp 22–3; G. Gilbert Scott, 'The Church on the Castle Hill, Dover,' *Arch. Cant.* 5 (1863), 1–18 (includes plan facing p 1).

107 W.A. Scott Robertson, 'The Old Church of St. Martin, at Dover,' *Arch. Cant.* 20 (1893), 297. See also F.C. Plumptre, 'Some Account of the Remains of the Priory of St. Martin's, and the Church of St. Martin-Le-Grand, at Dover,' *Arch. Cant.* 4 (1861), 21–6.

108 John Leland, Collectanea, Bodl.: MS. Top. gen. c. 3, p 128.

109 Jones, *Annals of Dover*, p 184.

110 Robertson, 'The Old Church of St. Martin, at Dover,' *Arch. Cant.* 20 (1893), pp 298–9.

111 Haines, *Dover Priory*, p 25; Jones, *Annals of Dover*, pp 216, 221; Hasted, *County of Kent*, vol 9, pp 540–1; S.P.H. Statham, *Dover Charters and Other Documents in the Possession of the Corporation of Dover* (London, 1902), 400–1.

112 John Leland, Collectanea, Bodl.: MS. Top. gen. c. 3, p 144.

113 F.F. Giraud, 'Faversham Town Charters,' *Arch. Cant.* 9 (1874), lxii.

114 Morgan (ed), *Domesday Book: Kent*, 2d. See also Tatton-Brown, 'The Towns of Kent,' pp 28–32.

115 R.C. Fowler, 'The Abbey of Faversham,' *VCH: Kent*, vol 2, pp 137–41.

116 See Murray, *The Constitutional History of the Cinque Ports*, p 236, and Giraud, 'Faversham Town Charters,' *Arch. Cant.* 9 (1874), lxiv, for the 1252 charter. F.F. Giraud, 'The Service of Shipping of the Barons of Faversham,' *Arch. Cant.* 21 (1895), 273–82, describes the royal demands for ship service from the thirteenth century to the defence against the Spanish Armada and the exploits of Faversham sea captains. A later article, F.F. Giraud, 'Cinque Ports: Notes from Minute Books of the Corporation of Faversham,' *Arch. Cant.* 28 (1909), 28–74, discusses the summons to meetings of the General Brotherhood, assessments for ship money, and other administrative payments from 1570 to 1740.

117 Giraud, 'Faversham Town Charters,' *Arch. Cant.* 9 (1874), lxv–lxvi.

118   For discussion of the abbey and its disputes with the town, see Edward Jacob, *The History of the Town and Port of Faversham* (London, 1774; rpt Sheerness, 1974), 8–14; Giraud, 'Faversham Town Charters,' *Arch. Cant.* 9 (1874), lxiii; F.F. Giraud, 'Faversham Town Accounts, Anno 33 Edw. i,' *Arch. Cant.* 10 (1876), 221–32; and Francis F. Giraud, 'Municipal Archives of Faversham, A.D. 1304–24,' *Arch. Cant.* 14 (1882), 186–7.

119   Giraud, 'Faversham Town Charters,' *Arch. Cant.* 9 (1874), lxviii; Jacob, *History of Faversham*, pp 69–74; Martin Weinbaum, *British Borough Charters 1307–1660* (Cambridge, 1943).

120   *Calendar of the Patent Rolls, Elizabeth i*, vol 7 (London, 1982), 202–3 (item 1411); Jacob, *History of Faversham*, pp 53–9.

121   Jacob, *History of Faversham*, pp 37–8. See R.C. Fowler, 'The Hospital of Ospringe,' *VCH: Kent*, vol 2, pp 222–4; Charles H. Drake, 'The Hospital of St. Mary Ospringe Commonly Called Maison Dieu,' *Arch. Cant.* 30 (1914), 35–78.

122   Jacob, *History of Faversham*, pp 39–52.

123   Tittler, *Architecture and Power*, p 55; Jacob, *History of Faversham*, pp 60–3.

124   Lambarde, *A Perambulation of Kent*, p 64.

125   Giraud, 'Faversham Town Charters,' *Arch. Cant.* 9 (1874), lxviii–lxix; Jacob, *History of Faversham*, pp 89–90.

126   Jacob, *History of Faversham*, pp 94–7, 75–88.

127   Gibson, 'The 1566 Survey of the Kent Coast,' *Arch. Cant.* 112 (1994 for 1993), 349.

128   Willan, *The English Coasting Trade 1600–1750*, pp 137–9; Thirsk, 'Agriculture in Kent, 1540–1640,' *Early Modern Kent 1540–1640*, Zell (ed), pp 101–2.

129   Peter Clark and Jean Hosking, *Population Estimates of English Small Towns 1550–1851*, rev ed (Leicester, 1993), 77. Chalklin, *Seventeenth-Century Kent*, p 30, gives lower figures of about 1,000 in 1570 to about 1,500 in 1670; Patten, *English Towns 1500–1700*, p 106, estimates between 1,000 and 2,500 in 1649–50.

130   *Holinshed's Chronicles of England, Scotland, and Ireland*, vol 3 (London, 1808; rpt New York, 1965), 1024–31; Hugh Macdonald (ed), *Arden of Feversham, 1592*, Malone Society Reprints (Oxford, 1947).

131   C.H. Bishop, *Folkestone: The Story of a Town* (London, 1973), 13–17. See also R.C. Jenkins, 'On a Roman Hypocaust Discovered at Folkestone A.D. 1875,' *Arch. Cant.* 10 (1876), 173–7; S.E. Winbolt, 'Roman Villa, Folkestone,' *Arch. Cant.* 37 (1925), 209–10; S.E. Winbolt, *Roman Folkestone* (London, 1925); S.E. Rigold, 'Roman Folkestone Reconsidered,' *Arch. Cant.* 87 (1972), 31–41.

132   Bishop, *Folkestone: The Story of a Town*, pp 21–4, 39–41; W.A. Scott Robertson, 'Church of St. Mary and St. Eanswith, Folkestone,' *Arch. Cant.* 10 (1876), liv–lxviii; W.L. Rutton. 'Folkestone Parish Church,' *Arch. Cant.* 28 (1909), 1–9; R.C. Fowler, 'The Priory of Folkestone,' *VCH: Kent*, vol 2, pp 236–8.

133   W.A. Scott Robertson, 'Mediaeval Folkestone,' *Arch. Cant.* 10 (1876), cvi, cviii–cix.

134   Hasted, *County of Kent*, vol 8, pp 176–7; Bishop, *Folkestone: The Story of a Town*, p 34.

135   Bishop, *Folkestone: The Story of a Town*, p 34.

136   Robertson, 'Mediaeval Folkestone,' *Arch. Cant.* 10 (1876), cix.

137   Bishop, *Folkestone: The Story of a Town*, pp 35, 42; S.J. Mackie, *A Descriptive and Historical Account of Folkestone and Its Neighbourhood* (Folkestone and London, 1856), 34–5.

138   Morgan (ed), *Domesday Book: Kent*, 9b–9c; Bishop, *Folkestone: The Story of a Town*, pp 29–30.

139   Gibson, 'The 1566 Survey of the Kent Coast,' *Arch. Cant.* 112 (1994 for 1993), 346.

140   Clark and Hosking, *Population Estimates of English Small Towns 1550–1851*, p 77. Chalklin, *Seventeenth-Century Kent*, p 30, suggests a static population during that period of about 500.

141   Tatton-Brown, 'The Anglo-Saxon Towns of Kent,' *Anglo-Saxon Settlements*, Hooke (ed), p 215.

142   Tatton-Brown, 'The Anglo-Saxon Towns of Kent,' *Anglo-Saxon Settlements*, Hooke (ed), p 229. See also Morgan (ed), *Domesday Book: Kent*, 12b; and Tatton-Brown, 'The Towns of Kent,' pp 16–22.

143   Darby and Campbell, *The Domesday Geography of South-East England*, p 554.

144   Anne Roper, 'Fordwich and the Cinque Ports,' *Fordwich: The Lost Port*, Kinn Hamilton McIntosh (ed) (Canterbury, 1975), 157; see also Woodruff, *A History of the Town and Port of Fordwich*, pp 32–5.

145   C. Eveleigh Woodruff, 'Fordwich Municipal Records,' *Arch. Cant.* 18 (1889), 81.

146   Woodruff, *A History of the Town and Port of Fordwich*, pp 8–13, 36.

147   Woodruff, *A History of the Town and Port of Fordwich*, p 53; Murray, *The Constitutional History of the Cinque Ports*, pp 236–9.

148   Woodruff, *A History of the Town and Port of Fordwich*, pp 12n, 52–8.

149   Woodruff, *A History of the Town and Port of Fordwich*, pp 37–8, 201–9.

150   Clark and Hosking, *Population Estimates of English Small Towns 1550–1851*, p 77.

151   In a series of articles Gordon Ward shows that the River Limen appears in Anglo-Saxon charters for Romney Marsh as late as the ninth and tenth centuries: Gordon Ward, 'Sand Tunes Boc,' *Arch. Cant.* 43 (1931), 39–47; 'The River Limen at Ruckinge,' *Arch. Cant.* 45 (1933), 129–32; and 'The Saxon Charters of Burmarsh,' *Arch. Cant.* 45 (1933), 133–41.

152   Tatton-Brown, 'The Anglo-Saxon Towns of Kent,' *Anglo-Saxon Settlements*, Hooke (ed), p 226; Tatton-Brown, 'The Towns of Kent,' pp 24–6; Maurice Beresford, *New Towns of the Middle Ages: Town Plantation in England, Wales and Gascony*, 2nd ed (Gloucester, 1988), 457; Duncan Forbes, *Hythe Haven: The Story of the Town and Cinque Port of Hythe* (Hythe, 1982), 13–35.

153   Morgan (ed), *Domesday Book: Kent*, 4a, 4c; Darby and Campbell, *The Domesday Geography of South-East England*, p 553.

154   Murray, *The Constitutional History of the Cinque Ports*, pp 233–4, 237–9.

155   Hasted, *County of Kent*, vol 8, p 239.

156   John Leland, Collectanea, Bodl.: MS. Top. gen. c. 3, p 141.

157   William Camden, *Britain, or a Chorographicall Description of the Most Flourishing Kingdomes, England, Scotland, and Ireland…Written first in Latine by William Camden… Translated newly into English by Philemon Holland* (London, 1637), 349.

158   Gibson, 'The 1566 Survey of the Kent Coast,' *Arch. Cant.* 112 (1994 for 1993), 346.

159   See A.J.F. Dulley, 'Four Kent Towns at the End of the Middle Ages,' *Arch. Cant.* 81 (1966), 99, 104–8, for analysis of the surviving Hythe wills prior to 1558, as transcribed by Arthur Hussey in 'Hythe Wills: First Part. A to F,' *Arch. Cant.* 49 (1938), 127–56; 'Hythe Wills: Second Part. G to M,' *Arch. Cant.* 50 (1939), 87–121; 'Hythe Wills: Third Part and Final Part,' *Arch. Cant.* 51 (1940 for 1939), 27–65.

160   Clark and Hosking, *Population Estimates of English Small Towns 1550–1851*, p 79. Chalklin, *Seventeenth-Century Kent*, p 30, however, estimates 700–800 in 1570 falling to 350–450 in 1670.

161   Herbert D. Dale, *St. Leonard's Church Hythe from Its Foundation with Some Account of the Life and Customs of the Town of Hythe from Ancient Sources* (London, 1931), 7–8; Herbert D. Dale, 'Notes on Hythe Church,' *Arch. Cant.* 30 (1914), 263–4. A court case in 1625 refers to the 'common hall or town hall' (PRO: E.134/19 Jac. I/mic. 25, Defendants Interrogatories, no. 5); however, the location of this hall is unknown (this reference was provided by Robert Tittler).

162   Dale, 'Notes on Hythe Church,' *Arch. Cant.* 30 (1914), 263–72.

163   G.M. Livett, 'The Architectural History of the Church of St. Leonard, Hythe,' *Arch. Cant.* 30 (1914), 307; W.A. Scott Robertson, 'St. Leonard's Church, Hythe,' *Arch. Cant.* 18 (1889), 403–20.

164   Gordon Ward, 'Saxon Lydd,' *Arch. Cant.* 43 (1931), 29–37; see also Grevile Mairis Livett, 'Lydd Church,' *Arch. Cant.* 42 (1930), 87–92.

165   F.C. Elliston Erwood, 'Notes on the Churches of Romney Marsh in the County of Kent, 1923,' *Arch. Cant.* 37 (1925), 177–90; Livett, 'Lydd Church,' *Arch. Cant.* 42 (1930), 72–87. For a summary of evidence, see Tatton-Brown, 'Church Building on Romney Marsh in the Later Middle Ages,' *Arch. Cant.* 107 (1990 for 1989), 254.

166   Morgan (ed), *Domesday Book: Kent*, 4c.

167   A facsimile of this charter forms the frontispiece in Arthur Finn (ed), *Records of Lydd* (Ashford, 1911), and a translation appears on pp xxix–xxxii.

168   John Leland, Collectanea, Bodl.: MS. Top. gen. c. 3, p 142.

169   Lambarde, *A Perambulation of Kent*, p 64; Hasted, *County of Kent*, vol 8, p 422; Clark and Hosking, *Population Estimates of English Small Towns 1550–1851*, p 79; Murray, *Constitutional History of the Cinque Ports*, pp 240–1.

170   W.A. Scott Robertson, 'Churches in Romney Marsh,' *Arch. Cant.* 13 (1880), 427–3; Arthur Hussey, 'Further Notes from Kentish Wills,' *Arch. Cant.* 31 (1915), 29–30.

171   Peter Clark and Lyn Murfin, *The History of Maidstone: The Making of a Modern County Town* (Stroud, 1995), 9–14; D.B. Kelly, 'The Mount Roman Villa, Maidstone,' *Arch. Cant.* 110 (1993 for 1992), 177–235. For earlier archaeological investigations, see Beale Poste, 'Observations on the Supposed Site of Ancient Roman Maidstone,' *Arch. Cant.* 1 (1858), 154–75; C. Roach Smith, 'On a Roman Villa Near Maidstone,' *Arch. Cant.* 10 (1876), 163–72; and W.A. Scott Robertson, 'Traces of Roman Occupation in and near Maidstone,' *Arch. Cant.* 15 (1883), 68–88.

172   Morgan (ed), *Domesday Book: Kent*, 3b; Clark and Murfin, *The History of Maidstone*, p 20.

173   Clark and Murfin, *The History of Maidstone*, pp 16, 20–1.

174   Lambarde, *A Perambulation of Kent*, pp 50–4.

175   Russell, *History of Maidstone*, pp 13–16; Clark and Murfin, *The History of Maidstone*, p 22.

176   Clark and Murfin, *The History of Maidstone*, p 22.

177   Clark and Murfin, *The History of Maidstone*, pp 28–31.

178   Clark and Murfin, *The History of Maidstone*, pp 26–7.

179   *Calendar of Patent Rolls, Richard II*, vol 5 (London, 1905), 635; Clark and Murfin, *The History of Maidstone*, pp 24–6; R.C. Fowler, 'The College of Maidstone,' *VCH: Kent*, vol 2, pp 232–3.

180   Russell, *History of Maidstone*, pp 162–71; Clark and Murfin, *The History of Maidstone*, pp 35–7.

181   Russell, *History of Maidstone*, pp 183–95; Clark and Murfin, *The History of Maidstone*, pp 32, 38, 56–7; Zell, 'The Establishment of a Protestant Church,' *Early Modern Kent 1540–1640*, Zell (ed), pp 206–44; Bindoff, *The House of Commons 1509–1558*, vol 1 (London, 1982), 116–17.

182   Tittler, *Architecture and Power*, pp 18, 164.

183   Clark and Murfin, *The History of Maidstone*, p 44, give the dates of the June fair as 'Midsummer (19–21 June).' The 1549 Maidstone charter (*Calendar of Patent Rolls, Edward VI*, vol 2 (London, 1924), pp 174–6), however, says the eve to the morrow of St Edmund. Lambarde, *A Perambulation of Kent*, p 64, lists this as 9 June, the Translation of St Edmund, making the dates of the fair 8–10 June.

184   Russell, *History of Maidstone*, pp 307–31; Clark and Murfin, *The History of Maidstone*, pp 43–52.

185   Bower, 'Kent Towns, 1540–1640,' *Early Modern Kent 1540–1640*, Zell (ed), pp 150–1. Clark and Murfin, *The History of Maidstone*, p 42, using a slightly lower multiplier for these sixteenth-century parish returns suggest a population of 1,900 in 1548 rising in 1557 to 2,100 in the town and 2,330 in the parish. Chalklin, *Seventeenth-Century Kent*, pp 30–1, reports only a general increase from about 2,000 in 1570 to over 3,000 in 1670.

186   R.D. Green, *Soils of Romney Marsh* (Harpenden, 1968) remains the standard study of the geology of the marsh. See also C.J. Gilbert, 'The Evolution of Romney Marsh,' *Arch. Cant.* 45 (1933), 246–72, who has identified three successive periods of depression of the earth's crust interspersed by two upheavals extending from the paleolithic period to the Roman and Saxon periods, resulting in submerged forests, shingle banks, and extensive alluvial deposits.

187   The existence of this river channel is demonstrated from the evidence of Anglo-Saxon charters by Gordon Ward in a series of articles: 'Sand Tunes Boc,' *Arch. Cant.* 43 (1931), 39–47; 'The River Limen at Ruckinge,' *Arch. Cant.* 45 (1933), 129–32; and 'The Saxon Charters of Burmarsh,' *Arch. Cant.* 45 (1933), 133–41; and from geological evidence by Green, *Soils of Romney Marsh*, pp 35–7. Nicholas Brooks, 'Romney Marsh in the Early Middle Ages,' *Romney Marsh: Evolution, Occupation, Reclamation*, Jill Eddison and Christopher Green (eds) (Oxford, 1988), 95–8, offers a useful summary.

188   Gordon Ward, 'The Saxon History of the Town and Port of Romney,' *Arch. Cant.* 65

(1953 for 1952), 12–24, demonstrates the existence of this channel from historical sources, but Green, *Soils of Romney Marsh*, pp 33–4, disputes that another branch of the Rother flowed through Walland Marsh to reach Romney from the southwest. Recent re-evaluations support Ward's interpretation; see Brooks, 'Romney Marsh in the Early Middle Ages,' *Romney Marsh: Evolution, Occupation, Reclamation*, Eddison and Green (eds), pp 98–102, and Tim Tatton-Brown, 'The Topography of the Walland Marsh Area between the Eleventh and Thirteenth Centuries,' *Romney Marsh: Evolution, Occupation, Reclamation*, Eddison and Green (eds), pp 105–11.

189   Green, *Soils of Romney Marsh*, p 40; Tatton-Brown, 'The Towns of Kent,' p 26.

190   Tatton-Brown, 'The Topography of the Walland Marsh Area between the Eleventh and Thirteenth Centuries,' *Romney Marsh: Evolution, Occupation, Reclamation*, Eddison and Green (eds), pp 105–11. W.V. Rendel, 'Changes in the Course of the Rother,' *Arch. Cant.* 77 (1963 for 1962), 63–76, describes further changes to the course of the River Rother by the commissions of sewers during the early seventeenth century.

191   Described by Matthew Paris, Holinshed, and Camden, as quoted by Margaret Brentnall, *The Cinque Ports and Romney Marsh* (London, 1972), 255–7.

192   *Calendar of the Patent Rolls, Henry III*, vol 4 (London, 1908), 635. Nineteenth-century writers assumed that the Romans had constructed the Rhee Wall in order to reclaim the marshland to the east. See, for example, Robert Furley, 'An Outline of the History of Romney Marsh,' *Arch. Cant.* 13 (1880), 181–2, and W.A. Scott Robertson, 'The Cinque Port Liberty of Romney,' *Arch. Cant.* 13 (1880), 271. Gordon Ward, 'The Saxon History of the Town and Port of Romney,' *Arch. Cant.* 65 (1953 for 1952), 15, however, demonstrated that the Anglo-Saxon Romney charters did not mention the Rhee Wall; and Green, *Soils of Romney Marsh*, pp 37–42, has further demonstrated from geological evidence that the Rhee Wall was constructed much later, partly before and partly after the storms of the thirteenth century. See also Robertson, 'Churches in Romney Marsh,' *Arch. Cant.* 13 (1880), 418, for evidence of construction of a sluice gate north of Romney at Snargate in 1254; and Tatton-Brown, 'The Topography of the Walland Marsh Area between the Eleventh and Thirteenth Centuries,' *Romney Marsh: Evolution, Occupation, Reclamation*, Eddison and Green (eds), p 108.

193   E.W. Parkin, 'The Ancient Buildings of New Romney,' *Arch. Cant.* 88 (1973), 117–28, has shown two categories of ancient buildings in New Romney: medieval timber-framed houses built at the present ground level and a second group, including the parish church of St Nicholas, standing on the lower pre-1287 level.

194   Robertson, 'The Cinque Port Liberty of Romney,' *Arch. Cant.* 13 (1880), 273.

195   For a summary of the documentary evidence, see Mark Gardiner, 'Old Romney: An Examination of the Evidence for a Lost Saxo-Norman Port,' *Arch. Cant.* 114 (1995 for 1994), 339–44.

196   Gordon Ward, 'The Saxon History of the Town and Port of Romney,' *Arch. Cant.* 65 (1953 for 1952), 25, gives a photographic reproduction and translation of the charter. See also R.C. Fowler, 'The Abbey of Lyminge,' *VCH: Kent*, vol 2, p 146.

197   Ekwall, *Concise Oxford Dictionary of English Place-Names*, p 392; see also Ward,

'The Saxon History of the Town and Port of Romney,' *Arch. Cant.* 65 (1953 for 1952), 18.

198 Ward, 'The Saxon History of the Town and Port of Romney,' *Arch. Cant.* 65 (1953 for 1952), 21–2. See also the note by S.E. Rigold in Parkin, 'The Ancient Buildings of New Romney,' *Arch. Cant.* 88 (1973), 118, note 7.

199 Morgan (ed), *Domesday Book: Kent*, 4a, 4c, 10d, 11a; Darby and Campbell, *The Domesday Geography of South-East England*, p 553.

200 W.A. Scott Robertson, 'Romney, Old and New,' *Arch. Cant.* 13 (1880), 349–73; Tatton-Brown, 'The Topography of the Walland Marsh Area between the Eleventh and Thirteenth Centuries,' *Romney Marsh: Evolution, Occupation, Reclamation*, Eddison and Green (eds), p 106; Mark Gardiner, 'Old Romney: An Examination of the Evidence for a Lost Saxo-Norman Port,' *Arch. Cant.* 114 (1995 for 1994), 339–44.

201 This theory has recently been revived. Beresford, *New Towns of the Middle Ages*, p 459, for example, without much support states that the town was re-sited sometime before 960. Tatton-Brown, 'The Towns of Kent,' pp 26–7, first suggested a date of 1000 for the development of a new town under the direction of the archbishop, a date coinciding with the establishment of the mint. In later articles – 'The Anglo-Saxon Towns of Kent,' *Anglo-Saxon Settlements*, Hooke (ed), pp 229–31; 'Church Building on Romney Marsh in the Later Middle Ages,' *Arch. Cant.* 107 (1990 for 1989), 255; and 'The Topography of the Walland Marsh Area between the Eleventh and Thirteenth Centuries,' *Romney Marsh: Evolution, Occupation, Reclamation*, Eddison and Green (eds), p 106 – he has revised this date, arguing that the Saxon port and mint were located at Old Romney, the new town not having been founded until the twelfth century when St Nicholas' Church was built and the distinction between old and new began to be made in the historical records. In the nineteenth century W.A. Scott Robertson disputed the theory of relocation on historical evidence in 'Romney, Old and New,' *Arch. Cant.* 13 (1880), 349–73, and on archaeological evidence in 'Churches in Romney Marsh,' *Arch. Cant.* 13 (1880), 408–87. More recently, reviewing both the documentary and archaeological evidence, Mark Gardiner, 'Old Romney: An Examination of the Evidence for a Lost Saxo-Norman Port,' *Arch. Cant.* 114 (1995 for 1994), 329–45, also argues against the relocation of the town.

202 Tatton-Brown, 'Church Building on Romney Marsh in the Later Middle Ages,' *Arch. Cant.* 107 (1990 for 1989), 253–65, gives a useful summary of the evidence.

203 See Robertson, 'Churches in Romney Marsh,' *Arch. Cant.* 13 (1880), 408–18 for Old Romney Church (St Clement's) and 466–79 for St Nicholas', New Romney. Tatton-Brown, 'Church Building on Romney Marsh in the Later Middle Ages,' *Arch. Cant.* 107 (1990 for 1989), 255, while acknowledging that there is no evidence, suggests an eleventh-century date for St Clement's.

204 W. A. Scott Robertson, 'Destroyed Churches of New Romney,' *Arch. Cant.* 13 (1880), 237–45, 249; C. Everleigh Woodruff, 'Some Early Kentish Wills,' *Arch. Cant.* 46 (1934), 27–30; J. Bradshaw, 'Investigations and Excavations during the Year: Ashford Area,' *Arch. Cant.* 84 (1970 for 1969), 235; J. Bradshaw, 'Investigations and Excavations during the

Year: Ashford Area,' *Arch. Cant.* 85 (1971 for 1970), 179; Mark Gardiner, 'Old Romney: An Examination of the Evidence for a Lost Saxo-Norman Port,' *Arch. Cant.* 114 (1995 for 1994), 330–8.

205   Murray (ed), *Register of Daniel Rough*, p xxxix.

206   John Leland, Collectanea, Bodl.: MS. Top. gen. c. 3, p 142.

207   Clark and Hosking, *Population Estimates of English Small Towns 1550–1851*, p 79. This figure, however, may be too low. A list of Old Romney and New Romney heads of households assessed for a tax levied on 1 April 1559 (EKAC: NR/FAc 6, ff 57v–8v) includes 102 names, suggesting a population closer to 400.

208   Robertson, 'Romney, Old and New,' *Arch. Cant.* 13 (1880), 372–3.

209   Edward Bacheler Walker, 'The Town and Port of New Romney,' *Arch. Cant.* 13 (1880), 205.

210   Hasted, *County of Kent*, vol 8, p 450.

211   F.C. Elliston Erwood, 'Notes on the Churches of Romney Marsh in the County of Kent,' *Arch. Cant.* 37 (1925), 197–202; Robertson, 'Churches in Romney Marsh,' *Arch. Cant.* 13 (1880), 408–18, 466–79.

212   Robertson, 'Destroyed Churches of New Romney,' *Arch. Cant.* 13 (1880), 238–45; W.L. Rutton, 'St. Martin's Church, New Romney: Records Relating to its Removal in A.D. 1550,' *Arch. Cant.* 20 (1893), 155–60; Tatton-Brown, 'Church Building on Romney Marsh in the Later Middle Ages,' *Arch. Cant.* 107 (1990 for 1989), 255.

213   R.C. Fowler, 'The Hospital of St. John the Baptist, Romney,' and 'The Hospital of St. Stephen and St. Thomas, Romney,' *VCH: Kent*, vol 2, p 225; Robertson, 'Destroyed Churches of New Romney,' *Arch. Cant.* 13 (1880), 245–9; and K.M.E. Murray, 'Excavations on the Site of the Leper Hospital, New Romney,' *Arch. Cant.* 47 (1935), 198–204. Andrew F. Butcher, 'The Hospital of St. Stephen and St. Thomas, New Romney: The Documentary Evidence,' *Arch. Cant.* 96 (1981 for 1980), 17–26, however, cites some evidence for the hospital's continued existence in the early sixteenth century.

214   Murray (ed), *Register of Daniel Rough*, pp liv–lv; Murray, *The Constitutional History of the Cinque Ports*, pp 232, 237–9; John Stokes, 'The Barons of New Romney in Parliament,' *Arch. Cant.* 27 (1905), 44–63.

215   *Calendar of Patent Rolls, Elizabeth*, vol 7, pp 202–3; Felix Hull (ed), *A Calendar of the White and Black Books of the Cinque Ports*, pp xii–xiv.

216   F.W. Hardman and W.P.D. Stebbing, 'Stonar and the Wantsum Channel. Part I. Physiographical,' *Arch. Cant.* 53 (1941 for 1940), 62–80; F.W. Hardman and W.P.D. Stebbing, 'Stonar and the Wantsum Channel. Part II. Historical,' *Arch. Cant.* 54 (1942 for 1941), 41–55; Gordon Ward, 'The Saxon History of the Wantsum,' *Arch. Cant.* 56 (1944 for 1943), 23–7; Tatton-Brown, 'The Anglo-Saxon Towns of Kent,' *Anglo-Saxon Settlements*, Hooke (ed), pp 217–20.

217   Helen C. Bentwich, *History of Sandwich in Kent* (Deal, 1971), 11–14; Tatton-Brown, 'The Towns of Kent,' pp 16–22; Tatton-Brown, 'The Anglo-Saxon Towns of Kent,' *Anglo-Saxon Settlements*, Hooke (ed), p 226; Morgan (ed), *Domesday Book: Kent*, 3a; Darby and Campbell, *The Domesday Geography of South-East England*, p 552; E.W. Parkin, 'The Ancient Cinque Port of Sandwich,' *Arch. Cant.* 100 (1985 for 1984), 189–92.

218   Justin Croft, 'An Assault on the Royal Justices at Ash and the Making of the Sandwich Custumal,' *Arch. Cant.* 117 (1997), 13–36.

219   Parkin, 'The Ancient Cinque Port of Sandwich,' *Arch. Cant.* 100 (1985 for 1984), 194; Charles A. Wanostrocht, 'Discovery of a Thirteenth-Century Hoard of Silver Coins in the Chapel of St. Bartholomew's Hospital, Sandwich,' *Arch. Cant.* 110 (1993 for 1992), 153–9; R.C. Fowler, 'The Hospital of St. Bartholomew, Sandwich,' *VCH: Kent*, vol 2, p 226.

220   Parkin, 'The Ancient Cinque Port of Sandwich,' *Arch. Cant.* 100 (1985 for 1984), 199.

221   Lambarde, *A Perambulation of Kent*, pp 63, 65; Hasted, *County of Kent*, vol 10, p 164.

222   Gardiner, *Historic Haven*, pp 161–70; R.C. Fowler, 'The Hospital of St. John, Sandwich,' and 'The Hospital of St. Thomas, Sandwich,' *VCH: Kent*, vol 2, pp 226, 227; A.G. Little, 'The Carmelite Friars of Sandwich,' *VCH: Kent*, vol 2, pp 204–5. Although Gardiner and Little both give the dates of 1272 and 1292 for early endowments of the Carmelite friary, Elizabeth Deighton, 'The Carmelite Friary at Sandwich,' *Arch. Cant.* 114 (1995 for 1994), 317–27, gives the evidence for the now generally accepted date of 1268 (see especially p 317).

223   Parkin, 'The Ancient Cinque Port of Sandwich,' *Arch. Cant.* 100 (1985 for 1984), 199–200, 211–12.

224   Clark and Hosking, *Population Estimates of English Small Towns 1550–1851*, p 81, although these diocesan figures would not have reflected the immigrant population; Gibson, 'The 1566 Survey of the Kent Coast,' *Arch. Cant.* 112 (1994 for 1993), 347.

225   PRO: SP 12/18/9 as quoted by Yungblut, *Strangers Settled Here Amongst Us*, pp 48–9. See also Gardiner, *Historic Haven*, pp 174–85.

226   Bower, 'Kent Towns, 1540–1640,' *Early Modern Kent 1540–1640*, Zell (ed), pp 160–5; Chalklin, *Seventeenth-Century Kent*, p 30.

227   Ekwall, *Concise Oxford Dictionary of English Place-Names*, p 463.

228   Gordon Ward, 'Saxon Records of Tenterden,' *Arch. Cant.* 49 (1938), 229–40.

229   A.H. Taylor, 'The Rectors and Vicars of St. Mildred's, Tenterden,' *Arch. Cant.* 31 (1915), 207; Ward, 'Saxon Records of Tenterden,' *Arch. Cant.* 49 (1938), 241–3; see also R.C. Fowler, 'The Abbey of Minster in Thanet,' *VCH: Kent*, vol 2, p 151; DNB, s.v. 'Mildred.'

230   Thirsk, *The Rural Economy of England*, p 225.

231   Robert Furley, 'The Early History of Tenterden,' *Arch. Cant.* 14 (1882), 37–60; A.H. Taylor, 'The Municipal Records of Tenterden. Part I,' *Arch. Cant.* 32 (1917), 283–302; A.H. Taylor, 'The Municipal Records of Tenterden. Part II,' *Arch. Cant.* 33 (1918), 91–112; A. H. Taylor, *The Chronicles of Tenderden* (Rye, [1924]), [4].

232   Michael Zell, 'Population and Family Structure in the Sixteenth-Century Weald,' *Arch. Cant.* 100 (1985 for 1984), 257; Bower, 'Kent Towns, 1540–1640,' *Early Modern Kent 1540–1640*, Zell (ed), p 160; Chalklin, *Seventeenth-Century Kent*, p 32. Clark and Hosking, *Population Estimates of English Small Towns 1550–1851*, p 83, suggest a population of only 1,010 in 1563.

233   A.H. Taylor. 'The Grammar Free School at Tenterden,' *Arch. Cant.* 44 (1932), 129–46. See also A.F. Leach, *The Schools of Medieval England* (New York and London, 1915), 326.

234 Lambarde, *A Perambulation of Kent*, pp 12–13.

235 This description relies on the analysis of the gentry and nobility of the sixteenth century in Zell, 'Landholding and the Land Market in Early Modern Kent,' *Early Modern Kent 1540–1640*, Zell (ed), pp 39–74, and of the seventeenth century in Alan Everitt, *The Community of Kent and the Great Rebellion 1640–60* (Leicester, 1966), 20–55. Everitt's analysis is based on some 800 to 1,000 gentry families including all the peers (10) and baronets (31) and most of the knights (50) in the county.

236 Hasted, *County of Kent*, vol 7, pp 465–70.

237 Everitt, *Community of Kent*, pp 36–7.

238 Zell, 'Landholding and the Land Market in Early Modern Kent,' *Early Modern Kent 1540–1640*, Zell (ed), pp 47–9.

239 Everitt, *Community of Kent*, p 41.

240 Everitt, *Community of Kent*, pp 27, 41.

241 Everitt, *Community of Kent*, p 35.

242 Everitt, *Community of Kent*, p 43.

243 Zell, 'Landholding and the Land Market in Early Modern Kent,' *Early Modern Kent 1540–1640*, Zell (ed), pp 49–62; Everitt, *Community of Kent*, p 38.

244 Zell, 'Landholding and the Land Market in Early Modern Kent,' *Early Modern Kent 1540–1640*, Zell (ed), pp 62–9.

245 Zell, 'Landholding and the Land Market in Early Modern Kent,' *Early Modern Kent 1540–1640*, Zell (ed), pp 58–9.

Drama, Music, and Ceremonial Customs

1 Excluded from this figure are payments to all borough and parish players and bann criers identified by place, payments to travelling waits and ceremonial musicians, and payments to local civic waits or musicians, all of which will be considered in other sections of the Introduction.

2 See Peter H. Greenfield, 'Touring,' *A New History of Early English Drama*, John D. Cox and David Scott Kastan (eds) (New York, 1997), 253–6; and Dawson, *Collections* 7, pp xxvi–xxvii.

3 For further analysis of the meaning of the performance terms discussed here, see Abigail Ann Young, 'Plays and Players: The Latin Terms for Performance,' *REEDN* 9.2 (1984), 56–62, and 10.1 (1985), 9–16; and Dawson, *Collections* 7, pp x–xv. A handful of payments to performers that do not easily fall into either of the main categories has been excluded from this classification, such as the payments at Dover for 'a player on the Rope before the maire' in 1465–6, for 'A playrre thurow hopys' in 1477–8, for 'the sworde players' in 1507–8, and half a dozen payments for 'player*es* with popett*es*' between 1475 and 1610 in Dover and for another 'popett player' at Lydd in 1519–20.

4 EKAC: NR/FAc 3, f 76v.

5 The low number of payments to travelling minstrels in the late thirteenth and fourteenth centuries may reflect the absence of sources rather than the absence of minstrel

activity since minstrels were already numerous enough in 1315 for Edward II to regulate their activities by royal proclamation (see pp 928–9).

6   An earlier payment to 'cuidam lusori' of Edmund Beaufort, 2nd marquess of Dorset, at Canterbury in 1446–7 illustrates the difficulty of distinguishing with certainty between minstrels and players. It is probable, however, that this single performer was a minstrel either playing an instrument or incorporating mimetic activity in his entertainment.

7   Greenfield, 'Touring,' pp 256–61.

8   For payments at Rye, see Cameron Louis (ed), *Sussex*, REED (Toronto, 2000), 133–4.

9   See also Scott McMillin and Sally-Beth MacLean, *The Queen's Men and Their Plays* (Cambridge, 1998), 178–9.

10   This second tour took place in late summer after the close of the 1588–9 accounts in these towns.

11   Gibson, 'Stuart Players in Kent: Fact or Fiction?', pp 1–12.

12   Louis (ed), *Sussex*, pp 330–6.

13   For payments at Rye, see Louis (ed), *Sussex*, pp 75, 78.

14   The unfortunate gap in the Lydd borough accounts between 1485 and 1511 results in artificially lower figures for the last quarter of the fifteenth century and first quarter of the sixteenth century.

15   The payments in Lydd to players of Canterbury in 1526–7 and 1535–6 are probably payments to the Canterbury waits since payments to the Canterbury waits or minstrels routinely appear in the Lydd and New Romney accounts between 1526 and 1540.

16   See Eamon Duffy, *The Stripping of the Altars: Traditional Religion in England c. 1400–c. 1580* (New Haven and London, 1992), 379–423, for a general account of the attack on traditional religion during this period.

17   Gibson and Harvey, 'A Sociological Study of the New Romney Passion Play,' pp 203–21.

18   EKAC: NR/FAc 6, ff 57v–8v.

19   CKS: PRC 17/29, f 254; PRC 17/39, f 211; PRC 32/28, f 30; PRC 32/34, f 82; PRC 17/33, f 221.

20   Gibson, '"Interludum Passionis Domini": Parish Drama in Medieval New Romney,' pp 137–48.

21   For a discussion of such hybrid plays, see David M. Bevington, *From Mankind to Marlowe* (Cambridge, 1962), 10, 170–8.

22   Compare the banns of the Chester plays in Lawrence M. Clopper (ed), *Chester*, REED (Toronto, 1979), 31–9, 240–7.

23   For payments at Rye, see Louis (ed), *Sussex*, p 76.

24   For payments at Rye, see Louis (ed), *Sussex*, pp 71, 78.

25   For payments at Rye, see Louis (ed), *Sussex*, pp 71, 88, 96, 106, 117.

26   For a discussion of the provenance of these two manuscripts, see Thomas Symons (trans), *Regularis Concordia* (London, 1953), liii–lix.

27   George B. Bryan, *Ethelwold and Medieval Music-Drama at Winchester: The Easter Play, Its Author, and Its Milieu* (Berne, 1981), 38–9, argues from circumstantial evidence that Æthelwold may have been the author of the *Visitatio Sepulchri* and suggests that the

liturgical play may have been performed at Abingdon, where Æthelwold was a monk before he became bishop of Winchester in 963.

28 A.G. Little, 'The Trinitarian Friars of Mottenden in the Parish of Headcorn,' *VCH: Kent*, vol 2, pp 205–8.

29 For further discussion of this manuscript and Dering's library, see Lennam, 'Sir Edward Dering's Collection of Playbooks, 1619–1624,' pp 145–53; *The History of King Henry the Fourth*, facsimile ed, George Watton Williams and Gwynne Blakemore Evans (eds) (Charlottesville, 1974); and Yeandle, 'The Dating of Sir Edward Dering's Copy of "The History of King Henry the Fourth,"' pp 224–6.

30 A.F. Leach, *The Schools of Medieval England* (London, 1915; rpt New York, 1969), 223–4.

31 Edwin Nungezer, *A Dictionary of Actors* (New Haven, 1929), s.v. 'Symcockes'; R.A. Foakes and R.T. Rickert (eds), *Henslowe's Diary* (Cambridge, 1961), 194; Peter Roberts, '"The Studious Artizan": Christopher Marlowe, Canterbury and Cambridge,' *Christopher Marlowe and English Renaissance Culture*, Darryll Grantley and Peter Roberts (eds) (Aldershot, 1996), 17–37.

32 Gostling, *A Walk in and about the City of Canterbury*, p 87. The dean and chapter treasurer's accounts contain frequent payments to the King's School students for declamatory exercises during the sixteenth and seventeenth centuries. A volume of plays, speeches, songs, and other exercises performed by the school before the dean and chapter on the anniversary of the birthday and restoration of Charles II, on Guy Fawkes Day, and on other occasions survives from the later seventeenth century. See CCA: DCc/Miscellaneous Accounts 41, f 426v; DCc/TA 17, f 189v; DCc/TA 18, f 196v; DCc/TA 19, f 204v; DCc/TA 20, f 217v; DCc/TA 22, f 223v; DCc/TA 23, f 229; DCc/TA 24, f 235; DCc/TA 25, f 240v; DCc/TA 26, sheet 2v; DCc/TA 27, sheet 3; DCc/TA 28, sheet 2v; DCc/TA 29, sheet 4v; DCc/TA 30, sheet 4; DCc/TA 31, sheet 4; DCc/TA 32, sheet 4v; DCc/TA 33, sheet 5v; DCc/TA 34, sheet 3v; DCc/TA 35, sheet 4; DCc/TA 36, sheet 3v; DCc/TA 37, sheet 4; DCc/TA 38, sheet 2; DCc/TA 39, sheet 4; DCc/TA 40, sheet 3v; DCc/TA 41, sheet 3v; DCc/TA 42, sheet 3v; DCc/TA 43, sheet 4; DCc/TA 45, sheet 3v; DCc/TA 46, sheet 3; DCc/TA 47, sheet 3; and Literary MS E41.

33 Charles Roach Smith, *The Antiquities of Richborough, Reculver, and Lymne, in Kent* (London, 1850), 161–6.

34 P. Bennett, 'The Topography of Roman Canterbury: A Brief Re-Assessment,' *Arch. Cant.* 100 (1984), 47–56, discusses the latest evidence and gives a revised plan correcting the earlier assumptions of Sheppard Frere, 'The Roman Theatre at Canterbury,' *Britannia* 1 (1970), 83–113.

35 CCA: CC/Woodruff's List XVI/5, 14, 17, and 27.

36 CCA: CC/Woodruff's List XVI/3. See also Edward Wilmot, *Eighty 'Lost' Inns of Canterbury* (Canterbury, 1992), 56.

37 CCA: CC/Woodruff's List XVI/8, 12, 13, 16.

38 CCA: CC/Woodruff's List XVI/5, 15, and 19.

39 CCA: CC/Woodruff's List XVI/10.

40 Peter Clark and Lyn Murfin, *The History of Maidstone: The Making of a Modern County Town* (Stroud, 1995), 30, 48–9.

41 Robert Tittler, *Architecture and Power: The Town Hall and the English Urban Community c. 1500–1640* (Oxford, 1991), 139–50, gives a useful survey of the performance of plays in town halls.

42 CCA: CC/Woodruff's List LVIA/7.

43 For the history and description of the guildhall, I am indebted to an unpublished paper by Anne M. Oakley, June 1999, in the pamphlet file of the Canterbury Cathedral Archives.

44 Tittler, *Architecture and Power*, p 164.

45 Tittler, *Architecture and Power*, p 145, following Glynne Wickham, *Early English Stages, 1300 to 1600*, vol 2, pt 1 (London and New York, 1963), 183–4, interprets the payment at Maidstone 'for layeng the tymber off ye stage to gether' in 1567–8 as an example of the erection of a stage in the town hall. The chamberlains' accounts, however, give no clue where this stage was erected or the purpose for its construction.

46 John M. Wasson, 'The English Church as Theatrical Space,' *A New History of Early English Drama*, Cox and Kastan (eds), pp 25–7, draws attention to churches as possible venues for performance; however, the Kent records do not confirm the evidence surviving in some other counties.

47 Peter Roberts, 'Politics, Drama and the Cult of Thomas Becket in the Sixteenth Century,' *Pilgrimage: The English Experience from Becket to Bunyan*, Colin Morris and Peter Roberts (eds) (Cambridge, 2002), 221–2, argues that this performance took place not in the church but in the Hackington rectory where Cromwell had acquired a share in 1535. Paul Whitfield White, *Theatre and Reformation: Protestantism, Patronage, and Playing in Tudor England* (Cambridge, 1993), 149–62, admits that there is no proof that Bale's plays were actually performed in St Stephen's Church (p 152) but, nevertheless, gives a useful plan of the church (p 153) and discusses the possible staging of these plays, employing the rood screen and rood loft that separated the nave from the choir. For an architectural discussion of the church with plans and nineteenth-century drawings of the rood screen, see Kenneth H. Jones, 'St. Stephen's Church, Hackington, and its Possible Connection with Archbishop Baldwin,' *Arch. Cant.* 44 (1932), 253–63, and the appendix by Aymer Vallance, 'The Rood-Screen at St. Stephen's, Hackington,' pp 264–8.

48 Alfred Harbage, *Annals of English Drama 975–1700*, Samuel Schoenbaum (rev) (London, 1989), 26–7, indicates a performance of all three of these plays at St Stephen's.

49 This play, probably a Protestant or humanist interlude, does not belong with the late medieval tradition of biblical plays and saints' plays that were suppressed during the Henrician Reformation. For a discussion of the evidence, see p 1377, endnote to CCA: DCb/J/X.3.6 pt 2 ff 158v, 159.

50 Ronald Hutton, *The Rise and Fall of Merry England: The Ritual Year 1400–1700* (Oxford and New York, 1994), 37–44.

51 John Stow, *A Survey of London*, Charles Lethbridge Kingsford (ed), vol 1 (Oxford, 1908), 101–4.

52 Roberts, 'Politics, Drama and the Cult of Thomas Becket in the Sixteenth Century,'

pp 199–237, gives a detailed account of the political and religious manoeuvring that preceded and followed the suppression of the veneration of St Thomas Becket in September 1538.

53 James Gairdner (ed), *Letters and Papers, Foreign and Domestic, of the Reign of Henry VIII*, vol 13, pt 2 (London, 1893), 49.

54 Gairdner (ed), *Letters and Papers of Henry VIII*, vol 13, part 2, p 354.

55 David Cressy, *Bonfires and Bells: National Memory and the Protestant Calendar in Elizabethan and Stuart England* (London, 1989), 67–92, discusses these celebrations generally and on pp 90–2 provides a list of such occasions from 1558 to 1702.

56 Cressy, *Bonfires and Bells*, pp 50–66.

57 Frank Streatfeild, *An Account of the Grammar School in the King's Town and Parish of Maidstone in Kent* (Oxford, 1915), 3–31.

58 Cressy, *Bonfires and Bells*, pp 141–55.

59 The records quoted in these volumes do not include all royal visits to Kent but only those visits known to have been accompanied by dramatic or musical entertainment or civic ceremony. The specific circumstances of each visit, if known, are discussed in the Endnotes.

60 The Dover accounts for 1572–3 are missing; however, since the accounting year ended on 8 September shortly after her visit, some of the expenses were included in the 1573–4 accounts. See also Nichols, *The Progresses and Public Processions of Queen Elizabeth*, vol 1, p 336.

61 Ronald Hutton, *The Stations of the Sun: A History of the Ritual Year in Britain* (Oxford, 1996), 9–24.

62 Hutton, *The Rise and Fall of Merry England*, pp 9–12, 53–4; Hutton, *The Stations of the Sun*, pp 95–111.

63 A.R. Wright, *British Calendar Customs: England*, T.E. Lones (ed), Publications of the Folk-Lore Society, vol 102 (1936; rpt Nendeln/Liechtenstein, 1968), 32–5, 50–5; Hutton, *The Stations of the Sun*, pp 13–14.

64 It is possible that the king and queen of Fordwich may have been elected during summer games rather than at Twelfth Night. The presence of tables, forms, tablecloths, and a wassail bowl in the inventory, however, suggests an organized, indoor, seated ceremonial custom, in which drinking was important, and supports the assignment of this mimetic custom to Twelfth Night festivities.

65 Wright, *British Calendar Customs*, pp 34, 60–8, 87, prints many such songs for wassailing the orchards still in use in the nineteenth century.

66 Lambarde, *A Perambulation of Kent*, p 137.

67 For a discussion of the general nature of this festival, see William Carew Hazlitt, *Faiths and Folklore of the British Isles* (New York, 1965), s.v. 'Hoke-tide'; A.R. Wright, *British Calendar Customs: England*, T.E. Lones (ed), Publications of the Folk-Lore Society, vol 97 (1936; rpt Nendeln/Liechtenstein, 1968), 124–8; and Hutton, *The Stations of the Sun*, pp 207–13.

68 Arthur Hussey, *Testamenta Cantiana: A Series of Extracts from Fifteenth and Sixteenth Century Wills Relating to Church Building and Topography, East Kent* (London, 1907), xvi.

69 Samantha Riches, *St George: Hero, Martyr and Myth* (Stroud, 2000), 101–39; Hutton, *The Stations of the Sun*, pp 214–17.

70 F.C. Elliston Erwood, 'Notes on the Churches of Romney Marsh in the County of Kent, 1923,' *Arch. Cant.* 37 (1925), 200; and W.A. Scott Robertson, 'Churches in Romney Marsh,' *Arch. Cant.* 13 (1880), 472, 476.

71 Robertson, 'Churches in Romney Marsh,' *Arch. Cant.* 13 (1880), 433.

72 EKAC: LY/ZP 4/1, pp 125, 198.

73 Dorothy Gardiner, *Historic Haven: The Story of Sandwich* (Derby, 1954), 161–2.

74 EKAC: SA/FAt 8, sheet 3; SA/FAt 11, sheet 3b; SA/FAt 12, sheet 3; SA/FAt 13, sheet 3; SA/FAt 15, sheet 1; SA/FAt 16, sheet 4; SA/FAt 17, sheet 4; SA/FAt 17A, sheet 5; SA/FAt 20, sheet 5; SA/FAt 21, sheet 2; SA/FAt 22, sheet 4; SA/FAt 23, sheet 4; SA/FAt 24, sheet 4; SA/FAt 25, sheet 5; SA/FAt 27, sheet 6; SA/FAt 28, sheet 9; SA/FAt 32, sheet 2; and SA/FAt 33, sheet 12.

75 James Gairdner and R.H. Brodie (eds), *Letters and Papers, Foreign and Domestic, of the Reign of Henry VIII*, vol 18, pt 2 (London, 1902), 309.

76 Hutton, *The Rise and Fall of Merry England*, pp 27–34; David Wiles, *The Early Plays of Robin Hood* (Cambridge, 1981), 1–30; John Forrest, *The History of Morris Dancing 1458–1750* (Toronto, 1999).

77 Hutton, *The Rise and Fall of Merry England*, pp 37–40; Hutton, *The Stations of the Sun*, pp 311–21.

78 Peter Clark, 'Reformation and Radicalism in Kentish Towns c. 1500–1533,' *Publication of the German Historical Institute* 5 (1979), 111. Apart from the payments for dancers in 1643, these payments do not include any further expenses for musical or mimetic entertainment.

The Documents

1 Paul S. Seaver, *Wallington's World: A Puritan Artisan in Seventeenth-Century London* (London, 1985), 199–208, provides an appendix listing all of Wallington's notebooks.

2 For general historical background, see R.C. Fowler, 'The Cathedral Priory of the Holy Trinity or Christ-Church, Canterbury,' *VCH: Kent*, vol 2, pp 113–21; and Patrick Collinson, Nigel Ramsay, and Margaret Sparks (eds), *A History of Canterbury Cathedral* (Oxford, 1995).

3 See R.C. Fowler, 'The Abbey of St. Augustine, Canterbury,' *VCH: Kent*, vol 2, pp 126–33; and Richard Gem (ed), *English Heritage Book of St Augustine's Abbey Canterbury* (London, 1997).

4 See Thomas Symons (trans), *Regularis Concordia* (London, 1953), liii–lix; and Lucia Kornexl, *Die Regularis Concordia und ihre Altenglische Interlinearversion* (Munich, 1993), for discussion of the manuscripts, their dating, and their connection with the Canterbury scriptorium.

5 For a full list of officers of the priory in 1435, see C. Eveleigh Woodruff, 'The Chronicle of William Glastynbury, Monk of the Priory of Christ Church, Canterbury, 1419–1448,' *Arch. Cant.* 37 (1925), 129–30.

6   See also J. Wickham Legg and W.H. St John Hope, *Inventories of Christchurch Canterbury* (Westminster, 1902), 125–37; and G.H. Rooke, 'Dom William Ingram and his Account-Book, 1504–1533,' *Journal of Ecclesiastical History* 7 (1956), 30–44.

7   For a discussion of the relationship between the two manuscripts, see M.A.F. Borrie, 'The Thorne Chronicle,' *British Museum Quarterly* 31 (1967), 87–90.

8   Joseph Foster, *Alumni Oxonienses*, Early Series, vol 1 (Oxford, 1891).

9   See Edward Arber (ed), *A Transcript of the Registers of the Company of Stationers of London: 1554–1640 A.D.*, vol 1 (London, 1875), 155.

10 See R.C. Fowler, 'The Priory of Dover,' *VCH: Kent*, vol 2, pp 133–7.

11 See the *General Report to the King in Council from the Honourable Board of Commissioners on the Public Records*, Parliamentary Sessional Papers 34 (1837), Appendix, p 452.

12 John English, 'Folkestone in Olden Times. Gleanings from the Municipal Records,' *The Folkestone Express* (16 September 1882), 6.

13 Derek Ingram Hill, *The Six Preachers of Canterbury Cathedral* (Ramsgate, 1982), 52–4.

14 For further description of the New Romney records, see 'Mr. Edward Salisbury's Report on the Records of New Romney,' *Arch. Cant.* 17 (1887), 12–33; and Major Teichman-Derville, 'The New Romney and Cinque Ports Records,' *Arch. Cant.* 42 (1930), 1–36.

15 See William Boys, *Collections for an History of Sandwich in Kent* (Canterbury, 1792), 197–275; John Cavell and Brian Kennett, *A History of Sir Roger Manwood's School Sandwich 1563–1963 with a Life of the Founder* (London, 1963), 1–48; and P.W. Hasler, *The House of Commons 1558–1603*, vol 3 (London, 1981), 15–17.

16 See R.C. Fowler, 'The Abbey of Boxley,' *VCH: Kent*, vol 2, pp 153–5.

17 See R.C. Fowler, 'The Priory of Leeds,' *VCH: Kent*, vol 2, pp 162–5.

18 See R.C. Fowler, 'The Priory of Minster in Sheppey,' *VCH: Kent*, vol 2, pp 149–50.

19 See A.G. Little, 'The Trinitarian Friars of Mottenden in the Parish of Headcorn,' *VCH: Kent*, vol 2, pp 205–8.

20 See R.C. Fowler, 'The Hospital of Ospringe,' *VCH: Kent*, vol 2, pp 222–4.

21 See Hasted, *County of Kent*, vol 7, p 355.

22 See C.S. Orwin and S. Williams, *A History of Wye Church and Wye College* (Ashford, [1913]), 134–55, for an abstract of these statutes.

23 Hasted, *County of Kent*, vol 7, p 468.

24 C.R. Cheney, 'The so-called Statutes of John Pecham and Robert Winchelsey for the Province of Canterbury,' *Journal of Ecclesiastical History* 12 (1961), 14–34, discusses the authenticity of this statute (pp 23–5) and lists the twenty-seven surviving manuscripts that contain the statute (pp 33–4).

25 See Cheney, 'The so-called Statutes of John Pecham and Robert Winchelsey,' pp 14–34.

26 See Powicke and Cheney (eds), *Councils and Synods*, vol 2, pt 1, pp 23–36.

27 For a discussion of these statutes and comparison with Richard Poore's statutes for the diocese of Salisbury, see Powicke and Cheney (eds), *Councils and Synods*, vol 2, pt 1, pp 57–96, 165–7.

Editorial Procedures

1 Sometimes entertainers were prosecuted in the ecclesiastical courts or appeared before magistrates for reasons other than musical or dramatic performance. In 1593, for example, William Jennings, musician, was presented by the churchwardens of St Peter's, Canterbury, and St Paul's, Canterbury, for fornication (CCA: DCb/J/X.3.9, ff 27–7v). In the Canterbury court of quarter sessions John Bemon, wait, was presented for assault (CCA: CC/J/Q/333/x); Lebarde, another wait, was fined for fighting (CCA: CC/FA 13, f 111); William Thorneborough, musician, forfeited his recognizance to appear at the court of quarter sessions to answer a charge of bloodshed in 1600 (CCA: CC/AC 3, f 360); and Thomas Myddelton, minstrel, was prosecuted in 1585 for buggery (CCA: CC/J/Q/384).

2 EKAC: Ly/2/1/1/1, f 158.

Select Bibliography

This list includes all books, articles, and published facsimiles that contain primary transcriptions from the records edited in this volume and general reference works that have proved particularly useful.

Baker, Oscar. *History of the Antiquities of Sandwich and Richborough Castle, in Kent* (London, 1848).

Bale, John. *The Complete Plays of John Bale*. Vol 1. Peter Happé (ed) (Cambridge, 1985).

– *King Johan*. John Henry Pyle Pafford (ed). Malone Society Reprints (Oxford, 1931).

Barrett, J.P. *A History of the Ville of Birchington, Thanet, Kent*. 2nd ed (Margate, 1908).

Boggis, R.J.E. *A History of St. Augustine's Monastery, Canterbury* (Canterbury, 1901).

Borough of Folkestone. *Municipal Records: Report by Mr. E.G. Atkinson of the Public Record Office* (Folkestone, 1904).

Boys, William. *Collections for an History of Sandwich in Kent* (Canterbury, 1792).

Brayley, Edward Wedlake. *Delineations, Historical and Topographical, of the Isle of Thanet and the Cinque Ports*. 2 vols (London, 1817–18).

Brent, John. *Canterbury in the Olden Time*. 2nd ed (London, 1879).

Bunce, John Bowes [V.S.D.]. 'Church Goods of St. Dunstan's, Canterbury, 1500,' *Gentleman's Magazine* ns 8 (December, 1837), 569–71.

Burn, John Southerden. *The History of Parish Registers in England*. 2nd ed (London, 1862; rpt East Ardley, Wakefield, 1976).

Carlisle, N. *A Concise Description of the Endowed Grammar Schools in England and Wales*. 2 vols (London, 1818).

Chambers, E.K. *The Elizabethan Stage*. 4 vols (Oxford, 1923).

– *The Mediaeval Stage*. 2 vols (London, 1903).

Clark, Peter. *English Provincial Society from the Reformation to the Revolution: Religion, Politics and Society in Kent 1500–1640* (Hassocks, Sussex, 1977).

– 'Josias Nicholls and Religious Radicalism, 1553–1639,' *The Journal of Ecclesiastical History* 28 (1977), 133–50.

– and Philip Morgan (eds). *Towns and Townspeople 1500–1780: A Document Collection* (The Open University Press, 1977).

Cotton, Charles. 'Churchwardens' Accounts of the Parish of St. Andrew, Canterbury, from A.D. 1485 to A.D. 1625: Part I, 1485–1509,' *Arch. Cant.* 32 (1917), 181–246.

– 'Churchwardens' Accounts of the Parish of St. Andrew, Canterbury, from A.D. 1485 to A.D. 1625: Part II, 1509–1523,' *Arch. Cant.* 33 (1918), 1–62.

– 'Churchwardens' Accounts of the Parish of St. Andrew, Canterbury, from A.D. 1485 to A.D. 1625: Part III, 1524–1557,' *Arch. Cant.* 34 (1920), 1–46.

– 'Churchwardens' Accounts of the Parish of St. Andrew, Canterbury, from A.D. 1485 to A.D. 1625: Part IV, 1553–4–1596,' *Arch. Cant.* 35 (1921), 41–108.

– 'Churchwardens' Accounts of the Parish of St. Andrew, Canterbury, from A.D. 1485 to A.D. 1625: Part V, 1597–1625,' *Arch. Cant.* 36 (1923), 81–122.

– 'St. Austin's Abbey, Canterbury, Treasurers' Accounts 1468–9, and Others,' *Arch. Cant.* 51 (1939), 66–107.

Cowper, J[oseph] M[eadows]. 'Accounts of the Churchwardens of St. Dunstan's, Canterbury, A.D. 1484–1580,' *Arch. Cant.* 16 (1886), 289–321.

– 'Accounts of St. Dunstan's, Canterbury,' *Arch. Cant.* 17 (1887), 77–149.

– 'Notes from the Records of Faversham, 1560–1600,' *Transactions of the Historical Society* 1 (1872), 324–43; rpt in *Transactions of the Royal Historical Society* 1 (1875), 218–38.

– (ed). *The Diary of Thomas Cocks March 25th, 1607, to December 31st, 1610. From MS E.31 in the Library of Canterbury Cathedral* (Canterbury, 1901).

– (ed). *The Register Booke of the Parish of St. George the Martyr within the Citie of Canterburie of Christenings, Mariages and Burials, 1538–1800* (Canterbury, 1891).

Cox, J. Charles. *Canterbury: A Historical and Topographical Account of the City* (London, 1905).

Cranmer, Thomas. *Miscellaneous Writings and Letters of Thomas Cranmer, Archbishop of Canterbury, Martyr, 1556.* John Edmund Cox (ed). Parker Society (Cambridge, 1846).

Cross, Francis W. 'The Early Minute Books of the Dean and Chapter of Canterbury,' *The Archaeological Journal* 53 (1896), 235–48.

– *History of the Walloon and Huguenot Church at Canterbury.* Publications of the Huguenot Society of London 15 (Canterbury, 1898).

Dawson, Giles E. (ed). *Collections* 7. Malone Society (Oxford, 1965).

Dorman, Thomas. 'The Sandwich Book of Orphans,' *Arch. Cant.* 16 (1886), 179–206.

Duncan, Leland L. *Testamenta Cantiana: A Series of Extracts from Fifteenth and Sixteenth Century Wills Relating to Church Building and Topography. West Kent* (London, 1906).

Edwards, D.L. *A History of the King's School, Canterbury* (London, 1957).

Fairfield, Leslie P. *John Bale: Mythmaker for the English Reformation* (West Lafayette, Indiana, 1976).

Finn, Arthur (ed). *Records of Lydd.* Arthur Hussey and M.M. Hardy (trans and transcr) (Ashford, 1911).

Frere, W.H. (ed). *Registrum Matthei Parker Diocesis Cantuariensis A.D. 1559–1575.* E. Margaret Thompson (transc). 3 vols (Oxford, 1928–33).

– (ed). *Visitation Articles and Injunctions of the Period of the Reformation.* 3 vols. Alcuin Club Collections 14–16 (London, 1910).

Gardiner, Dorothy (ed). *The Oxinden Letters 1607–1642: Being the Correspondence of Henry Oxinden of Barham and His Circle* (London, 1933).

Gibson, James M. '"Interludum Passionis Domini": Parish Drama in Medieval New Romney,' *English Parish Drama*, Alexandra F. Johnston and Wim Hüsken (eds) (Amsterdam, 1996), 137–48.

– 'Stuart Players in Kent: Fact or Fiction?' *REEDN* 20.2 (1995), 1–12.

– and Isobel Harvey. 'A Sociological Study of the New Romney Passion Play,' *Research Opportunities in Renaissance Drama* 39 (2000), 203–21.

Gostling, W. *A Walk in and about the City of Canterbury, with Many Observations not to be found in any Description hitherto Published* (Canterbury, 1774).

Graham, Rose (ed). *Registrum Roberti Winchelsey Cantuariensis Archiepiscopi A.D. 1294–1313*. 2 vols. Canterbury and York Society 51–2 (Oxford, 1952–6).

Greatrex, Joan. *Biographical Register of the English Cathedral Priories of the Province of Canterbury c.1066 to 1540* (Oxford, 1997).

Haines, Charles Reginald. *Dover Priory: A History of the Priory of St Mary the Virgin, and St Martin of the New Work* (Cambridge, 1930).

Halliwell-Phillipps, J.O. *The Visits of Shakespeare's Company of Actors to the Provincial Cities and Towns of England, Illustrated by Extracts Gathered from Corporate Records* (Brighton, 1887).

Happé, Peter. *John Bale* (New York, 1996).

Haslewood, Francis. *The Parish of Benenden, Kent: Its Monuments, Vicars, and Persons of Note* (Ipswich, 1889).

Hasted, Edward. *The History and Topographical Survey of the County of Kent.* 12 vols (Canterbury, 1797–1801).

Hinde, Thomas. *Imps of Promise: A History of the King's School, Canterbury* (London, 1990).

The Historical Manuscripts Commission. Fraser, William. 'Report on the Manuscripts of Charles Stirling-Home-Drummond Moray,' *The 10th Report of the Manuscripts Commission.* App 1 (London, 1885), 81–199.

– Poole, Reginald L. 'The Muniments of the Dean and Chapter of Canterbury,' *Report on Manuscripts in Various Collections.* Part 1 (London, 1901), 205–81.

– Riley, Henry Thomas. 'The Corporation of Lydd, Kent,' *The 5th Report of the Manuscripts Commission.* Part 1 (London, 1876), 516–33.

  – 'Court Books of the Corporation of New Romney,' *The 6th Report of the Manuscripts Commission.* Part 1 (London, 1877), 540–45.

  – 'The Manuscripts of the Corporation of New Romney,' *The 4th Report of the Manuscripts Commission.* Part 1 (London, 1874), 439–42.

  – 'The Manuscripts of the Corporation of New Romney (Second Notice),' *The 5th Report of the Manuscripts Commission.* Part 1 (London, 1876), 533–54.

– Sheppard, J. Brigstocke. 'The Records of the City of Canterbury,' *The 9th Report of the Manuscripts Commission.* Part 1 (London, 1883), 129–77.

Hussey, Arthur. 'Visitations of the Archdeacon of Canterbury,' *Arch. Cant.* 25 (1902), 11–56.

[Hussey, Robert]. *Excerpta E Compoto Thesaurariae Monasterii Sancti Augustini Extra Muros Cantuariae A.D. 1432* (London, 1881).

Hyde, Patricia. *Thomas Arden in Faversham: The Man behind the Myth* (Faversham, 1996).

Jacob, Edward. *The History of the Town and Port of Faversham, in the County of Kent* (London, 1774).

Jacob, E.F., and H.C. Johnson (eds). *The Register of Henry Chichele, Archbishop of Canterbury 1414–1443*. Vol 2. Canterbury and York Society 42 (Oxford, 1938).

Jenkins, R.C. 'Gossip from the Municipal Records of Folkestone,' *Arch. Cant.* 10 (1876), lxix–lxxxv.

Jones, John Bavington. *The Records of Dover* (Dover, 1920).

Knocker, Edward. 'On the Municipal Records of Dover,' *Arch. Cant.* 10 (1876), cxxxiv–cl.

Lambarde, William. *A Perambulation of Kent: Conteining the Description, Hystorie, and Customes of that Shyre*. 2nd ed (London, 1596; stc: 15176).

Larking, Lambard B. (ed). *Proceedings, Principally in the County of Kent, in Connection with the Parliaments Called in 1640, and Especially with the Committee of Religion Appointed in that Year*. Camden Society ([Westminster], 1862).

Lennam, T.N.S. 'Sir Edward Dering's Collection of Playbooks, 1619–1624,' *Shakespeare Quarterly* 16 (1965), 145–54.

Mackie, S.J. *A Descriptive and Historical Account of Folkestone and Its Neighbourhood* (Folkestone, 1856).

Maidstone Corporation. *Records of Maidstone: Being Selections from Documents in the Possession of the Corporation*. K.S. Martin (ed) (Maidstone, 1926).

Mercer, Francis R. (transcr). *Churchwardens' Accounts at Betrysden 1515–1573*. Kent Records 5 (Ashford, 1928).

Murray, John Tucker. *English Dramatic Companies 1558–1642*. 2 vols (London, 1910; rpt 1963).

Murray, K.M. Elizabeth (ed). *Register of Daniel Rough: Common Clerk of Romney 1353–1380*. Kent Records 16 (Ashford, 1945).

Nichols, John. *The Progresses and Public Processions of Queen Elizabeth*. 3 vols (London, 1823).

Plomer, Henry R. 'Plays at Canterbury in 1570,' *The Library*, 3rd ser, 9 (1918), 251–4.

Powicke, F.M., and C.R. Cheney. *Councils and Synods with Other Documents Relating to the English Church*. 2 vols (Oxford, 1964).

Robertson, W.A. Scott. 'The Passion Play and Interludes at New Romney,' *Arch. Cant.* 13 (1880), 216–26.

Rooke, G.H. 'Dom William Ingram and His Account Book, 1504–1533,' *The Journal of Ecclesiastical History* 7 (1956), 30–44.

Rozmital, Leo of. *The Travels of Leo of Rozmital*. Malcolm Letts (trans). Hakluyt Society, 2nd ser, no 100 (Cambridge, 1957 for 1955).

Russell, J.M. *The History of Maidstone* (Maidstone, 1881; rpt 1978).

Searle, William George (ed). *Christ Church, Canterbury. I. The Chronicle of John Stone, Monk of Christ Church 1415–1571. II. Lists of the Deans, Priors, and Monks of Christ Church Monastery* (Cambridge, 1902).

Selby, Elizabeth. *Teynham Manor and Hundred (798–1935)* (Ashford, 1935; rpt Rainham, Kent, 1982).

Sheppard, J. Brigstocke. 'The Canterbury Marching Watch with Its Pageant of St. Thomas,' *Arch. Cant.* 12 (1878), 27–46.

Smith, R.A.L. *Canterbury Cathedral Priory: A Study in Monastic Administration* (Cambridge, 1943; rpt 1969).

Somner, William, and Nicholas Battely. *The Antiquities of Canterbury: In Two Parts*. Part 2, *Cantuaria Sacra*. 2nd ed revised and enlarged by Nicholas Battely (London, 1703).

Statham, S.P.H. 'Dover Chamberlains' Accounts, 1365–67,' *Arch. Cant.* 25 (1902), 75–87.

– *The History of the Castle, Town, and Port of Dover* (London, 1899).

Tatton-Brown, Tim. 'The Towns of Kent,' *Anglo-Saxon Towns in Southern England*, Jeremy Haslam (ed) (Chichester, 1984), 1–36.

Toynbee, Margaret. 'King Charles I at Canterbury in 1625,' *Arch. Cant.* 71 (1958 for 1957), 241–2.

Urry, William. *Christopher Marlowe and Canterbury*. Andrew Butcher (ed) (London, 1988).

Victoria History of the Counties of England. *History of the County of Kent*. Vols 2, 3. William Page (ed) (London, 1926, 1932; rpt 1974).

Walcott, Mackenzie E.C. 'Inventories of (I.) St. Mary's Hospital or Maison Dieu, Dover; (II.) The Benedictine Priory of St. Martin New-Work, Dover, for Monks; (III.) The Benedictine Priory of SS. Mary and Sexburga, in the Island of Shepey, for Nuns,' *Arch. Cant.* 7 (1868), 272–306.

Wood, A.C. *Registrum Simonis Langham Cantuariensis Archiepiscopi*. Canterbury and York Society 53 (Oxford, 1956).

Wood-Legh, K.L. (ed). *Kentish Visitations of Archbishop William Warham and His Deputies, 1511–1512*. Kent Records 24 (Maidstone, 1984).

Woodcock, Brian L. *Medieval Ecclesiastical Courts in the Diocese of Canterbury* (London, 1952).

Woodfill, Walter L. *Musicians in English Society from Elizabeth to Charles I* (Princeton, 1953; rpt New York, 1969).

Woodruff, C. Eveleigh. 'Fordwich Municipal Records,' *Arch. Cant.* 18 (1889), 78–102.

– *A History of the Town and Port of Fordwich, with a Transcription of the xvth Century Copy of the Custumal* (Canterbury, 1895).

– 'A Monastic Chronicle Lately Discovered at Christ Church Canterbury: With Introduction and Notes,' *Arch. Cant.* 29 (1911), 47–84.

– 'Notes on the Inner Life and Domestic Economy of the Priory of Christ Church, Canterbury, in the Fifteenth Century,' *Arch. Cant.* 53 (1941 for 1940), 1–16.

– and H.J. Cape. *Schola Regia Cantuariensis: A History of Canterbury School, Commonly Called the King's School* (London, 1908).

– and William Danks. *Memorials of the Cathedral and Priory of Christ in Canterbury* (London, 1912).

Wright, Thomas. 'On the Municipal Archives of the City of Canterbury,' *Archaeologia* 31 (1846), 198–211.

Yeandle, Laetitia. 'The Dating of Sir Edward Dering's Copy of "The History of King Henry the Fourth,"' *Shakespeare Quarterly* 37 (1986), 224–6.

Zell, Michael (ed). *Early Modern Kent 1540–1640* (Woodbridge, 2000).

Kent, from John Speed, *Theatre of the Empire of Great Britaine* (1611). This item is reproduced by permission of The Huntington Library, San Marino, California.

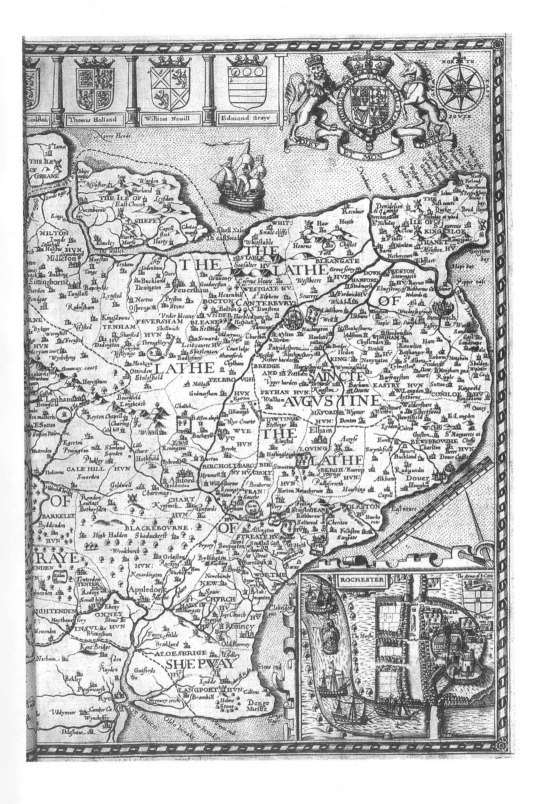

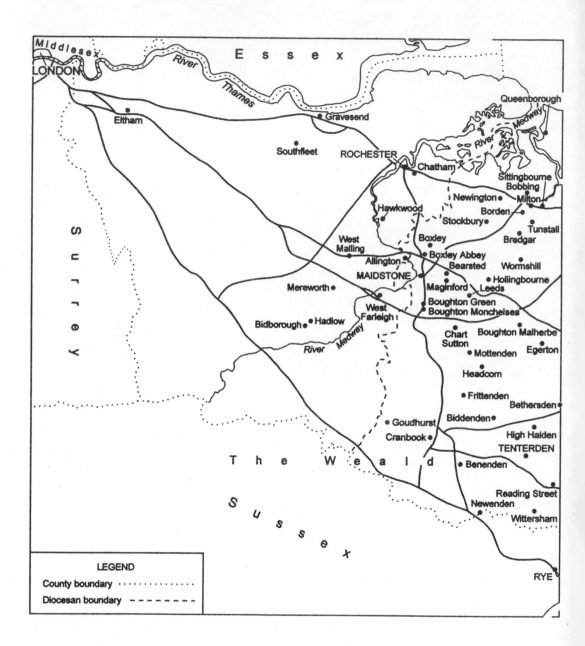

Kent with renaissance roads (derived from Philip Symonson's *A New Description of Kent*, 1596).

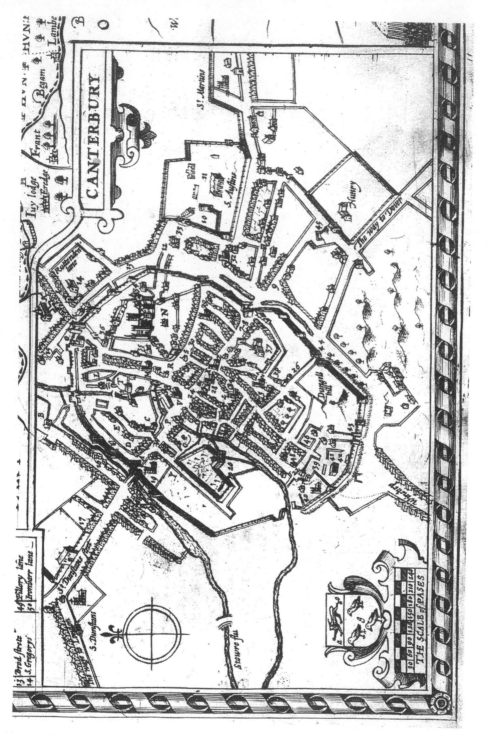

Canterbury, from John Speed, *Theatre of the Empire of Great Britaine* (1611). This item is reproduced by permission of The Huntington Library, San Marino, California.

RECORDS OF EARLY ENGLISH DRAMA

Symbols and Abbreviations

BL	British Library	EKAC	East Kent Archives Centre
Bodl.	Bodleian Library	Folger	The Folger Shakespeare Library
CCA	Canterbury Cathedral Archives	LPL	Lambeth Palace Library
CKS	Centre for Kentish Studies	PRO	Public Record Office

A	Antiquarian Compilation
AC	Antiquarian Collection
Arch. Cant.	*Archaeologia Cantiana*
DNB	*Dictionary of National Biography*
PTC	Patrons and Travelling Companies
REED	Records of Early English Drama
STC	A.W. Pollard and G.R. Redgrave (comps), *Short-Title Catalogue ... 1475–1640*
VCH	*The Victoria History of the Counties of England*
Wing	D.G. Wing (comp), *Short-Title Catalogue ... 1641–1700*
*	(after folio, membrane, page, or sheet number) see endnote
⟨...⟩	lost or illegible letters in the original
[ ]	cancellation in the original
(blank)	a blank in the original where writing would be expected
° °	matter in the original added in another hand
⌈ ⌉	text written above the line
⌊ ⌋	text written below the line
^	caret mark in the original
...	ellipsis of original matter
|	change of folio, membrane, page, or sheet in continuous text
®	right-hand marginale
†	marginale too long for the left-hand margin

Boroughs and Parishes

ALKHAM

1581
Archdeacon's Court Book   CCA: DCb/J/X.2.1
f 65*   *(22 November)*

Proceedings of the court held in St Margaret's Church, Canterbury, before Robert Bishopp, LLD, the archdeacon's official, and in the presence of Thomas Cranmer, notary public and registrar

Elmestede

We presente one Iames Todman of Elmested for that he commeth verye seldome the sondayes to his paryshe churche, but often goeth to other parysshes with his Instrumente beinge a rebeck or kytt to call companye together to prophane the Sabothe daye by wanton dauncynge, and was at Alkeham aboute such a matche on sondaye the first daye of this presente monethe of october as we have learned
°Quo die comparuit personaliter Todman, [qui cui d] qui fatetur detecta/ vnde dominus iniunxit ei quod publice agnoscat culpam suam in facie ecclesie de Elmested iuxta schedulam tempore divinorum/ et ad certificandum in proximo/ et monuit ipsum ad comparendum in proximo, ad audiendum voluntatem domini°
°Sexto [N] decembris 1581 preconizatus Todman [citatus] non comparuit/ vnde dominus pronunciauit ipsum contumacem [p] et in penam excommunicauit in scriptis°
°Introducte sunt litere excommunicationis denuntiate contra dictum Todman in ecclesia ⌈de⌉ Elmested predicta vltimo die mensis decembris anno domini iuxta &c. 1581. per dominum Iohannem ffarbrase vicarium ibidem pro vt in certificatorio &c/°
°xviij Ianuarij Anno domini iuxta &c 1581 comparuit personaliter predictus Todman et humiliter petijt beneficium absolucionis sibi impendi ad cuius

18/ iniunxit: *5 minims in* MS

°dimiss*io*°#

humile*m* petic*ion*em d*ominus* eu*m* absoluit et restuit etc deinde d*ict*us
cer*tificaui*t se *p*eregisse penit*enti*am iniunctam &c/ vnde d*omin*us eu*m* ab
officio dimisit/°

1611

Archdeacon's Court Book   CCA: DCb/J/X.5.4
f 32v   *(3 May)*

Swinfeelde

Heele:

Detectum est, that Richard Heelie did vpone a sondaye w*i*thin this moneth
laste paste come into the Churche of Alkham in tyme of Divine service and
then & there w*i*th a lowde voice beeing as it ys thowght in drincke, crye or
singe owt, Hay downe deree, deree, deree, to the greate disturbance and
[admiripac*i*on] admirac*i*on of the minister and p*a*rishioners assembled
iij° die mensis Maij 1611 farlie appar*itor* &c cer*tificaui*t se debite quesivisse
dictum Rich*ard*um Heelie 25 die Aprilis vlt*imi* &c a*n*imo citand*i* &c et quod

vijs et modis:

non potuit &c preconizat*o* d*ict*o Heelie non comp*aru*it vnde vijs et modis in
prox*imum* &c
°xx° Maij 1611 ffarlie app*ar*itor &c cer*tifica*v*i*t se debite citasse d*i*ctum
Heelie per affix*ion*em 15 die mens*i*s instan*ti*s &c preconizat*o*° °heelye non
comp*aru*it vnde d*ominus* p*ro*nuntiavit ips*um* contumacem et in pena*m*

excom*muni*ca*tur*

excom*mun*icand*um* fore decrevit et excom*municavi*t in scriptis°
°Introducta est excom*mun*icatio pred*i*c*t*a denunciat*a* 30° die Iunij 1611 p*er*
Edwardu*m* Chiselbury ministru*m*°
26 Martij 1613 cora*m* d*omi*no Offic*i*ali &c iudicial*iter* seden*te* &c p*re*sente Thoma
Lillicitt no*t*ario pub*li*co &c Comp*aru*it d*i*ctus Heelee al*i*as excom*mun*icatus &c
quem d*omin*us [monuit] a d*i*cta S*enten*c*i*a excom*muni*cationis &c absolvit et
restituit &c prius iura*m*ento ad tacta &c Tunc d*omi*nus obiecit ei detecta
qui r*e*spondend*o* fatebatur et submisit se &c vnde d*omi*nus iniunxit ei ad
agnoscend*um* Culpam sua*m* pub*li*ce in ecc*l*esia de Swingfeelde pred*i*c*t*a tempore

sched*ula*

diui*n*orum &c [vnace] vnica vice iuxta schedulam &c citra prox*imum* &c et
ad Cer*tifica*nd*um* d*i*cto p*ro*ximo &c hoc in loco hora &c alioquin &c

ASHFORD

1578

Archdeacon's Court Book   CCA: DCb/J/X.2.2
ff 26–6v*   *(18 September)*

Beatresden

Detectu*m* est that Peter waterman & Nathanyell loder mynstrells. dyd playe

---

1/ restuit: *for* restituit   1/ d*ic*tus: *for* dictus Todman

waterman
&
lodar/

all the after noone on sondaye. beinge the xxxth of August last past/ & dyd
cause the youthe of the paryshe to absente them selves from evening prayer
that Day & they them selves dyd abyde in an ale howse all evening prayer
the daye abovesayde/

xviij⁰ Septembris 1578 *preconizati* waterman et loder comp*arui*t waterman   5
[comp*arui*t] et fatetur that he did play thesaid daye before evenyng prayer/
and, after evenyng prayer but he saythe that he did not play in the evenyng
prayer tyme et quoad negata d*omi*nus assignau*i*t ei ad purgand*um* se quarta
manu honestor*um* viror*um* de Aishforde in prox*imo*/ et vlterius affirmauit
that he was sicke in the servyce tyme/   10
Preconizatus loder non comp*arui*t vnde d*omi*nus pronunciau*i*t ips*u*m
contumace*m* et in pena*m* excom*municaui*t in script*is*
Postea comp*aruerun*t loder ∧⌈et waterman⌉ cui d*omi*n*us* obiecit pr*out* detectu*m*
est qui fatentur that they were not at servyce the same day neyther at the
mornyng prayer nor the evenynge prayer et submiserunt se correc*cion*i d*omi*ni   15
Iudicis/ vnde d*omi*nus iniunxit eis et eor*um* vtriq*ue* ad penitend*um* se die
d*omi*nica prox*ima* in ecclesia de Aishforde/ et ad cer*tificandum* in prox*imo*
post/ et moniti sunt ad tunc comp*arendum* ad audiend*um* voluntate*m* domini
°xvj⁰ octobris 1578. [*preconizati* waterman] Mr Pett cer*tificaui*t ips*os*

dimiss*io*

satisfecisse &c vnde d*omi*nus ips*os* ab offitio suo dimisit⌐°   20

Asheford

Detectu*m* est that Robert wallopp of hothefyld dyd here the mynstrells

Robert
wallopp

aforesayd to playe at Asheford on Sonday the xxxth of august & there by
his meanes dyd cause the youth of the parishe to loose evening prayer &   25
also he hym selfe to the evell example of others/

excommunicatur

xviij⁰ Septembris 1578. *preconizatus* wallopp non comp*arui*t vnde d*omi*nus
pronunciau*i*t ips*u*m contumace*m* et in pena*m* excom*municaui*t in script*is*
Postea comp*arui*t wallopp. cui d*omi*n*us* obiecit detecta. qui fatetur that he
requested the mynstrells to come to Asheford to playe & that he emongest   30
others viz Penbrokes sonne of Asheford ffydges sonne of westwell one of mr
Edollfes men & dyu*er*s others. dyd paye them their wagyes. & sayth that
[he dyd ff] he was [not] not at morning prayer at Asheford where he then
dwelte, but he wente vnto Westwell for certen clothes that he had there
lyeing & there he hyred fore noone servyce/ as he saythe & evening prayer   35
he herde at Asheford. vnde d*omi*n*us* monuit eu*m* ad proband*um* allega*cion*em
in prox*imo* sub manib*us* fidedignor*um* ib*id*em/ et ad tunc comparend*um*
ad audiend*um* vlteriorem voluntatem d*omi*ni

°*excommunicatur*°

°xvj⁰ Octobris 1578 *preconizatus* walloppe non comp*arui*t vnde D*omi*n*us*
pronunciau*i*t ips*u*m contumace*m* et in pena*m* excom*municaui*t in script*is*/° 40
Introducta est l*itt*era excom*munica*cionis denu*n*ciata in ecclesia p*re*d*i*cta xix⁰

13/ cui: *for* quibus

Octobris *anno* pre*dicto*

°solu*tio*°   °xiij° Novembris 1578 comp*aruit* p*er*sonali*ter* Wallopp que*m* d*omi*nus ad
eius peti*cio*nem eu*m* a S*enten*cia excommunicaci*on*is absoluit et restituit &c
°dimiss*io*°   et tunc d*omi*nus eu*m* dimisit cu*m* monici*one*°

1640
Nehemiah Wallington, Historical Notes and Meditations
BL: Additional MS. 21,935
f 90

1640

OF the Exploites that the Solgers did in Kent

Att Ashford their was a Solger his name was Bishop (and he was a uery peuish
man) and the rest of the Solgers went and apparelled him like a Bishope with
a Goune, White sleeues and a flat Cape, Then they Called for a Sessions
among them selues, and this Bishop was accused of the troubles that were
Come on the Church and Commonwelth, and so they Condemed him to
dye, and as they were hanging him in Iest (he striuing with them) and they
had like to haue hanged him in earnest for he was almost strangled, And after
this the Solgers went into the Church and pulled vp the Rayles

...

BARHAM

1613
Archdeacon's Court Book   CCA: DCb/J/X.5.8
f 52*   *(13 December)*

*Proceedings arising from the archdeacon's general chapter held in St Margaret's
Church, Canterbury, on 28 October 1613*

pre*sented from*   Kingston
Barham
Boyken   To the 57th article wee present one Boyken of the p*ar*ishe of kingston (a
minstrall for playeinge one the sabboth dayes after eveninge prayer:/:
13° decembris 1613: Browne appar*rit*or &c cer*tificaui*t se p*er*sonali*ter* Citasse
*dict*um Boyken 10° instan*tis* &c preconizat*o* dict*o* Boyken °comp*aruit* [quem
d*omi*nus] cui d*omi*nus obiecit detecta qui r*espondend*o fate*tur* That being a
very poore man ⌐&¬ hauing a great chardge of children he doth sometimes
for his releife being requested play on his instrument on Sondaies after

33/ the 57th article: *one of the visitation articles*   39/ instrument: u *corrected over* a
34/ minstrall: *5 minims in* MS; *closing parenthesis*   39/ Sondaies: *3 minims in* MS
   omitted after minstrall

euening prayer at some honest yeomens houses, Tunc dominus inhibuit
dicto Boykin [cui posthac] That he play noe moore on the Sabaoth day,
°dimissio°   eundemque cum pia monicione dimisit, [mon]°

BENENDEN   5

1612
Archdeacon's Court Book   CCA: DCb/J/X.5.5
f 160v   *(22 October)*

                                                                                10
*Proceedings arising from the archdeacon's general chapter held at Ashford on
28 September 1612*

...

To the 64 wee present Edward Morlene for that hee being vnlicensed keepeing
Morlene./   a blynde Alehouse & suffereth danceing in his howse on the holydaies in   15
service tyme & as wee greate suspecte on the Saboath daies alsoe
22 die Octobris 1612 Bull Certificavit ipsum debite quesivisse dictum
Edwardum Morlene 16 die instantis &c infra parochiam de Benenden
Archidiaconatus Cantuarie animo citandi &c et quod non potuit &c
preconizato dicto Morlene °comparuit personaliter cui dominus obiecit   20
detecta qui fatetur that vpon Ste Peters day last in service tyme he did suffer
one Henrie Tomkyn Roberte Ierrard Iohn Woodman and certen women
°schedula   ∧⌜whose names he knowes not⌝ to daunce in his howse et submisit se &c Tunc
emanauit°   dominus iniunxit dicto Morlen quod agnoscat culpam suam publice in ecclesia
parochiali predicta iuxta schedulam citra proximum &c ⌜vnica vice⌝ et ad   25
certificandum in proximo ei hoc in loco hora causarum &c [vnde] vlterius
dominus decrevit prefatos Tomkyn Ierrard et Woodman citandos in proximum
°decretum°   ad respondendum articulis°
2do die Novembris 1612 coram magistro willelmo Walsall Clerico Substituto
Woodman   &c in eius edibus &c presente Polycarpo Tangett notario publico &c   30
Comparuit personaliter dictus Iohannes Woodman alias Citatus &c qui
consentijt &c Cui dominus obiecit that vpon St Peters daye last hee did
daunce in the house of Edward Morlene abouesaid in ye tyme of divine
service qui respondendo fatetur that hee comeing [to] by Chaunce to the saide
Morlenes howse aboute [a] xj or xij of the Clocke in the foorenoone of the   35
said daye did there daunce but whether yt were then service tyme or noe he
doth not knowe et submisit se &c Tunc dominus ex causis &c cum monicione
&c ipsum Woodman ab Officio suo dimisit &c
6to die Novembris 1612 preconizato dicto Morlene °introduxit certificatorium
°dimissio°   de peraccione penitentie &c vnde dominus eundem Morlen dimisit°   40

14/ the 64: *one of the visitation articles*   17/ Bull: *a summoner*
16/ greate: *for greatlie*

f 170   *(19 November)*

...

Martine

Also I presente Philipp Martine for playeing vpone his fiddle vpone vnlawfull
tymes, as vpone St Peeteres daye laste paste, whereby to drawe the yownger
sorte of people, to spende those tymes vnlawfullye   5
19o Novembris 1612 Bull apparitor &c certificavit se personaliter Citasse
dictum Martine 9o die instantis &c preconizato dicto Martine °comparuit cui
domino obijciente detecta fatetur that he was on the day detected in the
housse of one Edward Morlyn in Bendenden and there did playe vpon a fiddle
of his owne makinge, but whether it were in tyme of devine service or not this 10
respondente doth not certenly knowe et submisit se &c and promiseth
°dimissio°   hereafter he will never doe the like, tunc dominus cum monicione &c dimisit°

f 171v

...   15

Smithe:

Detectum est that these persons whose names are heerevnder seuerallye sett
downe & expressed togeather with others allreadye called & dischardged for
the same matter, did vpone St Peeters daye laste paste 1612, in the tyme of
divine service celebrated the same daye in the parishe Churche of Benenden
aforesaide dawnce in the howse of one Edward Morlen of ye same parishe: to   20
the offence of god contrarye to the kinges Maiesties ecclesiastical lawes and
evill exsample of otheres: vizt: George Smithe Abraham Hodge, Iohn Hedge,
and Daniell Gorham
19o Novembris 1612 Bull apparitor &c certificavit se debite quesivisse dictum
Smithe apud edes 9o instantis &c animo citandi &c et quod non potuit &c   25
preconizato dicto Smith °comparuit cui domino obijciente detecta fatetur that
he was in the housse detected on the day detected in the fore noone but
whether it were in divine service or not he cannot answere [et submisit] ∧⌜but
did not daunce as is detected⌝ & was not at dyvine service in the forenoone of
that day et submisit se &c Tunc dominus [iniunxit ∧⌜dicto Smith⌝ quod solvit   30
ad manus ad causam ⌜&c⌝ summam xij d. ad vsum pauperum parochie
predicte citra proximum &c et ad certificandum in proximo &c] ex gracia &c
°dimissio°   eundem Smith cum monicione &c dimisit°

f 172   35

...

Hodge:

Abrahamus Hodge detectus vt contra Smithe folio precedenti:/
19o Novembris 1612 Bull apparitor &c certificavit se personaliter Citasse
dictum Hodge 9o die instantis &c preconizato dicto Hodge: °comparuit
cui domino obijciente detecta expresse negavit et obtulit se promptum et   40

38/ 1612: *underlined*

　　　　　　　　　*p*aratu*m* ad faciendu*m* fidem ad tacta &c [sem] se inocentem *esse* quoad
°dimiss*io*°　　detecta &c vnde d*omi*nus decreuit sup*er* sedend*o* fore &c dimiss*um* gratis°
　　　　　　　　　…

Hedge　　　　　Iohannes [Hedge] ⌈°Hodge°⌉ detect*us* vt con*tra* Smithe pa*gina* preceden*ti* /
　　　　　　　　　19o Novembris 1612 Bull p*re*dict*us* cer*tifi*cav*it* se p*er*sonali*ter* Citasse d*ictum*　5
　　　　　　　　　Hedge 9o instan*tis* &c preconizato d*icto* Hedge °comp*ar*uit cui d*omi*no
°dimiss*io*°　　obijcien*te* detecta &c expresse negavit eade*m* esse vera vnde d*omi*nus decrevit
　　　　　　　　　sup*er* sedend*o* fore &c°

　　　　　　　　　f 172v　　　　　　　　　　　　　　　　　　　　　　　　　　　　10
　　　　　　　　　…

Gorham:　　　Daniell Gorham detect*us* vt Smithe fol*io* preceden*ti*
　　　　　　　　　19o Novembris 1612 Bull appa*ritor* &c cer*tifi*cav*it* se [p*er*sonali*ter*] debite
　　　　　　　　　quesivisse dictum Gorham apud edes &c 9o instan*tis* &c a*nim*o citandi &c
　　　　　　　　　et quod non potuit &c *pre*conizat*o* d*icto* Gorham °non comp*ar*uit vnde vijs　15
　　　　　　　　　et modis in prox*imum* &c postea seden*te* Curia Comp*ar*uit cui d*omi*no
°dimiss*io*°　　obijcien*te* detecta &c expresse negavit &c vnde d*omi*nus decrevit sup*er*
　　　　　　　　　sedendu*m* fore &c°

BETHERSDEN　　　　　　　　　　　　　　　　　　　　　　20

1520–1
St Margaret's Churchwardens' Accounts　Bethersden: St Margaret's Church
p 116　*(1 January 1519/20–3 February 1520/1)*
　　　　　　　…　　　　　　　　　　　　　　　　　　　　　　　　　　　25
Memorandum　the remayn to the Cherch of the pley aboue all thyng*es* Cownted and alowyd
　　　　　　　　　xlv s. vj d. therof Robert Glou*er* ouyth vj s. viij laur*ence* dewar iij s. iiij d.
　　　　　　　　　W. Poryn vj d.

　　　　　　　　　p 117　　　　　　　　　　　　　　　　　　　　　　　　　　　30
　　　　　　　　　…
　　　　　　　　　It*em* paid to Iohn dyn for caryng of plank*es* fro the stage　　　　ij d.
　　　　　　　　　…

1521 2　　　　　　　　　　　　　　　　　　　　　　　　　　　35
St Margaret's Churchwardens' Accounts　Bethersden: St Margaret's Church
pp 9–12*

　　　　　　　　　Compit*us* Thom*e* bresynden Iun*ioris* Ioh*an*nis clerke Will*el*mi Glou*er* Edw*ard*i
　　　　　　　　　holnerst gardianoru*m* lude beate Cristine a*n*no *regni* regis henr*ici* viij *post*　40
　　　　　　　　　conq*uestu*m anglie xiijo

　　　　　　　　　27/ viij: *for* viij d.　　　　　　40/ lude: *possibly* ludo; *final letter corrected by overwriting*

℃ In primis receyued at the ffyrst pleye daye   xlij s.
℃ Item receyued at the ijᵈ pleye daye   lij s. j d.
℃ Item receyued at the iijᵈ pleye daye   xxxix s. vij d.
℃ [Item receyued of William byshoppe]   vj s. viij d.
℃ [Item receyued of laurence Brodstret]   vj s. viij d.   5
    …

                                                                Summa vij li. vij s.l
℃ In primis payed at charrynge for william Taberares dennar   ij d.
℃ Item payed for a Chamber to Raye vs yn   ij d.
℃ Item payed at Tenterynden for horsmete and pleyeres   ix d.   10
℃ Item payed to William Taberar ther   v d.
℃ Item payed to the Clerke for Wrytyng   v s.
℃ Item payed for mete ∧⌈&⌉ drynke at the fyrst for bannoke
    and Iohn moyse   x d.
℃ Item payed for Iamys pers dennar when he carryed   j d. ob.   15
℃ Item payed for a C of iiij peny nayle   iiij d.
℃ Item payed for bannokes moysys and quersted dennar the
    fyrst playe daye   [vj] ⌈viij⌉ d.
℃ Item payed for a C prygge   j d.
℃ Item payed to Robert Selke for glovys   iij s. ij d.   20
℃ Item payed to William tuyssnoth for pynnys and laces   viij d.
℃ Item payed for mete and drynke at mendynge of þe stage   ij d.
℃ Item payed to Water at nashe to Ryde with our banys   viij d.
℃ Item payed for drynke in the stage   v d.
℃ Item payed for mete and drynke for them þat worke vppon   25
    the Stage at dyuerse tymes   iij s.l
℃ Item payed to Iohn Mapyllysden and to William Marchall   ij s. viij d.
℃ Item payed for drynke at our reherse   iiij d.
℃ Item payed to William Taberar   iij s. iiij d.
℃ Item payed to Rychard abraham   ij d.   30
℃ Item payed for asherst dennar   ij d.
℃ Item payed for quersted dennar   ij d.
℃ Item payed to Thomas Mapyllysden and to William turnor   x d.
℃ Item payed for their Sopperes that were getheres þe ijᵈ pleye   xij d.
℃ Item payed to Iamys peres for Carryenge   xxij d.   35
℃ Item payed to Iohn lodar for carryenge of þe packes   xij d.
℃ Item payed for menys bordynge at deweres   xx d. ob.
℃ Item payed to the menstrelles the ijᵈ pleye daye   iij s.
℃ Item payed to Iohn a Vale for workynge on the stage   xij d.
℃ Item payed to Iohn Dyne   ix d.   40
℃ Item payed to Iohn lesse   xxiij d.

℃ It*em* payed for nayle   ij d.
℃ It*em* payed to Iohn dewar   ij s. iiij d.
℃ It*em* payed for a quart of wyne   ij d.
℃ It*em* payed to Ryc*hard* bannoke for a ffachan   iij d.|
℃ It*em* payed to Thom*as* Elsey for borde   xvj d.   5
℃ It*em* payed to Ierme*n* Glou*er*   ij d.
℃ It*em* payed for the gether*es* dennar the iij^d playe daye   iiij d.
℃ It*em* payed to quersted   ij d.
℃ It*em* payed to Elsey wyfe   xiij d. ob.
℃ It*em* payed to iij boyes to fetche clothes   iij d.   10
℃ It*em* payed for Iohn a Vale and Thom*as* a Vale Sopper the
       iij^d pley dayes evyn   ij d.
℃ It*em* payed for mete and drynke the sayd playe daye   xj d. ob.
℃ It*em* payed to Ryc*hard* bannok*es* iij boyes   iij d.
℃ It*em* payed to Thom*as* bregge for Corde   iiij d.   15
℃ It*em* payed to Iohn lodar for bere   xvij d.
℃ [It*em* payed to Iamys per*es*   iij s. iiij d.]
℃ It*em* payed to Will*i*am Glou*er* for carryenge vp and down
       of the devysor*es* gere   iij s. iiij d.
℃ It*em* payed for fatchons and ʌxc*es*   iiij s.   20
℃ It*em* payed to the devyser for h*is* labor   iij li. x s.
℃ It*em* payed to the clerke for wryttyng of the accompt*es*   iiij d.
                    Su*mm*a vj li. v s. xj d. ob.

1572   25
Archdeacon's Court Book   CCA: DCb/J/X.1.11
f 145v   *(19 June)*

Proceedings of the court held in St Margaret's Church, Canterbury, before Thomas
Lawse, deputy of the archdeacon's official, and in the presence of Thomas Cranmer,   30
notary public and registrar

...

holnest   Also we p*re*sente one Stephen holnest a mynstrell for playenge on his
                    Instrument on the sabothe dayes. and the most parte of the youthe passe
Ex*communicatur*   the daye in daunsynge. wherfore we desyre some good order herein   35
                    Quo die p*re*conizatus holnest non comp*aruit*, vnde d*omi*n*us* pronu*n*ciau*it*
                    ip*su*m contumace*m* ⌐et in pena*m* excom*municaui*t in script*is*⌐ [pena reseruata
                    in pro]

...

11/ Vale¹: *altered from* Wale

BIDDENDEN

1580/1
Archdeacon's Court Book   CCA: DCb/J/X.2.2
f 98   *(10 February)*

Proceedings of the court held in St Margaret's Church, Canterbury, before Richard Beseley, STB, deputy of the archdeacon's official, and in the presence of Thomas Cranmer, notary public and registrar

...

danyell lamben of halden *presented in* Biddenden byll   We pr*e*sent danyell lamben of the paryshe of halden Mynstrell for that on the xvj^th day of october beinge sonday he played ymedyatly after eveninge prayer/ & so dyd cause dyu*er*s of o*ur* paryshe to profane the Sabaothe We woulde be verye gladd to have it reformed for that it maketh greate dysorder in o*ur* paryshe/

solu*tio*   ℂ Quo die Taylor cer*tifi*caui*t* se citasse dictu*m* lamben p*er*sonalite*r* pr*e*conizat*us* Lamben comp*aru*it cui d*omi*n*us* obiecit vt supra/ qui fate*tur* detecta// vnde d*omi*n*us* eum cum monici*o*ne dimisit &c/

dimiss*io* #

BIRCHINGTON

1540
All Saints' Churchwardens' Accounts   CCA: U3/76/5A/2
p 68*   *(Receipts)*

...

Item R*e*ceiv*e*d of the hoctyd monye   viij s. ij d.

...

1606–7
All Saints' Churchwardens' Accounts   CCA: U3/76/5A/3
p 62*   *(25 March–24 March)* *(Expenses)*

...

It*e*m for takinge downe the maypole   viij d.

...

1622
Consistory Court Book   CCA: DCb/J/Z.4.2
f 171v   *(19 September)*

Proceedings of the court held in St Margaret's Church, Canterbury, before George Newman, LLD, the archdeacon's official

...

Wyhall   I pr*e*sent Nathaniell Wihall of Birchington aforesaid for not resorting to

our parish Church but he doth not onely absent himselfe but being a
drummer doth draw away our youth on thc Saboath day to vnseemely
pastimes as namely he goeth dumming with them following him about the
Isleland on the Saboath daies in time of diuine seruice

19o Septembris 1622 Hards apparitor certificauit se 2o 7bris instantis debite   5
quæsiuisse dictum Wihall apud ædes suas infra parochiam de Birchington
⌈prædicta⌉ animo citandi &c quodque non potuit &c facta fide &c
præconizatus non comparuit vnde vijs et modis in proximum

3o Octobris 1622 Hards apparitor exhibuit decretum vijs et modis executum
per ipsum contra dictum Wihall 24o Septembris per afficcionem eiusdem   10
super valuis exterioribus domus seu solitæ habitacionis eius infra parochiam
prædictam facta fide &c præconizatus non comparuit vnde dominus [de]
pronunciauit ipsum contumacem et in penam excommunicandum fore decreuit

excommunicatio   et excommunicauit in scriptis

Introductæ fuerunt litteræ excommunicacionis per Robertum Hards apparitorem   15
denuntiatæ in ecclesia prædicta contra dictum Wihall vicesimo die Octobris
1622 tempore diuinorum per Magistrum Stancomb ibidem Curatum

°9o decembris 1623 coram domino Richardo Clerke clerico sacræ Theologiæ
professore Surrogato &c ac in ædibus magistri Iohannis Sandford vnius   20
prebendariorum ecclesiæ Christi Cantuariæ præsente me Willelmo Somner
Iuniori notario publico

Comparuit personaliter dictus Wyhall in diem locum et Iudicium consensos et
humiliter petijt beneficium absolucionis a sententijs excommunicacionis alias
contra eum latis sibi impendi ac Ius &c Ad cuius peticionem dominus   25
eundem absolvit et restituit ecclesiæ prius facta per ipsum fide de parendo
Iuri et stando mandatis ecclesiæ et desuper decrevit ei litteras testimoniales
&c Vlterius dominus obiecit ei detecta qui humiliter submittendo se &c
fatetur vnde dominus iniunxit ei penitenciam Canonicam vnica vice post
preces coram Ministro Iconomis et duobus vel tribus alijs parochianis   30
parachiæ prædictæ iuxta schedulam et ad Certificandum in proximo &c°

1628
Consistory Court Book   CCA: DCb/J/Z.4.5
f 91   *(10 July)*   35

Cramp ⎦   Officium domini contra Iohannem Cramp Oeconomum ibidem, for that he
               (to the prophanacion of the Saboath, & evill example of others he being a

3/ dumming: *for* drumming   24/ sententijs: *apparently corrected over* sententia
4/ Isleland: s *apparently added later; Isle of Thanet*   30/ vel: *apparently written over* et
5, 9, 17/ 1622: *underlined*

sworne officer) did on Easter day last past teene ˄⌈or mend⌉ hedges or an
hedge, And likewise for that he on the sunday next after Whitsonday, not
onely absented himselfe from divine service in his parish Church both
forenoone & afternoone, but also (which was worse) mispent & prophaned
the same Saboath day, by being with his sonne & daughter dancing at a   5
garland at the house of George Bennett in the afternoone of the sunday
aforesaid, with much other Company./.

10º Iulij 1628 Hardes apparitor certificavit se 4º instantis Iulij debitè
quæsivisse dictum Cramp apud ædes &c infra parochiam prædictam, animo
Citandi &c quodque non potuit &c facta fide &c præconisatus °Comparuit   10
et fatetur that he was absent from church on the forenoone of the sunday

dimissio detected et quoad cetera negavit detecta vnde dominus eundem cum pia
monicione dimisit°

1636–7   15
All Saints' Churchwardens' Accounts   CCA: U3/76/5A/3
p 176   *(25 March–24 March)*
…

Item giuing to Vallentine Archer towards ye setting vp
of ye May-pole   00 06 08   20
…

BONNINGTON

1594   25
Archdeacon's Court Book   CCA: DCb/J/X.3.3 pt 2
f 58*   *(10 May)*

Proceedings of the court held to hear cases arising from the archdeacon's visitation
on 5 April 1594 and sitting in St Margaret's Church, Canterbury, before Stephen   30
Lakes, LLD, the archdeacon's official, and in the presence of William Watmer,
notary public

…

Peercivall Detectum est that William Peercivall was at a dauncing in the house of Iohn
Diggins in tyme of divine service the third of Marche 1593.   35
xiijº [M] Iunij 1594 Cosbye certificavit ipsum [per] debite quesivisse dictum
Peercivall animo citandi &c vjº instantis, quodque non potuit &c preconizatus
Peercivall °comparuit cui dominus obiecit detecta qui respondendo fatetur
that he was at a dauncing as is presented [after ev] but it was after evening
prayer, and sayth that he was that evening at [e] Allington at evening prayer   40

1/ Easter day last past: *13 April*   19/ Vallentine Archer: *churchwarden*
2/ sunday next after Whitsonday: *8 June*   36/ Cosbye: *a summoner*

ac super veritate allegacionis offert se promptum ad faciendum fidem vnde
dominus iniunxit ei ad solvendum xij d. pro absentia ab ecclesia sua parochiali
die predicto ad manus Iconomorum ibidem, et ad agnoscendum culpam suam
coram ministro Iconomis et parochianis iuratis post preces vespertinas iuxta

schedula
emanauit

schedulam citra proximum et ad certificandum in proximo postea dictus   5
Percivall deposuit apud acta pro absentia predicta xij d.°
°xxvij° Iunij 1594 comparuit et certificavit ipsum satisfecisse &c vnde

°dimissio°

dominus ipsum ab offitio suo dimisit°

f 60*   10

Limpne

Stowe

detectum est That Iohn Stowe was at a dauncing in the house of Iohn diggins

°solutio predicta°

of Bonnington in time of divine service the iij^d of marche 1593./
xxvij° Iunij 1594 Cosby certificavit ipsum debite quesivisse eundem animo   15
citandi &c xxij° instantis quodque non potuit &c preconizatus Stowe
°comparuit qui negauit detecta et allegauit that the said daye viz the thirde
of he was at the divyne servyce in the parish church of lympne/ Vnde dominus
assignauit ei ad probandum duos dies Iuridicos proximos° °postea Stowe
humiliter petijt se ab officio domini iudicis dimitti et obtulit se promptum   20
et paratum ad faciendum fidem that hee was present both forenoone and
afternoone at divine service In the parishe church of of Limpne where
hee is parishe clarcke, according to his duetie in that beehalfe: vnde quia
constat domino Substituto ipsum non esse detectum per aliquos Iconomos
parochianosve iuratos ideo prestito prius iuramento per dictum Stowe iuxta   25

°dimissio°

&c dominus eum dimisit cum monicione°

Consistory Court Book   CCA: DCb/J/X.8.8
f 211v*   *(12 November)*

30

*Proceedings of the court held to hear cases arising from the archbishop's visitation
and sitting in the consistory of Canterbury Cathedral before Stephen Lakes, LLD,
commissary general*

Smethe   35

Hewit

Detectum est yat Osmonde Hewit ministrell & his boye did playe vpon their
instrumentes in the tyme of devyne service, at a daunsing in Bonnington
parishe on sonday the third of marche 1593
xij° novembris 1594 coram Domino Commissario &c loco Consistoriali &c
Cosbie exhibuit mandatum originale executum personaliter quarto novembris   40

15/ Cosby: *a summoner*   22/ of of: *dittography*
18/ of¹: *for* of March   40/ Cosbie: *a summoner*

Andree

instan*tis* *preconizatus* hewit non comp*aruit* vnde D*omi*nus pro*nun*ciavit ip*sum* cont*umacem* pena reservata in *proximum* Andree *proximum*

Decimo Decembris 1594 cora*m* D*omi*no Commissario &c loco Cons*istoriali* &c cont*inuatu*r in *proximum*

xiiij Ianuarij a*nno* do*mi*ni iuxta &c 1594 loco Cons*istoriali* &c cora*m*   5
D*omi*no Commissario &c °*preconizatus* hewyt non Comp*aruit* vnde do*mi*nus pro*nun*ciavit ip*sum* con*tumacem* pena reservata in *proximum*

°*excommunicacio emanavit*°

xxviij Ian*uarii* loco Cons*istoriali* &c *preconizatus* hewit non comp*aruit* vnde do*mi*nus pro*nun*ciavit ip*sum* cont*umacem* et in penam excommu*ni*cavit in scriptis   10

viij°° ffebruarij 1594 Cora*m* m*agist*ro Iacobo Bissell Cl*er*ico substituto &c In ædibus suis &c *presente* me Will*elm*o Somner not*ar*io pu*bli*co Comp*aruit* *personalite*r Hewyt quem do*mi*nus ad eius petic*ionem* absoluit et restituit fac*ta* fide &c et tunc do*mi*nus monuit eu*m* ad Comp*arendum* in *proximum* secundu*m* loco Cons*istoriali* &c ad audiendu*m* vol*unta*tem do*mi*ni Iudicis   15
quoad detecta

Annunciacionis

xxv°° ffebr*uarij* 1594 Cora*m* do*mi*no Commissario &c loco Cons*istoriali* &c *preconizatus* hewyt non comp*aruit* vnde Cont*inuatur* in *proximum* post Annunciac*i*onis *proximum*°

...   20

BORDEN

1582
Archdeacon's Court Book   CCA: DCb/J/X.2.4   25
f 67   *(13 December)*

Proceedings of the court held to hear cases arising from the archdeacon's visitation
of Sittingbourne deanery in 1582 and sitting in St Margaret's Church, Canterbury,
before Stephen Lakes, LLD, the archdeacon's official, and in the presence of Thomas   30
Cranmer, notary public and registrar

...

Carter

Item we p*resent* Arthure Carter minstrell for refusing to paie the forfayture of xij d. A sondaye for ij sondayes being asked by the churchwardens according to the Statute.   35

°*dimissio*°
°*solutio*°

°xiij° decembris 1582 comp*aruit* *personalite*r Cartar qui [negauit] allegauit that he was not absent eny two sondayes, and therfore he hath not payde/ postea submisit se correc*cioni* et soluit ad manus meas duos solidos no*m*ine penet*encie*/ vnde do*mi*nus ip*sum* ab offitio suo dimisit°

...   40

2/ in *proximum*: *for* in proximum post   36/ qui: *corrected from* que *or* qua
14–15/ in *proximum* secundu*m*: *for* in proximo secundo

f 67v*

…

Harrys. Pett.
Norrys. Carter.
Clerk

Item Robert Harrys & Thomas Pett & Gilbert Morrys of Bobbing for
dauncing ye morris and ye minstrels William Clerk & Arthur Carters
servauntes　　　　　　　　　　　　　　　　　　　　　　　　　　　　5
°xiij° decembris 1582 comparuit personaliter Morrys qui fatetur detecta, et
allegauit that he was from servyce at his own parishe but yn another parishe
[they were] he was at servyce/ vnde [dominus iniunxit] submisit se correccioni
[dominus] domino Iudicem/ vnde dominus iniunxit ei ad reconciliandum
se publice in [facie] ecclesia de Bobbynge die dominica proxima et ad　　10
certificandum in proximo post postea soluit et
Preconizatis Pett et harrys non comparuerunt vnde dominus pronunciauit
ipsos contumaces, pena reservata in proximum

vide plura folio
5 sequenti

Preconizato Willimo Clerke comparuit, et fatetur that his servauntes &
he did Playe at a certeyne morryce daunce/ vnde dominus iiuxit ei ad　　15
comparendum in proximo ad dicendum causam quare puniri non debet°

…

f 73*

　　　　　　　　　　　　　　　　　　　　　　　　　　　　　　　　　20

vide plura folio
5 sequenti

postea [comparuit pers] dictus Clerke submisit correccioni domini Iudicis
vnde dominus iniunxit ei ad soluendum Iconomis ibidem citra proximum

Epiphanie

post Epiphanie et ad certificandum in proximo post

dimissio

°xvij° Ianuarij 1582 certificatum est ipsum satisfecisse &c. vnde dominus
ipsum ab offitio suo dimisit°　　　　　　　　　　　　　　　　　　　25

…

BOUGHTON MONCHELSEA

1582　　　　　　　　　　　　　　　　　　　　　　　　　　　　30
Archdeacon's Court Book　CCA: DCb/J/X.2.4
f 60v*　(29 November)

*Proceedings of the court held to hear cases arising from the archdeacon's visitation
of Churing deanery in 1582 and sitting in St Margaret's Church, Canterbury,　35
before Stephen Lakes, LLD, the archdeacon's official, and in the presence of Thomas
Cranmer, notary public and registrar*

…

<table>
<tr><td>4m/ Norrys: for Morrys</td><td>15/ iiuxit: for iniunxit; abbreviation mark missing</td></tr>
<tr><td>9/ domino Iudicem: for domini Iudicis</td><td>16/ puniri: 4 minims in MS</td></tr>
<tr><td>10/ ecclesia: corrected from ecclesijs</td><td>22m/ sequenti: for precedenti</td></tr>
<tr><td>11/ et: for etc</td><td></td></tr>
</table>

Younge

Thomas younge a mynstrell is vehemently suspected to be of our parishe vseth to play vpon the saboth dayes but he sayth that he hath a messuage at hedcern

solutio

xxix° Novembris 1582 comparuit personaliter younge, qui fatetur detecta/ vnde dominus [assig] iniunxit ei quod posthec non vtatur fidibus, diebus   5

dimissio

sabotis vel dominicis sub pena Iuris, et sic ipsum ab offitio suo cum monicione dimisit

…

BOUGHTON UNDER BLEAN   10

1535
Sts Peter's and Paul's Churchwardens' Accounts   CCA: U3/221/5/1
f 6v*

15

Edward Songer was borne on Witsonday yven in Anno domini Millesimo Quingentesimo Tricesimo quarto and was one hole yere old whan Corpus Christi play was playd in Boughton strete per me Edwardum Songer 1578

…

20

f 7*
…

°This yere Corpus christi play was plaid at boughton strete° †
                anno domini Millesimo d xxxvti
Memorandum stevyn Wylles hayth cowntytt for the fyrst play day iiij li. v s.   25
x d. & xx s. for rychard folke

…

1640/1
Complaint against Samuel Smith   BL: Additional MS. 26,785   30
f [1]*   (9 February)

to proue [his] ⌜mr Samuell Smithes⌝ hanting of Alehouses & playing at tables & continuing there by night is Edmon Pachingham & Anthony Edwards   35

2/ messuage: expansion conjectural
5/ fidibus: first i written over e
18/ Edwardum Songer: Songer has drawn his mark, resembling a notarial knot, between the 2 words
    of his signature
25/ stevyn Wylles: churchwarden

To proue his drinking of healths & singing of idle catches is William Abraham
and Ezeckiell Maxsted

...

BOXLEY   5

1586
Archdeacon's Court Book   CCA: DCb/J/X.2.9 pt 1
f 48*   *(2 June)*

...   10

Record

Offitium domini merum *contra* Iohannem ⌈Willimum⌉ Record œconomum de
Boxlye [detectum per] notatum per Richardum Shawe et Iohannem Payne, for
that the sonday before St Markes daye, and vpon St Markes the said Record
kept dauncyng yn his howse yn the tyme of divyne servyce/ viz. vpon Saynt
Markes day bothe yn the mornyng and evenyng prayer tyme/ and the sonday   15
before yn the evenyng prayer tyme vnde dominus decreuit Record citandum
fore in proximum ad respondendum articulis/
°Secundo die Iunij 1586° comparuit personaliter Record, qui fatetur that vpon
St Markes day yn the evenyng prayer tyme he kept dauncyng yn his howse,
[yn] but as vpon the sonday before he [k] had no dauncyg yn his howse [yn]   20
but towardes the evenyng after evenyng prayer tyme/ and sayth that one
(blank) wodley was the mynstrell there dwellyng in westfairly yn the dyoces
of Rochester/ and one Thomas Burbage the sonne of Iohn Burbage was one
that did daunce who dwelt at Boxlye/ and one howtynges sonne of Barsted did
also then daunce vnde dominus monuit ipsum ad comparendum in proximo   25
ad dicendum causam si &c quare penitentia canonica ei non debeat iniungi
et decreuit Thomam Burbage et Thomam howtyng citandos fore in proximum
ad respondendum articulis et decreuit Richardum Shawe et Iohannem Payne
citandos fore in proximum ad [respondendum articulis] iustificandum notata
per ipsos   30

Record

xvj° die Iunij 1586 °comparuit personaliter Record, qui interrogatus per
dominum causam nullam allegauit, vnde dominus iniunxit ei iniunxit ei
penitentiam canonicam more solito iuxta schedulam vnica vice in ecclesia

---

1/ drinking: k *corrected over* g
1/ William: W *corrected from* N
13/ the sonday before St Markes daye: *18 April*
20/ dauncyg: *for* dauncyng; *abbreviation mark missing*
22–3/ westfairly ... Rochester: *although in the neighbouring diocese of Rochester, West Farleigh is only*
    about 5 miles from Boxley
26/ iniungi: *5 minims in* MS
32/ iniunxit¹: *5 minims in* MS
32/ iniunxit ei iniunxit ei: *dittography*

de Boxlye tempore divinorum/ et ad certificandum in proximo post/ et vltius
dominus iniunxit ei soluendum œconomis ibidem xij d. in vsum pauperum &c
et ad certificandum in proximo post/°
[ix° die Iulij ad peticionem dicti Record dominus] †

°vide pagina
tertia sequenti°

5

f 49v*

…

°Record°   °ix° Iulij comparuit dictus Record ad cuius peticionem dominus [negavit]
⌐iniunxit⌐ penitentiam [suam] ⌐ei⌐ forma sequenti vz. quod publice agnoscat
culpam in ecclesia parochiali de Boxlie tempore divinorum iuxta schedulam   10
°Crucis°   absque linteis et ad solvendum pixidi pauperum iij s. iiij d. et vltra pro absentia
vide pagina   eius ab ecclesia xij d. provt in priori acta et ad certificandum in proximo
tertia precedenti   secundo°
°solutio mathew°   xxij° Septembris 1586, preconizatus Record non comparuit/ vnde dominus
pronunciauit ipsum contumacem et in penam decreuit ipsum excoicandum   15
fore
°xxviij°   °in visitatione apud ffauersham Introducte fuerunt littere certificatorie in
Septembris   quibus certificatum fuit ipsum record peregisse penitentiam suam iuxta &c
1586°   et absolutus est et dimissus satisfecit iniunctioni 24 Iulij 1586°
°dimissio°

20

f 48v*

…

xvj° Iunij 1586   Offitium domini merum contra Thomam Burbage parochie de Boxlye notatum
[Mast] Burbage   [contra] for dauncyng, yn the tyme of common prayer on St Markes ⌐day⌐
last past, citatum per Mastall qui certificavit &c preconizatus Burbage   25
comparuit qui domino obijciente fatetur that vpon St Markes day last past yn
the evenyng prayer he was not at his parishe churche, but was yn company
of dauncers & mynstrells yn the tyme of dyvyne prayer/ vnde dominus
monuit ipsum ad comparendum in proximo ad dicendum causam si &c quare
penitentia canonica ei non debeat iniungi   30
°Primo Iulij 1586 comparuit, et quia causam nullam° °sed submisit se
correctioni Iudicis &c comissum vnde dominus monuit eum ad agnoscendum
culpam suam in Ecclesia parochiali de Boxley aliquo die dominico siue

---

1/ vltius: *for* vlterius; *abbreviation mark missing*   25/ Mastall: *a summoner*
2/ iniunxit: *4 minims in* MS   28/ dauncers: *3 minims in* MS
2/ soluendum: *for* ad soluendum   30/ iniungi: *5 minims in* MS
13/ priori: *for* priore   31/ nullam: *for* nullam &c
15/ excoicandum: *for* excommunicandum;
   abbreviation mark missing
23m/ Iunij: *3 minims in* MS

festiuo *proximo* temp*ore* divinor*um* solempnia et ad certificand*um* in *proximo*
post hoc in loco et ad soluend*um* pixidi pauper*um* eodem temp*ore* xij d. et
simil*iter* ad certificand*um* de soluci*one* eiusdem die *predicto* certificat*um*
est ip*sum* satisfecisse Iniunctioni Iudicis et solvisse *dictam* Su*m*mam Vnde

°dimiss*io*°   dominus eu*m* dimisit°
                                                                                    5

                                   Barstedd

Howtyng   *Similiter contra* Thomam howtyng de eadem/ preconizatus Thomas Howtyng,
                 ⌈non⌉ comp*aruit* [qui negauit q*uod* [⟨.⟩] cui d*ominus* obiecit pr*ov*t superius
                 Burbage est obiectum, qui negauit] vnde d*ominus* [pronunciauit ip*sum*   10
                 contumacem] decreuit ip*sum* citand*um* fore in prox*imum* ad resp*on*dend*um*
                 art*icu*lis
                 °xiiij° Iulij, 1586 [comp*aruit*] Tho*mas* howtyng citat*us* personalit*er* p*er*
                 mastall comp*aruit* p*er*sonalit*er* cui d*ominus* obiecit that vppon St Mark*es*
                 day last he was absent from his paryshe churche at the tyme of devyne   15

°solut*io*°   servyce/ qui fatet*ur* obiecta [Vnde d*ominus*] et allegauit that he hathe p*aid*
                 xij d. to the churche wardens there for his said defalt/ vnde d*ominus* monuit
                 eu*m* ad comp*ar*end*um* in *proximo* hoc in loco ad cer*tificandum* de soluc*ione*
                 eiusd*em* su*m*m*ae*°
                 ...   20

vide pag*ina*   °xxij° Septembris 1586° continuatur in *proximum*
sequen*ti*   °xxj° die Octobris 1586°

                 f 49
                                   Barstedd   25
Howtyng   Offitiu*m* d*omini* meru*m contra* Willimu*m* Howtyng, de Barstedd *presentem*
                 in iudicio, cui d*ominus* obiecit that vpon St Mark*es* day last past he was
                 absent from co*m*mon prayer, bothe yn the mornyg & also yn the evenyng,
                 qui fatetur obiecta et allegauit that he was so lame that he was not ablc
                 to go out of the doores by a blowe gyven to hym yn runyng for a matche   30
                 vnde d*ominus* iniunxit ei ad soluend*um* œcon*omis* de Barstedd ad vsu*m*
                 pauperu*m* ib*idem* xij d. citra *proximum* et ad cer*tificandum* in *proximo*
                 post
                 °decimo quarto Iulij 1586 Preconiz*atus* howting non comp*aruit* vnde d*ominus*
                 pronunciau*it* ipsum contumacem pena reservata in *proximum*°   35
dimiss*io*   °xxviij° die Iulij anno d*omini* 1586° certificatum est et di*missus*
                 ...

                 1/ solempnia: *for* solempnium
                 28/ mornyg: *for* mornyng; *abbreviation mark missing*

BRABOURNE

1607
Archdeacon's Court Book   CCA: DCb/J/X.4.7
f 128   *(14 December)*   5

*Proceedings arising from the metropolitical visitation held in Canterbury
Cathedral on 14 September 1607 before Richard Bancroft, archbishop of
Canterbury*

...   10

Detectum est, that Iohn Brickenden of Braborne a victuler doth ofte prophane
the Saboth daye by enterteyning fidlers or musitions into his house, with
diverse other persons there daunceing & keepeing ill rule: and namelie on
the xiijth of September last past being sondaye:

14to Decembris 1607 Cappit certificauit se personaliter Citasse dictum   15
Iohannem Brickenden viijo die mensis instantis &c preconizato dicto
Brickenden °comparuit cui dominus obiecit detecta qui respondendo negavit
eadem esse vera saving hee saith that one sondaye abowte michaelmas laste
hee had fydling and dawnseing in his howse after evening prayer: Tunc
dominus ex confessatis per Brickenden et propter evidentiam detectionis   20
iniunxit eidem Brickenden quod agnoscat culpam publice in ecclesia de
Braborne iuxta shedulam aliquo die dominico citra proximum:
xviij Ianuarij 1607 coram domino doctore Newman aucthoritate reverendissimi
&c preconizatus Brickenden non comparuit: pronuntiatur contumax pena
reservata in proximum:°   25
4to ffebruarij 1607 iuxta &c introductum est certificatorium [ac] de peraccione
penitentie &c vnde dominus ipsum Brickenden ab Officio suo dimisit:/.

Brickenden *(left margin, line 13)*
dimissio *(left margin, line 27)*

BREDGAR

                                                             30
1579
Consistory Court Book   CCA: DCb/J/X.8.10
f 137v   *(11 November)*

Proceedings of the court held in the consistory of Canterbury Cathedral before   35
Thomas Lawse, LLD, *commissary general*

...

°excommunicatur° *(left margin)*   [Iohn Quylter played at Bredgar vpon the Saboth day with his tabor to the
[off] breach of the Saboth daie vt informatur]

15/ Cappit: *a summoner*   38m/ °excommunicatur°:   *reading conjectural*

1579/80
Archdeacon's Court Book   CCA: DCb/J/Y.4.18 pt 2
f 93v*   *(12 January)*

Proceedings of the court held in St Margaret's Church, Canterbury, before Robert 5
Bishopp, LLD, the archdeacon's official, and in the presence of Thomas Cranmer,
notary public and registrar

...

Iohn Collyar

we present Iohn Collyar a mynstrall of our paryshe for playeng at our paryshe
the xx^th daye of September being sonday all the tyme of common prayer at 10

°evocetur°

after noone/
°Quo die *(blank)*
xxvj° Ianuarij 1579 iuxta &c *(blank)*
ix° ffebruarij anno domini 1579 predicto *(blank)*°

...   15

BROOKLAND

1527
Will of James Hoggelyn of Old Romney   CKS: PRC 17/17   20
f 250   *(2 April; proved 3 June)*

...To william Ealdishe if he playe yn brokeland playe on penticost next
commyng to the makyng of his hoses xij d....

25

CANTERBURY

c 970
Regularis Concordia
*(Instructions for Easter observance)**   30

...

on dæge þam halgum easter tide   seofon preostlice tida   fram
In die sancto Paschae   septem canonicae horae a

munecum on cyricean godes æfter þeaɣe preosta   for   35
monachis in aecclesia Dei   more   canonicorum, propter

Collation with BL: Cotton Faustina B.III, ff 188–9v *(F)* and Cotton Tiberius A.III,
ff 21–1v *(T)*: 33 die] d⌈i⌉e *T* 33 Paschae] Paschaeae *F*

23–4/ penticost next commyng: *9 June*

ealdorscype þæs eadigan gregorius papan setles þæs ap*ost*olican
autoritatem beati   Gregorii papae sedis apostolicae

þa   hesylf on þam antefne dihtnode to ᵹyrþienne synd
quam ipse   antiphonario   dictauit, celebrandae sunt.   5

þære sylfan on timan nihte ær þam þe dægred sanga becnu beon gestyrude
Eiusdem   tempore noctis antequam matutinorum signa moueantur

niman   þa cyricᵹerdes þa rode & settan on stoᵹe hyre gedafenlicre   10
sumant editui   crucem & ponant in loco sibi congruo.

on fruman to nocterne   fra*m* abbude oððe sumum mæssepreoste
In primis ad nocturnam, ab   abbate seu   quolibet sacerdote

                                                                            15

þænne byþ asteald lof godes on cyrcean cᵹeþe
dum initur   laus Dei, in ecclesia dicat 'Domine labia mea

                   syþþan
aperies' semel tantum; postea 'Deus in adiutorium meum   20

                   þa*m* sealme
intende' cum gloria. Psalmo autem 'Domine quid multiplicati

           forlætenu*m*   ongynne   þænne ðry   25
sunt' dimisso, cantor incipiat inuitatorium, tunc tres

antefnas   mid þrim sealmas þam   geendudu*m* fers
antiphonae cum tribus psalmis. Quibus finitis,   uersus

                                                                            30

gebyrigende si gecᵹeden syþþan sᵹa fela rædinga mid repsum
conueniens dicatur,   deinde tot lectiones   cum responsoriis

to þam on riht belimpendum þonne seo þridde byþ gerædd ræding
ad hoc rite   pertinentibus. Dum tertia   recitatur   lectio,   35

Collation continued: 5 celebrandae] celebranda*æ* F   11 sumant] sumat *F*
14 ab] *T omits* 20 aperies] *F adds* et os meum   32 conueniens] conuenies *F*
32 lectiones] lectionis *T* 35 Dum] um *F (initial elaborated capital missing)*

17–20/ 'Domine labia ... aperies': *Ps 51.15 (50.17 Vulgate)*
20–3/ 'Deus ... intende': *Ps 70.1 (69.2 Vulgate)*
23–6/ 'Domine ... sunt': *Ps 3.1 (3.2 Vulgate)*

feoƿer gebroþru scrydan hi þære   an   mid alban gescrydd
iiii^{or} fratres   induant se quorum unus alba   indutus

sƿylce elleshƿæt to donne inn ga   &   diglice þæs byrgenes
ac si   ad aliud agendum ingrediatur atque latenter sepulchri   5

stoƿe   togange & þam mid handa healdende palmam gedefe sitte & þænne
locum adeat   ibique manu   tenens   palmam quietus sedeat. Dumque

se þridda byþ gesungen reps   þa oþre ðry æfterfylian ealle   10
tertium   percelebratur responsorium, residui tres succedant omnes

ƿitudlice mid kappum gescrydde storcillan mid recelse   on handum
quidem cappis   induti,   turribula cum incensu manibus

                                  15
berende & fot mælum & gelicnysse   secendra   sum þincg
gestantes, ac pedetemptim ad similitudinem quaerentium quid

cuman to foran stoƿe   þæs byrgenes synd gedone soþlice þas
ueniant ante   locum sepulchri.   Aguntur   enim   haec   20

to gcefenlæcincge þæs engles sittendes on byrgene   &   þæra ƿifa
ad imitationem   angeli   sedentis in monumento atque mulierum

mid ƿyrtgemangum cumendra   þæt hi smyredon lichaman þæs hælendes   25
cum aromatibus   uenientium ut ungerent   corpus   ihesu.

þænne earnustlice se sittende þry sƿylce ƿorigende & sum þinc
Cum ergo   ille residens tres uelut erraneos ac aliquid

                                  30
secende   gesihþ him togenealæcean ongynne he mid medumre stefne
quaerentes uiderit sibi approximare, incipiat   mediocri   uoce

ƿerudlice | singan   þam gesungenum oþ ende
dulcisone cantare 'Quem queritis.' Quo decantato   fine tenus,   35

Collation continued: 2 alba] abba *T* 5 latenter] latentur *F*

35/ 'Quem queritis': *incipit for first line of trope, 'Quem quaeritis in sepulchro, Christicolae?'*

andsƿarian þa ðry anum muþe   þam
respondeant hi tres uno   ore 'Ihesum Nazarenum.' Quibus

he
ille 'Non est hic, surrexit sicut predixerat. Ite nuntiate quia   5

                þare   hæse   stefne ƿendan
surrexit a mortuis.' Cuius iussionis uoce   vertant

hi þa ðry to chore   cƿeþende   10
se illi tres ad chorum dicentes 'Alleluia. Resurrexit

                gecƿedenum þysum eftsona se sittenda sƿylce
dominus.' Dicto   hoc   rursus ille residens uelut
                                                                         15
ongenclypiende hi   cƿeþe antefn
reuocans   illos dicat antiphonam 'Uenite & uidete locum.'

þas soþlice cƿeþende arise   & hebbe upp þæne claþ & geoƿige   him
Hec uero   dicens   surgat & erigat   uelum   ostendatque eis   20

þa stoƿe rode abarude ac þæt an   þa linƿæda gelede mid þam
locum   cruce nudatum sed   tantum linteamina posita quibus

seo rod befealden ƿæs þam geseƿenum settan   25
crux   inuoluta erat. Quo uiso,   deponant

þa storcillan þa hi bæran   on þære sylfan byrgene & niman
turribula   quae gestauerant in eodem   sepulchro sumantque
                                                                         30
þæt lin & aþenian   ongea þæne hired & sƿilce ætyƿende
linteum et extendant contra clerum   ac, ueluti ostendentes

Collation continued: 2 Nazarenum] *F omits*   8 surrexit] surre‸⌐x⌐it *F*
8 iussionis] iussimus *T*   23 nudatum] nudata *F*   26 inuoluta] inuolata *F*
26 deponant] deponat *F*   29 sumantque] sumanque *F*   32 contra] concra *F*

2/ 'Ihesum Nazarenum': *incipit for second line of trope, 'Iesum Nazarenum crucifixum, o caelicolae'*
5–8/ 'Non est hic … a mortuis': *third line of trope*
11–14/ 'Alleluia … dominus': *incipit for fourth line of trope, 'Alleluia, resurrexit dominus hodie, leo fortis, Christus, filius dei, deo gratias dicite, eia'*
17/ 'Uenite … locum': *incipit for fifth line of trope, 'Venite et videte locum ubi positus erat dominus, alleluia, alleluia'*

þæt aras   drihten   eac   he na si þar befealden
quod surrexerit dominus & iam non   sit illo inuolutus,

þysne singan antefn
hanc canant antiphonam 'Surrexit dominus de sepulchro'   5

& ofer lencgan þ*æt* lin þa*m* ƿeofode geendedu*m* antefne yldra
superponantque linteum altari.   Finita antiphona,   prior

geblissigende for sige   cynincges ures þ*æt*   ofercumennu*m* deaþe   10
congaudens   pro triumpho regis nostri,   quod deuicta   morte

he aras   ongynne þæne ymen   þa*m* ongunnenum samod
surrexit, incipiat ymnum 'Te Deum laudamus.' Quo incepto,   una
                                                       15

beoþ gehringde ealle becnu...
pulsantur   omnia signa....

1272–3
Christ Church Treasurers' Accounts   LPL: MS. 242   20
f 9v col 1   *(Miscellaneous business)*

...It*em* histrionib*us* ad festu*m* *s*an*c*ti thom*e* .ix s....
...
                                                       25

1274–5
Christ Church Treasurers' Accounts   LPL: MS. 242
f 21 col 2   *(Miscellaneous business)*

...It*em* histrionib*us* *per* priorem .v s....   30

f 22 col 1
...
...It*em* histrionib*us* *per* man*us* iii s....
...   35

Collation continued: 2 surrexerit] surrexit *F*   2 & iam] etiam *T*

5/ 'Surrexit ... sepulchro': *incipit for seventh line of trope, 'Surrexit dominus de sepulchro qui pro nobis pependit in ligno, alleluia'*
23/ festu*m* *s*an*c*ti thom*e*: *probably Martyrdom of St Thomas Becket, 29 December*

1275-6
Christ Church Treasurers' Accounts LPL: MS. 242
f 26 col 1   *(Miscellaneous business)*
...

Item histrionibus per Capellanum prioris [xviij d.] xxx. d.   5
...

col 2
...

Item pro histrionibus per manus Domini capellani .ix. d.   10
...

1277-8
Christ Church Treasurers' Accounts LPL: MS. 242
f 38 col 1*   *(Miscellaneous business)*   15
...

Item Datum ystrionibus domini regis per preceptum prioris xij. d.
...

col 2   20
...

...Item hystrionibus vj d.
...

f 38v col 2   25
...

...Item datum Cuidam istrioni xij d. per priorem...
...

1279-80   30
Christ Church Treasurers' Accounts LPL: MS. 242
f 51 col 1 *(Miscellaneous business)*
...

Item cuidam ystrioni .xij. d. precepto prioris per manus eiusdem
...   35

col 2
...

Item Cuidam histrioni .xij. d.
...   40

1284–5
Christ Church Treasurers' Accounts   LPL: MS. 242
f 86v col 1   *(Miscellaneous business)*
...

¶ Item dat*um* cuida*m* istrioni .xij d. p*er* prior*em*...   5

1286–7
Christ Church Treasurers' Accounts   LPL: MS. 242
f 92v col 2   *(Miscellaneous business)*
...   10

¶ Item Dat*um* histrionib*us* harpat*oribus* & aliis menestrall*is* diuersis ad festu*m*
translacio*n*is .vij. so. vj d.
...

1287–8   15
Christ Church Treasurers' Accounts   LPL: MS. 242
f 97v col 1   *(29 September 1287–30 November 1288) (Miscellaneous business)*
...

¶ Diuersis histrionib*us* i*n* festiuitate sa*n*c*t*i thom*e* p*er* manus Ioha*n*nis de
hardr*es* .vj. s. viij d. ⌊Item aliis v so. p*er* prior*em*⌋   20
...

f 98
...

Datu*m* diuersis Istrionib*us* & Citharedib*us* ad Translacio*n*em be*at*i Thome   25
.vj. so. viij. d. p*er* Ioha*n*n*em* de hardr*es*
...

1288–9
Christ Church Treasurers' Accounts   LPL: MS. 242   30
f 105v col 1*   *(1 December–29 September) (Miscellaneous business)*
...

...Ite*m* diu*er*sis istrionib*us* in festiuitate sa*n*c*t*i thom*e* martir*is* vj. so. viij d....

f 106v col 1   35

Histrionib*us* ad transl*ac*ion*em* sa*n*c*t*i thom*e* martir*is* vj so. viij d....

11–12/ festu*m* translacio*n*is: *ie, Translation of St Thomas Becket, 7 July*
19/ festiuitate sa*n*c*t*i thom*e*: *probably Martyrdom of St Thomas Becket, 29 December*
19–20/ Ioha*n*nis de hardr*es*: *prior's chaplain*
33/ festiuitate sa*n*c*t*i thom*e* martir*is*: *probably Martyrdom of St Thomas Becket, 29 December*

1289-90
Christ Church Treasurers' Accounts   LPL: MS. 242
f 110 col 1   *(Miscellaneous business)*
...

Item dat*um* diu*er*sis histrionib*us* die s*an*c*t*i thome martir*is* viij s. viiij d....   5

col 2*
...

...It*em* hystrionib*us* i*n* festiuitate vid*elicet* i*n* translacione d*e*i martir*is* pro ij ⟨...⟩
vij so. achard & p*ro* sp*e*cieb*us* die tr*an*slacionis be*a*ti th*om*e xx. s. iiij d. wngel   10
...

1290-1
Christ Church Treasurers' Accounts   LPL: MS. 242
f 153 col 1*   *(Miscellaneous business)*   15

...It*em* histrionib*us* i*n* festo s*an*c*t*i thome martir*is* vj so....
...

col 2   20
...

Item dat*um* histrionib*us* ad translac*i*o*n*em [v s.] vij so.
...

1291-2   25
Christ Church Treasurers' Accounts   LPL: MS. 242
f 157 col 1   *(Miscellaneous business)*
...

Item histrionib*us* die passionis s*an*c*t*i thome .iiij. s. .vj d.
...   30

1292-3
Christ Church Treasurers' Accounts   LPL: MS. 242
f 163 col 1   *(Miscellaneous business)*
...   35

Item histrionib*us* die passion*is* s*an*c*t*i thome v s. vj d.
...

5/ die s*an*c*t*i thome martir*is*: *probably Martyrdom of St Thomas Becket, 29 December*
10/ achard: *John Acharde, monk of Christ Church Priory*
17/ festo s*an*c*t*i thome martir*is*: *probably Martyrdom of St Thomas Becket, 29 December*
23/ translac*i*o*n*em: *ie, Translation of St Thomas Becket, 7 July*

col 2

...

Item histrionibus quando iusticiarii comederunt cum domino priore xv. s. iiij d.

...

5

1298–9
Christ Church Treasurers' Accounts LPL: MS. 242
f 199v col 1* *(Miscellaneous business)*

...

Item datum trumpatoribus domini Regis euntibus ante processionem   10
conuentus in vigilia assencionis per preceptum supprioris   iiij. so.

...

1299–1300
Christ Church Treasurers' Accounts LPL: MS. 242   15
f 209v *(Miscellaneous business)*

...

Datum Gauterio ystrioni eunti ad priorem ad expensas per
Manus Andree   ij so. vj d.

...   20

1300–1
Christ Church Treasurers' Accounts LPL: MS. 242
f 216 col 1 *(Miscellaneous business)*

...   25

Datum Gauterio de flandria ystrioni per suppriorem .iii. so.

...

Datum ystrionibus die passcionis sancti thome vj so. per priorem

...

30

1301–2
Christ Church Treasurers' Accounts LPL: MS. 242
f 224 col 1* *(Miscellaneous business)*

...

Datum ystrionibus domini Regis ⌈quando⌉ fuit cantuarie in festo   35
sancti michaelis per mannus alexandri   vj so. vj d.

...

11/ in vigilia assencionis: *Ascension Eve, 27 May*
18/ priorem: *Henry de Eastry, prior 10 April 1286–8 April 1331*
19/ Manus: *-us sign corrected over* n *or* u
19/ Andree: *Andrew de Hardys, monk of Christ Church Priory*
36/ alexandri: *Alexander de Sandwyco, prior's chaplain*

1303–4
Christ Church Treasurers' Accounts   LPL: MS. 242
f 235 col 1   *(Miscellaneous business)*

...

Item ystrionibus   vj so. iij d.   5

...

1306–7
Christ Church Treasurers' Accounts   LPL: MS. 242
f 256 col 1   *(Miscellaneous business)*   10

...

Datum ystrionibus eodem die   x. so.

...

f 256v col 2   15

...

Item datum ystrionibus In translacione sancti thome   dimidiam marcam

...

1307–8   20
Christ Church Treasurers' Accounts   LPL: MS. 242
f 115 col 1   *(Miscellaneous business)*

...

Item ystrionibus eodem die   xl d.

...   25

Item Datum ystrionibus die translacionis sancti thome
per priorem   x s.

...

1308–9   30
Christ Church Treasurers' Accounts   LPL: MS. 242
f 264 col 2   *(Miscellaneous business)*

...

Item ystrionibus eodem die   xi so. x d.

...   35

12*l* eodem die: *Martyrdom of St Thomas Becket, 29 December*
24*l* eodem die: *Trinity Sunday, 9 June*
34*l* eodem die: *Martyrdom of St Thomas Becket, 29 December*

f 265 col 1

...

Datum ystrionibus die sancte trinitatis xiij s. iiij d.

...

5

col 2*

...

¶ Item ystrionibus die quo dominus Guillelmus inge & alii iusticarii
ad assisas comederunt cum priore x so.

... 10

¶ Datum ystrionibus die translacionis sancti thome per supriorem ij. so.

Item ystrionibus die translacionis sancti thome xx so.

...

15

f 265v col 2

...

Item ystrionibus die sancti michaelis dimidiam marcam

...

20

1309–10
Christ Church Treasurers' Accounts LPL: MS. 242
f 273 col 2* *(Miscellaneous business)*

...

Item ystrionibus xiij so. iiij d. 25
Item ij. vigilis castri douorie xl d.

...

f 273v col 2

...

30

Datum ystrionibus per suppriorem die assencionis xij d.

...

f 274 col 1

...

35

Item Datum ystrionibus diebus sancti dunstani et sancte
trinitatis per Manus eiusdem viij. so.

...

3l die sancte trinitatis: *Trinity Sunday, 25 May*   36–7l sancte trinitatis: *Trinity Sunday, 14 June*
31l die assencionis: *Ascension Day, 28 May*   37l eiusdem: *Alexander de Sandwyco, prior's chaplain*

col 2*

...

Item datum diuersis ystrionibus Regis per constamentum
episcopi Eliensis ⌐per manus eiusdem⌐   x s.

...   5

William Thorne's Chronicle of St Augustine's Abbey
Corpus Christi College, Cambridge: MS. 189
f 143*   (16 November)

...   10
...ℭ Et quia tempora moderna in rerum copijs & affluencia terrenarum
facultatum temporibus elapsis minime valeant comparari prouidenciam circa
predictam installacionem factam non vt sequentes eam paralitate imitentur
sed vt eam pocius admirentur expediens duxi ad scribendum que fuit talis
de frumento liij summe precio xix li. de brasio lviij summe precio xvij li. x s.   15
de vino xj dolea precio xxiiij li. de Auena pro hospitibus tam infra portus quam
in villa xx summe iiij li. pro speciebus xxviij li. De Cera CCC libre precio viij li.
De amygdalis D libre precio lxxviij s. de carcoisis boum xxx precio xxvij li.
de porcis C precio xvj. li. de Multonibus CC precio xxx li. de aucis Mille
precio xvj li. de caponibus & Gallinis D precio vj li. v s. de pulonibus iiijᶜ   20
lxiij precio lxxiiij s. de porcellis CC precio C s. de cygnis xxxiiij precio vij li.
de cuniculis vjᶜ precio xv li. de sceutis de braun xvij precio lxv s. de perdicibus
Madlardis bittores alaudis precio xviij li. de ollis terreis Mˡ precio xv s. De sale
ix summe precio x s. de ciphis Mˡ iiijᶜ & de discis & platellis Mˡ Mˡ Mˡ CCC
de stopis & Gachis viij li. iiij s. de pisce caseo lacte alleis precio L s. de ouis   25
ix Mˡ vj ᶜ precio iiij li. x s. In croco & pipere xxxiiij s. In carbonibus doleis
& furnasiis locatis xlviij s. In CCC vlnis de caneuasio iiij li. in tabulis trestalis
dressoris faciendis xxxiiij s. Item datum cocis & eorum garcionibus vj li. &
Menestrallis lxx s. ℭ Summa CC iiijˣˣ vij li. v s. cum allocacione exenniarum Et
fuerunt tam viri potentes quam alij diuersis in locis primo discumbentes vj   30
Mille hominum & eo amplius ad tria millia ferculorum quo respondentes...

...

1310–11
Christ Church Treasurers' Accounts   LPL: MS. 242   35
f 280 col 2   (Miscellaneous business)

...

¶ Datum ystrionibus eodem die per alexandrum capellanum   xiij s. iiij d.

...

4/ episcopi Eliensis: *John de Ketene, bishop elect of Ely from 2 March 1309/10*
4, 38/ eiusdem, alexandrum capellanum: *Alexander de Sandwyco, prior's chaplain*
38/ eodem die: *probably Martyrdom of St Thomas Becket, 29 December*

f 280v col 1

...

¶ Item datum ystrionibus eodem die per eundem   ij s.

...

Datum ystrionibus comitis de Valenscia   v so.   5

...

1311–12
Christ Church Treasurers' Accounts   LPL: MS. 242
f 122 col 1   (Miscellaneous business)   10

...

Datum trupatoribus die concepcionis beate Marie per suppriorem   ij so.

...

col 2   15

...

¶ Datum diuersis ystrionibus per manus eiusdem Alexandri   xiij s.

...

f 122v col 1   20

...

¶ Item ystrionibus eodem die   xx s.

...

1312–13
Christ Church Treasurers' Accounts   LPL: MS. 242   25
f 287 col 1   (Miscellaneous business)

...

Item datum truppator' & aliis ystrionibus eodem die   x s.

...   30

1313–14
Christ Church Treasurers' Accounts   LPL: MS. 242
f 297 col 1   (Miscellaneous business)

...   35

Item eodem die datum ystrionibus per alexandrum   x s.

...

3, 22/ eodem die: *Translation of St Thomas Becket, 7 July*
3, 17, 36/ eundem, eiusdem Alexandri, alexandrum: *Alexander de Sandwyco, prior's chaplain*
12/ trupatoribus: *for* trumpatoribus; *abbreviation mark missing*
29/ truppator': *for* trumppator'; *abbreviation mark missing*
29, 36/ eodem die, eodem die: *Martyrdom of St Thomas Becket, 29 December*

f 297v col 1

...

Item Datum ystrionibus eodem die per eundem   iij so.

...

5

1314–15
Christ Church Treasurers' Accounts   LPL: MS. 242
f 301v col 1   *(Miscellaneous business)*

...

Item datum ystrionibus per spicer in festo pentecostis   vj s. viij d. 10

...

col 2

...

Datum ystrionibus eodem die   xj. s. vj. d. 15

...

1316–17
Christ Church Treasurers' Accounts   LPL: MS. 242
f 316v col 1*   *(Miscellaneous business)*

20

...

Item Datum ystryonibus die sancte trinitatis per dominum
hugonem capellanum   viij. so.

...

25

1317–18
Christ Church Treasurers' Accounts   LPL: MS. 242
f 324v col 1   *(Miscellaneous business)*

...

Item datum ystryonibus die passionis beati thome   iij. so. 30

...

col 2

...

Item istrionibus die martis post circumcisionem   v. so. 35

...

3, 15/ eodem die: *Translation of St Thomas Becket, 7 July*
3/ eundem: *Robert de Dover, subprior*
10/ spicer: *John le Spycer, archbishop's chaplain*
10/ festo pentecostis: *11 May*
22/ die sancte trinitatis: *Trinity Sunday, 29 May*
35/ die ... circumcisionem: *3 January*

1318–19
Christ Church Treasurers' Accounts LPL: MS. 242
f 331 col 2 *(Miscellaneous business)*

...

Item datum ystrionibus in festo Natalis domini per   5
Iohannem de Gore ⌈priori⌉   vj. so.

...

1319–20
Christ Church Treasurers' Accounts LPL: MS. 242   10
f 337v col 1 *(Miscellaneous business)*

...

Item Datum istrionibus die translacionis sancti Thome per priorem   xlij so.

...

                                            15

1322–3
Christ Church Treasurers' Accounts LPL: MS. 242
f 135 col 2 *(Miscellaneous business)*

...

Item datum ystrionibus die translacionis sancti thome   vj s. viij d. 20

...

1323–4
Christ Church Treasurers' Accounts LPL: MS. 242
f 141 col 2 *(Miscellaneous business)*   25

...

Item datum ystrionibus in passione sancti thome   x. s. per priorem

...

f 141v col 2   30

...

Item datum istrionibus die sancte trinitatis & translacionis   vj s. viij d.

...

1324–5   35
Christ Church Treasurers' Accounts LPL: MS. 242
f 147 col 1 *(Miscellaneous business)*

...

Item datum ystrionibus die omnium sanctorum & in passione sancti thome   x s.

...   40

6/ Iohannem de Gore: *John de Goore, prior's chaplain*   32/ translacionis: *ie, Translation of St Thomas*
32/ die sancte trinitatis: *Trinity Sunday, 10 June*   *Becket, 7 July*

f 147v col 1

...

Item ystrionibus die sancte trinitatis & festo translacionis
sancti thome   vj s. viij d.

...   5

1325–6
Christ Church Treasurers' Accounts   LPL: MS. 242
f 352   *(Miscellaneous business)*

...   10

Item datum ystrionibus in passione sancti thome   v s.

...

Item ystrionibus die sancte trinitatis & translacionis   vj s. viij d.

...

                                                                                              15

1326–7
Christ Church Treasurers' Accounts   LPL: MS. 242
f 361 col 1   *(Miscellaneous business)*

...

Item datum ystrionibus die passionis sancti thome ⌈per priorem⌉   vj s. viij d. 20

...

f 361v col 1

...

Item datum ystrionibus die sancte trinitatis & beati thome   25
⌈per capellanum⌉   x s.

...

1327–8
Christ Church Treasurers' Accounts   LPL: MS. 243   30
f 2v col 1   *(Miscellaneous business)*

...

Item datum Istrionibus .die Natalis domini passionis sancti
thome pasche & pentecostis   .x. s.

...   35

3/ die sancte trinitatis: *Trinity Sunday, 2 June*
13/ die sancte trinitatis: *Trinity Sunday, 18 May*
13/ translacionis: *ie, Translation of St Thomas Becket, 7 July*
25/ die sancte trinitatis: *Trinity Sunday, 7 June*
25/ die ... beati thome: *probably Translation of St Thomas Becket, 7 July*
34/ pasche: *3 April*
34/ pentecostis: *22 May*

1329–30
Christ Church Treasurers' Accounts   LPL: MS. 243
f 16v col 1   *(Miscellaneous business)*
…

® *per suppriorem*   Item datum istrionibus in die translacionis beati thome martiris   xl d.   5
…

1330–1
Christ Church Treasurers' Accounts   LPL: MS. 243
f 24v col 2*   *(Miscellaneous business)*   10
…

per Ricardum   Item datum Istrionibus die introitus domini prioris   lx s.
priorem
…

f 25v col 1   *(Subprior's payments)*   15
…

Item datum ystrionibus cum aliis dictis per dominum Ricardum
de Ikham Capellanum domini Ricardi prioris   xxxvj s.
…

                                                                                          20

1331–2
Christ Church Treasurers' Accounts   LPL: MS. 243
f 32v col 2   *(Miscellaneous business)*

Item datum Istrionibus domini Regis die Iouis post octabas   25
natiuitatis beate marie   x s.
…

f 33 col 1*
…   30
Item datum Istrionibus eodem die per dominum priorem   iij s.
…

1332–3
Christ Church Treasurers' Accounts   LPL: MS. 243   35
f 40 col 2   *(Miscellaneous business)*
…

per priorem   Item datum istrionibus die passionis sancti thome martiris   vj s. viij d.
…

17–18/ Ricardum … Capellanum: *Richard de Ikham, monks' warden*
25–6/ die Iouis … marie: *17 September*
31/ eodem die: *Translation of St Thomas Becket, 7 July*

f 40v col 1

...

per priorem

Item datum Istrionibus die translacionis beati thome martiris
per priorem   xiij s. iiij d.

...   5

1333-4
Christ Church Treasurers' Accounts   LPL: MS. 243
f 49 col 2   *(Miscellaneous business)*

...   10

®*suppriore*

Item datum Istrionibus ad mesam magistri per Robertum de
douor' die sancti thome   vj d.

...

1334-5   15
Christ Church Treasurers' Accounts   LPL: MS. 243
f 57 col 1   *(Miscellaneous business)*

...

Item datum diuersis Istrionibus in camera domini prioris die
martis proxima post intronisasionem domini Archiepiscopi   xx s. 20

...

col 2*

...

Item datum istrionibus die passionis beati thome martiris   25
per priorem   xl d.

...

Item datum diuersis Istrionibus domini Regis in aduentu
domini in camera domini prioris die Mercurii proxima
post festum sancti benedicti   xxv s. per priorem 30

...

f 57v col 2

...

Item datum istrionibus die translacionis sancti thome   vij. s. ij. d. 35

...

11/ mesam: *for mensam; abbreviation mark missing*
11-12/ Robertum de douor': *Robert de Dover, subprior*
12/ die sancti thome: *probably Martyrdom of St Thomas Becket, 29 December*
19-20/ die martis proxima post intronisasionem: *11 October*
20/ domini Archiepiscopi: *John Stratford, archbishop of Canterbury 1333-48*
29-30/ die Mercurii ... benedicti: *7 December*

1337–8
Christ Church Priors' Daybook CCA: DCc/DE 3
f 40*

...

℃ Item dat*um* ystrionib*us* die Intronizac*i*onis n*os*tre   xl. s.   5

...

1339–40
Christ Church Priors' Daybook CCA: DCc/DE 3
f 42* *(4 December–16 February)*   10

...

℃ Item diu*ersis* Nunciis et ystrionib*us* ducis Cornubie
Com*itum* Warruici et Arundell et alior*um* magnat*um*
temp*ore* Parliam*en*ti   xlvj. s.

...   15

1340–1
Christ Church Priors' Daybook CCA: DCc/DE 3
f 46v* *(19 February–1 June)*

...   20
Item diu*ersis* ystrionib*us* apud Eastry*am*   iiij. s.

...

℃ Item dat*um* quib*us*dam ystrionib*us* die Pentecost*is*   .vj. s. .viij. d.

...

                                                                        25

f 47 *(1 June–17 August)*

...

℃ Item dat*um* ystrionib*us* die s*an*cte Trinitat*is*   .v. s.

...

                                                                        30

f 47v *(17 August–18 October)*

...

℃ Item dat*um* ystrionib*us* apud Eastry*am*   .iiij. s.

...

5/ die Intronizac*i*onis n*os*tre: *ie, celebration of anniversary of archbishop's enthronement, 9 October*
5, 12–14, 23, 28, 33/ Item ... xl. s., Item ... xlvj. s., Item diu*ersis* ....vj. s. .viij. d., Item ....v. s.,
   Item ....iiij. s.: *pages administratively cancelled*
23/ die Pentecost*is*: *27 May*
28/ die s*an*cte Trinitat*is*: *Trinity Sunday, 3 June*

1341–2
Christ Church Priors' Daybook   CCA: DDc/DE 3
f 48   *(18 October–24 December)*

...

℃ Item dat*um* ystrionibus die om*nium* s*a*nctorum   .vj. .s. .viij. d.   5

...

f 48v   *(24 December–26 March)*

...

℃ Item dat*um* ystrionib*us* die s*an*c*ti* Thome   xiij. s. .iiij. d.   10

...

f 49   *(26 March–13 May)*

...

℃ Item dat*um* cuidam ystrioni die ascenci*o*nis d*o*m*i*ni   .iij. s. .iiij. d.   15

...

f 50   *(26 June–9 August)*

...

Item dat*um* ystrionib*us* apud Eastriam   .v. s. .iiij. d.   20

...

(9 August–28 September)

℃ Item dat*um* Nunc' et ystrionib*us* d*o*m*i*ni R*e*gis   .xiij. s. .iiij. d.   25

...

℃ Item cuid*am* ystrioni .xij. d....

f 50v

...   30

Item dat*um* ystrionib*us* apud Ryssebergh   vj. s. .viij. d.

...

5, 10, 15/ Item ....vj. s. .viij. d., Item ... xiij. s. .iiij. d., Item ....iij. s. .iiij. d.: *pages*
   administratively cancelled
10/ die s*an*c*ti* Thome: *Martyrdom of St Thomas Becket, 29 December*
15/ die ascencionis: *Ascension Day, 9 May*
20/ Item ....v. s. .iiij. d.: *section administratively cancelled*
31/ Ryssebergh: *Monks Risborough, Buckinghamshire, site of one of the priory's manors*

1350–1
Christ Church Treasurers' Accounts LPL: MS. 243
f 74 col 2 *(Prior's payments)*
...

Item dat*um* histrionib*us per* uices x s. 5
...

f 74v col 1 *(Miscellaneous business)*
...

Item dat*um* istrionib*us* die s*an*c*ti* th*om*e mart*iris* xx s. 10
...
Item harpator' d*omi*ne Regin*e* vj s. viij d.
...

f 75 col 1* *(Prior's payments)* 15
...

Item dat*um* histrionib*us* d*om*ini ducis lancast*rie* v s.
...

col 2 *(Miscellaneous business)* 20
...
℃ Item Cuid*a*m histrioni ij. s.
...
Item dat*um* histrionib*us* die t*r*anslac*ionis* xl s.
... 25
Item q*ui*busd*a*m histrionib*us* xiij. s. iiij d.
...

1351–2
Christ Church Treasurers' Accounts LPL: MS. 243 30
f 78 col 1 *(Miscellaneous business)*
...
Item dat*um* histrionib*us* v s.
...
Item cuid*a*m histrioni vj s. viij d. 35
...

10/ die s*an*c*ti* th*om*e mart*iris*: *probably Martyrdom of St Thomas Becket, 29 December*
24/ die translac*ionis*: *ie, Translation of St Thomas Becket, 7 July*

col 2   *(Prior's payments)*

...

Item dat*um* cuid*am* histrioni   v. s.

...
                                                                               5

f 78v col 1   *(Prior's payments)*

...

℃ Item dat*um* histrio*nibus* ducis Lan*cast*rie   iij. s. iiij. d.
℃ Item dat*um* histri*oni*bus die *translacionis* b*eati* thom*e*   xxvj s. ⌐viij d.⌐

...
                                                                               10

1352–3
Christ Church Treasurers' Accounts   LPL: MS. 243
f 83 col 1   *(Miscellaneous business)*

...
                                                                               15
Item dat*um* histrio*nibus* ducis lancastrie   vj s. viij d.

col 2

...

Item dat*um* histrio*nibus* die passio*nis* s*anc*ti thom*e*   〈...〉 20

...

f 83v col 1   *(Prior's payments)*

...

℃ Item dat*um* histrio*nibus* die passio*nis* s*anc*ti thom*e*   xxvj s. viij d. 25

...

℃ Item dat*um* cuid*am* histrioni   xviij d.

...

℃ Item dat*um* I. harpour existenti cu*m* Regina   vj. s. viij d.

...
                                                                               30

f 84 col 1

...

Item cuid*am* histrioni   ij s.
Item in alijs   ij. s. 35

...

col 2   *(Miscellaneous business)*

...

℃ Item dat*um* cuid*am* histrioni   v s. 40

...

℃ Item dat*um* cuid*am* histrioni   xij d.

...

1353–4
Christ Church Treasurers' Accounts   LPL: MS. 243
f 87 col 1   *(Miscellaneous business)*
...

Item dat*um* menistrall' ducis Lancaustrie   v s.   5
...

Item dat*um* histrionib*us* die *sancti* thom*e*   xxxvj s. viij d.
...

col 2   10
...

℃ Item dat*um* diuers*is* amicis & histrionib*us*   xxxvj s. viij d.
...

f 87v col 1   15
...

Item dat*um* histrionib*us* die Translac*i*onis *sancti* thom*e*   xlvj s. viij d.
...

col 2   20
...

℃ Item dat*um* histrionib*us*   vj s. viij d.
...

f 88 col 1   25
...

Item in histrionibus   xx d.
...

Item cuid*am* histrioni   iij s. iiij d.
Item histrionib*us* do*m*ini Com*itis* oxon*iensis*   vj s. viij d. 30
...

1354–5
Christ Church Treasurers' Accounts   LPL: MS. 243
f 92 col 2   *(Miscellaneous business)*   35
...
℃ Item cuid*am* histrioni   xij d.
...
℃ Item histrionib*us* die be*ati* Thome   xxvj s. viij d.
...   40

7, 39/ die *sancti* thom*e*, die be*ati* Thome: *probably Martyrdom of St Thomas Becket, 29 December*

f 92v col 1   *(Prior's payments)*
...

℃ Item dat*um* histrio*n*ib*us*   iij. s. iiij d.
...

5

(Miscellaneous business)

Item dat*um* histrio*n*ib*us* die tnslaci*on*is be*ati* Thom*e*   xx. s.
...

10

col 2   *(Prior's payments)*
...

℃ Item dat*um* histrio*n*ib*us*   vj s.
...

15

1355–6
Christ Church Treasurers' Accounts   LPL: MS. 243
f 97 col 2   *(Miscellaneous business)*
...

℃ Item dat*um* histri*on*ib*us* die s*an*c*t*i Thom*e*   xxvj s. viij d. 20
...

f 97v col 2

℃ Item dat*um* histrio*n*ib*us* d*o*mi*n*i Ep*iscop*i Wynton*i*e   vj s. viij d. 25
...

Item dat*um* histrio*n*ib*us* d*o*mi*n*i lyonell*i*   iij s. iiij d.
...

Item dat*um* histrio*n*ib*us* die ∧⌈translaci*on*is⌉ s*an*c*t*i
Thom*e* martiris   xxvj s. viij d. 30
Item dat*um* eodem die coco abbatis s*an*c*t*i augustini   .xiij. s. .iiij. d.
...

(Prior's payments)

35

℃ Item histri*on*ib*us* die translaci*on*is be*ati* Thom*e* & cocis   xl s.
...

8/ tnslaci*on*is: *for* translaci*on*is; *abbreviation mark missing*
20/ die s*an*c*t*i Thom*e*: *probably Martyrdom of St Thomas Becket, 29 December*

f 98 col 1

...

Item dat*um* histrionib*us* die t*r*anslacio*n*is *sanct*i Thome   vj s. viij d.

...

5

1356–7
Christ Church Treasurers' Accounts   LPL: MS. 243
f 102 col 2   *(Prior's payments)*

...

Item ystrionib*us* in *f*esto *sanct*i thome   xxvj s. viij d. 10

...

Item dat*um* cocis in eodem *f*esto   .x. s.

...

Item ystrioni d*om*ine p*hilippe* regine   x. s.

...

15

f 102v col 1   *(Miscellaneous business)*

...

Item dat*um* istrionib*us* die t*r*anslacio*n*is beati thom*e*
per pri*o*rem   xxvj s. viij d. 20

...

col 2   *(Prior's payments)*

...

℃ Item cuid*am* histrioni   iij s. iiij d. 25

...

℃ Item histrionib*us* in *f*esto t*r*anslacio*n*is be*ati* Thom*e*   xxvj s. viij d.
℃ Item in Iunc*is* empt*is* co*n*tra id*e*m *f*est*um*   .ij. s. iiij d.
℃ Item diu*er*sis cocis in eod*e*m *f*esto   .x. s.

...

30

f 103 col 1*

...

Item histrionib*us* d*om*ini principi*s*   vj s. viij d.

...

35

Item trib*us* histrionib*us* d*om*ini principi*s*   viij s. viij d.
Item in aliis *per* vices   iij d.

...

10/ *f*esto *sanct*i thome: *probably Martyrdom of St Thomas Becket, 29 December*

1358-9
Christ Church Treasurers' Accounts   LPL: MS. 243
f 107 col 1   *(Miscellaneous business)*
...

Item datum hystrionibus die passionis sancti thome   xxvj s. viij d.   5
...

col 2   *(Prior's payments)*
...

☾ Item datum histrionibus comitisse de holstre   vj s. viij d.   10
...

☾ Item datum histrionibus die passionis sancti Thome   xxvj s. ⌐viij d.⌐
☾ Item datum eodem die nuncio domini Regis   xiij s. iiij d.
☾ Item datum Coco abbatis sancti Augustini & alijs eodem die   viij s.
...
                                                                                            15

f 107v col 1
...

☾ Item cuidam histrioni   iij s. iiij d.
...
                                                                                            20
☾ Item vigili domini archiepiscopi   iij s. iiij d.
...

☾ Item histrionibus domini principis & ducis Lancastrie   vj s. viij d.
...

☾ Item Harpour de scocia   v s.   25
...

f 108 col 1   *(Miscellaneous business)*
...

Item datum cuidam hystrioni [die]   v s.   30
...

Item datum diuersis ystrionibus die translacionis   xl s.
Item datum diuersis cocis   x. s.
Item Roberto ffol & gerardo   xiij s. iiij d.
...
                                                                                            35

col 2   *(Prior's payments)*
...

☾ Item cuidam ystrioni existenti cum comite de richemond   vj s. viij d.
...
                                                                                            40

32/ die translacionis: *ie, Translation of St Thomas Becket, 7 July*

1359–60
Christ Church Treasurers' Accounts   LPL: MS. 243
f 111v col 1   *(Prior's payments)*

...

C Item datum ystrionibus contra eundem festum   xxvj s. viij d. 5

...

col 2

...

C Item datum ystrionibus domini principis apud suthcherch   vj s. viij d. 10

...

C Item ystrionibus in eodem festo   xxvj s. viij

...

1360–1   15
Christ Church Treasurers' Accounts   LPL: MS. 243
f 115 col 1   *(Prior's payments)*

...

Item datum ystrionibus in die passionis sancti thoma martiris   xxvj s. viij d.

...   20

Item iiij ystrionibus domini Regis ibidem   iij s. iiij d.

...

f 115v col 1*

...   25

Item ystrionibus existentibus cum filio Regis francie   x s.

...

col 2

...   30

C Item ystrionibus comitis de Warewyk   vj s. viij d.

...

Item ystrionibus in festo translacionis beati thome   xiij s. iiij d.
Item aliis in eodem festo   vj s. viij d.

...   35

Item datum histrionibus die translacionis beati thome   xl s.

5/ contra: *sign for ra written twice in* MS
5, 12/ eundem festum, eodem festo: *Translation of St Thomas Becket, 7 July*
10/ suthcherch: *Southchurch, Essex, site of one of the priory's manors*
12/ viij: *for* viij d.
19/ thoma: *for* thome
21/ ibidem: *Eastry, site of one of the priory's manors*

f 116 col 1

...

Item dat*um* ystrionib*us* d*om*ini principis   x s.

...

Item dat*um* istrionib*us* d*om*ini Principis & al' *per* Eund*em*   xvj s. viij d. 5

...

1362–3
Christ Church Treasurers' Accounts   LPL: MS. 243
f 120 col 2   *(Prior's payments)*   10

...

Item dat*um* cuid*am* Istrioni   iij s. iiij d.

...

Item dat*um* istrionib*us*   iij s. iiij d.

...   15

f 120v col 1

...

Item dat*um* quibusd*am* istrionib*us*   vj s. viij d.

...   20

col 2

...

Item dat*um* quib*us*d*am* istrionib*us* in *fes*to Translaci*onis*
be*at*i Thome   lxvj s. viij d. 25
Item quib*us*d*am* Cocis & al' in eodem *fes*to   xiij s. iiij d.

...

1363–4
Christ Church Treasurers' Accounts   LPL: MS. 243   30
f 124 col 1   *(Prior's payments)*

...

Item dat*um* hobbe ffol & socio suo   x. s.

...

Item dat*um* ystrionib*us* d*om*ini reg*is* Cipr*i*   x. s. 35

...

col 2

...

Item dat*um* cuid*am* ystrioni existe*nti* cu*m* d*om*ina Regina   xiij s. iiij d. 40

...

5/ Eund*em*: *the prior, Robert Hathbrande*

f 124v col 1

Item ystrionibus domini Regis apud Chartham	x. s.
...	
Item datum ystrionibus die sancte Trinitatis	vj s. viij d. 5
...	
Item datum quibusdam ystrionibus venientibus cum domino Rogero Beauchamp'	vj s. viij d.
...	
Item datum famulie & ystrionibus domini ducis Lancastrie	xxvj s. viij d. 10
...	
Item datum Istrionibus per priorem die sancti Thome	xl. s.
...	
Item Datum ystrionibus in festo translacionis beati Thome	xxx. s.
Item diuersis cocis in eodem festo	viij s. 15
...	

col 2

...

| Item ystrionibus domini Comitis herfordie & al' | xxvj s. viij d. 20 |
| ... | |

1364–5
Christ Church Treasurers' Accounts LPL: MS. 243
f 129 col 2   (Prior's payments) 25

...

Item datum familie & Istrion' domine Isabelle filie Regis	xiij s. iiij d.
...	
Item datum Istrionibus die Purificacionis beate Marie	v. s.
...	30

f 129v col 1*

...

Item datum Istrionibus die Translacionis beati Thome martiris	L. s. 35
Item datum diuersis cocis in eodem festo	xiij s. iiij d.
Item datum Istrionibus dominica Septuagesime	vj s. viij d.
...	

5/ die sancte Trinitatis: *Trinity Sunday, 19 May*
12/ die sancti Thome: *probably Martyrdom of St Thomas Becket, 29 December*
37/ dominica Septuagesime: *9 February*

Item cuid*am* Istrioni   v s.

...

Item dat*um* cuid*am* Istrioni cu*m* d*om*i*n*o Reg*e*   vj s. viij d.

...

                                            5

col 2

...

Item dat*um* Istrionib*us* die Pasch*e*   x s.

...

Item dat*um* Istrion' d*om*ini Reg*is*   vj s. viij d. 10

...

Item dat*um* Labikyno Istrioni   vj s. viij d.

...

Item Dat*um* Roberto ffool   vj s. viij d.

...   15

f 130 col 1

...

Item dat*um* Istrionib*us* d*om*i*n*e Ph*illi*pe Regine   v s.

...   20

Item dat*um* cuid*am* ystrioni   iij s. iiij d.

...

col 2

                                            25

℃ Item dat*um* Istrionib*us* p*re*cept*o* Prioris   v s.

...

1365–6
Christ Church Treasurers' Accounts LPL: MS. 243   30
f 134 col 2   *(Prior's payments)*

...

Item dat*um* Istrionib*us* die Translac*ionis* bea*t*i Thome
p*re*cept*o* Prioris   xlvj s. viij d.

...   35

Item dat*um* Istrionib*us* London*ie*   x s.

...

Item dat*um* cuid*am* Istrioni   ij s.

...

8/ die Pasch*e*: *13 April*

f 134v col 1

...

Item ystrionib*us* d*omi*ni Reg*is* in f*es*to Translac*ionis*   xx s.

...

Item ystrionib*us* in festo Natiuit*atis sanc*ti Ioh*anni*s Bapt*iste*   iiij. s.

...

col 2

...

Item I. harpatori d*omi*ne Phi*lipp*e Regine & ei*us* garc*ioni*   viij s. viij d. 10

...

Item trib*us* ystrionib*us* d*omi*ni de Spenser   x s.

...

Item dat*um* cuid*am* ystrioni d*omi*ni R*egis*   vj s. viij d.

...   15

1366–7
Christ Church Treasurers' Accounts   LPL: MS. 243
f 138 col 1   *(Prior's payments)*

...   20

Item dat*um* ystrionib*us* d*omi*ni duc*is* Lancastrie   vj s. viij d.

...

Item ystrionib*us* in eodem festo   xxvj s. viij d.

...

Item dat*um* ystrionib*us* de villa   vj s. viij d. 25

...

col 2

...

Item dat*um* Istrionib*us* ⌐ut p*atet*⌐ per compot*u*m feretr*iarii*   xx s. 30

...

Item dat*um* trib*us* Istrionib*us* d*omi*ne Reg*ine*   vj s. viij d.

...

f 138v col 1   35

...

Item dat*um* cuidam histrioni d*omi*ni R*egis*   iij s. iiij d.

...

Item dat*um* Hobbe fool existent*i* cum d*omi*no Reg*e*   vj s. viij d.

...   40

23*l* eodem festo: *probably Martyrdom of St Thomas Becket, 29 December*

col 2

...

Item datum diuersis istrionibus & nunciis per vices   vj s. iiij d.

...

Item datum Hanekyno Libekyn istrioni   viij s. viij d. 5

...

f 139 col 1

...

Item istrionibus in festo assumpcionis beate Marie   iij s. iiij d. 10

...

Item datum cuidam Istrioni domini Regis   vj s. viij d.

...

Item cuidam Istrioni   vj s. viij d.

... 15

1367–8
Christ Church Treasurers' Accounts LPL: MS. 243
f 143 col 2*   *(Prior's payments)*

... 20

Item datum istrionibus domini principis xx s. per dominum priorem

...

Item datum clericis sancti Nicholai apud godmersham   xij d.
Item datum hankyn lepekyn   xiij s. iiij d.

... 25

f 143v col 1

...

Item datum histrionibus in festo epiphanie   iij s. iiij d.

... 30

Item datum ystrionibus domini principis venientibus
de garsconia   xiij s. iiij d.

...

Item datum diuersis ystrioibus & Wafratoribus vna cum aliis   v s.

... 35

Item datum cuidam ystrioni   ij s.

...

5, 24/ Hanekyno Libekyn, hankyn lepekyn: *royal entertainer (see p 55, l.16)*
34/ ystrioibus: *for ystrionibus; abbreviation mark missing*

Item datum Nunciis & ystrionibus domini Regis in festo
pentecostis   vij s. vj d.

...

Item datum cuidam ystrioni   ij s.

...   5

col 2

...

Item datum thome fustulatori domini prioris   iij s. iiij d.

...   10

Item cuidam ystrioni   xx d.

...

Item datum ystrioni domini Regis   vj s. viij d.

...

Item cuidam ystrioni   ij s. 15
Item datum hanekyno lybekyn ystrioni domini Regis   xiij s. iiij d.

...

1368–9
Christ Church Treasurers' Accounts   LPL: MS. 243   20
f 148 col 2   (Prior's payments)

...

Item datum cuidam ystrioni   ij s.

...

     25

f 148v col 2

...

Item datum histrionibus   iij s. iiij d.

...

Item datum cuidam histrioni   iiij s. 30

...

Item datum cuidam histrioni constabularij douorie   vj s. viij d.

...

Item datum histrionibus domini Walteri mauny   vj s. viij d.

     35

f 149 col 1

...

Item histrionibus in festo translacionis beati Thome   xxiij s. iiij d.

...   40

1–2/ festo pentecostis: 28 May

col 2

...

Item quibusdam histrionibus   ij s.

...

                                                                          5

1369-70
Christ Church Treasurers' Accounts   LPL: MS. 243
f 153 col 2*   *(Prior's payments)*

...

Item datum histrion' in festo sancti Thome   vj s. viij d. 10

...

Item histrionibus domini regis in festo epiphanie
domini   vj s. viij d.
Item datum histrioni cuiusdam magnatis   iij s. iiij d.

...

                                                                          15

f 153v col 1*

Item datum cuidam histrioni Ducis Lancastrie   vj s. viij d.

...   20

Item datum histrionibus   iij s. iiij d.

...

Item cuidam histrioni domini Regis   vj s. viij d.

...

                                                                          25

col 2*   *(3 August–29 September)*

...

Item datum cuidam histrioni   ij s.

...

Item histrioni domini regis   iij s. 30

...

f 154 col 1*   *(20 April–14 July)*

...

Item datum hystrionibus & aliis in festo sancti   35
Iohannis Baptiste   v s.

...

10/ festo sancti Thome: *Martyrdom of St Thomas Becket, 29 December*

1371–2
Christ Church Priors' Accounts   CCA: DCc/Prior 22
sheet 1   *(Rendered December 1372)*

...

Item dat*um* histrion' in festo s*an*c*t*i Thome vz. transl*acione*   5
et Wafrat*or'* d*om*ini Archiep*iscopi* eodem die   xxxiij s. iiij d.

...

Item dat*um* histrion' die assumpc*ionis* be*a*te Marie   iij s. iiij d.

...

Item dat*um* histrion' d*om*ini Principis   xiij s. iiij d. 10

...

1372–3
Christ Church Treasurers' Accounts   LPL: MS. 243
f 159 col 2*   *(Prior's payments)*   15

...

Item dat*um* histrionib*us* die Omn*ium* s*an*c*t*orum   iij s. iiij d.

...

f 159v col 1   20

...

Item dat*um* histrionib*us* d*om*ini Reg*is* die Passion*is* be*ati*
Thom*e* martir*is*   xxvj s. viij d.

...

Item dat*um* Thome Skynn*er*e Stulto d*om*ini R*egis*   vj s. viij d. 25

...

Item dat*um* histrionib*us* d*om*ini Reg*is* ap*ud* Westwell   vj s. viij d.

...

Item dat*um* histrionib*us* d*om*ini Ducis Lancastr*ie*   iij s. iiij d.

...   30

Item dat*um* histrionib*us* d*om*ini Regis   iij s. iiij d.

...

Item p*ro* pannis lineis & laneis p*ro* stulto   vj s. viij d.

...

Item dat*um* histrionib*us* d*omi*ne de Mann   ij s. 35

...

Item dat*um* histrionibus in festo Pasch*e*   iij s. iiij d.

...

Item dat*um* histr*ion'* d*om*ini Com*itis* March' in festo Pasche   xiij s. iiij d.

...   40

37, 39/ festo Pasch*e*: *17 April*

Item histrion' apud Broke   ij s.
Item datum histrion' die Pentecostis   iij s. iiij d.
...

1374–5   5
Christ Church Treasurers' Accounts   LPL: MS. 243
f 164v col 1   *(Prior's payments)*
...
Item datum Istrionibus domini Regis & Principis   xxvj s. viij d.
...   10
Item datum Istrionibus domini Regis   xiij s. iiij d.
...
Item datum cuidam Perciual' Istrioni domini Regis   vj s. viij d.
Item datum Istrionibus domini Principis   vj s. viij d.
...   15

1375–6
Christ Church Treasurers' Accounts   LPL: MS. 243
f 170v col 1*   *(Prior's payments)*
...   20
Item datum histrionibus die Lune post dominicam in
ramis palmarum   vj s. viij d.
...
Item datum histrionibus die translacionis beati thome   xxxiij s. iiij d.
...   25

col 2*
...
Item datum familie eiusdem & histrionibus domini
Regis & ducis lancastrie   xxx s. iiij d. 30
...
Item datum histrionibus domini Regis & ducis lancastrie &
Waffrer & Marssiote in festo Sancti thome   L. s.
...
Item datum histrionibus in festo sancti thome   xx s. 35
Item datum histrionibus dominica septuagesime   iij s. iiij d.
...

2/ die Pentecostis: *5 June*
21–2/ die Lune ... ramis palmarum: *7 April*
29/ eiusdem: *Simon Sudbury, archbishop of Canterbury 1375–81*
33, 35/ festo Sancti thome, festo sancti thome: *probably Martyrdom of St Thomas Becket, 29 December*
36/ dominica septuagesime: *10 February*

1376–7
Christ Church Treasurers' Accounts   LPL: MS. 243
f 171v col 1*   *(Prior's payments)*

...

Item datum histrionibus quando dominus archiepiscopus   5
comedit priore   xvj s. viij d.

...

col 2*

...   10
Item histrionibus & familie comitis cantabrigie   xxiij s. iiij d.

...

1377–8
Christ Church Treasurers' Accounts   LPL: MS. 243   15
f 175v col 2*   *(Prior's payments)*

...

Item datum clericis ecclesie in honore sancti Nicholai   xij d.

...

Item datum histrionibus die passionis sancti thome   xiij s. iiij d. 20

...

Item datum histrionibus matris domini regis   xiij s. iiij d.

...

Item datum histrionibus domini Regis   xiij s. iiij d.

...   25
Item datum histrionibus in festo translacionis beati Thome   xxx s.

...

Item datum histrionibus comitis de march'   iij s. iiij d.

...

Item datum ȝeuan Wallico histrioni   xx d. 30

...

1380–1
Christ Church Treasurers' Accounts   LPL: MS. 243
f 179v col 2   *(Prior's payments)*   35

...

Item pro histrionibus die sancti thome in natale   xx s.

...

5/ archiepiscopus: *Simon Sudbury, archbishop of Canterbury 1375–81*
6/ priore: *for* cum priore

Item *pro* histrionib*us* die ascenc*io*nis   x s.

...

1394–5
City Jurats' Accounts   CCA: CC/FA 1   5
f 41v*   *(Allowances)*

...De quib*us* allocat*um* est dicto Ric*ar*do *pro* minstrall' temp*ore* reg*ni* reg*is*
Ric*ar*d*i* qu*an*do Ioh*ann*es Proude & idem Ric*ar*d*us* fuer*unt* Ball*iui* adinuicem
xij s. iiij d....   10

1401–2
City Jurats' Accounts   CCA: CC/FA 3
f 19*
...   15
...Et Ioh*an*i pirye vni Ballior*um pro* custa⟨...⟩ iij scutor*um* argent*eorum* de
armis ciuitat*is* liberat*orum* histrionib*us* d*ic*te ciuitat*is* xxvj s. viij d....

1402–3
City Jurats' Accounts   CCA: CC/FA 3   20
f 19v*   *(Costs and alms by the bailiffs)*
...
...Et dat*um* Menstrall' & wafer*ar*' d*om*ini reg*is* in *pre*senc*ia* reg*is* in Cantuar*ia*
xj s. viij d. Et in vino dat*o* Comitisse de Rochland vz. j galon*e* de bastard &
j galon*e* de vini albi ij s. Et in vino dat*o* Comitisse de Somersete vid*elicet* ij   25
galon*ibus* vini de Romene bastard & malmesyn & j galon*e* vini rub*ei* &
j potel*lo* vini albi iij s. iiij d.
Et in vino dat*o* will*elm*o Brenchisle vz. j galon*e* vini rub*ei* &
j galon*e* bastard & malmesyn   ij s.
Et in vino ∧⌈& piris⌉ dat*is* will*elm*o Rikhill & vx*or*i ei*us* vz.   30
ij galon*ibus* bastard & malmesyn   iij s.
Et d*om*ino Guidoni Mane j galon*e* bastard xvj d. Et in lib*er*atura dat*a* Petro
atte Chambre xj s. Et *pro* furur*a* eiusdem ij s. iiij d.
                                                                                    ℭ S*um*ma lxviij s. x d.
ℭ Item Costag*ia* Regine eodem anno   35

Prim*is* in j eq*u*o conducto *pro* Thom*a* Cokeman equitant*e* vsq*ue* Roffa*m*

1/ die ascenc*io*nis: *Ascension Day, 23 May*
8/ dicto Ric*ar*do: *Richard Gerweys*
16/ custa⟨...⟩: *for* custagiis
25/ de vini albi: *for* vini albi *or* de vino albo
30/ will*elm*o Rikhill: MP *for Kent 1420*

*pro cer*citudi*ne* h*abend*a de aduentu Regine xij d. Et in exp*ensis* eiusd*em*
Tho*me* ead*em* vice xx d. Et in diu*ersis* exp*ensis* ad arraiand*am* porta*m* de
westgate fact*is* ij s. Et op*er*ari*is* ac laborari*is* conduct*is* p*er* Tho*mam* Ikham
ad eande*m* ij s.

Et in vino albo empt*o* cu*m* will*elm*o Halyngherst vz. xiij gal*onibus* & di.   5
miss*is* in le Blen ix s.

Et in vino rub*eo* empt*o* cu*m* Ioh*ann*e Petham in ij barell*is* ferers xxiiij
gal*onibus* & j quart*erio* xvj s. ij d.

Et in vino dulci empt*o* cu*m* eode*m* vid*elicet* in iij botell*is* bastard &
Romen*e* ij s.   10

⌐Et in vino d*u*lci empt*o* cu*m* Thoma Lane & misso in le blean vz. iij gal*onibus*
bastard & Romen*e* iiij s.⌐

Et in vino rub*eo* deliberat*o* pinc*er*ne regine p*ro* ore regin*e* & al*iarum*
domi*narum* misso ad palaci*um* lxvj galon*es* xliiij s.

Et in pane empto cum Ioh*ann*e Noreys miss*o* in le blean   v s.   15
Et in pane empto cum Ric*ard*o Maydestan   iiij s.

Et in vino dat*o* quib*us*cum venient*ibus* de familia regine ad Tab*er*nam Ioh*ann*is
Petham vid*elicet* vij^xx xviij galon*es* v li v s. iiij d. Et in ciphis empt*is* & miss*is*
in le blen v d. Et in pecuni*a* dat*a* Wafer*ar'* regi*ne* v s. Et dat*um* Ministrall*is*
Commu*n*itatu*m* Cantu*arie* & Sandwici vj s. viij d.   20

Et dat*o* Waferar' Regine v s. Et in v*n*a caruc*a* conduct*a* ad cartand*um* vinu*m*
in le blen xij d.

                                        ⫶ Su*m*ma x li. xiiij s. iij d.

...
                                                                                            25

1406–7
St Augustine's Treasurers' Accounts   BL Harley Roll Z 19
mb 6d   *(Gifts and grants)*

...
Et dat*um* diu*ersis* ministrall*is* diu*ersis*   v. s. 30

...

1407–8
Christ Church Chronicle   CCA: Literary MS C14
f 31 *(reversed)*   *(24–5 August)*   35

...
Item Anno p*ri*oratus sui xix° Anno *regni* *regis* henrici iiij^ti ix° Anno d*om*ini

---

3/ Tho*mam* Ikham: *Thomas Ikham, bailiff*
11/ Thoma Lane: *Thomas Lane, jurat; bailiff 1407–8*
11–12/ Et in vino … iiij s.: *interpolated beginning at
    end of previous line and continued interlinearly*

15, 16/ Ioh*ann*e Noreys, Ric*ard*o Maydestan:
    bakers and mill-suitors
30/ diu*ersis*: *for* diuersis vicibus *(?)*
37/ sui: *Thomas Chillenden, prior 1391–1411*

M¹ CCCCviij° isto anno de assensu *domi*ni Thome Arundel Archiep*iscopi* &
cap*itul*i dimisit & *t*radidit administracion*em omni*um temporalium ecc*lesie*
Alumpno suo *domi*no Ioh*an*nis Wodenysbergh ecc*les*ie Elemosin*ario* & ipse
ad sacr*um* concilium pisanum p*re*fectus *est* primo die Aprili*s* An*n*o sup*ra*dic*t*o
& in die *sanct*i Bartholomei post c*re*acion*em* d*omi*ni Alex*andri* pape v*ti* qui   5
fu*er*at de ordi*ne* minor*um* ap*ud* sandwic*um* aplicuit & in crastino cu*m omni*
clero p*o*p*u*lique tripudio ad ecc*les*iam sua*m* est re*u*ersus

…

1416–17   10
City Jurats' Accounts   CCA: CC/FA 1
f 124*   *(Waits' pledges)*

…

Pleg*ij pro* lez
skochonz

⊂ *Memo*randum q*uo*d liberatum fuit ∧⌈anno sup*ra*dicto⌉ Iacob*o* Gylot I. skochon
arg*en*teum & deamelatum q*uia* fatebatur se fore pleg*ium pro* langle menstrall*o*   15
vt ip*s*e Iacob*us* respondeat in camer*a* xij Iur*atorum pro* eodem
⊂ It*em* consim*i*li modo liberat*um* fuit I. skochon Will*el*m*o* Chilton spycer
pleg*io* ∧⌈pro⌉ Thom*a* Wodelond me*n*strallo vt ip*s*e &c
⊂ It*em* consim*i*li forma liberatum fuit I skochon Thome Payntor pleg*io* ∧⌈pro⌉
Will*el*m*o* ffordmell menstrallo. Et ip*s*e Thomas postea reliberauit in camer*am*   20
xij Iur*atorum* [v] & ponitur vna cu*m* vna obligacione Ioh*an*nis lymton
seruient*is* camere in magna cista cerat*a* cu*m* iij^b*us* ceruris. Et rem*an*sit
ib*ide*m &c

1429–30   25
City Jurats' Accounts   CCA: CC/FA 1
f 198

…Et solut*um* Ioh*an*ni langle Ric*ard*o Belle & Ric*ard*o Barton Mynstrall*is*
voc*atis* les waytes p*ro* eor*um* liberatura tog*arum* suar*um* de vna secta   30
vestiend*o* ob honorem d*ict*e Ciuitatis in Cam*er*a xij Iur*atorum* p*er*soluend*o*
xiij s. iiij d.…

1431–2
St Augustine's Treasurers' Accounts   CCA: DCc/Charta Antiqua A 218a   35
mb 4*   *(Clothing)*
…
Et dat*um* diu*er*s*is* generosis & valett*is pro* robis emend*atis*
erga aduentu*m* d*omi*ni Reg*is*   lxj s.
…   40

(Gifts)

Et dat*um* menstrall' do*m*ini Reg*is*	vj s. viij d.
…	
Et dat*um* menstrall' Comit*is* Staffordi*e*	iij s. iiij d. 5
…	
Et dat*um* iiij menstrall*is* in die Natal*is* do*m*ini	vj s. viij d.
Et iiij menstrall*is* in vigil*ia* san*c*ti Thome	iij s. iiij d.
Et dat*um* vic*ecomiti* in Nat*a*li	xx s.
Et dat*um* Subvic*ecomiti*	vj s. viij d. 10
Et dat*um* fam*u*lis vic*ecomitis*	iij s. iiij d.
Et dat*um* Th*ome* Champion coronat*ori* do*m*ini Reg*is*	iij s. iiij d.
Et dat*um* mag*istro* chr*isto*foro Bacallar*io* in Theolog*ia*	vj s. viij d.
Et dat*um* Thome nuncio do*m*ini Archiep*iscop*i in Nat*a*li	iij s. iiij d.
…	15
Et dat*um* ludent' in aula in Nat*a*li *per* vices	vj s. viij d.
Et dat*um* Promo do*m*ini duc*is* Glouc*estrie*	vj s. iiij d.
Et dat*um* menstrall' do*m*ini duc*is* Glouc*estrie*	vj s. viij d.
…	
Et dat*um* cursori do*m*ini Reg*is*	iij s. iiij d. 20
Et dat*um* Clerico fori	vj s. viij d.
Et dat*um* valett' Panetrie do*m*ini Reg*is*	xx d.
Et dat*um* menstrall' do*m*ini Reg*is*	xiij s. iiij d.
F*.*t dat*um* valett' equor*um* do*m*ini duc*is* Glouc*estrie*	vj s. viij d.
Et dat*um* valett' [d] equor*um* do*m*ini Reg*is*	iij s. iiij d. 25
Et dat*um* valett' auen*e* do*m*ini duc*is* Gloucestri*e*	iij s. iiij d.
…	
Et dat*um* menstrall' eod*em* die	iij s. iiij d.
…	
Et dat*um* menstrall' do*m*ine ducisse Westm*er*land*ie*	iij s. iiij d. 30
…	

1436–7
City Jurats' Accounts CCA: CC/FA 1
f 243v *(Wages and rents paid)* 35

…

…Et solut*um* Ioh*ann*i langle Ioh*ann*i molys & Will*elm*o Makefare Ministrall*is* & Waytes anni instantis di*c*te Ciuitatis p*ro* togis suis de Camera xij Iurat*orum* *per* ordinacio*n*em in Cur*ia* de Burgemoto fact*am* xiij s. iiij d.…

… 40

8/ in vigil*ia* san*c*ti Thome: *eve of Martyrdom of St Thomas Becket, 28 December*

28/ eodem die: *Ascension Day, 29 May*

30/ ducisse: *for* comitisse

Christ Church Priors' Accounts   CCA: DCc/Prior 7
mb 2   *(Offerings and gifts)*
...

Et in donis dat*is* Ministr*i*s d*o*m*i*ni Regis. d*o*m*i*ni Duc*is*
Gloucestr*i*e & al*i*orum d*o*m*i*norum & magnatum   5
histrionib*us* nuncijs & al*ijs* fistulatorib*us* venient*ibus*
per vices hoc anno   xij. li. xiiij. s. v. d.
...

1439–40   10
City Jurats' Accounts   CCA: CC/FA 1
f 269*   *(Wages and rents paid)*

...Et solut*um* Ioha*n*ni harnhell Taillor *pro* panno ab eo empt*o* *pro* togis
Ioh*ann*is lengle & socior*um* suor*um* Ministrall*orum* Ciuitatis nom*in*e eiusdem   15
Ciuitatis hui*us* anni xviij^i xiij s. iiij d....

1440–1
City Jurats' Accounts   CCA: CC/FA 1
f 276v   *(Wages and rents paid)*   20

...Et solut*um* Ioha*n*ni langle Mynstrall*o* *pro* toga sua hui*us* anni xix^i vj s.
viij d....

1442–3   25
Christ Church Priors' Accounts   CCA: DCc/Prior 6
mb 2*   *(Offerings and gifts)*
...

Et in donis dat*is* Ministr*is* d*o*m*i*ni Regis. d*o*m*i*ni duc*is* Gloucest*i*e
& al*i*orum d*o*m*i*norum & magnat*um* histrionib*us* nuncijs &   30
alijs fistulatorib*us* hoc anno   ⟨...⟩
...

1444–5
Christ Church Treasurers' Accounts   CCA: DCc/Miscellaneous Accounts 4   35
f 41   *(Gifts)*
...

℃ Et dat*um* Ministrall' [d*o*mini] Comit*is* Exon*ie* ap*u*d Chartham   vj s. viij d.
...

31/ ⟨...⟩: *edge of membrane damaged; sum lost*   38/ Comit*is*: *for* ducis *(?)*

f 41v

…

℃ Et dat*um* lusoribus die pascionis *sancti* Thome   iij s. iiij d.

℃ Et dat*um* famil*is* Thome kyrell, Will*elmi* Saye & Thome
Brydde *pro* exhennijs deportat*is* d*omi*no priori erga die*m*   5
pasc*ionis sancti* Thome   v s.

Et dat*um* fistilatorib*us* eodem die   iij s. iiij d.

…

Et dat*um* cleric' Elemosinar*ij* ludent' coram d*omi*no priore   v s. ij d.

…   10

f 42

…

Et dat*um* Ric*ardo* harpo*ur* Ministrallo d*omi*ni Cantuar*iensis*   vj s. viij d.

…   15

f 43

…

℃ Et dat*um* Ministrallis de Sandewico ap*u*d Eastry   ij s.

…   20

f 43v

…

℃ Et dat*um* Bartholomeo Ministrallo d*omi*ni Cardinal*is*
ap*u*d Eastry   iij s. iiij d. 25

℃ Et dat*um* Ministrall*is* d*omi*ni duc*is* Glouc*estrie* duc*is* Exon*ie*
& al*iorum* d*omi*no*rum* die Translac*ionis sancti* Thome Martiris   xxj s. viij d.

…

℃ Et dat*um* p*ar*ochianis *sancte* Mildrede in coexibic*i*onem ludi   vj s. viij d.

…   30

f 44

…

℃ Et dat*um* Ministrall' d*omi*ni Ioh*ann*is Bowcher ap*u*d
Chartham   vj s. viij d. 35

…

4/ Thome kyrell: *Sir Thomas Kyriell, lieutenant of Dover Castle 1454–60; MP for Kent 1459–60*
4/ Will*elmi* Saye: *William Say, lord warden of Cinque Ports and constable of Dover Castle 1457–60*
9/ Elemosinar*ij*: *John Wodnesburgh, almoner*
9/ d*omi*no priore: *John Salisbury, prior 9 March 1437/8–9 January 1445/6*

f 44v

...

Et datum ministrall' domini Regis die sancti Edwardi   vj s. viij d.

...

1445–6
Civic Accounts   CCA: CC/FA 2
f 7v   *(Wages and rents paid)*

¶ Et solutum Iohanni langle Mynistrallo pro toga sua de anno xxiijᵒ Regis
henrici vjᵗⁱ vj s. viij d.... Et solutum Iohanni langle Menstrallo Ciuitatis
Cantuarie de anno xxiiijᵗᵒ regis henrici vj anglie pro toga sua &c vj s. viij d....

...

Christ Church Treasurers' Accounts   CCA: DCc/Miscellaneous Accounts 4
f 93   *(External expenses)*

...

℃ Et solutum henrico pykot pro interludijs erga Natale domini in presencia
domini Cardinalis [xxvj s. viij d.] lx⟨...⟩

...

(Gifts)

℃ Et datum Ricardo Citheredi domini Cantuariensis   vj s. viij d.

...

f 93v

...

℃ Et datum lusoribus ludentibus coram domino tempore
Natalis domini   viij. s. .viij. d.

...

Et datum Ministrall' domini Cardinalis & al' Ministrall'
pro tempore Natalis domini conductis   xxj. s. .viij. d.

...

f 94

...

℃ Et datum Ministrall' domini Ducis Gloucestrie apud Charteham   xx. s.

...

℃ Et datum Ministrall' domini Comitis dorsette apud Chartham   vj. s. viij. d.

...

18/ henrico pykot: *prior's chamberlain*   19/ lx⟨...⟩: *edge of folio damaged by burning, rest of sum lost*

f 95

...

℃ Et dat*um* histrioni de london   iij s. iiij d.

℃ Et dat*um* [d] cuidam Ministrall*o* d*om*ini Cardinal*is*   xvj d.

...   5

Et dat*um* Ministrall' d*om*ini Regis & al*ijs* ministrall*is*
diu*ersorum* d*om*in*orum* in die Translac*io*nis *sanct*i
Thome Martiris   xliij. s. .iiij. d.

Et dat*um* pu*er*is ludentib*us* coram d*om*ino Priore eod*e*m die   iij. s. iiij. d.

...   10

f 95v

...

Et dat*um* diu*ersis* Ministrall*is* ap*u*d Monketon die *sanct*e
M*ari*e Magdalene   iij s. iiij d. 15

...

f 96

...

Et dat*um* Ministrall' d*om*ini Gloucestr*ie* ap*u*d Estry mens*e*   20
Semptembr*is*   xiij. s. .iiij. d.

...

1446–7

Civic Accounts CCA: CC/FA 2   25
f 14v   *(Wages and rents paid)*

...

...Et sol*utum* Ioh*ann*i lengle will*elmo* Rampen & Will*elmo* Ionson
Ministralib*us* Ciuitat*is* Cant*uarie* pro tog*is* suis de lib*er*ato Camere xij
Iur*atorum* de anno xxv° Regis h*e*nrici vj xiij s. iiij d....   30

Christ Church Treasurers' Accounts CCA. DCc/Miscellaneous Accounts 4
f 141v   *(Gifts)*

...

℃ Et dat*um* Ricard*o* Berton Ministrall*o* d*om*ini archiep*iscop*i   35
ap*u*d Chartham   vj .s. viij .d.

...

9/ domino Priore: *John Elham, prior 13 April 1446–19 February 1448/9*
21/ Semptembr*is*: *for* Septembris

f 142*

…

℃ Et datum Ministrallis diuersis die translacionis
sancti Thome   vj .s. viij .d.

…   5

℃ Et datum lusoribus in die Circumsionis domini   vj .s. viij .d.

℃ Et datum diuersis personis tripudiantibus in nocte
tnslacionis sancti Thome   xiij .s. iiij .d.

…

℃ Et datum pueris cantantibus die Epiphanie   iij .s. iiij .d. 10

…

℃ Et datum diuersis lusoribus ludentibus coram domino
Priori apud Chartham   iij .s. iiij .d.

…

                                                                              15

f 142v

…

℃ Et datum Bartholomeo Citheriste domini Cardinalis
apud Chartham   iij .s. iiij .d.

…   20

Et datum lusoribus apud Chartham & lusoribus coram
domino priore die Purificacionis beate Marie   iiij .s. iiij .d.

…

Et datum Ministrall' ville Cantuarie   xx .d.

…   25

f 143v

…

℃ Et datum Ministrall' ducis Excestrie apud Chartham   vj .s. viij d.

…   30

℃ Et datum Ministrall' Episcopi Deuolensis apud Chartham iij s. iiij d.

…

f 144

…   35

Et datum Ministrallis diuersis in die Translacionis sancti Thome   xx .s.

…

3/ Ministrallis: 5 minims in MS
6/ Circumsionis: for Circumcisionis
8/ tnslacionis: for translacionis; abbreviation mark missing
12–13/ domino Priori: for domino Priore; John Elham, prior 13 April 1446–19 February 1448/9
31/ Episcopi: for Archiepiscopi (?)

f 144v

...

℃ Et dat*um* cuidam lusori d*omi*ni [d] Mar*chi*onis dorsett*e*   iij s. iiij d.

...

℃ Et dat*um* Ministrall' d*omi*ni mar*chi*onis dorsett*e* ap*u*d Eastry   vj. s. viij. d.   5

...

℃ Et dat*um* Ministrall' d*omi*ni de Say ap*u*d Eastry   xx. d.

...

St Augustine's Treasurers' Accounts   LPL: Estate Document 2058   10
mb 3d*   *(Gifts)*

...

Et dat*um* Ri*card*o harpero   iij s. iiij d.

...

Et dat*um* Ministralis d*omi*ni cardinal*is*   iij s. iiij d. 15

...

Et in v ⌜du*od*enis⌝ viij Capon*ibus* dat*is* d*omi*no cardinal*i*
Marchioni dors*ette* & expendit*is* tempore *p*arliamenti   xxx s. x d.
Et dat*um* lusor' in ffesto Natal*is* d*omi*ni   xx s.

...   20

Et dat*um* Ministrall' d*omi*ni Regis   xiij s. iiij d.
Et dat*um* Ministrall' d*omi*ni dors*ete*   vj s. viij d.

...

1447–8   25
Civic Accounts   CCA: CC/FA 2
f 20v   *(Wages and rents paid)*

...

...Et Ioh*an*ni langle Will*elmo* Ionson et Will*elmo* Rampeyn Minnistral*ibus*
hui*us* Ciuitat*is* *pro* lib*er*ato suo xiij s. iiij d....   30

Christ Church Treasurers' Accounts   CCA: DCc/Miscellaneous Accounts 4
f 187*   *(Gifts)*

...

℃ Et dat*um* lusor*ibus* de ffevyrsham ludentib*us* cora*m*   35
d*omi*no Priori die *sancti* Steph*ani*   vj s. viij d.

...

36/ d*omi*no Priori: *for* domino Priore; *John Elham, prior 13 April 1446–19 February 1448/9*

C Et dat*um* Ministrall*is* & al*ijs* lusorib*us* die pasc*ionis* *sancti* Thome   x .s.

...

Et dat*um* lusorib*us* de villa ludent*ibus* die Circumsic*ionis* dom*ini*   iij s. iiij .d.

...

C Et dat*um* pu*eris* ludentib*us* & tripudiant*ibus* coram d*omi*no   5
Priori   vj .s. viij .d.

C Et dat*um* pu*eris* Tome Ware ludentib*us* coram d*omi*no priori   x .s.

...

f 187v   10

...

C Et dat*um* diuers*is* lusorib*us* de ffeversham   iij s. iiij d.

...

f 188   15

...

C Et dat*um* Ric*ard*o Citheriste d*omi*ni archiep*iscop*i Cant*u*ariensis   iij s. iiij d.

...

C Et dat*um* Ministrall' d*omi*ni ducis Bukk*ingham*ie   xiij .s. iiij d.

...   20

C Et dat*um* lusorib*us* ludentib*us* coram d*omi*no Priori die
Ascenc*ionis* dom*i*ni   vj .s. viij .d.

...

f 188v   25

...

C Et dat*um* Ministrall' d*omi*ni Regis apud Ikham   xiij s. iiij d.

...

C Et dat*um* diu*ers*is Ministrall*is* die translac*ionis* *sancti* Thome   xlvj s. viij d.

...   30

1448–9
Civic Accounts   CCA: CC/FA 2
f 26v   *(Wages)*

    35

...Et sol*utum* Iohann*i* langley Will*elmo* Ionsson et Will*elmo* Rampeyn
Ministralib*us* Ciuitat*is* Cant*u*arie *pro* eo*rum* togis de vna secta emend*atis*
ad honorem d*ic*te Ciuitat*is* xiij s. iiij d.

...

1/ Ministrall*is*: *5 minims in* MS   7/ Tome Ware: *Thomas Ware, master of the almonry school*
6, 21/ Priori: *for* Priore   21–2/ die Ascenc*ionis* dom*i*ni: *2 May*
7/ priori: *for* priore

Christ Church Treasurers' Accounts CCA: DCc/Miscellaneous Accounts 4
f 225v *(Gifts)*

...

℃ Et dat*um* Ministrall' d*om*ini ducis Bukk*inghamie*   xiij .s. .iiij .d.

...   5

f 226

...

℃ Et dat*um* Ministrall' die *sancti* Thome   vj .s. viij .d.

...   10

f 227

...

℃ Et dat*um* iij histrionib*us* d*om*ini duc*is* Som*er*sette   v .s.

...   15

f 227v

...

℃ Et dat*um* histrionib*us* d*omi*norum & al*iorum* die
translaci*onis* s*an*c*t*i Thome   xxvj .s. viij .d. 20

...

Et dat*um* iij histrionib*us* ville Cant*uarie* die tnslaci*onis*
s*an*c*t*i Thome   v .s.

...

                                                                       25

f 228

...

℃ Et dat*um* Ric*ard*o harpor die translaci*onis* s*an*c*t*i Thome   iij .s. iiij .d.

...

℃ Et dat*um* Bartholomeo Mynystrall*o* d*om*ini Sumersette   xx .d. 30

...

℃ Et dat*um* histrihonib*us* london*ie* die Nat*iuitatis* sancte
[Ioh*an*ni] Marie   xviij .d.

...

                                                                       35

f 228v

...

℃ Et dat*um* histrionib*us* d*om*ini ducis Suff*olicie* ap*u*d Chartham   iij s. iiij d.

...

4/ Ministrall': *5 minims in* MS
9/ die s*an*c*t*i Thome: *probably Martyrdom of*
  St Thomas Becket, 29 December

22/ tnslaci*onis*: *for* translaci*onis*; *abbreviation*
  mark missing
32/ sancte: *corrected from* sancti

1449–50
Civic Accounts   CCA: CC/FA 2
f 30   *(Wages and rents paid)*

...Et sol*utum* Ioh*ann*i langley menstrall*o pro* toga sua de anno xxvij^mo R*egis*   5
henr*ici* sexti vj s. viij d....

...

1450–1
Civic Accounts   CCA: CC/FA 2   10
f 34   *(Necessary and external costs)*
...

...Et sol*utent*' do*mi*ni R*egis* exist*ent*' apud Cantuar*iam* iiij die
Augusti xx d....

15
Prior Goldston's Daybook   CCA: Literary MS E6
f 53   *(Gifts)*
...
Item dat*um* histrionib*us* do*mi*ni de Arundell ap*ud* Chartham   ij s.
...   20

f 53v
...
Item dat*um* ludentib*us* in nocte s*an*c*ti* Stephani   xx d.
...   25
Et dat*um* histrionib*us* ville Cant*uarie* s*an*c*ti* s*an*c*ti* Thome   iij s. iiij d.
Et histrionib*us* & al*ijs* de patria eod*em* die   ix s. iiij d.

f 54
...   30
Item dat*um* ix die Ianuar*ij* diu*ersis* histrionib*us* & alijs   xj .s. iiij d.
...

f 54v
...   35
Et sol*utum* v histrionib*us* do*mi*ni regis primo die mayy   xx .s.
...

26*l sanc*ti *sanc*ti: *dittography in *MS; *for die sancti*
26*l sanc*ti *Thome: *probably Martyrdom of St Thomas Becket, 29 December*

f 55

...

Et da*tum* histrionib*us* d*omi*ni ducis Bokynhamie xvj° die Iulij   vj s. viij d.

...

Item decim histrionib*us* die *sancti* Thome   xvj s. viij d.   5

1452-3
Christ Church Priors' Accounts   BL: Sloane MS. 4074
single mb*   *(Offerings and gifts)*

...   10

Et in donis dat*is* Ministris d*omi*ni Regis d*omi*ne Regine
& al*iorum* Magnat*um* Histrionibus nunc*ijs* & al*ijs*
fistulat*oribus*   xij li. xviij. s. ix d.

...   15

1453-4
Christ Church Priors' Accounts   CCA: DCc/Prior 9
mb 2   *(Offerings and gifts)*

...

Et in donis dat*is* Ministris d*omi*ni Regis d*omi*ne Regine   20
& al*iorum* Magnat*um* histrionibus nuncijs & alijs
fistulatorib*us* sup*er*uenient*ibus* hoc anno   xij li. vij s. iiij d.

...

1455-6   25
Christ Church Priors' Accounts   CCA: DCc/Prior 10
mb 3   *(Offerings and gifts)*

...

Et in donis dat*is* Ministris d*omi*ni Regis d*omi*ne Regine
& al*iorum* magnat*um* histrionib*us* nuncijs & al*ijs*   30
fistulatorib*us* sup*er*uenient*ibus* hoc anno   xvij li. iij s. xj d.

...

1456-7
Christ Church Priors' Accounts   CCA: DCc/Prior 15   35
mb 3*

...

Et in donis dat*is* Ministris d*omi*ni Regis & al*iorum*
magnat*um* histrionib*us* nuncijs & al*ijs* fistulat*oribus*
sup*er*uen*ientibus* hoc a*n*no   x li. xvj .s. iiij d. 40

...

5*l* die *sancti* Thome: *probably Translation of St Thomas Becket, 7 July*

1459–60
St Augustine's Treasurers' Accounts LPL: Estate Document 298
f 15 (Gifts)

...

Et dat*um* Ministrall' d*om*i*n*i Reg*is*   iij s. iiij d.   5
Et ministrall' in festo Natal*is* d*om*i*n*i   vj s. viij d.

...

f 15v

10

Et ministrall' d*om*i*n*i Reg*is* london*ie*   x s.

...

1461–2
City Jurats' Accounts CCA: CC/FA 4   15
f 9 (4 November)

...

℃ Pleg*ius* pro   *M*emorandum quod iiij die Nouembr*is* anno primo Reg*is* Edwardi iiij.ᵗⁱ
lez Scochons   liberata fuer*un*t Iohan*n*i langle de Cantuar*ia* Mynstrallo .iij. Skochons
Argent*ea* & dealmelat*a* q*ui*a fatebat*ur* se fore pleg*ium* pro seipso Will*elm*o   20
Rampayn & Ioh*ann*e Sclough Mynstrall*is* vt idem Ioh*ann*es langle respondeat
pro lez iij. Skochons in Camera xij. Iur*atorum* Sub pena xv .li. st*er*lingorum.
Nou*er*int &c me Ioh*ann*em langle de Cantuar*ia* Mynstrall*um* teneri &c
Ioh*ann*i Wynter Will*elm*o Sellow & Thome Prowde in xv li. st*er*lingorum
solu*endas* in festo Natal*is* d*om*i*n*i p*ro*ximo futur*o* &c dat*um* die & anno   25
supradict*o*.

...

1464–5
St Augustine's Treasurers' Accounts CCA: DCc/Charta Antiqua A 66e   30
f 27v* (Gifts)

...

Et dat*um* Ministrall' Cant*uarie* in die Natal*is* d*om*i*n*i   xx d.

...

Et dat*um* Ministrall' d*om*i*n*i Reg*is*   xij s. iiij d.   35
Et dat*um* Ministrall' d*om*i*n*i de warwyk   viij s. iiij d.

...

Et dat*um* Ministrall' d*om*i*n*i Reg*is*   xiij s. iiij d.
Et dat*um* Ministrall' Cancellar*ij*   iiij s. ij d.
Et dat*um* Ricard*o* Ministrall*o*   ij s. j d.   40

...

24/ Iohanni Wynter Willelmo Sellow & Thome Prowde: *3 of the 12 jurats for 1461–2*

John Stone's Chronicle of Christ Church Priory
Corpus Christi College, Cambridge: MS. 417
f 73v*   *(6 December)*

...

                  Episcopus de scola Cantuarie   5
Item hoc anno in festo sancti Nicholai non erat Episcopus in Scola gramaticali
in ciuitate Cantuarie et hoc ex defectu Magistrorum. videlicet Iohannis Gedney
& Thome hikson/

...

                                                  10

1466–7
John Stone's Chronicle of Christ Church Priory
Corpus Christi College, Cambridge: MS. 417
ff 78–8v   *(8 December)*

...   15

...et eodem die fratres sancti augustini comederunt in aula domini prioris in
presenlcia episcopi sancti Nicolai & prioris ecclesie Christi Cantuarie. Et in
eodem anno Thomas Burbage episcopus erat sancti Nicolai–

...

                                                  20

1467–8
City Chamberlains' Accounts   CCA: CC/FA 5
f 60   *(Wages and rents paid)*

...

•   Et solutum Iohanni harnell nuper Maiori Ciuitatis Cantuarie   25
   pro vestura histrionum   xiij s. iiij d.

...

Christ Church Priors' Accounts   CCA: DCc/Prior 16
mb 1*   *(Offerings and gifts)*   30

...

Et in donis datis Ministris domini Regis & alijs Magnatum histrionibus
nuncijs & alijs fistulatoribus superuenientibus hoc anno vt patet per
librum domini prioris de particulis   ⟨...⟩
                                                                                           35
...

1468–9
Christ Church Priors' Accounts   CCA: DCc/Prior 11
mb 3   *(Offerings and gifts)*

...   40

Et in donis datis Ministris domini Regis & alijs Magnatum histrionibus

---

25/ Iohanni harnell ... Maiori: *John Harnell, mayor 1466–7*   32, 41/ alijs: *for* aliorum

Nuncijs & alijs fistulatoribus superuenientibus hoc anno vt patet
per librum de particulis domini Prioris   viij⟨...⟩
...

St Augustine's Treasurers' Accounts   CCA: DCc/Charta Antiqua A 66d   5
f 14   *(Gifts)*

...

Et Ministrall' domini Regis   · vj s. viij d.
Et Ministrall' in die sancti Augustini   xij d.
...   10

1471–2
City Chamberlains' Accounts   CCA: CC/FA 5
f 131*   *(External expenses)*

...   15
℃ Item solutum le Mynstrallys domini Regis   vj s. viij d.
℃ Item solutum pro vino dato eisdem mynstrallys   xvj d.
...
℃ Item datum le [D] Menstrallys Domini Ducis Clarencie   v s.
℃ Item datum in vino & pane eisdem   xij d. 20
...

1472–3
City Chamberlains' Accounts   CCA: CC/FA 5
f 142v*   *(External expenses)*   25
...
℃ Nota   Et solutum le Mynstrellys domini Regis   x s. iiij d.
    ℃ Et solutum le Mynstrellys domini Ducis Clarencie   v s. iiij d.
...

                                                                              30

Christ Church Priors' Accounts   CCA: DCc/Prior 12
mb 3   *(Offerings and gifts)*
...

Et in donis datis Ministris domini Regis & alijs magnatum
histrionibus Nuncijs & ffistulatoribus superuenientibus hoc   35
anno vt patet per librum domini Prioris   lxxiij. s. ij. d.
...

34/ alijs: *for* aliorum

1473–4
City Chamberlains' Accounts   CCA: CC/FA 5
f 158*   *(External expenses)*

…

In primis solutum le Mynstrellis domini Ducis Clarencie	v s.	5
Et solutum pro .vj. Caponibus pinguioribus datis Duci Clarencie in suo aduentu	viij s.	
Et solutum [Stephano] [Iohanni] ⌈Thome⌉ lyndregge pro ij lagenis de Claret wyne ⌈datis eidem domino⌉	xx d.	
Et solutum willelmo Ingram pro pane leui dato eidem domino ·	xij d.	10
Et solutum iiijor hominibus ferentibus eidem domino dona predicta	iiij d.	
Et solutum .viij.[or] hominibus ferentibus dona & munera domino Camerario ⌈regis⌉ existenti in hospicio Signi	viij d.	
Et solutum pro quodam Iantaculo siue potacione dato Maiori Rogero Brent & alijs Aldermannis cum alijs viris honestis proponentibus representare predicta dona & munera coram prefato domino Camerario		15
	viij d.	
Et solutum pro vino dato Magistro [Iacobo] Iakys hawtes in domo Thome Morys	iiij d.	
Et solutum Pincerne dicti domini Camerarij regis pro bona gubernacione vini dati prefato domino		20
	xx d.	
Et solutum Iohanni Frennyngham pro .ij. Signis datis eidem domino	x s.	
Et solutum Iohanni Frennyngham pro duobus Caponibus pinguibus datis eidem domino	v s.	
Et solutum eidem Iohanni Frennyngham pro alijs duobus Caponibus datis predicto domino		25
	ij s.	
Et solutum Ricardo wellys pro duobus Caponibus datis eidem domino	ij s. viij d.	
Et solutum pro lvj lagenis & j potello de vino rubeo emptis de Iacobo kynggesmell. precio vnius lagene x d.	xlvij s. j d.	30
Et solutum Iacobo kyngesmell pro j potello dulcis vini vocati Muskadell	viij d.	
Et solutum pro quodam Iantaculo facto in hospicio Solis dato Maiori & alijs generosis predicti domini in exitu prefati domini de Ciuitate Cantuarie	x d.	35
Et solutum Thome holt equitanti pro vna fera ⌈vocata Buk⌉ equitanti apud westynghanger pro equo expensis & Cariagio eiusdem	xiiij d.	

10/ willelmo Ingram: *one of the city's common bakers*
15/ Rogero Brent: *mayor, 1471–3*
15/ honestis: h *corrected over* g
22/ Iohanni Frennyngham: *alderman; mayor 1462–3, 1468–9*

36/ Thome holt: *common serjeant*
36–7/ equitanti … equitanti: *dittography*

Et sol*utum* Parkario ib*ide*m pro regardo suo   ij s.

Et sol*utum* pro pistura eiusdem vide*lice*t [in spe*ciebus*] pro [di. b]

vno b*ushello* di. ∧⌈de le ffflowre⌉ di. li. piperis & vno denariat*o*

Salis & pro labore pistoris in om*nibus*   ij s. xj d.

Et sol*utum* histrionib*us* d*omi*ni Regis   vj s. viij d.   5

Et sol*utum* Maiori pro iiij^or ffasianis dat*is* predict*o* d*omi*no

Camerario   *(blank)*

…

Christ Church Priors' Accounts   CCA: DCc/Prior 14   10

mb 3*

…

Et in donis dat*is* diu*ersis* Ministr*is* d*omi*ni Reg*is* & al*iorum*

magnat*um* histrionib*us* Nunc*ijs* & al*ijs* fistulat*oribus*

superuen*ientibus* hoc anno vt patet p*er* libru*m* d*omi*ni   15

prior*is*   lij .li. x .s. vj .d.

…

1474–5

City Chamberlains' Accounts   CCA: CC/FA 5   20

ff 171–1v*   *(External expenses)*

…

…It*em* sol*utum* pro vasto iij li*brarum* Cere in Torticib*us* ecclesie s*ancte* andree

Cantuar*ie* illuminat*is* & accensis in adventu d*omi*ni Regis in nocte xij d.

Et sol*utum* vj ho*minibus* deferentib*us* eosd*em* Tortic*es* vj d.   25

Et sol*utum* in ∧⌈victu &⌉ potu dat*is* eisdem ho*minibus* ap*ud* Westgate

ne sep*ar*arent*ur*   vj d.

Et sol*utum* le Menstrallys d*omi*ni Regis   vj s. viij d.|

⊄ Et sol*utum* le Menstrallys Duc*is* Clarencie   vj s. viij d.

⊄ Et sol*utum* le Menstrallys Duc*is* Glocestrie   vj s. viij d.   30

⊄ Et sol*utum* Custodi leonis d*omi*ni Regis pro vno ariete   xx d.

…

f 172

…   35

⊄ Et sol*utum* le Mynstrallis D*omi*ne Regine   v s.

…

1/ regardo: o *corrected over illegible letters*

23/ *sancte* andree: *for* sancti andree

1476–7
City Chamberlains' Accounts   CCA: CC/FA 5
f 193v*   *(External expenses)*

...

per holt   ℭ Et solutum Edmundo Mynot pro [Remuneracione] eo quod ipse soluit   5
le Mynstrallis [ad] domini Principis ad mandatum Maioris pro eorum
remuneracione   v s.
ℭ Et solutum pro vna lagena vini data eisdem   viij d.

...

10

f 194   *(Delivery of scutcheons)*

...

ℭ Memorandum quod xvjᵒ die Ianuarij Anno regni regis Edwardi .iiijᵗⁱ
xvjᵒ willelmus Sellow & willelmus Bele Camerarij Ciuitatis Cantuarie
deliberauerunt Iohanni Chaldan de Cantuaria Mynstrall vnum Skochon   15
precio C s. per plegium Thome Goldsmyth
ℭ Ac etiam eodem die & anno predicti Camerarij deliberauerunt willelmo
Massyng de Cantuaria Menstrall vnum aliud Skochon precio C s. per plegium
Nicholai Sheldwich tunc presentis & Edwardi payabill vt asserit predictus
Willelmus Massyng   20

...

f 195   *(External expenses)*

...

ℭ Et solutum le Mynstrallis domine Regine   v s. 25
ℭ Et solutum pro vino & pane expositis circa eos   viij d.
ℭ Et solutum le Mynstrallis Ducis Clarencie   v s.
ℭ Et solutum pro pane & vino datis eis   viij s.

...

ℭ Et solutum le Mynstrallis domini Regis   vj s. viij d. 30
ℭ Et solutum le Mynstrallis domini Ducis ∧⌈Glocestrie⌉
[Clarencie] & pro vino eis dato   v s. [v] iiij d.

...

f 198   *(Wages and payments)*   35

...

ℭ Item solutum Willelmo Massyng & Iohanni Chaldan vigilibus
Cantuarie pro feodo suo [& pro Togis suis] hoc anno   xl s.
ℭ Item solutum eisdem vigilibus pro ijᵇᵘˢ Togis hoc anno   xvj s.

...

40

5m/ holt: *Thomas Holt, common serjeant*
5/ Edmundo Mynot: *chamberlain 1486–8*

1477–8
City Chamberlains' Accounts   CCA: CC/FA 5
f 206*   *(External expenses)*

...

Et sol*utum* histrionib*us* d*o*m*i*ni Reg*is* vj s. viij d. & p*ro* vino   5
dat*o* eis viij d.   vij s. iiij d.
Et sol*utum* histrionib*us* d*o*m*i*ne Regine v s. & in vino viij d.   v s. viij d.
Et sol*utum* histrionib*us* Duc*is* Glocestrie v s. & in vino iiij d.   v s. iiij d.
Et sol*utum* histrionib*us* Ducisse Eboraci iij s. iiij d. & p*ro*
vino iiij d.   iij s. viij d. 10
Et sol*utum* histrionib*us* equestrib*us* D*o*m*i*ne Regine   xx d.
                         Su*m*ma xxiij s. viij d.
...

f 210

...   15
It*em* trib*us* histrionib*us* voc*atis* le wayt*es* p*ro* Tog*is* suis hoc anno   xx s.
It*em* sol*utum* eisdem trib*us* p*ro* feod*is* suis hoc anno   xl s.
...

                                                                                 20
1478–9
Civic Accounts   CCA: CC/FA 2
f 191v   *(Wages and payments)*
...
...Et sol*utum* Iohan*n*i Chaldan Will*elm*o Skarlett & Will*elm*o Powlyng   25
vigilib*us* Ciuitat*is* Cantuar*ie* p*ro* Tog*is* suis hoc a*n*no xx s. Et sol*utum* eisd*em*
trib*us* vigilib*us* p*ro* eor*um* feod*is* hoc anno xl s.
...

City Chamberlains' Accounts   CCA: CC/FA 5   30
f 194   *(Delivery of scutcheons)*
...
℃ Et idem Will*elm*us Massyng .v*to*. die Nouembr*is* a*n*no *regni regis* Edwardi
.iiij*ti* .xviij*o*. relib*er*auit le Scocchon suu*m* will*elm*o Sellowe & Ioha*n*ni
whitlok Cam*er*arijs Ciuit*atis* p*re*dict*e*   35
...

f 223   *(External expenses)*
...
℃ It*em* sol*utum* [ₐ⌈le⌉ mynstrallys] ₐ⌈Tubicinis⌉ d*o*m*i*ni Reg*is* in   40
pecun*ijs* & vino dat*is* eis in domo Maior*is*   ij s.
...

5/ vj s. viij d.: *this sum and other internal subtotals underlined*

f 223v*

C Item solutum le Mynstrall*is* Domini principis in pecun*ijs* &
vino in domo maior*is*   v s. viij d.
...   5

C Et solut*um* le Mynstrallis d*om*ini Duc*is* Glocestrie   v s.
C Et solut*um* pro j lagena vini dat*a* eisdem   viij d.
...

1479–80   10
City Chamberlains' Accounts   CCA: CC/FA 6
f 6v*   *(Schedule of payments made by Thomas Atwood, mayor)*
...
...Et sol*utum* histrionib*us* d*om*ini Principis in remun*er*acione & in vino dat*o*
eisdem v s. viij d. Et sol*utum* histrionib*us* d*om*ini Duc*is* Glocestrie & in vino   15
v s. iiij d. Et sol*utum* histrionib*us* d*om*ine Ducisse Eboraci *pro* consi*m*ili iij s.
viij d....

...

f 7   *(External expenses)*   20
...
histriones   Et solut*um* histrionib*us* d*om*ini Reg*is* vj s. viij d./ Et in pane & vino dat*is*
eisdem x d./ vij s. vj d. Et solut*um* histrionib*us* d*om*ine Regine v s./ Et in
vino dat*o* eisdem iiij d./ v s. iiij d. Et sol*utum* pro quadam potac*i*one dat*a*
Maiori hamoni Bele & Ioh*ann*i Whitlok in domo Ioh*ann*is wower vacantib*us*   25
sup*er* histriones d*om*ini Reg*is* iiij d....
...

f 11   *(Wages and payments)*
...   30
Item solut*um* Ioh*ann*i Chaldan Will*el*mo Skarlet & Will*el*mo
Pawlyng histrionib*us* seu vigilib*us* pro eorum Tog*is* hoc Anno   xvj s.
Item solut*um* eisdem trib*us* [f] histrionib*us* a f*esto* s*ancti*
Michaelis archangel*i* a*n*no *regn*i reg*is* Edw*ard*i iiij.^ti vsque
festu*m* annu*n*ciacionis beat*e* Marie virg*in*is proximum sequ*entem*   35
pro feod*is* eor*um*   xx s.

22/ vj s. viij d./: *this sum and other internal subtotals underlined*
25/ hamoni Bele: *mayor 1478–9*
25/ Ioh*ann*i Whitlok: *one of the 2 city chamberlains this year*
25/ Ioh*ann*is wower: *one of the city's common bakers*
34/ anno ... iiij.^ti: *page dated 19 Edward* IV

Item solutum Iohanni Chaldan & Willelmo Pawlyng pro feodis
ipsorum duorum a predicto festo annunciacionis beate Marie vsque
festum sancti Michaelis archangeli tunc proximum sequentem   xiij s. iiij d.
...

5

1480–1
City Chamberlains' Accounts   CCA: CC/FA 6
f 19*   *(Wages and payments)*
...
Et solutum Iohanni Chaldan [Willelmo Scarlet] & willelmo   10
Pawlyng ij.bus vigilibus Ciuitatis Cantuarie pro Togis suis
hoc anno   xiij s. iiij d.
Et solutum eisdem vigilibus pro stipendio suo hoc anno   xl s.
...

15

f 21v
...
Et solutum le Mynstrellis domine [Regis] Regine in pecunijs
& vino   v s. viij d.
...   20
Et solutum le Mynstralis domini Regis & pro vino eis dato   vij s. iiij d.
Et solutum le Mynstrelys Ducisse Eboraci   iij s. iiij d.
...

1481–2   25
City Chamberlains' Accounts   CCA: CC/FA 6
f 32*   *(External expenses)*
...
Et solutum histrionibus domini Regis in pecunijs & vino vij s. iiij d. Et
solutum histrionibus domini Principis in pecunijs & vino v s. vj d. Et solutum   30
histrionibus domini Ducis Glocestrie v s. Et pro vino dato eisdem vj d.
Et solutum histrionibus domini ducis Eboraci iij s. iiij d. Et solutum pro
vino iiij d....
...

35

f 35   *(Wages and payments)*
...
℃ Et solutum Iohanni Chaldan Willelmo Pawlyng & Thome
Pawlyng fratri suo pro Togis suis hoc anno   xx s.
℃ Et solutum eisdem vigilibus pro stipendio suo hoc anno   xl s. 40
...

11/ ij.bus: *apparently added in left margin*   11/ Ciuitatis: s *written over another letter, possibly* b

1482–3
Civic Accounts   CCA: CC/FA 2
f 208   *(External expenses)*

℃ Et solut*um* histrionib*us* do*m*ini Reg*is* Edwardi quarti & histrionib*us* do*m*ini   5
Ducis Glocestrie in vino & argento xiiij s. viij d....

(Wages and payments)

...Et Ioha*n*ni Chaldan Will*el*mo Paulyng & Thome Paulyng vigilib*us* Ciui*tatis*   10
Cant*uari*e p*ro* eor*um* Tog*is* hoc anno xx s. Et p*ro* eor*un*de*m* stipend*ijs* viz. p*ro*
iij^b*us* quart*er*ijs huius anni & non vltra xxx s.
...

City Chamberlains' Accounts   CCA: CC/FA 7   15
f xxvij verso*   *(14 July 1485)* *(Settlement of mayor's accounts)*
...
M*em*orandu*m* qu*od* xiiij.º die Iulij a*n*no Reg*ni* Reg*is* Ricard*i* t*er*cij t*er*cio
Nichol*a*us Sheldwych armig*er* exhibuit in C*om*mu*n*i Camera Ciui*tatis*
Cant*uar*ie ij. Quitus est habit*a* de s*c*accario do*m*ini Reg*is* pro ij.^b*us* [M⟨.⟩]   20
annis Maioratus ipsius Nichol*a*i viz. p*ro* anno xxij.º Reg*ni* Reg*is* Edwardi .iiij.^ti
Et p*ro* anno Reg*ni* Reg*is* Ricardi t*er*cij primo Et tunc solut*um* fuit eidem
Nichol*a*o p*er* manus Camerarior*um* liij s. iiij d.
Et sol*utum* eidem Nichol*a*o p*ro* histrionib*us* D*om*ine Elizabethe nup*er* Regine
anglie v s. [p*ro*] in xxij.º anno Reg*ni* Reg*is* Edwardi .iiij.^ti Et sol*utum* eidem   25
Nichol*a*o eodem anno p*ro* histrionib*us* D*om*i*n*e Ducisse Eboraci matris d*om*ini
Reg*is* nu*n*c iij s. iiij d.
...

1483–4   30
City Chamberlains' Accounts   CCA: CC/FA 7
f xj verso   *(External expenses)*
...
Et solut*um* histrionib*us* Ducisse Eboraci iij s. iiij d....
...   35

f xxvij verso*   *(14 July 1485)* *(Settlement of mayor's accounts)*
...
Et sol*utum* [histrionib*us* do*m*ini] eidem Nichol*a*o p*ro* expens*is* suis fac*t*is
histrionib*us* do*m*ini Reg*is* anno Reg*ni* Reg*is* Ricard*i* t*er*cij primo vj s. viij d.   40

20/ Quitus est: *underlined*
39/ eidem Nichol*a*o: *Nicholas Sheldwich, mayor 1482–4*

Et sol*utum* eidem Nich*o*l*ao* [pro] eodem anno *pro* expens*is* suis fact*is*
histrionib*us* Do*m*ini Comit*is* Northumbrie iij s. iiij d. in primo aduentu
do*m*ini Reg*is* Ricard*i* tercij apud Cantuar*i*am Et sol*utum* eidem Nich*o*l*ao*
pro expens*is* suis fact*is* histrionib*us* Do*m*ine anne regine anglie v s. eod*em*
primo a*n*no R*egni* R*egis* Ricard*i* tercij...   5
...

1484–5
St Dunstan's Churchwardens' Accounts   CCA: U3/141/4/1
p 5   *(April/May–April/May) (Receipts)*   10
...
Item Ress*eyvyd* by vs the seyde wardeynes of hockemoney at ester   ix s. x d.
...

1485–6   15
City Chamberlains' Accounts   CCA: CC/FA 7
f xlj   *(External expenses)*
...
℃ Et sol*utum* histrionib*us* Do*m*ine Regine v s....

                                                                                   20
St Andrew's Churchwardens' Accounts   CCA: U3/5/4/1
f 7
...
It*em* recept*um* die de hokemunday p*er* manus mulier   ix s. vj d.
It*em* recept*um* die de hoketuysday de mulierib*us*   iij s. iiij d. 25
...

1486–7
City Chamberlains' Accounts   CCA: CC/FA 7
f lxiij*   *(May) (External expenses)*   30
...
...Et sol*utum* histrionib*us* do*m*ine Regine existen*tibus* apud le Swan Cantuar*ie*
in p*re*sencia Maioris & confr*atrum* suor*um* in pecun*ijs* & vino v s. vj d....
...

12/ vs the seyde wardeynes: *William Balle and John Thomas*
12/ at ester: *Hocktide, 11–12 April*
24/ hokemunday: *3 April*
24/ mulier: *for* mulier*um; abbreviation mark omitted*
25/ hoketuysday: *4 April*
33/ Maioris: *Thomas Atwode*

1487–8
City Chamberlains' Accounts   CCA: CC/FA 7
f liiij verso*   *(30 September)*   *(Waits' badges)*

ℭ M*emor*and*um* quod vltimo die Septembr*is* anno r*egni* r*egis* henrici septimi post   5
conq*uestu*m angl*ie* tercio Edm*und*us Mynott & Ric*ard*us wellys Camerarij
liberauerunt tres skochynnes argenti & deaurat*i* voc*atos* le Mynstrall skochynnes
huius Ciuitat*is* videl*icet* vn*um* inde ponder*antem* x vnnc*iarum* di. quart*erio*
vnc*ie* carente Ioh*ann*i Chaldan saluo custodiend*um* p*er* plegi*u*m Ioh*ann*is
walkar de Cantuar*ia* Plomer Thome Paulyn de Cantuar*ia* Mynstrall & will*el*mi   10
Paulyn de Cantuar*ia* Mynstrall Et alt*er*um inde d*ic*to Thome Paulyn
ponder*antem* x vnnc*iarum* dimid*ij* quarterio unc*ie* carente p*er* plegiu*m* Thome
Quy de Cantuar*ia* ffuller ∧⌈predictorum⌉ Ioh*ann*is Chaldan & will*el*mi Paulyn
saluo custodiend*um* Et t*er*cium inde ponder*antem* ix vnnc*iarum* & dimid*ij*
quart*er*ij unc*ie* p*re*fato will*el*mo Paulyn saluo custodiend*um* p*er* plegiu*m* Thome   15
Goldsmyth de Cantuar*ia* p*re*d*ic*torum Ioh*ann*is Chaldan & Thome Paulyn./.
...

f lxxxvj verso   *(External expenses)*
...   20
ℭ Et sol*utum* histrionib*us* d*omi*ni Reg*is* recept*is* p*er* Petru*m* Casenowe   vj s. viij d.
...

f lxxxvij
...   25
ℭ Et sol*utum* histrionib*us* D*omi*ne Regine   v s.
...

f lxxxix   *(Wages and payments)*
...   30
per Camer*arios* +   Et sol*utum* iij^bus histrionib*us* & vigilib*us* Ciuitat*is* Cantuar*ie*
pro eor*um* stipend*io* hoc Anno Et p*ro* eor*um* Tog*is*   lx s.
...

1488–9   35
City Chamberlains' Accounts   CCA: CC/FA 7
f Cj   *(External expenses)*

...Et sol*utum* histrionib*us* d*omi*ni Reg*is* per manus Thome Propchaunt vj s.
viij d....   40
...

39/ Thome Propchaunt: *one of the 2 chamberlains*

f Cv*   *(Wages and payments)*

+   It*em* Ioh*ann*i Chaldan Thome Paulyn & will*elm*o Paulyn
      histrionib*us* seu [C] vigilib*us* Cantuar*ie pro* eor*um* stipendio
      hoc anno eo qu*od* Ioh*ann*es Chaldan moriebat*ur* circa festu*m*   5
      sanc*t*i Ioh*ann*is bap*t*iste   xxxvj s. viij d.
+   It*em pro* Togis d*i*ctorum histrionu*m* seu vigilium hoc anno   xx s.
      ...

1489-90   10
City Chamberlains' Accounts   CCA: CC/FA 7
f liiij verso   *(29 September) (Waits' badges)*
...

¶   Me*morandum* quod xxix° die Septembr*is* anno quinto *regni regis* henrici vij^mi
    Ioh*ann*es walker Thomas Paulyn & will*elm*us Paulyn fideiussores Ioh*ann*is   15
    Chaldan iam defuncti reliberauerunt ˰⌈Camerarijs⌉ le Scochone d*i*c*ti* Ioh*ann*is
    Chaldan sanu*m* integru*m* & in eod*em* statu quo receperu*n*t &c

(5 December)
                                                                             20
¶   Me*morandum* quod quinto die Decembr*is* a*n*no *regni regis* henrici vij^mi quinto
    Thomas Quy fideiussor Thome Paulyn iam defuncti relib*er*auit Camerarijs le
    Scochon d*i*c*ti* Thome Paulyn sanu*m* integru*m* & in eod*em* statu quo recepit

f Cvij verso   *(22 December)*   25
...
Me*morandum* quod xxij° die Decembr*is* anno quinto *regni regis* h*en*rici septimi
Thomas Propchaunt & Thomas Sare tradiderunt will*elm*o Cuttyng vni
histrionu*m* seu vigilium Ciuitat*is* Cantuar*ie* vnu*m* le Scocchon [p] argenteu*m*
& deauratum ponder*antem* x. unc*iarum* j qu*arterij* sanu*m* & integru*m*   30
[*preterquam* quod idem Scocchon caret ij^bus] cu*m* xvj Clauis argenteis no*n*
deaurat*is* & iij^bus Coronis deaurat*is* & ij^bus auricu*l*is argent*eis* & no*n* deaurat*is*
viz. ad salua*m* custodia*m* per pl*e*giu*m* Thome Quy ffuller tu*n*c no*n* pr*e*sent*is*
sed prius Camerarijs pr*o*mittent*is*
                                                                             35
f Cxv verso   *(External expenses)*
...
Et sol*utum* histrionib*us* d*om*ini Reg*is* mens*e* augusti in
pecun*ijs* & vino   vij s. ij d.
...   40

28/ Thomas Propchaunt & Thomas Sare: *chamberlains*

f Cxix verso   *(Mayor's accounts)*

    Recepte de ffinib*us* Carnificu*m* & ffrunitor*um* voc*atorum* Tannors
In p*rimis* rece*ptum* de Thoma Breux p*ro* fine vni*us* Tauri int*er*fecti
& p*er* eum venditi sine licencia maioris & Camerarior*um*   viij d.   5
Item rec*eptum* de eode*m Thoma* Breux p*ro* fine alt*er*ius Tauri p*er* eum
int*er*fec*ti* & vend*iti* cu*m* licen*cia* &c   viij d.
Item rec*eptum* de Ioh*anne* Russlyn p*ro* fine ij*orum* Tauror*um*
int*er*fectorum & vend*itorum* j. cu*m* licen*cia* & p*ro* alt*ero* s*ine*   xvj d.
Item rece*ptum* de eode*m* Ioh*anne* p*ro* fine vni*us* Tauri p*er* eum   10
int*er*fec*ti* & venditi sine licen*cia*   viij d.
It*em* rec*eptum* de Thoma Breux p*ro* consim*i*li causa cu*m* licencia ·   viij d.
…

f Cxxj verso   *(Wages and payments)*   15
…
☾ Et sol*utum* p*ro* Tog*is* duor*um* histrionu*m* ho*c* anno   xiij s. iiij d.
☾ Et sol*utum* will*elm*o Pawlyn p*ro* feod*o* suo ho*c* anno   xiij s. iiij d.
☾ Et sol*utum* Will*elm*o Cuttyng alt*er*i histrioni in p*artem* feodi sui   vj s. viij d.
Et sol*utum* Relicte Thome Pawlyn qui decessit in die *sancti*   20
Martini ho*c* est p*ro* medio q*uarterio* int*er festum sancti* Mich*ae*lis
& Nat*alis* dom*ini*   xx d.
…

Ordinance for Regulating the Markets   BL: Stowe MS. 850   25
f [2v]*   *(Market regulations)*

Bocher*es*   Item that no man*er* of Bocher foren nor deynsyn sell no bull flesshe till it be
chasyd or baytid at the Bulstake and that they sle no kene grete w*ith* calf
Ewes grete w*ith* lambe nor no man*er* of flesshe but it be holsome for mannys 30
body & that they cast no fylth vnder their shamell*es* ne in the kyng*es* strete to
infect the kyng*es* people vppon payne vt s*up*ra
…

St Dunstan's Churchwardens' Accounts   CCA: U3/141/4/1   35
p 12   *(May/June–May/June)* *(Receipts)*
…
Item R*eceyvid* of hocke money in the p*a*ryshe   ix s. vj d.
…

38/ hocke money: *gathered 19–20 April*

1490-1
City Chamberlains' Accounts   CCA: CC/FA 7
f Cxxix verso   *(20 April)*   *(Waits' badges)*

...

Willelmus Paulyng

ℂ Memorandum quod xx° die aprilis anno regni regis henrici vij.mi vjto Thomas   5
Sare & Thomas Morys Camerarij Ciuitatis Cantuarie deliberauerunt iij. le
Scocchons argentea & deaurata cum armis eiusdem Ciuitatis quorum vnum
Scutiferorum predictorum ponderantem ix unciarum iiij quarteriorum vnius
vncie quod tunc [tradid] traditum fuit willelmo Pawlyng in salua custodia
habendum per plegium Thome Goldsmyth vt prius continetur in anno   10
Edmundi Mynot

Willelmus Cuttyng

ℂ Item eodem xx° die aprilis traditum fuit vnum aliud Scutiferum argenteum
sanum & integrum willelmo Cuttyng vni vigilium dicte Ciuitatis Cantuarie in
salua custodia habendum per plegium Thome Quy vt prius vltimo fuit anno
ponderantem ix vnciarum & iij quarteriorum vnius vncie   15

Nicholaus Reps

ℂ Item dicto xx° die aprilis traditum fuit tercium Scutiferum argenteum &
deauratum ac nouiter emendatum & reparatum per predictos Camerarios
Nicholao Reps in salua custodia habendum per plegium Iohannis Grafton
Inholder quod quidem Scutiferum ponderauit viij vnciarum dimidij.

    20

f Cxlj   *(Payments and wages)*

...

+ ℂ Item solutum pro iijbus Togis histrionum seu vigilium viz. willelmi
Paulyn willelmi Cuttyng & Nicholai Reps hoc anno erga festum
Natalis domini   xx s.   25

+ ℂ Et solutum willelmo Cuttyng vni vigilium pro plena solucione
stipendij sui de vltimo anno   vj s. viij d.

+ ℂ Item solutum dictis willelmo Paulyng willelmo Cuttyng & Nicholao
Reps vigilibus predictis in partem solucionis eorum stipendij anni
instantis viz. cuilibet eorum vj s. viij d.   xx s.   30

...

+ ℂ Et solutum dictis willelmo Pawlyng willelmo Cuttyng & Nicholao
Reps vigilibus Ciuitatis Cantuarie xxiiij° die Septembris Anno
instanti in plenam solucionem [h] eorundem huius anni   xx s.

...   35

f Clxj verso*   *(Payments of arrears from past years)*

...

...Et solutum eidem Iohanni Carlyll pro anno vjto Regis henrici vijmi quo anno

---

9/ custodia: *corrected from* custodiend'
10–11/ in anno ... Mynot: *chamberlain, 1486–8;*
   see p 85, ll. 14–16 above

30/ vj s. viij d.: *sum underlined*
39/ Iohanni Carlyll: *mayor; chamberlain 1491–2*

ipse extitit Maior eo quod soluit histrionibus diuersis id est le Mynstrels quibus
non fuit solutum per Camerarios viz. histrionibus domini Regis vj s. viij d.
histrionibus Regine v s. Et soluit histrionibus domini Principis iij s. iiij d....

St Dunstan's Churchwardens' Accounts   CCA: U3/141/4/1   5
p 17   *(Rendered 28 May) (Receipts)*

...

Item resyuyd of the hocke money good & bad   ix s. viij d.

...

                                                                                    10

1491-2
City Chamberlains' Accounts   CCA: CC/FA 7
f Clix   *(External expenses)*

...Et solutum histrionibus domini Regis vj s. viij d....   15

...

f Clxij   *(Wages and payments)*
...

Item solutum pro vj. Togis viz. xij. virgis panni lanei Thome Sare   20
pro iijᵇᵘˢ vigilibus Thoma holt Iohanne andrew Myller & Elizeo
Strangbow Melwreght precio j virge iij s.   xxxvj s.

...

ℂ Item solutum willelmo Pawlyn willelmo Cuttyng & Nicholao Reps
vigilibus Ciuitatis Cantuarie in plenam solucionem eorum stipendij   25
hoc anno   xl s.

...

St Dunstan's Churchwardens' Accounts   CCA: U3/141/4/1
p 21   *(May/June—May/June) (Receipts)*   30

...

Item receyuyd of the hockemoney   vj s. ix d. ob.

...

2/ vj s. viij d.: *this sum and other internal subtotals underlined*
8/ hocke money: *gathered 11–12 April*
20/ Thome Sare: *chamberlain 1489–90; mayor 1498–9*
22/ iij s.: *sum underlined*
32/ hockemoney: *gathered 30 April–1 May*

1492–3
City Chamberlains' Accounts   CCA: CC/FA 7
f Clxxiiij   *(External expenses)*

…Et sol*utum* histrionib*us* d*o*m*i*ni Reg*is* vj s. viij d.…   5
…

f Clxxviij verso   *(Wages and payments)*
…
Et sol*utum* will*elm*o Paulyng will*elm*o Cuttyng & Nich*o*l*a*o Reps   10
vigilib*us* Cantuar*ie* p*ro* eor*um* feod*is* & Tog*is* ho*c* anno   iij li.
…

1493–4
City Chamberlains' Accounts   CCA: CC/FA 7   15
f 198*   *(External expenses)*

Item sol*utum* Edwardo Bolney Maiore p*er* man*um* Roberti
Heutton Smyth p*ro* histrionib*us* d*o*m*i*ni Reg*is*   vj s. viij d.
…   20

f 199v   *(Wages and rents paid)*
…
Item sol*utum* will*elm*o Paulyn will*elm*o Cuttyng & Nich*o*l*a*o Reps
vigilib*us* Ciuitat*is* p*ro* eor*um* feod*is* & Togis   lx s. 25
…

St Andrew's Churchwardens' Accounts   CCA: U3/5/4/1
f 9   *(Easter and Hocktide receipts)*
…   30
Item R*eceived* on hopmu*n*day a tuysday   xxviij s. iiij d.
…

1494–5
City Chamberlains' Accounts   CCA: CC/FA 7   35
f 218*   *(Wages and payments)*
…
Item sol*utum* will*elm*o Paulyn Nich*o*l*a*o Reps Ioha*n*ni Cuttyng
& Relicte eiusdem Ioha*n*nis vigilib*us* d*i*c*te* Ciuitat*is* p*ro* eor*um*
feod*is* & tog*is*   iij li. 40
…

18/ Maiore: *for* Maiori   31/ hopmu*n*day a tuysday: *Hock Monday and Tuesday, 7–8 April*

St Andrew's Churchwardens' Accounts CCA: U3/5/4/1
f 11 *(Easter and Hocktide receipts)*

...

Item Reseyuyd at hopetyd of men and women — xvij s. vj d.

... 5

1495–6
City Chamberlains' Accounts CCA: CC/FA 7
f 230v* *(External expenses)*

... 10

Item sol*utum* Edwardo Bolney nup*er* Maiori *pro* histrionib*us*
dom*i*ni Regis *pro* annis ix & x° R*egis* nunc — xiiij s. iiij d.
Item sol*utum* eid*em* Edwardo *pro* histrionib*us* dom*i*ne Regine
pro eisd*em* ann*is* — x s.
Item sol*utum* ∧⌐histrionib*us*⌐ dom*i*ni Principis *pro* isto anno 15
per Cameras*ios* — xl d.
Item sol*utum* Thome Wode Maiori *pro* histrionib*us* dom*i*ni
R*egis* *pro* isto a*n*no — vj s. viij d.

... 20

f 231v *(Wages and rents paid)*

...

Item sol*utum* will*elm*o Paulyn & Nich*ol*ao Reps vigilib*us* d*ic*te
Ciuitat*is* *pro* vad*ijs* & togis hoc Anno — xl s.
... 25
Item sol*utum* Ioh*an*ni Rafe vigili d*ic*te Ciuitat*is* *pro* j q*ua*rterio — iij s. iiij d.

...

St Andrew's Churchwardens' Accounts CCA: U3/5/4/1
f 13 *(Receipts)* 30
...

Reseyuyd hopmu*n*day & hoptuysday — xvij s. ix d.

...

1496–7 35
City Chamberlains' Accounts CCA: CC/FA 7
f 244v* *(Wages and payments)*

In p*r*imis sol*utum* Istrionib*us* dom*i*ni Reg*is* — vj s. viij d.

... 40

4/ hopetyd: *Hocktide, 27–8 April* 39/ primis: *6 minims in* MS
32/ hopmu*n*day & hoptuysday: *Hock Monday and Tuesday, 11–12 April*

Et sol*utum* will*elm*o Paulyn Ioh*an*ni Raffe Nich*ola*o Ryps vigilibus
d*ic*te Ciuitat*is* pro vad*ijs* & tog*is* suis hoc anno   iij li.
...

St Dunstan's Churchwardens' Accounts   CCA: U3/141/4/1   5
p 28*   (May/June–May/June)
...

Item rec*eyuyd* that was gatheryd at hoctyde S*um*ma   iij s . viij d.
...

                                                                                    10

1497–8
Civic Accounts   CCA: CC/FA 2
f 282   (Wages and rents paid)
...

Et sol*utum* will*elm*o pawlyn Ioh*an*ni Rawff & Nich*ola*o Ripys   15
vigilib*us* dict*e* Ciuitatis pro vad*ijs* & togis suis   lv s.
...

Et sol*utum* histrionib*us* d*om*ini principis   iij s. iiij d.
...

Et sol*utum* histrionib*us* d*om*ini Regis & Regine hoc anno   xj s. viij d. 20
...

St Dunstan's Churchwardens' Accounts   CCA: U3/141/4/1
p 31*   (May/June–May/June) (Receipts)
...   25
Item of hockemoney of p*a*ryshyns & strangers   xiiij s. iij d.
...

1498–9
Civic Accounts   CCA: CC/FA 2   30
f 295   (Wages and rents paid)
...

Et sol*utum* will*elm*o paulyn & Nich*ola*o Ryps vigilib*us* d*ic*te
Ciuitatis pro vad*ijs* & tog*is* suis hoc anno   xlvj s. viij d.
Et sol*utum* Maiori p*ro* histrionib*us* d*om*ini Regis hoc anno   vj s. viij d. 35
Et sol*utum* eidem Maiori p*ro* histrionib*us* d*om*ine Regine in regardo   v s.
...

8/ hoctyde: *3–4 April*
26/ hockemoney: *gathered 23–4 April*
35/ dom*i*ni Regis: *corrected from* dom*i*ne Regine

f 299v *(Mayor's accounts)*

...

Et re*ceptum* de xij d. de ffine vni*us* tauri in*ter*fecti cu*m* licencia sine
inquietac*i*one siue vexac*i*one canu*m* p*er* Thomam Ridar Carnificem
Et de xvj d. *pro* consi*m*ili ffine duor*um* tauro*rum* Thome Broux & hugonis
Clarke in*ter*fect*orum*
Et de viij d. *pro* consi*m*ili ffine vni*us* tauri Ri*card*i Pesemede Carnific*is*
in*ter*fect*i*

Su*m*ma iij s.

...

St Dunstan's Churchwardens' Accounts CCA: U3/141/4/1
p 31* *(May/June–May/June) (Receipts)*

...

Item of hockemoney in the xiiij yere of the seyde kyng of
p*ar*ysshens & straungers v s. iij d.

...

1499–1500
Civic Accounts CCA: CC/FA 2
f 308 *(Wages and rents paid)*

...

Et sol*utum* histrionib*us* d*om*ini R*egis* hoc anno vj s. viij d.
Et sol*utum* histrionib*us* d*om*ine Regine hoc anno v s.

...

f 313v *(Mayor's accounts)*

...

Et re*ceptum* de xx d. *pro* [firme] ⌈ffine⌉ duor*um* tauror*um* in*ter*fect*orum* sine
inquietac*i*one canu*m* p*er* Thomam Breux & hugonem Clark Carnifices
cu*m* licencia
Et de xx d. *pro* consi*m*ili fine *pro* duob*us* Tauris in*ter*fect*is* cu*m* lice*n*c*i*a p*er*
Ioh*ann*em Russhelyn
Et de viij d. *pro* consi*m*ili fine *pro* vno Tauro in*ter*fect*o* cu*m* licenc*i*a p*er*
Ioh*ann*em Edmond Carnificem

Su*m*ma iiij s.

...

15/ hockemoney ... kyng: *gathered 29–30 April*

St Dunstan's Churchwardens' Accounts   CCA: U3/141/4/1
p 33*   *(May/June–May/June)*

Item of hockemoney last passid of p*a*ryssens & strangers   viij s. ij d.
…   5

A   **St Dunstan's Church Inventory**   Bunce: 'Church Goods'
p 571 col 1   *(1 May)*
…
A vestment, for Saint Nicholas tyme, w*ith* crosyar and myter.   10
…

1500–1
Civic Accounts   CCA: CC/FA 2
f 331   *(Wages and rents paid)*   15
…
+   Item to the kyng*es* Milstrell*es*   vj s. viij d.
+   It*em* to the Quenys mynstrell*es*   v s.
Item to the prync*es* Mynstrell*es*   v s.
…   20
+   Item paied to the iij wayt*es* for their wag*es* by half ayere endyng at
Mighelmas &c   xx s.
Item for their gownes by thesame tyme   x s.
…

25

f 346v   *(Mayor's accounts)*
…
ffin*e* pr*o* tauris ¶   Et r*eceptum* de iij s. iiij d. recept*is* pr*o* finib*us* Tauror*um* i*n*terfector*um* cum
sccis*is* &c   licenc*ia* &c p*er* comm*un*es Carnifices Ciuitat*is* p*re*dic*te* hoc anno &c
Su*m*ma iij s. iiij d.   30
…

f 349*   *(External expenses)*
…
®Mynstrell*es*   Et sol*utum* histrionib*us* d*omi*ni R*egis* eis in regard*is* dat*is*   vj s. viij d. 35
Et sol*utum* histrionib*us* d*omi*ne Regine &c   v s.
Et sol*utum* histrionib*us* d*omi*ni de Oxforde ex p*re*cepto Maioris   xx d.
…

4/ hockemoney last passid: *gathered 27–8 April 1500*

1501–2
Civic Accounts CCA: CC/FA 2
ff 360v–1*

Expences for +
makyng of
the bankett
in the Courte +
hall
+

ffyrst paied to Richard Iuner for the makyng of ij bestes and for
the Towre in the yeldehall

Item for xij elles of Canvas for the iij bestes

Item for payntyng of thesame iij bestes

Item for hoopys lathe and nayle for thesame iij bestes

Item in meate & drynke for the seid Richard Iuner and Thomas
a Courte and also for Candill by the space of vj daies and
vj nyghtes

Item for orsedue for to make with the kynges garmentes and
their henshemennys syluer papers golde papers and synaper
papers for thesame &c and monkes frokkes with other thynges
necessary therto

Item for the heddyng of the hensshemen and gyldyng of a Starre
°xxxvij s. iiij d.° Summa

x s.

iiij s.

iij s.

iij s.

vj s. viij d.

vj s. viij d.

v s.

5

10

15

Bankett vz. v
die Ianuarij

+
+
+
+
+

Item paied to Iohn Shorte & ij of his men and to andrewe atkynson
Thomas alowe & another Carpenter by ij daies & di.

Item for ij hoopys for the castell

Item for jC of iiij peny nayle & jC of iij peny nayle

Item for ijC of ij peny nayle

Item paied for one hundreth of paten nayle

Item to Richard Redhode paynter for payntyng of the Castell
in the Courtehall & his Colowers

Item paied to theseid Redhode for payntyng of the Trapper for the
best of one of the iij kynges of Coleyn the whiche cloth is in the
handes of Mr wode

Item for the deners of theseide Redhode Courte & the Carver

Item to ij Sawyers by a day & a half

Item for a dosyn of brede

Item to Roger Clarke for a kylderkyn of Bere

Item to Thomas ffoox for a dosyn of Candill

Item to Burges for v galonz of wyne

Item to Thomas wainflet for iij galons of wyne

Item to william prior for ij galonz

vij s. vj d.

ij d.

vij d.

iiij d.

I d.

iij s. iiij d.

iij s.

iiij d.

xviij d.

xij d.

xviij d.

xij d.

iiij s. ij d.|

ij s. vj d.

xx d.

20

25

30

35

37/ Thomas wainflet: *common councillor*
38/ william prior: *common councillor; sheriff 1503–4*

Item paied to theseid william prior for wyne for my lorde of seint
austyns seruantes and the lorde prior of Cristischurche seruantes that
dranke not in the halle the whiche were hadde to his house at the
brekyng vppe of the bankett   vij d.
Item for a Rynge of ale   xiiij d.   5
Item paied the same nyght at the Swanne for the souper of the
pleyers and other that were occupied aboute theseid bankett   iiij s. iiij d.
Item spent on theym in wyne at william priors   x d.
Item paied to andrewe atkynson and Thomas alowe for takyng doun
of the Scaffoldes and settyng vp of the barre in the yeldehall   xij d.   10
Item for brusshyng of the clothys & makyng clene of the hall   ij d.
                              Summa xxxvij s.

...

f 364v   (External expenses)   15

...

¶ Item the seid Thomas wode axith allowance for his charges
don in theseid Mr huettes yer for midsomer wacche after
your discresion .s.   x s.
...   20
Item paied to ij fflemmynges that were hurte with gunne powder
in theseid wacche by theseid commaundement   xij d.
...

ff 366v–7   25

...

Reparaciones
apud le
Bullestake

¶ Item paid to Richard asshynton for castyng of vj lodes of
Sande for pavieng ther   xij d.
Item to Iohn Tempill for cariage of the same   ix d.
Item to thesame Iohn Tempill for a lode of smalle sande   30
to thesame   vj d.
Item for bolder and gutter stone for the same   ij s.
Item to Iohn Pavyer for pavieng of the same   iij s. vj d.
Item in surplusage of seint mighelles gate   iij s. iij d.
                              Summa xj s.   35

...

1–2/ lorde of seint austyns: *John Dygon, abbot 1497–1510*
2/ lorde prior of Christischurche: *Thomas Goldston, prior 19 January 1494/5–16 or 17 September 1517*
17/ Thomas wode: *chamberlain*
18/ Mr huettes yer: *1501–2, year of John Huett's mayoralty*
21/ fflemmynges: *5 minims in MS*
22/ theseid commaundement: *ie, master mayor's commandment*

(Wages and rents paid)

Item paied to the Mynstrelles for their wages and gownys	xlvj s. viij d.
Item to the kynges mynstrelles	vj s. viij d.|
Item to the quenys mynstrelles	v s.
Item to the prynces mynstrelles	v s.

…

1502–3
Civic Accounts CCA: CC/FA 2
f 379v *(Expenses and rents paid)*

…

Et solutum Thome pygeon vigilibus et socijs suis pro vadijs
& Togis suis hoc anno ... xlvj s. viij d.

…

f 384 *(External expenses)*

…

Et de vj s. viij d. solutis histrionibus domini Regis Et de v s. solutis histrionibus
domine Regine Et de v s. solutis histrionibus domini principis…

…

1503–4
Civic Accounts CCA: CC/FA 2
f 395*

…

A gyfte to
my lorde
prynce Artur

¶ Item in a gyft gevyn to theseid lorde prynce artur at his first
comyng to Caunterbury that is to say a gylte Cuppe weyng
xxiij vnces price the vnce iiij s. ij d. *Summa* iiij li. xvj s. ij d.
and in mony paied to Iohn Alcock Goldesmyth for the byeng
of thesame iiij s. and ouer that xiij li. vj s. viij d. in nobilles in
theseid Cuppe *Summa* totalis ... xviij li. vj s. x d.
Item paied to the pursyvaunt bryngyng the Commyssion
for the ayde xx d. Item to the kynges Desers xx d. to the
kynges Mynstrelles xx d. to the kynges ffotemen vj s. viij d.
to thesaid prynces fotemen vj s. viij d. Item to the kynges
henshmen and the prynces henshmen iij s. iiij d. And to
the Clerk of the markett vj s. viij d. vnde summa ... xxviij s. iiij d.
Summa xix li. xv s. ij d.

…

13/ vigilibus et socijs suis : *for* et socijs suis vigilibus f 395v   *(Payments)*

…

Item for the wages of the waytes	xl s.
Item for their lyuerey	xx s.

…

f 399v   *(Mayor's accounts)*

…

ffynes of
Bullys

¶ Item of v s. for licence gevyn to sle Bulles without Baytyng

Summa v s.

…

1504–5
Civic Accounts   CCA: CC/FA 2
ff 411–11v

…

seynt
Thomas
pageant

¶ Item paied to Sampson Carpenter and hys man hewyng and squaryng of tymber for theseid pagent by one day	viij d.
Item paied to Iohn Stulpe for makyng of seint Thomas Carte with a peyr of whylis	v s. viij d.
Item to Thomas Starke Carpenter and his felowe makyng of the pageant by iiij daiez takyng bitwene theym by the day fyndyng theymself xiiij d. *Sum*ma	iiij s. viij d.
Item to Richarde harte for ij yaxronges weyeng iiij li. & di.	v d.
Item for C & xiiij fote of borde bought for the floryng of thesame pagent	ij s. viij d.
Item in C of iij peny nayle iij d./ in C & di. of ij d. nayle iij d. and in smalle nayles j d. ob. *Sum*ma	vij d. ob.
Item in talowe for the whiles	j d.
Item in ale spent j d. to iiij men to help to cary the pagent viij d. & to Iamys Colman for his horse hyre iiij d. *Sum*ma	xiij d.
Item paied for ij bagges of leder to Gyllam	xviij d.
Item to Gylbert payntor for payntyng of the awbe & the hedde	vj d.
Item to arnold lokyer for gunpowder bought at Sandewiche	iij s. iiij d.
Item for fettyng of borde from Northgate	ij d.
Item for lynen cloth bought for seint Thomas garment	vj d.|
Item for a dosyn and a half of tynen syluer	ix d.
Item for di. li. of glewe j d. ob. in an erthyn potte ob. packthrede j d. *sum*ma	iij d.
Item for iij Calve skynnys xiiij d. in syse bought j d. viij dosen of Cades poyntes viij d. in goldefoyle j d. *Sum*ma	ij s.

Item in Colys for to mylt the glewe ob. in a rewarde yevyn to Thomas
ffleccher for forgyng and makyng of the knyghtes harnes vj d. to Iohn
a Tent for the hyre of a swerde ij d. and for Wasshyng of an Albe and
a amys ij d. *Summa*   x d. ob.
Item in Candillis   j d.   5

Summa xxv s. x d.

f 413v   *(External expenses)*

...   10

Item paied to the waytes of london for their attendunce on seint
Thomas evyn   vj s. viij d.

...

Item in a rewarde gevyn to the prynces Mynstrelles   iij s. iiij d.

...   15

f 414   *(Wages and payments)*

...

Item paied to pygeon and Ryppis waytes of the Cetie for their
wages for the terme of Cristmas   vj s. viij d. 20

...

Item paied to the kynges Mynstrelles at the enstallyng of the
lorde archiebisshop of Caunterbury   vj s. viij d.

...

Item paied to the seid waytes for our lady day terme   vj s. viij d. 25

...

Item paied to theseid waytes for Midsomer terme   vj s. viij d.

...

f 426v   *(Mayor's accounts)*   30

...

Item of hugh Bocher for a fine for bulle kyllynges   xlj d.
Item of Thomas Brewes bocher for ij bulles kyllynges   ij s.
Item of yong pesemede j bulle   xij d.

20/ terme of Cristmas: *25 December–24 March*
22–3/ enstallyng … Caunterbury: *9 March 1504/5, enthronement of Archbishop William Warham*
25/ lady day terme: *25 March–23 June*
27/ Midsomer terme: *24 June–28 September*

St Andrew's Churchwardens' Accounts   CCA: U3/5/4/1
f 17v*   *(25 December 1504–25 December 1506)* *(Receipts)*
...
R*eceived* of the wyvys for hokke monday yn the same yere   xiiij s. ix d. ob.
...   5

A   ***O Quantum in Rebus Inane***   STC: 25073
sheet [9] cols 1–2*   *(9 March)* *(Enthronement banquet for Archbishop William Warham)*
¶ ...   10

Prouisiones & Emptiones
circa dictam Intronizationem.

De Frumento. liiij. quart*eria* prec*io* qu*arterij* v. s. viij. d.	xv. li. vj. s.
De simula pura & pro operatione le Wafers	xx. s. 15
De vino rubeo vi. dolea prec*io* dol*ei* iiij. li.	xxiiij li.
De Vino claret*o* iiij. dol*ea* prec*io* dol*ei* lxxiij. s. iiij. d. xiiii. li. xiii. s. iiij. d.	
De Vino alb*o* elect*o* unum dol*eum* iii. li. vj. s. viij. d.	
De Vino alb*o* pro coquina i. dol*eum*	iii. li.
De Maluesey. i. but*ta*	iiij. li. 20
De Ossey i. pipe.	iij. li.
De Vino de Reane. ii. almes.	xxvj. s. viij. d.
De Ceruisia Londini. iiij. dol*ea*	vj. li.
De Ceruisia Cant*uariae* vj. dol*ea* prec*io* dol*ei* xxv. s.	vij. li. x. s.
De Ceruisia ang*lice* bere. xx. dol*ea* prec*io* dol*ei*	25
xxiii. s. iiij. d. xxiij. li. vi. s viii. d.	
De Speciebus in gross*o* simul cum le Sokettes.	xxxiii. li.
De Cera operat*a* & divers*is* luminar*ibus* iijC. li. le C.	
xlvi. s. viij. d.	vii. li.
De Candel*is* albis liiii. dd. le dd. xv. d.	iiij. li. 30
De Pan*no* lineo & Canuas*io* viC. vln*ae* le uln*a* v. d.	xiiij. li. x s.
De Lynge iijC. prec*io* C. iij. li.	ix li.
De Coddes viC. le C. xxvi. s. viii. d.	viii li.
De Salmon*ibus* salss*atis* vij. bar*el*li le bar*rel* xxviij. s.	ix. li. xvj. s.
De Salmon*ibus* recent*ibus* xl. prec*io* cap*itis* vij. s.	xiiij. li. 35
De Halec*e* alb*o* xiiij. bar*el*li le bar*rel* viij. s.	v. li. xii. s.
De Halec*e* rub*eo* xx. cades. le cade iiij. s. viii. d. iiij. li. xiii. s. iiij. d.	
De Sturgion salss*ato* v. bar*el*li le bar*rel* xxx. s.	vii. li. x. s.
De Anguil*lis* salss*atis* ii. bar*el*li le barrel xlvi. s. viii. d. iiii. li. xiii. s. iiij. d.	
De Anguil*lis* recent*ibus* vi.C. prec*io* c. xl. s.	xii. li. 40
De Welkes viii.M. prec*io* M. v. s.	xl s.

4/ hokke monday yn the same yere: *20 Henry VII; hence 31 March 1505*

De Pykes v.C. le C. v. li. xxv. li.

De Tenches iiii.C. precio C. iii. li. vi. s. viii. d. xiij. li. vj. s. viii. d.

De Carpes C. precio capitis xvi. d. vj. li. xiii. s. iiii. d.

De Breames viii. c. precio c. xl. s. xvi. li.

De Lampreys salssatis ii. barelli le barel xx. s. xl. s. 5

De Lampreys recentibus lxxx. precio capitis xxii. d. vii. li. vi. s. viii. d.

De Lamprons recentibus xiiii.C. precio in grosso lii. s.

De Congre salssato Cxxiiii. precio capitis iii. s. xviij. li. xii. s.

De Roches grossis CC. precio C. iij. s. iiii. d. vj. s. viij. d.

De Seales & Porposses precio in grosso xxvi. s. viii. d. 10

De Pophyns vi. dd. le dd. iiii. s. xxiiij. s.

De Piscibus marinis xxiiii. seames. le seame xi. s. iiii. d. xiij. li. xij. s.

De Sale albo & grosso iii. quarteria le quarter x. s. xxx. s.

De Oleo Rape. ii. barelli le barel xxxvi. s. viii. d. iij. li. xiii. s. iiii. d.

De Oleo Oliui v. lagenae precio lagenae ii. s. x. s. 15

De Melle i. barellus precio xliii. s.

De Sinapio in grosso xiii. s. iiii. d.

De vino acri i. hoggshead viii. s.

De Vergez i. pipe. xvi. s.

De Carbonibus. cc. quarteria precio v. li. 20

De Talshide & Fagotes ii.M. precio liij. s. iiij. d.

De conductione vC. garnishturarum vasorum
electrinorum capiente pro le garnish. x. d. xx. li. xvi. s. viii. d.

De vasis ligneis lx. dd. precio dd. viii. d. xl. s.

De ciphis ligneis albis iii.M. precio v. li. 25

De Ollis terreis lxij. dd. precio iii. li. ii. s.

In cariagio stauri per terram & aquam xlii. li.

In stipendiis Cocorum Londini & aliorum. xxiij. li. vi. s. viij. d.

In regardis Haraldorum armorum le Trumpets, &
aliorum mimorum. &c. xx. li. 30

In pictura Throni & operatione de le Sotilties in saccharo
& cera. xvj. li.

In expenssis necessarijs vnacum regardis datis diversis
personis venientibus cum diversis exhenniis x. li.

35

Summa vC.xiij. li. iij. s.

Vltra.   Compositionem cum Duce pro feodis suis, & regardis expensis circa famulos
suos, & vltra dietam suam per tres dies, in manerijs Archiepiscopi
Et vltra conductionem lectorum. &c. Vltra ea quæ missa sunt a   40
Londino, & conductionem vasorum coquinariorum preter sua propria Et
recompensationem vasorum electrinorum id est. iiij. garnishturarum

ii. dd. & vii. peces deperditor*um* Et xviij. peces northen russettes Et alias
multas prouisiones de suo. &c.

…

1505–6
City Chamberlains' Accounts   CCA: CC/FA 9   5
f 42   *(External payments)*
…

Item paide to Richard waren for to speke with [e] ∧⌈the⌉ wayt*es*
att Camb*er*ege to brynge the*m* to Cant*er*bury   vj s. viij d. 10

…

f 43*
…

Item paide to the prinses Crouders by the hand*es* of Mr Cro*m*pe   15
in the tyme of his maieralte   xx d.

…

Item in Reward youen to the kyng*es* Mynstrell*es* the xth day of
May & spent on the*m* at the Rede lion in red wyne vj d. ther
beyng M*aster* Maier & certen of his bretherne   vij s. ij d. 20

…

f 43v
…

Item in rewarde youen to the wait*es* of londen on seint Thomas   25
Night goyng before the wacche   x s.
Item paide for iij yard*es* & j q*uarter*ne of fustien for Iohn
park*es* Iakett p*ri*ce the yard iiij d. xiij d. & in grene teweke
for the same parke j virg*e* dimid. & di. q*uarter*ne *price* le
virg*a* xij d. xxj d. in toto   ij s. x d. 30
Item for Iohn Heies Iakett ij yard*es* & di. of fustien iiij d. x d.
& on elle of grene tewke xv d.   ij s. j d.
Item paide to Thomas Iohnson for makynge & refresshynge of
+   the knyght*es* hernes xx d. for an horse herid & iij men for to
conueye seint Thomas pagente xij d. to Redehode for a newe   35
myghter ij s. to Gilberd payntour for payntyng of seinte Thomas
hede vj d. for the supper of the knyght*es* & the seide iij men viij d.   v s. x d.
+   Item paide to peter Gose for ij lib. & di. of gunpouder   xx d.
+   Item paide to arnolde fremer for ij lib. & di. of gunpouder   xx d.
…   40

15/ Mr Crompe: *William Crompe, mayor*
31/ iiij d.: *sum underlined*

f 47v   *(Wages and rents paid)*

...

Et sol*utum* histrionib*us* do*mi*ni Reg*is* hoc anno   vj s. viij d.
Et sol*utum* histrionib*us* do*mi*nj ⌈principis⌉ [Regine] hoc anno
& in vino   v s. [iiij d.]   5

...

f 66v   *(Mayor's accounts)*

...

ffin*es* for bull*es* to be Slayne   Item p*ro* fin*ibus* iij tauror*um* p*er* man*um* Will*el*mi Chapman   v s.   10
                                                    S*um*ma v s.

St Andrew's Churchwardens' Accounts   CCA: U3/5/4/1
f 18*   *(25 December 1504–25 December 1506)*

...   15

Rec*eived* of hokke monday folowyng   xvj s. ij d.

...

1505–7
St Dunstan's Churchwardens' Accounts   CCA: U3/141/5/1   20
p 4*

...

Item receyvid of hoktyde money for iij yere   xxiij s. viij d.

...   25

1506–7
City Chamberlains' Accounts   CCA: CC/FA 9
f 8v   *(External payments)*

...Et sol*utum* mymys do*mi*ni Reg*is* apud signu*m* solis x die mensis Iunij in   30
regard*o* in p*re*senci*a* maioris & al*terum* aldermann*orum* cu*m* iiij d. p*ro* I
potello vino vij s. Et sol*utum* p*er* man*um* Ioh*ann*is parke a lez waytes london*ij*
existent*ibus* apud Cantuari*am* in vigilia s*anct*i Thome app*os*toli x s. Et
sol*utum* a lez Crouders principis & prinsesse ad idem f*estum* iij s. iiij d. Et in
iij virg*is* & [di] ⌈j q*uar*t*er*ne⌉ de fustien ⌈xx d.⌉ I elne of grene tewke ⌈viij d.   35
ob.⌉ & I q*uar*terne empt*is* p*ro* le Iakett Ioh*ann*is parke iij s. ij d. ob. Item
sol*utum* p*ro* j elne de Tewke [price] & ij virg*is* & di. de ffustien p*ro* j Iakette
empt*o* p*ro* Ioh*ann*e hey ij s. vj d. Et sol*utum* p*ro* le wasshyng & le hurting
panni linei p*ro* le pagent s*anct*i Thome martiris vj d. Et sol*utum* p*ro*

4/ do*mi*nj: *corrected from* do*mi*ne   31/ iiij d.: *sum underlined*
16/ hokke ... folowyng: *20 April 1506*   32/ vino: *for* vini
31/ maioris: *Henry Goseborne*   36/ q*uar*terne: *3 minims in* MS

conduct*ione* j equi & iiij hom*inum* haurient*ium* & cariant*ium* le pagent s*ancti* Thome martir*is* xij d. Et in tynne foyle nayle & threde & emendac*ione* hernesie Milit*um* s*ancti* Thome pagent xvij d. ⌈Et sol*utum* pro x libr*is* of gunpouder empt*is* de Will*elmo* Rutland *(blank)*⌉ Et in expens*is* Milit*um* p*ro* cena s*ua* viij d. Item in vno gross*o* of poynt*es* empt*o* p*ro* le hernesing de lez   5 knyght*es* & lac*es* vij d....

f 10   *(Fees and wages paid)*

...Et sol*utum* histrionib*us* do*m*ini R*egis* hoc anno vj s. viij d. Et sol*utum*   10 histrionib*us* do*m*ini principis hoc anno v s....

...

Register of Christ Church Penitentiarian   CCA: Literary MS C11
f 115*   *(20 June–26 September)*   15
...
Ite*m* eide*m* in argent*o* p*ro* le clavic*ord*   ij s. [v] iiij d.
...

St Andrew's Churchwardens' Accounts   CCA: U3/5/4/1   20
f 30v   *(6 January 1506/7–6 January 1507/8)* *(Receipts)*
...
Item *received* at hokmonday & hoktuysday of the wyvis of
the seid parisshe   xvij s.
...   25

1507–8
City Chamberlains' Accounts   CCA: CC/FA 9
f 94v

...   30
Custu*s* pagine
s*ancti* Thome

In primis ij dd. & dj. de Tynfoyle vij d. ob. dimid. dd. de goldefoyle ij d. ob. Item glewegh empt' I d. iij lib. gunpouder xviij d. p*ro* clauis j d. ob. Item in packethrede ob. in [dimid.] ∧⌈vij⌉ dd. poynt*es* ij d. ob. p*ro* labore vni*us* hom*inis* p*ro* emendac*ione* harnisi*e* milit*um* xx d. p*ro* le yettyng sanguynis iiij d. in pane & seruisi*a* p*ro* duob*us* hom*i*nib*us* p*ro* le dressing eiusdem pagine   35 cu*m* expens*is* Milit*um* xij d. le Iakett Ioh*ann*is parke ij s. xj d. stac*ione* de le

---

4/ Will*elmo* Rutland: *common councillor; chamberlain 1508–10; alderman from 1513; mayor 1518–19, 1528–9*

17/ eidem: *Ralph Ewyn*

23/ hokmonday & hoktuysday: *12–13 April 1507*

31–6/ vij d. ob., ij d. ob., I d., j d. ob., ob., ij d. ob., xx d., iiij d., xij d., ij s. xj d.: *sums underlined*

pagient ij s. j equo conducto pro le pagent ˰⌈& conduccione ij hominum⌉
xvj d. le payntyng capitis sancti Thome iiij d.

in toto xij s. iiij d. ob.

...

f 97   *(Wages and payments)*

...

...Et solutum histrionibus domini Regis hoc anno vj s. viij d....

f 97v

...Et solutum histrionibus domini principis iij s. iiij d....

...

f 110v   *(Receipts from fines)*

...

ffines pro
Tauris
Inquietandis

Et de xij d. de ffine j Tauri interfecti cum licencia sine Inquietacione de
Stephano Bocher Item xij d. de ffine j Tauri interfecti cum licencia sine
inquietacione siue vexacione

Summa ij s.

...

St Andrew's Churchwardens' Accounts   CCA: U3/5/4/1
f 35v*   *(6 January 1507/8–6 January 1508/9) (Receipts)*

...

Item received vppon hokmonday & hoktuysday ·   xiiij s. vj d.

...

1508–9
City Chamberlains' Accounts   CCA: CC/FA 9
ff 154v–5

...

Repuraciones   ¶
pageanti sancti
Thome martiris

Et solutum pro clauis   ij d.
Et pro [j li.] ⌈j dosyn⌉ de Tynnefoyle   iij d.
Et solutum pro Glewe   ob.
Et solutum pro [j] ⌈dimidio vnius⌉ duodena punctorum   iiij d.
Et in filo vocato pakthrede   ob.|

26/ hokmonday & hoktuysday: *1–2 May 1508*
36/ duodena: *for* duodene

Et solutum Thome Iohnson pro labore suo in emendacione
harnisie Militum cum alijs   xx d.
Et solutum Thome Courte seniori pro ministracione sanguinis
extra capud sancti Thome martiris   viij d.
Et solutum pro vno saculo correo pro sanguine   viij d.   5
Et solutum pro payntyng capitis & Tunice sancti Thome   iiij d.
Et solutum pro pane potu & cibarijs &c   xij d.
Et solutum Iacobo Colman pro stacione pageanti predicti in
orreo suo per annum   ij s.
Et solutum pro conduccione vnius eque ad cariandum pageantum   10
predictum cum duobus hominibus adiuuantibus   xvj d.
Et solutum Iohanni Parke pro Tunica sua curta   iij s. iiij d.

                    Summa reparacionis pageanti predicti xj s. x d.

                                                                      15

f 157   *(Wages and payments)*
...
Et solutum histrionibus domini Regis venientibus vsque
Cantuariam in regardo   vj s. viij d.
...   20

f 157v

Et solutum histrionibus domini Principis in regardo   iij s. iiij d.
...   25

St Andrew's Churchwardens' Accounts   CCA: U3/5/4/1
f 40v*   *(6 January 1508/9–6 January 1509/10) (Receipts)*
...
Item vppon hokmonday & hoktuysday   xiiij s. x d. 30
...

1508–14
St Dunstan's Churchwardens' Accounts   CCA: U3/141/5/2
p 51*   *(Receipts)*   35
...
Item of hokmony   vj s. iiij d.
...

1/ Thome Iohnson: *keeper of the archbishop's palace*   30/ hokmonday & hoktuysday: *16–17 April 1509*

1509–10
City Chamberlains' Accounts CCA: CC/FA 9
ff 133–3v

...

Reparaciones ¶ Item solutum homini conducto ad reparandum & newe tynne		5
pageanti sancti le harnes iiijᵒʳ Militum	xvj d.	
Thome		

¶ Item solutum homini conducto ad reparandum & newe tynne
le harnes iiijᵒʳ Militum   xvj d.
Item pro quinque duodenis & di. de Tynnefoyle   xvj d. ob.
Item pro x paupiris deauratis ad renouandum le harnez   xx d.
Item pro j li. de Glewe   iij d.
Item in Carbonibus   I d.
Item pro j pipe de Orsady   ij d.
Item pro cibo & potu pro eo qui renouauit le harnes per
spacium iiijᵒʳ dierum   viij d.
Item solutum *(blank)* Stark pro emendacione pageanti predicti   xvj d.
Item pro pergameno pro eadem   iij d. ob.
Item in clauis pro eadem   iij d.
Item pro iijᵇᵘˢ duodenis [puct] punctorum   iij d.
Item pro pakthrede & nedylles   j d.
Item in pane & potu datis Iacobo Colman & iiijᵒʳ Militibus
in preparacione eorum   iiij d. ob.
Item solutum homini conducto ad ministrandum sanguinem
extra Capud sancti Thome   viij d.
Item solutum Nicholao hunt pro Tunica sua curta   iij s. iiij d.|
Et solutum Iacobo Colman pro stacione pageanti predicti
per idem annum in orreo   ij s.
Et pro conduccione vnius equi & duorum equorum pro
cariacione pageanti predicti   xvj d.
Item solutum a lez waytes de loundres pro suis laboribus   x s.
Item pro li. de redde lede   ij d.
Item pro xiij vlnis de Canvas pro eodem pageanto le
vlna iij d. ob. Summa   iij s. ix d. ob.
Item pro tincione eiusdem le vlna iij d. Summa   iiij s.
Summa xxxiij s. v d.

f 135   *(Wages and payments)*

...

Et solutum histrionibus domini Regis venientibus vsque
Cantuariam in regardo   vj s. viij d.

...

23/ Nicholao hunt: *Nicholas Hunt, serjeant of the chamber*
26/ equorum: *for* hominum *(?); compare previous year's account, p 106, ll.10–11 above*

St Andrew's Churchwardens' Accounts   CCA: U3/5/4/1
f 45*   *(6 January 1509/10–6 January 1510/11) (Receipts)*
...

Item vppon hokmonday & hoktuysday   xij s. iij d.
...   5

1510–11
Register of Christ Church Penitentiarian   CCA: Literary MS C11
f 1   *(7 June) (Inventory of goods of Dom Henry Arundel)*
...   10
Item ij lewtes with casis ⎫
Item ij par clavicordis   ⎬ domino priori
...

1511–12   15
St Andrew's Churchwardens' Accounts   CCA: U3/5/4/1
f 51   *(6 January 1511/12–6 January 1512/13) (Receipts)*
...

Item vppon hokmonday and hoktuysday of the wyvys   xvij s. ij d.
...   20

1512–13
City Chamberlains' Accounts   CCA: CC/FA 10
f 29v

                                                                                25
Reparaciones ¶ Item paied for nayle nedillys and threde to amende and
pageanti sancti   sowe the clothys of the pageant   iij d.
Thome &c   Item paied to Colbrande for his horse hyre to cary the
                pageant and his labour   ix d.
                Item in mete and drynk to theym that holpe to dresse   30
                the pageant   xij d.
                Item for standyng of the same pageant in the barne &c   ij s.
                            probatur Summa iiij s.

f 38v   *(Wages and payments)*   35
...

Item paied to theseid William May for his Cote ayenst seint
Thomas evyn   iij s. iiij d.
...

4/ hokmonday & hoktuysday: *8–9 April 1510*   37/ William May: *serjeant of the chamber*
19/ hokmonday & hoktuysday: *19–20 April 1512*

f 39*

¶ ffyrst paied to the kyngys trumpettes   vj s. viij d.

Item to the kyngys haroldys of armys   vj s. viij d.

Item to the kyngys pursevauntys   vj s. viij d. 5

Item to the kyngys hensshemen   vj s. viij d.

Item to the kyngys ffote men   iij s. iiij d.

Summa xxx s.

Regarda data seruientibus domine Regine thesame tyme &c †

¶ Item paied to the quenys fote men   [iij s. iiij d.] v s. 10

Summa v s.

Regarda data seruientibus [S] domini Senescalli hospicij domini Regis &c
eodem tempore &c †

¶ Item [pa] gevyn to the trumpettourys of theseid lorde Steward
in reward   iij s. iiij d. 15

probatur Summa iij s. iiij d.

f 41   (External expenses)

...

Item gevyn to the waytys at their first comyng in a reward   ij s. 20

...

1513–14
City Chamberlains' Accounts CCA: CC/FA 10
ff 85–5v   25

¶ Item paied for a Calves skyn to mende the knyghtes harnes
therwith   iiij d.

₵ Item paied for glue and a pot to melt yt in and for pakthrede
& paknedylles   iij d. 30

₵ Item paied for iij dosen of syluer foyle to mende the knyghtes
harnes   xij d.

₵ Item paied for iij dosen & a skynne of golde foyle for mendyng
of theseid harnesse   xiiij d.

₵ Item paied to Colyn for helpyng of Thomas to mende the knyghtes   35
harnes by the space of a day   iiij d.

₵ Item payed for ossydew and browne paper   ij d. ob.

₵ Item payed for a leffe of synaper and for a golde papir for theseid
harnes   iij d.

₵ Item paied for iiij peny naile iij peny naile and takyt nailes for   40
mendyng of the pagent   iiij d. ob.

₵ Item paied for rede lede   j d.

℃ Item paied for ij alder polys for mendyng of the pagent to
Rychard Sparkewell   ij d.

℃ Item paied for a payer of new gloves for seynt Thomas   j d.

℃ Item paied to Whitebrede for fetchyng downe of the gunnes
fro Westgate Seynt Georges gate and fro the Towers and   5
beryng of them in to the Store house   v d.|

℃ Item paied to Thomas a Court senior for makyng & mendyng
of the knyghtes harnesse and other thynges a bowte the pagent
for hys labour and mete and drynke by the space of v dayes   ij s. viij d.

℃ Item paied to Robert Goldwych for yaxyng and Cloutyng of   10
the pagent   viij d.

℃ Item paied to Iohn Latter for payntyng of the hede and the
Angell of the pagent   xxij d.

℃ Item payed to Rychard Layston for mendyng the Pagent
by a day   iiij d. 15

℃ Item paied to Temple for hymselfe and hys for cariage a
bowte of the Pagent   xij d.

℃ Item paied for stondyng of the same pagent in the barne   ij s.
Summa xiiij s. ij d.

                                                                                 20

f 87   (Wages and payments)

…

℃ Item paied for ix yardys of cloth for iij gownes to the iij waytes
price the yard iij s. iiij d. Summa   xxx s.

…   25

f 87v

…

Item paied to the foreseid Vmfray Walys for hys Cote at seynt
Thomas tyme   iij s. iiij d. 30

…

f 88*

Rewardes
gevyn to the
kynges
seruantes
when he
cam out of
ffraunce

¶ Item paied to the kynges waytes   vj s. viij d. 35
℃ Item paied to the kynges ffotemen   vj s. viij d.
℃ Item payed to the kynges trumpettes   vj s. viij d.
℃ Item paied to the kynges hynsemen   vj s. viij d.

16/ hys: for hys horse with a laborer (?); compare p 111, ll.32–3
29/ Vmfray Walys: serjeant of the chamber

C *Item* paied to the ffrenche quenys ffotemen in seynt austyns a
Crowne *summa*   iiij s.

           probatur Sum*ma* xxx s. viij d.

Register of Christ Church Penitentiarian   CCA: Literary MS C11   5
f 124v   *(25 March–24 June)*

...

It*em* p*ro* le clauicord wyr*e*   iiij d.

...

                                                     10

1514–15
City Chamberlains' Accounts   CCA: CC/FA 10
f 139v

Reparaciones   ¶ It*em* paied to Iohn Kenet Carpent*er* for mendyng of the   15
pagianti sancti   pageant by iij dayes   xviij d.
Thome &c
C *Item* for C of iiij peny naile   iiij d.
C *Item* paied for small nayl*es* & taynt*er*hokes   ij d.
C *Item* paied for beryng of bord & tymber fro the store
  house to the Pagent   j d. 20
C *Item* paied for x yard*es* of new canvesse to hang a bowte
  the pagent price l*e* yard iij d. ob. Sum*ma*   iij s. ij d. ob.
C *Item* paied for payntyng of theseid canves to Iohn latter
  paynter price l*e* yard payntyng ij d. Sum*ma*   xx d.
C *Item* paied to the seid Iohn for payntyng of seynt Thomas hede   x d. 25
C *Item* paied for pakthrede   j d.
C *Item* paied for white threde and sowyng togeder of the
  paynted Clothese   j d. ob.
C *Item* paied to Thomas a Court thelder for helpyng p*re*payre
  the pagent   xij d. 30
C *Item* paied to hym that turned the vyce   ij d.
C *Item* paied to Iamys Colman & hys hors wit*h* a laborer to
  Cary a boute the pagent   xij d.
C *Item* paied for stondyng of the pagent   ij s.
C *Item* paied for cariage of the pagent to the Nunry from there   35
  hit stode   ij d.
C *Item* paied for mete & drynke to the Children & the Cariers
  of the pagent   vj d.
           probatur Sum*ma* xij s. x d.

1/ the ffrenche quenys: *Mary, sister of Henry VIII*   36/ hit: t *corrected over* s
35/ the Nunry: *St Sepulchre's Priory*

f 144   *(Wages and payments)*

...

℃ It*em* paied to Will*i*am Thomson for ix yard*es* of Tawney
gevyn to the wayt*es* of theseid Citie for lyvery p*r*ice l*e* yard
iij s. ij d. S*um*ma   xxviij s. vj d.   5

...

f 145   *(Rewards to royal servants)*

...

It*em* paied to the kyng*es* waite*s* the ix^th day of August   vj s. viij d.   10

...

ff 148v–9*   *(External expenses)*

...

℃ Item paied for a hors for Vmfray walys to Dou*er* to know the   15
Dukys pleasur how Maist*er* Mayer shoulde receyve the frenche
quene comyng oute of ffraunce to Cant*er*bury &c   xij d.

℃ It*em* for hys expenc*es* at Dovour then   iij d.

gevyn to the   ℃ It*em* paied for a grete base .x. lopsters and .iij. turbott*es* gevyn
ffrench quene   to the ffrenche quene for a p*re*sent at her comyng out of ffraunce   vj s. v d.   20

℃ It*em* paied for a potell of white wyne for M*aster* Mayer &
the aldermen aft*er* they had rec*eived* the ffrenche quene   iiij d.

℃ Item paied for a hors to stonstrete to wayte the Ryppers for a
dysshe of ffysshe to p*re*sent the quene that hyt should not be
takyn byfore &c   iiij d.   25

℃ Item paied for a hors hire for will*i*am Milys Towne Clark to ryde
wi*th* Mr Rutlond to Dou*er* to mete the ffrenche quene   xij d.l

℃ It*em* paied to the Duke of Bukkynghams j mynstrell in reward
gevyn them   ij s.

℃ Item gevyn & paied to the ffrenche quenys fote men   iij s. iiij d.   30

...

St Andrew's Churchwardens' Accounts   CCA: U3/5/4/1

f 55   *(Receipts)*

...   35

It*em* receyvyd off the money gadderyd be the p*a*ryshons aswell
be the men [&] ⌈as by⌉ the wome*n* att hocktyde   xx s. iiij d.

...

15/ Vmfray walys: *serjeant of the chamber*
27/ Mr Rutlond: *William Rutlande, alderman*
29/ them: *for* him *(?)*
37/ hocktyde: *16–17 April*

1515–16
City Chamberlains' Accounts CCA: CC/FA 10
f 199v

Reparaciones
pagianti
sancti
Thome &c

¶ Item paied to Iohn latter for payntyng of the hede iiij d. 5

℃ Item paied for wyre for the vyce of ye angell j d.

℃ Item paied for whipcord & pakthrede j d.

℃ Item for paknedylles tenthokes ⌈&⌉ takett nailes ij d.

℃ Item for j quarter of lambe and brede and drynk gevyn to the
Children that played the knyghtes and for them that holpe stey
& convey the pagent a bowte xj d. 10

℃ Item paied to Thomas Plomer for Turnyng of the vyce ij d.

℃ Item paied to Iohn Temple for carieng of the pagent a bowte the Citie xij d.

℃ Item paied to ij men that holpe lyft and stay the pagent a bowte
ye watche iij d. 15

℃ Item paied to Iohn hartes wyfe for wasshyng of the olbe & other
clothes a bowte the auter & settyng on agayn of thapparell iiij d.

℃ Item paied for drynk to the children byfore their goyng furth & for
candell to lyght the turner of the vyce ij d.

℃ Item paied to Thomas a Court senior for helpyng to prepayre the 20
pagent xij d.

Summa iiij s. vj d.

f 204 *(Rewards to royal and other servants)*

25

¶ Item paied to the kynges Iogler the xx^th day of May gevyn to
hym for reward ij s.

℃ Item paied to the kynges Mynstralles the xxviij^th day of May vj s. viij d.

...

℃ Item paied to the waytes of london by the handes of Mr Nailer 30
then Mayer iij s. iiij d.

...

St Andrew's Churchwardens' Accounts CCA: U3/5/4/1
f 60v *(Receipts)* 35

...

Item received in money gaderyd as well be the men as the
women att hocktyd xviij s. j d. q^a

...

7m/ *sancti*: i *corrected over* e
38/ hocktyd: *31 March–1 April*

1516–17
St Andrew's Churchwardens' Accounts   CCA: U3/5/4/1
f 65v   *(Receipts)*

Item rec*eived* in money gaderyd att hocktyd   xviij s. iiij d.   5

...

1517–18
City Chamberlains' Accounts   CCA: CC/FA 10
f 244v   10

Rep*araciones*
pagianti
sancti
Thome
Martir*is*

¶ Item paied for ij Calveskynnes for the repayryng & mendyng
  of the knyght*es* harnes   viij d.
℃ Item paied for white threde   j d.
℃ Item for white leder   ij d.   15
℃ Item paied for ix dosen & di. of tyn [fu] foyle for garnysshyng
  of the seid harnes p*r*ice l*e* dosen iiij d. S*um*ma   iij s. ij d.
℃ Item for di. dosen gold foyle   ij d.
℃ Item for vj li. of glue the li. iij d. s*um*ma   xviij d.
℃ Item for ij quayer of broune papyr   ij d.   20
℃ Item for pacthrede   ij d.
℃ Item for vj dosen buckyll*es*   vj d.
℃ Item paied for a nother li. of glue   iij d.
℃ Item paied for taket nail*es*   ob.
℃ Item paied to Iohn Colyn by the Grete for new makyng &   25
  trymmyng of the seid harnesse   vj s.
℃ Item paied to my lady of seynt Sepulcres for the stangdyng
  of the pagent in her barne this yere   xx d.
℃ Item paied for hopyng of a grete Tonne that Iohn levak capper gave
  to putt in seynt Thomas hede the harnes & other p*er*teynyng to   30
  ye pagent   vj d.
                              S*um*ma xv s. ob.

f 250v   *(External expenses)*
...   35
It*e*m paied to Robert lewys for x li. of gunpowder ayenst the
watche on seynt Thomas evyn l*e* li. viij d. S*um*ma   vj s. viij d.
...

5/ hocktyd: *20–1 April*
27/ my lady of seynt Sepulcres: *Mildred Hale, prioress from c 1511*
27/ stangdyng: *for* standyng
36/ Robert lewys: *common councillor; alderman 1542–3; mayor 1529–30, 1536–7, 1540–1*

f 251v

...

℃ Item the xxth day of august gevyn in reward to the kyng*es* wayt*es*   vj s. viij d.

...
5

ff 265–5v   *(Mayor's accounts)*

...

Recepc*iones*
fin*ium* pro
tauris
mactand*is* &c

¶ ffirst the seid Chamberleyn yeldyth accompt of xij d. receyved
of the wedow of Thomas Edynden Bocher for lycence of one
bull to be sleyn wit*h*⌈out⌉ baytyng at the Bulstake   xij d. 10

℃ Item receyved of Iohn Chapman Bocher in lykewyse for one
Bull slayne   xiiij d.

℃ Item rec*eyved* of Iohn wakefeld Bocher for a yong Bulchon   x d.

℃ Item rec*eyved* of the same Iohn wakefeld for a Bull &c   xij d.

℃ Item rec*eyved* of Robert Gray Bocher for ij Bullys in lykewyse
by hym sleyn   15
ij s.

℃ Item rec*eyved* of Thomas Brewxe Bocher for a yong bulkyn &c   ix d.

℃ Item rec*eyved* of Iohn hobbys Bocher for a Bull by hym so sleyn &c   xij d.⎮

℃ Item rec*eyved* of the foreseid Iohn wakefeld for a Bull &c   xvj d.

                              *Sum*ma ix s. j d.   20

...

f 274v   *(Officers' wages and livery)*

...

Item paied for ix yardys of Tawney gevyn to Thomas Newnam and   25
hys ij felowes C*om*en wayt*es* of theseid Citie eu*er*y of theym .iij.
yard*es* pr*ice* the yarde as it is aboueseid iiij s. iiij d. *Sum*ma   xxx s.

...

St Andrew's Churchwardens' Accounts   CCA: U3/5/4/1   30
f 69   *(Casual receipts)*

...

resseyvid yn mony gaderid by the p*ar*yschons aswell by men
as by the wymen at hoptyde   xvijj s. viij d. ob.

35

1518–19
City Chamberlains' Accounts   CCA: CC/FA 10
f 311

Expens*e*
rep*aracio*nis
pagian*ti sancti*
Thome Martir*is*

¶ Item paied for taket nailes and whipcord   j d. ob. 40

34/ hoptyde: *Hocktide, 12–13 April*

Item paied for brede & drynk for the children that pleyed in the
pagent byfore the wacche   ij d.
Item for Sope and Candell   j d. ob.
Item paied for mete & drynk for the seid Children and other
that holpe convey and cary a boute the pagent after the wacche   5
was don   xij d.
Item paied to Iohn Temple for caryeng a bowte of the seid pagent   xij d.
Item paied to hym that turned the vyce in the vyce in the pagent   ij d.
     Summa ij s. vij d.

                     10

f 319v *(External expenses)*

...

to the kynges + Item the ix^th day of Iune paied & gevyn in reward to the
mynstralles kynges mynstalles   vj s. viij d.

...   15

ff 329–9v *(Mayor's accounts)*

...

Recepciones ¶ Item ffirst the seid Chamberleyn yeldyth accompt of xij d receyved
pro tauris of [the wedow] of Thomas [Edynden] ⌈Brewx⌉ Bocher for a fyne   20
mactandis &c for one bull sleyn not bayted at the Bulstake   xij d.
   ⊂ Item receyved of Iohn Chapman bocher for a Bull in lyke wyse
   not bayted   xij d.
   ⊂ Item receyved of Iohn Iamys Bocher for ij Bulles euery of them xij d.
   Summa   ij s. 25
   ⊂ Item receyved [for] of the wedow of Iohn Guston for one Bull   xij d.
   ⊂ Item receyved of Iohn hobbyes for ij Bulles &c   ij s.
   ⊂ Item receyved of Robert Gray Bocher for one Bull by hym in
   lyke wyse sleyn   xij d.
   ⊂ Item receyved of Edward Guston bocher for one bull &c   xij d. 30
   ⊂ Item receyved of Iohn wakefelde Bocher for one Bull by hym
   in lyke maner &c   xij d. |
   ⊂ Item receyved of william Brome Bocher for one Bull not
   Bayted &c   xij d.
   ⊂ Item receyved of hym for half a yong Bulchon   iiij d. 35
      Summa xj s. [v] iiij d.

8/ the vyce in the vyce in: *dittography*
14/ mynstalles: *for* mynstralles
20/ of ... of: *dittography*

f 338v   *(Officers' wages and livery)*

...

℃ Item paied for ix yard*es* of theseid Cloth gevyn to Thomas Newnam
and hys ij felowes Comen wayt*es* of theseid eu*ery* of them .iij. yard*es*
p*ri*ce vt supra   xxx s.   5

...

f 343   *(Final allowances)*

...

and of xxx s. paied to Thomas Newman & hys ij felowes Comen   10
wayt*es* of theseid Citie for their wag*es* in theseid last yere and not
allowed in the same yere &c   xxx s.

...

St Andrew's Churchwardens' Accounts   CCA: U3/5/4/1   15
f 74v   *(Casual receipts)*

...

Item Receyued in money Gadered by the p*ar*ysshons aswell by
men as by women att hoktyde   xxj s. xj d.

...   20

Register of Christ Church Penitentiarian   CCA: Literary MS C11
f 131*

...

It*em* p*ro* le cokfyhtyng T. R. & R*eginaldo* borage   iiij d. 25

...

1519–20
City Chamberlains' Accounts   CCA: CC/FA 10
f 378   30

Expense
rep*ar*acio*nis*   ¶ Item paied for ij yard*es* of white Canves for a new Chemer for
pagiant*i*   seynt Thomas   ix d.
sanc*ti*   ℃ Item for di. yard of blak tuke for the typpet   v d.
Thome   ℃ Item for ij yard*es* of grene saten of cyp*er*s for ij Curtens p*ri*ce   35
Marti*ris*   le yard viij d. S*um*ma   xvj d.
                   ℃ Item paied to Thomas Rede paynter for payntyng of the foreseid
                     ij yard*es* of white clothe in to rede   viij d.
                   ℃ Item paied for makyng of theseid Curtens   iij d.

4/ theseid: *for theseid Citie (?)*   25/ T.R.: *possibly error for Thomas Saxon*
19/ hoktyde: *2–3 May*   25/ Reginaldo borage: *a scholar at the almonry school*

ℂ Item paied for payntyng of an ymage of our lady *with*
ij angell*es* gylt to hang ayenst the ymage of s*eynt* Thomas
vppon the auter   iij s. iiij d.

ℂ Item for di. C of iij d. naile & iiij d. naile for mendyng
of the pageant   ij d. ob.   5

ℂ Item for mete & drynk to the Carpent*er* henry Ebbeney
that gave ye mendyng therof   ij d.

ℂ It*em* for taket nailes taynt*er* hook*es* and pak threde   ij d.

ℂ It*em* for j li. soope for the whel*es*   j d.

ℂ Item for mendyng of the mytre   iiij d. ob.   10

ℂ It*em* paied to Barow for Caryeng a bout of the pagent on
s*eynt* Thoma*s* evyn   xij d.

ℂ It*em* for turnyng of the vyce   ij d.

ℂ Item for mete & drynk for the Children & other that holpe
convey ye pagent   vj d.   15

Su*m*ma ix s. v d.

ff 394–4v   *(External expenses)*
...

ℂ Item paied the xvj^th day of aprill for ij galons of wyne Rede   20
& Claret gevyn to my lord Chief Iustice & my lord warden
for their good advyces and Counsell gevyn for the orderyng
of the Citie ayenst the kyng*es* co*m*yng   xvj d.

ℂ Item for spyced brede sent theym   xviij d.

ℂ Item paied to a man that went to hern to shew my lord   25
Chief Iustice that my lord warden wold be at Cant*er*bury
the xvj^th day of april   v d.
...

ℂ Item paied for thexpenc*es* of will*i*am Milys towne Clark
rydyng to london the vth day of May for a Co*m*myssion   30
that no vytaile shulde be takyn nygh Cant*er*bury for the
kyng*es* comyng &c as it apperith by a byll of hys hand   vij s. iiij d.|

ℂ Item the xix^th day of May gevyn in Reward to my
lord of Arundell*es* Mynstrall*es*   xx d.
...   35

ℂ Item paied to Iohn lewgor for the hire of a hors to Charryng
for Iohn Toft*es* rydyng to Charryng ij dayes to Inquyre & know
by what way the kyng*es* grace wold come to Cant*er*bury   ij s. viij d.
Item for hys expenc*es* & hors mete ther   iiij d.

37/ Iohn Toft*es*: *common clerk of the chamber*

ℭ Item the xxviijth day of May paied for iij pottell*es* of wyne gevyn to the kyng*es* hynchemen the kyng*es* wayt*es* and to my lord Cardynall*es* fote men   xij d.

...

ℭ Item paied to anthony knyght for x li. of gune powder for the watche on seynt Thomas evyn p*ri*ce *le* li. viij d.   vj s. viij d.   5

...

ff 395v–6*

...   10

+ ℭ Item paied to my lady Pryor*es* of seynt Sepulcres for the stondyng of seynt Thomas pagent in her barne this yer   xx d.

...

Reward*es* gevyn to dyue*r*se of the kyng*es* seruaunt*es* &c	ℭ Item paied to the kyng*es* hynchemen for a reward	vj s. viij d.
	ℭ Item to the kyng*es* fotemen	vj s. viij d. 15
	+ ℭ Item to the kyng*es* Trumpett*es*	vj s. viij d.
	ℭ Item to the kyng*es* wayt*es*	vj s. viij d.
	ℭ Item to the quenys fote men	vj s. viij d.
	ℭ Item to my lord Cardynall*es* fotemen	iij s. iiij d.

Munera dat*a* diue*r*sis officiar*iis* d*i*cte Ciu*it*atis erga aduent*um* d*omi*ni R*egis* ad eandem Ciu*itatem*

ℭ Item paied to will*ia*m Myl*ys* C*om*en Clark of the Citie toward a Cote ayenst the comyng of the Kyng*es* grace to the Citie graunted by Bourmote   x s.   20

The Kyng*es* grace cam to the Citie the thursday byfore Whitsonday

ℭ Item paicd to Ioh*n* Toft*es* Clark of the Chamber toward hys Cote &c   vj s. viij d.| 25

ℭ Item paied to Mark*es* Olford Seryeant of the Mace toward hys Cote the same tyme   vj s. viij d.

ℭ Item to Robert hunt *ser*ieant toward hys Cote   vj s. viij d.

ℭ Item to Iohn yomanson *ser*ieant toward hys Cote the same tyme   vj s. viij d.

ℭ Item to Robert Sturdy *ser*ieant toward hys Cote eod*em* temp*ore*   vj s. viij d. 30

ℭ Item to Vmfray wal*es* C*om*en *ser*ieaunt of the Chamber toward hys Cote the same tyme   vj s. viij d.

f 403   *(Mayor's accounts)*

...   35

Recepc*iones* p*ro* tauris mactand*is* &c

ℭ first the seid Chamb*er*leyn yeldyth accompt of the receyt*es* of dyue*r*se fyn*ez* for bull*es* sleyn this yere by dyue*r*se botcher*es* vsyng the seid Citie not bayted at the bulstak ffirst of Iohn hobbys Bocher for .v. bull*es* by hym sleyn this yere ⌈euery bull xij d. *summa*⌉   v s.

2/ my lord Cardynall*es*: *Thomas Wolsey, archbishop of York*   23/ thursday byfore Whitsonday: *24 May*
5/ anthony knyght: *common councillor*
11/ my lady ... Sepulcres: *Mildred Hale, prioress from c 1511*

C Item of William Canon Bocher for j bull   xij d.
C Item of Iohn Wakefelde for j bull   xij d.
C Item of Iohn Chapman Bocher for j bull   xij d.
C Item of Iohn hayman Bocher for a yong bulkyn   x d.
Summa viij s. x d.

St Andrew's Churchwardens' Accounts   CCA: U3/5/4/1
f 78v   *(Casual receipts)*

...

C Item in money Gadered by the parysshons on hokmunday
and Tewysday aswell by men as by women   xiiij s. viij d. ob.

...

C Item of the wardens of the Grocerres paieaunte for vij lb. & a half in
Torches wasted aboute there paieaunte price le lb. iiij d. Summa   ij s. vj d.

Summaries of Letters from the Venetian Ambassadors
Venezia, Biblioteca Nazionale Marciana: It. vII, 256 (=9243)
f 369*   *(28 May)* *(Written from Canterbury)*

...

Furono heri queste majestate cesarea & de ingaltera a la messa con Tanta
comitiua di signori & donne richissimamente vestiti & finita la messa
disnorono insieme in la caxa doue era alozata la cesarea majesta con la qual
sedeteno a Tauola qesto Serenissimo re le regine et la sorela & il Reuerendissimo
legato cardinal eboracense et per quanto Intendeno el conuito fu lautissimo
con balli & piaceri assai Da poi la sera fossemo mandati a chiamar per dui
Gentilhomeni inglesi insieme con l orator dil re christianissimo menati in vna
sala richamente adornata de razi d oro & di seda: veni le dite majestate &
Data l acqua a le man a tuti doi li re vnitamente & poi a le regine sorella &
Reuerendissimo legato Tutti sentorono ad vna Tauola: Da poi poco distante fu
posta vna altra tauola longissima doue sentassemo l orator dil re christianissimo
& noi & molti signori & Gentilhomeni fin al numero di 200 duro il bancheto
piu di tre hore fu lautissimo & finito si ballo per la majesta dil re di Ingalterra
ma la cesarea majesta non ballo ma stete a parlar con dame e duro tal festa fino

...

f 365v   *(29 May)* *(Written from Canterbury)*

...

dil bancheto fato a la cesarea majesta qual duro 3 hore poi balato fino di
ma l imperador non ballo ben il re d'ingaltera eraui la rezina et la sorella e
altre dame/ poi a di *(blank)* l imperador si leuo & ando verso santuzi a

10–11/ hokmunday and Tewysday: *16–17 April*

montar in naue il re lo acompagno /5/ mia rasonando ne volse niun di
oratori vi andasse...

Charles v's Visit to Canterbury

Venezia, Biblioteca Nazionale Marciana: It. VII, 257 (=9244)   5
f 147   *(27 May)*

...finita la messa il *Reuerendissi*mo car*dina*le legato si vesti d un piuiale di
soprarizzo d oro & dette la beneditione & indulgentia plenaria et his peractis
leuati li Re et ordinatame*n*te acompagnati perueuer*unt* iter*um* alla camera   10
doue rimasero le m*aje*sta *pre*fate & la regina et licentiati Tutti iui disnorono
assetati a messa ambi li re a dextra lo imp*er*atore la regina & madama maria
soli Da poi pranso si da*n*zo & al tardo fece la intrata la Regina sua sorella et
dame a cauallo 60 sopra chinee bia*n*che & sellate Di Drappo d oro incontrata
tra le altre da madama maria ol*im* regina di fra*n*za era etia*m* acompagnata da   15
200 dame di natione hyspane et di habito il capo di le qualle vellato alla
usanza fiame*n*ga con uelli sotilissimi & lo*n*gi con berette piciole in capo pur
co*n* le coste & doppie piege pur a la fiamenga di color qual bia*n*che qual verde
qual lionato Queste Dame no*n* erano belle ma Gratiate & p*er* li costumi
hispani atratiue molto...   20

ff 147v–8v*   *(28 May)*

...La messa fu solen*n*e finita & aco*m*pagnati li rc alla stantia de lo Imperatore
Qui le M*aje*sta sue disnorono insieme lo imperator fu in megio la me*n*sa   25
apresso quello a sinistris El sere*n*issimo anglese a dextris apresso lo imp*er*atore
la reina anglese a sinistris ap*re*sso el re anglese madama maria a dextris
ap*re*sso la raina anglese la reina Germana Disnato che hebbe si ballo
allongamente & el re anglese impersona ma non | Gia lo imperatore la sera
poi ad hora*m* circa vna de notte furno ambi li oratori veneti ma*n*dati a   30
leuar de casa nomine regio p*er* dui caualieri & andati a corte in vna salla
molto Gra*n*de al basso nel palaggio doue era alogiato la cesarea m*aje*sta
doue erano *pre*parate me*n*se tre due *per* longo vna in testa de la salla et qui
ritrouorono etia*m* l orator franceso Da poi expectato vn pezo discesero li
re & reine & fu data la aqua alle mano in questa forma lauaro*n*si insieme   35
lo Imperatore lo re la regina anglese & no*n* altri Fu portato per il duca di
sopholch cognato dil re vn gra*n* bazil d oro coperto sopra il qual coperto
era vna corona et nel mezo di quella corona era vna tazza piccola qual
prese il duca di buchingan Poi el fradello del m*ar*chexe di bra*n*deburg
venuto con lo Imperatore scoperse il bazil & poselo sotto laltro che era in   40
ma*n* del duca di sopholch De inde p*er* il duca preditto di buchingan Presa
la aqua fu data a bere al duca *pre*fato di sopholch & fatta la crede*n*za poi

effuse con el bazil suo che hauea alla banda el forame ouer bocca atta de
funder l aqua alle mani de dicti re et lauate le mani el fratello del conte
pallatino del reno, ancor lui venuto con lo Imperatore porse la Touaglia
ad sugar le mani poi Questi re & raina si posero a Tauola lo imperatore in
mezo a sinistris el re anglese Ambi sopra sedie indorate et molto pompose   5
a destris sedete la raina anglese ma sopra vna sedia bassa Da poi fu portato
il segondo bazil d oro pur coperto ma senza corona per el figliolo del conte
de nort Tamburlan che vno deli primi signori del regno de anglia la Taza
de far credenza hebbe el sopraditto duca di buchingan: la scoperse il
marchese d anghelteram: la Touaglia de asugar le mani porse el duca   10
vechio di norfolch anglese lavaronsi le mani insieme il *Reuerendissi*mo
cardinal eboracense la raina Germana & madama maria assentaronsi a
mensa el *Reuerendissi*mo *cardinal* apresso la raina anglese a destris ma
distante da lei quanto potea capir vna sedia apresso el *cardinal*e pur a
dextris la reina Germana & a sinistris apresso el re di anglia la raina | 15
maria sua sorela & questi sei sederono ne la mensa al capo de la sala posta:
poi ne la segonda mensa a dextris primo fu posto lo orator francese con
vna dama spagnola nominata signora dona maria figlia de vno conte hyspano
secundo fu posto lo orator veneto Suriano con la duchessa di norfolch
seguiua poi il fratello del conte pallatino con la figlia del ducha Di   20
buchingan & poi altri signori successiue con dame spagnole & anglese
Da parte sinistra Primo fu posto l orator veneto cornario e appresso la
cesarea majesta con vna Dama & poi il duca di alba con li signori &
dame: el conuiuio fu lautissimo Circumdauano le mense & peidi Giouani
innamorati & tra li altri alcuni hyspani che faceuano lo innamorato Tanto   25
brauamente che nihil supra vno fo tra li altri nominato conte de capra che
fece lo innamorato Tanto di core che se ne ando in sincopi ouero angossia
per la Innamorata soa Di maniera che fu portato a piedi et mani via fin
che si rihebbe Finito il bancheto che duro da horre quarto Tante viuande
ui fu & leuate le mense si ballo et la prima danza pur alla spagnola fu dil   30
duca di alba vechio di anni quasi sesanta ma innamorato ancora el qual
ballo con vna soa fauorita hyspana non bella ma sopramodo Gratiata in
ogni parte & maniera il ballo fu li Guanti di spagna con certa piua in fine
molto Galante: l habito Di la dama era questo che saria longo ma lui duca
portaua vna bareta picolla di pano Tane con vna cordelina di seda verde   35
che trauersaua la bereta la quale portaua pendente alla banda sinistra alla
gibellina Da poi questo duca ballo lo innamorato conte di capra Da poi
vno altro hyspano conte Quarto ballo el *Serenenissi*mo re anglese vltimo
ballo el principe de bisignano molto bello Tutti questi ballorono alla
spagnola finito il ballo era l alba & di chiaro onde Tutti se ne ritornorono   40
finita la festa a casa/
...

1520-1
City Chamberlains' Accounts   CCA: CC/FA 11
ff 28-8v

Expens*e*
Rep*ar*aci*onis*
pagiant*i*
sanc*ti*
Thome
m*artiris*

Item paied to Will*ia*m Bradle for xx fote of tymber for the new   5
makyng of seynt Thomas Pagent   iij s. iiij d.
℃ Item paied to Brusshyng & his mate for sawyng of theseid tymber   xv d.
℃ Item for beryng of theseid tymber to the Sawstage   j d.
℃ Item paied to will*ia*m haryson yoynor & hys ˄⌐ij⌐ mates for [iiij]
˄⌐fyve⌐ dayes workyng vppon the Pagent takyng by the day for   10
eu*er*y one of them iij. vij d. *Sum*ma   viij s. ix d.
℃ Item paied to the same will*ia*m haryson & hys seid ij mates for
v dayes & half more in the same work*es* takyng by the day for
theym iij xxj d. *Sum*ma   ix s. vij d. ob.
℃ Item paied for CC of iij peny naile   vj d. 15
℃ Item for C & di. of iiij peny naile   vj d.
℃ Item paicd for ij ell*es* & a quarter of cloth for a surples for ye
ymage p*r*ice the ell vij d. ob. *Sum*ma   xvj d. ob.
℃ Item paied to Richard Colbrond for a new Cart & new whel*es*
for the pagent   viij s. 20
℃ It*e*m for ij li. of Sope   ij d. ob.
℃ Item paied for v quarter pec*es* of asshe for stanchonyng of the pagent   xvj d.
℃ Item to my lady of Seynt Sepulcres for the standyng of the pagent
in her barne   xx d.
℃ It*em* paied to Henry Gyldwyn for di. C of bord for the pagent   xvj d.l 25
℃ Item for iij yard*es* of wyre for the vyce   ij d.
℃ Item for whipcord taket nail*es* & teynt*er*hook*es*   ij d.
℃ Item for ij asshe hoopys to bere vp the clothes ou*er* the hors bak   j d.
℃ Item for turnyng of the vice   ij d.
℃ Item for mete & dryng for the knyght*es* and other that holp convey   30
the pagent   xij d.
℃ Item paied to Trussell for caryage of the pagent a boute the tyme
of the wacche   xij d.
℃ Item paied to M*rez* Symon for ij ell*es* & half of white clothe for
an alter clothe p*r*ice the ell vij d. *sum*ma   xvij d. ob. 35
℃ It*em* paied to her for makyng of the surplyce a fore wreten   iiij d.
℃ Item paied for a dosen & di. of [gold]⌐tyn⌐ foyle for mendyng
of the harnes   iiij d. ob.
℃ Item for half a dosen of gold foyle   ij d.

23/ my lady of Seynt Sepulcres: *Mildred Hale, prioress from c 1511;* p *of* Sepulcres *corrected from* y
34/ Mrez Symon: *Mistress Symon, wife of Nicholas Symon, alderman*

℃ Item for j li. & half of glue iiij d. ob.
℃ Item paied to Iohn Colyn for mendyng of theseid harnes xij d.
    Item for Candell & wasshyng of the clothes of the pagent ij d.

Su*m*ma xliiij s. v d. 5

f 42v   (*Wages and payments*)

...

℃ Item paied to vmphrey wales Comen se*r*ieaunt of the Chamber
    for hys Cote ayenst St Thomas evyn this yere iij s. iiij d. 10

...

℃ It*em* paied to Thomas waren Iohn waren & Iohn Eton Com*m*en
    way*tes* of theseid Citie to eu*er*y of theym for their wag*es* this yere
    xiij s. iiij d. Su*m*ma xl s.
℃ It*em* paied to harry se*r*uant & app*r*entyce of the foreseid Thomas 15
    waren for hys wag*es* this yere vj s. viij d.

...

f 44v   (*External expenses*)

...   20

℃ Item paied to anthony knyght for xj li. of gunpowder
    [ayenst] for the watche on seynt Thomas evyn p*r*ice
    the li. viij d. Su*m*ma vij s. iiij d.

...

25

f 45

...

℃ It*em* the iij^de day of August paied & gevyn in reward to
    the kyng*es* way*tes* vj s. viij d.
℃ Item gevyn to the kyng*es* pleyers iij s. iiij d. 30

...

f 60   (*Mayor's accounts*)

...

Recep*ciones*
fin*ium* pro
tauris
mactand*is*

¶ ffirst the seid Chamb*er*leyn yeldyth accompt of the Receyt*es* of dyu*er*se 35
    ffynez for bull*es* sleyn this yere by dyu*er*se Bochers vsyng theseid Citie
    not bayted at the Bulstak ffirst of Iohn hobbys Bocher for iij bull*es* by
    hym sleyn this yere for eu*er*y bull xij d. Su*m*ma iij s.

5/ xliiij: l *corrected over* i
21/ anthony knyght: *common councillor*

℃ Item of the wedowe of Thomas Pett for one bull   xij d.
℃ Item of Robert Gray Bocher for j bull   xij d.
℃ Item of william Canon Bocher for one bull   xij d.
℃ Item of Robert Sampson Bocher for ij bulles   ij s.
℃ Item of·Richard Goorde Bocher for one bull   xij d.   5
              Summa ix s.

f 69v   *(Officers' fees and livery)*

...

℃ Item paied for xij yardes of theseid Clothe gevyn to Thomas   10
waren Iohn waren Iohn Eton and to harry seruant of the foreseid
Thomas waren Comen waytes of theseid Citie to euery of them
iiij./ iij yardes summa   xl s.

...

    15

St Andrew's Churchwardens' Accounts   CCA: U3/5/4/1
f 82v   *(Casual receipts)*

...

Item Received in money gathered aswell by men as by women
at hoktyd this yere   xv s. j d. ob. 20

...

1521—2
City Chamberlains' Accounts   CCA: CC/FA 11
f 104v   25

Expense
Reparacionis
pagiantis sancti
Thome martiris
&c

¶ Item paied for j li. of Sope for the yaxe   j d.
Item for pakthrede & taket nailes   j d.
Item for drynk to the children at the dressyng of them   j d. ob.
Item for turnyng of the vyce   ij d. 30
Item paied to Iohn pvtt for carying of the pagent a bowte
in the watche   xij d.
Item for a quarter of lambe & brede & drynk for the knyghtes
& other that holp to convey the pagent after the watche   xij d.
Item for wasshyng of the auter clothes & albe & emperrellyng   35
a gayn therof   ij d.
Item paied to the Priores of Seynt Sepulcre for the stondyng of
the pagent in her barne this yere   xx d.
            Summa iiij s. iij d. ob.

19/ hoktyd: *8—9 April*
34/ the Priores of Seynt Sepulcre: *Mildred Hale, prioress from c 1511*

ff 111–11v

Reparaciones
Crucis apud le
Bulstake

¶ Item paied for makyng of one of the lytyll crosses in the top of the
seid Crosse by the grete   iij s. iiij d.
Item paied to Iohn Bunse & hys laborer for .v. dayes labour mendyng   5
of theseid Crosse takyng by the day for them both x d. Summa   iiij s. ij d.
Item paied to a nother laborer for one day helpyng theseid Bunse in
the seid workes   iiij d.
Item paied for the burnyng of the playster of parys for the same Crosse   viij d.
Item paied to the forseid Iohn Bunse & hys man for iij dayes work   10
makyng of the skaffold a boute the Crosse   ij s. vj d.
Item paied to a laborer for a day beryng of tymber & other stuff
from the storehouse to the Crosse for theseid skaffold   iiij d.
Item for iij quartrons of C of vj d. naile   iiij d. ob.
Item for di. C of iiij peny naile   ij d.   15
Item for C of iij peny naile   iij d.
Item paied to Thomas Mathew mason for iij fre stones and keying
of them   xij d.
Item paied for xiij fote of tymber for the raylys   xiij d.
Item for sawyng of the same tymber   vij d.   20
Item for caryage of the same tymber fro the Bulstake to the sawe
stage & a gayn   ij d. |
Item paied to iij Carpenters for makyng of the seid Raylys by one
day & more   xx d.
Item paied to a laborer for ij dayes in theseid workes beryng of   25
tymber & stuf & makyng of hooles iiij d. le day summa   viij d.
Item paied for v li. of lede for the starres and castyng of them   v d. ob.
Item paied for xxx fote of tymber for postes a boute the Crosse
after v the tonne   iij s. ix d.
Item for a quarte of Oyle for the postes   iiij d.   30
Item for di. li. of wax & rosen for symonyng of the starres   vj d.
Item paied for C of golde bought of Maister Rutland for gyldyng   vj s. viij d.
Item paied to Anthony knyght for a nother C of gold for the
same workes   vj s.
Item for di. C of iiij peny naile   ij d.   35
Item paied for ij li. of rede lede   iij d.
Item for oyle & glue   ij d.
Item for mendyng of the pament a boute the Crosse & the postes
that was brokyn   vj d.
Item paied to Mr Rutland for j li. of byce   vj s.   40

32, 40/ Maister Rutland, Mr Rutland: *William Rutlande, alderman; mayor 1518–19, 1528–9*
33/ Anthony knyght: *common councillor*

Item paied to ffloraunce the Paynter by the grete for the workmanship
therof he fyndyng all man*er* stuf for the payntyng of the Crosse/
except gold & byce to the same & gyldyng of the starr*es*   lviij s. viij d.

                        *Sum*ma v li. ix d.

f 113v   *(Wages and payments)*

...

ℂ Item paied to Thomas waren Iohn waren Iohn Eton Comen wayt*es*
of theseid Citie to eu*ery* of theym for their wag*es* this yere xiij s. iiij d.
*Sum*ma   xl s.

ℂ It*em* paied to harry s*er*uant & apprentyse of theseid Thomas waren for
hys wag*es* this yere   x s.

...

f 115   *(External expenses)*

...

Item paied to danyell Smyth for mendyng of one of the Rodd*es* of the
Canapye brokyn at my lord Cardynall*es* comyng home from beyonde
the see   ij d.

ff 115v–16v*

...

Item the xvj^th day of apryll paied to Iohn Burgrove for hys labour &
expens*es* rydyng to my lord of Canterbury w*ith* a lett*er* to know of
hym the kyng*es* pleasure what *pr*eparac*i*on shoulde be made ayenst the
Emp*er*ours comyng   iiij s.
Item paied for making clene of the king*es*strete w*ith*out seynt
Mighell*es* gate   v d.
Item the iij^de day of May paied to the kyng*es* wayt*es* in rewarde   vj s. viij d.

...

Item the xxv^th day of May paied to will*i*am Canone for the hire
of ij hors for M*aster* Chamberleyn & Iohn Toft*es* to waite on hym
to london for a Canape to grauesende & home a gayne   iij s. iiij d.|
ℂ Item paied for their expens*es* & hors mete in the same yourney out
& home agayne   ij s. xj d.
ℂ It*em* gevyn in reward to the Sextayn of seynt Dunstons in thest at
london that delyu*er*ed the Canape borowed ther   xij d.

to the king*es*   ℂ Item xxviij^th day of May paied to the kyng*es* fotemen for the discharge
seruant*es*   of the Canape whiche they cleymed to be to the Emp*er*ours fotemens
                 of dutie and by grete meane and entreaty was had a gayn &c.   liij s. iiij d.
                 ℂ Item paied to the kyng*es* Trumpett*es*   vj s. viij d.

23/ Iohn Burgrove: *commoner*   32/ Iohn Toftes: *common clerk of the chamber*

℃ Item paied for brede & ale at the metyng of the king at harbaldowne   v d.

remanet in Camera

℃ Item paied for a grete box for comfettes that should haue ben gevyn to the Emperour   x d.

℃ Item paied for a hors hire & the expenses of yong Iohn alcok to dovour to bere a letter theder to my lord Cardynall   xviij d.   5

℃ Item for a nother hors hire for Iohn Taillour to dovour to bryng knowlege of to Master Mayer of the Emperour & kynges comyng   xij d.

℃ Item paied to ij laboreres for dyggyng of grauell for the stretes by one day   viij d.

℃ Item paied for a hors hire to Sandwych to fett another Canape ther with ye expenses   x d.   10

℃ Item paied for iij bordes for ledgyng of the Canape & makyng therof   viij d.

℃ Item paied for prepayryng of the Canape for white lyre and sylk poyntes   ij s.l

Item paied for a hors hire & the expenses of a man that caryed home the Canape agayn to london   iij s. iiij d.   15

Item paied for gyldyng of the staves of the Canape that were hurte by the kynges fote men for hast in Cuttyng of the Canape from the staves   xij d.

Item paied to Iohn haslast for rydyng ij tymes to douour in one day to bryng certen knowlege of the Emperour & the kynges comyng   ij s.

...   20

Item paied for a hors hire & the expenses of hym that caryed home the Canape to Sandwyche   xij d.

...

f 117*   25

℃ Item paied to william Mylys Towne Clerk in reward toward hys Gaberden ayenst the Comyng of the Emperour & the kynges grace to the Citie &c.   vj s. viij d.

Munera data diuersis Officiarijs dicte Ciuitatis erga aduentum domini Regis & imperatoris ad eandem Ciuitatem

℃ Item to Iohn Toftes Comen Clark of the Chamber toward a Gaberden in lykewyse   vj s. viij d.   30

℃ Item to Vmfray wales Comen serieant of the Chamber toward his gaberden   vj s. viij d.

℃ Item to Markes Olford serieaunt of the Mace in lyke wyse toward hys gaberden   vj s. viij d.   35

℃ Item paied to Robert Sturdy serieant of the mace toward hys Gaberden   vj s. viij d.

℃ Item paied to Iohn yomanson serieaunt toward hys gaberden the same tyme   vj s. viij d.

℃ Item to Thomas Gere serieant the same tyme toward hys gaberden   vj s. viij d.   40

℃ Item to Iohn Bradley Iayler toward a Gaberden   vj s. viij d.

6/ Iohn Taillour: *common councillor*   7/ knowlege of ... of: *dittography*

℃ Item paied for j quarte of malvesey gevyn to *Master* Champneys of
london for the kyndnes that he lent the Canape that ⌈was⌉ borowed
at london of hys owne mynde beyng then churche warden of seynt
dunston in the East wherunto the Canape bylonged   iiij d.
℃ It*em* for j li. of confett*es* gevyn hym the same tyme   x d.   5
...

f 117v
...
℃ Item paied for x li. of gunpowder for the watche on seynt Thomas   10
Evyn price the li. vij d. *Summa*   v s. x d.
...
Item paied for a staf & a baner to bere byfore the Mores pyk*es*
ₐ⌈& the gunners⌉ on seynt Thomas eve   xij d.
...   15

f 127   *(Mayor's accounts)*
...

Recepc*iones* fin*ium* pro tauris mactand*is*

¶ ffirst theseid Chamberleyn yeldyth accompt*es* of the receyt*es* of
dyu*er*se fynes for bullys sleyn this yere by dyu*er*se Boch*er*s vsyng &   20
occupyeng theseid Citie not bayted at the Bolstake &c/ ffirst of
Thomas Shipston Boch*er* receyved for ij bull*es*   ij s.
℃ Item of Robert Sampson Boch*er* for j bull   xij d.
℃ Item of Iohn hobbys Boch*er* for one bull   xij d.
℃ Item of Iohn Chapman boch*er* for j bull   xij d.   25
                 Summa v s.

f 135v   *(Mayor's fee and officers' livery)*
...
℃ It*em* paied for xij yard*es* of theseid cloth gevyn to Thomas waren Iohn   30
waren Iohn Eton and to harry s*er*uaunt of theseid Thomas waren Comen
wayt*es* of theseid Citie to eu*er*y of them fower iij yard*es* *Summa*   xl s.

St Andrew's Churchwardens' Accounts   CCA: U3/5/4/1
f 88   *(Casual receipts)*   35
...
Item Rec*eived* in money gathered aswell by men as by women
at hoktyd thys yere   xviij s. vj d.
...

38/ hoktyd: *28–9 April*

1522–3
City Chamberlains' Accounts   CCA: CC/FA 11
f 169v

...

Expense
Pagianti sancti
Thome

Item paied to the priores of seynt Sepulcre for the stondyng of   5
the seid pagent in her Barne   xx d.

Summa patet

...

f 176v   (Wages and payments)   10

...

℃ Item paied to Thomas waren Iohn waren Iohn Eton and harry
(blank) seruant of theseid Thomas waren Comen waytes of theseid
Citie to euery of them for their wages this yere xiij s. iiij d. Summa   liij s. iiij d.

...   15

f 179v   (External expenses)

...

℃ Item paied to Edmunde Goodlad for rydyng into Tenet at tyme
of the surmyse of the landyng of the danes   xx d. 20
℃ Item for iij vessell of Bere gevyn to the Citizens the same tyme   iiij s. vj d.
℃ Item gevyn to Mynstrall the same tyme   xij d.

...

f 186*   (Mayor's accounts)   25

...

℃ ffirst theseid Chamberleyn yeldeth accomptes of the Receytes of dyuerse
fynez for bullys sleyn by dyuerse Bochers vsyng and occupyeng theseid
ᴧ⌈Citie⌉ not bayted at the bulstake &c ffirst receyved of Iohn
℃ Iamys for one bull this yere   xij d. 30
℃ Item of Iohn Chapman Bocher for j bull   xij d.
℃ Item of Robert Sampson Bocher for j bull   xij d.

Summa iij s.

f 193v   (Mayor's wages and officers' livery)   35

...

℃ Item paied for xij yardes of the seide clothe gevyn to Thomas waren
Iohn waren Iohn Eton & harry (blank) seruant of theseid Thomas
waren Comen waytes of theseid Citie to euery of theym ffower
iij yardes Summa   xl s. 40

5/ the priores of seynt Sepulcre: *Mildred Hale, prioress from c 1511*

St Andrew's Churchwardens' Accounts   CCA: U3/5/4/1

f 92   *(Casual receipts)*

...

Item received in money Gadered by the parysshons on hockmunday
and Tewysday aswell by men as women   xxj s. vj d.   5

...

1523–4
City Chamberlains' Accounts   CCA: CC/FA 11

f 234v   *(Wages and payments)*   10

...

ℂ Item payd to Thomas waren Iohn waren Iohn Eton and harry *(blank)*
seruant of the seid Thomas waren Comon waytes of theseid Citie to
euery of them .iiij. for their wages this yere xiij s. iiij d. Summa   liij s. iiij d.

...   15

f 236v   *(External expenses)*

...

ℂ Item the iiijth day of Iune gevyn in reward to the kynges waytes   vj s. viij d.

...   20

f 237

Item the xvjth day of Iuly payd to my lady of seynt Sepulcres for the
stondyng of seynt Thomas pagent in her barne   xx d.   25

...

f 245   *(Mayor's accounts)*

...

Recepciones   ¶ ffirst theseid Chamberleyn yeldeth accomptes of the receytes of dyuerse fynez   30
taurorum   for bullys sleyn by dyuerse Bocheres vsyng the market of theseid Citie not
               bayted at the bulstake &c
ℂ ffirst receyved of Robert Sampson Bocher for I bull by hym sleyn
   this yer   xij d.
ℂ Item of Iohn hobbys Bocher for j bull   xij d.   35
ℂ Item receyved of Iohn Chapman for ij bulles   ij s.
ℂ Item receyved of Iohn Vance Bocher for j bull   xij d.
ℂ Item receyved of Iohn Iamys Bocher for j bull   xij d.
                              Summa vj s.

4–5/ hockmunday and Tewysday: *13–14 April*
24/ my lady of seynt Sepulcres: *Mildred Hale, prioress from c 1511*

St Andrew's Churchwardens' Accounts   CCA: U3/5/4/1
f 97   (Casual receipts)

Item receyued in money Gadered by the parysshons on hockmunday
and Tewysday as well by the men as by the women   xxj s. viij d.   5
...

1524–5
City Chamberlains' Accounts   CCA: CC/FA 11
f 295   (Wages and payments)   10
...

℃ Item payd to Thomas waren Iohn waren Iohn Eton & harry knyght
seruant of theseid Thomas Comen waytes of theseid Citie to euery
of theym for ther wages this yere xiij s. iiij d. Summa   liij s. iiij d.
...   15

f 296v   (External expenses)
...

to the kynges   ℃ Item the first day of Iuly gevyn in reward to the kynges Mynstralles   vj s. viij d.
Mynstralles   ...   20
                 ℃ Item payd to the priouresse of seynt Sepulcre for the standyng of
                 seynt Thomas pagent ther this yere   xx d.
                 ...

f 302   (Mayor's accounts)   25
...

Recepciones   ¶ ffirst theseid Chamberleyn yeldyth Accomptes of the Receytes of dyuerse
finium   ffynes for bulles sleyn this yere by dyuerse Bochers vsyng & occupyeng
Taurorum &c   theseid Citie not bayted at the Bulstake ffyrst receyved of Iohn hobbys
                for one bull this yere   xij d. 30
                ℃ Item receyved of Iohn Chapman Bocher for one Bull   xij d.
                ℃ Item receyved of theseid Iohn hobbys for another bull   xij d.
                ℃ Item of theseid Iohn Chapman for a nother Bull   xij d.
                                Summa iiij s.

                                                                           35
f 307   (Mayor's wages and officers' livery)
...

℃ Item for xij yardes of theseid cloth gevyn to Thomas waren Iohn waren

4–5/ hockmunday and Tewysday: 4–5 April
21/ the priouresse of seynt Sepulcre: Mildred Hale, prioress from c 1511

Iohn Eton and harry knyght *seruant* of theseid Thomas Comen *waytes*
of the seid Citie to eu*ery* of the same iiij. iij yard*es* for their leu*ery*   xl s.
...

St Andrew's Churchwardens' Accounts   CCA: U3/5/4/1   5
f 101v   *(Casual receipts)*
...

It*em* Rec*eived* in money Gadered by the p*a*rysshons on hokmu*n*day
and tuysday aswell by men as by women   xxvij s. ij d. ob.
...   10

1525–6
City Chamberlains' Accounts   CCA: CC/FA 11
f 342v   *(Wages and payments)*
...   15
℃ Item payd to Thomas waren Iohn waren Iohn Eton and harry *(blank)*
seruant of theseid Thomas waren Comen *waytes* of the seid Citie to
eu*ery* of theym xiij s. iiij d. for their wag*es* this yere Su*m*ma   liij s. iiij d.
...
                                                                                     20
f 343v   *(External expenses)*
...

gevyn to my   ℃ Item the xxvij^th day of apryll payd for a reward gevyn to my lord
lord Cardynall*es* . Cardynall*es* wayt*es*   vj s. viij d.
wayt*es*
...   25

f 344
...

℃ Item the xxix^th day of Iuly payd to the kyng*es* wayt*es* in reward   vj s. viij d.
...   30

f 350   *(Mayor's accounts)*
...
Recepc*iones* ¶ ffirst theseid Chamberleyn yeldyth accompt of the Receyt*es* receyved of
fin*ium*   dyu*er*se fynez for Bull*es* sleyn by dyu*er*se Bocher*es* vsyng & occupyeng the   35
Tauror*um* &c   m*a*rkett*es* with*in* the seid Citie not Bayted at the Bulstake &c/ ffirst
℃ Receyved of a Straunge Bocher for half a Bull put to sale   vj d.
℃ Item rec*eyved* of Rychard Saunder Bocher for half a Bull   vj d.
℃ Item receyved of Iohn Chapman Bocher for a Bull   xij d.
℃ Item rec*eyved* for a quarter of a Bull   iij d. 40

8–9/ hokmu*n*day and tuysday: *24–5 April*

℄ Item rec*eyved* of Iohn hobbys for a Bull   xij d.

                                      *Sum*ma iij s. iij d.

f 357v   *(Mayor's wages and officers' livery)*

...

Item for xij yard*es* of theseid clothe gevyn to Thomas waren Iohn waren
Iohn Eton and henry *(blank)* ser*u*aunt of the seid Thomas waren Comen
wayt*es* of theseid Citie to eu*er*y of them iij yard*es* for their leverey s*um*ma   xl s.

St Andrew's Churchwardens' Accounts   CCA: U3/5/4/1

f 105v   *(Casual receipts)*

...

Item yn monye gaderyd by the p*a*rysheons on hocke mundaye and
tewysdaye as well bye men as bye wemen   xvij s. ix d.

...

1526-7
City Chamberlains' Accounts   CCA: CC/FA 11

f 399   *(External expenses)*

...

Item payd & gevyn in reward to the kyng*es* trumpett*es* goyng ou*er*
wi*th* my lord Cardynall   iij s. iiij d.
Item gevyn to the kyng*es* Mynstrall*es* the xv^th day of Iuly   vj s. viij d.

...

Item payd to Thomas Iohnson kepar of the palys in the p*r*ice of a
payer of shose for the stondyng of seynt Thomas pagent in the palys
hall this yere   ix d.

...

f 405   *(Mayor's accounts)*

...

Recepc*iones*
fin*ium*
Tauro*rum* &c

ffirst theseid Chamberleyn yeldyth accompt*es* of the receyt*es* receyved of
dyu*er*se ffynez for Bull*es* sleyn by dyu*er*se Bochers vsyng & occupyeng the
m*a*rkett*es* wi*th*in theseid Citie not bayted at the Bulstake &c ffirst
℄ Receyved of Iohn hern Bocher for ij bull*es* by hym sleyn this yere   ij s.
℄ Item receyved of Iohn hobbys for j bull   xij d.
℄ Item receyved of Iohn Chapman Bocher for j Bull   xij d.
℄ Item receyved of willi*a*m deryng Bocher for ij Bullys   ij s.
                                  *Sum*ma vj s.

...

13-14/ hocke mundaye and tewysdaye: *9-10 April*   25/ the palys: *ie, of the archbishop of Canterbury*
22/ my lord Cardynall: *Thomas Wolsey*

f 410v   *(Mayor's wages and officers' livery)*

...

℃ Item for iij yard*es* & di. of theseid clothe gevyn to Iohn Eton
Comen wayte of the seid Citie by Bourmote   xj s. viij d.

...   5

St Andrew's Churchwardens' Accounts   CCA: U3/5/4/1
f 109v   *(Casual receipts)*

...

Item Rec*eived* in money Gaderred by the p*a*rysshons on   10
hockmu*n*day and Tewysday as well by the men as By
the wemen   xvij s. vj d.

...

St Dunstan's Churchwardens' Accounts   CCA: U3/141/5/2   15
p 43*   *(25 November—25 November)*

...

℃ Item resceyued of hokmony [th] of the wemen gadryng of the
fyrst yere   iiij s. j d.

...   20

1527–8
City Chamberlains' Accounts   CCA: CC/FA 11
f 438v

                                                                                                                     25

Expens*e*   Item payd for ij lood*es* of Bolder price the lode ij s. vj d. Su*m*ma   v s.
pauagij Reg*is*   Item payd for iij lood*es* of Sand   xv d.
strate iux*t*a   Item payd for pavyng of xx yard*es* ther price *le* yard pavyng j d. ob.
Cruce*m* ap*u*d   su*m*ma   ij s. vj d.
le Bulstake
                                                    Su*m*ma viij s. ix d.   30

...

f 442v   *(External expenses)*

Item paid to the kyng*es* pleyers the xvj^th day of Ianuary   iij s. iiij d. 35

...

Item paid to Iohnson in the price of a paire of shose for the
standyng of seynt Thomas payent in the pales   ix d.

...

11/ hockmu*n*day and Tewysday: *29–30 April*
18–19/ hokmony ... of the fyrst yere: *gathered Hock Monday, 29 April*
37/ Iohnson: *keeper of the archbishop's palace*

f 443

...

Item gevyn to the kynges waytes the ix^th day of Iuly   vj s. viij d.

...

f 449   *(Mayor's accounts)*

...

fines taurorum ¶ ffirst theseid Chamberleyn yeldyth accomptes of the Receytes of ffynes for
mactandorum   bulles sleyen by the Bochers vsyng & occupyeng theseid Citie not bayted at
&c   the Bulstake &c ffirst
                 Of william deryng for one Bull this yere   xij d.
                           Summa patet

...

f 454v   *(Mayor's wages and officers' livery)*

...

[Item for iij yardes ⌐& di.⌐ of the same Clothe gevyn to Iohn Eton
Comen wayte of theseid Citie by bourmote   xj s. viij d.]

...

Item payd for ix yardes of theseid Clothe gevyn to Iohn Eton & hys
ij seruantes Comen waytes of theseid Citie for their lyuerey this yer   xxx s.

...

St Dunstan's Churchwardens' Accounts   CCA: U3/141/5/2
p 43*   *(25 November–25 November)*

...

℃ Item resceyued of hokmony of the ij^de yere   [iiij s. j d.] v s. vj d.

...

1528–9
City Chamberlains' Accounts   CCA: CC/FA 12
f 29   *(External expenses)*

...

Item gevyn in reward to the kynges Mynstrelles   vj s. viij d.

...

f 29v

...

Item payd for a payer of Shose gevyn to Thomas Iohnson of the
palys for the standyng of seynt Thomas pagent in the palys   ix d.

...

18/ wayte: a corrected over y   27/ hokmony of the ij^de yere: *gathered Hock Monday, 20 April* f 35   *(Mayor's receipts)*

...

Recepc*iones*
fin*ium*
Tauror*um* &c

¶ ffirst theseid Chamb*er*leyn yeldyth accompt*es* of the receyt*es* of dyu*er*se
ffynes for bull*es* sleyn this yere by dyu*er*se bochers vsyng & occupying
theseid Citie not Bayted at the bulstake ffirst receyved of will*i*am deryng
for one bull this yere   xij d.   5

Su*m*ma xij d

...

f 42v   *(Mayor's wages and officers' livery)*   10

...

Item paid for x yard*es* of theseid Cloth gevyn to Iohn Eton &
his ij s*er*uant*es* Comen wayt*es* of the seid Citie for their lyu*er*ey
this yere   xxxiij s. iiij d.

...   15

St Dunstan's Churchwardens' Accounts   CCA: U3/141/5/2
p 55*   *(6 December–6 December)*

...

Item the furst yere of hopmu*n*day of strayngers and the   20
p*ar*rysshyns   vij s. iij d.

...

1529–30
City Chamberlains' Accounts   CCA: CC/FA 12   25
f 77

Expens*e*
pagiant*i* °of°
[*sancti* Thome]
°Thomas beket°

¶ It*em* payd to Dandyson & his man for ij days work a
bowte ye pagent   xviij d.
Item payd to Nycolas harte for ij alder polys   iiij d. 30
Item payd for taynt hook*es* & wyre   vj d.
Item for a payer of new gloves & buckyll*es* for the harnes   iij d.
Item for a new typpet of Buckeram   vj d.
Item for a new leder bag for ye blode   vj d.
I*tem* payd to Iohn hay paynter by the grete for makyng of the   35
knyght*es* harnes & payntyng of the Pagent   v s.
Item payd for di. ownce of Byce   ij d.
Item payd for a dosen & half of tyn foyle & golde foyle   iij s. ij d.
Item for a li. of rede lede   ij d.
Item for x ownc*es* of vermyl*i*on   x d. 40

20/ hopmu*n*day: *Hock Monday, 4 April*
30/ Nycolas harte: *commoner*

Item for ij skynnes to make harnes   v d.
Item for ij dosen of poyntes   ij d.
Item for paktrede & white threde   iij d.
Item for paynters oyle   ij d.
Item for a quartron of Rosett   iij d. 5
Item for a quartron of partie gold   vj d.
Item for ij li. of glue   vj d.
Item for remevyng of the pagent   iij d.
Item to Wodrof for cariage of the pagent a bowte the watche   xij d.
Item for drynk & on to turne ye vyce   v d. 10

Summa xvj s. x d.

f 78v   (External expenses)
...   15
Item gevyn in reward to the kynges waytes   vj s. viij d.
Item gevyn in reward to the kynges players   iij s. iiij d.
...
Item paid for a paire of shose gevyn to Thomas Iohnson of the palys
for the standyng of seynt Thomas pageaunt there   x d. 20
Item paid for nyne pownd of Corne powdre for the gunners on seynt
Thomas nyght price the li. ix d. summa   vj s. ix d.
...

f 83   (Mayor's receipts)   25
...
Recepciones   Item theseid Chamberleyn yeldyth accomptes of the receytes
finium   of dyuerse ffynes for bullys sleyn this yere by dyuerse bochers
Taurorum &c   vsyng & occupying theseid Citie not Bayted at the Bulstake
                ffirst receved of Thomas Bocher for sellyng of Bullflesshe in   30
                the market   ix d.

Summa ix d.
...

35

f 89v   (Mayor's wages and officers' livery)
...
Item paid for x yardes of the seid Cloth gevyn to Iohn Eton &
his ij seruantes Comen waytes of theseid Citie for their lyuerey
this yere   xxxiij s. iiij d. 40
...

Burghmote Orders CCA: CC/AB 1
ff 5–6*

...

the wacche

® The acte ⟨..⟩ the wacche ⟨..⟩ the Ci⌈te⌉ of ⟨...⟩

ffor as moche as all maner of harnes with in the Cite of Canterbury is decaied
and rustid for lacke of yerly wacche the whiche wacche be fore [ty] this tyme 5
haue bene yerly contynewed by oure predecessours to the grete honour of
theseide Cite & proffyte of the fense of the reme by makyng clene & purchesing
yerly of harnes within the same Cite and by cause nowe of late summe Maiers
in ther yere haue full honourably kepte the seide wacche and summe Maiers
none. wherfor it is enactid and agreed by the auctorite of the same Burgemote 10
that frome hensforth yerly euery maier shall contynewe & kepe the seide
wacche in the Euen of the Translacion of seint Thomas the Martier. And in the
seide wacche the sheryfe of theseide Cite to Ride in harnes with an hencheman
aftir hym onestly emparellid for the honour of the same Cite. And the Maier to
ride att his plesuer and yf the Maiers plesure be to ride in harnes the aldermen 15
to ride in lyke maner and yf he ride in his Scarlett goone the aldermen to ride
aftir thesame wacche in scarlett & Crymesyn gownes. And yf any Maier here
aftir for slowe or of wilfulnesse wille not obserue this acte in contynewyng the
seide wacche with the premysses he to forfett to the Comenalte of theseide
Cite .x. li. and yf I any sherife of the same Cite her aftir for slowe of wilfulnesse 20
refuse to do as is aboueseide he to forfett to the comenalte as is aboueseide
.xl. s. and yf eny alderman of theseide Cite herafter by sloweth or wilfulnesses
ride not with the seide Maier he to forfette to theseide comenalte xl. s. also it
is enactid and agreed that euery alderman of thesame Cite shall fynde too
cressetes brennyng in the seide wacche and euery [tweyne] ⌈one⌉ the comen 25
counsell & euery Constable and towne clerke of the same Cite on Cressett to
brenne in lyke forme and yf eny of theseide persons lacke eny cresset that nyght
he to forfette for euery Cresett soo lackyng iij s. iiij d. whiche amerciamentes to
be leuyed by theseide Maier to his owne vse towarde his charges susteyned in
thesame wacche. also the Mayer of of thesame Cite for the tyme being to fynd 30
too Cresettes & vj torches or moo att his plesure

⟨.⟩he play of ⟨...⟩pus Christi

Be it remembered that wher be fore this tyme ther hath bene by the moste
honourable and worshypfull of the Cite of Canterbury vsid & continued
within the same Cite a play called Corpus Christi play as well to the honour of 35
the same Cite as to the profite of all vitelers & other occupacions within the
same whiche play before this tyme was meynteyned and plaide att the costes
and charges of the Craftes & Mistiers within the same Cite. And wher as nowe
of late daies it hath bene lefte & laide aparte to the grete hurte & decay of the
seide Cite. and for lacke of goode orderyng of certeyn craftes within the same 40

20/ of²: *for* or *or* or *of*   30/ of of: *dittography*

Cite nott corporatt wherfor it is ennactid ordeyned and establisshed that frome hensforth euery crafte within theseide Cite beyng not corporat for ther non sufficience of ther crafte be associatt Incorporatt & adioynyng | to summe other crafte moste nedyng of supporte yf they wille not labore tobe corporatt within them selfe as shalbe thought conuenient & moste necessary by this Courte And that alle maner Craftes & Mistiers within the same Cite be so Incorporat for the sustentacion & contynuance of theseide play by the feste of seint Michel next comyng And yf eny suche crafte or Crates be obstynatt or wilfulle & wille not make sute to the Burgemote for the performacion of theies premissis by theseide feste to forfett to theseide Chamber .xx s. and their bodies to be punysshed furthermore att the plesure and by discrescion of this Courte

pena

...

1530–1
City Chamberlains' Accounts   CCA: CC/FA 12
f 122

Expense
pagianti sancti
Thome

¶ Item paid to Iohn Hay paynter by the grete for mendyng of the knyghtes harnes payntyng of the pageaunt & turnyng of the vyce   ij s.

Item paid for half a pownd of vermylion a pownd of glew ij dosyn of goldfoyle & tynfoyle   xx d.

Item payd for new yaxing of the same & for makkyng of holys in the same   viij d.

Item paid for makyng of a new Crosse   iiij d.

Item paid to Iamys Colman for cariage of the pageant abowte the wacche   xvj d.

Item paid for lyftyng of the pageant ouer the Barres in the palys in & out   vj d.

Summa vj s. vj d.

ff 124–4v   *(External expenses)*
...

Item paid for xiiij li. of [Corne] ʌ⌈Gonne⌉ powder for the Gunners on seynt Thomas evyn   x s. vj d.

gevyn to the
kynges waytes

Item gevyn in reward to the kynges waytes   vj s. viij d.|
Item gevyn to the kynges players in reward   iij s. iiij d.
...

8/ Crates: *for* Craftes
28/ Barres: B *corrected over illegible letters*

Item paid to Thomas Ionson for the standyng of seynt Thomas
pageaunt in the palys   x d.
Item paid to the iiij serieantes of the Mace & to the serieaunt of the
Chamber toward the beying of their Cootes ayenst seynt Thomas
nyght to euery of them iij s. iiij d. summa   xvj s. viij d. 5
Item paid for a hatt gevyn to vmfray wales the same tyme   xvj d.

...

f 129*   (Mayor's receipts)

...   10

Recepciones   ¶ Item theseid Chamberleyn yeldyth accomptes of the receytes of dyuerse
finium   ffynes for bullys sleyn this yere by dyuerse Bochers vsyng & occupying
Taurorum &c   theseid Citie not bayted at the Bulstake ffirst receyved   nil

...

                                                                                               15

f 136v   (Mayor's wages and officers' livery)

...

Item paid for x yardes of theseid Cloth gevyn to Iohn Eton & his
ij seruantes Comen waytes of theseid Citie for their lyuerey
this yere   xxxiij s. iiij d. 20

...

1531–2
City Chamberlains' Accounts   CCA: CC/FA 12
f 173v   25

Reparaciones   ¶ Item payd to Iohn hay paynter for mendyng of the pagent & kepyng
Pagianti sancti   of the vyce   xij d.
Thome   Item payd to Thomas wodrof for Caryage of the pagent a boute
               the watche   xij d. 30
               Item payd for mete & drynk for the knyghtes croyser & other helpyng
               furth the pagent after the watche   xij d.
               Item for wasshyng of the albe the auterclothes & settyng on a gayn
               of the apparell   iiij d.
               Item for a new payer of gloves   j d. 35
               Item for payntyng & trymmyng of the hede   iij d.
               Item payd for mendyng of the wheles with stayes & nailes   vj d.
               Item payd for cariage of pagent to and from the place where
               it standyth   vij d.

1/ Thomas Ionson: *keeper of the archbishop's palace*
6/ vmfray wales: *serjeant of the chamber*

Item payd for stondyng of the pagent   x d.

                *Summ*a v s. vij d.

f 176v   *(External expenses)*

...

gevyn to the
kyng*es* wayt*es*

Item gevyn to the kyng*es* wayt*es*   vj s. viij d.

Item gevyn to the kyng*es* players   xl d.

...

f 177

...

Item paid to iiij *ser*ieant*es* of the mace and to the *ser*ieant of
the chamber toward the bying of their cot*es* ayenst seynt
Thomas nyght   xvj s. viij d.

Item paid for xij li. of [gonne]ᴧ⌈corne⌉ powdre for hand gonnys   x s.

Item paid for hatte gevyn to Vmfray wales aynst the watche   xvj d.

...

Item spent vppon the Carpenters in Bred & drynk at ordeiners at
the makyng of the frame a a bowte the Crosse at the Bulstake   ij s.

...

f 186   *(Mayor's wages and officers' livery)*

...

It*em* payd for x yard*es* of theseid cloth gevyn to Iohn Eton and
hys ij [*ser*ieaunt] *ser*uant*es* Comen wayt*es* of the seid Citie for
their levery this yere   xxxiij s. iiij d.

...

1532–3
City Chamberlains' Accounts   CCA: CC/FA 12
f 213v

Expens*e*
Pagiantis
*san*c*ti* Thome
&c

¶ Item payed to Will*ia*m Gylbert paynter by the grete for payntyng
of dyv*er*se thyng*es* a boute the pagent & the hede   xij d.

Item payd for golde foyle & tynfoyle   xij d.

Item payd for wyre taynt hook*es* nailes blak soope & pactherde   vj d.

Item payd to a Carpent*er* by the grete for mendyng & trymyng of
the pagent   xij d.

16/ Vmfray wales: *serjeant of the chamber*
16/ aynst: *for* ayenst
19/ a a: *dittography*

Item payd to Semark Couper for ij hoopys to bere vp the clothe ou*er*
the hors bak   ij d.
Item payd for mete & drynk spent vppon the children af*ter* the watche   xij d.
Item payd for cariage of the Page to & from the place where it stondyth   iiij d.
Item paid to wodrof for cariage of the pagent a bowte the watche   xvj d.   5
Item paid for a payer of new shose gevyn to Thomas Iohnson for the
stondyng of the Pagent in the palys   x d.
Item for a payer of new shose this yere bought for seynt Thomas   vij d.
                                 *Summ*a vij s. ix d.

                                                                                          10

f 216v*   *(External expenses)*

…

+ Item payd to the kyng*es* fote men for a reward in two Crowne
   ⌈of ye some⌉   ix s. iiij d.
+ Item gevyn to the kyng*es* trumpettors   v s. iiij d.   15
+ Item gevyn to the kyng*es* Clark of the m*a*rket in reward   vj s. viij d.
+ Item gevyn to the kyng*es* harbenger in reward   vj s. viij d.
+ Item paied for a dosen spyced bred ij li. of Orrenget & sucket
   bake gevyn to M*r* Crumwell at hys comyng to Caun*ter*bury   ij s. iiij d.
   Item for quynce*s* & spices for the seid M*r* Crumwell   ij s.   20
   Item paied for iiij Coupell of Capons sent to M*r* Crumwell
   to Calys   vj s. viij d.
   Item for ij dosen of Bake wardens   iiij d.
   Item for a galon of ypocr*a*s gevyn to the seid M*r* Crumwell   iiij s.

…   25

gevyn to
dyu*er*se
the kyng*es*
s*er*uantes

f 217

…

gevyn to the +   Item gevyn in reward to the kyng*es* pleyers   iij s. iiij d.
kyng*es* pleyers
…   30

ff 217v–18

…

gevyn to the +   Item gevyn to the kyng*es* wayt*es* in reward   vj s. viij d.
kyng*es* wayt*es*   Item payd for xij li. of fyne corne powder for hand*es* gunnes   35
                 ayenst seynt Thomas evyn   x s.

1/ Semark: *John Semarke, cooper*
4/ Page: *for* Pageant (?)
6/ Thomas Iohnson: *keeper of the archbishop's palace*
14/ some: *extra minim in* MS
20–3/ Item for … vj s. viij d.: *entries written in reverse order but marked for inversion by clerk*

Item for a hat gevyn to the serieant of the Chamber humfray wales   xvj d.|
Item toward the Cootes of the iiij serieantes and the serieant of the
Chamber ayenst seynt Thomas evyn euery of them iij s. iiij d.
Summa   xvj s. viij d.
...   5

f 222   *(Mayor's receipts)*

...

finium   ¶ Item receyved of Thomas ffarthyngton Bocher for half of one Bull
taurorum   by hym sold in the market and not Bayted at the Bulstake &c   vj d. 10
Mactatorum   Item receyved of Robert Bocher for half a Bull in lykewyse sold in
&c   the Market   vj d.
             Item receyved of william Iope Bocher for one Bull   xij d.
                          Summa ij s.

                                                                                                15
Order of the Marching Watch   CCA: Literary MS C13
f 10*

                          The order of the [ware] watche the tyme of *Thomas* bele
                          with the number of bowmen byll men Moryspykes hand 20
                          gonnys and Cressettes
          In the wardes of westgate in byll men xxxiiij
          Item xiij bowe men
          Item [xij] Cressettes xvj
Norgate   In bowez xiiij In bylles lxviij Cressettes xvj   25
      ℂ Newyngate In bowez xxv In bylles xvj Cressettes xij
      ℂ Redyngate In bowez vj In bylles x Cressettes iij
      ℂ woorgate bowez xxiij bylles xxvij Cressettes xiij
      ℂ burgate bowez xxiij bylles xxxix Cressettes xv
                          Summa of bow men Ciij byllmen CC Cressettes lxxviij   30

          Item Moryce pykes and hand gonnys *(blank)*
the order ffyrst the gyantes/ then the gyttern then the gunneres then the moryce pykes/
          Then the salutacyon/ Then the stander(.) then xl byll men/ Then the
          Cunstable of Redyngate/ saynt George then xl byll men/ The Cunstable of 35
          worgate the Natyuyte/ a standard xxx bowez the Cunstable of Northe gate
          the assumpcyon xxx bowmen the Counstabl(.) of westegate saynt Thomas xl
          bowmen/ Then the Cunstables of burgate and Newyngate with there
          henchemen/ Then the Cunstable of saynt marteynys Then the too handyd
          swerdes the Moryce the seriauntes Master Mayor the aldermen dd. byll men 40
          a Moryce the shreue the resydue of the bylle men

the ordereres of the Cressettes Iohn ambrose Robert hunt C Carpynter Iames
Tompson Mark olford Richard barker
the orderes of the watche Christopher Levyns Iohn Coppyn Iohn Toftes henry
gere Iohn starky Iohn hobbys Iohn burgroue

St Dunstan's Churchwardens' Accounts   CCA: U3/141/5/2
p 39

...

℃ In primis Receyvyd of gethyryng at hoptyd   vj s. j d.

...

1533–4
City Chamberlains' Accounts   CCA: CC/FA 12
f 249

Reparaciones
Pagianti sancti
Thome

Item Payd to hocchon Carpenter by grete for trymmyng of the pagent and nailes	xv d.
Item payd to william Stephynson paynter by the grete for payntyng of seynt Thomas hed & other apparell and for trymmyng of the knyghtes harnes kepyng the vice & other necessaries	iiij s.
Item payd for vij dosyn ^⌈& di.⌉ of Goldfoyle and tynfoyle for the harnes	[ij s.] ij s.
Item payd for glue partie gold with dyuerse other colours for the payntyng of the hed & the garmentes & other	ij s. ij d.
Item payd for mete & drynk for the knyghtes & other that holp furth the pagent after the watche	xij d.
Item payd for cariage of the pagent in and out to the palys & fro	v d.
Item payd for stondyng of pagent ther to Iohnson the kepar	x d.
Item payd to wodrof for carieng a boute of the pagent in the watche	xij d.
Item for wyre & taynter hookes	iiij d.

Summa xiij s.

f 252v   *(External expenses)*

...

Item gevyn in reward to the kynges pleyers   iij s. iiij d.

...

Item gevyn to the kynges waytes   vj s. viij d.

...

9/ hoptyd: *21–2 April*

f 253

...

Item payd toward the Cootes of the iiij serieauntes and and the serieaunte of the Chamber euery of them iij s. iiij d. Summa ayenst the watche on seynt Thomas evyn   xvj s. viij d. 5

Item payd for xij li. of fyne Corne powder ayenst the watch on seynt Thomas evyn for hand gunnes   x s.

Item payd for a hatt for the serieaunt of the Chamber ayenst the watch   xiiij d.

...   10

f 258v   (Mayor's receipts)

...

finium
taurorum
mactatorum &c

¶ Item receyved of Rychard Saunder Bocher for half a Bull sold in the market & not Bayted at the Bulstake   vj d. 15

Item receyved of Thomas ffarthyngton Bocher for a quarter of a Bull in lyke wyse sold vnbayted &c   iij d.

                    Summa ix d.

...

                                                                                                                                    20

f 262   (Mayor's wages and officers' livery)

...

Item payed for xiij yardes of [Cloth] the seid Cloth gevyn to Iohn Beamond & his iiij seruantes Comen waites of the seid Citie for lyuereys   xliij s. iiij d. 25

...

1534–5
City Chamberlains' Accounts   CCA: CC/FA 12
f 284   30

Reparaciones
pageanti sancti
Thome

Item paid for the knyghtes souper   xij d.

Item paid for a hors to cary the pageant   viij d.

Item paid for wyre   ij d.

Item paid for standyng of the pageant   x d. 35

Item payd for a hatt gevyn to humfray to ryde in the watche on seynt Thomas evyn   xiiij d.

                    Summa iij s. x d.

...

3/ and and: *dittography*   36/ humfray: *Humphrey Wales, serjeant of the chamber*

f 287   *(External expenses)*

...

Item gevyn to the kyng*es* pleyers	vj s. viij d.
Item gevyn to the kyng*es* wayt*es*	vj s. viij d.
Item gevyn to the kyng*es* Mynstrell*es*	v s.
Item gevyn to the quenys Mynstrell*es*	v s.
Item gevyn to my lord Chamberleyns Menstrell*es*	xij d.

...

f 296v   *(Mayor's wages and officers' livery)*

...

Item paid for xiij yard*es* of theseid Cloth gevyn to Iohn Beamond
and his iiij *seruantes* Comen wayt*es* of theseid Citie for lyu*er*eys   xliij s. iiij d.

...

f 327v*   *(External expenses)*

...

Item paid to v *serie*aunt*es* toward their cot*es* ayenst seynt Thomas
tyme in the xxvij^th yere of theseid kyng which was not allowed in
the accompt of the same yere   xvj s. viij d.

...

1535-6
City Chamberlains' Accounts   CCA: CC/FA 12
f 327v*   *(External expenses)*

...

Item paid to the seid *serie*ant*es* toward their Cot*es* ayenst seynt
Thomas tyme in the xxviij^th yere of the reigne of kyng henry the
viij^th which was not allowed in the accompt of the same yere   xiij s. iiij d.

...

1536-7
City Chamberlains' Accounts   CCA: CC/FA 12
f 324v

*Repar*aei*on*es ¶ Item paid for payntyng of xxix yard*es* of Cloth to hang aboute
pageanti *sancti* the pageant price le yard j d. ob. *Sum*ma   iij s. ix d.
Thome martiris

Item paid for the knyght*es* souper	xij d.
Item paid for cariage abowte of the pageant	xij d.
Item paid for pacthrede and nedill*es* ⌈& wyre⌉	iiij d.
Item paid for nayles and Brasell	ij d.
Item paid for standyng of the pageaunt	x d.

Item paid for gonpowder spent on seynt Thomas evyn   vj s. viij d.
Summa xiij s. ix d.
…

f 327   (External expenses)
…
Item gevyn to the kynges players   iij s. iiij d.
…

f 327v*

Item paid to the iiij serieauntes toward their Cotes ayenst seynt
Thomas evyn now last past   xiij s. iiij d.
…

f 335v   (Mayor's wages and officers' livery)

Item paid for ix yardes of theseid Cloth gevyn to the iij waytes of
theseid Citie for their lyuereys this yere   xxx s.
…

St Dunstan's Churchwardens' Accounts   CCA: U3/141/5/3
p 21*
…
Item receyvyd of hoktyde money the last yere   iiij s. j d.
…

1537–8
City Chamberlains' Accounts   CCA: CC/FA 12
f 360v
…
ffines for Bulles   Item receyved of Iohn Iamys Bocher for the fyne of ∧⌈half⌉ a Bull not
Bayted &c   v d.

f 369v
…
Reparacions of   Item payd to Thomas hall plomer for mendyng of the ledys & for
the Crosse at   ij li. of sowder   viij d.
the Bulstake   Item payd to Robert ffryer for viij li. more of sowder for mendyng
of the seid ledys   ij s. [v] x d.
Summa iij s. vj d.

25/ hoktyde money the last yere: *gathered 16–17 April 1537*

The
expenses
of Bysshop
Beckettes
pagent

¶ Item payd for x li. of gonpowder price le li. x d. Summa   viij s. iiij d.
Item for caryage of the same pagent & all charges spent vppon
the same   iij s. ij d.

                                        Summa xj s. vj d.

f 373v   (External expenses)

…

Item gevyn to my lord Chauncellers players ouer and aboue vj s.
viij d. gathered at the play   iij s. iiij d.
Item paid for Candell at the same play   iiij d.
Item the ijde day of Marche gevyn to the pryncys players   v s.

…

f 374v

…

Item gevyn to the kynges Trompettours   vj s. viij d.

…

Item the xth day of September paid to the players of hadley   xx d.

…

f 375

…

Item paid to the iiij serieauntes towardes their Cootes on bysshop
Bekettes nyght   xiij s. iiij d.

…

f 383v   (Mayor's wages and officers' livery)

…

vacat   [Item paid for ix yardes of theseid cloth gevyn to the iij waytes of
theseid Citie for their lyvereys this yere   xxx s.]

…

Burghmote Court Minutes   CCA: CC/AC 1
f 93v   (9 July)

…

Memorandum that at this burgemote Robert Brigeman Henry ade and
Iohn lyberd were admyttyd to be waytes of thys Citie and not to haue
any lyuere

…

St Dunstan's Churchwardens' Accounts   CCA: U3/141/5/3
p 21*

...

℃ It*em* rec*eyvyd* of hoktyde money this yere   iij s. v d.

...   5

Thomas Cromwell's Accounts   PRO: E 36/256
f 140*

...

the trumpet*tes*   The viij^th of the same monethe gyven to them at Saint Stephyns   x s.   10

Balle and his   The same daye gyven to them by my Lord*es* comm*aundement* at saynt
ffelowes   Stephens besyd*es* Caunturbury ∧⌈for playing before my Lorde⌉   xl s.

...

1538–9   15
City Chamberlains' Accounts   CCA: CC/FA 13
f 25

...

expens*es* of   ¶ It*em* payd for a lode of Stone   xvj d.
pavage at the   It*em* for a lode of Sand   vj d.   20
Bulstake   It*em* for pavyng of vj yardes ther iij d. the yard S*um*ma   xviij d.
                                  S*um*ma iij s. iiij d.

...

f 27v   *(External expenses)*   25

...

It*em* the xxviij day of Ianuary gevyn to the prync*es* pleyers   vj s. viij d.

It*em* the xx^th day of Marche payd to the kyng*es* trumpettours   vj s. viij d.

...

                                                                                          30

f 29

...

It*em* the xxj^th day of september payd in reward to the kyng*es*
pleyers   iij s. iiij d.

...   35

4/ hoktyde money this yere: *gathered 6–7 May*
10/ the same monethe: *September 1538*
10, 11–12/ Saint Stephyns, saynt Stephens besyd*es* Caunturbury: *St Stephens, Hackington*
11, 12/ my Lord*es*, my Lorde: *Archbishop Thomas Cranmer*

St Andrew's Churchwardens' Accounts   CCA: U3/5/4/1
f 148   *(Casual receipts)*

...

It*em* R*eceived* of hoctyd al thing*es* gadderyd the ij days and
at supper   xvij s. x d.   5

...

Thomas Cromwell's Accounts   PRO: E 36/256
f 153v   *(31 January)*

...   10

Bale & his
ffelowes

The last of Ianuary gyven to him & his ffelowes for playing before
my Lorde   xxx s.

...

Depositions Concerning Henry Totehill of London   PRO: SP 1/142   15
ff [1–1v]*   *(10 January)*

Witnes examined the xth daye of Ianuary in the xxx yere of the Reign of our
sou*er*aign Lorde King Henry the viii^th, of certen wourdes, whiche one Henry
Totehill of the parishe of saincte kateryns bisid*es* the Tower hill shipman   20
should speake in the house of one Thomas Brown of Shawlteclyf wi*th*in the
Countie of kente, co*n*cerning the bisshop of Rome and Thomas Becket some
tyme Archebisshop of Canterbury

Iohn Alforde of thage of xviij yeres examined saith that by reason that he had   25
ben in Christmas tyme at my lorde of Canterburys and y*er* had harde an
enterlude co*n*cernyng king Iohn/ aboute viij or ix of the clocke at nyght on
thursdaye the seconde daye of Ianuarye last paste, spake, theis wourdes
folowing in the house of the said Thomas Brown That it ys petie, that the
bisshop of Rome should reigne any lenger, for if he should, the said Bisshop   30
wold do wi*th* our king as he did with king Iohn. Whervnto (this deponent
saith) that Henry Totehill answered and said That it was petie, and nawghtelye
don to put down the pope and saincte Thomas, ffor the Pope was a good
man, And saincte Thomas savid many suche as this deponet was from*e*
hangyng, whiche wourdes were spoken in the presence of Thomas Browne   35
and one Will*iam (blank)* ser*u*ante vnto the said Totehill

Thomas Brown of the age of .l. yeres examined, saith that about viij of the
clocke on ffridaye the iij daye of Ianuarye laste paste as he remembereth,
one Henry Totehill beyng in this deponent*es* house at Shawlteclyf, this   40

4/ hoctyd: *14–15 April*   34/ deponet: *for* deponent; *abbreviation mark missing*
12/ my Lorde: *Archbishop Thomas Cranmer*

deponent tolde that he hadde ben at my lorde of Canterburys, and there hadd
hard one of the best matiers that euer he sawe towching king Iohn and than
sayd yat he had harde diuers tymes preistes and clerkes say, that King Iohn did
loke like one that hadd rune frome brynnyng of a house, butt this deponent
knewe now, that yt was nothing treu, for as farr as he perceyued, king Iohn   5
was as noble a prince as euer was in England, And therby we myght perceyve
that he was ye begynner of the puttyng down of the bisshop of Rome,
and thereof we myght be all gladd, Than answerd the said Totehill that
the bisshope of Rome was made Pope by the Clergie and by the consent
of all the kinges christen, Than said this deponent holde your peace for   10
this communicacion ys nawght, Than said Totehill, I am sorye, if I haue said
amysse, ffor I thoughte no harme to no man This | Communicacion was
in the presence of Iohn Alforde and a laborer of the said Totehill/ and this
deponente And this deponente saithe, that the said Totehill was dronken
This deponent examyned wherfore he thought the wourdes of Thotehill   15
so nawght, saith, [that] by cause he thought that he spake theym in the
mayntenance of the bysshop of Rome/
Also concernyng the wourdes spoken of Thomas Beckette This deponente
aggreeth with the firste witnes

20

Antony Marten examyned what he harde spoken of Henry Totehill syns
he was in his custodie or at any tyme bifore/ Saith that he harde Iohn
halforde reporte, that Henry Totehill should saye, that it was petie that
saincte Thomas was put down, and yat the olde lawe was as good as the
newe/ And farther sayth, that the said Iohn Halforde reported, That   25
Totehill said, that the Bisshop of Rome was a good man, and this he harde
the said Halford reporte bifore he toke hym/ And farther the forsaid
Antony marten, saith, That he demanded one Thomas Brown (in whose
house the said Totehill spake theis wourdes aboue rehersid) what said
Totehill/ And he saithe that the said Brown said, that the said Totehill   30
hath spoken very evill, and whan he shoulde be examined, he would tell
the trueth

1539–40
City Chamberlains' Accounts   CCA: CC/FA 13   35
f 62v   *(Casual receipts)*
...
Item receyved of Stevyn apsley for the Cart of Bysshop
bekettes pageant   iij s. iiij d.
...   40

38/ Stevyn apsley: *alderman*

f 69v*   *(External expenses)*

...

Item paid to the Duk*es* Trompetours	xij d.
+ Item Gevyn to the lady anne of Cleve in mony	vj li.
Item paid for Burnyshyng of a Cup	vj d. 5

...

f 70*

...

Item paid to the Gonners at the lady annys comyng	xvj d. 10
Item paid to the kyng*es* trompettours thesame tyme	v s.

...

Item paid to Mast*er* Mayer that he gave to a p*ur*seuante that brought
a le*tt*re from my lord p*ri*vye seale for the receyte of the duke   xij d.

Item paid to Mast*er* Mayer that he gave to one that caryed a letter to   15
Calays conc*er*nyng the lady annes comyng   iiij d.

...

f 70v*

...   20

Item paid for the cariage of Bysshop Beket*tes* Pageant from the palays
to apsleys   iiij d.

...

Item paid to Mr ffreman for that he lent toward*es* the gyft gevyn to
the lady anne   xl s. 25

...

Item paid to the kyng*es* players   v s.

...

f 71   30

Item paid to my lord Chauncellours Mynstrell*es*   ij s. viij d.

...

1540–1   35
City Chamberlains' Accounts   CCA: CC/FA 13
f 106v   *(External expenses)*

...

It*em* payd for fetchyng of Gyaunt*es* & the gonnes from ye store house
in to the Court hall   ij d. 40

...

24/ Mr ffreman: *John Freeman, alderman; mayor 1543–4, 1549–50*

f 109

…

Item payd to the kyng*es* pleyers   iij s. iiij d.

…

Item gevyn in reward to the kyng*es* trumpettours   v s.   5

…

1541–2
City Chamberlains' Accounts   CCA: CC/FA 13
f 141   10

…

Recepc*iones*   Item receyved of Iohn Basshe Bocher for a fyne of a bull by hym
fin*ium*   sleyne and not Bayted at the Bulstake   xij d.
tauro*rum*   *Sum*ma *patet*

                                                                             15

f 146v

…

Repar*aciones*   Item payd to Iohn pavyer for pavyng of vj yard*es* price l*e* yard
ap*ud* le   ij d. ob. *sum*ma   xv d.
Bulstake   Item for a lode of Sand   v d. 20
                   Item for Canell ston a certen   x d.
                                *Sum*ma ij s. vj d.

f 148   *(External expenses)*

…   25

Item payd to the prync*es* Mynstrell*es*   iij s. iiij d.

…

f 148v

…   30

Item payd in reward to Peryn the kyng*es* Bereward   iiij s.
Item payd & spent at the fflower de lyce vppon *Master* Mayer of
Dovorr & dyu*er*se other honest men of the same Town byfore the
tyme of ye pley   iiij d.
…   35

Burghmote Court Minutes   CCA: CC/AC 1
f 103v   *(20 December)*

…

wayt*es*   *Memorandum* that at this Court of Bourmote yt was fully agreed & pr*o*mysed 40

32–3/ *Master* Mayer of Dovorr: *Thomas Foxley*

by the hole Court that the Wayt*es* of the Citie should haue lyverays of the
Citie the next yere aft*er* this/ as they were wont to haue &c

...

1542–3   5
City Chamberlains' Accounts   CCA: CC/FA 13
f 185v

...

Recepc*iones*
fin*ium*
Tauror*um*

¶ It*em* receyved of Iohn Iamys for a fyne of a Bull by hym sleyn and not
Bayted at the Bulstake   xij d.   10
It*em* receyved of Iohn wythyer for a fyne of a bull by hym sleyn &
not bayted   xij d.

Su*m*ma ij s.

f 186v*   *(Casual receipts)*   15

...

It*em* receyved of henry Gere of the money that remayned in his
hand*es* vppon his accompt at the ende of the play [th] in M*aste*r
Copyns yere in good mony and badde   xxx s.
It*em* receyved of Richard Waller vppon hys accompt the   20
same tyme   ix s. iiij d.

...

f 187

25

It*em* receyved of M*aste*r Batherst for the hole stage of the pley to
hym sold   xl s.

...

f 190v   30

Repar*aciones*
de le Bulstake

It*em* paid for makyng clene of the leed*es* ther & serchyng of the
same to Thomas hall   iiij d.

Su*m*ma iiij d.

...   35

17/ henry Gere: *common councillor; sheriff of Canterbury 1539–40*
18–19/ M*aste*r Copyns yere: *William Copyn, mayor 1541–2*
20/ Richard Waller: *commoner*
26/ M*aste*r Batherst: *Thomas Batherst, deputy mayor 1542–3*

f 192   *(External expenses)*

...

Item paid to Bryce Shomaker for iiij paire of Shoes for the
tormentours in the pley   ij s. viiij d.
Item paid to father William for certeyne thynges had of hym for   5
the pley at the laste pley day   v s.
Item paid to Robert Brome in full payment of certeyn stuffe by
hym bought at london for the pley   xv s.
Item gevyn to pyrryn the kynges berward in reward   v s.
...   10
Item paid to Iohn Williams for certeyn stuffe & makyng of the
clothes for the tormentours for the pley ⌈as appearith by hys bill⌉ xxiij s. iij d.

f 192v

...   15
Item paid for drynk gevyn to the pleyers at dyuers tymes in the Courthall   x d.
...

f 193

...   20
Item gevyn to the kynges pleyers in reward   iiij s.
Item gevyn to my lord Wardens pleyers pleying in the Courthall   iij s. iiij d.
Item gevyn in reward to the kynges mynstrelles   vj s. viij d.

f 193v   25

...

Item paid to Master lewys due to hym of the mony of the pley   xij d.
...

f 201v   *(Mayor's wages and officers' livery)*   30

...

Item paid for x yardes of theseid Cloth gevyn to the waytes of
the Citie for their lyuereys this yere   xxxiij s. iiij d.
...

                                                                                    35

f 205   *(Final allowances)*

...

Item of viij s. which was of evill mony gathered of the pleys
⌈which was nought⌉   viij s.
...   40

7/ Robert Brome: *common councillor; deputy mayor 1541-2*
27/ Master lewys: *Robert Lewys, alderman; mayor 1529-30, 1536-7, 1540-1*

Item of ij s. viij d. spent at the sonne vppon Master pacche &
Master wyngfeld for ther benyvolence shewed to the Citie
concernyng the Cities pley   ij s. viij d.

...

                                                                                  5

Burghmote Court Minutes   CCA: CC/AC 2
f 1v   *(11 September)*

...

Item at this Court was bought a mitre of mr Robert lewes for xxx s. whiche
money was had out of the boxe xiiij s. and the rest was had out of the play   10
money &c

1543–4
City Chamberlains' Accounts   CCA: CC/FA 13
f 220*   *(Admission of freemen)*   15

...

Item the xxiiijth day of aprill in the xxxvjth yere of the reigne of our
wode   seid souereigne lord kyng henry the viijth Thomas wode of Caunterbury
Syngyng man was admytted and sworne to the liberties of the seid Citie
for the whych he paid nothyng because it was gevyn hym by Bourmote   nil 20

...

f 225v

...

Recepciones   ¶ Item receyved of Iohn Corser Bocher for a fyne of a bull by hym sleyn   25
finium   and not bayted at the Bulstake   xij d.
Taurorum   Item receyved of Iohn wydyer bocher for a fyne of a bull by hym sleyn
              and not bayted   xij d.
              Item receyved of Iohn Iamys for a fyne of a Bull by hym sleyn and not
              Bayted   xij d. 30
              Item receyved of Iamys Draper Bocher for a fyne of a Bull by hym sleyn
              and not Bayted   xij d.
                          Summa iiij s.

f 236   *(External expenses)*   35

...

Item paid to the kynges Berward in reward ouer and besides the
benyvolens of Master Mayre and his Brethern   iiij s.

...

1/ Master pacche: *Thomas Patche, MP for Sandwich 1539, 1547, 1553*
2/ Master wyngfeld: *Thomas Wingfield, MP for Sandwich 1529, 1536*

Item paid to my lord Daubnes bereward in reward   ij s.

Item paid to Master Tresurers pleyars in rewarde   ij s.

...

Item gevyn to my lord wardens Mynstrell*es* in reward   xvj d.

Item gevyn to the quenys pleyars in reward   v s.   5

Item gevyn to the pryncys pleyers in reward   v s.

...

f 236v*

...   10

Item gevyn in reward to the mynstrell*es* of leyceter   viij d.

...

+   Item gevyn to the kyng*es* fotemen in reward   viij s.

Item gevyn to the kyng*es* Trompettours   viij s.

Item paid for the hire of a hors to send to the Co*ur*t to knowe   15

the kyng*es* plesure whether he wold come thorowe the towne

or nay   xvj d.

...

f 237v   20

...

Item paid to my lord of Norfolk*es* Trompetto*ur* at Master

Mayres   iij s. iiij d.

...

                                                                                        25

f 244v   *(Mayor's wages and officers' livery)*

Item paid for x yard*es* of theseid Cloth gevyn to the Comen

wayt*es* of the Citie for their lyu*er*eys this yere   xxxiij s. iiij d.

...   30

Burghmote Court Minutes   CCA: CC/AC 2

f 5v   *(26 February)*

...

m*emorandum* at the seyd Court of Boroughmote it was agreed that the   35

wayt*es* of the seyd Citie for the tyme beyng shall haue all suche lyb*er*ties as

heretofore hath ben vsed & accustomed

...

1/ Daubnes: D *written over another letter (?)*

1544–5
City Chamberlains' Accounts CCA: CC/FA 13
f 260 *(Admission of freemen)*

…

Bryggeman

Item the iij^the day of October and yere aboueseid Robert Bryggeman 5
of Caunterbury Mynstrell was admytted and sworne to the liberties of
the seid Citie for the which he paid x s. wherof the seid Chamberleyn
yeldyth accomptes x s.

…

10

f 269

…

Recepciones ¶ Item receyved of Iohn hobbys for a fyne of a Bull by hym sleyn and
finium not bayted at the Bulstake xij d.
Taurorum Item receyved of Iohn Iamys for a fyne of a Bull by hym sleyn and not 15
Bayted xij d.
Item receyved of Iohn kyngesdowne for a fyne of ij bulles by hym sleyn
and not bayted ij s.
Summa iiij s.

20

f 270 *(Casual receipts)*

Item receyved of the waytes for a fyne of two straungers offendyng
the statutes of their corporacion xvj d.

… 25

f 275v *(External expenses)*
…
Item paid in reward to pyryn the kynges Bereward v s.
… 30
Item gevyn in reward to the kynges lester ij s. viij d.
…
Item gevyn in reward to the pryncys pleyers iiij s.

f 282v *(Mayor's wages and officers' livery)* 35
…
Item paid for x yardes of theseid Cloth gevyn to the Comen
waytes of theseid Citie for their lyuereys this yere xxxiij s. iiij d.
…

13/ hobbys: h *written over* B

St Andrew's Churchwardens' Accounts   CCA: U3/5/4/1
f 114   *(Casual receipts)*

…

Item Received at hoctyd gadaryd as well be ye men as the women   viij s. j d.

…   5

Minstrels' Guild Deed of Incorporation   CCA: CC/Woodruff's List LIV/20
single sheet*

Be yt knowen to all Men by thys presentes that we Iohn alcok Maire of the Cytye   10
of Canterbury and the aldermen of the sayd Cytie by vertue of the letteres
patentes of the progenytours of our souereigne lord the kyng to vs granted and
of an estatuyt Made concernyng the liberties & privileges of the seyd Cytye doo
orden in maner & fourme folowyng that is to say ffyrst we orden that all waytes
and mynstrelles that nowe doo inhabyte or hereafter shall inhabyte in the sayd   15
Cytye or the suburbis of the same Cytie shalbe one ffelowshyp and called by
the name of the ffelowshyp of the Craft & mystery of Mynstrelles & so shall
conteynewe frome hensforth foreuer also we orden that yt shall not be laufull to
any ffreman vsyng or exercisyng the Craft or Mystery of mynstrelles to Ioyn them
silfes to any foren mynstrell to thentent to occupye there Instrumentes within   20
the sayd Cytye or lyberties of the same except he be hys apprentice vppon payn
to forfett for euery suche default vj s. viij d. also we orden that it shall not be
laufull to no freman vsyng or practysyng the seyd Craft or mystery of Mynstrelles
in no Dedycacion within the seyd Cityе to prevent the Waytes in any alderman
or comen counsellours house vppon payn to forfett for euery suche default iij s.   25
iiij d. also we orden that yt shall not be laufull to any ffreman vsyng or practysyng
the seyd Craft or mystery of mynstrelles to take any May game Garland Chyldale
or Weddyng out of an other ffreman hand vppon payn to forfett for euery suche
default iij s. iiij d. also we orden that yt shall not be laufull to any foren Mynstrell
to take any suche Weddynges Dedycacions Maye games or garlondes from any   30
freman vsyng or practysyng the seyd Craft or mystery of Mynstrelles within the
seyd Citie vppon payn to forfett for euery such default vj s. viij d. also we orden
that no man of the seyd mystery shall tak any apprentice for no lesse tyme then
seven yeres vppon payne to forfet for euery yere lackyng of vij yeres xx s. and that
euery master takyng apprentice within the seyd Cytie shall within xij monethes   35
& a day next after the takyng of the apprentice Inroll the Indentures &
Couenantes concernyng hys apprentishyp in the comen Chamber of the seyd
Cytye vppon payne to forfett vj s. viij d. also we orden frome hensforth that

Collation with CCA: CC/Woodruff's List LIV/18 *(B)*:   20 foren] forener *B*   23 mystery]
Mynstery *B*   28 an] any *B*   31 mystery] Mynstery *B*   33 mystery] Mynstery *B*

4/ hoctyd: *13–14 April*

any personne of the foresayd mystery shall not take any Iournyman into hys
seruyce but he to be of the age of xviij yeres or eles to be seasyd for one holle yere
vppon payne to forfett for euery suche default vj s. viij d. also we orden that yf
any that haue ben apprentice in the seyd Cytie for the time of vij yeres or More
be dysposid to abyde within the seyd Citie and occupie wyll pay to hys felowshyp   5
at thend of hys apprentishod vj s. viij d. that then he shalbe admytted to be ffree
of the seyd Mystery & felowshyp that he was apprentice of also we orden that yf
any of the seyd ⌈Craft⌉ or Mystery of Mynstrelles from hensforth doo entyce any
other mannes seruant Iournyman or apprentice beyng of the seyd Cytye orelles
where to lose and forfett for euery suche default xl s. also we orden that from   10
hensforth yt shall not be laufull to any personne or personnes of the seyd Craft or
mystery of Mynstrelles to play of any Instrument on the Sonday in tyme of Masse
or evynsong in any Inne Tavern or any other place Except it be at a weddyng or
a place where he ys hyred or at the Comaundement of Master Mayre of thys Citie
for the tyme beyng or any other wurshypfull man and also except yt be a freman   15
syttyng at hys owen house to tune hys instrument or a foren Mynstrell syttyng
at hys ostes house tunyng his Instrument vppon payne to forfett for euery tyme
doyng the contrary iij s. iiij d. also we orden that yf any of the seyd Craft or
mystery at any tyme hereafter in sport or in malice doo call one a nother knave
or any other vyle wordes then euery personne of the seyd Craft or Mystery so   20
offendyng shall lose & forfett for euery tyme that he shall so offend xij d. also we
orden that yf any foren Mynstrell resortyng thys Cytye shall offend in any of the
articles herein comprysed after that they shalbe warned by the waytes of the seyd
Citie after what wayes they shalle haue them sylfes that then they & euery of them
shall suffer suche penaltye as ys before expressyd accordyng to the quantetye of   25
there offensys also we orden that yf any Mynstrelles yea though[t] the be ffree
admytted with the waytes of thys Cytie to be in any Inne or other place within
the seyd Cytye wher any noble man shall repayre and they not hauyng entred or
begone to play that then they shall geve place to the waytes of thys Cytie and
shall not excercise any melody tyll they haue begon or otherwyse haue leve of   30
them vppon payne to forfett for dysobedyens or contrary doyng for euery tyme
nota   vj s. viij d. provyded always that nothyng in thys ordynance before rehersyd shalbe
at any tyme hereafter any thyng preiudiciall or hurfull to any of the kynges
Mynstrelles the queenes my lord princes or any honorable or wurshypfull manns
Mynstrelles of thys realme also we orden that yf yt shall fortune any personne or   35
persones freman & Inhabytauntes of the seyd Citie to hire the waytes of the seyd
Citie for any weddyng Mayegame or other suche like thynge by the space of one

Collation continued: 16 tune] tyme *B*   17 tunyng] tymyng *B*   22 resortyng]
resortyng to *B*   31 or] *B omits*   32m nota] *B omits*   33 hurfull] hurtfull *B*
37 for] of *B*

33/ hurfull: *for* hurtfull

two or thre dayes that then euery suche personne & persones that shall so
hire the waytes of the seyd Citie shall paye & geve to euery of the seyd waytes
for euery daye xij d. & nomore and yf yt fortune the seyd waytes at any tyme
hereafter be not able or refuce to serue in Manner & fourme next before
mencioned that then yt shalbe laufull to euery of the inhabitauntes of the seyd   5
nota   Cytie that shall fortune to haue any suche nede to take any other Mynstrell
mete & able for the same also we orden that all such somes of money that
shalbe forfett by any Meanes or occasion aboue sayd shalbe levyed by the comen
seriant of the seyd Citie for the tyme beyng and by suche personne as for the
tyme beyng shalbe called the Bedyll of the sayd mystery of Mynstrelles and   10
the seyd Comon seriant to haue for gatheryng of euery xij d. iiij d. and so
vpward after the ratte also we orden that yf any Manner of some of money by
any Meanys or occasyon aboue mencioned shalbe forfetted that the one half
therof shalbe to thuse of the Maire & Comynaltye of thesayd Citie for &
toward the comen Charges of the seyd Citie & the other half therof to thuse   15
of the felowshyp of the seyd Craft or mystery and also that the wardens &
masters of the seyd Craft or mystery shall within xv dayes next after any somme
of money forfetted by Meanes or occacion abouesayd make certificat therof to
the Maire & Chamberlyen of the seyd Citie for the tyme beyng vppon payne
of forfettyng to the comen Chamber of the seyd Citie for euery tyme duryng   20
the contrary xx s. provided always that yf yt shall happen any master wardens
or other personne or persones beyng in thys ffelowshyp or in any other that
will take vppon hym to adde subtra or ther to enfrynge any thyng in thys boke
conteyned or in any other liberties given by the kyng to the maire & aldermen
of the seyd Citie Then the seyd partie or parties so doyng shall forfett to the   25
Chamber xl s. and these contentes to stand in as muche power & effect as they
dyde before foreuer Provided also that thys boke or any thyng therin conteyned
shall not be at any tyme hereafter any thyng preiudiccyall or hurtfull to the
Maire & other hys bretheren & there successours nor agenst the Comen welth
in any act or graunt heretofore made & graunted by the kyng our souereigne   30
lord & hys progenytours.

Drapers' and Tailors' Memoranda Book   CCA: U12/A1
ff 1v–2*   (Rendered 25 October)

...   35

The Chardges of the dynner for the sayd ffelowshippe expended

Collation continued: 6m nota] *B omits*   13 that] that then *B*   18 by] by any *B*
20 duryng] doyng *B*   22 or other] or any other *B*   23 adde subtra] adde or
subtra *B*

20/ duryng: *for* doyng

and layde out by me the sayde henry geyre in the xxxvij^{th}
yere of our sayde Soueraigne Lord the kinges reigne |

ffyrst A vessell of beere	xix d.
Item iij gallons of Ale	iij d.
Item iiij^{or} Geese	iij s. iiij d. 5
Item iiij^{or} Pygges	iij s. viij d.
Item iiij^{or} Capons	iiij s.
Item Pygeons	xvj d.
Item in Bochery meate	v s. iiij d.
Item Suett for Pyes v li.	v d. 10
Item fflowre a tolvett	xvj d.
Item Butter for basting and egges for the past	vj d.
Item mylke and wheat	xij d.
Item Suger	ij d.
Item Mustard salt and sawce	iij d. 15
Item Saffron	ij d.
Item half a loode of Woode	xij d.
Item great Raysinges ij li.	viij d.
Item small Raysinges ij li.	vj d.
Item Prunes iiij li.	x d. 20
Item ij dosen and a half of bread	ij s. vj d.
Item Cloves and mace iij^e ounces	xv[j] d.
Item Pepper two ounces	iiij d.
Item Malmesey a quarte	iiij d.
Item to the Mynstrelles	iiij d. 25
Item Peeres	viij d.
Item to the Cooke	ij s. iiij d.
Item to Danyell for cleaving of woode and the next day for	
turnyng the Spytt	vj d.
Item to A Woman	iiij d. 30
Item to a woman cooke for scalding	vj d.

...

Receiptes the same yere by the sayde Henry geyre
of certayn of the occupacion and other beinge at
the saide Dynner whose names folowe. 35

ffyrst of the sayde mr ffreman	viij d.
Item of mr Thompson	viij d.
Item of Iohn Wydoppe	vj d.
Item of Nicholas ffyshe	vj d.
Item of Iohn Cawell	vj d. 40

36/ mr ffreman: *John Freeman, alderman; mayor 1543–4; master of Drapers' and Tailors' Company*
39/ Nicholas ffyshe: *commoner*

Item of Iohn yemans   vj d.
Item of Iohn Richardson in Saynct Margaretes parishe   vj d.
Item of Thomas Walker   vj d.
Item of Christopher Scotte   vj d.
Item of henry Harte   vj d.   5
Item of william Watson   vj d.l
Item of Roger ffowler   vj d.
Item of Iohn Steward   vj d.
Item of Iohn Brompson   vj d.
Item of Iohn ffrenche   *(blank)* 10
Item of george Geffrey   *(blank)*
Item of Iohn yonge drap*er*   vj d.
Item of the Skynner   vj d.
Item of Iohn yonge taylor   vj d.
Item of two Taylors in wynchepe   xij d. 15
Item of Iohn walker   iiij d.
Item of Thomas Applegate   vj d.
Item of Iohn Richardson   vj d.
Item of Roger Litlewoode   *(blank)*
Item of Iohn Molte   *(blank)* 20
Item of Angell Elyng   vj d.
Item of Iohn Nightingale   vj d.
Item of Iohn Copper   vj d.
Item of Bonaventure Rydar   vj d.
Item of humfrey Dunkyn   vj d.   25
Item of william Swetyng   vj d.
Item of william Geyre   vj d.
Item of Eustace ffrencham   *(blank)*
Item of Robert Byckerstaf   vj d.
Item of Robert Reade   vj d.   30
Item of Roger Colbrand   vj d.
Item of Robert Collens   vj d.
    The whole su*mm*e of the Receipt*es* for the dynn*er*   xvj s. viij d.
...

35

1545–6
Burghmote Court Minutes   CCA: CC/AC 2
f 25v   *(26 January)*
...

M*emorandum* at the seid Court of burmote it was enacted ordeyned and   40
establysshed by the assent of the hole court of burmotte that all & eu*er*y suche
wait*es* & mynstrell*es* ffremen wi*th*in theseid Citye ffrom hensforth shall be

of the ffelowshype of Barbours & Surgions and so shall contynewe from
hensforth for euer/ and also that theseyd Mynstrelles shall be at the direccion
[of] and stand at the Controlment of the Master of Barbours & Surgeons &c/
...

5

St Andrew's Churchwardens' Accounts CCA: U3/5/4/1
f 118v* (Casual receipts)
...

Item Received at hoctyd as well be ye men as be the women   vij s. j d.
...

10

St Dunstan's Churchwardens' Accounts CCA: U3/141/5/1
p 19*
...

Item Recevyd of the wyvys yat they did gather at hoktyd   iij s. ix d. 15
...

1546–7
City Chamberlains' Accounts CCA: CC/FA 14
f 10v (Admission of freemen)

20

Item the xxixth day of Ianuary in theseid yere Peter Nycols of
Caunterbury wayte was admytted and sworne to the liberties

Nycols   of the seid Citie for the which he paid xiij s. iiij d. wherof the
seid Chamberleyn yeldyth accomptes   xiij s. iiij d. 25
...

f 17v

Recepciones   Item receyved of Richard day for a fyne of ij bulles by hym sleyn and   30
finium   not bayted at the Bulstake euery of them vj d. summa   xij d.
Taurorum   Item receyved of austyn Coke for the fynes of v Bulles by hym sleyn
              and not Bayted   ij s. vj d.
              Item receyved of Thomas wythyer for a fyne of one bull by hym sleyn
              and not Bayted   vj d. 35
              Item receyved of Iohn kyngesdowne for a fyne of ij bulles by hym sleyn
              and not bayted   xij d.
              Item receyved of Thomas Ongley for a fyne of ij bulles by hym sleyn
              and not bayted   xij d.
                                        Summa vj s.   40

9, 15/ hoctyd, hoktyd: 3–4 May

f 22

Reparacions of
the Bulstake

Item paid to the plomer for serchyng and makyng clene the leedes
and gutters therof   viij d.

Summa viij d.   5
...

f 25*   (External expenses)
...

Item gevyn in reward to the prynces pleyers at the Cheker pleying   10
before Master Mayre & his brethern   v s.
...

Item gevyn in reward to the kynges pleyers pleying at the Courthall
before Master Mayre & his brethern   vj s. viij d.
...   15

f 25v
...

Item gevyn in rewarde to the kynges Berward   iiij s.
...   20
Item gevyn in rewarde to the kynges Iestour   ij s.
...

f 31v   (Chamberlain's payments for mayoral charges)
...   25
Item paid for x yardes of the seid cloth gevyn to the Comen
waytes of the seid Citie for their lyuerey this yere   xxxiij s. iiij d.
...

St Andrew's Churchwardens' Accounts   CCA: U3/5/4/1   30
f 124v   (Casual receipts)
...

Item receuyd of money gatheryd at hoktyde at the suppr in the
Corne markett   viij s. viij d.
...   35

1547–8
City Chamberlains' Accounts   CCA: CC/FA 14
f 58

Recepciones
finium
Taurorum   40

Item receyved of Iohn Molde Bocher for a fyne of a Bull   vj d.

11, 14/ Mayre: *Thomas Batherst*   33/ hoktyde: *18–19 April*

Item rec*eyved* of willi*a*m Clerk for one bull vj d.
Item rec*eyved* of Thomas Ongley Bocher for ij bulls xij d.
Item rec*eyved* of Iohn kynge*s*down for iiij bull*es* [xviij d.] ij s.
Item rec*eyved* of Iohn Iamys for j bull vj d.
item rec*eyved* of Iohn wydyer for j bull vj d. 5
Item rec*eyved* of willi*a*m Capon for j bull vj d.
      Sum*m*a v s. vj d.

f 65

10

Reparaci*on*s of   Item paid to a Carpenter for makyng of dyu*er*se fourmes for the
the Bulstake   m*a*rkett folk*es* to sett on   xiiij d.
      Sum*m*a xiiij d.
...

15

f 67* (External expenses)
...
Item gevyn in reward to the kynge*s* Berward   iij s. iiij d.
...
Item paid to my lord prot*ec*to*ur*s pleyers playing in the 20
Courth*a*ll   iij s. viij d.
...
Item gevyn to [thenquest] in reward to *th*e kynge*s* Iester   iij s. iiij d.

f 67v

25

...
Item paid in reward to the kynge*s* pleyers   vj s. viij d.
...

f 68

30

...
Item gevyn in rewarde to the duchesse of Suffolk*es* pleyer*s*   ij s.
...

f 74v (Chamberlain's payments for mayoral charges)

35

...
Item payd for x yard*es* of theseid cloth gevyn to the Comen
Wayt*es* of theseid Citie for their lyu*er*eys this yere   xxxiij s. iiij d.
...

1548–9
City Chamberlains' Accounts   CCA: CC/FA 14
f 104

Recepciones
finium
Taurorum

ffirst receyved for a fyne of [a] ⌈iij⌉ bulles of austyn Coke bocher   xviij d.   5
Item receyved of Iohn kyngesdowne for iiij bulles   ij s.
Item receyved of Iohn wydyer for ij bulles   xij d.
Item receyved of william Capon for ij bulles   xij d.
                              Summa v s. vj d.

...   10

f 109

...

Reparaciones
de le Bulstake

Item payd for v li. of sawder spent ther   xx d.
[Item paid to the plomer for a days work ther   x d.] 15
                              Summa xx d.

f 113v   *(External expenses)*
...
Item gevyn in reward to my lord protectours mynstrelles   iij s. iiij d. 20
...

f 114*
...
Item gevyn in reward to my lord protectours pleyers pleyng in the   25
Courthall ouer and besydes the benevolens of the people   iij s. viij d.
...

f 120v   *(Chamberlain's payments for mayoral charges)*
...   30
Item payd for x yardes of the seid cloth gevyn to the Comen
waytes of theseid Citie for their lyuereys this yere   xxxiij s. iiij d.
...

1549–50   35
City Chamberlains' Accounts   CCA: CC/FA 14
f 148

Recepciones
finium
Taurorum

¶ Item receyved of william Capon for a fyne of iij bulles by hym
sleyn and not bayted   xviij d. 40
Item receyved of Iohn wydyer for ij bulles   xij d.

Item rec*eyved* of austyn Coke for ij bull*es*   xij d.
Item rec*eyved* of Iohn kyng*es*downe for iij bull*es*   xviij d.
Item rec*eyved* of Thomas Ongley for ij bull*es*   xij d.
Item rec*eyved* of Gylbert Bland for one bull   vj d.
Item rec*eyved* of Iohn Kyng*es*downe for iij bull*es*   xviij d. 5
                    Su*m*ma viij s.

...

f 152v

...   10

Reparaciones   Item paid for sawyng of a rayle for the bulstake & the post*es*   xiiij d.
de le Bulstake Item paid to the Carpenter & hys man for settyng of theseid Rayle
                 & post by grete   xx d.
                 Item paid for makyng of the hole for the post   iiij d.
                 Item paid to paule Rychemond for xvj fote of tymber for the same   ij s. 15
                    Su*m*ma v s. ij d.

f 156   *(External expenses)*
...
Item gevyn in reward to my lord of huntyngdons mynstrell*es*   xx d. 20
...

f 156v

...
Item gevyn in reward to the King*es* Iester   xx d. 25
Item gevyn in rewarde to *sir* George Som*er*sett*es* pleyers   xx d.
...

f 157
...   30
Item gevyn in reward to the dewke of suffolk*es* mynstrell*es*   xx d.
...
Item gevyn in rewarde to the wayt*es* of lyncoln   xij d.

                                                                                35

f 163v   *(Chamberlain's payments for mayoral charges)*
...
Item payd for x yard*es* of the seid cloth gevyn to the Comen
wayt*es* of the seid Citie for their lyu*er*eys this yere   xxxiij s. iiij d.
...   40

1550–1
City Chamberlains' Accounts   CCA: CC/FA 14
f 189v

Recepciones
finium
Taurorum

Item receyved of william Capon for a fyne of iij bulles by hym sleyn   5
and not bayted at the Bulstake euery of them vj d. summa   xviij d.
Item receyved of austyn Coke Bocher for iij bulles   xviij d.
Item receyved of Iohn Kyngesdowne for v bulles   ij s. vj d.
Item receyved of Gylbert Bland for j bull   vj d.
            Summa vj s.   10

...

f 194v

...

Reparaciones
de le Bulstake

Item paid to Robert pavyer for mendyng the pament abowt the Bulryng   xiiij d.   15
            Summa xiiij d.

f 197v*   (External expenses)

...

Item gevyn in reward to the kynges pleyers   x s.   20

...

Item gevyn in reward to my lord of Rochefordes pleyers   xx d.

...

Item gevyn in reward to my lord wardens Mynstrelles   xij d.
...   25

f 198

...

Item gevyn in reward to the waytes of lyn   xviij d.
...   30

f 204v   (Chamberlain's payments for mayoral charges)
...

Item paid for x yardes of the seid cloth, gevyn to the Comen
waytes of the seid Citie for their lyuerey this yere   xxxiij s. iiij d.   35
...

1551–2
City Chamberlains' Accounts   CCA: CC/FA 14
f 229   40

Recepciones
finium
Taurorum

¶ Item receyved of william Capon for a fyne of one bull by hym
sleyn & nott bayted at the Bulstake   vj d.

Item rec*eyved* of Iohn Iamys for ij bull*es*   xij d.
Item rec*eyved* of Iohn Kyngysdowne for one bull   vj d.
Item rec*eyved* of Iohn Beynton for one bull   vj d.
Item rec*eyved* of Iohn wythyer for one bull   vj d.
Item rec*eyved* of will*i*am Dalton for one bull   vj d.   5
Item rec*eyved* of Gylbert Bland for one bull   vj d.

Summa iiij s.

…

f 235v   *(External expenses)*   10

…

Item paied in reward to the kyng*es* bererard   vj s. viij d.

…

Item gevyn [to] in reward to my lorde wardens Mynstrell*es*   iij s. iiij d.

…   15

f 242v   *(Chamberlain's payments for mayoral charges)*

…

Item paied for x yard*es* of the seid Cloth gevyn to the Comen
Wayt*es* of the seid Citie for their lyu*er*y this yere   xxxiij s. iiij d.   20

…

1553–4
City Chamberlains' Accounts   CCA: CC/FA 15
f 19v   25

Recepciones | ¶ Item rec*eyved* of austen Cooke for a fyne of ij bull*es* by hym slayn
fin*ium* | & not bayted at the bulstake   xij d.
tauror*um*

Item rec*eyved* of Gilbert Bland for one bull   vj d.
Item rec*eyved* of Iohn wythyer the yong*er* for ij bull*es*   xij d.   30
Item rec*eyved* of Iohn kyngysdowne for ij bull*es*   xij d.
Item rec*eyved* of will*i*am Capon for ij bull*es*   xij d.
Item rec*eyved* of Iohn wythyer thelder for ∧⌈one⌉ [ij] bull[*es*]   [x] vj d.

Summa v s.

…   35

f 26v

…

Reparaciones | Item payed to Stevyn Redbo*ur*ne for Sowderyng & mendyng the
de le Bulstake | Crosse at the Bulstake   ij s.   40

Summa ij s.

ff 31–1v   *(External expenses)*

...

Item payed to Danyel pottier Smyth for vj li. of gun*n*powder
& for di. vessell of bere for the guners to drynk at the watche   vj s. viij d.

Item payd to peter hacneyman for fetchyng of c*er*teyn pyk*es*   5
at Syttyngbo*ur*ne of M*r* Rychard Monyng*es* for the watche   ij s. viij d.

Item payd for [fetchyng of xx pyk*es*] a newe Cressett for
the watche   ij s. iiij d.

Item payd for ij torches for the seid watche   ij s. viij d.

Item payd for lyght*es* for the seid Cressett   viij d.   10

Item payd to Raffe albryght for the hyre of Syx horses to bere the
⌈iij⌉ Charyott*es* in the watche & for lyght*es* for them & for their
labo*ur*s y*at* sett them fourth   iiij s.

Item gevyn to my lord wardens trompet*er* & M*r* Monyng*es*
trompet*er* of the Castell of Dovorr for their reward blowyng   15
in the watche   x s.

...

Item gevyn to S*ir* will*i*am walgraves mynstrell*es* beyng one
of the Counsell in reward   [xx d.] xviij d.|

Item payd to Thomas yomans Cappar & to Thomas Dyxson   20
Cappar for lendyng of c*er*teyn Cappes for the pykemen in the
watche & for one that was lost   xx d.

Item payd to Thomas Brymstone for a yelowe Cote that was
lost in the watche   iiij s.

Item gevyn in reward to M*r* Spylmans ser*u*ante for bearyng   25
of the Cities flag   viij d.

...

Item gevyn [to] in reward to my lord Russell*es* mynstrell*es*   xx d.

Item payd to M*r* lovelas for borowyng of certeyn vysers &
Coot*es* at london for the watche & for y*at* ij of the vysers   30
were broken   xiij s. iiij d.

Item payd to will*i*am Iohnson paynt*er* for payntyng of c*er*teyn
vysers & hatt*es*   ij s.

...

Item payd to ij labourers for fetchyng of c*er*teyn stuffe as app*ar*ell &   35
harnes from M*aste*r Iustyce hales   viij d.

Item for mendyng of the Cities dru*m*me & settyng in of ij newe
hedd*es* & for his paynes that playd vpon it in the watche   ij s.

20/ Thomas Dyxson: *capper, freeman from 1550*
29/ M*r* lovelas: *William Lovelace, gentleman, freeman from 1555*
36/ M*aste*r Iustyce hales: *Sir James Hales, justice of the court of Common Pleas*

f 32

...

Item payd to ij men for bearyng of ij Cressettes in the watche viij d.

...

Item gevyn in reward to my lord wardens mynstrelles iij s. iiij d. 5

...

f 32v

...

Item payed to certeyn Mynstrelles ⌈of my lord wentforth⌉ at 10
Master Mayors commaundement xx d.

...

f 38v *(Chamberlain's payments for mayoral charges)*

... 15

Item payed for x yardes of the said Cloth gevyn to the Comen
waytes of the seid Citie for their lyuery this yere xxxiij s. iiij d.

...

1554–5 20
City Chamberlains' Accounts CCA: CC/FA 15
f 69

...

Recepciones ¶ Item receyved of Iohn Redy bocher for a fyne of a bull by hym slayne
finium & not bayted at the bulstake vj d. 25
taurorum Item receyved of Iohn kyngysdowne bocher for [one] ⌈ij⌉ bulles xij d.
  Item receyved of austyn Cooke bocher for one bull vj d.
  Item receyved of Iohn wythyer senior bocher for one bull vj d.
  Item receyved of a straunge bocher for one bull vj d.
     Summa iiij s. 30

...

f 76 *(External expenses)*

...

Item gevyn in reward to my lord wardens Mynstrelles iij s. iiij d. 35

...

f 76v

...

Item gevyn to a trumpeter that blewe in the watche before the 40
horsemen xx d.

Item payed for a newe Cressett & for lyghtes for ij Cressettes &
bearyng of them in the watche   iiij s. vj d.

…

Item gevyn to one that played vpon a drumme of the Cities in
the watche   viij d.   5

Item payed for ix li. of gunne powder ayenst the watche & gevyn
besyde to the gunners to drynk at the appoyntment of Master
Mayer [price] xviij d. & price the li. of gunne powder xij d.   x s. vj d.

…

Item gevyn in reward to the kyng & the quenys Iesters   ij s.   10

…

f 77

…

Item payed the makyng Cleane & oylyng of xiiij payre of harneys   15
[aft] & mendyng the buckelles & lethers after the watche   ij s. j d.

…

f 77v

                                                                                     20

Seynt Thomas   Item payed for xxiiij^{ti} elles of Canvas and iij quarteres at vj d. ob.
pagent in the   the ell   xij s. vj d.
watche   Item for xij dossen of Goldfoyle   iiij s.
                 Item for buccles for the knyghtes harnys   xij d.
                 Item for lether[s] to make the seid harneys   xviij d. 25
                 Item for a payer of newe wheles the yex & the makyng of the
                 Carte & for Clowtes of yron for the same Cart   xiij s. iiij d.
                 Item payed to Rychard Bellynger Ioyner for vij dayes work at
                 viij d. the day   iiij s. viij d.
                 Item payed to Wylson Carpynter for viij dayes work aboute   30
                 the same payent at x d. the day   vj s. viij d.
                 Item payed for nayles for the same   xj d.
                 Item payed to a turner for turnyng of vj postes & x lylly pottes   ij s.
                 Item for v li. of Candell at ij d. ob. the li.   xij d. ob.
                 Item payed for iij horse hire to cary the seid pagent   ij s. 35
                 Item payed to William Ionson paynter by grete for payentyng the
                 Cloth about the pagent & for flowers & trymmyng the same   xxv s.
                 Item payed for wyre & Cord   iiij s. ob.
                 Item for a C small nayles   ij d.
                 Item for tymber for the hole pageant for sawyng & for bordes   40
                 for the same   xvij s. viij d.
                 Item payed more to hilles for Sawyng   ij s.

Item payed for makyng of certeyn noses [for] of Canstyke*s* & for
settyng them on   vj d.
Item payed for settyng on of the buccles & trymmyng on of the
harneys for the seid knyghte*s*   xij d.
Item for makyng of a mould for to make the helmette*s* for the knyghte*s* xiiij d. 5
Item paied to ij men for bearyng of torche*s* about the same pagent   viij d.
Item paied for caryeng the same pagent aft*er* the watche to the palayce   ij d.

...

f 78*   10

...

gevyn to kyng
phylyp & to his
offycers at his
ffirst comyng to
the Citie

Item gevyn to the kyng on his ffirst comyng to Caun*ter*bury of the
money that was rec*eived* of George webbe alderman   xx li.
Item gevyn to the kynge*s* herawd*es* at armys of the benevolence of
the Citie   x s. 15
Item gevyn to the kynge*s* s*er*iaunte*s* at armys   vj s. viij d.
Item gevyn to the kynge*s* trumpeters   vj s. viij d.

...

f 83v   *(Chamberlain's payments for mayoral charges)*   20

Item payed for x yardes of the seid Cloth gevyn to the Comen
wayte*s* of the seid Citie for their lyu*er*y this yerc   xxxiij s. iiij d.

...

                                                                            25

Burghmote Court Minutes   CCA: CC/AC 2
f 93v   *(4 June)*

...

and also it is agreed that the wacche vsed to be kept on seynt Thomas
Evyn shalbe kept and sett fourth on seynt Thomas evyn now next   30
comyng

...

St Andrew's Churchwardens' Accounts   CCA: U3/5/4/1
f 134   *(Receipts)*   35

...

Item receyued at hoptide in money gathered by wemen   x s.

...

37/ hoptide: *Hocktide, 22–3 April*

Letter from Antonio Maria di Savoia to the Bishop of Arras
Wien, HHStA: England, Varia 4
ff [1–2v]*

...

il di di natale 5
1554 in cantuberi
Reverendissimo et Illustrissimo signor mio osservandissimo

...

Il signor Duca me ha detto di uoler' scriuere hoggi a Uostra Signoria Illustrissima
et che mi dara la lettera la quale uenendo sara con questa et perche soa Altezza 10
li dira della peregrination' nostra sin qui non li saro per hora molto prolisso,
ma li diro solamente, che in xx hore di passaggio da cales a doura, per il uento
contrario, se ben al partire ne fu fauoreuole, tutta la compagnia che si trouo
con predetta soa Altezza stette[ro] sempre piu morta che uiua, fuor' che il
duca, il quale non patti molto, io solo fui quei che consolaua et aiutaua tutti, 15
ne mai senti il mare, ma si ben' la fame, et il freddo. Gionti a doura trouamo
milord Uarden, qual con tanta artellaria et accoglienze gratissime receui
l'Altezza sua in nome del Re et Regina, che ci dono la uitta a tutti, et gionti
allo allogiamento combattuti dal freddo dalla fame et dal sonno, si scaldassemo,
facessemo | facemmo colatione et si dormi, doppo uista la messa, il milord 20
condusse sua Altezza con la compagnia a pranso nel castello di doura et
fu alle spese Reale. il giorno seguente che fu Heri partimmo, e gionsemo
qui et sua Altezza fu receuuta da xij. uechij uestiti di scarlato sin ai piedi
con una stola di ueluto negro [sin] al collo sin al genochio con molte sorte
de instrumenti, et cossi accompagnorno sua Altezza sin all'allogiamento, 25
et licentiatosi sua Altezza se retiro, et un'hora Doppo uenne il milord et
⌈la⌉ condusse al suo allogiamento a pranso, molto solenne, come sara quello
di hoggi ancora, pero io uoglio andar' a corte et uedere se sua Altezza ha
scritto, et poi me ne ritorno a serrare questa, ma li diro in questo mezo
che sua Altezza non partira hoggi di qua, et io me uoglio incaminare hoggi 30
inanzi accio che sua Altezza sia tanto piu commoda de caualli et con le
susseguenti mie da londra li daro ogni minuto raguaglio, et in tanto li bascio
le sacratissime manni, et prego dio che la feliciti | et conserui longamente.
datum ut supra
Doppo hauer' scritto questa ho accompagnato sua Altezza alla messa, la quale 35
de camino me disse non hauer' scritto ma che scriueria questa sera et che non
uoleua ch'io partisse, ma che lassase andar' prima i miei seruitori et che non
tenesser se non uno, et cossi ho fatto, Sua Altezza fu alla messa alla chiesa
maggiore, accompagnata dal milord, il qual portaua l'ordine grande di san
georgio, et monsignor il grande, l'ordine della toison, sua Altezza portaua 40

20/ facessemo | facemmo: facessemo *acts as catchword*

quello di san georgio con la giarettiera: nella chiesa per ordine del milord ui
haueuano fatto il dosalet serrato per sua Altezza la quale ui entro, ma non
uolse che si lassase serrato, et poi tutti gl'altri con i suoi banchi tapezzati con
cosini etc.

Si fece oratione nella messa per il Re et la Regina, et poi una oratione, che ha   5
composto il vescovo di uinceltre, perche dio dia felice parto alla Regina, et
dicono che hora si dice quella oratione in tutte le messe che se dicono in questa
isola, finita | la messa andamo col milord a disnare et si fece un solenne brindes
con tutti questi alemani conti, et hor hora andamo a caccia in un barco regio
ai daini con leureri et archibusi,   10
Il Duca non fa altro che dire in alta uoce, io sono molto amico al monsignor
d'Arras, et li sono molto obligato et uoglio che ogni homo il sapia, che sara
il fine doppo hauerli basciato un'altra uolta la mano
Di Uostra Signoria Reverendissima et Illustrissima
Humilissimo et Affettiosissimo   15
Servitore Antonio Maria di Sauoija

1555-6
Burghmote Court Minutes   CCA: CC/AC 2
ff 103v-4*   *(22 September)*   20
…

Memorandum that at this Court of Bourmote ∧⌐it⌐ is graunted and agreed
that Thomas wood of the seid Citie Mynstrell shall haue the Roome of one
of the Comen waytes of the same Citie and from hensforth shalbe one of
the waytes of the same Citie/   25
Also at the same Courte it is agreed (that not withstandyng ther is an
auncyent lawe that yerely ther shoulde be a wacche at seynt Thomas tyme/
and who that shoulde neglect or laye downe the same wacche sholde forfayte
x li./ and for asmoch as theseid wacche for dyuerse consideracions this present
yere by order of this Courte was not hadd and kept/ It is cleerly agreed and   30
concluded at | this Court of Bourmote that theseid summe of ten poundes
shall for this tyme cleerly be remytted and discharged not withstandyng
theseid act/ to [theseid] Edward Carpynter now Mayer of theseid Citie/
…

                                                                                     35
St Andrew's Churchwardens' Accounts   CCA: U3/5/4/1
f 137*   *(Receipts)*
…
Reseued att hoptyde for gadderynge   ix s. ob.
…   40

39/ hoptyde: *Hocktide, 13-14 April*

1556-7
Burghmote Court Minutes CCA: CC/AC 2
f 107v   *(6 April)*

...

         also at this Court of Bourmote it is agreed that Robert Bryggeman shalbe   5
discharged of the beyng of one of the wayt*es* of the Citie/ and that Thomas
wade and Robert alderson assocyatyng one other to them shalbe from

the wayt*es*   hensforth the wayt*es* of the Citie/ and that theseid Robert Briggeman in the
opyn Court of Bourmote hath delyu*ered* vp his iiij scochons and his bond
made for the delyu*ery* of the same to be voyd   10

...

St Andrew's Churchwardens' Accounts CCA: U3/5/4/1
f 138v   *(Receipts)*

...   15

Item Rec*eived* at hopetide for gathering   xviij s. v d.

...

Drapers' and Tailors' Memoranda Book CCA: U12/A1
f 8v*   *(Charges)*   20

...

Item p*a*yd for boles of wex and too Lytill tapers   xij d.
Item p*a*yd to the berr*e* of the torche   iiij d.
Item p*a*yd for bred and bere apon Synt peters yeven   iiij d.
Item p*a*yd for Cresset Lyght   xiiij d. 25
Item p*a*yd to the bears of the Cresset*es* and to aboye   ix d.
...
Item p*a*yd to the payntor for the torche   iiij s. iiij d.

...

                                                                   30

f 9*   *(Expenses)*

...

Item p*a*yd for gold foyle and gold pap*er*   vj d.
Item p*a*yd for nales   j d.
Item p*a*yd for [gover] govre pap*er* & vardgrese   iiij d. 35
...
Item p*a*yd to the beres of the torche   iiij d.
...
Item p*ai*d to horshe for caryng the pagent   viij d.

...   40

16/ hopetide: *Hocktide, 26-7 April*   34/ nales: *3 minims in* MS

Letter from the Privy Council to the Mayor and Aldermen
CCA: CC/Woodruff's List LII/29
single sheet*   *(27 June)*

After our hartie comendac*i*ons, we haue receuid your le*tt*res toguithers with a   5
lewde boke, plaied of late, by *pe*rsonnes of like sorte in that Cittie of Caunterbury
and other places thereaboutes, And vnderstande by your said le*tt*res your diligence
vsed in thapprehending of the plaiers and comitteng them to warde, ffor ∧⌈the⌉
w*h*ich we giue yow our verie hartie thank*es*, And praye yow to cause them to be
so kepte, and diligentlye examined who was the maker of the playe and where   10
he dwelleth w*i*th suche furder circumstances as ye shall thinke convenient, And
to signifye what ye shall lerne herein hither vnto vs, we haue taken order in the
meane tyme that the King and Quenes Ma*iestes* lerned Counsell shall consider
what the matters contained in the said lewde play boke do way vnto in lawe,
vpon thunderstanding wherof we shall furder signifye vnto yow what furder   15
order ye shall take w*i*th them, And this we bid yow hartely well to fare, ffrom
Westminster the xxvij^th of Iune 1557

Your loving frend*es*

 (signed) Nico*laus* ebor*acensis* Cance*llarius*   Winchester   20
          PENBROKE
 Anthony Mountague   Thom*a*s Elye*nsis*
 E Clynton:
 Io*h*n Bourne

                     25

The mayor of Canterbury

Letter from the Privy Council to the Mayor and Aldermen
CCA: CC/Woodruff's List LII/27
single sheet*   *(11 August)*   30

After our hartie commendac*i*ons, we haue receyved your Le*tt*res of the seconde
of this pr*e*sent, wherin ye require vs, tadvertise yow by le*tt*res, what ordre ye
shall take, w*i*th the lewde *pe*rsonnes, that played the sedic*i*ouse playe there at
Canterburye, about whitsontyde laste./ ffor aunswer wherunto, we haue thought   35
goode to signifie vnto yow, that considering, we wrote vnto yow allreadie in that
matter, and willed yow, to lerne of som*m*e men of lawe nere about yow, what
their offence wayed vnto in lawe, and to cause them therupon, be *p*roceded
w*i*thall according to iustice: we moche m*e*rvaile ye haue not so doon, or that
ye will eftsones trouble vs, ageine, w*i*th the self same matter, wherin I the Lord   40

26/ The mayor of Canterbury: *in display script*

Stuarde, also, tolde yow syns by mouthe, what was expedient to be doon,
for their punyshement./ And therfore thies be in the Kinges and Quenes
Maiestes names to require yow, in eny wise, to see our former ordre duely
executed without delaye, so as having conferred, with somme men of
knowlege theraboutes (for whiche purpose, we returne yow herewith   5
aswell the playe itself, as the players examinacions) ye cause them to be
proceded withall according to their desertes./ And thus ffare ye well ffrom
Richemound, this xjᵗʰ of August 1557.

Your lovinge frendes,

10

(signed) Nicolaus eboracensis Cancellarius   Arundell
                                                    Thomas Elyensis
Iohn Mason   Richard Southwell

Post scriptum:/ The booke of the playe, semeth vnto vs very   15
     sediciouse, and therfore we thinke, the parties are to be
     punyshed as persons that sette furthe sedicion./

The Maiour & Aldremen of Canterburye./

20

1557–8
City Chamberlains' Accounts   CCA: CC/FA 16
f 21

Recepciones   Item Recevyd of Iohn wyt bwtcher ffo ye ffyen of one Bwll by hym   25
finium   slayn & nott baytyd at ye Bwllstake   vj d.
Taurorum   Item Recevyd off Iohn wytt/ more ffor jᵒ bull by hym slayne & not
                baytyd at the Bwllstake   vj d.
                               Summa xij d.
                ...   30

f 30*   (External expenses)
...
Item payd ffor a Cowrtt To Carry iij harlottes abowtt the town   vj d.
Item payd to hym yat Carryd ye basson   j d. 35
Item payd to ye paynter ffor wrytynge off iij papers   vj d.
...

19/ The Maiour & Aldremen of Canterburye: in display script
25/ ffo: for ffor

f 30v

...

Item p*a*yd ffor a Cowrtt to Carry iij harlott*es* abowt ye towne &
to a pore ma*n* y*at* Carryd the basson   vij d.

... 5

f 31

...

Item p*a*yd so mvtche yevyn to ye erle off oxffor*des* players at
M*aster* mayers Com*m*and*m*entt   iij s. iiij d. 10

...

f 32

...

Item yevyn To ye qwenes trw*m*pyt*eres*   vj s. viij d. 15

...

f 32v

...

Item yevyn to my lord wardyns mynstrell*es* at ye Com*m*andmen*t* 20
off M*aster* mayer   iij s. iiij d.

...

f 33

... 25

Item p*a*id more to M*r* ffuller by Co*n*sentt off burmvthe ffor
so mvtche layd owt by hym to ye Kyng*es* trwmpyt*eres*   vj s. viij d.

...

St Andrew's Churchwardens' Accounts   CCA: U3/5/4/1 30
f 140   *(Receipts)*

...

It*em* reseyved for gatheryng at hoptide   xv s.

...

35

St Dunstan's Churchwardens' Accounts   CCA: U3/141/5/3
p 14   *(8 August–8 August)*

...

Item of the wyef*es* of the p*a*rishe in Money Gatheryd at
hoptydd last past   vij s. vj d. 40

...

33/ hoptide: *Hocktide, 18–19 April*   40/ hoptydd last past: *Hocktide, 18–19 April*

1558–9
City Chamberlains' Accounts   CCA: CC/FA 16
f 67

Recepc*iones* fin*ium* Tauror*um*	¶ Item R*ecevy*d off Iohn wytt Bwtcher ffor *ye* ffyene off one bull slayn & not baytyd	vj d.	5

Su*m*ma vj d.

...

f 71v   10

...

Rep*ara*ciones de Le bwllstake	¶ Item paid to Stevyn Redborne ffor vj li. off Sawder & ffor his workyng there w*i*th his *ser*vant	iij s.

Su*m*ma
3 s. } iij s.   15

...

f 75   *(External expenses)*

...

Item gevyn to ye qwenes players playng at ye Town hawll at mast*er*   20
mayers Com*m*a*n*dyme*n*t   x s.

...

Item p*a*yd for ij pap*er*s payntyd ffor one y*at* Spaeke sedyssyws word*es*   iiij d.
Item gyvyn to one y*at* Range ye basson beffore hym   ij d.
    25

f 75v

...

Item gyvyn to one y*at* Range ye basson beffore *ser* Loye   ij d.

...
    30

f 82   *(Chamberlain's payments for mayoral charges)*

...

Item paid ffor viij yard*es* ∧⌈j q*uarter*⌉ off clothe yevyn to ye iij waytt*es*
off this Cytte ffor ther lyu*er*y this yere at v s. viij d. ye yarde   xlvj s. ix d.
...
    35

Burghmote Court Minutes   CCA: CC/AC 2
f 120v   *(29 November)*

...

wayt*es*	M*em*orand*um* also that at this Courte of Bourmote Thomas wood Richard 40

34/ xlvj s. ix d.: *corrected from* xlv s. iiij d.

Dorney and william ffoster were admytted to be waytes of the seid Citie
and to haue their lyuereys nowe at this tyme/

...

f 124v   *(13 June)*   5

...

at this Court of Bourmote it is agreed that the comon wacche vsed to be
kept on seynt Thomas Evyn next shall not be then done with pageantes
but Master Mayor that nowe is to be discharged of eny act made heretofore
to the contrary [not withstandyng]/ and of euery fyne contained in the   10
same/

...

St Andrew's Churchwardens' Accounts   CCA: U3/5/4/1
f 141   *(29 September 1558–3 December 1559)*   15

...

Item recevyd at hoptyde of ye gatheryng [vij]   vij s. x d.

...

1559–60   20
City Chamberlains' Accounts   CCA: CC/FA 16
f 110

Recepciones   ¶ Item Recevyd off awstyn Cooke Bwtcher ffor ye ffyen off one Bwll
finium   slayn & not Baytyd   vj d.   25
Taurorum   Item Recevyd gylbard bland Bwtcher ffor ye fyen off one bwll slayn
                 & not baytyd   vj d.
                              Summa xij d.

...

                                                                                                       30

f 118   *(External expenses)*

...

Item gyvyn to ye marqwes off northamtons players   vj s. viij d.

...

[Item gyvyn to ye lord marqwes off northamptons players   vj s. viij d.]   35

...

Item gyvyn to my lord Robert dudles players   vj s. viij d.

...

17/ hoptyde: *Hocktide, 3–4 April*

f 126   *(Chamberlain's payments for mayoral charges)*

...

Item paid to Thomas Wood one off ye wayttes ffor his lyuery &
the Rest off his fellows ffor his & ther lyueryes this yere   xlij s. viij d.

...   5

Examinations in John Bale con. Richard Ugden   CCA: DCb/J/X.10.7
ff 36–9v*   *(27 May)* *(Examination of John Poole, aged 22, of St Alphege's,
Canterbury, on interrogatories on behalf of Richard Ugden)*

10

Examinatus virtute Iuramenti sui alias prestiti dicit apon friday Last he was
present in [the] ⌈his⌉ shope [of a taylor] within christes church yard in thafter
none the same day at which tyme ther cam by one Pylkyngton and asked one
phillip hall ther also presente whether he wolde work cui hall yea; have you
cutt anny work, [no] cui pilkington noo, I will by and by cut owte a fryers   15
garment which you shall work/ cui hall well I am content Then Richard
okeden standyng also ther, said country man make it not [I will give to]
tunc hall what will you give me then, cui Okeden I will give you ij d. Then
said Okeden wherfor shall this fryers garment be made to whom pilkinton
answered Mr Bale settith furth ⌈a play⌉ wherin ther is a fryer, cui Okeden   20
respondendo dixit, I nowe, he doth well for that [I] ⌈he⌉ cannot preach anny
more he settith furth and inventith plaies to speke against fryers and monckes
and other religious people that haue ben in the tymes past. Examined touching
the callyng of mr bale knave he cannot depose nether that he spake of mr cole.
Saving as he remembrith that he said that mr cole sholde say in the pulpit that   25
he did know a papist/ I Well ynough by his face. for they loked like dronckers
but whether at that ⌈tyme⌉ he cannot tell but sure he is he spake the same wordes
or the like in effect ∧⌈then⌉ or a wednesday when he cam from his sermon Other
wordes to his remembraunce he spake not of mr bale nor cole And further
examyned saith he herd not him the said okeden threaten pilkington but he   30
saith ∧ that okeden met with pilkington at the conduit and what talk they had
he cannot depose But/ at ther comyng backe pilkington requested okden to
Let him a lone; and okeden said he wolde for he had nothing to do with him
Et hec deponit de auditu visu et scientia proprijs et aliter nescit deponere

35

(Examination of Robert Barnes, aged 24, on the same interrogatories)
...

Examinatus dicit that apon friday last past in the after none in the shope of
Iohns within christes church yard wher ther was also presente hughe Iohns

40

12/ ⌈his⌉: *for* Iohns *(?)*
31–2/ that okeden ... backe: *added in left margin with caret to show insertion point in text*
39/ Iohns': *Hugh Johns, tailor, freeman from 1561*

Richard Okeden and [hugh pilkington] ⌜pole⌝ at which tyme ther cam to the
shope one phillip hall requiryng poole to com to | Mr darrell to take measure
of an aps cote And therat the company their presente laughed And incontinent
pilkyngton cam and requested hall to worke with him for he said he had a
plaiers garmentes to make and lacked helpe To whom hall aunswered that he   5
cold not for his masters busynes/ And then okeden said to hall will thowe goo
to make a fryers cote ⌜make it not⌝ come to me I will ∧⌜giue⌝ the too pence
for to worke somwhat with me, And apon wordes multiplied betwyne him
and pilkyngton okeden called him knave And said to him the said Pilkyngton
will you make a fryers cote in derison And pilkyngton said he muste make   10
such worke as was brought vnto him and declarid that he made the same
for mr bale And therapon Okeden said nowe mr bale can Preach no more
he settith furth plaies And ⌜said⌝ mr cole that preached the last day and so
lefte of [speach] speaking of him/ and som of theis mynystres be Smythes
shoemakers and droken knaves. Et examinatus ac interrogatus per Iudicem   15
an aliquam habuit communicacionem aliquo quid et qualiter deponeret et
deponere potuit dicit respondebat that he was asked by mr Okeden the father
of the said Richard and mr Byngham the alderman what he colde depose to
whom he declared his deposition aforesaid and no otherwise; And examyned
saith that he doth not nowe remember the hole communication betwyne   20
p⌜i⌝lkington and the said okeden | Because he gave no hearyng therunto/ Et
hec deponit de auditu et visu proprijs et aliter nescit deponere de scientia sua

*(Examination of Philip Hall, servant of Mr Darrell, aged 19, on the same
   interrogatories)*   25

...

Examinatus dicit apon fryday last past one hughe pilkington somtyme this
deponentes master cam to this deponent to the shop of Iohns within christes
church gate being then and ther presente Iohns poole Barnes Richard okeden
and this deponent And requested him to helpe to worke to whom this   30
deponent said he wolde if his master did ⌜not⌝ set him aboute his busines
wherapon this deponent asked what worke he sholde do/ to whom pilkington
said he sholde choise whether he wolde make a gowne which was cut owt or a
fryers cote. Tunc okeden dixit vnto this deponent rather than thowe shallt [do
it], make a fryers cote, I will giue the somwhat my self, vz. ij d. towardes thie   35
supper, therfore if thowe Love me do it not And then said okeden said further
to pilkington wherfor shall the cote sarve cui/ | Pilkington it is for mr Bale for
a play which he settith forth and then Richard okeden Answered and said

10/ derison: *for derision; abbreviation mark missing*   28/ deponent: d *written over* p
15/ droken: *for dronken; abbreviation mark missing*   36/ then said: *for then the said (?)*
17/ mr Okeden: *John Ugden, alderman*
18/ mr Byngham: *George Byngham, alderman; chamberlain 1560–2*

mr Bale doth well ∧⌈practise himself⌉ to sett furth playes against religious men
and not com in to the pulpit to make sermons, And saith further apon
communication he the said okeden called pilkington knave with an oth or
twayne beyng in a greate Rage and angre And further examyned saith that
they had mutche more talke and communication and were in grete rage and   5
⌈okeden⌉ called knave twyse or thrise but ⌈[bye]⌉ whom he so called bicause he
this deponent went over the way to se legges of sliuer made for a game he
cannot tell for he [po] departed a way [from] ⌈to⌉ kesham his shop. Et hec
deponit deponit de auditu visu et scientia proprijs Et aliter nescit deponere Et
dicit se nullam habuisse communicationem cum aliquo ut deponeret &c   10

(Examination of Hugh Pilkington, aged 40, of St Andrew's, Canterbury, on the
   same interrogatories)

…

Examinatus dicit apon fryday last past in the after none he this deponent   15
beying sent for to mr willowby the prebendary/ And as he went into christe
church at Iohns shop ther in the church yard founde hall his servaunte
standinge in the shope And willed him to goo home to worke | And the said
hall asked what work he sholde do and pilkington said ther is a womans
gowne and other worke ther is the friers cote you may make vpe that, tunc   20
okeden presens eodem tempore et loco dixit to hall godes blode thow arte my
contry man [if thow will] make it for if thowe make a fryers cote thowe shalte
be my contry man no more, And here is ij d. bicause yow shalt not medle
withall And will set the a worke thowe shallt be vtherwise occupied in the
meane while tunc vlterius interogauit Is it mr bales doyng cui pilkinge   25
respondendo said yea; it shall be played at mr mays house tunc okeden they
arre Ryche ynough howe saist thowe will they take anny mony I will be ther,
And then ymmedyatly sayd nay goddes blode I will not com ther I will goo to
Romney wher ther is good playe, And said mr Bale doth well to occupie him
self with such trompery And speaking against fryers, yet the ∧⌈knave⌉ him self   30
was a fryer And knewe ther knavery well ynoughe To whom Pylkyngton
answered and said I knowe not him to be such aman Cui okeden yes by godes
blode he is as the rest are knaves all the mayny of them to whome one barns
said all priestes be not knaves, tunc okeden I do not meane priestes I meane
mynysters | And said is cole a priest, no saith he with an oth: he is a Raylyng   35
knave [for] And this deponent asking him whie he said so Okeden answered
and said I may as well rayle apon him as he to rayle apon his betters And
further sayd what arre they anny better then tinckers souters tylers and

---

9/ deponit deponit: *dittography*
16/ mr willowby the prebendary: *Thomas Willoughby, canon of Canterbury Cathedral*
22/ make it: *for* make it not (?)
26/ mr mays: *George May, alderman; mayor 1557–8 and 1565–6*

dronkyn knaves ∧⌐all⌐ arre they anny other Et hec deponit de auditu visu et
scientia proprijs et aliter nescit deponere

1560–1
City Chamberlains' Accounts   CCA: CC/FA 16   5
f 159v   *(External expenses)*

Item paid to my lord Robert dwdles players ye xvij^th off martche   vij s.
...

Item paid to ye qwenes maiesties players at ye comandment off   10
Master mayer   xiij s. iiij d.
...

f 160
                                                                         15
Item paid to my lord off oxffordes players at Master mayers
Comandment   v. s.
...

f 161   20
...
Item paid to my lord off arrondelles players   vj s. viij d.
Item paid to my lord ambros dwdles players   vj s. viij d.
...
Item paid to ye quenes Berward   x s. 25
...

f 166v   *(Chamberlain's payments for mayoral charges)*
...
Item paid to Mr tomsson ffor sertyn brood clothe of hym bowght &   30
gyvyn to ye wayttes ffor yer lyuerys yis yere   l s.
...

John Bale, 'A retourne of James Canceller's raylinge boke'   LPL: MS. 2001
ff ii–iii*   *(Dedicatory epistle)*   35
...

    As the preachers haue bene in the pulpett, with a very small numbre of
hearers afore them, the cytie neuerthelesse beynge populouse and great, they
haue mocked them with their maye games, troubled them with their
tombrelles, greued them with their gunnes, and molested them with their   40
other mad mastryes: they settynge fourth those vnruly pageauntes, whose
dewtye it had bene, to haue seane best rule, and vpon the sondaye to haue
sought the glorye of God with edifycatyon of sowle. An other lyke facte of

contemptuouse mockerye agaynst Gods truthe and the preachers therof, was
shewed there but now of late also. Vpon mydsomer even, whych is otherwyse
called the vigyll of *Saint* Iohan Baptistes natiuyte, there were bonefyers made
in the stretes, yea, afore some | of the Aldremennys dores for good examples
sake, doubtlesse in contempte of the Christen religyon, and for vpholdynge   5
the olde frantyck supersticyons of papistrye. The next daye, preached one
maistre Clarke, a man sober, godly and learned: and amonge other talke,
he towched the origynall of superstityouse bonefyers, and declared that
they first came from Iulianus apostata, whych tyrannously brent the bones
of *Saint* Iohan Baptyst, as witnesseth Sigebertus Gemblacensis and other   10
historiographers, whome he there alleged.

   The saturdaye folowynge, they made bonefyers agayne for *Saint* Peter, yea,
twyse so manye as afore, some of the Aldremen not beynge behynde with their
partes, in spyght of that whych the preacher had spoken afore, stubbernely
vsynge their olde superstityons. The next daye beynge sondaye and *Saint*   15
Peters daye, as they call it, maistre Bysley preached, and in hys sermon very
charitably, peaceably and godly exhorted the Mayer and Aldremen, to see
suche superstitiouse and mockynge customes, as were the bonefyers, abolyshed:
and the true religyon of God, as becommeth Christyanes, maynteyned,
accordynge to the Quenes maiesties godly expectatyon. Moreouer, he   20
requyred in Gods holy name, that nothynge from thens fourth were done in
contempte of the preachers of Gods sacred wurde, as were those bonefyers the
nyghte afore. All thys notwithstandynge, on the same daye at nyght, one
called raylynge dycke, otherwyse Richarde Borowes, an vnshamefast ribalde
and commen smelfeast, a generall iester or mynstrell also for baudy songes at   25
all bankettes of the papistes, and an ydle vagabonde, vpholden amonge them
only to that ende: for other wurke he doth none, as the commen fame goeth.
Thys ribalde (I saye) gote vnto hym a dromme, with more then an hundred
boyes at hys tayle, and commaunded a great fyer to be made at the Bulstake,
where commenly there is most resort of people.   30

   And vnto that sedicyouse fyer, some of the offycers were most busye to
mynystre wode and other matter els. One Lewes the shrieue, threwe them
out .ij. fagottes, and the constable Randolf a pytchebarell, and diuerse other
papistes brought fuell therunto. Two honest mennys wyues, perceyuynge thys
to be done in contempte of religyon and of that the preachers had spoken [of]   35
afore, asked what it ment. Thys kynde of doynge (sayd they) hath bene spoken
agaynst by the preachers. yea marry (sayth raylynge dycke) and therfor I
do it, euen in spyght of them. And with that he uttered in hys madnesse
most vnhonest, shamefull and fylthie wurdes agaynst them and ⌈all⌉ their
maynteyners, whych are not with honestie to be ones named: concludynge   40
thus. Thys | fyer (sayd he) is made for *Saint* Paule. Come to it all yow that be

---

12/ The saturdaye folowynge: *28 June*

poullers, for it is for yow. With that the boyes made an excedynge great
shought, mockynge and gaudynge at them, whome they knewe to be
protestauntes: myndynge that nyghte as apereared, to haue made a tumulte.
But men of discressyon and Christen honestie, smellynge out their wycked
attemptes, gaue place, and so peaceably departed thens, and by and by went   5
home to their owne howses. Then made he the boyes to sytt downe on their
knees, and to counterfett a mockynge of God in holdynge vp their handes, in
maner of the olde superstition of *Saint* Iohans nyght sumtyme vsed.

   And that done, he arose and went with them abought the fyer as in
processyon, with burchyne bowes in their handes, syngynge most fylthie   10
songes of baudrye. And with these mockeryes of the Christen religyon and
preachers, the Mayer and most of the Aldermen hys bretherne were nothynge
offended, but both in sylence and in other aperaunce wele pleased. God sende
that cytie better and more godly gouernours....

...   15

1561–2
City Chamberlains' Accounts   CCA: CC/FA 16
f 192v

                                                                             20
Recepciones   ¶ Item Recevyd off gylbard bland for ye fyen of one Bwll not baytyde   vj d.
finium   Item Recevyd off william pottyer for ye lyeke   vj d.
taurorum   Item Recevyd off Iohn heethe ^for^ ye fyen off a quarter off Bwlles
                Beeff Sowld in ye markytt   j d. ob.
                              Summa xiij d. ob.   25

...

f 197v   *(External expenses)*
...
Item paid to my lord off warwyckes players   x s. 30
...

f 198
...
Item paid to my lord Robert dwdleys players ye vᵗʰ day off may   x s. 35
...

f 199

Item paid to a mynstrell [for] at ye iij sessions dyner at Master mayers   ij s. 40

40/ Master mayers: *Richard Furner*

Item paid to my lord off arrondelles players at Master mayers
comandment   v s.

...

f 199v   5

Item paid to my Lord of oxefordes players at Master mayers
comandyment   viij s.

...

                                                                                                                          10

Cathedral Chapter Act Book   CCA: DCc/CA 1
f 21*

...

note scholerij   Item yt ys agreed that ⟨...⟩ of the Grammer Scole ⟨...⟩ of theyre charges
hades⟨...⟩ settyng furthe of Interludes ⟨...⟩ towardes theyre said cha⟨...⟩   15

...

1562–3
City Chamberlains' Accounts   CCA: CC/FA 16
f 232v   20

...

Recayttes   ¶ Item Recevyd off gylbard bland ffor the ffyen off bwll by hym sowld
off ffyenes   and not baytyd   vj d./
off Bwlles   Summa vj d.

                                                                                                                          25

f 239v   (External expenses)

...

Item ffor staelyng off a fforme at ye bwllstaek   iiij d.

...

Item paid ye xixth off november to the qwenes berwardes at   30
Master mayers Comand   vj s. viij d.

...

Item paid to my lord of warwykes players at Master mayers
Comandyment   x s.

...   35

f 240

...

Item gyvyn to sertyn players apertaynyng to one syr hwmffrey of
ye north contre at master mayers Comandyment   iij s. iiij d. 40

...

f 240v

...

Item paid to ye Qwenes players at Master mayers
Comandyment   x s.

...   5

f 241

...

Item gyvyn to ye Dwtchis off suffolkes players at Master mayers
Comandment   viij s. 10

...

Item paid ffor a Cart & one yat Range ye basson beffore a
harlott   viij d.

...

                                                                      15

f 248v   *(Chamberlain's payments for mayoral charges)*

...

Item paid to Thomas brown ye Taylor/ ffor sertyn Clowght bowght
off hym/ ffor ye wayttes   xl s.

...   20

New Foundation Treasurers' Accounts   CCA: DCc/Miscellaneous Accounts 40
f 218*   *(Extraordinary expenses)*

°By me Anthonye
Ruesshe°   ...

®allowed   To mr Ruesshe for reward geuen him at settynge out of his   25
              plays yn Christmas per capitulum   iij li. vj s. viij d.

              ...

Cathedral Chapter Act Book   CCA: DCc/CA 1
f 28v*   *(27 October)*   30

...

⟨...⟩ yt ys agreed that the Scolemaister and ⟨...⟩ shall haue lvvj s. viij d.
towardes such ⟨...⟩ges as they shall be at in settyng furthe of ⟨...⟩gedies
Commedyes and interludes this next ⟨...⟩mas and the same to be done
by thadvise ⟨...⟩ consent of master vicedeane   35

...

24–5m, 25, 32/ Anthonye Ruesshe, mr Ruesshe, Scolemaister: *Anthony Rushe, schoolmaster of the King's
School July 1561–June 1565*

1563–4
City Chamberlains' Accounts   CCA: CC/FA 16
f 277v   *(Casual receipts)*

…

Item *Recevy*d off M*r* arden ffor a payer off wheell*es* & ye bedd   5
off an old pagent   ij s. [x d.] viij d.

…

f 283   *(External expenses)*

…   10
Item gyvyn to ye erle of warwyk*es* players at M*aster* mayers
coma*n*dmentt   x s.

…

f 283v   15

Item paid ffor Carryng off Sartyn owld*es* off a padgantt/ ffrom
ye pallys to ye cowrt hall   viij d.

…

It*em* paid to ffetherston ffor his sufferyng ye paigons to stand in   20
ye pallys hawll   ij s.

…

Item gyvyn to my lord Rob*er*t dwdles players at M*aster* mayers
Comau*n*dyment   x s.

…   25
Item paid to my lord off lwrborthes berward at M*aster* mayers
Coma*n*dyment   iij s. iiij d.

…

f 284v   30

…

Item gyvyn to ye Qwenes berward at M*aster* mayers
Coma*n*dyment   vj s. viij d.

…

                                                                    35
Burghmote Court Minutes   CCA: CC/AC 2
f 177   *(19 May)*

…

M*emorandum* that yt is agreed at this Court of burgemote by hole assent of
thys Court that whereas at act was made heretofore by this Court that their   40

17/ owld*es*: *corrected from* owld (?)   40/ at: *for* an

shulde be yerely a wathe at beckett*es* tyme vpon payne of forfeyture of ten
pound*es* [to] ⌐by¬ the Mayor for the tyme beyng to the chamber/ [which
act] that the same act & eu*er*y thyng article & clause therin shalbe & ys
by this Court clerely repealed ∧⌐°made°¬ voyde & of none effect from
hensfourth &c/   5
...

1564–5
City Chamberlains' Accounts   CCA: CC/FA 16
f 324   *(External expenses)*   10
...

Item p*ai*d to ye erlle off wossyt*es* players at M*aster* mayers
Comandyment   v s.
...

15

f 324v
...

Item p*ai*d To my lord strayndg players at M*aster* mayers
Comandyment   x s.
...   20
Item p*ai*d to ye qwenes players   x s.
Item p*ai*d to ye Qwenes berward   iij s. iiij d.
...

New Foundation Treasurers' Accounts   CCA: DCc/Miscellaneous Accounts 40   25
f 293v   *(Alms)*
...

To ⌐Iohn¬ Iohnson yn tyme of the playe   iij s. iiij d.
...

30

1565–6
City Chamberlains' Accounts   CCA: CC/FA 16
f 361v*
...

Recaytt*es* off
ffyenes oft
bull*es*

Item R*ecevy*d off Thomas kyng butcher ffor ye fyene off one but   35
slayne & not Baytyd   vj d.
Item R*ecevy*d off awstyn Cooke butcher ffor ye ffyene off one ∧⌐bull¬
slayn & not baytyd   vj d.
                         Su*m*ma xij d.

1/ wathe: *for* watche; *altered from* wattes   28/ ⌐Iohn¬ Iohnson: *painter, freeman from 1552*
18/ players: e *corrected over* d   35/ but: *for* bull

f 368   *(External expenses)*

...

Item p*ai*d ffor a Court y*a*t Carryd ij wom*en* & a Man/ abowt y*is*
Citte/ & ffor one y*a*t Carryd ye baeson   vj d.

...   5

f 368v

...

Item p*ai*d to my lord off hwnsdons players   viij s.

...   10

f 369

...

Item p*ai*d ffor staelyng off a fforme   iiij d.
Item p*ai*d to ye pavyor ffor pavyng of xx yard*es* off grownd at   15
the bullstaeke at iij d. ye yard   v s.
Item p*ai*d ffor ij lood*es* off stone w*it*h ye Carryng off them   ij s. viij d.
Item p*ai*d ffor ij lood*es* off Sand   xvj d.

...

                                                                                                   20

Burghmote Court Minutes   CCA: CC/AC 2
f 198   *(4 December)*

...

It*em* it is further ordered & decreed that from hensfourthe it shall not be
lawfull for any p*er*son or p*er*sones to vse any co*m*men dansyng at any Garland   25
where vnt*o* any resort of youthe shall come w*it*hin the libert*es* of this Cytty
vpon payne of Imprisonment and also that the m*aste*r & keep*er* of eu*er*y Tavern
Inne or typlyng housse suffryng any co*m*men daunsyng for youthe in his or
ther housys shall forfet for eu*er*y offence xl s. to the Chamber of this Cytty &c

                                                                                                   30

1566–7
City Chamberlains' Accounts   CCA: CC/FA 16
f 406   *(External expenses)*

...

Item p*ai*d to ye Qwenes playars at M*a*ster mayers coma*n*dyme*n*t   35
with other ye masters off this Citte   xiij s. iiij d.

...

f 406v

...   40

Item p*ai*d to my lord off Hwnsdons players   x s.

4/ vj: *corrected from* ij

Item p*ai*d to ye Qwenes berward   vj s. viij d.

...

f 407v

...   5

[Item gyvyn in Reward to my lord off leysters players   iij s. iiij d. x s.]

...

Item p*ai*d to my lord off leyst*eres* players   x s.

...

                                                                                                 10

Quarter Sessions Jury Presentments CCA: CC/J/Q/366
f [1]

...

xij d. The Iury present*es* wyllyam bery of ⟨...⟩ ward of newing gat for sufferyng
dawnsyng bulbatyng in his howse one the Saboth Day in the tyme of the   15
Devine Sarvis to wit the viij day of Iune an*no* nono/ Elyzabeth Regine

...

1567–8
City Chamberlains' Accounts CCA: CC/FA 16   20
f 444v *(External expenses)*

Item ffyrst p*ai*d ffor ye ∧⌈last⌉ Cownty dyn*er* to M*r* lee off
ye *Sum*ma ye last yere   iij li. ij s. iiij d.
Item p*ai*d to ye mvsyssyons y*at* day by ye comandyme*nt*   25
off M*aster* mayor   iij s. iiij d.

...

f 445

                                                                                                 30

Item p*ai*d xj lood*es* off Sand ffor ye pavyng at ye bullstaek at
viij d. ye lood   vij s. iiij d.
Item p*ai*d ffor Carryng off vj lood*es* off stones beyng Carryd
ffro*m* ye Roziars to ye paviors woork at vj d. ye lood   iij s.
Item p*ai*d ffor y*e* Carryeng off iiij°ʳ lood off bowllder owt off   35
the sellar to ye pavyors work/ at iiij d. ye lood   xvj d.

...

f 446

...   40

Item p*ai*d to ye pavior ffor pavyng off vjˣˣ xiiij yard*es* at ye

23/ M*r* lee: *Thomas Lee, vintner, freeman from 1564*

bullstaek// at ij d. ob. ye yard   xxvij s. xj d.

...

f 446v

...   5

Item p*ai*d to w*illia*m Swetyng ffor mendynge & sowderyng off
ye leed*es* & gwt*ere*s over ye Crosse at ye bullstaek/ w*i*th his labourar
& allso ffor Sowder & leed & workma*n*ship   xxvj s. viij d.

...   10

1568–9
City Chamberlains' Accounts   CCA: CC/FA 17
f 27v   *(External expenses)*

...

Item p*ai*d to my lord off worssetor*es* playars at M*aster* mayor*es*   15
Comandyme*n*tt   xiij s. iiij d.
Item paid to ye Qwenes maiesties players/ at M*aster* maior*es*
comandyment   xx s.

...   20

f 28v

...

It*e*m gyvyn to my lord off sussex players at M*aster* maior*es*
comandyment   v s.

...   25

Item p*ai*d to my lord strayngys players   x s.

...

f 29v

...   30

Item ∧⌈p*ai*d &⌉ alowyd to edward ansell ffor s*er*ten poost*es* at
ye bulstaeke in thand*es* off *(blank)* pollyn   iiij s.

1569–70
City Chamberlains' Accounts   CCA: CC/FA 17   35
f 61v

Resayt*tes*   ¶ Recev*i*d off awstyn Cooke ffor the ffyene/ off one bull/ by hym
off ffyenes   kyllid & not bayted   vj d.
off bull*es*
                              S*um*ma vj d.   40

...

6/ w*illia*m Swetyng: *plumber, freeman from 1559*   15/ lord: d *corrected over illegible letter(s)*
7/ labourar: *corrected over* labor

f 69v* *(External expenses)*

...

Item paid to Iaeffery the Taylar ffor a drvm ffor this Citte whoo hathe
promysid to kepe the saeme well ffor ye vse off y*is* Citte   xij s.

...   5

f 70

...

Item paid to my lord wardens plaior*es* at ye comandyment off
M*aster* maior[*es*]   x s.   10

...

Item p*aid* to my lord Ritchis plaiers at M*aster* maior*es*
Comandyme*nt* & his brethern   xiij s. iiij d.

...   15

f 70v

...

Item p*aid* ffor a newe Rym*m* ffor ye ∧⌐Cittes⌐ drvm   xij d.

...

Item paid to my lord mvngis playars at M*aster* maior & his brethens
comandyme*nt*   x s.   20

...

Item paid to my lord of lessetarys pleyars at M*aster* maior &
his brethrens comandyme*n*tt   xiij s. iiij d.

...   25

Item p*aid* to syr thomas beniars players M*aster* off the qwenes
maiesties [playar] Revell*es*   x s.

...

f 72   30

Item paid to Launselott*es* sone ffor playng on ye drwm at
sondry tyemes   xij d.

...   35

1570–1
City Chamberlains' Accounts   CCA: CC/FA 17
f 111v

Reparacions   ...
off ye cros at   ¶ Item paid ffor xij lli. ∧⌐C⌐ off Sawder   vj s. iij d.   40
ye Bulstaek

4/ well: w *corrected over* t
23/ lessetarys: ys *apparently corrected over other letters*

Item p*ai*d to ye plum*er* & his man/ ffor one days work   xix d.

Item p*ai*d to Mr Lee ffor wood ffor ye hetyng off ther Iernes   xij d.

Item p*ai*d bowrne ye carpynt*er*/ ffor iij dais & a hallff work/

in hewyng/ & layng off ij Selles vnder the Cros   iij s. vj d.

Item p*ai*d to a maeson ffor vnderpynyng off ye cros   viij d.   5

13 s.

*Sum*ma xiij s.

13 s.

f 113v   *(External expenses)*   10

...

Item paid the ffirst day off novemb*er* to my Lord of Sussex players   x s.

...

ff 114–14v   15

...

Item gyvyn to my lord off burgaynes players at m*aste*r maior*es*

& his brethrens comandym*en*t   xiij s. iiij d.

...

+   Item p*ai*d to Launselot vandepere/ ffor ij Ioyned fformes   20

ffor ye alderme*nn* to set on at the bulstak   viij s.|

Item paid to hym ffor staelyng off ye ould formes   xviij d.

Item gyvyn to my lord wardyns players   x s.

...

Item gyvyn to ye Qwenes maiesties playars   xv s. 25

...

Item gyvyn in Reward to my lord mvngys players/ ye 20

off august   vj s. viij d.

p*ai*d ye iiij^th off Iune at ye apoyntm*en*t off M*aste*r mast*er*

maier to s*er*ten morrys daunsers off the cuntre   v s. 30

...

Quarter Sessions Jury Presentments   CCA: CC/J/Q/370

f [3]   *(9 July)*

...   35

xij d.   Item the Iury dothe pr*e*sent laurens walker of wynchepe for that he kept

daunsyng in his howse on saterday the vij^th day of Iuly a*nn*o 1571/ at xj of

the clock at night contrary to order taken in that behalf/

...

1571–2
City Chamberlains' Accounts   CCA: CC/FA 17
f 145v

<table>
<tr><td>Receates of
fynes of Bulles</td><td>¶ Item for iij bulles killede not baytede
Some xviij d.</td><td>xviij d.</td><td>5</td></tr>
</table>

...

f 151   *(External expenses)*

...   10

Item paid for the last countye dynner to daile   iij li. xiij s. iiij d.
Item gyven to the waightes at that tyme   iiij s.

...

f 151v   15

...

Item for mending and newe ameling of the Skutchions
for the waightes   viij s.

...

                                                                             20

f 152

...

Item to Iohn Ionson for writing of certaine papers, for
wytches and others   vj d.
Item to the kepers man for Ringing the bason   iij d.   25

...

f 152v

...

Item to the pompmaker for his paynes taken at the Bulstake   xij d.   30

...

f 157   *('Chamberlain's allowances)*

...

Item for the lyveries of the three waightes being viij yardes   35
and a halfe of broode clothe at vij s. the yarde   iij li.

...

23/ Iohn Ionson: *John Johnson, painter, freeman from 1552*
25/ the kepers: *Ambrose Simpson, keeper of the city gaol at Westgate*

Burghmote Court Minutes   CCA: CC/AC 2
f 253v   *(16 October)*

…

Memorandum it is agreed in this cort of burgemote that there shalbe
appoynted a company of discrete & mete men & such as are able & quyet   5
personez to be the waytes of the Cytty as in tyme paste hathe byn vsed/ ffor
the worship of the Cytty &c

f 255   *(27 November)*

…   10

Memorandum that yt ys decreed & ordered that the waytes shall haue Gownes
for lyveres thys yere of the charges of the chamber of the Cytty &c/
…

Drapers' and Tailors' Memoranda Book   CCA: U12/A1   15
f 26v   *(Expenses)*

…

Item paid for the dyner   xl s.
Item to william maye for playinge att the diner   xij d.
…   20

f 27   *(Receipts)*

…

Item Receyued att the diner   xx. s. vj d.
…   25

Probate Inventory of Robert Betts   CCA: DCb/PRC 10/6
f 91*   *(31 October)* *(Bad debts owed to the deceased)*

…

Item william ffidge and whetstone owe the said bettes ffor   30
their portions in buyinge of certen playe bookes   xxxv s. iiij d.
…

1572–3
City Chamberlains' Accounts   CCA: CC/FA 17   35
f 193*   *(External expenses)*

…

Item gyven to the waytes at Master Mayers apoyntment
the xvij of Nouember   iij s. iiij d.
Item for the last countie dynner   iij li. xviij s.   40
Item to the waytes at that tyme   iiij s.
Item for Maulmesey then a pottell   xvj d.
…

f 193v

...

Item gyven to the Earle of worcesters players   vj s. viij d.

...

f 194v

...

Item for one to loke to the worcke at the bulstake   iiij d.

...

Item to Mr wyckes for his paynes in makyng the oration
to the quene   xx s.

Item to Swetyng for mendyng the leades at the bulstake   xvj d.

...

f 195

...

Item to theseid worckeman & his laborer for whytyng & trymmyng
the bulstake ruff for three dayes at xxj d. the day   v s. iij d.

...

f 196*

...

The charges to the quens maiestie & the offycers
at her commyng & beyng at caunterbury

+ Inprimis gyven to the quenes maiestie in money	xxx li.
+ Item to the kyng of herauldes	xl s.
+ Item to the serieantes at armes	xx s.
+ Item to the quenes footemen	xl s.
+ Item to the trompetters	xxx s.
+ Item to the messengers	xx s.
+ Item to the Cochemen	x s.
+ Item to the yoman of the bottelles	x s.
+ Item to the surveyer of the wayes	x s.
+ Item to the porters	xilJ s. iiij d.
+ Item to the black garde	x s.
+ Item to the Typstaves & knight marshalles men	xx s.
+ Item to the drummes & flutes	v s.
+ Item to the musitions	vj s. viij d.
+ Item to walter the Iester	iij s. iiij d.
+ Item to the Clarck of the marckett	xx s.

12/ Swetyng: *William Swetyng, plumber, freeman from 1559*

+ Item to his man   vj d.
+ Item to the quenes bererd   x s.
+ Item to Mr Beale for paynes by hym taken for the Cyte   x s.

...

5

f 200   *(Chamberlain's allowances)*

...

Item for the lyueries of the three waytes beyng viij yard*es* & a halfe
of broade cloth at vij s. the yarde   iij li.

...   10

Burghmote Court Minutes   CCA: CC/AC 2
f 270   *(13 August)*

...

M*emoran*dum it is agreed by m*aste*r Maior & the aldermen that eu*er*y of   15
them shall Ryde in the Scarlett gownes w*ith* foote clothes to mete the
quenes maiestie &c/ and all the com*m*en counsell to be a foote in their
best apparrell in decent gownes/ & lyke wyse so many of the cheeffe
com*m*eners as haue gownes to be assosyat together in desent order [&c]
to mete her grace &c/   20

...

f 270v   *(21 August)*

...

Item yt ys agreed that the quenes maiestie shall haue a gyfte of the Cytty at   25
her nowe com*m*yng hether in p*ro*cresse the Some of xxx li., wherof xx li. to
be of the chambers charge and x li. resydue to be levied otherwyse as this
howse shall hereafter devyse & agree/

...

30

f 271   *(4 September)*

...

Item it is agreed at this burgemote that certen of the quenes maiest*es*
offycers shalbe rewarded as hereafter ensuythe
ffyrst to the herrold*es*   xiij s. iiij d. 35
It*em* to the Trumpeters   x s.
It*em* to the Seriant*es* at armes   x s.
It*em* to her ma*iest*es ffootemen   x s.
It*em* to the gentleman Surveyar of the ways   v s.

...

40

26/ procresse: *for* progresse

f 271v   *(22 September)*

...

weyk*es* xx s.   It*em* it is agreed that mr weyk*es* shall haue for his paynes in makyng the
oracyon before the quene xx s.

...   5

New Foundation Treasurers' Accounts   CCA: DCc/TA 7
f 96v

Expen*se*
ext*ra*ordin*arie*
racione accessus
Regie ma*iestatis*
ad ecclesiam
hanc hac estate

Et in denarijs p*er* d*ictu*m Thesaurariu*m* hoc anno erga aduentum   10
do*mi*ne n*ost*re Elizabeth*e* Regine ad ecclesiam hanc delib*er*at*is*
m*a*gist*r*o decano p*er* ipsum p*er* consensu*m* tocius capituli eede*m*
do*mi*ne Regine ad primu*m* ingress*um* in ecclesiam p*re*d*ictam*
dat*is* et presentat*is* viz. in auro content*o* in quadam decente
Bursa de Serico cum filis argenteis context*a* sexaginta aureis   15
voc*atis* angell*es* in toto cum xxv s. de p*re*cio d*ic*t*e* burse   xxxj li. v⟨...⟩

...

Et in denarijs s*imiliter* p*er* d*ictu*m Thesaurariu*m* cum consensu
decani et capituli via regardi dat*is* diu*er*sis Seruientibus d*ic*t*e*
do*mi*ne Regine viz. Peditibus per compositio*n*em pro canabo qui   20
portat*us* fuit sup*r*a p*er*sonam Regie ma*iesta*tis in primo ingressu
in ecclesiam quem vendicabant eis ex consuetudine p*er*tinere x li.
et valectis garde C s. ac callentibus musicam voc*atis* music*i*ons xl s.
et Sonantibus tubas voc*atis* the trumpeters xl s. acetiam Gromettis
camere regie xvij s. ac Ianitoribus xx s. necnon Lixis voc*atis* the   25
black garde xx s. in toto ut patet p*er* libru*m* Thes*aurarij* sup*er*
hunc Comp*otu*m examinatu*m*   xxj li. xvij s.

...

The Life of Archbishop Matthew Parker   BL: Printed Book C.24.b.6   30
ff [19v–21]   *(3–7 September)*

...Postridiè*que* qui tertius Septembris fuit, Wingham*a*e in itinere pransa
accessit Cantuariam paulò post horam tertiam pomeridianam. Eiusq*ue* per
Occidentalem portam in Cathedralem Ecclesiam ingressus, ab adolescente   35
quoda*m* Schol*æ* grammaticalis discipulo oratione Latina celebrabatur. Qua
finita cum se ad Sca*m*mum genibus flexis inclinasset, preces consuet*æ* ab
Archiepiscopo, Lincolnensi Roffensiq*ue* Episcopis, & doueri Suffraganeo in
aduentum eius fundebantur. Tum Decanus vnà cum prebendarijs, canonicis,
ministris, & choro Ecclesi*æ* Cathedralis, nonnullisq*ue* sui sacelli cantoribus   40

16/ v⟨...⟩: *edge of sheet damaged; probably for* v s.   22/ quem: *minim missing in* MS

eam sub conopeo à quatuor Militibus erecto sequentem, per Chorum vsquè
ad oratorium suum præibant. Indeque finitis vespertinis precibus, reuersa per
vrbis plateas ad suum Palatium, quod antiquitus Augustinense dicebatur
transijt. Ac die Dominico ad eandem Ecclesiam, curriculo per plateas ducta,
rursus redijt. hoc die Decanus è Sacro suggestu concionatus est. Cumque is   5
perorauisset ad pallatium eadem via curriculo regressa est. Postridiè verò qui
septimus mensis septembris fuit, ad Conuiuium ab Archiepiscopo inuitata ad
Archiepiscopale palatium cum tota familia venit, Is natalis fuit Reginæ dies....

Nobiles soli Reginæ ministrabant, quæ simulatque manus abluisset,
accessit ad mensam in summo Aulæ Archiepiscopalis loco in latitudinem   10
extensam, ad cuius medium in veteri quadam Marmorea cathedra pannis
auro infusis ornata sub pretioso auroque fulgenti Regio conopeo descubuit.
Tum comes Retius Galliæ Mariscalcus qui paulò antè a Regie Galliæ ad
Reginam cum centum generosis Cantuariam le|gatus venisset, vna cum
Domino Moto eiusdem Regis ad Reginam Oratore a dextris Reginæ ad   15
eiusdem mensæ extremitatem, ore ad Reginam tergoque ad aulam, vt
convenientius familiariusque conferri sermones poterant, conuerso sedebant:
alteramque à sinistris mensæ extremitatem quatuor illustres fœminæ,
Marchionissa Northamptoniensis, Comitissa Oxoniensis, Comitissa
Lincolniensis, & Comitissa Varuicensis occupabant./   20
...

Reliquæ omnes aulæ mensæ conuiuis repletæ sunt. In proximis Reginæ
mensis à dextris discubuerunt cum Archiepiscopo Consilarij cum quibusdam
tum ∧⌈viris tum⌉ fœminis illustribus, & ex his præcipui illorum qui ex Gallia
cum Rhetio venerant: à sinistris nobiles ac illustres fœminæ: in remotioribus   25
vero mensis, Maior Cantuariensis cum illius Civitatis senioribus, & Cantiani
Comitatus generosi viri, & mulieres sederunt, Hisque omnibus ab
Archiepiscopi famulis toto conuivio servitum est./

Interea verò dum multi spectatum frequentes introissent, & aulam mediam
penè complessent, removeri eos et ad aulæ latera concedere subinde iussit   30
Regina, vt aulæ longitudinem & discumbentes per omnes mensas, conuiuas
intueretur. Epulis autem peractis, & remotis, mensis postquam assurectum est.
Regina cum Rhetio Legato, & Domino Moto Oratore Gallico ad longam illam
mensam secretum semonem habuit, interea dum inter Nobiles ad instrumenta
musica tripudia haberentur. Ac paulò post per viam secretam in Archiepiscopi   35
deambulatorium ascendit. Ibi cum eodem | Legato ad noctem ferè colloquium
perduxit./ Tum Archiepiscopum accersiuit, narrauitque quam gratum atquè
honorificum sibi vsum esset illius diei convivium, actisque summis gratijs ad
Palatium suum in curriculo per plateas reducta est./
...   40

13/ Regie: *for* Rege

1573–4
City Chamberlains' Accounts CCA: CC/FA 17
f 237v

Receytes of   ¶ Item rec*eyued* this yere of Thomas west bocher for kyllyng of a   5
fynes of bull*es*   bull not bayted   vj d.
...

f 243   *(External expenses)*
...   10
Item gyven to the waytes at the Maiors apoyntm*ent* the xvij
of Nouember   iij s. iiij d.
Item for the last countie dynner   liiij s. x d.
Item to the waytes at that tyme   iiij s.
...   15

f 243v
...
Item gyven by apoyntem*ent* to the *lord* chamb*er*leyn his players   xiij s. iiij d.
...   20

f 245v
...
It*em* payd to my lord wardens tru*m*mpett*es* that brought the veneson
that was gyuen to the cytie   iiij s.   25
...

f 250   *(Chamberlain's allowances)*
...
Item for the lyu*er*ies of the three waytes beyng   30
ix yard*es* & a halfe of broade cloth at vj s. viij d.
the yarde   iij li. [vj s. viij d.] ⌊iij s. iiij d.⌋
...

1574–5   35
City Chamberlains' Accounts CCA: CC/FA 17
f 291*   *(External expenses)*
...
Item gyven to the waytes at the maiors apoyntm*ent* the xvij
of Nouember 1574   iij s. iiij d. 40
Item for the last countie dynn*er*   xlix s. vj d.

41/ xlix s.: *corrected from some other figure, perhaps* xliiij s.

Item gyven to the Waytes at that tyme   iiij s.

...

Item fett at Mr ffysshers at the countie dynner in wyne at the
commaundment of Master Mayer   ij s. iiij d.
payd to Mr lee for wyne at that dynner   xj s. j d.   5
Item payd to the lord of leycester his players for playeng before
Master Mayer & his bretherne at the Courte halle the third of
December 1574   xviij s.
for Candelles & torches then spent   xvj d.
for iiij^or newe plates   xvj d.   10
Item payd to the Carter for Cartyng of Christofer & others   vj d.
to a boy that dyd ryng the bason   ij d.

...

f 292   15

...

payd to a carter [th] & to a boye that rong the bason for the
cartyng of Anne lockwood & other   vj d.

...
                                                                                20

f 300   (Chamberlain's allowances)

...

Item for the lyueries of the three Waytes beyng nyne yardes of
broade cloth at vj s. viij d. the yarde   iij li.

...   25

Burghmote Court Minutes   CCA: CC/AC 2
f 285v   (26 October)

...

Memorandum it is ordered & agreed that the waytes of the Cytty shall play   30
& contynue accordyng to the old custome/

f 290   (18 March)

...

Item also at this Cort yt ys graunted to Edmund Nycolson to be the wayte of   35
the Cytty and he to provyde for the vsyng & kepyng of that office Sufficiently
wherein he to take to hym the other [foure] musysyons that served before yf
they wyll serve reasonably & vsyng them selves well &c

...

3/ Mr ffysshers: *William Fysher, alderman;*   5/ Mr lee: *Thomas Lee, vintner, freeman from 1564*
mayor 1572-3   7/ Master Mayer: *John Rose*

Quarter Sessions Jury Presentments   CCA: CC/J/Q/374/i
mb 2   *(6 December)*

...

ponit se .R. austen

12   Item they present Robert lynsey for kepyng ill rule in his howse at all tymes &   5
xij d.   kepyth [a] one wylliams his tapster which goeth vp & downe the streates wyth
a fyddell & iij or iiij^{or} companyons folowyng hym daunsyng & syngyng at
one or two of the Clock after midnight very vnorderly & suspitiously

...

10

New Foundation Treasurers' Accounts   CCA: DCc/Miscellaneous Accounts 40
f 458   *(Extraordinary expenses)*

...

®°allowed°   To my Lord of Leacester players mandato magistri decani 7o decem   xx s.
...   15

1575–6
City Chamberlains' Accounts   CCA: CC/FA 17
f 348v   *(External expenses)*

...   20

Item to Mrs ffyssher for the last countie dynner   lvj s. viij d.
Item to the waytes at that tyme   iij s. iiij d.

...

Item gyven to the lord of pembrookes players att the apoyntment
of Master Mayer   vj s. viij d. 25

...

f 349v

Item gyven to the waytes at the fyrst session   iij s. iiij d. 30
...

f 350

...
Item to the waytes at that session   iij s. iiij d. 35

...

4/ ponit se .R. austen: *'R. Austen puts himself forward (as a pledge)'*
5/ Robert lynsey: *capper, freeman from 1561*
14/ decem: *for* decembris
21/ Mrs ffyssher: *wife of William Fysher, alderman; mayor 1572–3*
30/ fyrst session: *first (Christmas) quarter session*
35/ that session: *second (Lady Day) quarter session*

f 350v

...

Item payd to Bourley the Carpynter for mendyng the pulleye
& for footyng the fourmes at the bulstake & for the stuff   xvj d.

...

to the waytes at that tyme   iij s. iiij d.

...

f 351v

...

to the waytes at that tyme   iij s. iiij d.

...

f 355   *(Chamberlain's allowances)*

...

Item payd to Thomas long for the liueries of of the three waytes
beyng nyne yard*es* ∧⌈& a quarter⌉ of broade cloth at vj s. viij d.
the yarde   iij li. [x]j s. viij d.

...

1576-7
City Chamberlains' Accounts   CCA: CC/FA 17
f 391   *(External expenses)*

...

payd to the waytes at that sess*ion* dyn*er*   iij s. iiij d. 25

...

f 391v

...

It*em* payd to the waytes at that sess*ion*   iij s. iiij d. 30

...

f 392

...

It*em* payd to a worcke man that founde certen stuff to amend the   35
fourmes & caettes at the bulstake & whytstable m*ar*ckett & for
his paynes   xvj d.

...

6/ that tyme: *third (Midsummer) quarter session*
11/ that tyme: *fourth (Michaelmas) quarter session*
16/ Thomas long: *draper, freeman from 1569;*
    alderman; mayor 1594-5

16/ of of: *dittography*
25/ that sess*ion* dyn*er*: *first (Christmas) quarter*
    session
30/ that sess*ion*: *second (Lady Day) quarter session*

f 393v

...

Item payd to hym that was in the devylles clothes that whypped
the man & the woman   vj d.

...   5

f 394

...

Item payd to the waytes then   iij s. iiij d.

...   10

f 394v*

...

Item gyven to the Earle of leycester his men that played at the Courte
halle apoynted so by Master Mayer & hys brethern   xx s. 15

...

f 395v

...

Item payd to the waytes at that session   iij s. iiij d. 20

...

f 400   (Chamberlain's allowances)

...

Item payd for nyne yardes & a quarter of broade cloth for the   25
lyueries for the waytes this yere at vj s. viiij d. the yarde   iij li. j s. viij d.

...

New Foundation Treasurers' Accounts   CCA: DCc/TA 8
f 111v   (Necessary expenses)   30

...

Et in regardo per dictum Computantem hoc Anno Cum consensu Magistri
decani & prebendariorum dato diuersis personis viz.... Lusoribus prenobilis
Viri Comitis Leicestrie xl s....

                                                                                     35

Actes du Consistoire   CCA: U47/A1
p 31*   (8 November)

...

fuit arreste qu'on admonestreite wallerand cocquel de ce quil auait Compose
une chanson mondaine et au deshonneur des filles de la Compaignie   40

...

_____

9/ then: *third (Midsummer) quarter session*   20/ that session: *fourth (Michaelmas) quarter session* p 33   *(22 November)*

...

Item dappeller wallerand Cocquel pour luj remonstrer a bon escrire le mal en
la Composition de cest chanson ou bien quil cest a declarer Chaunteur

p 34   *(25 November)*

Du 25th

Walerand cocquel estant deuant Les freres apres auoit entendu La remonstrance
protesta nestre autheur de ceste chanson. Et Le personnage qui Lauoit fait   10
estoit passe par icj venant de Londres, et Lequel nestoit de Leglise et nestoit
aussi bien cognú de La Compaignie par quoj il prioit de nestre abstreint a le
nominer. Au cest il desaduouoit Ladite chanson et depuis quil auoit entendu
quelle estoit tiree en telle consequence Lauoit bruslee et sestoit abstenu de le
chanter auec protestation de ne le plus chanter ni autres par ailleur Suiuant   15
quoy Les freres furent content de luj

...

1577-8
City Chamberlains' Accounts   cca: CC/FA 18   20
f 30v*   *(External expenses)*

Item payd to the [mo] musitioners at the dynner made at Mr doddes
on the day of the chaunge of the quenes maiesties reign   ij s. vj d.
...   25

f 32v

...

Item payd to hym that playde on the drumme that dwelt wythoute
westgate   xij d. 30
Item payd to Edmond Mr palmers man for dromme & phyf   ij s. vj d.

...

f 33v

...   35

Item payd on may day to the dromme & phyfe & to Mr ower
for their dynners   ij s.

...

4l cest²: *for* sait
14, 15l le: for la
23l Mr doddes: *Sampson Dodd, linen-draper,*
  freeman from 1570; alderman

31l Mr palmers: *Henry Palmer, freeman from 1578*
37l dynners: *3 minims in* ms

f 37   *(Chamberlain's allowances)*

...

+ Item payd for a whole cloth for the lyueries of the town Clarck, the
 chamberlayns Clarck, the keper & the five *serieantes*   xj li. x s.

+ Item payd for the cloth of lyveries of the fyve waytes of the cytie vz.   5
 for xiij yard*es* & one quarter   iiij li. vij s.

...

Item fower of the companye of the waytes had iij yard*es* a quart*er* a pece w*hi*ch
came to xiij yard*es* and the other quarter therof was putt vnto two yard*es* halfe
quarter that was left of the fyrst cloth and that ij yard*es* quarter & di. serued   10
the boye Nicholsons sonne yet had eu*er*y of the fyrst eight offycers iiij yard*es* a
peece so that the cloth was xxxiiij yard*es* di. quarter

Burghmote Court Minutes   CCA: CC/AC 2
f 328v   *(5 November)*   15

...

ℂ Item at thys cort yt ys graunted & agreed by the hole consent of this housse
that whereas the company of the Musysyons [h] & wayt*es* of thys Cytty haue
accustomably had iij s. iiij d. in reward eu*er*y Sessyon day w*hi*ch co*m*mythe
to xiij s. iiij d. a yere & three Gownes for thre of them, and nowe ther   20
co*m*mpany [ys] ∧⌈beyng⌉ incressed from thre vnto fyve// wherfore yt ys
graunted & agreed that the sayd Musysyons & wayt*es* shall from hensfurthe
haue no more the said reward in mony geven them, but in recompense therof
beyng but (xiij s. iiij d.) [Thy] They shall haue yerely fyve gowne cluthes [s]
geven them at the charg*es* of the Cytty and they to haue & take the good   25
wyll*es* of eu*er*y man w*i*thin the libert*ies* of the Cytty in reward towardes their
paynes & travell &c as before they haue had

1578–9
City Chamberlains' Accounts   CCA: CC/FA 18   30
f 78   *(External expenses)*

...

Item payd to M*aste*r Maior iij s. iiij d. w*hi*ch before he had layd
owte to the quenes Bereward*es*   iij s. iiij d.

...   35

f 78v

...

It*em* gyven to Edward the ffyf & his fellow   ij s.

...   40

24*l* gowne: g *corrected from some other letter*
33*l* iij s.: *corrected from* iiij s.

f 80

...

for new heddyng the drumme to gossen   iij s. iiij d.

...

5

f 81

...

Item ∧⌜for⌝ ij peces of lead to cealle the fourmes at the bulstake   vj d.

...

10

f 84   *(Chamberlain's allowances)*

...

Item payd for cloth for the lyveries of the towne clarck the
Chamberleyns Clarck the keper the fyve serieantes & for the
fyve waytes   xv li. xij s. vj d. 15

...

New Foundation Treasurers' Accounts   CCA: DCc/TA 9
f 122   *(Necessary expenses)*

...

20

...Et in regardo dato diuersis Lusoribus vocatis therle of leicestres players
xxx s....

1579–80
City Chamberlains' Accounts   CCA: CC/FA 18   25
f 117*   *(External expenses)*

...

Item payd to Barbye for charges for the offycers & the waytes
there at the quenes day   iiij s.

...   30

f 118

...

Item gyven to the Earle of leicesters players   xx s.

...   35

f 119

...

Item payd to gossen for amendyng the drumme   ix s.

...   40

3, 39/ gossen: *Cornelius Gossen, joiner*

f 120

...

Item for the pavyng vnder the bulstake   vj d.

...

f 124   *(Chamberlain's allowances)*

...

Item payd for cloth for the lyueries of the towne clarck the
chamberleyns Clarck, the keper, the fyve serieantes & for the
fyve waytes   xvj li. x s. viij d.   10

...

Burghmote Court Minutes   CCA: CC/AC 3
f 14   *(1 December)*

...

a decre that
there shalbe but
iiij of the waytes

Item at this Courte yt is ordered and decreed that from hencefourthe there shalbe
but fower musicions to be waytes of the Citie & no more whereof davis to be one
nycholson the other william Hunte one other and Iames nower the other and that
they fower shall from hencefourthe Inioye and take all the Comoditie and proffytt
for the same. Item yt is ordered and decreed that yf at any tyme hereafter there doe   20
happen any contencion or variaunce betwene the said fower then yf three of the
same fower doe agree vppon any suche variaunce theire agreement shall stand in
effect notwithstandynge the dissente or not agreinge therevnto of the fowerthe.
And also yt ys ordered that he of the said fower whiche hathe moste cunninge in
the said musick of the waytes shalbe the Cheyfest of the said fower &c/   25

f 15   *(15 December)*

Item at this Courte yt is agreed that nycolson his sonne shalbe one of the
fyve musicions notwithstandinge any acte heretofore made &c/   30

...

1580–1
City Chamberlains' Accounts   CCA: CC/FA 18
f 166v   *(External expenses)*   35

...

Item gyven to my lord Straunges players   x s.

...

Item for makyng cleane [bulstake] the bulstake & for carryeng awey
the stones   vj d.   40

...

17/ davis: v *corrected from* y   23/ notwithstandynge: y *corrected over* e

f 170   *(Wages and payments)*

...

Item payd for cloth for lyueries of the towneclarck, the Chamberleyns
Clarck the keper the fyve serieantes & for the waytes   xviij li.

...   5

1581-2
City Chamberlains' Accounts   CCA: CC/FA 18
f 210   *(External expenses)*

...   10

to Iohn Bale for vndoyng the ventes vpon the bulstake & for makyng
it cleane   iiij d.

...

f 210v*   15

...

<table>
<tr><td rowspan="16" valign="top">The Charge
of Quene
Elizabeth
hyr comyng
to the
Cyty in the
tyme of
Mr Gaunt
beyng
Mayor</td><td>+</td><td>payd to a laborer to digg gravell to lay on the streates agen her maiestie was here</td><td>xij d.</td></tr>
</table>

The Charge
of Quene
Elizabeth   + payd to a laborer to digg gravell to lay on the streates agen her
hyr comyng   maiestie was here   xij d.
to the   + Item [payd for] gyven to the quenes maiestie at her beyng here at
Cyty in the   Caunterbury   xx li. 20
tyme of   + Item gyven to the quenes foote men at her maiesties beyng here xl s.
Mr Gaunt   + Item to the yeoman of the bottelles   x s.
beyng   + Item to the trumpettes   xxx s.
Mayor   + Item to the serieantes at armes   xx s.
               + Item to the surveyor of the wayes   x s. 25
               + Item to the yeoman of the robes   vj s. viij d.
               + Item to the knight Mershall his men   xiij s. iiij d.
               + Item to the black garde   x s.
               + Item to the quenes porters   x s.
               + Item to the Coche men   x s. 30
               + Item payd to Mr Berry for a syluer cup gyven to the quenes
                 maiestie at her beyng here   lvij s. vj d.
               + Item for burnysshyng of that cup   viij d.
               + Item to the Clarck of the markett at that tyme   xxx s.
               + Item to the noble men their trumpettes at that tyme   v s. 35

f 212

...

Item gyven to the lord morleys players   v s.

...   40

f 212v

…

Item gyven to the Earle of harteforde his players   x s.

…

                                                                          5

f 217   (Chamberlain's allowances)

…

Item payd for cloth for the lyveries of the towne clarck the
chamberleyns clarck the keper, the five serieantes & for the
fyve waytes   xviij li. 10

…

1582–3
City Chamberlains' Accounts   CCA: CC/FA 18
f 262   (External expenses)   15

…

Item payd for the serieantes & waytes dynner at the sunne at the
solempnizacion of the begynnyng of the quenes reign for this yere   v s. vj d.

…

                                                                          20

f 262v

…

Item payd to Newchurche the drumme graunted hym by
bourmowth   xiij s. iiij d.

…   25

f 265v*

…

Item payd to the players that fyrste came hyther by Master Maior
his [⟨..⟩] apoyntement   xiij s. iiij d. 30

…

Item payd to the quenes players that played before Master Maior
& his brethren at the courte halle   xl s.

…

                                                                          35

f 268   (Chamberlain's allowances)

…

Item payd for cloth for the lyueries of the towne clarck the
chamberleyns clarck the keper the fyve serieantes & for the
fyve waytes   xvij li. xiij s. viij d. 40

…

18/ the begynnyng … reign: *17 November*   29, 32/ Master Maior: *John Nutt*

Actes du Consistoire CCA: U47/A2
f 40 *(22 September)*

...

Du 22e

Antoine Cambier, Iacques de frissencourt et Le filz a Ian catel estans 5
appellez pour leur faire remonstrance sur ce qu'ilz auoient chante des
chansons mondaines et dissollues et qui plus est auoient Iniuries ceux
qui leur en auoient fait remonstrance recognurent Leurs fautes et
promirent de ne plus faire item de contenter ceux qui auaient este
offensez de ces choses 10

1583–4
City Chamberlains' Accounts CCA: CC/FA 18
f 311 *(External expenses)*

... 15

Item payd to ffowler Colebrand for the serieantes dynner & other
waytes at the dynner at the coronacion of the quenes day iiij s. vj d.

...

f 311v 20

...

Item to hym more for iij loades of Sand for the pavyng at
the bulstake iij s.

...

Item payd to atkynson for xlij yardes of pavyng at the bulstake x s.vj d. 25

...

Item payd to harnes for a loade of sand brought to the bulstake viij d.

f 312

... 30

Item payd to atkynson for xxiiij yardes of pavyng at the bulstake
& for helpyng to wey the stones vj s. iiij d.

...

Item payd to the players that playd in the courte halle xx s.
Item payd for the serieantes dynner at that tyme ij s. vj d. 35

...

16/ ffowler Colebrand: *tailor, freeman from 1574*
22/ hym: *William Harnes*
25, 31/ atkynson: *John Atkynson, paviour, freeman from 1569*

f 317 *(Wages and payments)*

...

Item payd for the Cloth for the lyueries of the towne clarck
the Chamberleyns Clarck, the keper, the fyve serieantes, &
for the fyve waytes   xvij l. xiij s. viij d.   5

...

Burghmote Court Minutes   CCA: CC/AC 3
f 75   *(12 May)*

...   10

Item at this Courte the Scutchions of the musitions of this Cittie beinge three
in number weyinge in the whole twentie Seauen ounces in Syluer ∧⌐were
deliuered to the Courte.⌐ and yt is decreed at the petition of the musicions
that the same Scutchions shalbe altered, and of those three to be made fyve
[So the fashion thereof] and that the Chamberleyn of this Cittie shalbe   15
appointe the makinge thereof at his discrescion bothe as touchinge the
worckeman and also for the ffasshion So as there be no Sylver dyminsshed
and so as the same musitions doe allowe all chardges in alteringe those three
Scutchions as is aboue said.

...   20

Actes du Consistoire   CCA: U47/A2
f 60v   *(1 May)*

...

                    Du premier de May   25
Sur le raport que Gilles mallebrance auoit este veu par La ville accoustre
comme vn fol fut arreste de sinformer de la cause qui Le mouuoit a
ce faire

...

                                                                                  30

1584–5
City Chamberlains' Accounts   CCA: CC/FA 18
f 362*   *(External expenses)*

¶ Item layd owte to hugh Iones for the offycers dynner & the waytes   35
the 17 day of November anno 27 regine Elizabethe   v s.

...

15/ shalbe: *for* shalle
17/ dyminsshed: n *corrected over* p; *for* dyminisshed

1585–6
City Chamberlains' Accounts   CCA: CC/FA 18
f 410*   *(External expenses)*

...

Item payd to mr prowde for the fyve serieant*es* the keper & the Cryer   5
their dynner at the day of the solempnac*i*on of her ma*i*esties reign   ij s. iiij d.
Item payd for the waytes dynner that day   xx d.
Item more for the dynner of certen s*er*vyngmen   xij d.
Item payd more for dynner had in to M*aste*r Maior   xij d.
Item more for a quarte of muskaden that ffoster fetched & suger that   10
was had in to the dynner   ij s.

...

f 410v

...   15

Item gyven to the *lord* chief baron his butler, his trumpett, his butler
& his porter   vij s.

...

f 411   20

Item payd to the scavenger for his courte for Carryeng of them that
ryde aboute the towne the 12 of ffebruary   xij d.
Item payd to hym that dyd whyp the woman the 12 of ffebruary   x d.
Item payd more to the boy that dyd ryng the basen   ij d. 25
Item payd more for iiij*or* papers of wrytyng*es* to putt on their head*es*   viij d.

...

f 412v

...   30

Item gyven to the ᴧ⌈quenes⌉ players that playd at the courte halle before
M*aste*r Maior & his brethren the xxvij of September   xxx s.

...

f 417   *(Chamberlain's allowances)*   35

...

Item payd to the fyve waytes in respect of their lyueries   v li.

...

5l mr prowde: *Henry Proude, gentleman, freeman from 1561; alderman*
6l the day ... reign: *17 November*
9, 32l M*aste*r Maior: *John Eastey*
16l his butler ... his butler: *dittography*

f 459v*   *(External expenses)*

Item payd to phillip the fyff & Edward newchurche the drumme
for their paynes in their seruyces for the cytie in the tyme of mr
Estey maior so agreed by bourmowth vpon their byll exhibyted   5
to the bourmowth   xiij s. iiij d.

...

Burghmote Court Minutes   CCA: CC/AC 3
f 101   *(15 March)*   10

...

Item at this Courte it is decreed that the five gownes for the waightes of
this Cittie shalbe deliuered to those five [waites] of them which haue
already hetherto doen the same Seruice the tyme of this yere [past]
Scithens mychelmas. And that vntill mychelmas nexte cominge they   15
whiche nowe remayne here namely Edmonde nycholson William hunte
nycholas Crosse & Roberte davies ⌈together with one other to be by
them prouided⌉ shall Serve oute theire tyme vntill mychelmas [aft] in
suche Sorte as they maye and so from thence fourthe so as the nomber
shalbe full & the persons mete & sufficient for that purpose otherwyse   20
the same musitions to be otherwise Appointed & prouided by this
house:

...

1586–7   25
City Chamberlains' Accounts   CCA: CC/FA 18
f 460v   *(External expenses)*

...

Item gyven to the Earle of Sussex his players apoynted so by mr nutt
the [Earle of] deputie to master maior   x s.   30

...

Item gyven to the Earle of leycester his players by order from Master
mayor & his brethren   x s.

...

                                                                                 35

f 462

...

Item payd to her maiesties players apoynted so by master mayor   xx s.

...

f 468   *(Chamberlain's allowances)*

...

Item payd to thomas long for cloth for the fyve waytes & the Cryer
beyng xx yard*es* & j quarter at 6 s. 8 d. the yarde   vj li. xv s.

...   5

1587–8
City Chamberlains' Accounts   CCA: CC/FA 19
f 30v*   *(External expenses)*

...   10

Item payd at the lyon the 17 day of nouember for the fower *serieantes*
the v waytes & the cryer their dynner   v s.

...

f 31v   15

...

Item payd to the quene*s* players the 27 of marche 1588   xx s.

...

Item payd to newchurche his wydowe for the fyne dru*m*m   xl s.

...   20

f 32

...

Item payd to may ∧⌈the boye⌉ one day playeng on the dru*m*me   iiij d.
Item payd the xx day of may to the wallen dru*m*me   xij d.   25

...

f 33

...

Item payd the first of Iuly for double heddyng ij dru*m*mes &   30
for the stuff   xiij s. iiij d.

...

Item payd to the walle*n* dru*m*me on St Iames day   viij d.

f 34   35

Item payd the xij day of August for heddyng ij syngle head*es* of
the dru*m*mes   vij s.
Item payd for double heddyng mr wyld*es* dro*m*me   vij s.
Item for a payer of dro*m*e styck*es* for launcelott*es* dro*m*me   ij s. iiij d.   40

3/ thomas long: *draper, freeman from 1569; alderman; mayor 1594–5*
40/ launcelott*es*: *Launcelot Vandepeere, joiner*

Item payd to Elias martyn for calue[s] skynnes for a case for the
dromme ⌈& makyng the same⌉   vij s.

...

f 37   (Chamberlain's allowances)   5

...

Item for xvj yardes ∧⌈one quarter⌉ of cloth for the fyve waytes of
this cytie at vij s. iiij d. the yarde euery one of theseid waytes
havyng three yardes & a quarter of cloth   v li. xix s. j d.

...   10

1588–9
City Chamberlains' Accounts   CCA: CC/FA 19
f 69   (External expenses)

...   15

Item for ij newe planckes for two newe fourmes at the bulstake   ij s.
Item to lyuerock the carpynter for one dayes worke & di. for
the same   xxj d.

...

Item payd the 5 of december to the lord of Sussex players   xiij s. iiij d.   20

...

f 70

...

Item gyven to her maiesties players aboute candlemas 1588 so   25
apoynted by Master maior & the aldermen   xx s.

...

f 71v*

...   30

Item payd to her maiesties players that played in the courte halle   xxx s.

...

f 73

...   35

Item payd to launcelott for heddying a drumme   v s.

...

1/ Elias martyn: *shoemaker, freeman from 1583*
36/ launcelott: *Lancelot Vandepeere, joiner*

f 79   *(Chamberlain's allowances)*

...

Item payd to nicholas yong for xxiiij yard*es* of broade cloth at viij s.
the yarde for p*ar*te of the lyueries of the towne clarck & other the
offycers wyth the waytes   ix li. xij s.   5

...

Quarter Sessions Examinations   CCA: CC/J/Q/388
single sheet*   *(10 May)*

10

henry parkes aged xxvj yers or ther about*es* ∧⌈the x of may 1589⌉ byf*or*
adryan Nycholls ∧⌈Iohis Rose⌉ gilb*er*t penny and Rychard Gaunt examyned
toching [the] his and his companies extraordynary comyng wi*th* a morrys
dance throwgh the Cyty the daye & yer [fore] ⌈aforesaid⌉ sayeth that/ ⌈the
last nyght beyng fryday nyght they were all at mr agers at Borne⌉ he beyng   15
a [mys] musycon was on may day last hyred by Iohn Turfrey nycholas
Saynt Iohn lychefyld Iames barby henry sere & Thomas yong [hyred] to
playe wi*th* them in ser*u*ing ther turne wi*th* the morrys dance for maye daye
& for [fryday last] thursday last being assencon daye and not for this day
[but] ⌈and⌉ doth thinke that they will hy⟨..⟩ hym for to morrowe ∧⌈beyng   20
sonday⌉ but dothe not certenly [knowe] knowe and [to] the said company
told hym that ∧⌈mr peter manwood⌉ my lord cheff barons sonne sent for
them to daunce at St Stephens this sayd daye ∧⌈beyng satterday⌉ and
sayethe further that [as] they cam from [fr] brydge to the ∧⌈Sygne of the⌉
george wi*th* out St georges gate [and] in Caunterbury and ther dyd adresse   25
and apparel them selves & put on ther bells & furnyture for the morryce
da*n*ce wi*th* mayd maryon being a boy in womans apparell/ [dated] wryt as
aboue he sayd that [yt] ∧⌈he hath [others sey] herd others sey⌉ yt was never
merry wi*th* Ingland sens men wer to go wi*th* l⟨..⟩ence beyng charged that he
wold not go a⟨...⟩t wi*th*out lycence   30
        (signed) henry parkes

3/ nicholas yong: *tailor, freeman from 1569*
12/ Iohis: *for* Iohn
15/ last nyght ... fryday: *Friday, 9 May*
15/ Borne: *probably either Bishopsbourne or Patrixbourne, both near Bridge (see p 223, l.31)*
16/ musycon: *for* musycion; *abbreviation mark missing*
19/ assencon daye: *for* assencion daye; *abbreviation mark missing; Thursday, 8 May 1589*
19/ this day: *Saturday, 10 May*
20–1/ to morrowe ... sonday⌉:   *Sunday, 11 May*
23/ St Stephens: *St Stephens, Hackington, just north of Canterbury*
28–30/ he sayd ... lycence: *written in blank space to right of Parkes' signature as continuation of text*

[xxv]

the xth of maye [15] 1589

Iohn Turfrey ∧⌈the vyce in the daunce⌉ seruant to george Ryder of herne/ aged
xx yers or theraboutes the day and yer abouesaid beyng one of the morryce
dauncers ∧⌈examyned⌉ sayeth that [he] Iohn lychefyld seruant with Ienick of   5
herne dyd [hyre] about xiiij dayes ⌈past⌉ as he thinketh byfore may day last
hyre henry parkes the fydler ∧⌈& his men⌉ to serue them for the morryce
dance tyll St peters day next for suche dayes as they shold caull hym and
[sayeth] gav[eth]e hym iiij s. aday for euery day and sayethe that on sonday
last they [day] daunsed at herne in the after noone and so dyd they then on   10
may daye and sayeth that this daye they all cam together to [St pet⟨.⟩
b⟨.⟩t parlo⟨.⟩ howse] ⌈the sygne of the george⌉ and ∧⌈that he⌉ was no wher
[yesterday] yesterday ⌈but⌉ about his mastars busynes ∧⌈at herne⌉ and cam to
the george ∧⌈aforesayd⌉ without St georges gate and there adressed them selves
in ther morrys ∧⌈daunsers⌉ [d] apparel and sayeth that they wer going to St   15
stevens to mr peter manwood to showe hym pastyme but sayeth that he dyd
not [soe] send for them as far as he knoweth

(signed) Ihon tvrfre

Quarter Sessions Examinations   CCA: CC/J/Q/388   20
f [1]

xth maij 1589

Nycholas Saynt aged xx^{ti} yeres or ther about/ the day and yere aforesaid
examyned byfor adryan Nycholls mayer & Gilbert penny and Rychard Gaunt   25
alderman sayeth that on may day [day] last they wer daunsyng at herne with
the company [at herne untill a lytle in the]/ and on sonday last they also
daunsed ther in the after noone and a lytle in the foorenone/ and sayeth that
on assencyon day they daunsed at reculver in the foornone and in the after
none at hode and sayethe that [they] the company of them went from hod   30
vpp in to east kent & yesternyght beyng fryday they cam to brydge to the ale
howse and ther laye/ and from thens cam to Caunterbury to the sygne of the
george// in St georges in Caunterbury and sayethe that they wer going to
St Stephens to mr peter manwood and that as [he knoweth dy] mr manwood
dyd not request [them but] ∧⌈to his knowlege but went of ther on myndes⌉   35
and that they began at St georges gate ∧⌈to daunce & so daunced⌉ till they
cam ∧⌈in⌉ to the highe streate and ther agaynst master mayer dore and they
daunsed once or twyse about tyll by the offycer ∧⌈the seria⟨..⟩t⌉ the musicyon

---

9–10, 27/ sonday last: *Rogation Sunday, 4 May*	30/ hode, hod: *probably Hoathe, between Herne*
11/ this daye: *Saturday, 10 May*	*and Chislet, south of Reculver*
13/ mastars: r *written over* s	31/ yesternyght … fryday: *Friday, 9 May*
29/ assencyon day: *Thursday, 8 May*	37/ master mayer: *for* master mayors

was [ta] called byfor master mayer & then the rest of the company and sayeth
that when they cam agaynst master mayers dore ther was one sayd here here &
thervppon they stayed & daunsed about once or twyse as byfor

nycholas + sayntes marke   5

                                    x maij 1589
Iohn lychefyld aged xix yers or theraboutes examyned as abouesayd on sonday
last all that day they daunsed at herne and that on may daye on foornone and
afternoone they daunsed at herne and that on assencyon day last they wer at   10
servyce at Chyslet and there daunsed a lytle & in the [aft] foornone & dansed
at hod ⌈in the afternone⌉ and further sayeth in all [the] as nycholas Saynt
hath said and further confessed that he dyd hyre the musicion as Iohn turfrey
hath said
                                    Iohn lyche + fyldes marke   15

f [2]

                                    x of may 1589
Iames barby aged xx yers or theraboutes examyned byfor adryan nycholls mayor   20
he sayeth/ that on may day they dansed both foornone and after noone at
herne on sonday last in the foornone & after non daunsed at herne & on on
thursday last bothe in the foornone & after at other parishes in east kent/ and
last nyght laye about halfe a score myles from Caunterbury and dyd com to the
george without saynt gorges gate ∧⌈that day⌉ and ther dyd adresse them selves   25
in the morrys daunsers apparell and began to daunse at St goorges gate &
so cam daunsyng downe tyll they cam into the hyghe streate agaynst master
mayors [dore] dore and ther they [byfor] of the company ∧⌈byfor⌉ steyng they
daunsed about or two byfor the mayors dore & then ment to go to mr [mand]
⌈Peter⌉ manwoodes but wer not by hym requested ⌈by hym⌉ or by any other   30
to his knowlege but of ther owne myndes.

                                    Iames barby + his marke

5/ nycholas + sayntes marke: *Saynt has signed with his personal mark*
8/ abouesayd on: *for* abousayd sayeth that on
8–9, 22/ sonday last: *Rogation Sunday, 4 May*
10, 23/ assencyon day last, thursday last: *Thursday, 8 May*
12/ hod: *probably Hoathe, between Herne and Chislet, south of Reculver*
15/ Iohn lyche + fyldes marke: *Lychefyld has signed with his personal mark*
22/ on on: *dittography*
30/ by hym requested ⌈by hym⌉: *second occurrence of phrase redundant*
33/ Iames barby + his marke: *Barby has signed with his personal mark*

[Iohn] ⌈henry⌉ Sere aged xxiiij yers or ther about*es* examyned as ⟨.⟩bouesaid
sayeth that Tymothy dunkyn one of the company of the morr⟨..⟩e Daunsers ys
syck & lyeth ∧⌈syck⌉ wi*th*out the [do] towne and that he [this] the day and yer
abouesai̯d [wer] was p*ro*cured in his place that was sycke & was not of them
byfor and ∧⌈that they⌉ wer dressed in the morryce dansers apparell ∧⌈at the   5
george wi*th*out St gorges gate⌉ & so went dansing to M*aste*r Mayors dore &
that ⌈he dyd [her] here that in the hyestrete⌉ the company [as the vyse or
one of them sayd here wold wyll] ⌈[they] they wod⌉ haue about or two &
so ment to go to St stephens but can not tell [wel] who requested or p*ro*cured
them therto   10

henry seers + m*a*rke

Thomas yong aged xij yers or therabout*es* [examyned by] beyng dressed in
womans apparell for mayd marryon wi*th* out any breches wi*th* Breyded here   15
sayeth that on maye day forenone & afternon ∧⌈the whole company⌉ daunsed
at [here at] ⌈herne on⌉ sonday [and] forenon and after none ⌈daunsed ther
aga̯in⌉ and on assencion day daunsed in the fornone ∧⌈at hode⌉ & after none
in other p*a*ryshes [and wer not at home sens] and hath gon in his womans
atteyre sythens fryday mornyng & further sayeth as the other have sai̯d &   20
no otherwyse
Thomas yong + his m*a*rke

1589–90
City Chamberlains' Accounts   CCA: CC/FA 19   25
f 110   *(External expenses)*
...
Item for [ij] iij newe fourmes at the bulstake m*a*rkett   iiij s.
...

30

f 111
...
Item payd to the quenes ma*ie*sties players the xth day of Auguste 1590   xx s.
...

12/ henry seers + m*a*rke: *Sere has signed with his personal mark*
17/ sonday: *Rogation Sunday, 4 May*
18/ assencion day: *Thursday, 8 May*
18/ hode: *probably Hoathe, between Herne and Chislet, south of Reculver*
20/ fryday mornyng: *Friday, 9 May*
22/ Thomas yong + his m*a*rke: *Younge has signed with his personal mark*

f 118   *(Chamberlain's allowances)*

...

Item payd to Iohn marten for xv yard*es* for the iiij waytes
for one gowne cloth of iiij yard*es* for Robert lee granted
by bourmouth   vj li. vj s. viij d.   5

...

Item payd to nower one of the waytes in respect of his gowne
cloth wyth them   xxv s.

...

10

New Foundation Treasurers' Accounts   CCA: DCc/TA 10
f 132   *(Extraordinary fees and rewards)*

...

Et in Denar*ijs* p*er* ips*um* similiter hoc anno solut*is*
quibusdam actorib*us* scænicis Anglice vocat*is*, the   15
Quenes players, and my Lord Admiralls players, sic
illis p*er* Capitulum via regard*i* dat*is*   xxx s.

...

1590–1   20
City Chamberlains' Accounts   CCA: CC/FA 19
f 158v   *(External expenses)*

...

It*e*m payd the xj day of Ianuary to the quenes players   xx s.

...   25

f 159v

...

Item allowed to davie newton for his [cost] ˄⌈carte⌉ &
makyng his souldyers coate that was gyven to Gaskyns   30
sonne that playd on the dru*m*me at the co*m*myng of the
Earle of Essex and fyrst wearyng of the coates   iij s.

...

f 167   *(Chamberlain's allowances)*   35

...

Item payd more for the lyueries of the fyve waytes   vj li.

...

3/ Iohn marten: *woollen-draper*
14/ ips*um*: *John Winter, the treasurer*

1591–2
City Chamberlains' Accounts CCA: CC/FA 19
f 204 *(External expenses)*

...

Item payd more to Colebrand for the dynner of the waytes & 5
seriantes at the quenes day lefte vnpayd ix s. iiij d.

...

f 205

... 10
Item payd to the quenes players the xxx day of marche 1592 xx s.

...

f 206*

... 15
players Item payd the xiij day of Iuly to the *lord* straunge his players
when they playd in the courte halle before Mr leedes maior &
other his brethren xxx s.

...

20

f 212 *(Chamberlain's allowances)*

...

Item payd more for the lyveries of the fyve waytes vj li.

...

25

Court of High Commission Act Book CCA: DCb/PRC 44/3
p 101* *(14 January)*

Proceedings of the court held before the bishop of Dover; William Redman,
archdeacon of Canterbury; and Thomas Lawse, LLD, high commissioners, in 30
the bishop's residence and in the presence of Richard Walleys, notary public

...

officium dominorum contra symcox
Quo die domini monuerunt willelmum symcox presentem in iudicio ad
comparendum in proxima sessione ad recipiendum articulos, et cum tunc 35
comparuerit quod non recedat e curia sine licentia &c/

...

pp 103–4* *(16 March)*

40

Proceedings of the court held before the bishop of Dover; William Redman,

archdeacon of Canterbury; and Thomas Lawse, LLD, *high commissioners, and
in the presence of Richard Walleys, notary public*

...

officium dominorum contra Edwardes et symcoxe
Quo die comparuerunt Edwardes et symcox quibus domini verbo tenus   5
obiecerunt, That they knowinge that the children of the schole were and
are vnder the government of the lord of dovor and other masters of this
churche/ and of the scolemaster and vssher of this scole, notwithstanding
haue inveigled the scolars or some of them to contemne the commandement
of theyr said Master, and in contempt of warnyng gyven them to go abrode in   10
the cuntrey to play playes contrary to lawe and good order/ And afterwardes
the said scolars beinge in pryson for theyr said contempte they the said
edwardes and symcox came to them and there dyd anymate the said children
to playe in contempte of the commandement of my Lord of dovor and other/
and hanged owte | a sho or a pott to beg wythall, and that they dyd anymate   15
the said boyes so ffarr that they were promysed ∧⌈that⌉ they shuld have as
good recompence as they shuld haue by the scole yf they dyd gyve over or lose
theyr place &c. et quia dicti edwardes et symcox negaverunt quam plurima
obiecta eis superius obiectis, ideo domini monuerunt eos ad comparendum in
proxima ad recipiendum articulos, et sic de curia in curiam donec &c.   20
...

p 108   *(11 May)*

Proceedings of the court held in Canterbury Cathedral before the bishop of Dover;   25
William Redman, archdeacon of Canterbury; and Thomas Lawse, LLD, *high
commissioners, and in the presence of Richard Walleys, notary public*

...

officium dominorum contra Edwardes et Symcox
Quo die comparuerunt personaliter Edwardes et symcox, et humiliter   30
submiserunt se &c et fatebantur se in hac parte deliquisse &c et
promiserunt imposterum se circumspectius in omnibus gesturos &c
vnde domini ad eorum humilem peticionem decreverunt eos ab offitio
dimittendos &c et dimiserunt &c

                                                                                  35

1592–3
City Chamberlains' Accounts   CCA: CC/FA 20
f 32   *(External expenses)*
...

Item geven by master Maior to the Quenes Maiesties players   x s.   40
Item paid for the seriauntes and other the officers dynners on
the Quenes daye   iij s.

Item for the Waytes dynner then   ij s. vj d.
Item for the dynner of the Quenes players then which were there
with Musyck   iij s.
...

                                                                              5

f 38v
...
Item paid back in allowance of mr ffrencheham his postes at the
bull stake   iiij s.
...   10

f 43   (*Chamberlain's allowances*)
...
Item paid more for the lyveryes of the fyve Waytes   vj li. v s.
...   15

Consistory Court Book   CCA: DCb/J/X.8.8
f 21v*   (*18 September*)

Proceedings of the court held in the consistory of Canterbury Cathedral to   20
hear cases arising from the archbishop's visitation before Stephen Lakes, LLD,
commissary general

                        St Alphege Canturbury
Weste   we presente one west having a chamber some good space in the sayd Iames   25
        Davyes howse came not orderlye to our parishe church as he oughte to do,
        but in the tyme of devyne service vsed to blowe or play vpon a pipe in his
        chamber to the offence to the offence of dyvers yat heard the same abuse
        xviij septembris 1593 Coram Domino Commissario &c loco Consistoriali &c
        Robins exibuit mandatum originale [exec] qui certificavit se fecisse diligenter   30
        &c preconizatus weste non comparuit vnde decretum est vijs et modis erga
        proximum
...

1593–4   35
City Chamberlains' Accounts   CCA: CC/FA 20
f 98v   (*External expenses*)
...
Item geven to the Musicians on the Countye daye at nyght   iij s. iiij d.
...   40

28/ to the offence to the offence: *dittography*   30/ Robins: *a summoner*

Item geven to the Quenes Maiesties players by master Maiors and
others their consentes   xx s.
...

f 99   5
...
Item for legging and mendyng of the formes in the markett at
the bull stake   viij d.
...
                                                                                                                  10
f 101

Item paid to goodman Vandapeere to buye ij payre of Dromme
heades at London for the ij Cityes drommes   viij s.
...   15
Item paid for makyng cleane the leades over the Bullstake   iiij d.
...
Item for Wood to legg the formes at the Bulstake and for
Carpenters worke   viij d.
Item for a newe chayne and a lock to lock in the   20
formes there   iij s. iiij d.
...
Item for iij plates of Iron and for nayles for the formes at
the Bulstake   vj d.
...   25

f 104
...
Item paid back in allowaunce of mr ffrencheham his postes at
the Bull stake   iiij s. 30
...

f 108   (Chamberlain's allowances)
...
Item paid for iij lyveries for iij of the Waytes viz. iij yardes   35
di. of clothe to every lyuery at xxiiij s. vj d. the lyverye   iij li. xiij s. vj d.
Item paid to Edward Haynes one other of the Waytes the
20 of Aprill 1594 at which tyme he went awaye, in parte
for his lyvery in respect of the tyme he had served vj s. and
I haue paid synce to Robert Stace who served in his steade   40
iij dayes of this yere synce his departure iij s. in all   ix s.

40/ Robert Stace: *apparently added in a lighter ink, possibly at a later time*

Item I paid to William Thorneback one other of the waytes the
ix^th of Iune 1594 at which tyme he went awaye in parte of his
lyuerye in respect of the tyme he had served xvj s. and I haue paid
synce to Iohn Browne who served in his steade iij dayes synce his
departure iij s. in all   xix s.   5
...

1594-5
City Chamberlains' Accounts   CCA: CC/FA 20
f 153   *(External expenses)*   10
...
Item geven to the Quenes Maiesties players   xxx s.
...

f 154   15
...
Item for wood to newe legg the formes at the Bulstake and the
workmanshipp   xviij d.
Item for mendynge A chayne there   ij d.
...   20

f 155
...
Item paid back in allowaunce of mr ffrencheham his postes at
the bulstake   iiij s.   25
...

f 161   *(Allowances)*
...
Item paid vnto Iohn Murton for the lyueryes of the .v. Waites viz.   30
Nycholas Crosse Robert Stace, Robert Dale, Iohn Browne, and
Ed. *(blank)* Warde allowing to euery of them iij yards di. for a
lyuerye at xxiiij s. the lyuerye   vj li.
...

                                                                               35

Burghmote Court Minutes   CCA: CC/AC 3
ff 261v-2   *(15 April)*

players &   Also ffor that to suffer players to playe on the Sabaothe daie ys a prophaninge
playes   of the Sabaothe & a matter highely displeasinge to god and the contynuance   40

4/ Iohn Browne: *apparently added in a lighter ink, possibly at a later time*
30/ Iohn Murton: *tailor, freeman from 1584*

of them so longe tyme as co*mm*only [ys] ⌈hathe byn⌉ vsed ys deemed verie
inconvenient and hurtefull to the state and good quiet of this Cittie and
Impouerishinge thereof especially the same beinge so late as vsually they haue
byn in the nighte tyme yt is therefore at this Courte of Burghemote holden
here on tuesdaie this fyftenthe of Aprill in the xxxvij^th yere of the Quenes   5
highnes reigne by full consent (as a matter for the good of the same Cittie
decreed and agreed from hence fourthe for eu*er* to be obserued and kept that
there shall not any playes enterludes tragedies or comedies be played or players
suffered to playe *wi*thin this Cittie or liberties of the same on any Sabaothe
daye nor aboue twoe daies together at any tyme. And no players ∧⌈so⌉ to be   10
suffered for any such twoe daies [*wi*thin twentie nether] to be suffered to playe
againe *wi*thin the said Cittie or libe*r*ties thereof *wi*thin twentie and eighte
daies nexte after suche tyme as they shall haue laste played [d] *wi*thin the said
twoe daies. And when soeu*er* any suche players shall fortune to playe in any
twoe Dayes as before they shall not exceede the hower of nyne of the clock in   15
the nighte of any of those daies. yf they doe then these players to be noted
what they are and not to be suffered at any tyme after to playe *wi*thin this
Cittie And for better *per*formance hereof m*aste*r maior of this Cittie for
the tyme beinge shall so often and whensoeu*er* any players doe come vnto
this Cittie disclose vnto them the tenor of this decree and geue to them   20
comaundem*ent* that they doe in eu*er*ye respecte accomplishe the same vppon
payne to them not to be suffered to playe againe at any other tyme. And that
the same maior doe send for the oste of the house where any suche players
shall haue theire Abode or be playinge and to lett hym also vnderstand the
tenor hereof | whiche yf he shall suffer to be in his house broken and not   25
obserued he shall forffecte and lose xl s. to the vse of the poore of the
Cittie and that of hym to be levied by distresse to be taken for eu*er*ye
suche contempte and offence by the Towne Sariaunte/

...

30

1595–6
City Chamberlains' Accounts   CCA: CC/FA 20
f 197v*   *(External expenses)*

Item gyven to the Earle of darbye his players by the consent of   35
m*aste*r maior & mr Gante   xviij s.

...

3/ the: th *corrected over* w
6/ (as ... Cittie: *closing parenthesis omitted*
15/ Dayes: *corrected over* ty*m*es (?)
36/ mr Gante: *Richard Gaunt, alderman*

f 198

...

for footyng of the formes at the bulstake xiij d.

...

5

f 199

...

Item [for] payd back in allowance of *ma*ster maior his post*es* at
the bulstake iiij s.

...

10

1596–7
City Chamberlains' Accounts CCA: CC/FA 20
f 237 *(External expenses)*

...

15

Item payd to mr Bussell in defrayeng the charge of the ses*sion*
dynner in december 1596 the so*mm*e of xxij s.
Item payd to the musitions by the consent of m*a*ste*r* maior and
the residue then p*re*sent at the ses*sion* dynner for their paynes ij s.
Item payd mr wetenhall alderman for a gallon of wyne that tyme ij s. viij d. 20

Quarter Sessions Jury Presentments CCA: CC/J/Q/396(a)
f [1] *(20 March)*

presentm*entes* by the graunde Iure the [xxviij^th] ⌈xx^th⌉ of m*a*rche 1596 25
we p*re*sent *(blank)* ffoscew for breikinge the peice and drawinge blude vppon
one of the Queenes plears.

...

f [2]

30

...

we p*re*sent Iohn blye for a noyinge the Queenes hey way w*i*th the solege of
Tow beares

...

35

Burghmote Court Minutes CCA: CC/AC 3
f 301v *(29 March)*

...

musitions &
weight*es*

Also at this Courte yt is granted w*i*th full consent that Iohn Iackson Iohn

20/ mr wetenhall: *Charles Wetenhall, vintner, freeman from 1581; alderman; chamberlain 1595–6;*
  mayor 1598–9
25/ 1596: *6 corrected over 7*

Basforde Iohn Stronge and Stephen ⌈stronge⌉ are Allowed to be the musytions
and waytes of the Cittie and theye to haue no gowndes but onely the [bel]
benevolence whiche they shall collect of the Inhabitant*es* of this Cittie

...

5

1597–8
City Chamberlains' Accounts   CCA: CC/FA 20
f 280*   *(External expenses)*

...

Item to the keeper of the Queens parke for his reward for brynging   10
+   the fate dowe by my *Lord* Cobham bestowed vppon m*aste*r maior
& his Company at the sonne one the Queens day   vj s. viij d.
Item payd the same day for wyne at the sonne expended by serving
men more then ordinary w*hic*h was by the maior & aldermen so
agreed one   iiij s. 15
Item payd the same daye to the Wayt*es* for their paynes in musike
their bestowed   v s.
Item payd more the same daye for the officers and the waytes
dinners at the sonne   v s.
...   20

f 281v
...
first for wood to lage the formes at the bulstacke   viij d.
...   25

f 282v*

Mydsomer   Item payd to mr gemmet at the lyon for two tables at xij d.
sessions   ordinary for xx^tie p*er*sones this *sessi*on dinner   xx s. 30
             Item more to him for M*aste*r Maior his table before agreed vpon   iij s. iiij d.
             Item payd for the dinners of the seriant*es* the serving men and
             the wayt*es* their this cessions to the nvmber of xiiij at viij d.
             ordinary   ix s. iiij d.
             Item payd more for iij pottels of clarret wyne [a qvart*er* of   35
             Sake] & a qvarter of Shewger   v s. iiij d.
             ...

11/ m*aste*r maior: *William Clarck*
29/ mr gemmet: *Warham Jemmett, innkeeper, freeman from 1590; alderman; mayor 1600–1*

f 284

...

Item payd for x yardes of rybond to hang the waytes scutchens
one vppon michalmas Day   xx d.

...   5

f 285v

...

Item for mending the formes at the bulstacke market   vj d.

...   10

1598–9
City Chamberlains' Accounts   CCA: CC/FA 20
f 328v*   *(External expenses)*

...   15

for all manner of Charges at the Countye dynner the xij^th of
december, Mr Manwood, Mr haddes, Mr ffynche, Mr Man,
Mr maije, Mr Cotton, Mr Parramore keepeinge Master maior
Companye, And the Charge beinge extraordynarye, bye reason
of some venison then eaten & geuen bye Mr Manwood and   20
other greate kyndenesses shewed by him vnto Master maior
and his brethren at St Stevens not longe before   vj li. viij s. viij d.
To the waytes bye the maiors Comaundment, in rewarde
for their musicke at the dynner that day   iij s. iiij d.

...   25

ff 332v–3

...

ffor the Bakeing of a Buck which my lord lyvetenant gaue to this
+   Cittye, Master maior, Master deane with the Prebendaryes, Mr Iohn   30
    Smyth Master Archdeaken, Master Comissarye, Master Recorder with
    the reste of the Counsell of this Cittye, with others to the nomber
    of fiftye, being by Master maior invyted to dyne at the Lyon   xv s.|
+   ffor x. ordinaryes at Master maiors Borde at that dynner   x s.
    ffor wyne at that Borde   v s. iiij d. 35
+   ffor v. ordinaryes for iij of the Prebendaryes Captayne Rogers
    and Thomas ffyneux gentleman whoe dyned at an other Borde   v s.
+   ffor wyne for those v.   ij s. vj d.
+   ffor ordynaryes for vj that wanted to make vppe the number
    of .50. beinge provided for   vj s. 40

18/ Master maior: *Charles Wetenhall*

+   ffor Ordynaryes for the officers and the gentlemens men that
wayted at viij d. beinge in nomber xv.   x s.

+   To the waytes by Master maiers order in rewarde for their
musick that day   v s.

...   5

the quarter
sessions at
st michaell
ffor the Sessions dynner at St michaell tharchangell beinge
xxijtie at the firste dynner, and xiij of the wayters, officers,
and musitians at the second dynner   xxxvij s.
ffor wyne and Suger at that dynner   xij s. iiij d.

    10

New Foundation Treasurers' Accounts CCA: DCc/Miscellaneous Accounts 41
f 158v   *(Extraordinary rewards and fees)*

...

Item to ye musitions for playinge at ye Commodies
ij nights ⌈etc⌉   [iij s. viij d.] ⌈x s. vj d.⌉ 15

memorandum
that master
deane must
answere this
[Item to ye musicions for an addicion to their stipend
ex mandato Decani & vicedecani   v s.]

...

St Andrew's Churchwardens' Accounts CCA: U3/5/4/1   20
f 188v*   *(4 December 1597–4 December 1598) (Charges paid)*

...

Item payed for Bread and Bere for the Tromppetors when
my Lord came to towne   viij d.

...   25

1599–1600
City Chamberlains' Accounts CCA: CC/FA 20
f 380   *(External expenses)*

...   30

17 nouember
ffor the dynners of the five waites the Seriantes And the Crier
they waytinge one Master maior & the Aldermen at the lyon,
they with Master Archdeakon and the prebendary dyninge
there one the Queenes daye   vj s. viij d.
ffor a pottel of Clarett wyne and a quart of Sacke for   35
their dynners   ij s. iiij d.
To the waytes in reward for their musicke that dynner   v s.

...

17–18m/ master deane: *Thomas Neville, dean 1597–1615*
32/ Master maior: *Robert Wynne*
33/ Master Archdeakon: *Charles Fotherby, archdeacon of Canterbury 1595–1619*

f 380v

ffor wyne Beere and bread in the Court halle after the readinge
of the laste Accompte   vj s. vj d.
ffor [that] the dynner that daye ffor Master maior And those   5
that kepte him Companie after the accompte ended   vij li. j s. vj d.
To the waytes that daye in rewarde for their musicke   iij s. iiij d.
…

To the waytes in rewarde for their musicke at the firste
quarter Sessions   v s.   10
…

f 382*

…

To the [Earle] lorde Admiralls players, in rewarde for A Playe which   15
they played before Master maior and [dyvers] manye of his frendes in
the Courte halle, And soe ordered bye [m] Master maior And the
Aldermen, vnder their handes, whose names ar here written, viz. Robert
wynne maior. Richard Gaunte. Marckes Berrye. Edward nethersoll.
Thomas longe. Ieames ffrencham. Charles wetenhall Aldermen   xl s. 20
…

f 382v

…

To the waytes in rewarde for their musicke at the Sessions at our   25
ladie daye   v s.
…

f 383*

…   30
ffor makeinge Cleane the Court halle after the playe   xij d.
…
ffor mendinge the formes at the bullstake   vj d.
…
                                                                            35

f 384

…

ffor all manner of Charges for midsommer Sessions dynner beinge
29. at the first dynner with Master maior, And 14. at the other
dynner of the officers Servingmen and Waytes   lviij s. x d. 40

9–10/ firste quarter Sessions: *ie, Christmas quarter sessions*

To the waytes for their musicke that dynner tyme bestowed
one M*aste*r maior and his Companie   v s.

...

1600–1   5
City Chamberlains' Accounts   CCA: CC/FA 20
f 430 *(External expenses)*

...

The Charges of the Contie Dinner at Mr Iemett*es* at the Read
lyon as it apereth vppon his byll of the p*a*rticulers   vij li. x s. vj d. 10
To the wayt*es* for their mvssicke that dinner   v s.
To the sayd Mr Iemett for the p*a*rticuler Charges of the Christmas
qu*a*rter Sessions dinner as it apeareth by his byll   xlvij s.
paid more their for the waytes dinners & other officers and
servaunt*es* their attending the same Daye and for one pottell of   15
claret wyne amounght them   vj s.

...

To the waytes for their paynes & reward at Christmas qu*a*rters
Sessiones Dinner   v s.
...   20

f 431

our ladye   to Mr Iemet late maior for o*u*r ladye qu*a*rters Sessiones Dinner   xlvij s.
Sessions   for the waytes & other the officers dinners the same day   v s. 25
              to the waites the same tyme for their reward & quarters pention v s.
...

f 432

                                                                              30
mydsomer   To Mr Iemete for mydsomer Sessiones dinner as apereth by
Sessions   the byll of the p*a*rticulers theirof   ij li. vj d.
             to the waytes In regard of their wayges the same dinner for
             their mvsike   v s.
...   35
for mendinge of formes at the Bullstake   vj d.
...

9/ Mr Iemett*es*: *Warham Jemmett, innkeeper, freeman from 1590; alderman and mayor*
16/ amounght: *for* amoungst
31/ Iemete: I *corrected over* G

f 432v

Mychalmas
Sessions

Item to mr Iemett late maior of this Cittie for mychalmas
Sessions dinner & the bakinge of venson & other ffees
w*hich* apere in his byll of the *particulers* theirof   v li. xvj s. iiij d.   5

...

To the waytes this Sessiones for their attendaunce & mussike
the same Dinner   v s.

...

ffor mendinge of formes at the bullstake   viij d.   10

...

1601–2
City Chamberlains' Accounts   cca: CC/FA 20
f 472v   15

Recept*es* of
fynes for bulles

Received of Thomas Ryene the Butcher in that respect for selling
of Bulles fleshe not being baythted at the Bulstacke   xij d.

...

20

f 478   *(External expenses)*

...

To mrs wheatenhall one the Countie day for the muskeden and
other wyne spent the same morninge at the Courte hall and for
the sayd coumptie Dinner w*ith* the wine the same dinner and   25
for the latter dinner of the officers gentelmens *servauntes* and

ye county
dinner

the wait*es* their dinner the same daye   v li. xj s. ix d.
To the waytes the same daye for their mussicke and
attendaunce their   v s.

...   30

1ª Sessio

To mrs watson at the fluerdeluce at Christmas q*uar*ters Sessions
Dinner for xxᵗⁱᵉ ordinaries their   xx s.
more to her for xj ordinaries at viij d. a pece   vij s. iiij d.
more to her for wyne   v s.
more to the Chamberlen for his attendaunce & for Shewger   35
w*hich* he fet thither   xviij d.

...

To the waytes the same daye for their attendaunce   v s.

...

23/ mrs wheatenhall: *wife of Charles Wetenhall, vintner and alderman*

f 478v

...

our Ladye
quarters
Sessions

To Mr Clyffe for our ladye quarters Sessions dinner and for wyne   ij li. ij s.

To the waytes for their attendaunce the same Daye   v s.

...   5

f 481

...

Sessiones at
St Iohn the
Babtiste

To mrs wheatenhall for xx^tie ordinaries

the same dinner   xx s.   10

more for wyne the same dynner   v s.

more for the waites and other officers &

waiters the same day for their Dinners   vj s. viij d.

⎫
⎬ xxxj s. viij d.
⎭

To the wayttes for their attendaunce and musicke

the same Daye   v s.   15

...

f 482

...

for iij qvarter of a hundred of Bryckes for to vnderpyn the bulstacke   xij d.   20

for lyme & sand   xx d.

payd the masone for his dayes woorke   xiiij d.

...

f 483   25

michalmas
quarters
Sesions

payd to mrs wheatnall at mychalmas quarter for the Sessiones

dinner with the wyne and officers dinners   ij li. ij s. x d.

...

To the waytes the same daye for ther musicke and attendunce   v s.   30

...

1602-3

City Chamberlains' Accounts   CCA: CC/FA 21

f 21v*   *(External expenses)*   35

...

Item paid to the waytes of the Cittie for their attendaunce &

musicke bestowed vpon master maiors deputy & such as dined

with him at the Swan on the Queenes holliday   v s.

Item to mr Prowde at the same time for the dinner of the Serieantes,   40

Waytes, & other officers & servinge men to the number of 18   xij s.

Item for a pottle of Clarett wine among them   xvj d.

...

f 22

…

Item to the waytes for their musicke & attendance at the first
quarter Sessions dinner   v s.

Item for wyne bread and beare in the towne hall vpon the
Countie day in ye morninge   vj s. vj d.

1ᵃ sessio

Item to mr Prowde for the Countie dinner and for wine as
by his bill of particulars appeareth   iiij l. xix s. vj d.

Item for the five Serieantes their dinners then, the Crior
waytes & other wayters & Servinge men attendinge vpon
their masters the same time   xij s.

…

f 23v

…

Item paid to Thomas Downton one of ye Lord Admiralles Players
for a gift bestowed vpon him & his company being so appoynted
by master maior & the aldermen becaus it was thought fitt they
should not play at all in regard that our late Queene was then
ether very sick or dead as they supposed   xxx s.

…

f 24

…

2 sessio

Item paid to mr Ellis for the quarter Sessions dinner being holden
in Lent   xxxviij s.

Item for wine at the same dinner   vj s. ij d.

Item to the waytes at the same time   v s.

…

f 24v

the Crosse and
Bulstake

Item to Marable ye mason for seeling and repayringe the penteys
of the Bulstake for setting vp the pinnacles which were broken
downe & ioyning in the vanes on the toppe   iij s. viij d.

Item to Gill the plummer for his paynes & worke about the
same 8 dayes di. in scowringe sowdringe & brightninge the
said Crosse & Bulstake ⌈at 14 d. a day⌉   ix s. xj d.

Item to him more for xv l. & quarter of sowder at vj d.
the pound   vij s. vij d.

Item to mr Bonnard the paynter for payntinge the same   iij li.

41/ mr Bonnard: *John Bonnard, painter, freeman from 1582*

Item to Gray the Smith for 300 di. of leade nayles vsed about
the Bulstake   iij s. vj d.
Item for 30 of v d. nayles   xv d.
Item for 3 doges of yron   xv d.
...   5

f 25

...

Item for tall wood & fagottes to heate the plummers yrons for ye
woorke at the [bl] Bulstake   xxiij d. 10
To Scull for his labour iij dayes and halfe in clearinge the Bulstake   ij s. xj d.

24 l. of lead   Item for xvj l. of lead   xx d.
was taken out
of the shop   ...
Item for wyre to binde the stones whereon the Vanes stande   iij d.
Item for coles to melte the leade   ij d. 15
Item to Gill for one dayes worke about settinge vp of the vanes &
mending ye leades   xiiij d.
Item to him more for a pound of sowder   vj d.
...
                                                                                 20

f 25v

...

3 sessio   To mrs wetenhall for Midsomer Sessions dinner vizt. for 20
ordinaries at xij d. and for 15 officers & others at 8 d. a peece   xxx s.
Item for wyne then spent   vj s. 25
Item to the waytes   v s.

...

Item to warde the Ioyner for mendinge of the Scutchions at the
Bulstake which were broken in takinge downe & for the settinge
them vp againe   xiiij d. 30
Item to the Paynters boy, and for nayles to sett vp the said
Scutchions   vj d.
...

f 27   35

...

4 sessio   Item to mr Cliffe for the Sessions dinner before michelmas vizt. for
20 ordinaries   xx s.
Item for 15 ordinaries more of the officers and serving men   x s.
and for wine   xj s. 40

1/ Gray: *Henry Gray, blacksmith, freeman from 1599*
23/ mrs wetenhall: *wife of Charles Wetenhall, vintner and alderman*

Item to the waytes for their attendance & musick   v s.

...

f 27v

...   5

Item for 4 vanes for the bulstake   x s.

...

f 28

...   10

Item to Gill for a dayes work at Bulstak   xiiij d.
Item for 2 pound of Sowder   xij d.
Item for wood for it   iiij d.

...
                                                                                 15

f 28v

...

Item to Richardson the Carpenter for makinge 4 new fourmes
at Bulstake & for legginge the old   ij s.
Item for a locke to locke vp the said formes at the Bulstake   vj d.   20
To Scull for his paynes in helpinge the said Carpenter   vj d.

...

Item for 4 silke Ribandes for the Scutchions to hange about the
waytes neckes   xx d.

...
                                                                                 25

1603–4
City Chamberlains' Accounts   CCA: CC/FA 21
f 72v   *(External expenses)*

...
                                                                                 30

County day.   Item to mrs wetenhall for a gallon of wine dronke the Countie
day in the morninge & for ye Countie dynner at the sune vizt.
for 50 ordinaries at 16 d. a peece & 16 ordinaries at 8 d. a peece
& for wine then   v li. vij s.
To the waytes for their attendance and musicke at the   35
County dinner   v s.
1 Sessions   Item to mr Ellis for the first Sessions dinner   xxiij s.
Item for 16 servingmen & officers at 8 d. a peece   x s. viij d.
Item for wine   vj s. ix d.

...
                                                                                 40

31/ mrs wetenhall: *wife of Charles Wetenhall, vintner*   34/ & for wine then: *possibly added later*
      and alderman   37/ first Sessions dinner: *ie, Christmas quarter sessions*

f 73

Item to the waytes for their musicke & attendance at the first Sessions   v s.
...

5

f 74

...

2 sessions   Item to mrs wetenhall for the Sessions dinner before Easter, for wine
and for the officers and servingmen their dynners at the same time   xxx s. ij d.
...

10

f 74v

Item to the waytes for their musicke and attendance at that Sessions   v s.
...

15

f 75*

...

Item deliuered to master Maior to giue vnto the Princes tumblers
and vnto the Duke of Lenox his players   xiij s. iiij d. 20
...

f 76

...

3 Sessio   Item to mrs wetenhall for the sessions dinner at midsomer vizt. for 27   25
ordinaries at 12 d. & 20 ordinaries at 8 d. for clarett wine vj s. vj d.
for white wine xviij d. for sacke & sugar xxij d. & for sturgeon
iij s. iiij d.   liij s. vj d.
Item to the waytes for that Sessions   v s.
...

30

ff 77–7v

...

Item paid to walter Hardes the Cooke for 27 ordinaries at 12 d. and
18 at 8 d. a peece at michaelmas Sessions   xxxvj s. 35
Item for a gallon of clarett & a pottle of sacke   iiij s.
Item for a pottle of clarett & an other of sacke more   ij s.
Item for a pottle of clarett for ye officers   xij d.
Item for a quart more   vj d.|
Item to the waytes for their attendance & musicke at that Sessions   v s. 40
...

8/ the Sessions ... Easter: *ie, Lady Day quarter sessions*

1604-5
City Chamberlains' Accounts   CCA: CC/FA 21
f 117v*   *(External expenses)*

County dynner   Item to mr wetenhall for the County dynner   iiij li. xij d. ⎫   5
more for wyne at *y*at dynn*er*   xviij s. viij d.   ⎪
Item more for xvj ordynaries for the Offycers   x s. viij d.   ⎬ v li. x s. iiij d.
Item then for wyne to them   xij d.   ⎭

…

Item payd the wayt*es* for plaing at the County dynn*er* & fyrst sess*ion*   x s.   10

…

f 119

…

Item to the wayt*es* on the king*es* daye   v s.   15

…

f 121   *(Vintner's bill)*

…

Item for the offycers dynn*ers* and the wayt*es* on the kyng*es* daye &   20
for a gallon of sack then   xij s.

…

1605-6
City Chamberlains' Accounts   CCA: CC/FA 21   25
f 161   *(External expenses)*

…

p*ai*d for cleanyng the leade over the bulstack   iiij d.

…

                                                                            30

Quarter Sessions Recognizance   CCA: CC/J/Q/405/vii/28
f 1*   *(17 February)*

…

Ewardus [hw] hewitt de Ciuitate Cantuar*ie* musit*io*n, ⌜recognovit in x li. &⌝
Andreas ffrenchburne de Ciuitate pred*icte* [Inhoulder] yeoman & henricus   35
Clarcke de Ciuitate pred*ic*ta husbandman, quilibet eor*um* ^⌜recognovit⌝ in
v li. pro p*er*sonal⟨.⟩ comp*arencia* d*ic*ti Edwardi ad p*roximum* &c & p*ro* pace

5/ mr wetenhall: *Charles Wetenhall, vintner; alderman; mayor, 1598–9*
10/ fyrst session: *ie, Christmas quarter sessions*
35/ pred*ic*te: *for* predicta
37/ personal⟨.⟩: *final letter corrected, now illegible; probably for* personali

erga &c & precipue erga Iohannem Basford de Ciuitate predicta musition
(signed) Markes berrey
Maior/

Drapers' and Tailors' Memoranda Book   CCA: U12/A1   5
f 42v   *(Receipts)*

…

Item receaved of 34 for theare ordinaryes vpon the ffeast daye
at viij d.   xxij s. viij d.

…   10

(Payments)

more he payd for expences at our ffeastes one our feast daye &
other tymes as appees the sum of   vj li. xj s.   15
…

more he payd to the wayttes   v s.
…

1606–7   20
City Chamberlains' Accounts   CCA: CC/FA 21
f 195*   *(External expenses)*

…

Geven to Iohn Buck one of ye waites for him selfe & the rest of
his companye for playing at the County dinner   v s.   25

…

Geven to Iohn Browne one of the waites for him selfe & the rest
of his companye for playinge master maior, at Chrismas Sessions   v s.

…   30

f 195v*

…

Geven to Iohn Baisford one of the waites for him self & the rest of
his company for playinge at Master Maiors at our Ladye Sessions   v s.
…   35

ffor settinge vp of the Cros on the bulstake   viij d.
ffor one to help him   iij d.
ffor vj li. of Lead to yote in yat Cros   vij d.
ffor wood to milte that Lead   ij d.
…   40

15/ appees: *for* appeers   28/ master maior: *Thomas Hovenden*
28/ playinge: *for* playinge before

f 196

...

To the waiths for playinge at master maior yat Sessions   v s.

...

5

f 196v*

...

Geven to Iohn [Bas] Baysford one of ye wayts for him self & the rest
of his company for playinge at master maiors at medsomer sessions   v s.

...

10

f 197

...

Geven to Iohn Buck one of the waytes for him self & the rest of
his company   iiij s. 15

...

f 197v

...

Item payd the fyft of November 1606 for ye sergiantes and waytes   20
dynner that daye at the Sonne   vj s.

...

Item payd to mr wetenhall for the County dynner   v li. ij s. vj d.

...

25

f 198v

...

Item for sylk Rybbons for ye waites   iij s. iiij d.

...

30

f 199

...

Item for new laging the foormes at ye Bulstack   xviij d.

...

35

Drapers' and Tailors' Memoranda Book CCA: U12/A1
f 43   *(Receipts)*

...

Item Received for ordynaryes at our feast   xxviij s. viij d.

...

40

3/ maior: *for* maiors   23/ mr wetenhall: *Charles Wetenhall, vintner;*
3/ yat Sessions: *third (Midsummer) quarter sessions*   *alderman; mayor, 1598–9*

f 43v   *(Expenses)*

...

It*em* payd at our feast for 65 ordynaryes at xij d.	iij li. v s.
It*em* payd for wyne y*at* tyme	j li. viij s. viij d.

...

It*em* payd to the musitians   v s.

...

Diary of Thomas Cocks   CCA: Literary MS E31
f 2

...

spent at the playe ⟨...⟩

...

f 4

...

paide for seyinge the playes yesterdaye & to daye   ij s. iiij ⟨.⟩

...

13   Spent goynge to the playe   xvj d.

...

f 7

...

Spent goynge into the playe   ij s. vj d.

...

12.   Spent goynge in to the playe   viij d.

...

paide for goynge into the Playe   iiij d.

...

f 7v

...

Spent goynge to the playe w*ith* j d. in damsons   v d.

...

12/ spent at the playe: *27 March expense*
12/ ⟨...⟩: *29mm tear in* MS
17/ yesterdaye & to daye: *11–12 April*
17/ ⟨.⟩: *15mm tear in* MS
19m/ 13: *13 April*
24/ Spent ... vj d.: *7 August expense*

26m/ 12.: *12 August*
28/ paide ... iiij d.: *15 August expense*
33/ Spent ... v d.: *24 August expense*

1607-8
City Chamberlains' Accounts CCA: CC/FA 21
f 231v* *(External expenses)*

…

Item paid to the weightes of this City for their attendance &   5
musicke vppon master mayor & such as dyned with hym on
the vth of November   v s.

…

County dynner   Item for the County dynner at ˄⌜the⌝ lyon vizt. for 50 ordynaries
at xij d. the peece & xv [d.] ordynaries at viij d. apeece and for   10
wyne then & for fyre   iij li. xix s. x d.
Item paid to the weightes for their attendance & musicke at the
County dynner   v s.

…
                                                                         15
f 232

…

Item gyven to Iohn Basforde one of ye weightes for hym & the rest of
his company for their musicke & attendance the same Sessions   v s.
…   20

f 232v

…

Item gyven to the lorde Chandoys players that played in the Courte
halle xxx s. so agreed by master Mayor & the Aldermen   xxx s. 25

…

f 233v

…

Item gyven to Iohn Bucke one of the weightes for hym self & the rest   30
of his Companie for playinge at the lady daye Sessions   v s.

…

f 236v

…
                                                                         35
Item payd by master mayors appoIntment vnto the Earle of Sussex
players vppon benevolence [&c]   xx s.

…

6/ master mayor: *Thomas Paramore*
6/ dyned: *3 minims in* MS
19/ the same Sessions: *first (Christmas) quarter sessions*

f 237

...

Item gyven to the weight*es* for playing at the same Sessions   v s.

...

5

f 237v

...

Item gyven to the weyght*es* for playing at michaelmas Sessions   v s.

...

Item for legginge of ye formes at the Bulstake   xj d. 10

...

f 238*

...

Item for the bakinge of 4 great pasties of venison of the bucke that   15
the lorde Treasurer gave to ye City   xvj s.
Item for the officers dynn*ers* & ye waight*es* w*ith* others at the
eatinge of ye same   vj s. viij d.
Item for a pottle of wyne for them   xvj d.
Item to Reve kep*er* of Canterburye p*ar*ke for his fee for the same   20
bucke of the lo*rd* Treasurers guift   x s.

...

f 238v

25

Item gyven to the weyghtes for playing at the eatinge of the bucke
of the lo*rd* Treasurers gyfte to this City   v s.

Robert Clark*es*   ffyrst for two bushell of flower to make pasties [ff] of the bucke
bill of ye lyon   that the lo*rd* Wotton gave to this City   xvj s.
Item for xx^tie pounde of suet at iiij d. ob. the pounde   vij s. vj d. 30
Item for xiij li. of butter   vij s.
Item for a li. of pepper   ij s. iiij d.
Item for salte   ij d.
Item for pap*er*   iiij d.
Item for l. egges   xviij d. 35
Item for wood the baker for bakinge the same pasties   ij s. iiij d.
Item for hard*es* the Cooke for his paynes makinge the pasties   iiij s.
Item for thirtye ordynaries for the ᴧ⌈knight*es* &⌉ gentlemen that
were byd to the eatinge of the same venison   xxx s.
Item for the dynn*ers* of the seriant*es* officers & waight*es* then   vj s. viij d. 40

3/ the same Sessions: *third (Midsummer) quarter sessions*
29/ lo*rd* Wotton: *Edward Wotton, first Baron Wotton, lord lieutenant of Kent*

Item for vij gallandes [of] apottle & one pynt of [wyne] claret wyne   xx s. iiij d.

Item for fower pottles of sacke   viij s.

Item for stronge beere   iij s. vj d.

the end of
his bill

Item gyven to the waightes for playing at the eatinge of ye same venison   v s.

...   5

Archdeacon's Court Book   CCA: DCb/J/X.5.2

f 21v*   *(4 July)*

Proceedings arising from the archdeacon's visitation held in St Margaret's Church,   10
Canterbury, on 8 April 1608

St Paules

Kingsnode 1   To the 57 article wee present the abouenamed william Kingsnothe, for a
disordered person, a contentious and unquiet lyver amonge his neighboures,   15
a swearer and blasphemer of the hollie name of god/

2   Item wee present the abouenamed william kingsnothe for prophaning of the
Saboath daye viz. for keepeing and maynteyning Mynstrells & daunsing in
his howse on sondaye the third day of Aprill 1608

Quarto die Iulij Haselwall apparitor &c certificavit se debite quesivisse   20
willimum Kingsnothe apud edes &c animo citandi &c [et quod no] 29 die
Iunij vltimi animo citandi &c et quod non potuit &c preconizato dicto
kingsnoth non comparuit vnde vijs et modis in proximum
18 die Iulij 1608 Haselwall certificavit se personaliter Citasse dictum kingsnode
xvjᵒ die mensis instantis &c preconizato dicto kingsnode °non comparuit vnde   25
contumax pena reservata in proximum &c°
xixᵒ die Septembris 1608 continuatur in proximum secundum &c

°Natalis Domini°   °vj octobris 1608 continuatur in proximum post natale domini &c°
16 die Ianuarij 1608 iuxta &c preconizato dicto kingsnode non comparuit

excommunicatur   vnde dominus pronuntiavit ipsum contumacem et in penam excommunicandum   30
fore decrevit et excommunicavit
°Introducta est excommunicatio denuntiata in ecclesia predicta 29 Ianuarij
1608 iuxta &c per magistrum william Walsall vicarium ibidem°

Diary of Thomas Cocks   CCA: Literary MS E31   35
f 14

26.   given the waytes of the towne ⟨...⟩
...

21–2/ *animo citandi &c ... animo citandi &c: second occurrence of phrase redundant*
38m/ *26.: 26 January*
38/ *⟨...⟩: 17mm tear in MS*

1608–9

City Chamberlains' Accounts   CCA: CC/FA 21

f 286v*   *(External expenses)*

...

Item paid to henry hamme executor of Iohn Launcelott Ioyner   5
ij s. vj d. for newe heddinge of one of the Cities drummes don by
the said Iohn in his lief tyme vppon the payment of this ij s. vj d.
the said henry delyuered to this Accomptant two drummes of the
Cities a payre of stickes and ⌈a⌉ souldiers coate that Launcelott had
in his lief tyme   ij s. vj d. 10

...

Item paid to Samuell Staples for one drumme which mr Paramore when
he was mayor agreed with hym for xl s. to serve for ∧⌈the⌉ Cities vse   xl s.

...

     15

f 287v*

...

Item paid for a dynner at the fflowre de luce for master Mayor master
Recorder mr ffynch & others then there to the number of xij beinge
that daye abowte the Cities busynes   xij s. 20
Item paid then for xvj ordynaries for ye officers waytes & servingmen
at viij d. a peece   x s. viij d.
Item payd then for wyne   viij s. ij d.

...

Item gyven to ye lorde Chandoys players for that they shoulde not playe   25
here by reason that the sicknes was then in this Cytye so appoynted by
master Mayor & the Aldermen twenty shillinges   xx s.

...

Item gyven to ye lorde Bartely his players for that they shoulde not playe
here in this citye by reason that the sicknes beynge her so appointed by   30
master Mayor and ye Aldermen twenty shillinges   xx s.

...

f 289*

...

     35

Item gyven to Basforde for hym self and the rest of his Companie for
playinge on the vth of November 1608   v s.

...

---

drummes (*left margin*)

5/ henry hamme: *joiner, freeman from 1600*   19/ mr ffynch: *Henry Finch, serjeant at law,*
12/ mr Paramore: *Thomas Paramore, mayor 1607–8*   *legal counsel for the city, and MP for*
18/ master Mayor: *William Watmer*   *Canterbury 1593, 1597*
18–19/ master Recorder: *Sir John Boys*

Item gyven to Iohn Basforde for hym self and the rest of his Companye
for playinge at the Countye dynner   v s.

…

Item gyven to Basforde & for the rest of his companye for playinge at
Christemas Sessions   v s.   5

…

Item gyven to Queenes maiestes players by master Mayor & the
Aldermens consent xx s. master Mayor & the Company with hym
beinge at the playe by them made at the Checkar and also spent
then in beere & byskettes viij d.   xx s. viij d. 10

…

f 291

…

Item gyven to two of the Queens trumpeters and other noble mens   15
Trumpeters with them being here in this Citye by master Mayor &
ye Aldermens appointment   iiij s. iiij d.

…

f 292v*   20

…

Gyven to the waytes for playinge at the fflowre de luce at the purchase
Sessions   v s.

…

ffor leggynge iiijor formes at bulstake   xij d.   25

…

Gyven to the waytes for playinge at the Sunne on the kinges daye   v s.

…

Gyven to the waytes at the ladye day Sessions   v s.

…   30

f 293

…

paid [for] to the pavior for pavinge 27 yardes at ye bulstake   vj s. ix d.

…   35

f 293v

…

paid for drumme heddes   iij s.
paid for heddinge the drummes   viij s.   40

…

paid more for legginge the formes at Bulstake   vij d.

…

f 294*

...

Gyven to the wait*es* for playinge when ye venison was eaten
at the post masters   v s.
Gyven more to them for playinge at mydsomer Sessions   v s.   5

...

Gyven to ye wait*es* at michaelmas Sessions when m*aste*r Mayor
and the Aldermen dyned at the .3. king*es*   v s.
p*ai*d for makinge cleane the leades at Bulstake   iij d.

...   10

Diary of Thomas Cocks   CCA: Literary MS E31
f 25v

...

given Besse walsall, ⌈12 d.⌉ & spent goyng in to the play ⌈6 d.⌉   xviij d. 15

...

14.   payde for my goynge in to the playe   v d.

...

Spent for my goyng in to the playe   iiij d.

...   20

f 28

...

given to the waightes of the towne   ij s.

...   25

f 29

...

Spent at the sonne for my v*alentines* supper, magge walsalls,
Tho*mas* Cockses, and myne, and for wyne and musicke   iiij s. viij d. 30

...

f 32

...

Spent at the playe for me & my man   vj d.   35

...

15/ given Besse ... xviij d.: *13 December expenses*
17m/ 14.: *14 December*
19/ Spent for ... iiij d.: *15 December expenses*
24/ given to ... ij s.: *27 January expenses*
29/ my v*alentines*: *Mrs Margaret Walsall, who cared*
   for the distracted wife of Thomas Cocks

29–30/ Spent at the sonne ... iiij s. viij d.:
   18 February expenses
30/ Thomas Cockses: *elder son of Thomas Cocks*
35/ Spent at the ... vj d.: *8 May expenses*

Spent at the playe for me and my man vj d.

...

Spent goynge in to the playe vj d.

...

5

1609–10
City Chamberlains' Accounts   CCA: CC/FA 21
f 334*   *(External expenses)*

...

ffyrst .2. Nouember 1610 to my lord bartlette his men for that they 10
should not playe by reason of the sicknes, & was appoynted by m*aste*r
mayor & ye alder*men* to geue them x s.

...

County dynn*er*

Item the 12^(th) of decemb*er* 1609 payd Robert turner for the
county diner at the checker for 50 ordinaryes at 12 d. & 16 15
ordinaryes at 8 d. & for wyne 21 s. 8 d. iiij li. ij s. iiij d.

...

Item to the waytes for ther attendance and musicke at the
county diner v s.

... 20

f 335

...

Item payd vnto basford & his company the mutisions for ther
service done at the sessions din*n*er at Christmas v s. 25

...

f 336

...

Item payd vnto basford for ye waytes for musicke at the quarter 30
sessions at our Lady day [sessions] v s.

...

f 337v

35

Item payd basford for hym self & his Companye for musick
at midsom*m*er sessions v s.

...

1/ Spent at the ... vj d.: *9 May expenses*
3/ Spent goynge in ... vj d.: *10 May expenses*
10/ 1610: *for* 1609

14/ 1609: *corrected from* 1610
14/ Robert turner: *vintner*
23/ mutisions: *for* musitions

f 338v

Item payd Basford for hym self & his Companye for musicke
performed at michaellmas quarters sessions   v s.
...   5

Drapers' and Tailors' Memoranda Book   cca: U12/A1
f 45   *(Receipts)*
...
R*eceaued* for ordinaries at our feaste day   xxv s. ij d. 10
...

(Allowances)

Imp*rimis* for the charges of our feast & at other seuerall   15
meetinges vppon sundry occasions about busines of the
company   vj ll. xij s. v d.
...
It*em* to the musitions   v s.
...   20

Diary of Thomas Cocks   cca: Literary ms E31
f 39v
        ...
30 given Bashford & his fellowes for theire nightely playenge   ij s. 25
        ...

f 49
        ...
p*aide* for goynge into the playe twise   viij d. 30
        ...

1610–11
City Chamberlains' Accounts   cca: CC/FA 22(1)
f 27*   *(External expenses)*   35
        ...
5th of november spent in wyne at mr Elvins   xiiij s. vij d.
& payd ther for the officers & wayghters   vj s. viij d.

25m/ 30: *30 January 1610*
30/ *paide* for ... viij d.: *27 September expenses*
37/ mr Elvins: *George Elvwin, vintner; alderman; mayor 1613–14*
38/ ther: r *corrected over* s

& payd to the mutisions ther   v s.

...

Item payd to Robert turner for the countye dinner at the
checker ther was 46 ordinaris at 14 d., & 20^ty seruitours
w*i*th the mutisions at 8 d. a piece & for the wynne there   iiij lib. vij s. ij d.   5

...

f 27v*

...

Item to basfoord & his companye at *y*at dynner   v s.   10

...

geven to the noblemens trompetours as vsually hathe benn geven   ij s. vj d.

...

f 28   15

...

Item payd basford & his company for ther service at Chr*ist*ma*s* sessions   v s.

...

f 28v*   20

...

payd a drom*m*er of lydd for ij days service the last som*m*er not
_∧_⌈[nott] sett downe in⌉ my former acount   v s. iiij d.

...

p*a*yd basford & his company for ther service done at our lady   25
day sessions   v s.

...

f 29*

...
                                                                                           30
payd for iij vella*m* or partchment*es* for the towne droomes   vij s. vj d.

...

payd Basford & his companye _∧_⌈for⌉ ther service at Easter sessions din*n*er   v s.

...
                                                                                           35
f 30

...

Item for a vellam for a drum*m*e head   ij s. vj d.
p*a*yd bona*m* for headdynge the ij drum*m*es   iiij s.

...   40

1, 5/ mutisions: *for* musitions   10/ yat dynner: *ie, the account dinner*
3/ Robert turner: *vintner*

f 30v*

...

Item for a vellam skyne for ye drum*me* head   xij d.

...

Item p*ay*d Basford & his company for ⌈there⌉ service service at   5
michaellmas sessions last   v s.

...

Item payd for headdyng a dru*mme*   ij s.

...
                                                                                   10

New Foundation Treasurers' Accounts   cca: DCc/TA 19
f 204v*   *(Necessary expenses)*

...

Et in denar*ijs* per dictum Computantem hoc Anno solut*is* cum concensu
Capit*u*li pro expens*is* h*a*bitis pro prandio in electione d*o*m*i*ni Georg*ij* in   15
Archiep*iscop*um Cantuar*ie* vij li. v s. vj d. et pro alio prandio ap*u*d
inthronizac*io*nem d*i*c*ti* d*o*m*i*ni Archiep*iscop*i xiij li. xiij s. iiij d. et pro ...
Musicis melodia*m* facientibus ad prandiu*m* inthronizac*io*nis Archiep*iscop*i x s....

...
                                                                                   20

Drapers' and Tailors' Memoranda Book   cca: U12/A1
f 45v*   *(Receipts)*

...

R*eceaued* for ordinaries at our feaste   xxix s. iiij d.

...   25

(Allowances)

[It*em* the charge of our feast for the diett   iij ll. x s. vj d.
It*em* for wine stronge beere & breaking of a glasse   xxx s.] 30

...

This sum*me* for some defaul*tes* was new written one th'other side

f 46

...   35

Imp*rimis* for the charges of our feast and at other seuerall
meting*es* of the company   vj ll. iiij s. v d.

...

It*em* to the waites   v s.

...   40

5/ service service: *dittography*
15/ d*o*m*i*ni Georg*ij*: *George Abbot, elected 18 March 1610/11, enthroned 9 April 1611*

Diary of Thomas Cocks CCA: Literary MS E31
f 49

...

Spent at the playe yesterdaye & todaye   xx⟨.⟩

5

1611-12
City Chamberlains' Accounts CCA: CC/FA 22(1)
f 67*   (External expenses)

...

Item paid mr Elvyn v s. for wyne and offycers dyett*es* when m*is*tris   10
mayres and of the aldermens wyves dyned at the swan at the day of
the gonpowder treason *pre*vented & that day solempnyzed   v s.
It*em* payd mrs whettenhall for xiij ordynaries ∧⌈as⌉ wayt*es* and *ser*iaunt*es*
and a pottle of wyne that they that daye had   ix s.
I payd one for trymmyng the hedd of one of the Cyttyes drom*es*   iiij s. 15
It*em* payd to the wayt*es* v of them playng that daye   v s.

...

Countye   The charge of the countye dynner ∧⌈at the lyon⌉ and
dynner   drynckyng in the morninge [bef] after the Accompt redd   iiij li. ij s. iiij d.
                 paid musycions at County dynner that day   v s. 20

...

f 67v

...

payd to the kyng*es* trumpeters sent to me by m*aste*r mayor on   25
crysmas daye   ij s.

...

f 69

...   30

coronacion   paid that daye for xij ordynaries of xij *ser*vyters offycers and wayt*es*
daye   w*i*th ther wyne to ther ordynaries   vij s. vj d.
                 payd that daye to the wayt*es* wh*i*ch Io*h*n browne receyved   v s.

...

4/ yesterdaye & todaye: *1-2 October*
4/ xx⟨.⟩: *12mm tear in* MS
10/ mr Elvyn: *George Elvwin, vintner; alderman; mayor 1613-14*
11/ of the aldermens wyves: *word or phrase missing before* of
13/ mrs whettenhall: *wife of Charles Wetenhall, vintner and alderman*
16/ playng: pl *corrected over other letters*
25/ me: *the chamberlain, Alderman Richard Gaunt*
25/ m*aste*r mayor: *Joseph Colfe*

the xj of aprill 1611 paid mr Colf mayor that he in my absence had
geven to the lady Elizabeth hyr players ·   v s.

...

f 72v   5

Mr Elvyns   ¶ [Item for a gallon of claret wyne bestoyed on master Attorney   ij s.]
Byll   Item for officers & musitians dynners the fyft of November being
            the daye of our delyverance from the gonn powder Treason   vj s. viij d.
            Item then for a pottle of claret wyne   xij d. 10
            Item for a quarte of sack   xij d.
            Item the suger then   iiij d.
            Item in fyre   xij d.
            Som   x s.

            ...   15

1612–13
City Chamberlains' Accounts   CCA: CC/FA 22(1)
f 99*   *(External expenses)*

...   20

paid the fyft of november 1612 ∧⌈vppon⌉ the good and iust cause of
praysyng god for delyverance of our kyng and nobylitie of [the]
pretended gunpowder treason when master mayer and the Aldermen
dyned at mr Elvyns at the Crowne ∧⌈wher⌉ mr wilson preacher then
ther dyned with them and paid for his ordynarye [to the waytes]   25
∧⌈then⌉ ther   xviij d.
paid more then v s. to the waites then that day playing and attendyng   v s.
paid more then ther for one pottle of wyne and a quart of sacke   ij s. iiij d.

...

                                                                                  30

f 100v*

County dynner   Paid for the County dynner kept at the lyon tewesday the viijᵗʰ of
            december 1612 for the yeare ended at St myghaell next before for
            the whole company of the mayor aldermen and common Counsell   35
            ∧⌈& audytors⌉ and for wyne & waytes yat day   iiij li.

            ...

7m, 24*l* Mr Elvyns: *George Elvwin, vintner; alderman; mayor 1613–14*
24*l* mr wilson: *Thomas Wilson, rector of St George's, Canterbury, 1586–1621*
35*l* the mayor: *Thomas Featherston*

f 101*

…

paid one wilson for velume for heddyng the drom ∧⌜that⌝ potter hathe   iiij s.

paid for brasyng cord for the same   xvj d.

paid Bonnam the phyffe for doyng ∧⌜therof/⌝ & to his sonne   ij s. vij d. 5

…

f 101v

…

Court hall + paid Iohn flackden mason for trymyng the court hall by washing and   10

Colloring the same whyt against the kyng and prynces commyng and

for stuffe as lyme and here and the workmanshyppe therof ther   iij s. viij d.

paid then to the smyth [to] ∧⌜for⌝ settyng to ryghtes in lead on the

topp of the postes at the Court hall dore   x d.

… 15

f 102*

…

paid more the xij^th daye of Aprill 1613 agayne to wilson for velumes

for heddyng the best drome that was brok at babes hill comaunded   20

to be newe amended against commyng of the Palsgrave & prynces   iiij s.

…

paid the xvj of Aprill 1613 ij s. iij d. for wyne when master mayer

mr yong the prynces gentleman ∧⌜vsher⌝ and one ∧⌜mr Grym one⌝

of his comissioners and of the kynges trumpettes wer present at   25

∧⌜mr⌝ lockles   ij s. iij d.

…

paid tewsday the xx^th of Aprill 1613 that mornyng prynce charles

went awaye hens from Caunterbury toward london for bred bere

& wyne at the lyon   xiiij d. 30

paid & geven to ffenner Iester to the lady Elizabeth the xx^th of

Aprill 1613 toward losse of his clothes and mony whearof he said

he lost and was here robbed   ij s.

…

paid to whit the bell rynger of chrystchuche [from] ∧⌜for⌝ brynging from   35

Christ churche home to the Courthall a pyke and ancient of the Cyties,

that was lent vppon request of the vycedeane & prebendaries to hang out

of the topp of bellharry steple to knowe when the wynd dyd shyft well/

for the palsgrave and the lady Elizabeth his wyf myght take shyppyng

at Margate   vj d. 40

10/ trymyng: *4 minims for* m *in* MS

26/ lockles: *Richard Lockley, vintner, freeman from 1602; mayor 1623-4*

paid to Georg Bailes for a drom Cord for the great dromm the last of
aprill 1613   xviij d.

+   paid v s. to the fyve waytes playing the lowd musycke on the topp of
all Saintes church in the highe streate at the commyng into the Cyttie
[coming in] at westgate of the prynce the lady Elizabeth his syster and   5
the pallsgrave hyr husbond   v s.

+ At this tyme they were receyved at westgate by ∧⌜the mayor⌝ all the

xxxix s.   ∧⌜[Mayor]⌝ aldermen and comon counsell (the ∧⌜mayor &⌝ aldermen in ther
Scarlett and comons in ther best attyre, when the prynce was presented with
a fayer great silver [Cub] Cupp, all gylt, and the palsgrave & his wyf the lyke,   10

Quod nota   of seuerall makynges or fassions, when mr mathewe hadd then recorder made
vppon delyuery of the presentes 2: seuerall oracions ∧⌜or speches⌝ fyrst to the
prynce and his sister the lady Elizabeth sytting in one Coche and an other
oracion to the palsgrave and the duke sytting in an other coche with all the
shott to the nomber of lxxx but with holberdes & partysayns in ther redd   15
soldiers Coats ⌜newe hattes & fethers⌝ half ⌜on the⌝ one side the streat &
∧⌜other⌝ half on the other so gardyng them ffrom westgate to the further gate
of chryst church, wher they went in to the deanes howse for the Court ther to
be for ⌜ther⌝ abod for the prynce ⌜& duke⌝ and docter fotherbe his howse for
the palsgrave & his ladye princes Elizabeth beyng in the church ∧⌜all full⌝ [all   20
the shott at ons gave them a gallant ⟨…⟩] of wellcvm
ther they contynewed ix daies

f 102v

…   25

drum   paid the xxvij of Iune 1613 to potter the drom parcell of his yerlie
wages of v s.   xij d.

…

f 103   30

…

paid the iiij^th of Iulie 1613 to the lady Elizabeth hyr pleyers who ⌜by
master mayer⌝ wer sent and brothe vnto me from Master Mayor by
edward foster keper   x s.

…   35

9/ attyre,: *comma used for closing parenthesis*
11/ mathewe hadd: *city recorder and MP for Canterbury*
15/ & partysayns: *added in right margin*
19/ docter fotherbe: *Charles Fotherby, prebendary and archdeacon of Canterbury*
33/ me: *Richard Gaunt, chamberlain*
34/ keper: *keeper of the city gaol at Westgate*

f 103v

paid the second of September 1613 to certeyn musicion waytes sent to
me as treasorer   vj d.

...   5

drum

paid the 2 of october 1613 to Iohn potter one of the dromes for his
ᴧ⌈two⌉ quarteredges of v s. a yere to beat the drome & at all tymes
to be reddy   ij s. vj d.

...

ffife

paid vnto *(blank)* Bonnam the phyffe ij s. vij d. for two quarters   10
pencion for beating the drom as above for potter all waies to be in
reddynes to do ye sam   ij s. vj d.

...

f 104   15

...

paid for woodd at one tyme to make drum styckes   xviij d. [xviij d.]
paid for turnyng of the styckes   iiij d.

...
                                                                            20

f 104v

...

paid for legging the formes at the bustack   ix d.

...
                                                                            25

1613–14
City Chamberlains' Accounts   CCA: CC/FA 22(1)
f 151*   *(External expenses)*

...

Item to the waightes for playeng on the vth of November 1613   30
being the gunpowder treason day, vnto the maior Aldermen
and Common Counsell at their dynner   v s.
Item to the sayd wayghtes for their attendance and musicke
on the County daie at dynner 1613   v s.
Item for the County dynner vpon the vij^th day of december   35
1613 at the Crowne   iij li. xiiij s. viij d.
Item for 2 gallons a pottle and a pinte of Clarett wyne   vij s.
Item for 9. quartes and a pint of sacke spent that dynner   ix s. vj d.

...

10/ vij d.: *for* vj d.   30, 34, 36/ 1613: *underlined in* MS
23/ bustack: *for* bullstack   31/ the maior: *George Elvwin*

Item for fire at the County dinner   xviij d.

...

f 151v*

Item paid for wyne at dynner on the vth day of November 1613
being the gun powder treason day, for the dynners of master mayor
Aldermen & Common Counsell vizt. 2 gallons of Claret v s. iiij d.
and a gallon of sack iiij s.   ix s. iiij d.
Item for fire then   vj d.
Item for the dynner of xij officers and servitors and waightes then viij s.
...
Item to Iohn Potter one of the drumms for the Citty for [y] his yeares
pencion allowed by Burghmot   v s.
To Thomas Bonnam the ffife for his yeares pencion likewise allowed v s.
Item to Iohn Warde an other of the drummes for his yeares pencion in
the like maner   v s.

f 152

...
Item to Robert Rawlins for a Corde for the drum in Iohn Potters
Custody   ij s.
Item to Iohn Wilson for taking downe the ij heades of that drum ij s. vj d.
Item to Thomas Bonnam for heading that drum   xvj d.
...

f 155

...
Item to warde the drumme for his chardges which he had layd out
vpon the drum vizt. for a head ij s. vj d. for 2 new hoopes viij d. for
setting on the same x d. in all   iiij s.
...

f 155v

...
Item for mendinge the formes at the Bullstack   xiij d.
...

6/ 1613: *underlined in* MS

1614–15
City Chamberlains' Accounts   CCA: CC/FA 22(1)
f 190*   *(External expenses)*

...

Item to the waytes of the Citty for their fee for attending and   5
playeng at dynner on the County day   v s.

...

Item to mr Elvyn Alderman for the County dynner kept in
his house as by his Bill of particulers therof may appeare   iiij li. x s. viij d.
Item to him for wyne and sugar and fire at that dynner   xxxiij s.   10

...

f 190v

...

Item to Potter the drum for his quarterage of v s. being his yearly   15
stipend allowed by Burghmot for his paynes   xv d.

...

f 191

...   20
Item payd to Iohn warde the drum for quarters stipend   xv d.

...

f 191v

                                                                                   25
Item payd to mr Elficke the Towne Serieant [wch] for his layenges
out the first quarter. vizt for the lengthening of a chayne to keepe the
formes at the Bulstacke   xv d.

f 192   30
...
Item for iiijor new foormes for the Bulstack   ix s.

...

f 193   35

...
Item to Potter the drum for his quarterage   xv d.
Item to Iohn warde the drum for his like quarterage   xv d.

...

                                                                                   40
f 195

...

Item to Potter the drum for his quarterage   xv d.

Item to warde the drum for the like   xv d.

...

Item for legging the foormes at the bulstake & for tymber to do them   xviij d.

...

5

f 195v

...

Item for legging of the foormes at the Bulstack ⌈& stuffe⌉   xvj d.

...

10

f 196

...

Item to Potter the drum   xv d.
Item to warde the drum   xv d.

...

15

f 197

...

Item to Tucker for ij drum stick*es*   ij s. vj d.

...

20

1615–16
City Chamberlains' Accounts   CCA: CC/FA 22(1)
f 237*   *(External expenses)*

...

25

Item to mr Elvin Ald*erman* for the County dinner w*hic*h was at
his house & for wynne suger & fier at that dinner   v li. xvj s.
Item to the waitts of the Citty for their atendinge and plaienge
y*a*t daye   v s.

...

30

f 237v

...

Item to Iohn Potter and Iohn ward the Cittys drums for their
qu*ar*ters stipend   ij s. vj d. 35

...

f 238

...

Item to Richard marable for amending the Burghmot horne   iij s. 40

...

19/ Tucker: *John Tucker, joiner, freeman from 1598*   40/ Richard marable: *brazier, freeman from 1605*

f 239

...

Item to Iohn Potter and Iohn ward the Cittyes drumes for their
quarters stipend   ij s. vj d.

...   5

f 239v*

...

Item to Iohn ward and Iohn Potter the Cittys drumes for their
quarters stipend dew at midsomer   ij s. vj d. 10

...

Item to Potter one of the Cittys drumes for puttinge in of a new head
in his drum   xij d.

...
                                                                               15

f 240*

...

Item for anew ho⌈u⌉ppe put one his drum   viij d.

...

Item to Iohn ward and Iohn Potter for their quarters stypend dew   20
at midsomer   ij s. vj d.

...

f 241

                                                                               25

Item to mr meryam for ∧⌈v⌉ [v] ells of ribbon to hange the waittes
scuchins one   iiij s.

...

Item to Iohn ward & Iohn Potter the Cittys [C] drumes for their
stipend that quarter   ij s. vj d. 30

...

1616-17
City Chamberlains' Accounts CCA: CC/FA 22(1)
f 289* *(External expenses)*   35

...

In primis [of] To the wayttes of the Citty for their fee atendinge and
playinge one the vth of november °1616°   v s.

...

18/ his: *John Ward, one of 2 city drummers*
26/ mr meryam: *John Meryam, haberdasher; alderman; mayor 1631-2*
30/ that quarter: *fourth (Michaelmas) quarter*

To mr Berry maior which he gave vnto my Lord woottons keeper, when
he brought hym the fatt dooe, the one halfe of which dooe was speent at
the county dinner   vj s.

...

To mr Elvin Alderman for wynne sugar and other Charges had one   5
the fifte of november   xvj s. x d.

...

To mr Elvin Alderman for the County dynner bakinge the venison
with wyne suger & fier & for vij quartes of muskyden had at the
Court hall in the morninge   vj li. v s. j d. 10

...

To the wayttes of the Citty for their atendance and musicke at the
County daye   v s.

...

                                                                           15

f 289v

To ward and Potter the Cittyes drumes for their Stipend dew
at Cristmas   ij s. vj d.

...   20

f 290v

...

To ward and Potter the Cittyes drumes for their stipend   ij s. vj d.

...   25

f 291v

To ward and Potter for their quartridge   ij s. vj d.

...   30

To Clarke the Seirgant that master Maior sent for to give the Lord of
Aubergaine his plaiers in respect that they should not playe in the Citty   xx s.

...

f 292*   35

...

To Potter for a hoppe for one of the Cittyes drumes   x d.

...

1/ mr Berry maior: *Mark Berry*
1/ Lord woottons: *Edward Wotton, first Baron Wotton, lord lieutenant of Kent*
5, 8/ mr Elvin: *George Elvwin, vintner; alderman; mayor 1613–14*
31/ Clarke: *Edward Clarke, one of 4 serjeants of the chamber*

To ward and Potter the Cittyes drumes for their pencion dew
at midsomar ij s. vj d.

...

1617–18 5
City Chamberlains' Accounts cca: CC/FA 22(1)
f 336* *(External expenses)*

...

To Mr Elvyn for Chardges that daie by order of Burmoth
likewise allowed x s. viij d. 10

...

To the wayttes of the Cyttie for their paynes playinge before the mayor
Aldermen and Comon counsell the ffifte of November att mr Elvyns v s.

...

To the wayttes of the Cyttie for their attendance and musique att 15
mr Elvyns att the County dynner v s.
To mr Elvyn for the countie dynner and for fyer suger and
iij pottles and one quarte of muskadell in the mornynge v li. vij s. vj d.

...

20

f 338v

...

To hym more for a Cord for his drumm ij s.
Layed oute for two payer of drumm hedes and for brynging
them downe vij s. iiij d. 25

...

f 339

...

ffor one payer of drum stickes for the base drum ij s. vj d. 30
To ward the drum for ffytinge fower hedes to the two drums and for
iij new hoopes with two pennyworth of nayles vsed about them vij s.

...

To Potter ʌ⌜for a better [h]⌝ hed on the Treble drum accordinge to order
of Burmoth which he said was putt on about two yeares synce ij s. 35

...

9, 13, 16, 17/ Elvyn, Elvyns: *George Elvwin, vintner; alderman; mayor 1613–14*
9/ that daie: *5 November*
12/ the mayor: *Thomas Hovenden*
23/ hym: *John Ward, one of the city's drummers*

1618–19
City Chamberlains' Accounts   CCA: CC/FA 22(1)
f 384*   *(External expenses)*

...

Inprimis paide for the ffee of a ffatt dooe sent by the Lord   5
Wotton to m*aste*r maior and the rest of the Company and for
bakinge and seasoning the same and for wyne and fyer and
other Chardges att the eatinge thereof vpon the fyfte of
November .1618 being allowed by order of Burghmoth on the
10th of November   iij li. iiij s. x d. 10
It*em* payde to the musitians for theire attendance on m*aste*r
maior that daye being the 5th of November   v s.

...

Payd for the County dynner and wyne to the same and for iij potles
and a quarte of Muskadyne in the morning at the Cort hall and   15
for fyer   v li. xv s.
Payd to the musitions for their attendance and playing that day   v s.

...

1619–20   20
City Chamberlains' Accounts   CCA: CC/FA 22(2)
f 445v

...

To Iohn Terrey Carpenter for his man j daye to legg the fourmes at
Bulstack [⟨..⟩] ix d., and for wood vj d. for a peece of tymber of   25
ix foote at ij d. the foote to make a barr for Northgate xviij d. for
workinge the same ix d. for xviijth pales for westgate pound xviij d.
ij peeces of Tymber to make rayles for the pound xxij d. for a
hundred of sixpeny nailes vj d. for workemanshipp ix d. in all   viij s. j d.
...   30

1620–1
City Chamberlains' Accounts   CCA: CC/FA 23
f 33*

...   35

To mr Elvyn for the Countye dynner w*hic*h was vppon the
xxviijth daie of Novembr*e* 1620   v li. v s. vj d.

...

5–6/ Lord Wotton: *Edward Wotton, first Baron Wotton, lord lieutenant of Kent*
6/ m*aste*r maior: *Avery Sabyn*
24/ Iohn Terrey: *John Terry, carpenter, freeman from 1614; mayor 1637–8*
36/ mr Elvyn: *George Elvwin, vintner; alderman; mayor 1613–14*

f 33v*

To the waytes of the Cyttie for their musique and attendance att the
said dynner   v s.

...   5

To Goodwiffe Bly for her Christide quartridg for sweeping the bulstake
and the whytstable markett   v s.

...

f 34v   10

...

To ward the drummer for two drumbhedes iiij s., for one newe Corde
xxij d. for two hoopes ij s./ for tryming the drumb iij s. iiij d./ in all   xj s. ij d.

...

                                                                                                                            15

1621–2
City Chamberlains' Accounts CCA: CC/FA 23
f 93*   *(External expenses)*

...

To william daniell the cheife of the Kinges Players to ridd them out   20
of the Cittie without actinge xx s. allowed by Burgmoth   xx s.

...

Paid the waightes for playinge at the Chequer the .5. of nouember   v s.

...

                                                                                                                            25

f 94v

To mr Lockley for the Countye dinner in december .1621. &
wine in the morninge   vj li. ix d.
And for bread, Beere Coles & Candles spent at the hall that   30
morninge   viij s. iij d.
To the waytes for musick that day   v s.

...

f 95v   35

To A Pavor for paving lix yardes of grownd at the bullstack
att iiij d. the yard   xiiij s. ix d.
for iij loades of stone for the [same] ⌈same⌉   vij s vj d.
for ij loades of sand theare   ij s. 40

28/ mr Lockley: *Richard Lockley, vintner, freeman*   37/ Pavor: *corrected over* laborer
    from 1602; mayor 1623–4   39/ [same]: s *corrected over* l

for Carying away of two load*es* of rubishe ther   viij d.

...

1622–3
City Chamberlains' Accounts   CCA: CC/FA 23   5
f 146*   (External expenses)

...

Item paied that was spente by the maior Aldermen and Comon
Counsell att the Chequer on the vth of November in wyne
xiiij s. vj d., for xiij ordinaris att viij d. for the Citties officers and   10
the musitians and for fier vj d., all   xxiij s. viij d.
Item paied to the musitians for musique that daie   v s.

...

f 146v   15

...

Item paied for /90/ foote of oaken plank for xiiij formes for the
markett folk*es* to sett att the Bulstake   xiiij s. iiij d.
Item for 84 foote of quarters for leg*es* for them   iiij s. ij d.
...   20
Item for xxij foote of Elme bord & five foote of quarters   ij s.

...

Item for a workman to legg the xiiij formes and to fitt the xxij foot of
Elme bord one the butchers stales where yt had went   vij s.

                                                                                   25
f 147v

...

Item to Barrett for A new Cheyne for the new formes made for the
markett folk*es* att the Bulstake and for a locke & key to locke them
together and for mending fower linck*es* of the ould Cheyne in all   v s. x d. 30
...

f 149

...

Item paied to the Paviors for pavinge xlv yard*es* of grownde att the   35
Bulstake the xiiij^th daie of march, for a load of sand vsed about that
worke, for Carriynge of two load*es* of stones from the bredwell one
loade to the Bulstake & the other load to the Streat against the
Courthall, and for Carrying awaie of one load of Rubbish that the
paviors made in bothe places, in [a] all   xj s. 40
...

8/ the maior: *George Clagett*   28/ Barrett: *Edward Barrett, locksmith, freeman from 1616*

f 150

...

Item paied that was gyven the king*es* players the xxiiij^th of Aprill by the
Appoyntment of the maior and Aldermen in regrad they should depart
the Cittie and not playe the some of   xxij s. 5

...

f 150v

...

Item paied to mr Colffe for A bancquett for the Spanish Embassador 10
that came in Iune 1623   vj li. xij s.

...

f 151

... 15

Item paied to Edward ffryerston for his Iornie he being sent by the
Maior and Aldermen to goe to meete the Spanishe Embassidor and to
retorne backe to gyve them notice by what howre he would come into
the Cittie   xviij d.

... 20

f 152

...

Item paied by the Appoyntment *of* m*aste*r mayor for fyve elles of
Ribbon to hang the Citties Scuchins that doe remayne with the 25
waithes of the Cittie   iij s. vj d.

...

Letter from Sir Lewis Lewknor to Sir Edward Conway
PRO: SP 14/146 30
ff [1–1v]* *(14 June)*

Right Ho*nor*able

I thought fitt according to the former direcc*i*ons receaued from you to 35
acquaint *you*r Honor with the perticulers of *our* voyage this day from Douer
to Canterburie. In ye morning my Lord of Rutlands fleete came from ye

4/ regrad: *for* regard
10/ mr Colffe: *Joseph Colfe, apothecary, freeman from 1589; alderman; mayor 1611–12*
16/ Edward ffryerston: *maltster, freeman from 1623*
37/ my Lord of Rutlands: *Francis Manners, earl of Rutland, admiral of the fleet*

Downes and roade before the to Towne of Douer not farre from ye shoare,
and when the Marquis went vp the hill with his Coaches the Admirall first
and then in order all the other shipps dicharged all theire Artillerie which was
seconded with the Artillery from ye Castle

Comming afterwardes to Barham Downes a braue Troupe of knightes &   5
gentlemen well horsed & ritchly apparelled mett him & lighted of their
horses. The Marquis the other Ambassador & the Spanish gentlemen did
the like out of their Coaches where after a Ciuill Complement past on
both sides with singuler contentment to the Marquis he went into ye
Coach & they toke theire horses and attended him into Canterburie   10
performing all kindes of respect & honor they could possibly do vnto
him. wherein Sir Dudley Diggs Sir Nicholas Tufton and Sir Edward
Hales did expresse the greate care they tooke in performing this service
according to his Maiesties commaundment so likewise did the other
knights and gentlemen and suerly your Honor shall do them a greate   15
deale of right to acquaint his Maiestie withall

vppon the Gates of Canterburie were placed by the Maior Hoboyes and
Sackbuttes that saluted his entrance into ye towne. within ye Gates stood
the Maior and all his bretheren in [y] theire Skarlett gownes tendring
vnto him theire service and desiring his permission that they might waite   20
vppon him in his lodging. which they did ^⌐afterwardes¬ presenting him
with 30 dishes of Marchpanes & other Costly sweete meates & because
the presse was greate they placed 20 handsome men with halbertes at the
Gate all apparrelled in the liuery of ye Towne. after the Maior had taken
his leaue & signified his Maiesties commaundment giuen vnto him & his   25
bretheren to do his excellence all the honor [th] and service the[y] towne
could aford. The Marquis went to see the Church where they were
Courteously receaued by some of the Channons & shewed euery thing
that was worthy to be seene especially the place where St Thomas of
Canterburie was murdred which they beheld with much curiosity. I   30
assure your honor that I haue seen many receptions in Kent but I neuer
saw any [so] performed so well & so orderly as these of this day. and I
should haue condemned my selfe of a greate neglect if I should haue left
it vnaduertised |

So remembring my humble respectiue service vnto your Honor I rest   35

Douer Saterday
14th of Iune 1623   Your most devoted servant to Commaund

1/ the to: *for* to the (?)
3/ dicharged: *for* discharged
31/ honor: *apparently inserted between* your *and* that
38/ 1623: *underlined in* MS

I thought fitt to let your Honor know yat the
former aduertismentes hold & yat ye Marquis will
certainely lodge to morrow night at Grauesend I
did yesternight write to my lord Chamberlaine to   (signed) Lewes Lewkenor
aduertise my Lord Kelley thereof & to send downe   5
Barges & do much desire to Know his Maiesties
pleasure touching his audience on Monday./

1623–4
City Chamberlains' Accounts   CCA: CC/FA 23   10
f 199*   *(External expenses)*
...

paid to Mr Penn the 18th of december ⌐1623¬ ffor the
County dynner   iiij li. xvj d.
paid to mr Hockley ffor 6 quartes of muskeden and a quart of   15
sacke spent on the County day in the morning and xij d. in strong
beere. and fower dozen and a halfe of manchett iiij s. vj d. in all   xij s. vj d.
paid to the waytes of the Citty for theire Musicke & attendance   v s.
...
                                                                                             20

f 204v

paid to Ward one of the Drummers of this Citty the 24th of September
1624 for three newe heades for one of the Cities drumes and for fower
newe hoopes for that drum and for putting them in according to an   25
order in Burmoth   xij s.
...

1624–5
City Chamberlains' Accounts   CCA: CC/FA 23   30
f 243*   *(External expenses)*
...

Paid by the appoyntement of master Maior the 16 of yat month that was
giuen to the princes plaiers to depart the Cittie and not to play   xj s.
...   35
Paid to mr Colfe the 2 of September for a march pane which was with a
Bonnett of sweet meates bestowed on monsier Deuile Core a french
Embassador the some of   xvij s.

13/ Mr Penn: *James Penn, innholder, freeman*   36/ mr Colfe: *Joseph Colfe, apothecary, freeman*
  from 1610   *from 1589; alderman; mayor 1611–12*
15/ Hockley: *for* Lockley *(?)*   37/ monsier Deuile Core: *probably the marquis*
33/ yat month: *November*   *de Villiaviler*

Paid to Mr Southwell for 2 torches vsed when m*aste*r Maior. the
Alder*men* & Co*mm*on Counsell went to the Chequior to Salute
ye *sai*d Embassador   xx d.

...

5

f 243v*

...

Paid the 16 of decem*ber* ˄⌈1624⌉ vnto Henry Bicraft for the
County dynner last   iij li. ij s. ij d.
Paid to the wait*es* of the Cittie for theire musicke and attendance   10
that day   v s.

...

f 246v*

15

...

paid to Potter and Ward Dummers for theire seruice 2 daies at the
king*es* coming from Douor w*it*h his Queene and at his dep*ar*ting from
this Citty   iiij s.

f 247*   20

...

paid to the musitians for theire musicke at his ma*ie*st*es* entrance into this
Citty: by appoyntem*ent* of m*aste*r maior   vj s.

...

25

f 247v*

...

paid for Caredg of a lather to St George*s* gate for the wait*es* at the
ffrench Embassandors coming into this Citty   iiij d.

...

30

f 248

...

paid to the painter in Christchurch yard for newe painting the armes at
the Bulstacke   xx s. 35

...

paid to S*ir* Iohn ffinches man for Coppying out of both the speaches
made to the king & Queene at theire being heere: by his mast   v s.

...

1/ Mr Southwell: *Walter Southwell, alderman; mayor 1634–5*
16/ Dummers: *for* Drummers
37/ Sir Iohn ffinches: *city recorder and* MP *for Canterbury*

paid to Rob*er*te Buchin the free mason for mending the pinnacles of ye
Bulstacke & for Smithes worke there   v s.

f 248v*

...   5

paid to Paule Wiggons for his worke and stuffe vsed about the Court
hall & Bulstake. as by bill appeareth the some of   xxx s.

...

f 249*   10

...

Fees due to the king*es* seruant*es* at his being here in Cant*erbury* Iune 1625 and
paid by the *sa*id Accompt*ant* vid*eli*c*et*
To the gent*lemen* vsshers daily Waiters   v li.
To the gent*lemen* vsshers of ye privey Camber   v li. 15
To the Sariant*es* at Armes   iij li. vj s. viij d.
To the gent*lemen* vsshers quarto Waiters   xx s.
To the Sewers of the Camber   xx s.
To the King*es* harbenger[s]   iij li. vj s. viij d.
To the ⌈knight⌉ marshall   xx s. 20
To the Yeomen vsshers   xx s.
To the Gromes & pag*es*   xx s.
To the ffootemen   xl s.
To the 4 yeomen of ye Mowth   xl s.
To the Porters of the gate   xx s. 25
To the Sariant Trumpeters   xx s.
To the Trumpeters them selucs   xl s.
To the Surueier of the waies   xx s.
To the Bottellmen of the feild   x s.
To the Cochemen   xx s. 30
To the yeomen Harbengers   xx s.
To the yeomen vsshers for ye sowrd   vj s. viij d.
To the King of Herrall*es* and Purssevant*es* at Armes at his ma*ies*t*es*
entring this Citty   v li.
To the king*es* musitions the auncient fee   x s. 35
To the King*es* drume and fife   v s.
To the Iester   x s.
To m*r* waller Deputy Clarke of ye markett for the virge as a Curtesey
from the Citty in forbering to execute his Aughtority here   xxx s.
                    The end of the *sa*id fees   40

...

f 250v*

...

p*ai*d to the waites of the citty for theire musicke at the king*es* Coming
heere, and at ye ffrench Embassendo*ur* whoe came in may last. for both
by order of Burmoth   x s.   5

...

f 251v

...

paid to Gibson the post for twoe paier of drume head*es* for ye Citty   10
drumes & for bringing of them downe   v s. vj d.

...

Privy Council Warrant   PRO: PC 2/33
f 80v*   *(9 July)*   15

...

A Warrant to S*ir* Willi*a*m Uuedale Kn*igh*t Treasurer of his M*aiesties* Chamber
to paie vnto Ierome Lanier and Anthony Bassano and eleuen other of his
M*aiesties* Musitians for the wind Instrum*entes* the som*m*e of 130 li. for their
attendance at Canterbury and Douer./.   20

1625–6
City Chamberlains' Accounts   CCA: CC/FA 23
f 292v*

...   25

p*ai*d for a quar*ter* of a load of stones to paue vnder St michaells gate,
and to the pauior for the paueing there & at bulstacke in may   ij s.

...

f 293   30

...

p*ai*d to ye Ropemaker for a Cord ffor whit*es* drume the 12 of Iuly
soe ordred by burmoth   ij s. ij d.

...
                                                                           35

f 295

...

p*ai*d for newe headding of one of the Citties drumes to Tucker the
ioyner xx d. for 2 newe hoopes for ye said drome ij s. & three newe
brac*es* iij d.   iij s. xj d. 40

...

38/ Tucker: *John Tucker, joiner, freeman from 1598*

f 295v

...

paid to mr whiting that he gaue to Certen[t] players to dep*a*rte the
Citty and not to play, and by Burmoth allowed x s.

...   5

1626–7
City Chamberlains' Accounts CCA: CC/FA 23
f 336* *(External expenses)*

...   10

p*ai*d for ye County dynn*er* ye 14 of decem*ber* 1626 to
Isaacke Barham iij li. iij s. vj d.

...

p*ai*d to the wait*es* of the Citty for theire seruice done at ye *said*
County dinner v s. 15

...

f 337v

...

p*ai*d to Goodman Tucker ye Ioyner for tryming vp of ye 20
Citties Drumes in ffebru*ary* putting in twoe newe head*es*
and 2 newe hoopes iij s. iiij d.

...

f 339v 25

...

p*ai*d to Richard white drume for a newe head for his Drume
ye 14 of may ij s.

...

30

1627–8
City Chamberlains' Accounts CCA: CC/FA 23
f 387v*

...

p*ai*d to mr Barham at ye Lion the 20 day of decem*ber* 1627 35
for the County dynn*er* as bye bill appeareth iij li. x s. x d.

...

3/ mr whiting: *William Whiting, mayor 1625–6*
12, 35/ Barham: *Isaac Barham, yeoman, freeman from 1614*
20/ Goodman Tucker: *John Tucker, joiner, freeman from 1598*

p*ai*d to the Cittie wait*es* for theire seruice at the County dynn*er* the
24 decem*ber*   v s.

...

f 389   5

...

p*ai*d to Iohn Ward for 2 paier of Dum*m* head*es* for the Citty drumes
wh*i*ch he bought at Sandw*i*ch in march the 7th day   vj s. ij d.

...

                                                                                 10

f 389v

...

p*ai*d to Tucker ye ioyner for putting on a snare head vppon the
Drum*m* y*at* potter vseth of the Citties in march   xviij d.

...   15

f 390

...

p*ai*d to Tucker the ioyn*er* the 24 of Iuly for mending of Potters
drume, and newe brac*es* thereto   ij s. vj d. 20

...

f 391

...

p*ai*d for 6 yard*es* ⌐½¬ of Crimson Ribon by the appoyntem*en*t   25
of mr ffurser maior for the wait*es* of the City to hang theire
scutchens on. the 29 Septem*ber* 1628   iij s. vj d.

...

Drapers' and Tailors' Memoranda Book   CCA: U12/A1   30
f 56v   *(Receipts)*

...

                                                                      li.   s.   d.

...

Rec*eued* for 42 ordinaries at our feast   1   8   0 35

...

7/ Dum*m*: *for* Drumm
13, 19/ Tucker: *John Tucker, joiner, freeman from August 1598*

(Payments)

	li.	s.	d.
Item paid for the charge of the feast and other meetinges of the componie this yere	7	1	7
Item paid the waites	0	5	0	5

…

1628–9
City Chamberlains' Accounts   CCA: CC/FA 23
f 438v*   10

…

paid to the Citty way*tes* for their service at the County dinner   v s.

…

paid to mr Barham at the Lyon for the County dinner
the 16. of december 1628 as appeareth by his Bill   iiij li. ij s. [vjj d.] vij d. 15

…

f 441

…

paid m*aste*r Maior the 9 of march 1629: x s. hee gaue to the king*es*   20
players for there forbearing to play in the Citty allowed by Burmoth   x s.

…

f 441v*
…   25
paid to Pott*e*r for setting in a snare head vpon on of the
Towne dru*m*mes   xij d.

…

Quarter Sessions Jury Presentments   CCA: CC/J/Q/428/ii   30
single sheet   *(23 March)*

Presentments of the Grand Inquest made at the general quarter sessions held in the
court hall of Canterbury before John Roberts, mayor; Lancelot Lovelace, recorder;
*and other j*r*s*   35

…

Item we p*re*sent Iohn webb of the parish of St Mildred of this Citty Musition
for that he the twentith daye of this Instant In the yeres a foresaid and diu*ers*
dayes before and sithence did and doth suffer many young men and youth to

14/ mr Barham: *Isaac Barham, yeoman, freeman from 1614*

be exercising daunceing on the saboth dayes drinckling and disordering in
vnseemly manner in his nowe dwelling house in wincheap in th⟨…⟩sh and
ward a fore said Contra &c

...

Drapers' and Tailors' Memoranda Book   CCA: U12/A1
f 57   *(Receipts)*

...

	li.	s.	d.
...			
Item for 51 ordinaries at .8. d. at our feast day.	1	14	0

...

(Payments)

	li.	s.	d.
Item Laid out at the feast and one the Countye night at super	8	1	2
Item paid the waites	0	5	0

...

1629–30
City Chamberlains' Accounts   CCA: CC/FA 23
f 496*   *(External expenses)*

...

Inprimis paid to Isaacke Barham at ye Lion for the County
dynner for 14 at xviij d. ordynary for 20 at xiiij d. ordynary
and for xvj at viij d. ordynary   ij li. xv. s.
Item for wyne in the mornyng and at dynner that daye   xiiij s.
Item for strong beere and fyer then   ij s. vj d.
Item paid to the waites of this Citty for theire seruice and
musicke at ye same dynner   v s.

...

f 497v

...

Item paid to a Company of Plaiers being denyed to p_⟨l⟩ay within
this Citty, x s. allowed by Burgmoth   x s./

...

25/ Isaacke Barham: *yeoman, freeman from 1614*

Burghmote Court Minutes CCA: CC/AC 4
f 5 *(6 July)*

...

At this Court yt ys ordered that the x s. geaven by m*aste*r Chamberlen by
Consent of m*aste*r maior and the Aldermen to the plaiers lately beyng in this 5
Cittie/ & desirous to plaie heere/ & denied but gratified by the said x s. shall
be allowed to m*aste*r Chamberlen in his accompt/

...

New Foundation Treasurers' Accounts CCA: DCc/TA 38 10
sheet 2* *(Necessary expenses)*

...

Et in denarijs *per* Ipsum s*imi*lite*r* solut*is* pro diu*er*sis rebus et necessarijs
Ecclesie pred*icte* vizt.... Scholar*ibus* pro eoru*m* act*ibus* in Comedia xiij s....

... 15

Drapers' and Tailors' Memoranda Book CCA: U12/A1
f 57v *(Receipts)*

...

It*em* for 44 ordinaries at 8 d.		1	9	4 20
It*em* of the M*aste*r for wine		0	3	6

...

(Expenses)

25

It*em* paid mr Torner at the feast		6	3	10
...				
It*em* to the waitys		0	5	0

...

30

1630–1
City Chamberlains' Accounts CCA: CC/FA 24
f 41v* *(External expenses)*

...

Item for the County dynn*er* 1630 at xvj d. ordynary for 35	
16 p*er*sons	xxj s. iiij d.
Item more for 28 p*er*sons at xiiij d. ordynary	xxxij s. viij d.
Item for wyne in the mornyng of y*a*t County day and for dynner	xv s. x d.
Item for strong beere and fyer then	vj s. iiij d.

13/ Ipsum: *John Simpson, the treasurer*
26/ mr Torner: *Robert Turner, vintner*

And for the officers dynner and others to the nomber of 16. at
viij d. ordynary   x s. viij d.
Item to the Citty wates for theire musicke that day   v s.
...

f 43

...

paid to the said Barnes for a batter head for his drome   xviij d.
...

New Foundation Treasurers' Accounts   CCA: DCc/TA 39
sheet 4*   *(Necessary expenses)*

Et in denarijs *per* Ipsum si*militer* hoc an*n*o solut*is* pro diu*er*sis rebus et
necessarijs Ecclesie p*redicte* vizt.... Pro Scena construenda pro scholar*ibus*
Schole gramatice ad duas vices iij li. xviij s. j d....
...

Drapers' and Tailors' Memoranda Book   CCA: U12/A1
f 58   *(Receipts)*
...

	li.	s.	d.
Item Rec*eiued* for 50 ordinaries at 8 d.	1	13	4

...

(Payments)

	li.	s.	d.
Item The whole Charge for the meetings of the Company at seuerall times this yeare is	08	03	10
...			
Item to the waites	00	05	00

...

1631–2
City Chamberlains' Accounts   CCA: CC/FA 24
ff 92–2v*   *(External expenses)*
...

Item for 13 ordinaries for ye County dynn*er* at ye Maiors table   0 17 4

8/ the said Barnes: *one of the city's drummers*
14/ Ipsum: *Thomas Anyan, the treasurer*

Item for 33 ordinaries for ye Common Counsell and Auditors of
ye said Accoumpt at 14 d. ordinary   1   18   6
Item for 11 quartes of sacke then   0   11   0
Item then 3 gallons of Clarett   0   8   0
Item then in the Morning a gallon and a quart of Muscaden   0   5   0   5
Beare and fier   0   8   0|
Item for 16 ordynaries for officers, sariantes and waites of ye Citty 0 10   0
And more for fier   0   2   6
Item given to the said waites for theire qualety that day   0   5   0
...   10

f 94*
...
Item for a newe head for Barnes Drome   0   1   8
Item for ye setting on of yat head   0   1   8   15
...

f 94v
...
Item for a Cord for potters Drome and a snare head   0   3   4   20
...
Item giuen to Potter the Drome for setting on a head & triming
his drome   0   1   8
Item for 2 newe heads for an other drome   0   3   0
for Cord & putting on ye said 2 heades   0   3   4   25
And for braces   0   1   8
...

f 95v
...   30
Item paid for a newe scochen for one of the waites and triming
the rest   1   14   0
...
Item for 6 yardes of Crimsen Ribon for the waites scutchens   0   4   6
...   35

Burghmote Court Minutes   CCA: CC/AC 4
ff 38-8v   *(22 November)*

Order
Towchinge the   ...
Musitions of   whereas some Controuersies haue risen betwene the musitions or waightes of   40
this Cittie   this Cittie which doe plaie with their musick in the morninges in the stretes of
                     this Cittie betwene the feastes of All Sainctes and the purificacion of the

virgyn Marie yeerelie especially what nomber of Boyes shall be kept amongest
them, and by which of them to bee trained vpp in the Sciens of Musick
which maie be hereafter fytt Musitions and waites for that and other purposes
in this Cittie (as occasion maie requir and what allowances shall be for
those Boyes | [shall be for those boyes] out of the money gathered for their   5
mornynges Musick And have peticioned vnto this howse for that purpose to
haue steddie Course therin for avoidyng of further Controuersies amongest
them/ which beynge referred vnto Certen of the aldermen and of the Comon
Counsell of this Cittie Comittees in that behalff/ To examyn and report
vnto this howse what ys fittest to be done therin, who havynge heard the   10
alligacions of their seuerall grevances haue retorned vnto this howse their
opinions and iudgementes therin/ And thervppon At this present Court of
Burgmot with full Consent yt ys ordered and decreed (as followeth) that ys
to saie/ That william Inwood nowe one of the said Musions and waites/
shall be the Cheefest of the waites (amongest them), and he to be allowed   15
to keepe one boye that hath sufficient Skill in Musick And he the said
[w]william Inwood to haue a share for him selff and a share for his boye
And so to Contynewe hereafter for the Chefest of the waites in the said
Cittie Company And that Robert wiltan and william wacher the second
and third waites of the Company To haue onely one boye betwene them   20
well instructed in Musicke and that boie to haue a share with the rest/
and that one musition and waite more of Sufficient Skill to be taken in
amongest them (as on of the waites of this Cittie/ So that ther shall be but
Six in nomber (that ys to saie) fower men and two boies which then (as
aforesaid) and that the said nowe Musitions and waites, and such as   25
hereafter shall be the Musitions & waites of this Cittie shall be Allwaies
ordered towching their procedynges/ and Controuersies as the musitions &
waites of this Cittie By the house of Burgmott of this Cittie/

f 51v   (31 July)   30

Also at this Court yt ys ordered and decreed that master Chamberlen shall
vppon the Citties Chardge Cause a Scutchin to be made for the musitions of
this Cittie to be the greatest Scutchyng of the ffower Scutchens for the said
musitions ⌃⌈in sted of that Scutchon lost⌉ to be borne by the Cheeff musitione 35
& the reste of the Scutchens to be amended wher nede shall be And that
william Inwood shall haue the kepyng of the said Scutchens & shall enter in
bond to the maior & Coialtie of this Citty [nye & the] for the saeff Custody

4/ requir: *closing parenthesis missing after this word*
14/ Musions: *for Musicions*
23/ (as on ... Cittie/: *virgule used as closing parenthesis*
38/ Coialtie: *for Cominaltie; abbreviation mark missing*

of them & for the [de] delyu*er*ye ther of them with the riband*es* to m*aste*r
Chamberlen of this Cittie for the Cytties vse in good sort & plight when he
shall be required them/

...

New Foundation Treasurers' Accounts   CCA: DCc/TA 40
sheet 3v   *(Necessary expenses)*

Et in Denari*j*s *p*er Ipsum si*milite*r hoc an*n*o solut*is* pro diu*er*sis rebus et
necessari*j*s Ecclesie pr*edicte* vizt.... Quatuordece*m* actoribus Scholar*ibus*
in Comedia *pro* eoru*m* incitamento xiiij s. pro expen*sis* circa d*ict*am
Comediam x li....

Drapers' and Tailors' Memoranda Book   CCA: U12/A1
f 58v   *(Receipts)*

...

It*em* Rec*eiued* of the wardens for 51 ordinarie at 8 d.   1 14 0

...

(Payments)

	li.	s.	d.
It*em* the whole Charg of the feast and other Meetinges of the company this yeare is	7	0	4
...			
It*em* paid the waites	0	5	0

...

1632–3
City Chamberlains' Accounts   CCA: CC/FA 24
f 140*   *(External expenses)*

...

Item paid to George Bridg for ye County dynner as followeth
for fier ij s. iiij d. for strong beere iiij s. for wyne xvij s. ix d. for
44 ordynaries at xvj d. ij li. xviij s. viij d. and for 15 ordynaries
*a*t viij d. x s. in all   4 12 9
Item then p*ai*d to ye wait*es* of this Citty   0   5 0

...

9/ Ipsum: *John Warner, the treasurer*
17/ ordinarie: *for* ordinaries
32/ George Bridg: *George Bridge, vintner, freeman from 1619*
35/ 4: *corrected over 3*

ff 143v–4*

...

Item paid to widowe Ieoffery for clening the bulstake markett in
Mr Midltones time of sicknes, by order of Burgmoth   0   7   6

...   5

Item paid to George Bridg for ye backing and ordering of the
venison sent from the Lady wotton   1   0   0
paid for 13 ordinaries extraordynarie at xiiij d. a peece then   0   15   2
paid for strong beere   0   2   0
Item for 10 ordynaries more for the waites at viij d.   0   6   8   10
And for wyne   0   16   0

...

Item paid to Mr Turnor of the Chequor for ordering and baking
the venison sent from the Countis of Winshallsea   1   0   0
paid then for wine   0   16   6   15
for strong beere   0   1   2
paid for 7 ordinaries extraordinary at xvj d. a peece   0   9   4l
Item paid for 8 ordynaries more for the waites at 8 d. a peece   0   5   4

...

Item for pauing about ye bulstake   0   1   6   20

...

Burghmote Court Minutes   CCA: CC/AC 4
f 55v*   *(9 October)*

...   25

Allso at this Court are appoynted mr watmer mr Sabin mr ffurser and mr
nicholson Aldermen mr Plaier & mr Branker to be Comittees to examyn &
determin towch 2/ peticions one exhibited Edward ward & Iohn Beck & the
other by the nowe Musitions/ or by any 4 of them at a time by them to be
agreed vppon   30

...

7/ Lady wotton: *Margaret, Lady Wotton, widow of Edward Wotton, first Baron Wotton*
13/ Mr Turnor: *Robert Turner, vintner*
14/ of: *followed by line filler covering originally blank space*
14/ Countis of Winshallsea: *Elizabeth Heneage, countess of Winchilsea, widow of Sir Moyle Finch,*
    a former sheriff of Kent
26/ and: *written over Ald*
28/ towch: *for towching*
28/ exhibited: *for exhibited by*

Drapers' and Tailors' Memoranda Book   CCA: U12/A1
f 59v   (Receipts)
...

	li.	s.	d.
...				5
Itim Receyved of the wardenes ffor 44 ordynaryes at 8 d.	01	09	04
...			

(Payments)

	li.	s.	d.	10
The whole charge of the feast and the countey Supper this yeare is the some of	06	11	02	
...				
To the waightes of the Cytye	00	05	00	
...				15

1633-4
City Chamberlains' Accounts   CCA: CC/FA 24
f 188*   (External expenses)

...				20
Item paid to Mr George Bridge for ye County dynner for 42 ordynaries at 16 d. a peece	2	16	0	
And to him for 12 ordinaries for ye waiters at viij d. a peece	0	8	0	
for strong beere then	0	8	3	
fyer	0	1	0	25
for wyne then as per bill appereth	1	6	6	
Item paid then to ye waites for theire paynes	0	5	0	
...				

f 190

...				30
Item paid to Iohn ward for a newe drum head and Cord	0	7	6	
...				

f 191

...				35
Item to Potter for a newe hoop for his drume	0	1	0	
...				

21/ George Bridge: *George Bridge, vintner, freeman from 1619*

f 191v

...

Item more to him for ye putting off of certen players   1   0   0

...

f 192

...

Item to Daniell Rigesbey for mending ye formes at ye Bulstake,
and one butchers stall, being ½ a dayes worke and for his stuffe   0   2   2

...

Burghmote Court Minutes   CCA: CC/AC 4
f 88   *(12 August)*

Also at this Court yt ys ordered that m*aste*r maior shall be allowed [xx s] &
paied to him by m*aste*r Chamberlen xx s. w*hi*ch he gave to Certen plaiers
w*hi*ch cam to this Cittie to plaie havyng com*m*ission in that behalff/ to the
end to avoyed disorders and night walkyng w*hi*ch myght come therby

...

Drapers' and Tailors' Memoranda Book   CCA: U12/A1
f 60v   *(Receipts)*

...

                                                           li.   s.   d.

...

Itim Receyved of mr Christop*er* Cossenes warden ffor 51
ordinaryes at 8 d.   01   14   0

...

f 61   *(Payments)*

...

                                                           li.   s.   d.

The whole Charge of the ffeast and the Countye Supper
this yeare   08   18   10

...

To the Cytye waightes   00   05   00

...

3/ him: *John Lade, mayor*
8/ Daniell Rigesbey: *carpenter, freeman from 1631*

1634–5
City Chamberlains' Accounts CCA: CC/FA 24
f 237v* *(External expenses)*

...

Item paid to George Bridge at ye Lion for ye County dynner as				5
followeth for strong beere iiij s. for sacke and Claret xxiij s. ij d.				
for fier xvj d. for 46 ordynaris at xvj d. a peece iij li. xvj d. for				
15 ordin*a*res at viij d. x s. in all	4	19	10	
Item then giuen to the Cook*es*	0	1	0	
And to the wait*es* of the Citty	0	5	0	10

...

ff 239v–40

...

Item p*ai*d to Iohn Mathewe for pauing 50 yard*es* at ye Bulstake			15
at ij d. ob. le yard	0	10	5

...

Item p*ai*d to Iohn Gouldsmith for 4 load*es* of stones for the			
said pauing	0	12	0
and to him more for 4 load*es* of sand for the same	0	4	0l 20
Item for ye Carrying awaie of 3 loads of Rubbedg left by			
the pauiers	0	1	0

...

Drapers' and Tailors' Memoranda Book CCA: U12/A1   25
f 61v *(Receipts)*

...

li.	s.	d.

...

Itim Receyved of Barthollmew Iohncock ffor 48 ordynaryes at			30
8 d. pece	01	12	0

...

f 62 *(Payments)*

...

li.	s.	d.	35

Itim ffor the whole ^⌈Charge⌉ of the dinner one our ffeast daye/			
wee haveinge noe countye Supper this yeare the some of	06	01	06

...

5/ George Bridge: *George Bridge, vintner, freeman from 1619*
18/ Iohn Gouldsmith: *cooper, freeman from 1636*

Itim paid to the waightes   00 05 00

...

1635–6
City Chamberlains' Accounts   CCA: CC/FA 24

f 285v*   *(External expenses)*

...

Item paid the 5 of Nouem*ber* 35 to Mr George Bridge at ye Lion at
a meeting there. for a gallon of sacke iiij s. three gallons and 3 pints
of Clarret vj s. ix d. for Mr Aldaies ordinarie xvj d. for the three
waite*s* ordinaries ij s. strong beere iij s. in all as p*er* bill appeareth   0 17   1

...

f 286

...

Item the 10 of decem*ber* 35 pa*i*d to mr merriam alderm*a*n for
ye waits a yard and ½ of Ribbon   0   1   6
Item more for 4 yar*ds* and ½ of Crimson Ribbon   0   3   4

...

Burghmote Court Minutes   CCA: CC/AC 4
f 112v   *(23 February)*

...

Lyneall: Cittie   vpon the petic*i*on of ffrancis Lyneall it is ordered that if the petic*i*oner before
Musique   Easter next present a newe Company of able Musitions to serue this Citty
the Court will vpon consideration had of them take such further order as
shalbe meete.

...

Letter from Mayor James Nicholson to Archbishop William Laud
PRO: SP 16/317
f [1]*   *(25 March)*

May it please yo*ur* grace
Certeyne Stage playere*s* came lately to this Citty and in obedience to his
Ma*iesties* Com*m*issi⟨..⟩ with my licence they pleyed heer 8 daies [in which
tyme alt] and although their night playe*s* contynued vntill neere Midnight to
the great disorder of the whole Citty and to the disquiet of many a citizen
whose seruante*s* without their masters lycence contynued at the playe*s* till
neere midnight whereof dayly complaynte*s* comyng vnto me and especially

---

8/ George Bridge: *George Bridge, vintner, freeman from 1619*
16/ mr merriam: *John Meryam, alderman; mayor 1631–2*

fynding that those plaies heere prooved a Nursery for drunkennes & disorder
[against the] especially in this tyme of abstynence & being from many persons
credibly informed that two honest mens daughters at that vnseasonably tyme
of the night were [carnally] made drunk & carnally abused at the play house
to the publick scandall of goverment I did require the players to desist from   5
playing any longer within this Citty wherevp⟨..⟩ one of them tould me he
would play without my leaue yet neuerthelesse they are gone & intend to
returne hither againe as I am informed & it is given out that they will
compleyne of me for prohibiting them. wherein I humbly beseech your
graces direction it is not my person but the office I beare and the affront to   10
goverment that makes me present this suite to your grace to whome as the
best friend this Citty hath vnder his Maiestie I am bould & incouraged by
your graces former fauoures to be [and] an humble suitor for redresse which
shall in all duty oblige this Citty and

Canterbury this 25th   your graces humble seruant   15
of Marche. 1635/   *(signed)* Iames Nicholson maior

Letter from the Privy Council to Mayor James Nicholson
PRO: SP 16/317
single sheet   *(29 March)*   20

After our harty Commendacions, By your lettres of ye 25th of this Moneth,
[wherewith] sent vnto our very good lord the Lord Archbishopp of Canterbury
his Grace, wee vnderstand with what respect [& obedi] yow proceeded with
the players that lately came to [your] that Citty, [with his Ma] in regarde of his   25
Maiesties Commission which they carryed, & [alsoe] wee likewise take notice
ˆ⌈not only⌉ of the[ir] disorders [there vnseasonable] occasioned by their
[vnseasonable] playing att soe vnseasonable a tyme in ye night, but alsoe of
their insolent behauiour to your self, for which they deserue punishement &
[will] shall smart [smart if] ˆ⌈when⌉ they ⌈shalbe⌉ [maybe] mett withall, to   30
which purpose wee pray yow to advertise the names of some of ye Cheefest
of their ˆ⌈Company⌉ that further inquiry may be here made after them: ˆ⌈also
as⌉ wee cannot but Comend the great Care yow [expresse] haue ˆ⌈[in that
particlar]⌉ expressed in the good & orderly gouernment of the Citty soe wee
must let yow know ˆ⌈for your encouragement that⌉ [that] ˆ⌈his Maiestie being   35
[represented to know]⌉ [wee have represented] ⌈by his Grace made⌉ acquainted
[his Maiestie therewith] with your [per] Carriage in this particular [he is pl]
hath commanded vs to giue yow notice of his gracyous acceptaunce thereof;
and [if ⟨..⟩] for the future [when] ˆ⌈if⌉ any ˆ⌈stage⌉ players [come] shall come
to play in your Citty [att ⌈the⌉ soe vnseasonable] ˆ⌈in ye⌉ tyme of lent, yow   40
are not to giue way vnto it without the speciall [privyty] privity [of our very

3/ vnseasonably: *for* vnseasonable

good lord thereto] of his Grace of Canterbury: And soe wee bid yow farewell
ffrom dated at Whitehall the 29th of March 1636. Signed

	Lord Keeper	Lord Newburgh
Mayor of Canterbury	Lord ArchBishop of Yorke	Master Comptroller
	Lord Treasurer	Master Secretary Coke
	Lord Privy Seale	Master Secretary Windebank

Letter from Mayor James Nicholson to the Privy Council   PRO: SP 16/318
f [1]   *(5 April)*

May it please your honores
That the iust compleyntes I latelie presented to my lordes Grace of
Canterbury haue from his Maiestie and your honores found redresse it is
a great Comfort to my selfe and the whole Corporacion nowe assembled
in Burgmott who haue heard your honores gracious letteres and they doe
all acknowledg your honores goodnes towardes them & retorne most
humble thankes for the reformacion of the abuse & establishment of the
goverment of this Cittie. And towching the playeres heere I am informed
they are of the Company of the fortune play howse the principall of
them [were] were Weekes and Perry the rest of their names I cannot yet
learne. Perry was the man that most affronted me in saying he would
play whether I would or not, and vpon the many compleyntes of honest
Citizens who could not restrayne their seruantes from being at the playes
till neer Midnight I desiered Perry to keepe better howeres or I would
acqueint your honores with their disorderes he replied he cared not. and
vpon Inquiry I fynd it was not a player but one mr Moseley who dwelles
neer Tower hill london who did inebriate and after carnally abuse ⌐one
of⌐ the two Maidens in the playe howse. And soe with the Seruice of the
Citty presented vnto your good honores I hast to subscribe my selfe as I
truely am.
                      your honores much bounden seruent
Canterbury. 5º. April
1636
                      (signed) Iames Nicholson maior

1636–7
City Chamberlains' Accounts   CCA: CC/FA 24
f 334v*   *(External expenses)*
...
for a Cord for Potteres drum   0 2 0
...

f 335

...

More to them at the entertaynement of the prince Palatine into
this Cittie 0 4 0

... 5

1637–8
City Chamberlains' Accounts CCA: CC/FA 24
f 380v* *(External expenses)*

... 10

...more to him for worke for mending and legging the formes of the
bullstake iij s. vj d....

...

f 381 15

...

Item to the Crier for blowing the burgmoth horne for one quarter 0 3 4

...

Item paid to Iustice ye plomer for a Cocke at St Georges gate and
simoning of it vj s. for simoning of the Cocke at Bulstake xij d. 0 7 0 20

...

Item paid to the Towne sariant for his 3 quarter vizt.... for a horslocke for the
foormes at bulstake vj d....

Burghmote Court Minutes CCA: CC/AC 4 25
f 134v* *(3 April)*

...

Musitions | Vpon the peticion of William Mathers of this Citty musition on the behalf
of himself & ffrancis Lyneall Richard Mounteere and Iohn Wright other
musitions of the said Citty It is ordered that the said persons shalbe the 30
City musique & keep two boyes And that master Alderman Sabyn master
alderman ffurser mr Branker & mr Bulkley or any two of them shall sett
downe orders for ye government of the said [Cittie] Musitians

...

35

f 135 *(17 April)*

...

Musitians | vpon the peticion of Sampson Wright Edward Berry Iohn [Westray] Westray
Iohn Floade and Edward Climer musitions desiring they may bee the Citty

---

3/ them: *the city drummers*
11/ him: *Goodman Quiles, a carpenter*
19/ Iustice ye plomer: *Nicholas Justice, plumber, freeman from 1622*

musick the consideracion thereof is also referred vnto the former comittees
for Matheres & otheres made ye last Court of Burgmott and out of both
companyes the said Comittees are desired to appoint one Company who
shalbe the waites for the publick seruice of this Citty and what orderes they
shall make shalbe confirmed by this Court   5

...

f 136v   *(26 June)*

...

Scutchions for
Musitians

vpon the peticion of william Matheres and Sampson wright on the behalf of   10
them selues & ye rest of the Cittie musique It is ordered that the Escutchions
of this City shalbe deliuered vnto them vpon good security to return them
to master Chamberleyn in as good case as they nowe are vpon demand

...

15

f 137*

vpon seuerall peticions this day receyued besides many other at former Courtes
by such as desired to be the Musick of this Cittie the matter of all the said
former peticions was referred vnto the consideracion of Master Alderman   20
Watmer master Alderman Sabyn master Alderman ffurser and to mr Thomas
Branker and Mr Ioseph Bulkly of the Comon Councell of this Cittie to
heer the parties & report vnto this Court [what] ⌈whome⌉ they thought fitt
personnes to make vp the company of waites And accordinglie the said
referres did this day bring in their report dated the 15th of this present Iune in 25
theis wordes following
Towching the waytes it is thought fitt by vs whose names are subscribed that
theis personnes herevnder named shalbe the waytes videlicet William Matheres
to be the chef soe longe as he shall behaue himself well and give noe iust cause
to the contrary   30
Sampson Wright the second soo longe as he shall well behaue himself and giue
noe iust cause to the contrary
Francis Lyneall the third vpon the same condicion
Ricard Mountier the fowerth vpon the same condicion
Edward Berry the fift vpon the same Condicion. Theis five are enough for   35
waytes by their owne confession with one boy skilfull in Musique which boy
shalbe allowed a share and that share shalbe paid to the two first personnes of
the waites and he that kepes the boy shall haue two third partes of the Share
and the other wayte to haue the other third parte which report ∧⌈nowe⌉ read
& considered is ordered & decreed from henceforth to be duly obserued   40
without any [further] alteracion vpon the further peticion of any of the said
fiue parties or of any otheres in that behalf

...

Drapers' and Tailors' Memoranda Book   CCA: U12/A1
f 64v   *(Receipts)*

...

	ll.	s.	d.

...

Receyved of Iohn Castle Wardenn ffor 45 ordynaryes at 8 d.
a pene and three pence over soe in all Rec*eyved*   01 10 03

...

f 65   *(Payments)*

	li.	s.	d.

...

Itim paid ffor the whole Charge one our ffeast daye ffor dinner
and the Charge of the Supper at our last account in all it dooth
come vnto 08 06 05 I say   08 06 05

...

Itim paid vnto the waightes   00 05 00

...

1638–9
City Chamberlains' Accounts   CCA: CC/FA 24
f 429v*   *(External expenses)*

...

Item paid on the 5 of No̩uem*ber* at the Chequ̩or for wine and
ordinaries according to order of Burgm*ote*   2 2 0
and to the shott of the selected band then   2 0 0
and to the wait*es* of the cittie   0 5 0
Item p*ai*d to ward ye drume for a skinne of vellum and putting
it on his drum for a head that was broken   0 4 0

f 431v

...

Item paid to Iohn ward for a Corde [head] for his drome   0 2 6

...

f 432

...

Item paid to the Smith for worke done at the bullstake and
setting vp the stone there ⌈at the Cocke⌉   0 2 6

...

7/ a pene: *for* a pece
39/ stone: *corrected over* formes

f 434

...

Item for sim*m*oning the cocke at the bulstake taking it downe and				
mending the same by Nicholas Iustice the plomer	0	2	0	
Item p*ai*d to Mr ffidge for Ribbon for the wait*es*	0	5	6	5

...

f 435

...

Item to alderm*an* Bridge that was giuen to the player*es* in				10
gratuity to depart the Citty. soe ordered by burgmoth	0	13	4	

...

Burghmote Court Minutes   CCA: CC/AC 4
f 146v   *(9 July)*   15

...

Alderman
Bridg 13 s. 4 d.

It is ordered that xiij s. iiij d. given by m*aste*r Alderman Bridge to discharg
one that had a shewe of the Creation from this Citty shalbe repaid him by
m*aste*r Chamberleyn.

...   20

Drapers' and Tailors' Memoranda Book   CCA: U12/A1
f 65v   *(Receipts)*

...

	li.	s.	d.	25
...				
Rec*ey*ved of Iohn mearser warden ffor 55 ordynaryes at 8 d.				
a pece	01	16	08	

...   30

f 66   *(Payments)*

...

	li.	s.	d.	
Itim paid ffor the whole Charge one our ffeast daye ffor dinner				
and ffor the Charge of our Supper at our last yeares accoumpt				35
in all it dooth amount vnto	07	17	06	
...				
Itim paid vnto the waightes	00	05	00	

...

4/ Nicholas Iustice: *Nicholas Justice, plumber, freeman from 1622*
5/ Mr ffidge: *Thomas Fidge, mercer and haberdasher, freeman from 1613*
10, 17m, 17/ Bridge, Bridg: *William Bridge, grocer, freeman from 1598; mayor 1636–7*

1639–40
City Chamberlains' Accounts CCA: CC/FA 24
f 478v *(External expenses)*

…

Item to mr Stanley maior that was giuen to a Company of plaiers,   5
not to play. soe ordered by Burgmoth   1   0   0

…

f 480v

…   10

Item to Thomas whineat*es* for his 3ᵈ q*uart*er at midsom*er* 1640 then ended …
Item for ½ a daies worke in lagging the formes of the bulstake and stuffe
ij s. vj d.…

…

       15

f 481*

…

Item to ward for a drume head & putting it on   0   3   6
…

Item to Iohn ward for a drum head   0   3   6   20
And for a newe drum for Cox   1   6   0

…

Burghmote Court Minutes CCA: CC/AC 4
f 148v *(29 October)*

       25

…

20 s. to It is ordered that xx s. paid to ye player*es* to discharge them shalbe repaid him
Player*es*
…

f 150v* *(21 January)*

       30

…

Mather*es* & At this Court willi*a*m Mather*es* [l] chief of the wayt*es* did refuse to be [at] one
Musitions of the wait*es* of this Cittie vnles he may haue his owne will & a full share for
his boy the matter is referred to further examynac*i*on hereafter to the old
Comit*ees* to examyne whether waite wright*es* demand of xxx s. from Mather*es*   35
be iust or not. & mr Glouer is added in stead of mr Branker dead & to
consider & settle the boye money

…

11/ Thomas whineat*es*: *serjeant of the chamber*
27/ him: *the chamberlain, Alderman John Lade*
36/ mr Glouer: *James Glover, grocer, freeman from 1613; common councillor*
36/ mr Branker: *Thomas Branker, linen-draper, freeman from 1601; common councillor*

f 152v*   *(12 May)*

...

Citty Musitions   It is ordered that Mr Sabyn mr ffurser & mr lade aldermen & mr Bulkley
& mr Sympson of ye common Counsell ⌈or any three of them⌉ shall examyne
ye differences & settle an order amongst the Musitians or waightes of   5
this Citty at shew the order by them made at the Court of Burgmott to
be entered.

1640–1
City Chamberlains' Accounts   CCA: CC/FA 25   10
f 43

...

Item paid the 14 of Aprill 41 for 2 newe hopes for Daniell
Coxes drome   0   2   0

...   15

f 44*

...

Item to the 4 Drumes for beating to the Companies at the
prince of Orang coming   0   8   0 20

...

f 44v

...

for mending the grat at the Bulstake and one of the cockes to   25
Goodman Hilderson in Iuly 1641   0   2   6

...

Item the 22 of Iuly 41 in dischardge of a Companie of plaieres
out of Towne by master maiores appointment   1   0   0

...   30

Burghmote Court Minutes   CCA: CC/AC 4
f 158*   *(19 January)*

...

Cittie musick   It is by this Court ordered and desired that master Maior master Alderman   35
Sabyn master Chamberlyn mr Bulkley & mr Sympson ⌃⌈or any 3 of them⌉
shall heere & settle the busines of the Cittie Musick [or discharge them] &
report their opynions.

...

26/ Goodman Hilderson: *Thomas Hilderson, blacksmith, freeman from 1625*

f 158v* *(2 February)*

...

Musick
dischardged

It is ordered that in respect of the misdemenor of this Citty musick the
Escutchons of the Citty shalbe called in by m*aste*r Chamberleyn & if they
refuse to deliuer the same then to be sued for them by m*aste*r Chamberlyn   5
& the said Citty musick & company are hereby absolutely dischardged &
dissolued.

...